PSYCHOLOGY
AND RACE

PSYCHOLOGY
AND RACE

edited by Peter Watson

with a foreword by M. Brewster Smith

ALDINE PUBLISHING COMPANY
Chicago

Published 1974 by
Aldine Publishing Company
529 South Wabash Avenue
Chicago, Illinois 60605

ISBN   0-202-25114-4   clothbound edition
       0-202-25115-2   paperbound edition
Library of Congress Catalog Number 73-89512

Printed in the United States of America

Foreword

Although race and racism pose a special "American dilemma" (as Myrdal put it), from a global perspective they are tangled in the snarl of world-wide problems that Man is now challenged to understand and solve if he is to preserve his place as passenger on a closed and shrinking planet. In contemporary American politics, specialists in race, poverty, and the urban crisis are tending to line up on opposite sides from environmentalists. Concern about the ecological crisis is seen as competitive with concern about the harm men and women do to one another when they are identified with social categories. That is an unfortunately narrow view: our common fate — and it is crucial we come to comprehend it as one we share as fellow passengers — depends on our ability to discover new patterns for sharing the limited resources of a finite planet before it is too late. We have to learn to live together. Otherwise, our dying will be most unpleasant.

Since the problems of race relations are worldwide, the international origins and perspective of this excellent and timely book are especially advantageous. More research has been done in the United States than elsewhere on the psychology of race relations, so it is appropriate that a plurality of the chapters are by American authors — a stellar group that includes leading contributors to our contemporary knowledge of the topic. Contributors from the English-speaking Commonwealth countries are next in number, followed by authors from the United Kingdom, where race-related issues have only recently become a salient concern of politics and social ethics. But the editor has assigned topics to his carefully chosen author-experts not by country or region, but by matching the expertise of each author against a need for coherent analysis of the important aspects of "psychology and race." The American literature is under competent view throughout, but many of the authors are not American and this imparts to the book a freshness of perspective and novelty of example that should be a substantial attraction to American readers.

Peter Watson, the editor, is a young Englishman whose roles with *New Society* and the *London Sunday Times* have given him rich experience in communicating the findings and competing claims of the social sciences to the intelligent general reader. The book benefits: it is as full of fact and theory and scholarly reference as a well-packed textbook, but for the most part it does not read like one. As an Englishman, Watson is located somewhat apart from the primarily American battleground of social science controversy concerning race. This stands him in good stead in his personal contribution as one of the many authors. His introductory essay on "psychologists and race" says some sharp but warranted things about the intrusion of ideological convictions on scientific judgment that are probably said more naturally, and surely more safely, from across the sea. What he calls the "actor factor" has entered into the social science literature about race to an embarrassing extent. The reader does indeed need to be warned to be alert to it, though I agree with Watson that he has managed to select authors who by and large avoid distorting science in the service of politics. Courageously, he assigned to himself the especially controversial chapter on race and intelligence (Chapter 17), in which I think he has dealt with the hot issues fairly and surefootedly.

A word about the scope of the book. The editor has taken a broad view of its domain, to include contributions by sociologists (and a psychiatrist) in addition to those by psychologists. (A wise decision, I think, since the social psychology of race and race relations cannot be sensibly divided up between the disciplines of psychology and sociology.) On the other hand, the biology of race, of concern to human geneticists and physical anthropologists as well as psychologists, is not treated, except for some appropriate attention to genetic issues in Watson's own chapter. The coverage in the areas treated is authoritative and up-to-date, and the references that follow each chapter provide the reader with ready entrance to the more technical literature.

My personal appraisal of the book may best be conveyed by saying that I believe a student or general reader can best get his bearings in the humanly important area of *Psychology and Race* by reading this book jointly with Gordon Allport's 1954 classic, *The Nature of Prejudice*. That is high praise indeed. Happily, both books are now available to the American audience in paperback.

M. Brewster Smith
University of California at Santa Cruz

Contents

Preface   11

Introduction   Psychologists and Race: The 'Actor Factor'   15

Part One
Aspects of Interracial Interaction   21
A Focus on the Majority Group

1 The Development of Racial Awareness and Prejudice
in Children   23
*Isidore Pushkin, Chiswick Polytechnic, London, and Thelma Veness,
Institute of Education, University of London*

2 The Measurement of Prejudice   43
Roger Jowell, Social and Community Planning Research, London

3 The Roots of Prejudice: Emotional Dynamics   57
Nevitt Sanford, The Wright Institute, Berkeley, California

4 The Roots of Prejudice: Cognitive Aspects   76
Henri Tajfel, University of Bristol

5 Techniques for Reducing Prejudice: Changing the
Prejudiced Person   96
J. Milton Yinger and George Eaton Simpson, Oberlin College, Ohio

6 Techniques for Reducing Prejudice: Changing the Situation   145
George Eaton Simpson and J. Milton Yinger

B Focus on the Minority Group

7 Colour: The Nature and Meaning of Negro Self-Identity   176
Harold Proshansky and Peggy Newton, City University, New York

8 Status: The Marginal Reaction – Mixed-Bloods and Jews   213
Jack Mann, University of Witwatersrand, South Africa

9 Migration: Problems of Adjustment and Assimilation
   in Immigrants 224
   Ronald Taft, Monash University, Australia

C Focus on the Interaction

10 Interpersonal Attitudes and Behaviour in Race Relations 241
   Harry Triandis, University of Illinois

11 Negro Performance in Interracial Situations 256
   Irwin Katz, City University, New York

12 Some Mechanics of Racial Etiquette 267
   Peter Watson, Sunday Times, London

13 Race Relations and Behaviour in Reality 286
   Anthony Richmond, York University, Toronto

Part Two
The Race Variable and Key Issues
in Social Psychology 309

D The Interaction of Personality and Culture

14 Culture, Personality and Prejudice 311
   James Ritchie, University of Waikato, New Zealand

15 Family, Marital and Child-Rearing Patterns in
   Different Ethnic Groups 330
   Oscar Ferron, Njala College, University of Sierra Leone

E Education

16 Education and Immigrants 343
   Ronald Goldman, La Trobe University, Australia

17 Race and Intelligence through the Looking Glass 360
   Peter Watson

18 Alternatives to a Personality-Deficit Interpretation of
   Negro Under-Achievement 377
   Irwin Katz

F Language

19 Learning Each Other's Languages   393
   John Macnamara, McGill University, Canada

20 The Sociolinguistics of Nationalism   403
   Joshua Fishman, Centre for East-West Studies, Hawaii

G A Miscellany of Other Key Issues

21 Psychiatric Disorders in Minority Groups   416
   Ari Kiev, New York Hospital

22 Crime and Delinquency in Immigrant and Minority Groups   432
   Anthony Bottoms, University of Sheffield

23 Tests as Inadvertent Sources of Discrimination in
   Personnel Decisions   453
   Sidney Irvine, Brock University, Ontario, Canada

Acknowledgements   467

Author Index   469

Subject Index   481

To Nick

Preface

This is a big book of twenty-three chapters involving authors in five continents and I would like to thank Miss Sally Nowell, my secretary when I was at *New Society*, and Miss Terry Parrish when I was at the Tavistock Clinic, for their spare-time help in coordinating the editorial progress. Inevitably, some chapters went ahead more quickly than others; and though all the contributors were given a chance to up-date their work at the end of 1971/beginning of 1972 when the last MS was delivered, for some of them (for example, especially, Professor Fishman's and Dr Bottom's), the bulk of the work was done more than a year previously. I would like to thank Harper & Row for permission to reproduce Chapters 5 and 6 (much abridged) and Holt, Rinehart & Winston for permission to reproduce Chapter 7 (entire).

Introduction
Psychologists and Race:
The 'Actor Factor'

Most areas of science have their element of theatre. That is, the course they run is at times determined more by the personalities of the 'actors' that people them and the relationships of these 'actors' with one another, than by the logic or objective needs of the scientific situation. These personal relations – affinities and antagonisms – can determine the scientific questions that are asked and the style of their asking. Of course, this is not always true: but it may happen more than we think.

Certainly, a number of well-known scientists – for example, J. D. Watson in biology and P. B. Medawar in medicine – have conceded that this may occur in all manner of sciences. In psychology, however, as with some of the other social sciences, there are reasons why this 'actor factor' is even more important. This is because, as several studies have now shown, a psychologists' *general world view* – his attitudes and political beliefs – and not only his relations with other psychologists in his chosen specialty, may determine the questions he asks in his professional life and the methods he adopts to find and interpret the answers.

Unfortunately, psychologists interested in racial problems are possibly among the worst offenders when it comes to letting personal relations determine the course or interpretation of scientific inquiry. It is therefore especially important for the beginner in the field to be aware of this, not only so that he or she may judge the evidence in this book and elsewhere on a better basis, but also because the reason *why* this has occurred so much should help to sensitize someone to the way different races may misunderstand each other, and trouble result.

Let's begin with the early research – for example, that on racial prejudice. One can discern in the studies published just before or after the Second World War a strong dose of the actor factor. Underneath all the reserved academic prose these early arguments were nevertheless presented as the 'good guy' psychologists versus the 'bad guy' bigots. The good guys would chase the bad guys with their questionnaires, trip them up with their attitude surveys and all but arrest them on 'charges' of bigotry.

Research of this sort was, in fact, part of an attack on a general way of life, one that psychologists, with the benefit of education, despised as near-criminal. Well-motivated though they may have been, their science was, in fact, pseudo-science – a basically political manoeuvre. And it was eventually exposed. The picture given by early research was that though everyone was more or less prejudiced there was a sizeable number of individuals who were extreme bigots; the view was, therefore, that race relations should concentrate on them, trying to change their attitudes.

We now recognize these claims as exaggerated, that extremes of prejudice are as rare as extremes of anything. In fact, our attention is no longer on the extremely prejudiced who are not usually taken seriously, but instead on the middle people – and even then on their *behaviour*, not their attitudes. For we have discovered that those who seem to be prejudiced according to tests may not discriminate, and those whom the tests say are tolerant, are less so when it comes to the crunch. But psychologists have been a long while getting to this point because they let their own preconceptions get in the way. Rightly, some have been discredited along the way.

Another area where the element of theatre and the personalities of the actors have often been apparent is in the 'nature-nurture' debate, where it concerns race and intelligence. In fact, this particular plot has somersaulted over the years – the roles of hero and villain changing hands every six years or so.

Just after the war, for example, the environmentalists played the good guys; the geneticists were the crooks – they had disreputable morals, used underhand techniques and had underworld ideals. In contrast the picture nowadays is reversed. Experimental psychologists and biologists with a genetic bent picture themselves as the cops, misunderstood by the public at large but right nevertheless. The social psychologists and sociologists, on the other hand, have been cast as the robbers – fiddling their results like tax sheets, criminally neglecting the statistics of their opponents and generally obstructing them in the course of their scientific duty.

Just as early researchers on prejudice seemed to be motivated by their *general* dislike of their subjects (not just the fact that they were bigoted) so, in the race and intelligence thriller, many seem to have been spurred on by a *personal* dislike of their theoretical opponents, not just a disagreement with their theories.

These two 'sub-subjects' are not the only ones in the general field of psychology and race where the 'actor factor' has operated. But they serve well enough to illustrate the general point. The scientific 'truths' concerning prejudice have changed beyond recognition since the actor factor was dealt with – but it still plagues race and intelligence, with the result that the conventional wisdom continues to turn on its head every so often.

One might think that, in a modern science, the actor factor would gradually disappear. But not so in psychology and race. In fact, it may very well be getting worse because the last couple of years have seen in psychology the development of a trend unique in all sciences – a *black psychology*.

A 'black physics' or a 'black algebra' – even a 'black medicine' – are unthinkable sciences: yet a black psychology has seemed not incongruous, to other psychologists certainly, but also to the general public in some cases (on the basis of black psychology theory, for example, in California in the summer of 1972, blacks managed to prevent white intelligence tests being used to place blacks in the state educational system). At the time of writing (November 1972) black psychology is essentially still an American phenomenon though there are stirrings of it in Britain and Europe.

The reason *why* black psychology has been accepted is because of certain failures in white psychology and white psychologists in the race field. I think this book avoids most of these failures but an understanding of the form black psychology takes cannot be had without knowing something about those failures. What is, however, ironic is that black psychology itself contains a strong dose of the actor factor.

So far, black psychology has concerned itself, in its theoretical work, with three principal areas: black family life and its effects on personality; mental health: and IQ.

Let's look first at what black psychology says about these three things, and how they differ in blacks from whites. Later we shall assess their significance.

Black family life was first to receive the attention of black psychologists – and it is easy to see why. The conventional (white) wisdom that grew up over many years but which culminated in the late sixties was that black family life was not merely different to whites, but inferior in nearly every way. It was more mother-dominated in an aggressive masculine world, offered its children little in the way of mental stimulation or love, was concerned only with what was happening in the present. The consequences of this were said to be that Negroes, particularly males lacking a permanent male model like a father, grew up with many feminine traits like dependancy or over-emotionality; lack of stimuli meant that the children were dull, lack of love made them brittle and incapable of sustaining lasting relationships; because the family was poor and oriented only in the present, adolescents grew up as impulsive, and incapable of planning . . . so the chronicles of woe went on. One way or another, blacks were thought of as psychologically impoverished, emotionally immature, culturally deprived compared with whites.

Given a white frame of reference, it is perhaps just understandable why this was the picture that white psychologists read into the test results of the black 'subjects' they researched. But given the pretty obvious fact that blacks could never have a white frame of reference this approach reveals an extraordinary insensitivity, an unforgivable ethnocentric scientific effort, especially among people who called themselves psychologists and specialized in the race field.

The second thing that black psychologists turned their attention to was the field of mental health. Here the prevailing picture was one of higher rates in blacks for some kinds of illness or crime, less success in treatment or imprisonment. The third field was the race and IQ issue where some psychologists maintained that the 15-point IQ difference between blacks and whites was mainly genetically based and others that it was produced by a variety of factors in the different backgrounds of races as well as in their genes.

Now the alternative explanations which black psychologists have provided in each of these cases differ markedly *in purpose*. What began as a sort of scientific watchdog exercise has since developed into the scientific wing of a political pressure group.

For example, the alternative picture which black psychologists were able to give about black family life, about the strengths it had but which were genuinely different to whites, about the different ways that blacks made out in their *own* world – all these, besides being morally welcome and timely, were scientifically correct. But the power that black psychologists discovered they had in being able to contradict white 'wisdom' has since been used for less scientific reasons.

The other two areas where they have been active both show this. In the field of mental health, for example, black psychologists in America have concentrated, deliberately it seems, on one aspect – white racism as the cause of black mental illness. As you will see from Chapters 12 and 21 of this book racism is only one cause of mental illness, and possibly even then only an indirect cause. (It follows that to reduce black mental illness through racism is inefficient). But blacks have chosen this because in so doing they have been able to caricature white racism itself as a sickness. And they have discovered an important political point about America – a point that is well illustrated by comparison with Britain.

In Britain, racism is viewed primarily as a crime. If you discriminate along racial lines you can eventually be brought before the courts. This is partly because Britain has a heavily centralized administration, one legal system, little variation between police forces. It also reflects a view that racism, at least in its mild form, is not 'unnatural' but a tendency which many people have, say like mild dishonesty, but which has to be curbed.

Racism is also seen as a crime in the United States but – more important – is now also seen by many predominantly as a sickness. This is not, in fact, because of any theoretical differences between psychologists in Britain and the US. It is because in America, by comparison with Britain, there are many different administrations, county laws, state laws, federal laws; and some forty thousand police authorities (compared with only forty in Britain). And there is, in any case, a different attitude to the law. All this means that, in America, *some forms of behaviour are better controlled by administrative techniques other than the law.* The medical and psychiatric professions are one such alternative. Think of their effect on upbringing. Dr Benjamin Spock (who in 1972 stood for President) has probably had more influence on children through his appeal to their parents than education departments have had through the schools under their control. And racism is another form of behaviour that can be dealt with by these 'extra legal' methods.

Make racism a sickness and three things happen. First, you take it out of the courts and it becomes the concern of doctors and psychiatrists/psychologists. Second, because of this, it is easier to deal with nationally in America – doctors share a more common frame of reference than policemen, are better organized across the country and more highly respected, too. Finally, it goes without saying that if racism is a sickness then, like all sicknesses, it is a state that should naturally be avoided – and people may accept 'treatment' for it when they wouldn't accept punishment. The contrast with Britain is marked.

A further, but different, point is illustrated by the black psychologists' involvement in the race and IQ saga. In August 1972, black psychologist Robert Williams released to the Annual Meeting of the American Association of Psychology, gathered in Honolulu, the first details of three black psychology tests he had developed.

The three tests were: a black awareness test, a black projective personality test, called Themes Concerning Blacks, and a Black Intelligence Test of Cultural Homogeneity (the BITCH test). These tests, especially the personality test and the IQ test, can be seen as a response to what was viewed as a growing racism not just in society at large but in the psychology profession itself.

And this development puts it in a class separate to that of the other developments. The alternative interpretations of black family life I have already said are scientifically appropriate: the picture of racism as a sickness is not necessarily wrong but its placing at the centre of black psychologists' activities is clearly politically motivated; but the development of black tests goes still further – a development in the scientific tools that is deliberately politically motivated.

The point at issue here is not whether these developments are right or wrong,[1] but to show how the actor factor operates in psychology and race at all levels and how this goes for black psychologists as much as for white ones.

The authors in this book were thus chosen not simply for academic excellence but also because, as far as is possible, they avoid identification with either the good guys or the bad guys in their particular specialty. Many have worked on more than one continent, between a third and a half are minority group members themselves – Jewish, Coloured, immigrants.

And it is my hope that in treating the actor factor in this way (many science books never mention it of course), drawing attention to it at the beginning of the book, it will prove especially useful to the beginner in the subject, and perhaps remind professional psychologists of a few pitfalls and home truths as well.

Certainly, the actor factor rubs in how people on opposing sides of any issue, be it political or scientific, can contrive to almost wilfully misunderstand each other, over-react, and behave in a limited frame of reference. And when it comes down to it, that's what the psychology of race relations is all about.

London, November 1972

1. Personally, I would argue that the development of black tests is wrong, not because they are a political manoeuvre (which may well be unavoidable in this field now), but because they seem to me to misunderstand the sociological trends of what is happening. Concern with I Q is high nowadays not because of any growth in racism but because general progress in genetics inevitably has had social repercussions. The concern about *group* differences in I Q signals a deeper worry by *individuals* about their own place on the ladder – how fixed is it, how much is it under or out of control? People are worried about this now due to the perpetual competition involved in urban living. This has given economic psychology its recent impact (witness also the interest in theories of achievement and motivation). It is as though the size of the black man's I Q has replaced the size of his penis as the object of wonder, as an urban economic psychology replaced the more rural family/sexual psychology (cotton-picking Freudianism) of the thirties. In other words, I believe that black psychologists would have more to offer if they attempted to show how the system bends the I Q, as is done bittily in this book, or how intelligence may have different patterns in different groups of people as has been recently shown by Marsh and Bogen (1971).

For an introduction to black psychology, see the following:

GRIER, W. and COBBS, P. (1968), *Black Rage*, Anchor Books.

THOMAS, A. and SILLEN, S. (1972), *Racism and Psychiatry*, Brunner/Mazel.

WILCOX, R. C. (ed.) (1971), *The Psychological Consequences of Being a Black American*, Wiley.

WILLIAMS, R. L. (1972), 'The problem of match and mis-match in testing black children', paper read to the Annual Meeting of the American Psychological Association, Honolulu, Hawaii, September.

For details of 'alternative forms of intelligence' see:

HEIM, A. (1070), *Intelligence and Personality*, Penguin.

MARSH, J. (1971), 'Are there two kinds of thinking?' unpublished Ph.D. thesis, University of California, Riverside.

WATSON, P. (1971), 'Is woman nigger?' *New Society*, 6 May.

Part One
Aspects of Interracial Interaction

The first half of the book looks at the interracial situation itself and analyses it by breaking it down into three sections. The first section concentrates on the majority – or dominant – group; the second focuses on the reactions of subordinate – or minority – groups; and the third deals with some specific aspects of interpersonal interaction, when the people concerned are of a different race.

Interracial interaction is, of course, a fluid process and so any breakdown for the purposes of analysis will be to some extent arbitrary. Here, however, an attempt has been made to prevent this happening too much – and several of the chapters overlap slightly and analyse the same evidence from a different perspective. The final chapter of this first part, by Professor Richmond, though not specifically written as an overview of what has gone before, does piece together the evidence in a helpful way.

Section A
Focus on the Majority Group

This first section deliberately focuses on prejudice and racial awareness. Other psychological factors in the majority group have been researched, but none is in any way as important as prejudice (though some are considered in Part 2 of the book).

An obvious starting point for this section is the development of racial awareness and prejudice in children. After this the section considers the origins of prejudice within the person: first the emotional reasons, second the cognitive or intellectual reasons. These three chapters show why people are prejudiced and why prejudice takes the form it does. This leads naturally on to the final two chapters of this section – on techniques for *reducing* prejudice. These chapters are by American authors since experience on that side of the Atlantic is much more extensive. A difficulty running through all this, however, is the definition and identification of prejudice. Roger Jowell, in his chapter on the measurement of prejudice, tackles the problem. Since this is a fundamental point the chapter has been placed second to enable the reader to encounter the arguments as soon as seems sensible.

Chapter One
The Development of Racial Awareness and Prejudice in Children

Isidore Pushkin and Thelma Veness[1]

Dr Pushkin has had a varied career in teaching, industry and welfare and is now Head of the Department of Social Studies at Chiswick Polytechnic. His research during the period 1961–3, based on the Birkbeck Psychology Department, into ethnic preferences of young children, has been subject to a follow-up study now being evaluated.

Thelma Veness lectured in psychology at Birkbeck College from 1959 to 1968, when she moved to a Chair at the London Institute of Education. Her main research interests were in social and applied psychology. She was editor of the *British Journal of Social and Clinical Psychology* for several years, and was engaged when she died in 1971 in follow-up studies of her *School Leavers: Their Aspirations and Expectations*, and (with Mrs V. Norburn and Dr Pushkin) on ethnic preferences in young children.

There are those who believe that young children are unaware of ethnic differences: it is a view which, in Britain at least, received what may well have been taken as authoritative confirmation in a pamphlet issued by the (then) Ministry of Education in 1963. 'Young children seem to be quite unconscious of colour differences,' this said, 'and there is no more pleasing sight than to watch in some of our primary schools groups of children of different racial origins working and playing happily together. Here has been created quite naturally and effectively the kind of social climate in which differences of race or of colour are accepted as a matter of course and are simply not noticed.' We shall show below that the evidence goes against this view. This is hardly surprising; after all children do imitate and copy, and absorb the attitudes and behaviour of their parents and of other individuals important to them.

Parents themselves may in their turn be conforming unconsciously to whatever attitudes are held generally by the people among whom they work or live; they may be treating a particular out-group, like immigrants, as scapegoats and as an excuse when lamenting their own ills; or they may be complying with specified attitudes for expediency; and their children are exposed to the results. The late Professor Allport (1954), discussing how the young child acquires ethnic prejudice, distinguished 'adopting'

1. Professor Veness died in November 1971; Dr Pushkin revised and up-dated the chapter after her death.

it – when the child takes over attitudes and stereotypes from his family or his cultural environment – and 'developing' it as a style of life because (perhaps through his parents' way of handling him) he acquires suspicions, fears and hatreds that sooner or later fix on minority groups. These two ways may be and often are combined, for parents who transmit specific prejudices may be likely to handle their children in such a way as to develop in them a prejudiced nature also. The complex and interrelated nature of the problem can well be seen.

In this chapter, we shall try to render this interrelatedness a little more clearly. We begin by discussing the child's process of putting this part of his experience into categories, how he does this, what his reasons are and at what ages he does it. We then go on to discuss how and when preferences arise in him for a certain group and why. Finally, we attempt to link awareness of differences between ethnic groups to preferences and their link to prejudices. We try too, at the end, to establish the importance of certain kinds of experience in the acquisition of such prejudices as do exist in the child.

Ethnic categorization

More than forty years have elapsed since Lasker (1929), in *Race Attitudes in Children*, concluded from a mass of evidence gathered from many sources that there was recognition of racial differences in individuals by the child from about five years of age. There have been surprisingly few studies since then of ethnic awareness in young children. What has been done (and this goes for several countries) confirms that it shows itself at an early age. In one of the first studies, Horowitz (1936) found strong preferences among five-year-old white boys for their own group, and reported adverse comments on black boys from a few three- and four-year-olds.

Recognition

In a well-known study of 253 Negro children, in nursery and primary schools in America which were integrated in the north and segregated in the south, Clark and Clark (1947) found the children well able to identify a doll that looked liked a white or a coloured child; the proportions of them choosing correctly were as high as 77 per cent at age three, and rose consistently year by year to reach 100 per cent at age seven. In another study, Mary Goodman (1952) observed 103 Negro and white boys and girls at play and tested them with jig-saw puzzles, pictures, coloured clay for modelling and dolls. Three quarters of the children were aged four, and the rest just over or under. She attributed 'high awareness' of overall differences to 32 per cent of the children because of their clear perception of and consistent attention to colour and other racial properties, their concepts of racial differentiation and separation, and their frequent use of racial terms whilst doing the tests. A further 52 per cent were 'medium aware', since their perception of and attention to colour and other physical properties was clear but not consistent, and they used racial terms fairly often but not always accurately. In all, then, 84 per cent of these four-year-old children displayed a considerable degree of racial awareness.

Further evidence of the early development of racial awareness was found by Stevenson and Stewart (1958). However, among the 225 Negro and white children, aged three to seven, whom they tested in America, the three-year-olds had difficulty in discriminating between Negroes and whites, which this time were represented by line and coloured drawings. The older children, though, showed a consistent rise, year by year, in the average number of correct choices they made, and the seven-year-olds chose with ease. The authors were surprised to find such young children responding in a manner which indicated not only awareness of racial differences but also the use of stereotyped concepts. In another American study, Morland (1958) tested children in nursery schools in the segregated city in Virginia bearing the suggestive name Lynchburg. The Negro and white boys and girls he tested there were aged mainly between three and five years, with a few aged six. They attended one Negro and five white nursery schools. Each child was asked whether he or she saw a white (or coloured) person in a set of pictures they were shown and, if the answer was yes, to point to that person. Each child had sixteen chances (eight pictures, two questions each), and was scored 'high' on recognition if he missed none, 'medium' if he missed two or three, and 'low' if he missed more than three. The results showed, again, a regular progression by age in ability to recognize racial figures accurately, with a rapid spurt during the fourth year. High recognition ability rose from 13 per cent at age three to 59 per cent at four and 82 per cent at five among the boys, and from 16 per cent to 63 per cent and then to 94 per cent among the girls.

Outside the USA there is evidence from New Zealand. In one set of tests conducted by Vaughan (1963) to investigate stages in the development of the concept 'Maori', nearly 200 white children in Wellington, aged from four to twelve, were asked to discriminate white from Maori in tests using pictures and dolls. Dolls were correctly distinguished by 70 per cent, 75 per cent, 95 per cent and 100 per cent of the children at ages four to seven years, though they were not so good with the pictures.

One may well ask, does the perceptual discrimination displayed by children in all these tests refer only to dolls and pictures, or does it apply to people? Such doubts are dispelled by the comments of many of the subjects. For the moment here is just one example, Joan G. She was a Negro girl aged four years and five months, and was one of the children studied by Goodman (1952). 'My daddy's coloured. My mommy's coloured. The people that are white, they can go up. The people that are brown, they have to go down.'

Self-identification

'Which is the doll that looks like you?' was one of the questions put by Clark and Clark (1947) to the Negro children in their study. Correct choices rose from 36 per cent at age three to 87 per cent at age seven. The proportions were higher among the Negro and white children in the Stevenson and Stewart study which we mentioned earlier: 72 per cent at age four, 96 at ages six and seven. An interesting result – because it was slightly different – was Morland's at Lynchburg (1963); 72 per cent of the white children (aged between three and six) identified themselves correctly with one of the figures in a picture, but only 41 per cent of the Negro children did so. (Though Judith Porter, 1971, in a study of 184 Negro and 175 white Boston children aged three to five, also found that the Negro children identified themselves less correctly than did the white.) Vaughan (1964a), in New Zealand, similarly found that self-identification with picture figures and dolls was proportionately lower, age for age, among Maoris than among whites. (This in the four-to-nine-year age range.)

How are we to explain the differences between white children and Negro or Maori children in self-identification found in these tests? The Clarks found themselves faced with this problem, for the rise in proportion of their Negro children identifying themselves correctly with the dolls was not consistent. There was a fall from 66 per cent at the age four to 48 per cent at age five, followed by a rise to 68 per cent at age six. Some children who could make the perceptual discrimination in the recognition test failed to identify themselves correctly. The key to solving this problem was found, in general terms, in the results of the Clarks' preference tests.

Preferences

When the Clarks requested the children in their study to choose: a doll to play with, the 'nice' one, the one with the nice colour and the one that looked bad, a *majority* of these children rejected the coloured doll. Sixty-seven per cent preferred the white doll for play, 59 per cent for being nice and 60 per cent for having a nice colour: yet 59 per cent chose the coloured doll as the one that looked bad. The preference was clear even in the three-year-olds and was strong among the four-year-olds. Stevenson and Stewart found much the same; Negro choices of a doll of their own race as a playmate fell from 50 per cent at age three, to 39 per cent, 35 per cent and 33 per cent at ages four, five and six, respectively, before rising to 65 per cent at age seven. White children's own-race choices for a playmate rose steadily during this time from 52 per cent to 82 per cent. Again, most of Morland's white children (73 per cent) preferred to play with children of their own race, but a majority of the Negro children (58 per cent) preferred children of the other race (Morland, 1962). Vaughan (1964b), in New Zealand, found a general tendency among the Maori children to favour other race figures as playmates, the boys being seen as less mean, less lazy and cleverer, and the girls as kinder, cleaner and more honest. The white children, on the other hand, tended significantly to favour the figures of their own race.

In a London study of 172 white children aged between three and seven carried out by Pushkin (1967), 45 per cent were rated as showing attitudes unfavourable to Negroes in a tea-party doll choice test; 33 per cent at age three did this with a peak of 82 per cent at age six, though with a fall to 61 per cent at age seven. In choosing a companion doll on a see-saw test, choices unfavourable to Negroes rose from 44 per cent to 83 per cent between ages three and seven, with a peak at age six. Fifty-four of the children were rated unfavourable to Negroes in both tests; among these the proportion was highest in the age six group (at 65 per cent).

The conclusion to which K. B. Clark (1955) was led, considering the light thrown by his preference tests on the self-rejection in his earlier tests, was plain. 'The child's first awareness of racial differences is found to be associated with some rudimentary evaluation of these differences.' He continued: 'The child ... cannot learn what racial group he belongs to without being involved in a larger pattern of emotions, conflicts and desires which are part of his growing knowledge of what society thinks about his race.' Self-identification is being mastered as a concept while the child is still learning about the evalution of his own and other ethnic groups.

The personal and emotional content of the child's evaluation was indicated by what occurred during the Clarks' 'Colouring test'. The children with medium-brown and dark-brown skin colour, constituting 29 per cent of the group, coloured their own figure white or yellow or even red or green – though they coloured the leaf, apple, orange and mouse correctly. Some children were so moved emotionally in the dolls and the colouring tests as to be unable to continue. 'One little girl who had shown a clear preference for the white doll and who described the brown doll as "ugly" and "dirty" broke into a torrent of tears when she was asked to identify herself with one of the dolls ... some children looked at the investigator with terror or hostility. Many of these children had to be coaxed to finish the tests' (K. B. Clark, 1955).

The explanation of the differences in self-recognition between the white and the Negro or Maori children emerges in terms of a self-rejection by members of the minority groups and their self-identification with the dominant, more privileged race. Many other examples of such self-rejection can be found in the research literature. Some of the Negro children in Morland's study responded reluctantly and with evident emotional strain. One little Negro boy hung his head and said quietly, 'I guess I's a kinda coloured.' The drawings of Ruby, a six-year-old Negro girl, studied by Robert Coles (1968), an American psychiatrist, reveal her self-denigration. She was the only Negro child to enter one of the previously segregated schools in New Orleans. The school was boycotted for weeks by angry whites, in protest, and the girl was harassed on the way to school by a mob who hurled insults and obscenities at her; one white woman threatened to poison her. For months Ruby never used brown or black in her drawings, except to indicate soil or the ground. She drew white people larger than Negroes and more intact; her own face lacked an eye or an ear, and other Negro children had fingers or whole sets of toes missing; but white girls which she drew always had all their features – even the proper number of fingers. Among Negro children at a residential treatment centre at Cleveland, Ohio, a distinct and common conflict involving racial identity was found. Clear and repeated modes of reaction ranged from a phase of special sensitivity (as if the child awaited and expected 'blame' for being a Negro), to one of 'colour blindness', (in which any differences from whites were denied) and, after some improvement, to one in which a loyalty struggle emerged ('as if saying "Each time I improve I get a little whiter"'). Tom, aged twelve, said "One day I'll wake up and be white" (Chethick, Fleming, Mayer and McCoy, 1967).

Contrast the white child's rejection of minority group members. When children in Philadelphia, studied by Radke, Trager and Davis (1949), were shown a 'Barrier picture' depicting a child in the foreground watching a group of others at play, and were asked 'Will they [the whites] ask him [Negro] to play?' the answer was 'No' from 43 per cent of the kindergarten group (aged five to six), 67 per cent of the first grade (six to seven years) and 75 per cent in the second grade (seven to eight years), among the white children. One of a number of examples reported by Mary Goodman tells of David J., a white boy just under five years old. 'Whenever a choice is asked for (or volunteered), David states *both* his preference and his rejection, as though to underscore the former.' Shown the picture of a solitary brown boy, he multiplies his rejections. 'He's black. He's a stinky little boy – he's a stinker – he sh—! Take it away! I want another little boy.' His attitude is not merely to this particular boy, since he adds, 'I don't like coloured boys' (Goodman, 1952). On the other side of the Atlantic, six-year-old B., a white boy in the London study by Pushkin, stated his view of a Negro classmate tersely: 'If I have to sit near him I'll have a nervous breakdown.' He had been reported by his teacher to Pushkin as having a 'down' on coloured children, and he was rated 'consistently unfavourable' in the 'tea-party' and 'see-saw' tests in which he had to choose, using dolls of different colours, who to invite and sit next to at a tea party and share a see-saw with.

Conceptual criteria

In what terms do young children identify themselves and others so far as race is concerned? Can they grasp the distinctions of such features as skin colour, culture and of nationality which define different ethnic groups?

Skin colour, as such, was plainly an important factor in the development of attitudes among the children in the studies which we have considered so far. Mary Goodman based the awareness categories into which she placed her subjects partly on the clarity of their perception of colour and the consistency of their attention to it. And the Negro children studied by the Clarks showed that they could colour certain objects correctly in spite of the fact that they chose bizarre colours when drawing themselves. They observed, too, that many more southern children (about 80 per cent) coloured their preferences brown, compared with a little over one-third (36 per cent) of the northern children, and that most of the remarks made by the children while they were drawing were about the desirability or relative prettiness of one or other skin colour. In yet another investigation, Landreth and Johnson (1953) found that both white and Negro children responded to differences of skin colour at age *three* although their responses became more accentuated during the succeeding two years.

Skin colour is a most prominent characteristic, as we might expect. Differentiation based on it hardly requires the kind of abstract concepts which the young child might find it difficult – if not impossible – to grasp. More obvious characteristics are, then, the ones used by the *young* child to classify people in racial terms.

But skin colour does not always have the same significance. Why did the children with medium-brown and dark-brown skins who were tested by the Clarks tend to prefer the Negro doll to the white doll more than did the Negro children with lighter skins? Perhaps because their own darker colour made it less possible for them to place themselves, even in fantasy, with the white children. Perhaps, also, because the majority of the children with darker skins attended southern segregated schools, and so had less contact with white children than did the lighter-skinned northern children who mainly attended integrated schools. Judith Porter, in her study of Boston children, found an interaction between the type of school and shade of skin colour: in the segregated set-up, light-skinned Negro children showed more preference for their own race than did those with dark skins, while in the integrated situations the relationship was reversed. Moreover, skin colour differences were found by Laishley, in another recent study, to be of little more significance than awareness of differences in colour; black or brown skin colour did not appear to be negatively evaluated by these English children, who ranged in age from three years to just over five, sixty-one of them white, four coloured and three light-skinned, of mixed parentage. The fact that none of the areas in which the children lived was a 'high tension' area in regard to colour prejudice was regarded as a probable factor. The contact which children have, and especially the kind of contact, will be considered later in this chapter.

What other children are actually doing is also important in the tests. In the Bronx district of New York, being *Jewish* or *Catholic* was understood by children primarily in terms of *doing something*. The children – they were aged between three and ten – were Jewish, Catholic and Protestant (some were Negroes), and the population of their neighbourhood consisted of a majority of East European Jewish immigrants, together with considerable numbers of Irish, Italians, Puerto Ricans and Negroes. When asked 'What are you?' the youngest children (aged three-and-a-half to four-and-a-half) tended to give their own names (44 per cent) rather than to describe themselves as belonging to a particular racial or ethnic group (only 6 per cent did this) or indeed any other self-designation. In the next age group – four-and-a-half to six-and-a-half – however, 60 per cent did label themselves as members of a racial group and in the group between six-and-a-half and eight-and-a-half 80 per cent did so. A similar pattern, i.e. related to age, was found when the questions referred instead to the children's parents. Being Jewish was understood as a matter of 'talking Jewish' or going to synagogue or not eating bacon, for example, while being Catholic meant 'taking communion'. However, some older children did use more abstractions. In the six-and-a-half to eight-and-a-half group, for example, some Jewish children defined Jewish as 'nice, kind, friendly' or as 'your religion', or as 'God made us'. Directed questions about ethnic identity were just not understood by the youngest children. One boy, aged three-and-a-half, when asked 'Are you American?' replied 'No, I'm a cowboy'. Another, four-and-a-half, said he was not a Catholic, he was 'Richie', and one child who was asked 'Are you Jewish?' answered 'No, I'm only four, I'll get Jewish.' A four-year-old girl denied being American: her father was American she said, she was a girl (Hartley, Rosenbaum and Schwartz, 1948a, 1948b).

The children in the study carried out in Philadelphia (mentioned earlier) were given a number of picture tests, in which race or religion was suggested by differences in skin colour or by religious symbols. In the 'Religious symbol' picture, for example, children stood on the step of a synagogue or a church. The increasing rejection of Negroes related to age which was found in other studies was found again, with hostile responses directed at Jews by non-Jews, rising from 14 per cent to 44 per cent between five- and eight-year-olds. Between Catholics and Protestants, hostility rose from 20 per cent to 40 per cent in the same age range. The Negro and Jewish children who were tested often displayed negative self-attitudes, personal conflicts and feelings of insecurity resulting from anticipated rejection. The tester questioned the children both before and after identifying the race or religion of depicted figures in the tests, and it emerged that even the act of labelling resulted in increased hostility and rejection of people of other groups – presumably by eliciting further knowledge, ideas and feelings associated with them (Radke, Trager and Davis, 1949).

The kind of houses people lived in and the kind of jobs they had also contributed to the differentiation between races which these children made. They were shown figures of Negro and white men and women, who differed only in being coloured brown and white. Both groups were shown wearing dressy, working or shabby clothes to suggest different social, economic and occupational backgrounds. They were also shown two-dimensional plywood houses, both the single-family, red-brick, white-trimmed type usually associated with the middle and lower classes in the community, and the red-brown multi-occupation house with the run-down appearance of the slum. The great majority of the children, Negro and white, allocated the poor house to the Negro doll and the better house to the white doll; they considered that the race represented by the doll belonged 'to that type of house'. In a similar way inferior jobs, e.g. maid or porter, were attributed to Negroes by 38 per cent of the 152 white children; among the ninety Negro children, 16 per cent attributed inferior roles and circumstances to Negroes, based mainly upon money and housing. The authors of this study, Radke and Trager (1950), commented that the Negro child might not be expected to express stereotypes of status as openly or freely as White children, since these stereotypes tended to be disparaging to his own group. Interestingly, when describing what the doll figures might be doing, work was given to the Negro doll and leisure to the white one by 24 per cent of the white children, though 37 per cent of the Negro children reversed the roles and gave leisure to the Negro doll.

The placing of self and others by nationality involves more complex and abstract categories, which can be only minimally based on personal experience. As evidence of this, consider a study in Geneva in which children aged seven and eight were found (by Piaget and Weil, 1951) to be thinking of town and nation to which they belonged as juxtaposed. Not until the ages of ten or eleven was there a concrete, realistic concept of 'Swiss' as something embracing 'Genevese'. And similarly among Glasgow children, Jahoda (1962) reported that at the ages of six and seven there was very little understanding of 'home country' and 'foreign'. Jahoda said that although the children aged eight to nine had mastered these concepts, it was not until ten or eleven that geographical and historical concepts of an adult kind were grasped and that political and economic ideas made their appearance. These tendencies were broadly characteristic of the age levels, though with a very wide variation. Some of the youngest children had never heard of Glasgow, or thought of it as something vaguely nearby, and which did not usually include their own geographical location (Jahoda, 1963). The next step, an awareness of being within Glasgow, was indicated by a statement such as 'It's here where we are' – but boundaries were still vague and Scotland was thought of as being outside Glasgow. When, in a further step, Glasgow was understood to be in Scotland, the children were still unable to place Scotland in its wider setting, e.g. 'Scotland is a country. It's beside Wales and Ireland. Britain is mostly called Great Britain. It's sort of Scotland, another name for it.'

Children's difficulties in handling concepts of nationality are under-standable for, as Jahoda has pointed out (in his critical study of Piaget's stages), spatial, geographical and linguistic relationships, as well as those of logical inclusiveness, are involved. There are historical, political and legal factors also to add to the complexities. (If we stop to think there are probably a good many adults who are uncertain themselves about the nationality of, for example, Silesians who lived in Germany until their territory became part of Poland in a post-war settlement, or about the precise distinction between French and English Canadians, or between the numerous linguistic nationalities in India.)

That increasing references to themselves in national terms is common in children as they grow older was clearly shown by a study of groups aged six, ten and fourteen in London, Louvain, Amsterdam and Montreal (both French and English speaking). This was carried out by Lambert and Klineberg (1959) who found that answers to the questions 'What are you?' and 'What else are you?' were increasingly given in terms of nationality, as age rose, and less as being a child of this or that sex. (References to religion were variable.)

The question of *preferences* for different nationalities is, however, a different matter. In Britain, for example, Tajfel (1966) found six- and seven-year olds to be more *polarized* in stating which nations they preferred than in putting them in correct size order. This polarization was more strongly marked among these *young* children than among others aged nine to eleven. (But see chapter 4, by Tajfel.)

In another research into national attitudes (testing children with mean ages seven years three months, nine years and eleven years) it was found that as age rose so did the preference for England among nations (the others being Australia, China, France, Germany, India, Italy, Japan, Russia and the United States). With increasing age, too, the children were more able to understand that the nationals of 'disliked' and 'neutral' nations would express preference for *their* own countries – a preference which already at age seven was attributed to the nationals of 'liked' countries.

The reasons given by Jahoda's young Glasgow children for their national preferences were often inaccurate or irrelevant. For the youngest, Africa was nice and hot and had coconuts, or had lions, tigers, elephants and polar bears; India was the warmest place and you could play Indians there; in Rome the buildings sometimes fell down and New Zealand butter was too salty. In the eight-to-nine group, Africa was disliked because of the head hunters and India because 'there's still natives there and you might catch your foot in an elephant trap'. Not all was irrelevancy, however – Germany was still disliked because, for example, Hitler was bad, and Japan because it was a wartime enemy. One nine-year-old disliked Czechoslovakia because 'they were pushing about when they played Rangers'. With the ten-to-eleven-year-olds, there was greater emphasis on people and their characteristics: Russia became most disliked because, as one boy put it, 'Some of them are communists, and if you are Russian you can't get out of the country. I don't like this trying to get to the moon – it might do something to the world' (Jahoda, 1963). If only one could ignore the inaccuracies, irrelevancies and nonsense in many adult stereotypes of out-groups. One would be tempted to do this with the comment on Negro immigrants which a young mother in Willesden made, that they 'tie curtains into a knot – makes me feel horrible inside' (Pushkin, 1967), were it not for the behaviour to which such thoughts and feelings might lead. It might be the case, of course, that ethnic concepts and preferences in childhood persist, in some ways, later in life, and this is an issue which clearly requires investigation.

Consistency

We have been seeing, then, that the development of inter-group attitudes may be regarded, on the one hand, as a matter of increasing differentiation by the child, as he learns the defining properties of groups, the characteristic stereotypes attached to them and the behaviour usually adopted towards them by members of his own group. On the other hand, there is gradual integration of ethnic attitudes within each individual child (Harding *et al.*, 1954). Evidence of this comes in the form of inter-correlations between the results of different tests applied to the same child. As far back as 1936, E. L. Horowitz found correlations which were positive and which increased with age from five years, between a 'Ranks' test (requiring pictures of children's faces to be placed in order of liking), a 'Social Situations' test (involving the willingness to include Negroes in certain situations) and a 'Show Me' test (involving choice of companions for a varity of activities). More recently, in New Zealand, Vaughan (1964b) found that between four and twelve-year-olds there was an increasing consistency between children's responses in three attitude tests (Stereotypes, Picture preference and Doll preference) administered to Maori and Pakeha (white) children.

Even seven-year-old children, in a study by Kutner (1958) of patterns of mental functioning associated with prejudice, showed a marked consistency of attitude when responding to questions about Mexicans, Jews, Catholics, coloured people and so on. When older white children (aged this time between ten and seventeen) in a school in Virginia were asked to compare Negroes and whites on sixty personality traits, the attitudes of the younger ones were more vague and less stereotyped than those of the older ones, but still almost exclusively negative to the Negro out-group. The attitudes of the older children were, however, more crystallized and more differentiated (including, for example, 'happy-go-lucky', 'laughs', and 'sense of rhythm', together with less desirable traits such as 'ignorant' and 'lazy') (Blake and Dennis, 1943). To take a further illustration, Frenkel-Brunswik (1948) found in her well-known study of prejudice in children aged between eleven and sixteen results which indicated that already 'at these age levels children's reactions to statements about men and society, as well as their spontaneous formulations about these topics, form a more or less consistent pattern'. From their questionnaire responses it would appear that the ethnic attitudes of over 500 adolescents living near Boston had become largely stable before the ages of seventeen or eighteen, and to be less varied between members of this age group than among the fifteen- and sixteen-year-olds (Wilson, 1963). It is well to remember, however, that while consistency may be taken as indicating crystallization of attitudes, a less-than-complete consistency in a child may indicate no more than his failure to report all his associations about a given group in each of a set of tests. The behaviour of adults may, after all, reflect only part of the overall picture regarding their underlying ethnic attitudes, which may consequently appear to lack some consistency from one occasion to another.

Older children

When Koch (1946) in the USA made a sociometric study of preferences about race, nationality and skin-pigmentation of children aged from eight to eighteen, preferences for whites by white children rose in strength up to age sixteen. Negro children's preference for Negroes, which was little displayed at eight, was very strong at fourteen. When testing boys and girls from kindergarten age upwards on their choice of classmate to stay in the same class, or to sit near, Moreno (1934) found no differences in black and white children's preferences for their own group until age eleven. Criswell (1939), too, found the eleven-year-old grade as that at which mutual withdrawal of the races characteristically crystallized. However, among the younger children, even when race withdrawal did not occur, colour preferences might still be present.

In a more recent sociometric study of social relations between British and immigrant children aged between seven and fifteen in the west midlands, the subjects were asked to choose someone to sit by in class, to play with in the playground and to invite home to tea or to a party. Ninety per cent of the British children of all ages preferred British friends for all three purposes. Seventy-five per cent of Indians and 60 per cent of the West Indians likewise chose their own nationality, and there was a slight tendency for these in-group choices to increase as the children grew older (Rowley, 1968). However, in another similar study, this time carried out in a comprehensive mixed school, a boys' secondary modern school and a primary school, all in London and where the majority of all the groups of children (British-born white and immigrant Cypriot, West Indian or African) preferred their own group, little or no evidence of an age-related pattern was found (Kawwa, 1968a).

Preference might, of course, differ for different purposes. This did occur in one study, though without disturbing the association already revealed between increasing age and increasing in-group choice (in the majority group). High-school students in the USA were tested by Lundberg and Dickson (1952). The whole group – 1360 strong – was composed of non-Jewish and Jewish whites, Japanese, Negroes, Chinese and others. Choices of students, from another ethnic group, for leadership, friendship, working together, taking part in a picnic together and representing the school at a national meeting, were significantly less frequent among older members of the non-Jewish white group than among their younger fellow-students; conversely, however, such out-group choices among those of the minority groups were made mostly by the older members. While every ethnic group showed an overall preference for its own members, ethnocentrism was strongest among the non-Jewish whites and weakest among Jews so far as the choice of leaders was concerned, and strongest among Negroes and weakest among non-Jewish whites so far as the choice of friends was concerned.

Awareness, preferences and prejudice

The child's differentiation between his self and others, together with his racial identification, is mastered, then, in a context of learning about the relative social importance of his own and other groups, with the appropriate conflicts and emotions. In this complex, achieving final mastery of a discrimination may provide a focus for familiar attitudes and a point of reference for an already-present emotional meaning. Lasker (1929), for example, quoted evidence bearing this out and cited a little coloured boy aged four who called any child who made him angry 'nigger'. He thought of the word as something to make one angry because he saw other children get angry when they were called 'nigger'. The story of Janet, told by Allport (1954), also illustrates this point; this six-year-old ran home to her mother to ask the name of the children she was supposed to hate.

In the Philadelphia study, too, it was found that labelling the figure in the picture increased hostility felt by children towards the out-group, and this was also found at Lynchburg, where among Morland's white school-children there was a greater preference for whites among those with 'high recognition ability'.

Are preferences prejudice?

Should young children's ethnic preferences, even when evidently attributable to conscious, mastered discriminations and imbued with emotions, be regarded as ethnic prejudice? A distinction has been drawn between preference for the in-group member when there is a choice, with rejection of the out-group member, and acceptance of the latter when no choice is available.

What is involved here is the definition of racial or ethnic prejudice, which should presumably allow for a range of intensity in the way it is shown. Moreover, if the definition is made, with Allport (1954), in terms of 'an antipathy based upon a faulty and inflexible generalization', then we might be very ready to agree that such a generalization by a child is faulty but reluctant to accept one so young as being inflexible. To find (as Kutner did) that mental rigidity and intolerance of ambiguity were two major and typical features of the seven-year-old prejudiced children he was testing, need not lead to the assumption that later personality change cannot occur. Follow-up studies of prejudiced and unprejudiced children could throw some light on this problem, and proposals for such studies have been detailed (Jahoda, Veness and Pushkin, 1966).

Should children's doll choices and responses to pictures be regarded as valid indicators of prejudice or the lack of it? Is doll play in general meaningful in real life terms, or is it wish-fulfilling in relation to real life? While evidence on this latter question is conflicting, the more important point is that the preferences displayed by children in the play situations might be as true an expression of underlying attitudes as would real-life actions. It is difficult to explain consistency in individual children's play responses, in tests of ethnic choice, and differences in these between children in different areas, without assuming some psychologically meaningful correspondence between play performance in tests and everyday life experience.

Acquisition: parental influence

That attitudes of children towards Negroes seem to have their origin with the parents. That was the conclusion drawn from a study of schoolchildren carried out in the southern USA in 1938. 'Apparently, the parents give direct instruction in the attitudes and cannot recall having done so; further, the children develop their attitudes, at first quite well aware of their sources, but towards adolescence, tending to lose conscious recollection of these origins, devise rationalizations of various sorts to support them, and maintain them little changed' (Horowitz and Horowitz, 1938). However, a majority (69 per cent) of 437 students tested by Allport and Kramer (1946) thought that they *had* been influenced by their parents' attitudes, the prejudiced students particularly reporting having done this.

In the Philadelphia study, in which children aged six and seven were compared with their parents in respect of ethnic attitudes, points of similarity of direction were found, but the children tended to be highly rejecting of Negroes regardless of their parents' reactions (Radke-Yarrow, Trager and Miller, 1952). Attitudes to Negro 'infiltration' into certain Minneapolis neighbourhoods were the subject of another study, also comparing parents with their children (aged in this case between nine and eleven). Questionnaires put to the children referring to Japanese, Indians, Negroes, Jews and non-Jewish whites asked which ones were most likely to cheat, to get into trouble with teachers and other boys or girls, which were the nicest families and whether they would be accepted as neighbours. The parents were questioned about their reactions to residence in the neighbourhood by members of these out-groups, to personal contact, friendship and association with them, and to their own children joining with children from those groups in play or membership of organizations. The resemblances between parents' attitudes and those of their children were strong – statistically reliable – but while the parents were more prejudiced towards Negroes than towards Jews, the children, (white and Negro) held both groups in equal disfavour. 'Since very few Jewish children lived in either of the two districts, it appears probable that both white and Negro children were orientated in their responses by an unconsciously held but subtle and pervasive stereotype of what Jewish children are expected to be like.' Parental attitudes were therefore clearly not the only source of influence (Bird, Monachesi and Burdick, 1952a). The same authors, however, in a further study (1952b), reported that the children who said that their parents had told them not to play with Negroes were more prejudiced than those who were not aware of such restraint.

Older children aged twelve and thirteen, in Ohio, were studied by Mosher and Scodel (1960), by means of a social distance test which focused on ten ethnic groups. Their ethnic attitudes were significantly related to those of their mothers. The questionnaires which the mothers completed also provided information about their child-rearing attitudes, but no significant relationship between these and the children's ethnic attitudes was found.

But this latter result runs counter to the general findings of *The Authoritarian Personality* study by Adorno *et al.* (1950) (see chapter 3 of this book) and of the associated study of adolescents aged between eleven and sixteen by Frenkel-Brunswik (1948). These claimed to show that harsh and rigid forms of discipline were a central feature in the upbringing of prejudiced adults and adolescents. An association between authoritarian parental attitudes to child control and intolerance of children's annoying behaviour on the one hand, and prejudice in their children on the other, was also found by Gough, Harris and Martin (1950) in a study of 242 Minneapolis children aged between ten and twelve years.

In the London study by Pushkin previously mentioned, the ethnic attitudes of 172 white children aged from three to seven, in nursery as well as infant schools, were compared with both the ethnic and the child-rearing attitudes of their mothers. The child was asked, first, to select from twelve Negro and white boy and girl dolls those to be invited to a tea party at home, and then those to share play on a see-saw; finally, the child played with six sets of family cards (mother, father, boy and girl) on which two white, two Negro, one Indian and one Mediterranean family were represented by line drawings, and was asked to place each boy or girl card against one of a row of eight picture-houses, in which a penultimate house was occupied by the child's 'self-card'. Structured interviews with the children's mothers were concerned mainly with their ethnic attitudes and their attitudes to child control. No association between the ethnic attitude of the child and the child-control attitude of its mother was found, nor any *general* relationship between the ethnic attitude of mother and that of the child. However, fifty-four children who were rated 'consistently unfavourable' to Negroes in the doll-choice tests tended significantly to have mothers rated 'very hostile' in ethnic attitude; from which it would appear that ethnic attitudes, if strongly expressed by the mothers, were reflected in their young children.

Contact

When white children in New York were found by Horowitz to be as prejudiced as those in the segregated south, he concluded that it was not the degree of contact with Negroes which chiefly influenced them, but their contact with the prevailing attitude towards Negroes. In the study in Philadelphia, the children showed a heightened awareness of Italian, Catholic and Jewish groups in the neighbourhood where tensions existed between these groups; in another neighbourhood, where differences between Protestants and Catholics were pronounced, these were the in- and out-groups. In New Zealand, white children aged eight, twelve and sixteen had much greater contact with Maori schoolfellows in Auckland (North Island), with its larger Maori population, than was true of the children in Christchurch (South Island); and whereas attitudes unfavourable to the Maoris increased significantly between eight and twelve years in both places, between twelve and sixteen it increased only in the low-contact Christchurch setting, leading Vaughan and Thompson (1961) to conclude that the greater amount of contact available to the white Auckland children was connected with the lesser prejudice there. In addition, the contact was between roughly equal status groups, since both white and Maori children came from predominantly working-class areas in both cities. (Support was provided, in this result, for Allport's view that contacts of equal occupational status tend to lessen prejudice – but see chapters 5 and 10 of this book.)

The kind of contact was found to be an important factor in Pushkin's London study. It was conducted in three areas, two of which (Willesden and Tottenham) contained immigrant Negro populations of approximately equal proportions and recency of arrival, while the third (North Finchley) had no Negro inhabitants. In one contact area (Willesden), pervaded by tensions and adult hostility to the Negro out-group, the white children tended to develop significantly greater hostility to the Negro, regardless of their mothers' ethnic attitudes, compared with the other contact area (Tottenham), where relatively harmonious inter-group relations prevailed. In Tottenham, with the better racial climate, the children were closer in their attitudes to those in the third, non-contact area, than to those in the tension area. Yet, older London children, in a comprehensive school in Islington, where they and their families were in constant contact with immigrants, both Cypriot and Negro, were found to be far more prejudiced in their responses to an open-ended questionnaire than were secondary modern school-children in Lowestoft who were the same age (eleven to seventeen), and in whose town immigrants were almost non-existent. However, the few Lowestoft children who displayed very marked prejudices mentioned relatives in London and Ipswich who had been badly affected by the existence of immigrants in their midst, so that here too it appears to have been not contact alone but the kind of contact which was influential (Kawwa, 1968b).

Exposure to prejudiced attitudes may lead to their adoption by the child despite parental admonitions of tolerance and brotherhood, as K. B. Clark has observed – and the school may be the contact medium. Negative ideas may be contributed by other parents through their children; or by teachers whose own prejudice or discrimination is noticed, or whose teaching may unwittingly nourish prejudices against those of other religions or against the allegedly innately inferior members of other 'races'. However, the teacher may make a positive contribution through the content of the teaching of history, geography, biology, social studies and religious ideas, setting straight the conventional but biased and inaccurate historical record, providing information about the details of daily life and problems of other peoples, disposing of invalid concepts of race and racial differences, valuing the cultural achievements of other nations in their diversities and upholding religious tolerance and co-operation as against exclusiveness. In Britain, for example, the Schools Council spent several thousand pounds producing a 'kit' for teaching 'race' in schools. No one as yet knows whether it will be successful and acceptable enough. Anyway there has been quite a lot of opposition to it. Critics believe the field to be inadequately researched, and that racial awareness may only be heightened by such methods and, possibly, tension increased.

Nevertheless, parents, teachers, religious leaders and others who make efforts to instil positive ethnic attitudes in children, based on concepts of equality and human rights, may be frustrated by forces of prejudice in society at large, which they cannot entirely ignore if their own efforts are not to be overwhelmed.

References

ADORNO, T. W., FRENKEL-BRUNSWIK, E., LEVINSON, D. J., and SANFORD, R.N. (1950), *The Authoritarian Personality*, Harper.

ALLPORT, G. W. (1954), *The Nature of Prejudice*, Addison-Wesley.

ALLPORT, G. W., and KRAMER, B. M. (1946), 'Some roots of prejudice', *Journal of Psychology*, no. 22, pp. 9–39.

BIRD, C., MONACHESI, E. D., and BURDICK, H. (1952a), 'Infiltration and the attitudes of white and Negro parents and children', *Journal of Abnormal and Social Psychology*, no. 47, pp. 688–99.

BIRD, C., MONACHESI, E. D., and BURDICK, H. (1952b), 'Studies of group tensions, 3. The effect of parental discouragement of play activities upon the attitudes of white children towards Negroes', *Child Development*, no. 23, pp. 295–306.

BLAKE, R., and DENNIS, W. (1943), 'The development of stereotypes concerning the Negro', *Journal of Abnormal and Social Psychology*, no. 38, pp. 525–31.

CHETHICK, M., FLEMING, E., MEYER, M. F., and McCOY, J. N. (1967), 'Quest for identity', *American Journal of Orthopsychiatry*, no. 37, pp. 71–7.

CLARK, K. B. (1955), *Prejudice and Your Child*, Beacon Press.

CLARK, K. B., and CLARK, M. P. (1947), 'Racial identification and preference in Negro children', in T. L. Newcomb, and E. L. Hartley (eds.), *Readings in Social Psychology*, Holt.

COLES, R. (1968), *Children of Crisis*, Faber.

CRISWELL, J. H. (1939), 'A sociometric study of race cleavage in the classroom', *Archives of Psychology*, vol. 33, no. 235, pp. 5–82.

FRENKEL-BRUNSWIK, E. (1948), 'A study of prejudice in children', *Human Relations*, vol. 1, pp. 295–306.

GOODMAN, M. E. (1952), *Race Awareness in Young Children*, Addison-Wesley.

GOUGH, H. G., HARRIS, D. B., and MARTIN, W. E. (1950), 'Children's ethnic attitudes, 2: relationship to parental beliefs concerning child training', *Child Development*, no. 21, pp. 170–81.

HARDING, J. *et al.* (1954), 'Prejudice and ethnic relations', in G. Lindzey (ed.), *Handbook of Social Psychology*, vol. 2, 1st edn., Addison-Wesley

HARTLEY, E. L., ROSENBAUM, M., and SCHWARTZ, S. (1948a), 'Children's use of ethnic frames of reference', *Journal of Psychology*, no. 26, pp. 367–86.

HARTLEY, E. L., ROSENBAUM, M., and SCHWARTZ, S. (1948b), 'Children's perception of ethnic group membership', *Journal of Psychology*, no. 26, pp. 387–98.

HOROWITZ, E. L. (1936), 'The development of attitudes towards the Negro', *Archives of Psychology*, no. 194.

HOROWITZ, E. L., and HOROWITZ, R. E. (1938), 'Development of social attitudes in children', *Sociometry*, no. 1, pp. 307–38.

JAHODA, G. (1962), 'Development of Scottish children's ideas and attitudes about other countries', *Journal of Social Psychology*, no. 58, pp. 91–108.

JAHODA, G. (1963), 'Children's concepts of nationality: a critical study of Piaget's stages', *Child Development*, no. 35, pp. 1081–92.

JAHODA, G., VENESS, T., and PUSHKIN, I. (1966), 'Awareness of ethnic differences in young children: proposals for a British study', *Race*, vol. 8, no. 1, pp. 63–74.

KAWWA, T. (1968a), 'Three sociometric studies of ethnic relations in London schools', *Race*, vol. 10, no. 2, pp. 173–80.

KAWWA, T. (1968b), 'A survey of ethnic attitudes of some British secondary school pupils', *British Journal of Social and Clinical Psychology*, pp. 161–8.

KOCH, H. L. (1946), 'The social distance test between certain racial, nationality and skin-pigmentation groups in selected populations of American schoolchildren', *Journal of Genetic Psychology*, no. 68, pp. 63–95.

KUTNER, B. (1958), 'Patterns of mental functioning associated with prejudice in children', *Psychology Monographs*, vol. 72, no. 460.

LAISHLEY, T. (1971), 'Skin colour awareness and reference in London nursery-school children,' *Race*, vol. 13, no. 1, pp. 47–64.

LAMBERT, W. E., and KLINEBERG, O. (1959), 'A pilot study of the origins and development of national stereotypes', *International Social Science Journal*, no. 11, pp. 221–38.

LANDRETH, C., and JOHNSON, B. C. (1953), 'Young children's responses to a picture and inset test assigned to reveal reactions to persons of different skin colour', *Child Development*, no. 24, pp. 63–80.

LASKER, B. (1929), *Race Attitudes in Children*, Holt.

LUNDBERG, G. A., and DICKSON, L. (1952), 'Selective association among ethnic groups in a high school population', *American Sociological Review*, no. 17, pp. 22–35.

MIDDLETON, M. R., TAJFEL, H. and JOHNSON, G. B. (1970), 'Cognitive and affective aspects of children's national attitudes', *British Journal of Sociology and clinical Psychology*, vol. 9, pp. 122–34.

Ministry of Education (1963), *English for Immigrants*, pamphlet no. 43, HMSO.

MORENO, J. L. (1934), *Who Shall Survive?*, Nervous and Mental Disorders Publishing Co.

MORLAND, J. K. (1958), 'Racial recognition by nursery school children in Lynchburg, Virginia', *Social Forces*, no. 37, pp. 132–7.

MORLAND, J. K. (1962), 'Racial acceptance and preference of nursery school children in a southern city', *Merrill-Palmer Quarterly*, no. 8, pp. 271–80.

MORLAND, J. K. (1963), 'Racial self-identification: a study of nursery school children', *American Catholic Sociological Review*, no. 24, pp. 231–42.

MOSHER, D. L., and SCODEL, A. (1960), 'Relationship between ethnocentrism in children and the ethnocentrism and child-rearing practices of their mothers', *Child Development*, no. 31, pp. 369–76.

PIAGET, J., and WEIL, A. (1951), 'The development in children of the idea of the homeland and of relations with other countries', *International Social Science Bulletin*, vol. 3, pp. 561–78.

PORTER, J. D. R. (1971), *Black Child, White Child*, Harvard University Press.

PUSHKIN, I. (1967), 'A study of ethnic choice in the play of young children in three London districts', unpublished Ph.D. thesis, University of London.

RADKE, M. J., and TRAGER, H. G. (1950), 'Children's perception of the social roles of Negroes and whites', *Journal of Psychology*, no. 29, pp. 3–33.

RADKE, M. J., TRAGER, H. G., and DAVIS, H. (1949), 'Social perceptions and attitudes of children', *Genetic Psychology Monograph*, no. 40, pp. 327–447.

RADKE-YARROW, M., TRAGER, H. G., and MILLER, J. (1952), 'The role of parents in the development of children's ethnic attitudes', *Child Development*, no. 23, pp. 13–53.

ROWLEY, K. G. (1968), 'Social relations between British and immigrant children', *Educational Research*, vol. 10, pp. 145–8.

STEVENSON, H. W., and STEWART, E. C. (1958), 'A developmental study of racial awareness in young children', *Child Development*, no. 29, pp. 399–409.

TAJFEL, H. (1966), 'Children and foreigners', *New Society*, no. 196, pp. 9–11.

WILSON, W. C. (1963), 'Development of ethnic attitudes in adolescence', *Child Development*, no. 34, pp. 249–56.

VAUGHAN, G. M. (1963), 'Concept formation and the development of ethnic awareness', *Journal of Genetic Psychology*, no. 103, pp. 119–30.

VAUGHAN, G. M. (1964a), 'Ethnic awareness in relation to minority group membership', *Journal of Genetic Psychology*, no. 105, pp. 119–30.

VAUGHAN, G. M. (1964b), 'The development of ethnic attitudes in New Zealand school-children', *Genetic Psychology Monograph*, no. 70, pp. 135–75.

VAUGHAN, G. M., and THOMPSON, R. H. T. (1961), 'New Zealand children's attitudes towards Maoris', *Journal of Abnormal and Social Psychology*, no. 62, pp. 701–4.

Chapter 2
The Measurement of Prejudice

Roger Jowell

Roger Jowell was born in South Africa and is now co-director of Social and Community Planning Research, an institute for social survey research in London. Over the past eight years he has been responsible for a variety of surveys into urban problems and has written articles in *Race, Race Today, New Society* and *Built Environment*. He also lectures frequently on survey research methodology.

It is already well established that the verb 'to be prejudiced' is hardly ever used in its first person singular – which renders its direct measurement extremely difficult. Yet, even without scientific measurement, we still know that prejudice has been around for a very long time, as the following extract from Dickens's *Little Dorrit* suggests:

In the first place they (the English) were vaguely persuaded that every foreigner had a knife about him; in the second, they held it to be a sound constitutional national axiom that he ought to go home to his own country ... In the third place, they had a notion that it was a sort of Divine Visitation upon a foreigner that he was not an Englishman, and that all kinds of calamities happened to his country because it did things that England did not, and did not do things that England did ... They believed that foreigners were always immoral and ... had no independent spirit ... Although he (the foreigner) could never hope to be an Englishman, still it would be hard to visit that affliction on his head. They began to accomodate themselves to his level ... but treating him like a baby, and laughing immoderately at his lively gestures and childish English – more, because he didn't mind it, and laughed too. They spoke to him in very loud voices as if he were stone deaf. They constructed sentences, by way of teaching him the language in its purity, such as were addressed by the savages to Captain Cook, or by Friday to Robinson Crusoe.

We also know that, with perhaps a few modifications, Dickens could have written a similar piece today. On this evidence, therefore, whatever the precise meaning of 'prejudice' may be, we certainly know that it is slow to change. And it is tempting to ask why on earth we should bother to measure it and not channel our resources instead into attempts at its reduction or elimination. So before describing some of the traditional and newer methods of quantifying racial prejudice, it is necessary to make the case for measurement in the first place.

The fact is that 'quantification' has become a kind of academic necessity; non-quantifiable phenomena are somehow regarded as less precise and to be taken less seriously. The development of measurement techniques within the social and behavioural sciences has, in many ways, corresponded to the development of the disciplines themselves and, in particular, to the mystique which surrounds them. Countless books and learned articles have been written about techniques of attitude measurement; arguments have been conducted *ad nauseam* about the relative reliability of different attitude scales; an inordinate amount of time has been taken up with the whole question of precision; and the magic of assigning numbers or scores to attitudes or behaviour has exercised social scientists for the last forty years or so. But, fruitless as the task may have appeared, the progress has been of considerable value far beyond the confines of academic endeavour. The fact is that there is a considerable investment – in both Britain and the United States – in policies and agencies designed to reduce the incidence of racial discrimination. What measurement techniques can now contribute is the ability to monitor the effectiveness of these policies, to see where they are inadequate, in what ways (if any) they are producing change, which categories of discrimination they are affecting and which groups of people they are influencing. Moreover, since the whole area of intergroup relations is subject to dramatic change as a result of different (and often conflicting) stimuli, the need to measure variations over time has become both socially and politically more important.

There may well be a case, however, for saying that the type of measuring tools needed are not finely calibrated instruments but rough-and-ready devices which can be used at short notice and are geared towards the identification of only broad movements in attitude or behaviour. And there is no doubt that social scientific measurement has often been much more concerned with the precision of its scaling techniques than with what the scales are trying to measure. There is a plethora of literature on the extent to which given attitude measurements may differ from the truth; yet all too often the truth itself remains ill-defined and open to a variety of interpretations.

C. W. Churchman (1971) suggests that measurement should be 'a decision-making activity designed to accomplish an objective'. And this not only implies a very careful definition of objectives but a deliberate assessment of whether or not the target in question is indeed capable of measurement. The view, neatly quoted by Abraham Kaplan (1971), that 'if you can measure it, that ain't it', has happily become less prevalent than it used to be. But there are still many sceptics – both within and outside the social sciences – who believe that human minds are too subtle or too varied to lend themselves to the type of systematic measurement which has, until recently, been the preserve of the pure sciences. Attitude measurements, they claim, do violence to the individuality of human beings and cannot hope to encapsulate the complexity of motivations, fears, prejudices and conflicts inherent in attitude formation. And their claim is, of course, correct. No single measurement can hope to encapsulate so many different abstractions; and, for this reason, the definition of objectives becomes even more crucial to the success or otherwise of the measurements themselves.

Attitude measurements are not, of course, designed to tell the whole story; nor indeed are any other kinds of measurement. When we measure the weight of an object it tells us little about its size or shape; when we measure intelligence (as has often been pointed out) it indicates very little about creativity or even perhaps potential intelligence. The objective of measurement is usually extremely limited – and should frequently be even more limited. Its application should always therefore be equally limited, and this is probably more true of racial attitude measurements than of most others. The first task is to decide precisely what aspect of race relations we are trying to measure. Then we need to ask whether or not it is capable of measurement by the techniques at our disposal and the constraints operating on their use. And only finally do we need to decide whether or not the likely levels of accuracy we will achieve are sufficiently high to meet our objectives.

All this implies an appreciation of at least some of the components of racial attitudes and behaviour. Later chapters will discuss in more detail the range of these variables, the motivations behind them and the extent of overlap between them. In this chapter my aim is to simplify (without, I hope, too much oversimplification) the categorization in order to illustrate some of the problems which beset any serious attempt to measure the intensity of racial prejudice or the incidence of racial discrimination.

In the first place, what are we trying to measure? Allport (1954) distinguished five degrees of antipathy to outgroups in terms of the extent of 'energy' displayed by the perpetrator:

Antilocution. This relatively harmless form of hostility simply involves talking about one's prejudices and may not go any further. But, of course, the antilocution can be mild or strong and provides real problems for the researcher: if he is measuring verbalized attitudes only, for example, he cannot be sure of whether or not the antipathy is restricted to verbal hostility.

Avoidance. If the antipathy is stronger, the individual will take steps to avoid members of the outgroup. This may often involve inconvenience to himself and does no direct harm to those he is avoiding.

Discrimination. This stage, in Allport's scale, marks the beginning of 'detrimental distinctions of an active sort'. The perpetrator takes steps to exclude members of the out-group from facilities, privileges or rights which others enjoy. When this form of antipathy becomes institutionalized, either legally or by custom, the society becomes segregated.

Physical attack. The antipathy between groups – under conditions of 'heightened emotion' – may lead to this further stage of violence or semi-violence.

Extermination. This is, of course, the ultimate stage of intergroup hostility, and includes genocide, lynchings and other mass violence.

Allport admits that his scale is not mathematically constructed and serves simply as an indicator of the diverse range of activities which group antipathy may generate. He points out that, while the individual may never move from one stage to the next, 'still it is true that activity on one level makes transition to a more intense level easier'. And he remarks on the 'fateful progression' during this century from one level to the next.

In practice, however, the suggestion of a continuum in Allport's scale is rather misleading. The five degrees of antipathy which he described need not be (and often are not) sequential. Active discrimination may take place – particularly when it is institutionalized – without first going through the intermediate stages of antilocution or avoidance; and even lynching (or other forms of Allport's ultimate stage) may be practised by some individuals, not on account of their own prejudice, but on the basis of compelling social pressures. So one cannot invariably assume that the existence of one of these stages in a particular population automatically implies that the population has passed through each of the other stages. Or, more accurately, one cannot assume that an individual (or group of individuals) will fit so neatly into any such sequential model. The first lesson we must learn is that there is no necessary correlation between an individual's attitudes and his behaviour, or between prejudice and dis-crimination.

There are at least four typologies – which derive simply from the two variables:

The non-prejudiced non-discriminator. This group, which probably forms a small minority of most populations, shows no signs of hostility towards groups or individuals (on account of their race or ethnic group) either in expressed attitudes or in behaviour.

The non-prejudiced discriminator. This group shows no attitudinal ten-dency to be hostile, but nevertheless behaves in a discriminatory way towards members of another racial group. The motivation may, of course, be the imputed prejudice of others, as, for example, in the case of non-prejudiced suburban dwellers who refuse to sell their houses to members of another racial group for fear of incurring the wrath of their neighbours – but not through any hostility on their own part. The British excuse for discrimination has frequently been along these lines, i.e. 'We don't mind at all, but what will our customers/neighbours/employees say!' In some cases this is probably a genuine stance and the role is that of the non-prejudiced discriminator.

The prejudiced non-discriminator. This group – despite its own hostility towards members of another racial group – does not translate its feelings into discriminatory actions. Again, the constraint may be imposed by social pressures or by other motivations, e.g. politeness or compassion. Nevertheless, the outward manifestations of prejudice (or the behavioural stages) are absent.

The prejudiced discriminator. Finally, within this group, there is a strong correlation between attitudes and behaviour. Like the first group, they behave as they feel; they act as they think.

This typology is again an oversimplification of the gradations of prejudice and discrimination: it takes no account of the different types of attitude which may constitute prejudice, or of the different levels of prejudice, or of the different types of target for prejudice. Nevertheless it makes the distinction between attitudes and behaviour which is a necessary starting-point for anyone researching in this area. The existence of a frequent dissonance between prejudice and discrimination is, of course, widely documented, but probably the two most celebrated examples of it are the studies by La Piere (1936) and Kutner, Wilkins and Yarrow (1952). In both these studies, the authors showed one set of behaviour patterns by hoteliers and restaurateurs in accommodating or serving members of minority groups; and a completely opposite set of attitude patterns when requested for a statement of their policy, either by telephone or letter. In both cases, the incidence of face-to-face refusals of service was extremely low, whereas the incidence of telephone and written refusals was strikingly high. What the hoteliers and restaurateurs were reflecting in their *policies* was a stereotype of the minority groups which made them unacceptable a clients. What they had reflected in their *behaviour*, however, was a pre-disposition to act in a polite and civil way when faced by polite and respectable clients.

But even the question of stereotyping – crucial to the measurement of prejudice – needs to be analysed and defined before it can be measured. Bettelheim and Janowitz (1950) drew a distinction between two different types of outgroup stereotyping, the first of which (the superego variety) ascribed traits such as over-ambition, craftiness, shrewdness, clannishness and slyness. By way of contrast, the id variety ascribed traits such as lack of ambition, stupidity, laziness, lack of inhibition, dirtiness, smelliness and over-sexiness. The prejudiced person thus projects his own feelings onto the target group. And, in practice, as Allport ingeniously illustrates, these two varieties of stereotyping are curiously interchangeable:

'MR X: The Jews think of nothing but money; that is why there are so many Jewish bankers.
MR Y: But a recent study shows that the percentage of Jews in the banking business is negligible, far smaller than the percentage of non-Jews.
MR X: That's just it; they don't go in for respectable business; they are only in the movie business or run night clubs.'

The same kind of interchangeable stereotyping is currently prevalent in Britain, where the contradictory complaint often expressed against immigrants is that 'they simply live off unemployment benefit and take all our jobs'.

So can we believe any verbal measurement of prejudice when it appears to be both inconsistent and imperfectly correlated with behaviour?

The fact is that we should not *anticipate* logical or rational responses to questions dealing with complicated phenomena like prejudice; and we should not even try to infer behaviour patterns from expressed attitudes. So we can 'believe' verbal measurements provided that we do not try to widen their application. In any case, measurement itself is an abstraction: any figure which purports to tell us the proportion of prejudice in the UK or USA tells us only what our definitions allow it to tell us. In a recent major survey in Britain (Abrams, 1969) arguments raged for months after publication over whether the 'true' proportion of prejudiced people in the British population was nearer 25 per cent or 50 per cent. In practice, of course, the critics were not arguing over 'true' proportions; they were arguing over the types of verbal expression which constituted prejudice. Abrams's definition of prejudice was simply different from their own, even though they were based on the same data derived from the same questionnaire.

In any case, the least interesting aspect of any *single* survey of racial prejudice is the figure indicating an overall level of its incidence. Prejudice is a relative concept: it is of little value to know that 50 per cent of the population is prejudiced, unless we intend to monitor the level over time. And, if we do, then it does not really matter whether we call the percentage

50 per cent or 25 per cent, as long as we use the same basis for calculating the percentage on the next occasion. So a series of surveys can be invaluable for looking at changes in the population over time; and they enable us to search for patterns which may emerge in response to external stimuli – such as legislation against discrimination, immigration controls, race riots, and so on. But a single survey tells us more about the distribution of prejudice than its incidence: which groups in the population are more prejudiced than others; what types of prejudice are more prevalent than others; which groups of people are the main targets for prejudice; in which situations prejudice is most likely to occur.

Nevertheless, the question still remains as to whether these measurements provide anything other than interesting material on the nature of our society. If prejudice and discrimination are not perfectly correlated, would it not be better to measure the levels of discrimination so that we know how to reduce their incidence?

In practice, of course, we need to do both. As the typology given earlier suggests, discrimination usually stems from prejudice (either one's own or other people's) and the two are integrally linked – if not perfectly correlated. If the level of prejudice is reduced, it will almost certainly have the (ultimate) effect of reducing the level of discrimination. More frequently, however, it seems to work the other way around: changes in behaviour (induced either by legislation or enforced contact) will usually generate changes in attitude which, in turn, will generate further changes in behaviour, and so on. A society determined to improve race relations therefore needs to be aware of the stimuli which best promote changes and those which are counterproductive. And this implies repeated and systematic measurements of both attitudes and behaviour. There are, in fact, several techniques which we can employ:

The opinion survey

In its simplest form, this type of attitude measurement consists of asking a series of questions of a representative group of respondents and tabulating the answers. It measures the existence and distribution of particular attitudes but does not usually concern itself with the intensity of feeling behind the expressed attitudes. The cursory version of this form of survey is the opinion poll, which has increasingly been adopted by the media as their very special form of attitude measurement. Do opinion polls actually tell us anything about attitudes?

In trying to assess opinion polls as a legitimate tool of attitude measurement, we need to accept that they are, at best, a very shorthand form of survey research, usually restricted to a handful of arbitrary questions. As an indicator of prevailing attitudes, therefore, the poll measurement is extremely suspect, despite its undeniable influence on government policies, or at least on the thinking of legislators. Few people would claim, however, that any reliable assessment of racial attitudes could conceivably be made on the basis of one or two questions, however closely analysed. Yet, if the same questions are repeated at regular intervals, the *trend* is certainly likely to be illuminating.

In the United States, for example, the first national survey of white attitudes towards Negroes was conducted in 1942 and a number of the same questions have been repeated in subsequent polls ever since. The trend, as reported by Hyman and Sheatsley (1964), tells a dramatic story. The following figures show the percentage of whites who said – in each of three different years – that whites and Negroes should attend the same schools:

Year of poll	All whites	Northern whites	Southern whites
1942	30	40	2
1956	49	61	14
1963	62	74	32

So, simply on the basis of one question – repeated at certain intervals – we can learn a great deal about both the direction and distribution of prejudiced attitudes. It tells us nothing, however, about changes in the intensity of racial prejudice or in the propensity to discriminate (tempting as it may be to draw one's own conclusions). Once we have an anchor (the 1942 figure) we can relate subsequent results to it, even though no real reliance can be placed on any of the precise percentages. All that the polls can discover is whether or not the situation is getting better or worse and whether or not the distribution is changing. Moreover, the fluctuations in attitudes (provided they are marked) can be related to particular events, e.g. a Supreme Court decision or a new piece of legislation, to monitor their effects.

Sheatsley (1966) used poll series data for this purpose in looking at the growth of white backlash in response to the progress of black militancy. He first looked at individual answers from white samples which suggested that the backlash was growing:

1964: 87 per cent felt that riots in New York, Rochester and Jersey City had hurt the 'Negro cause'.
1965: In the six months from November 1964 to May 1965, the proportion of Americans who thought that civil rights progress was moving 'too fast' had grown from 32 per cent to 41 per cent.

But, on examining the poll data on prejudice, he found that during the same period, racial hostility had continued its steady decline. In fact, the growth of black militancy had apparently produced the opposite of a backlash:

Our survey data persuasively argue that where there is little or no protest against segregation and discrimination, or where these have the sanction of law, racial attitudes conform to the existing situation. But when attention is kept focused on racial injustice and when acts of discrimination become contrary to the law of the land, racial attitudes change. Conversely, there is no persuasive evidence thus far that either demonstrations and other forms of direct action, or legal sanctions applied by government, create a backlash effect and foster segregationist sentiment. On the contrary ...

Sheatsley's analysis was based on time series data, which elegantly exploded the myth – based on single poll questions – that the backlash had arrived and was thriving. So the opinion poll is certainly a useful tool of measurement, but only for comparisons over time and for illuminating major differences between different sections of the population. It does not and cannot adequately distinguish between strong feelings and sloganizing.

The a priori *scale*

This type of scale is constructed essentially on the basis of 'logical' considerations and its first proponent was Bogardus (1925) with what he called social distance scales, which marked the beginning of systematic attitude measurement. What distinguishes *a priori* scales from other attitude scales (subsequently developed) is that their scoring is arbitrary. There is an assumption made about a continuum of positive or negative attitudes with an equal interval between each point on the scale.

The Bogardus scale asked respondents to indicate the degree of intimacy or closeness to which they would admit members of another race:

1. To close kinship by marriage.
2. To my club as personal chums.
3. To my street as neighbours.
4. To employment in my occupation in my country.
5. To citizenship in my country.
6. As visitors only to my country.
7. Would exclude from my country.

It is, of course, apparent that the interval between each of the above items is not necessarily equal, nor are the items themselves necessarily in the correct order for all respondents. In some circumstances, for example, admission to a neighbourhood relationship would be less threatening than admission to an occupational group. So while the *a priori* scale provided the first stimulus for systematic measurement, and is still frequently used in survey research, it does have certain practical drawbacks which need to be taken into account but which by no means render the method unacceptable in all situations. It is economical and easy to use and can often tell us something (but perhaps not enough) about the distribution of attitudes and their characteristics. Moreover, the correlation between the measures of prejudice obtained by the more mathematically based scaling techniques and those obtained by the more intuitive techniques is generally very high.

Other scaling methods

There is, of course, a plethora of different attitude-scaling techniques, most of which have direct relevance to the measurement of prejudice. Since the Bogardus scale (nearly fifty years ago) the development of new techniques for measuring attitudes has become a full-time occupation for some social scientists and a part-time pre-occupation for many others. Perhaps it is useful simply to mention some of the landmarks in measurement techniques.

Probably the most important development in attitude measurement was the application of psychophysical (or rational) scaling by Thurstone and associates (1929). The rationale behind the method is that attitudes towards an object or value lie along a continuum of favourableness to unfavourableness and can be ordered so that each statement of attitude is equidistant from the next one on the continuum. But the whole process of constructing a Thurstone scale is extremely laborious and involves the use of 'judges' (usually about 200) whose job it is to order the statements. The extent of agreement between them then determines the position of each statement in the continuum, and those that do not appear to be more or less equally spaced along the scale are discarded. It was, of course, the first of the mathematically constructed scaling techniques and has been widely used as a basis for many of the methods now employed to measure racial attitudes.

Likert's method of summated ratings (1932) followed close on the heels of Thurstone. It is much simpler to construct but very similar in other respects to the Thurstone method. The Likert scale is also made up of a series of statements relating to an object or value, but – unlike Thurstone's scale – it measures attitudes along a simple agree-disagree continuum. An individual's attitude score is then derived by adding together his individual ratings. No assumption is made about equal intervals, but the choice of statements is also based on a filtering process by a sample group of respondents who – in this case – reflect their *own* attitudes and do not attempt to act as 'judges'. The final list of statements comprises those which differentiate best between respondents with the highest and lowest scores and those which correlate best with the other selected statements.

From these two pioneering developments, it seemed only a short step to take scaling theory to its logical conclusion: if a scale represents a continuum of attitudes towards an object or value, there should be an 'unambiguous meaning to the order of attitude values' (Guttman, 1944). In other words, Guttman pointed out that if a set of statements were ordered according to their 'difficulty of acceptance', the acceptance of one item implies the acceptance of all those that precede it. One can therefore predict a person's attitude towards a range of items from a knowledge of the most 'difficult' item he will accept; or at any rate, the chances will be at least nine in ten that if he rejects one item he will also reject the others. The following Guttman scale on racial attitudes was constructed by the National Opinion Research Center, Chicago, in 1963 and was reported by Sheatsley (1966):

	Percentage giving a pro-integration response
1. Do you think Negroes should have as good a chance as white people to get any kind of job, or do you think white people should have the first chance at any kind of job?	82 (as good a chance)
2. Generally speaking, do you think there should be separate sections for Negroes in street cars and buses?	77 (no)
3. Do you think Negroes should have the right to use the same parks, restaurants and hotels as white people?	71 (yes)
4. Do you think white students and Negro students should go to the same schools or to separate schools?	53 (same schools)
5. How strongly would you object if a member of your family wanted to bring a Negro friend home to dinner?	49 (not at all)
6. White people have a right to keep Negroes out of their neighbourhoods if they want to, and Negroes should respect that right?	44 (disagree)
7. Do you think there should be laws against marriages between Negroes and whites?	36 (no)
8. Negroes shouldn't push themselves where they're not wanted.	27 (disagree)

Thus, there is at least a 90 per cent probability that the minority who gave an *anti*-integration response to the first question would have given it to all succeeding items; and that the minority who gave a *pro*-integration response to the last item will have given it to all preceding items.

In practice, however, Guttman scales are extremely difficult to construct and by no means all attitudes lend themselves to scaling in this way. As Guttman himself acknowledged, a population may not be scalable at any given time and 'perfect scales are not found in practice'. The degree of approximation to perfection should, however, be measured by a 'coefficient of reproducibility' and an 85 per cent perfect scale would be as efficient an approximation as is necessary.

Disguised and unstructured measurement techniques

The methods mentioned so far are all largely undisguised and structured (they are paper and pencil questionnaires); and there are, of course, many others, notably Osgood's semantic differential method (1965). But there is also a battery of disguised and unstructured techniques of attitude measurement, some of which have a particular bearing on the measurement of prejudice.

Unstructured studies may also be either direct or indirect, and the free-response interview is probably the most common form of undisguised method. Its value lies in its ability to determine the range of attitudes towards an object or value and the way in which those attitudes are expressed. It provides an appreciation of possible determinants of attitude sets, but affords no real opportunity to quantify or measure their prevalance in the population. The free-response interview is generally difficult to carry out and to analyse, but its greatest weakness is that it is often impossible to replicate. There are, however, other unstructured techniques – usually disguised – which are more systematic, such as 'sentence completion tests' (racial intermarriage is . . .); 'thematic apperception tests' (what does this picture represent?); 'doll play techniques' and other projective tests (what would you do?). In all these cases, the respondent is told that there are no right or wrong answers and the expression of attitudes derived from them is often more natural and spontaneous than from direct attitude scaling.

The disguised approach is also possible in structured tests of attitudes. 'Information tests', for example, have often been used as an indirect measure on the basis that, in a quiz situation, the direction of guessing is weighted towards the subject's attitude so that the process of answering tends to become an attitude test. The rationale behind these types of test is that, under the guise of collecting objective fact, the investigator is actually collecting subjective opinion; that errors in the answers are not random but systematic.

Much the same rationale lies behind structured projective techniques, which involve asking respondents not what their *own* feelings are, but what they estimate is the majority opinion on a particular object or value. The hypothesis here is that there is an automatic correlation between a person's own attitude and his estimate of majority opinion. In practice, however, this is by no means always true and may be more a measure of awareness – governed by limited experience – or of personality type, than of attitude, *per se*.

The greater availability of computers has, of course, enabled a range of new techniques to be employed. In principle, however, measurement tools such as factor analysis and cluster analysis do little more than the Thurstone and Likert scales were designed to do some four decades ago – but they do it more quickly and efficiently and almost certainly more accurately and objectively. Nevertheless, having described various classical and accepted approaches to attitude measurement, it would be wrong to end without repeating a stricture on all the techniques, including particularly those made practicable by the use of computers.

There are inherent inaccuracies, limitations and biases in all methods of attitude measurement: each of the techniques involves – to some extent – an underestimation of the complexity, subtlety and contradictions in human brains. All measurements are subject to change – which needs itself to be measured – and no measurement is universally applicable. Yet in the absence of measurement techniques for assessing racial prejudice, it is a fair guess that progress in reducing or checking its incidence would have been very much slower (if not non-existent). What has to be accepted is simply that – despite the jargon, despite the increasingly scientific terminology and despite the plethora of mathematical formulae – measurements of intergroup prejudice represent only the crudest approximation of the way in which people actually think and feel about each other and provide only a tenuous clue to the way in which they behave towards each other.

References

ABRAMS, M. (1969), 'The incidence of race prejudice in Britain', in E. J. B. Rose *et al.* (eds.), *Colour and Citizenship*, Oxford University Press.

ALLPORT, G. (1954), *The Nature of Prejudice*, Addison-Wesley.

BETTELHEIM, B., and JANOWITZ, M. (1950), *Dynamics of Prejudice*, Harper.

BOGARDUS, E. (1925), 'Measuring social distance', *Journal of Applied Sociology*, vol. 9, pp. 299–308.

CHURCHMAN, C. W. (1971), 'Why measure?', in B. J. Franklin and M. W. Osborne (eds.), *Research Methods and Insights,* Wadsworth.

GUTTMAN, L. (1944), 'A basis for scaling qualitative data', *American Sociologica Review.*

HYMAN, H. H., and SHEATSLEY, P. B. (1964), 'Attitudes towards desegregation', *Scientific American*, vol. 211, no. 1, pp. 16–23.

KAPLAN, A. (1971), 'Measurement in behavioural sciences', in B. J. Franklin and M. W. Osborne (eds.), *Research Methods and Insights*, Wadsworth.

KUTNER, B., WILKINS, C., and YARROW, P. (1952), 'Verbal attitudes and overt behaviour involving racial prejudice', *Journal of Abnormal Social Psychology*, vol. 47, pp. 649–52.

LA PIERE, R. T. (1936), 'Attitudes versus actions', *Soc. Forces*, vol. 13, pp. 230–37.

LIKERT, R. (1932), 'A technique for the measurement of attitudes', *Archives of Psychology*.

OSGOOD, C. E. (1965), 'Cross-cultural comparability in attitude measurement via multi-lingual semantic differentials', in J. D. Steiner and M. Fishbein (eds.), *Current Studies in Social Psychology*, Holt, Rinehart & Winston.

SHEATSLEY, P. B. (1966), 'White attitudes towards the Negro', *Daedalus*, vol. 95, no. 1, pp. 217–38.

THURSTONE, L. L. (1929), 'Theory of attitude measurement', *Psychological Review*.

Chapter 3
The Roots of Prejudice: Emotional Dynamics

Nevitt Sanford

Nevitt Sanford is one of the authors of the famous work of the 1950s, *The Authoritarian Personality*. Since then he has been director of the Wright Institute, a social science and education research organization near the Berkeley campus, and has carried out several reappraisals of that work and has also been concerned with the general study of human aggressive behaviour; and in 1971 he published, with Craig Comstock, *Sanctions for Evil*.

A man in San Francisco made headlines by refusing to sell his home to a prominent Negro and then, in the glare of unfavourable publicity, said he had nothing against Negroes but was simply doing what he thought was agreed among his neighbours. Three policemen were arrested in Detroit for torturing and killing three young black men whom they were questioning in connection with alleged sniping during a period of high racial tension; the young men and some of their friends had been found in a suite at the Algiers Motel; there was no evidence of sniping but they were in the company of two white girls. A young man was arrested in Gilroy, California, for trying to shoot a judge whose sentencing of a rapist he felt to be too lenient; he said that the judge, who had a Jewish name, was a 'legal criminal, the worst kind', and he added, 'the Jews don't like anybody who's against the Communist conspiracy. I've been threatened morally by the Jews by being called a queer. They threatened me bodily too.'

These episodes, which are of a sort that can be seen in the newspapers in America almost any day, suggest something of the complexity of our subject. It will probably be agreed that each episode is an example of racism, the crucial point being that in each case the victim of discrimination or violence was treated not as an individual but as a member of an ethnic minority, and that his treatment was different from what it would have been had he not been a member of such a group. But here the similarity between the episodes ends. They differ not only in their circumstances and their effects upon victims but, we may well believe, in their meaning to and implications for the people who carried out the hostile actions.

In trying to understand such happenings we may ask, first, whether or how far racist actions are carried out by 'racists' – that is to say, persons who, in disregard of facts, entertain negative beliefs about and hostile attitudes toward ethnic minorities and are disposed to behave towards them generally in discriminatory or aggressive ways. To put the question differently: is a given instance of racist behaviour due to factors in the situation of the moment – pressures that would induce almost anyone to behave in such a manner – or to persisting dispositions of personality? Or is it due to both?

In the case of the man who refused to sell his house to a Negro, we have no evidence that personality dispositions were important. His behaviour might very well have been in line with the norm for people in his circumstances in his area, and it could be accounted for largely on the basis of the human need to conform. Before we could be sure that personality factors had a significant role in determining his behaviour we should have to observe him in various situations and note that he consistently discriminated against minority groups; in addition, we should have to find independent evidence of tendencies that expressed themselves not only in racial discrimination but in other ways as well.

In the case of the policemen charged with murder the inference of aggressive personality dispositions is more readily made. Not many people, clearly, are capable of shooting unarmed men even when they have a licence to do so, and torture, far from being supported by any social norm, must spring from motives that are ordinarily suppressed. Still, situational factors are not to be discounted in this case either. Excitement was high. A policeman had been killed. Not only had the riot in Detroit been in progress for some time, but riots in other American cities had occurred only a short time before. It seems highly likely that the police were in a frame of mind that permitted them to believe almost anything about the black people they were supposed to control – certainly that they were highly dangerous, if not diabolical. It is important to note, too, that the actions of these officers were collective. Not only were they in a position to urge one another on, but each of them, acting in the presence of other representatives of the law, could feel that he had social sanction for what he did.

The young man who went gunning for the judge may safely be called 'disturbed'. Although his behaviour was triggered, so to speak, by his reading of a news item, there can be little doubt that he harboured within himself a set of fantastic beliefs about Jews, Communists and rapists, as well as a disposition to aggressive behaviour. The most interesting question concerns the interrelationships of these phenomena, and their connection, in turn, with the idea of being 'threatened morally'. Granted that in this case we deal with psychopathology, the fact is that anti-Communism, punitiveness toward sex offenders, generalized aggressiveness, and doubt about one's own sexual adequacy are regularly found to be associated in anti-semitic males, just as a characteristic pattern of sex, fear and violence – to refer again to the murderous policemen – is regularly found in people who are deeply prejudiced against Negroes (Adorno, Frenkel-Brunswik, Levinson and Sanford, 1950).

Our understanding of such patterns must derive from knowledge of personality – the organization within the individual of persisting dispositions that help to determine behaviour and that are inferred from the observation of behaviour in various situations. At the same time, there is much evidence that racist behaviour depends upon a wide range of situational and social factors – what other people are doing at the moment, what propaganda is in the air, pressures to conform, economic insecurity, lowered social status, lack of education, membership in groups in which negative beliefs and hostile attitudes toward particular outgroups are common, belonging to organizations whose policies are explicitly or implicitly racist, and so on. It is not with the intention of downgrading the importance of such factors that personality is accentuated in this chapter; the concern here, rather, is with how such factors interact with personality in the determination of racist actions, particularly actions carried out by groups that are more or less organized.

An account of personality and racism may well begin with the studies carried out by colleagues of mine and myself at the University of California, Berkeley, during the 1940s and published, for the most part, under the title *The Authoritarian Personality*. Attention will be given only to findings and conclusions that have held up through the years.[1]

Data for the research were collected by means of questionnaires and interviews. The questionnaires were designed to yield measures of social attitudes – for example, attitudes towards Jews – and they were administered to over 2500 Americans from various walks of life. Interviews, conducted usually with people whose attitudes were extreme, served as a check on the validity of the questionnaires and as a means for exploring the characters and backgrounds of key individuals.

Our attention was directed first to anti-semitism, then to attitudes toward a variety of other minority groups and then to various opinions, attitudes and values which appeared to be associated with anti-semitism and other forms of prejudice.

Some of the first findings concerned the essential irrationality of anti-semitism. Opinions about Jews, in people who are hostile toward them, are over-generalized and frequently contradictory: *all* Jews are said to have this or that fault, and any Jew who is found to be at fault in one respect is found to be at fault in all respects, even though some of the faults in question could not possibly coexist in the same person. Opinions so irrational could not derive from concrete experience with particular Jews, nor

1. For evaluations of *The Authoritarian Personality* in the light of more recent research see Brown (1965), Kirscht and Dillehay (1967) and Klineberg (1968).

are they likely to be modified by anything that Jews, singly or in groups, might do.

When we looked at opinions and attitudes with respect to various other minority groups we found prejudice to be highly generalized. A person who is prejudiced against a particular group is almost always prejudiced against numerous others. Although anti-semitism has some special features, it has to be regarded primarily as an aspect of generalized prejudice. The general disposition to prejudice does not confine itself to 'racial' or ethnic minorities; any group, be it social, economic, national, religious or ideological, that is seen as different from the prejudiced person's own, is likely to be the object of the same pattern of negative opinions and hostile attitudes. More than this, prejudice against various groups (outgroups) is so closely associated with bias in favour of the subject's own group (ingroup) that we were led to look upon the two as aspects of a single phenomenon. This phenomenon we called, reviving a term of Sumner's, *ethnocentrism*, and the instrument for measuring it was the 'E scale'.

It is ethnocentrism that describes what is common to anti-semitism, prejudice against people of colour, jingoistic nationalism, religious bigotry, and ideological fanaticism. In anti-semitism or in any other form of prejudice, what we have mainly to deal with is not an attitude toward a particular group developed through more or less rational processes, or out of experiences with members of that group but, instead, a way of thinking about groups and group relations. This way of thinking embraces at the least the following tendencies: to see all people as divided categorically into homogeneous groups or classes; to infer the essential nature of a person from a knowledge of what group he belongs to; to arrange all groups, and all people within groups, into hierarchies with the strong at the top and weak at the bottom; to solve most moral questions by assuming that the good is what good people do, good people – in contrast to bad people – being those who belong to the same group as oneself.

This way of thinking about groups and group relations is associated with characteristic views on politics, economics, religion, social relations, family and sex relations. Indeed, it seemed to us that in our extremely prejudiced subjects we were confronted with a way of looking at the world.

This outlook did not strike us as something that could have been learned at school, or something that had been taken over *in toto* from any existing agency of propaganda. Instead, we were led, mainly through interviews with highly ethnocentric individuals, to the view that the ethnocentric outlook was generated and maintained primarily because it served important needs within the individual personality. It was the hypothesis of an underlying character structure which, if it was expressed in ethnocentrism, would be expressed in various other ways as well, that became the concern of a third attitude scale. This was the 'F' or pre-Fascist scale, which we thought of as a measure of susceptibility to Fascist propaganda. With the use of this instrument we were able to demonstrate a close association between ethnocentrism and the following tendencies: rigid adherence to conventional values; submissive attitudes toward moral authorities of the ingroup; a readiness to punish the slightest violations of conventional values; opposition to the subjective, imaginative or tender-minded; belief in primitive, hereditarian theories and in mystical deter-mination of the individual's fate; the inability or the unwillingness to deal with the indefinite, the ambiguous or the probable; preoccupation with the dominance–submission aspect of human relationships and exaggerated exertions of strength and 'toughness'; cynicism with respect to 'human nature'; and a disposition to ascribe evil motives to people. A subject's score on this scale predicts his score on an anti-semitism scale with suf-ficient accuracy, so that for estimating how much anti-semitism there is in a population the former may be substituted for the latter. In other words, to obtain a rough estimate of the degree of a person's anti-semitism it is not necessary to ask him what he thinks about Jews.

Not every prejudiced person displays all of these tendencies, but it does appear that they form a coherent pattern each element of which is some-how related to all the others. This pattern has come to be called *authori-tarianism*. It would be a mistake to say categorically that some people possess the pattern while others do not; rather, it should be thought of as something that exists in different degrees in different individuals.

Almost as soon as *The Authoritarian Personality* appeared in 1950, it became the object of vigorous criticism, both for its methodological short-comings and for the left-liberal bias of the authors. Critics examined various technical inadequacies in sampling, in scale construction, and in procedures for quantifying interview material.

Some methodological issues have remained unresolved and of these the matter of 'response bias' deserves brief discussion. Setting out to study susceptibility to anti-semitic propaganda in the midst of the Second World War, Levinson and Sanford (1944) used only scale items that stated an anti-semitic position and offered at the same time a 'pseudo-democratic facade' or a rationalization for agreement: 'there may be some exceptions, but Jews . . .' The question was how far a subject would per-mit himself to be lured into agreement with anti-democratic sentiments. Interviews with subjects who had obtained high or low scores on this scale satisfied these authors that their instrument was effective in identifying individuals who were relatively anti-semitic and those who were the opposite. These same interviews taught the investigators a great deal about the personality characteristics that distinguished highly anti-semitic subjects from other people (Frenkel-Brunswik and Sanford, 1944) – knowledge that became the major basis for the construction of the F scale. This latter scale was composed in the same way as the original anti-semitism scale, using items which the authors thought were fascist in content – with varying degrees of explicitness – and with which subjects might agree without violating their democratic self-conceptions.

In reviewing this procedure for constructing the F scale, critics not surprisingly asked how we could tell how far high scores on the scale were due to authoritarianism and how far to response bias (a general tendency to acquiescence). There followed numerous studies, many of them highly ingenious, directed to finding out how much of the variance on the F scale was due to acquiescence. Conclusions have ranged from 'virtually all', for example, Peabody (1961), to 'none worth bothering about', for example, Gage and Chattergee (1960). The latter writers are among those who have argued that acquiescence is an expression of 'authoritarian submission' and that therefore the use of only positive items increases the validity of the scale. Kirscht and Dillehay, in their valuable 1967 survey of research on authoritarianism in personality, sum up the controversy as follows:

Even after fifteen years of research, the influence of acquiescence on scores from the F-scale is difficult to assess. This is due in part to mechanical problems in isolating acquiescence, but it is also due to the likelihood that the interaction between acquiescence and authoritarianism is complex.

To readers who have worried about authoritarianism in the individual and in society ever since Horkheimer (1936), Fromm (1941), Maslow (1943), Reich (1946) and others drew attention to the phenomenon, and who have never felt there was any difficulty about recognizing it when they saw it, this controversy about response bias might seem trivial. To more than a few psychologists, however, the question of how to formulate authoritarianism, how to resolve it into its constituent elements, has seemed important, for this has a heavy bearing on our understanding of its relations to intelligence, education, socio-economic background, and cognitive and emotional development.

The point about the left-liberal bias of the authors of *The Authoritarian Personality*, according to such critics as Shils (1954) and Rokeach (1960), was that it led the authors to focus on rightist authoritarianism to the neglect of 'authoritarianism of the left'. This criticism also led to a great deal of research which helped to make clear that racism, particularly political racism, is to be found on the extreme left as well as elsewhere on the political spectrum. It is questionable, however, whether the personality dispositions underlying rascism and irrationality in left-wing extremists form a pattern that is properly called authoritarianism. Adorno, in *The*

Authoritarian Personality, described a type of person scoring at the low extreme on the F scale – the 'rigid low scorer' – who had 'most in common with the overall high-scoring pattern' and were 'definitely disposed toward totalitarianism in their thinking'; and Rokeach (1960) and his co-workers found that subjects at the two extremes of the political spectrum scored higher on a scale for measuring dogmatism than did subjects in the middle. However, I have argued from time to time, on the basis of clinical material (Sanford, 1956; 1971), that the emotional appeals of fascism and of communism have fundamentally different sources in the dynamic structure of personality – at least in countries such as the United States where communist parties have been weak and generally despised. The issue may never be settled; for a resolution would require that an adequate sample of left extremists be studied as intensively and with as great a variety of methods as were the subjects of *The Authoritarian Personality*, and, of course, that the investigators be free of any kind of political bias.

In spite of the criticisms, evidence in support of the basic conceptions of *The Authoritarian Personality* has continued to accumulate. The F scale has been used by numerous investigators with various groups of respondents. As Brown (1965) says, 'On the level of covariation, of one variable correlated with another, the findings of *The Authoritarian Personality* seem to me to be quite well established. Anti-semitism goes with ethnocentrism goes with anti-intraception goes with idealization of parents and self goes with authoritarian discipline in childhood goes with a rigid conception of sex roles, etc.'

Many studies carried out since 1950 have served to widen the circle of covariation. For instance, high scores on the E or the F scale have been shown to be associated with high scores on various other attitude scales, such as scales for measuring rigidity, misanthropy, dogmatism, traditional family ideology, restrictiveness toward the use of alcohol, and punitiveness toward alcoholic patients; with characteristic behaviour in experimental situations, for example, ethnocentrism is associated with low tolerance for the ambiguity of visual stimuli and, under some conditions, with rigidity in problem-solving; with characteristic behaviour in various social roles – dominance and possessiveness in mothers, autocratic, totalitarian behaviour in school teachers, ineffectiveness in army officers, unreceptivity to psychotherapy in psychiatric patients, unwillingness to volunteer for psychological experiments and low tolerance for personal freedom in college freshmen.

These findings have strengthened the argument in favour of a central and relatively deep-seated personality structure which helps to determine prejudice and other behaviour in a wide variety of situations. These findings, however, like those reported in *The Authoritarian Personality*, are in the form of *general* relationships – correlations between or among variables in populations of people. It is important to note that although a coefficient of correlation is very high by ordinary standards, there will be some people in the sample who do not go with the majority. For example, the correlation between anti-semitism and ethnocentrism, as reported in *The Authoritarian Personality*, is 0·80 (where 1·00 is perfect correlation, i.e. the person scoring highest on anti-semitism also scores highest on ethno-centrism, the person scoring next highest on anti-semitism is next highest on ethnocentrism and so on), but this does not mean that there are not some people who are prejudiced against Jews but not against Negroes – or another ethnic minority – and vice versa.

Nevertheless, there has been a strong tendency among students of racism, including the authors of *The Authoritarian Personality*, to consider the object of their inquiries as *one thing* – a single all-of-a-piece phenomenon that varies in amount from one person to another. Thus Noel (1971) in a recent comprehensive review of studies of white anti-black prejudice in the United States, writes: 'A white person may fall anywhere on a continuum, which ranges from complete acceptance of blacks as equals to the other extreme – complete hate, rejection and social distance.' This single dimen-sion is the dependent variable in nearly 100 studies cited by Noel in which the object was to study anti-black prejudice, usually measured by a scale, in relation to one or more of a large number of independent or predictor variables. Studies of anti-semitism usually have these same characteristics. For example, in the massive, well-publicized research on anti-semitism funded by the Anti-Defamation League of B'nai B'rith, and carried out by the Survey Research Center of the University of California, Berkeley (Glock and Stark, 1966; Selznick and Steinberg, 1970), the focus is on the causes of generalized anti-semitism as measured by an 'Index of Anti-Semitic Belief'.

There is, to be sure, theoretical and empirical support for the idea of racism as a unitary phenomenon, but the fact remains that social scientists, despite their discovery of numerous social and psychological correlates of racism, have not been able to reach much agreement concerning the causes of the phenomenon. In these circumstances it seems not unreasonable to ask whether studies of prejudice do not suffer from a failure to sufficiently differentiate the dependent variables. Might it not be, for example, that some white people, when left to their own devices – not confronted with a set of ready-made items – will unjustifiably ascribe some but not other negative qualities to black people, while other white people will similarly ascribe other qualities? Might it not be, in other words, that there are qualitatively different conceptions, views, images of blacks which, despite some uniformity of outlook in all prejudiced persons, have different implications for action affecting black people and different sources in the background, situation, or personality of the prejudiced person?

Actually, the literature affords some suggestions that the answer to this question might be yes; and the work which is, in this respect, most suggestive is, perhaps paradoxically, that which took the strongest position in favour of the generality of prejudice, namely *The Authoritarian Personality*. This probably is mainly due to the fact that the authors of this work had time to allow their subjects to talk freely about what they thought of various minority groups. As Adorno says in Chapter 16:

Although the correlation between anti-semitism and anti-negroism is undoubtably high, a fact which stands out in our interviews as well as in our questionnaire studies [actually the correlation was 0·80], this is not to say that prejudice is a single compact mass. Readiness to accept statements hostile to minority groups may well be conceived as a more or less unitary trait, but when, in the interview situation, subjects are allowed to express themselves spontaneously it is not uncommon for one minority more than the others to appear, for the moment at least, as an object of special hatred.

He later goes on to suggest, on the basis of interviews, that lower class and middle class gentiles see Jews differently:

To the true proletarian, the Jew is primarily the bourgeois. The working-man is likely to perceive the Jew, above all, as an agent of the economic sphere of the middle-man, as the executor of capitalist tendencies. The Jew is he who 'presents the bill.'

To the anti-Semitic members of the middle classes, the imagery of the Jew seems to have a somewhat different structure ... They are themselves on the defensive and struggle desperately for the maintenance of their status. Hence, they accentuate just the opposite of what working-men are likely to complain about, namely, that the Jews are not real bourgeois, that they do not really 'belong'.

If conceptions of minorities differ according to the socio-economic class of the prejudiced person, they may also differ according to whether they derive from adult experiences – of economic exploitation or competition, of religious group memberships, of pressure from family and friends, of frustrated progress, and so on – or from inner conflicts having their origins in childhood. And different childhood conflicts, with their accompanying misperceptions, fantasies and defensive strategies, may be sources of different conceptions of 'the bad people'. Thus Cohn (1967) has argued, on the basis of historical and clinical studies, that traditional European anti-semitism and contemporary anti-black prejudice in the United States have different psychodynamic sources – anti-semitism being a displacement of hostility toward the 'bad father' of childhood, anti-black prejudice being largely a projection onto blacks of reprehensible sexual and aggressive tendencies which the prejudiced person has to suppress.

That white Americans differ in their conceptions or images of black people can be verified not only by commonsense observation, but also by at least one systematic study. In open-ended interviews with a sample of white subjects, May (1972) asked what black people as a group might do, what they might desire, what they were like in terms of personal characteristics; he also asked what the causes were of racial problems in the United States. May found that different people seemed to have different images of blacks – for example, 'happy-go-lucky', 'a retiring type of people', 'sexually undisciplined', 'highly religious', 'full of hate for the white man'. It was his impression that different views of blacks were associated with different dispositions to action affecting them. May is presently engaged in an effort to find out if distinguishable patterns of imagery of blacks can be discovered and, if so, what their determinants and consequences are.

This is in line with Levinson's analysis of what he calls 'ethnocentric ideology' (Chapter 4 in *The Authoritarian Personality*). After making his case for the unitary structure of ethnocentrism, he considers three ethnocentric solutions to problems of group conflict: the liquidation, the subordination, or the segregation of outgroups. On this basis he distinguishes between 'politicized ethnocentrism' as in Nazism or Fascism, which is represented by the first solution, and 'American ethnocentrism' of which subordination and segregation are characteristic. Levinson does not say so explicitly, but there are strong suggestions in his writing and in that of his co-authors, that different kinds of imagery of outgroups, as well as different degrees of devotion to democratic values, lie behind the different solutions favoured; if Jews are believed to be like germs, and as naturally incorrigible, then liquidation might be the 'only solution to the Jewish problem'; but if they are seen as greedy children then it might seem best to keep them in a subordinate position until they 'learn to be like us'.

When you consider the situation of black people in the United States today and ask, with them, what is *their* best strategy, it would seem to be highly important to know whether and to what extent they are up against people who think they are non-human and should be eliminated, people who think they are children who should be brought up in the way they (the whites) should go, people who think they are dissident adolescents who need strict control, or people who think they are 'the hope of the world'.

It seems clear, then, that to conceive of racism as a 'single compact mass' and to correlate measures of this 'variable' with various psychological and social factors is not likely to yield the whole truth about the phenomenon nor tell all we need to know of what to do about it.

There is need for a broad-scale survey, designed to discover anew people's imagery of 'good' people and 'bad' people. The past decade has brought vast and significant social changes in most parts of the world, yet most of our research continues to use conceptions of prejudice and instruments for measuring it that were developed more than twenty years ago. Careful analysis of the data gathered in a national survey could reveal and delineate major patterns of imaging of other people. New instruments for measuring such patterns will then be needed, so that they may be studied in relation both to what causes them and their possible consequences for action and policy making.

Work of this kind will lead to a more differentiated and more expanded picture of prejudice than is now available; it will not, however, lead to the discarding of what has been established concerning authoritarianism as a major psychodynamic source of generalized prejudice. Knowledge of both the specific and the general will be necessary to the development of a general theory of prejudice – one that gives due attention to both cognitive and psychodynamic processes (see the next chapter).

But let us return to authoritarianism; first, to the theory we worked out in *The Authoritarian Personality* to explain the origins and development of ethnocentrism and authoritarianism within the individual personality. This theory was based largely upon differences in what individuals scoring at opposite extremes on our scales said about their backgrounds and histories, upon general psychoanalytic theory, and upon our clinical experience with highly prejudiced and relatively unprejudiced individuals. I still favour our original formulation which, in brief, is as follows.

Most important is the pattern of discipline to which the individual is subjected in childhood. Crucial for the development of the character structure within which ethnocentrism has a functional role is an authority that is at once stern, rigid, unreasonable and unaccompanied by love. The hostility aroused by this authority, instead of being directed against the strong and – the child must believe – 'good' people who wield it, is suppressed and displaced onto substitutes, eventually – with some assistance from parents and educators – onto outgroups. The child, through submitting to the authority, sometimes even 'protesting too much,' does not really accept it. This has far-reaching consequences for the personality. First of all it makes for defectiveness in the individual conscience. Authority remains, as it were, 'out there', to be obeyed, self-pityingly, if it is strong enough and unavoidable enough, to be ignored under other conditions. Unless the child is affected directly he need not concern himself with what 'they' – the powers that be – do. Again, the individual is left with a continuing sense of impotence, which is the more infuriating because its sources are unrecognized. He tends to strike out wildly, finding all manner of possible 'causes' for his troubles: people are against him, he is being persecuted, 'it's the Jews.' In attempting to overcome his sense of weakness he insists upon his superiority and presents himself to the world as a strong and hard-headed fellow. Since weakness is contemptible, he cannot admit it in himself nor tolerate it in others. It is because the perceived weakness of others reminds him of his own that he becomes more violent the more pitiable and the less able to strike back his victim becomes. The device of projecting onto others that which cannot be admitted in oneself is used not only for managing weakness but for putting from oneself various other unrecognized tendencies. This explains why a group, once it has been placed in the role of outgroup, may be seen as the embodiment of all manner of evil.

The few studies relevant to this formulation that have been reported are, as far as they go, consistent with it. Harris, Gough and Martin (1950), for example, using questionnaires in their study, found that ethnic prejudice in children was associated with an accent on obedience, strict control, and inculcation of fear on the part of their parents. Frenkel-Brunswik and her associates measured prejudice in children, aged ten and eleven, and obtained information on family background, handling of discipline, and childhood events by means of visits to homes and interviews with parents. Children were found to differ in the degree of their prejudice much as adults do, and the more prejudiced children showed personality characteristics very similar to those that make up adult authoritarianism. Prejudice and the correlating personality characteristics were associated with family relationships 'characterized by fearful subservience to the demands of the parents and by an early suppression of impulses not acceptable to adults' (Frenkel-Brunswik, 1954). Lyle and Levitt (1955) developed a children's anti-democratic scale, like the F scale, and found that high scores on it were associated with parental punitiveness as measured by a sentence completion test. Baumrind (1968) conducted careful observational studies of nursery school children and their parents, singly and together, and was able to distinguish and describe in detail three patterns of parental behaviour toward children: authoritative, authoritarian and permissive. She did not describe the behaviour of the children in terms of prejudice or authoritarianism, but concluded that the authoritative pattern was most favourable to the development of various desirable traits in children while the authoritarian pattern tended to give rise to distrust, withdrawal, discontent – traits that may be thought of as forerunners of authoritarianism. These conclusions are consistent with Frenkel-Brunswik's finding that unprejudiced children more often showed conformity to adult values and with her observation that, 'this conformity to adult values is based on genuine love and identification with the parents and is to be differentiated from the fearful submission of the ethnocentric child' (Frenkel-Brunswik, 1954).

This research goes quite a long way toward laying the basis for a usable account of the origins of authoritarian dispositions in childhood. It provides little, however, in the form of tests of the above theoretical propositions concerning dynamic relations among processes on different levels of the personality. There is a great need for research in this area.

Some additional understanding of the development of authoritarianism in the individual has been gained from studies of college students. Marked differences in E and F scale scores have been found among college freshmen, and careful clinical studies have shown that the high scorers, in contrast with the low scorers, are still under the influence of the kind of authoritarian parental behaviour noted above. Hopeful from the point of view of possible remedial actions is the evidence that personality continues to develop during the four years of college. The E and F scales have been administered to large samples of students, in all classes in various kinds of higher educational institutions. According to the summary of this work by Newcomb and Feldman (1969), ethnocentrism and authoritarianism are significantly reduced in most colleges. There is thus the possibility that education which succeeds in giving self-insight and building self-esteem and the confidence to criticize authority can effectively reduce racism.

We must, however, take note of the possibility that changes in E and F scale scores during a period in college are due to adaptation to the campus culture as well as – or, perhaps, rather than – to changes in the personality itself. This raises the whole question of whether ethnocentrism and authoritarianism are not simply cultural norms of which individuals serve as 'carriers'. In the case of change in college, the argument seems to favour personality theory since, as Freedman (1962) has shown, changes wrought in college tend to be maintained even after graduates have begun to live in quite different cultures. Culture, on the other hand, would seem to be a main determinant of the fact that mean E and F scale scores differ, in all classes, from one institution to another, being higher, for example, in church-related colleges than in secular ones; higher in vocationally-oriented institutions than in those in which the liberal arts are accentuated. Culture comes very much to the fore when these scales, properly translated, are used in different nations. University students in Germany, Egypt and Lebanon, for example, obtain significantly higher scores than do their counterparts in the United States. The same may be said for various studies in which ethnocentrism and authoritarianism have been found to be associated with low income, low education and religious fundamentalism. In all these cases it is possible to understand how an individual could agree with any item expressive of ethnocentrism or authoritarianism because he had learned this response from his parents, teachers or friendship group – had, in other words, accepted a cultural norm. It is even possible to conceive of an 'ethnocentric' or 'authoritarian culture' in which the whole set of dispositions expressed in the E and F scales go together to form a pattern.

This, however, is only to push back the question of what makes the dispositions go together. Why should racism be associated with anxiety about sex, self-glorification, and submissiveness toward authority? The question is the same whether we are talking about a culture or about an individual. The argument in *The Authoritarian Personality*, and here, is that the component dispositions are related dynamically; they constitute a working system – in an individual or in a social group. In an authoritarian culture there are primitive impulses which are widely shared; and ways of coping with these impulses which prove to be effective are adopted generally. In any culture there will be individuals who accept prevailing values and social codes without necessarily needing them for defensive purposes; there will also be others who develop methods for coping with the problems of life in the same way as they were originally developed in that culture. Culture and personality continuously interact, in mutually supporting ways (see Chapters 14 and 15).

The idea of widely shared personality needs seems necessary to explain why the policemen who committed the murders in *The Algiers Motel Incident* (Hersey, 1968), like the official murderers of civil rights workers in Mississippi, cannot be convicted by local courts; why these policemen, whom Hersey interviewed, remained confident that nothing very serious would happen to them and even felt aggrieved that they were 'singled out' in a way that led to their suspension from the force. As Friedenberg (1965) writes in his review of Hersey's book, 'It is not, after all, customary to fire a dedicated officer for zeal beyond the call of duty; and, certainly not for volunteering to participate, at some danger to himself, in a civic pageant designed to act out the fantasies of the populace.' In the prevailing culture of the United States aggressive impulses are strong, though largely unrecognized, and a viable way of handling them is to participate vicariously in the aggression of officials against people who have been defined as morally low – usually, today, people of colour, though students are another prominent target. This 'fantasy', however, is not acted out except under special conditions, the most important of which are emotional excitement sufficient to impair the functioning of the higher mental processes and a barrage of propaganda depicting the people who become victims as less than human.[2]

[2] For a comprehensive discussion of this phenomenon see Sanford and Comstock (1971).

The Algiers Motel Incident is a vivid example of how cultural trends express themselves in racial violence in critical situations, but Hersey makes it clear also that the three policemen most directly involved were, as personalities, strongly disposed to take their roles in the drama. Not only were they prejudiced against Negroes but, because of their inner conflicts (they were each backward in their relations with women and had been over-enthusiastic in their work as members of the vice squad), unusually aggressive, particularly toward people perceived as violators of moral standards.

Personality and social processes also interact in what is known as organizational or institutional racism, of which the Nazi system of persecution and the American institution of slavery are familiar examples. The striking fact here is that apparently ordinary people, even those who profess opposition to the general trend of the system, contribute merely by 'doing their jobs' to effects that are discriminatory or destructive. Hannah Arendt (1963) has dramatized this phenomenon in her book *Eichmann in Jerusalem*. She used the term 'banality of evil' to describe a state of affairs in which an apparently ordinary man, bent on doing his job efficiently and winning his promotion, could participate effectively in systematic mass murder.

Sociologists have long stressed the idea of the replaceability of individuals in bureaucratic roles, and used this conception to explain those common instances of 'corporate immorality' in which blame can be attached to no individual. Organizational processes are clearly of enormous importance in maintaining racial discrimination in education, employment, housing, medical care, and the administration of justice. Small wonder that in much writing on this subject it is assumed that personality makes no difference. There is no doubt that organizations go their own way and that individuals adapt themselves to the requirements of their roles, but this is far from saying that personality factors do not enter into the determination of racist effects. They influence the selection of the individual for, and his selection of, the role (Eichmann was well suited for his job), his adaptation to it, the way he carries out his responsibilities, the surrender of his individual conscience in favour of the organization's 'morality'. Individuals who cannot adapt themselves to the requirements of work in a school, hospital, social agency or industrial organization leave, often after prolonged periods of unhappiness, and when organizations are caught in some blatant manifestation of discrimination or destructiveness, there will almost always be some individuals who resisted the corporate action.

It is nevertheless understandable that people who are or have been victims of organizational discrimination or destructiveness are not disposed to draw fine distinctions among the people who make up that organization. The white liberal who is shocked at being called a 'racist' may, in fact, be taking his assigned role in a 'racist institution', and may be quite unprepared for the costs of doing something to change it. It seems not unlikely that such tolerance of organizational racism is among some of the more subtle forms of prejudice not taken into account by existing ethnocentrism or anti-semitism scales.

One way of approaching these phenomena would be to study ways in which individuals adapt to life in organizations. It may be supposed that some individuals, under the requirements of some kinds of role, are more disposed than others to abandon their individuality and to become more cynical, to become, in other words, more de-humanized, and that this kind of adaptation is accompanied by the tendency to see other people as less than human. More concretely, we may expect that as young school teachers, welfare workers and nurses lose their idealism and autonomy through convincing themselves that institutional actions – however contrary to principle – are really all right, become increasingly frustrated in their efforts to do anything for their charges or clients, in other words, become less human; they will take increasingly negative views of those they are supposed to help, and obtain higher scores on scales for measuring prejudice.

In the early 1950s during the period of McCarthyism in the United States the authors of *The Authoritarian Personality* had reason to hope that popular writers, commentators and opinion makers would seize upon this work and go on to make the mechanisms of prejudice familiar to every housewife and high school student. It still seems remarkable that there is so little public understanding of the text-book cases of authoritarianism and ethnocentrism being presented by high officials in, for example, the state of California in the 1970s. Unconscious resistance to this kind of understanding is perhaps greater than we thought; certainly we underestimated the power of massive cultural trends and organizational role structures to prevent this kind of understanding. Still, it must be admitted that an important reason why our findings and formulations did not become more influential is because they were not well enough established. The effort to supply the needed empirical support must be continued. There are great opportunities for research along the lines indicated above.

But this is not to suggest that we meet the racial crisis of today merely by conducting more studies. Action, long overdue, must be of several kinds:

1. *The Authoritarian Personality* was generally thought to take a pessimistic view by stressing character and its formation in early life. In fact,

we sought to make clear that we were talking about readiness or suscepti-bility in the individual, that what actually happened depended upon con-temporary circumstances, and that it was possible to control behaviour without modifying personality. Probably, the main situational determinant of discriminatory and destructive behaviour is propaganda. This, in theory at least, can be controlled by leaders and opinion-makers, and understood and defended against by the rest of us.

Legal restraints upon overt expressions of racism have in some instances been effective; and this is consistent with what is known of authoritarian-ism – highly prejudiced people tend to be conforming, and very respectful of the law. The racist person admires and fears power, tends to identify himself with it and does not oppose it unless he is sure of ample support. This same kind of attention to situational factors leads to the conclusion that in trying to curb the racism of policemen it is far more practical to use authority to encourage them to live up to professional standards than to undertake a modification of their racist attitudes.

Nothing that we know of personality in relation to racism contradicts the principle that overt manifestations of prejudice depend upon socio-economic conditions, and that such manifestations will be reduced in frequency and severity as the individual gains a sense of social and economic security and of general well-being.

2. A highly important social determinant of an individual's participation in racial behaviour, or behaviour that is racist in its effects, is his role in an organization. Anything that serves to make an organization more human will reduce its racism, and racial actions by its individual members. Organizations can be changed in this way. It is largely a matter of making arrangements that allow individual autonomy and self-expression, rather than insisting on rigid adherence to narrowly defined role requirements. There is evidence that such arrangements do not decrease, but may actually increase, productivity (Bennis, 1966; Trist *et al.*, 1963).

3. As for dispositions to racism within the individual, it is possible, with present knowledge, to work out a programme of child training and education that could prevent the development of ethnocentrism and authoritarianism in personality. Such a programme would centre on love, appreciation of the child's humanity, and a pattern of discipline that took seriously the child's increasing capacity to govern himself.

It is encouraging to know that racist attitudes can be modified even at the college level, by a kind of education that develops the whole person through giving him insight into himself and the world. Such education is not uncommon today; it is vividly expressed in the United States, for example, in the mainstream of student protest. Liberation from authoritarianism at the college level is not infrequently followed by anarchism; this, however, is usually short-lived; in any case, it is not as dangerous to ethnic minorities as authoritarianism.

4. The task of changing culture in the direction of more humanistic values seems even more formidable than that of modifying, or preventing the development of, authoritarian personality structures in individuals. Yet culture does change. It alters as a result of such changes in society as urbanization and industrialization, and it changes – more slowly to be sure – with the spread of enlightenment. It is changing rapidly in the west today, due to accelerating technological development and the affluence associated with it. Indeed, there is in these countries today a cultural crisis: traditional values, such as the Protestant work-ethic, future orientation, the belief that all good things are in short supply and must be distributed according to merit, competition and property ownership are becoming increasingly inappropriate if not irrelevant in nations' part-industrial phase of over-production and overwhelming power. These traditional values are being effectively challenged by students and by people at the bottom of the economic heap. This challenge has aroused authoritarian reactions from those who man established institutions, and the issue will not be settled for some time. The future, however, belongs to the youth, who have the benefits not only of numbers but of relative freedom from indoctrination in the traditional values and increaisngly easy access to education and enlightenment.

References

ADORNO, T. W., FRENKEL-BRUNSWIK, E., LEVINSON, D. J., and SANFORD, N. (1950), *The Authoritarian Personality*, Harper & Row.

ARENDT, H. (1963), *Eichmann in Jerusalem*, Viking Press.

BAUMRIND, D. (1968), 'Authoritarian *v.* authoritative parental control', *Adolescence*, vol. 3, pp. 255–72.

BENNIS, W. (1966), *Changing Organizations*, McGraw-Hill.

BROWN, R. (1965), *Social Psychology*, Free Press.

COHN, N. (1967), *The Myth of the Jewish World-Conspiracy: A Case Study in Collective Psychopathology. A Commentary Report*, American Jewish Committee.

FREEDMAN, M. B. (1962), 'Studies of college alumni', in N. Sanford (ed.), *The American College*, Wiley.

FRENKEL-BRUNSWIK, E. (1954), 'Further explorations by a contributor', in R. Christie and M. Jahoda (eds.), *Studies in the Scope and Method of 'The Authoritarian Personality'*, Free Press.

FRENKEL-BRUNSWIK, E., and SANFORD, N. (1944), 'Some personality correlates of anti-semitism', *Journal of Psychology*, vol. 20, pp. 271–91.

FRIEDENBERG, E. Z. (1965), 'Motown justice', *New York Review of Books*, vol. 11, no. 2, pp. 24–8.

FROMM, E. (1941), *Escape from Freedom*, Farrar & Rinehart.

GAGE, N. L., and CHATTERGEE, B. B. (1960), 'The psychological meaning of acquiescence set: further evidence', *Journal of Abnormal and Social Psychology*, vol. 60, pp. 280–83.

GLOCK, C., and STARK, R. (1966), *Christian Beliefs and Anti-Semitism*, Harper & Row.

HARRIS, D. B., GOUGH, H. G., and MARTIN, W. E. (1950), 'Children's ethnic attitudes: 2. Relationships to parental beliefs concerning child training', *Child Development*, vol. 21, pp. 169–81.

HERSEY, J. (1968), *The Algiers Motel Incident*, Bantam Books.

HORKHEIMER, M. (ed.) (1936), *Studien über Authorität und Familie*, a publication of the Institute of Social Research, Felix Alcan, Paris.

KIRSCHT, J. P., and DILLEHAY, R. C. (1967), *Dimensions of Authoritarianism*, University of Kentucky Press.

KLINEBERG, O. (1968), 'Prejudice: the concept', in *International Encyclopedia of the Social Sciences*, vol. 12. Macmillan and the Free Press, pp. 439–48.

LEVINSON, D. J., and SANFORD, N. (1944), 'A scale for the measurement of anti-semitism', *Journal of Psychology*, vol. 17, pp. 339–70.

LYLE, W. H., and LEVITT, E. E. (1955), 'Punitiveness, authoritarianism, and parental discipline of grade school children', *Journal of Abnormal and Social Psychology*, vol. 51, pp. 42–6.

MASLOW, A. H. (1943), 'The authoritarian character structure', *Journal of Social Psychology*, vol. 18, pp. 401–11.

MAY, M. (1972), *Images of Negroes and Personality Development*, doctoral dissertation, Graduate Theological Union, Berkeley, California.

NEWCOMB, T. M., and FELDMAN, D. (1969), *Impacts of College*, Jossey-Bass.

NOEL, J. (1971), 'White anti-black prejudice in the United States', *International Journal of Group Tensions*, vol. 1, pp. 59–77.

PEABODY, D. (1961), 'Attitude content and agreement set in scales of authoritarianism, dogmatism, anti-semitism and economic conservatism', *Journal of Abnormal and Social Psychology*, vol. 63, pp. 1–12.

REICH, W. (1946), *The Mass Psychology of Fascism*, Orgone Institute Press.

ROKEACH, M. (1960), *The Open and Closed Mind*, Basic Books.

SANFORD, N. (1956), 'The approach of the Authoritarian Personality', in J. L. McCary (ed.), *Psychology of Personality: Six Modern Approaches*, Logos Press.

SANFORD, N. (1971), 'Authoritarianism and social destructiveness', in N. Sanford, and C. Comstock (eds.), *Sanctions for Evil*, Jossey-Bass.

SANFORD, N., and COMSTOCK, C. (eds.) (1971), *Sanctions for Evil*, Jossey-Bass.

SELZNICK, G., and STEINBERG, S. (1970), *The Tenacity of Prejudice*, Harper and Row.

SHILS, E. A. (1954), 'Authoritarianism: right and left,' in R. Christie and M. Jahoda (eds.), *Studies in the Scope and Method of 'The Authoritarian Personality'*, Free Press.

TRIST, E. L., HIGGIN, G. W., MURRAY, H., and POLLACK, A. B. (1963), *Organizational Choice*, Tavistock Publications.

Chapter 4
The Roots of Prejudice: Cognitive Aspects[1]

Henri Tajfel

Henri Tajfel is Professor of Social Psychology at the University of Bristol. He studied in Paris, Brussels and London. After two years teaching at the University of Durham, he went to Oxford where he was Fellow of Linacre College and University Lecturer in Social Psychology. In 1958–9 he was a Visiting Lecturer at Harvard University, in 1966–7 a Fellow at the Center for Advanced Study in the Behavioral Sciences ot Stanford, California and in 1970 a visiting professor at the École Pratique des Hautes Études in Paris. In 1969–72 he was President of the European Association of Experimental Social Psychology and still works on several committees concerned with international developments in social psychology. He has published many articles in British, European and American psychological journals and contributed to several books. Recently he published (with others) '*The Context of Social Psychology: A Critical Assessment*', a volume in the collection of 'European Monographs in Social Psychology' of which he is general editor. He is also one of the editors of the *European Journal of Social Psychology*.

Introduction

Man has always had a variety of notions about his place in nature and about his own nature. In the past, these 'images' and ideas drifted slowly from various specialist groups to the population at large. Today, with the unprecedented growth of the means of public information available to us, ideas which catch the fancy or the imagination of the new myth makers can sometimes spread more quickly and widely than an epidemic; and often they have a longer life-span. This revolution in the diffusion of ideas presents an entirely new problem to social scientists, and particularly to social psychologists. The massive assimilation and simplification of new points of view about human nature, human society, and the physical and biological environment of man, is capable of affecting attitudes and behaviour of large populations as never before.

The general image of man as a creature coming to terms with the physical and biological constraints of his environment is essentially that

[1] This chapter is a revised version of a contribution to the Symposium, organized by the Eugenics Society, on the 'Biosocial Aspects of Race' published in its original form as part of Supplement no. 1 to the *Journal of Biosocial Science*.

of an exploring and rational being stumbling heavily on his way, pulled back by his insufficiencies and stupidities, but still imperfectly rational, still engaged in what Sir Frederick Bartlett (1932) called the 'effort after meaning'. It is interesting to see that this 'rational' model is extended, in contemporary social anthropology, to societies which were earlier considered as using a 'primitive' and non-rational approach to the exploration of the world about them. The eminent French anthropologist, Claude Lévi-Strauss, recently wrote:

To transform a weed into a cultivated plant, a wild beast into a domestic animal, to produce, in either of these, nutritious or technologically useful processes which were originally completely absent or could only be guessed at; to make stout water-tight pottery out of clay which is friable and unstable, liable to pulverize or crack; to work out techniques, often long and complex, which permit cultivation without soil or alternatively without water; to change toxic roots or seeds into foodstuffs or again to use their poison for hunting, war or ritual – there is no doubt that all these achievements required a genuinely scientific attitude, sustained and watchful interest, and a desire for knowledge for its own sake. For only a small proportion of observation and experiments (which must be assumed to have been primarily inspired by a desire for knowledge) could have yielded practical and immediately useful results (1966, pp. 14–15).

But there seems to be one exception to this model, one set of problems for the consideration of which we seem to have adopted a very different set of ideas. It is as if we were suddenly dealing with a different and strange animal that uses some of his abilities to adapt to some aspects of his environment, and is quite incapable of using them in order to adapt to others. The prevailing model of man as a creature trying to find his way in his social environment seems to have nothing in common with the ideas of exploration, of meaning, of understanding, of rational consistency. We have the rational model for natural phenomena; we seem to have nothing but a blood-and-guts model for social phenomena. In the new blood-and-guts romanticism so fashionable at present in some science and semi-science, man's attitudes and beliefs concerning the *social environment* are seen mainly as a by-product of tendencies that are buried deeply in his evolutionary past or just as deeply in his unconscious.

And this seems to be particularly true in a field in which the acquisition of knowledge about the springs of human behaviour is perhaps the most urgent and ominous task confronting us at present. This is the field of relations between large human groups which includes, of course, race relations, but encompasses international relations as well. The psychological aspects of intergroup relations include the study of behaviour in intergroup situations, of behaviour related to these situations, and of beliefs and attitudes concerning an individual's own group and various other groups which are relevant to him. The competitive or co-operative, hostile or friendly, relations between groups are determined, to a very large extent, by the logic of the situations within which they arise. Once this is taken for granted it is equally true that these situations have their effects on the motives and attitudes of millions of individuals, that these motives and attitudes in turn determine behaviour, and that this behaviour partly determines in turn the subsequent relations between the groups.

A psychological theory of intergroup relations must provide a two-way link between situations and behaviour, and it can do this through an analysis of the motivational as well as the cognitive structures which intervene between the two. But it is in this analysis that man's search to understand his environment often seems to be forgotten, and a peculiar one-way causation is established. In this, ideas and beliefs seem to be considered as no more than projections and rationalizations of powerful motivational forces; and somehow or other, it has implicitly been taken for granted that inferences can be made directly from motivation and the evolutionary past of the species to complex intergroup behaviour without paying much attention to the flimsy cognitive by-products thrown out as if at random by the subterranean springs of emotion and 'instinct'. Our image of the social man is that of a man who has lost his reason. Otherwise, the argument usually runs, how can we explain the perennial hostility of man to man? Less attention has been paid to the fact that co-operation between groups also needs to be explained; or that hostility need not be based on unconscious motivational factors, that it can also follow as a result of attempts to explain to oneself in the simplest and most convenient way the causal sequence of relations between groups.

Two intellectual traditions form the background from which arises this denial of the autonomy of cognitive functioning. One consists of extrapolating from the background of animal behaviour to human behaviour in complex social situations; the other, of assuming that theories of unconscious motivation provide the necessary and sufficient basis for the understanding of social attitudes. In both these trends of thought certain authors, like Tinbergen (1968), exhibit a proper methodological caution. But it is just as true that the general climate of opinion favours the blood-and-guts model which at present is having quite a run. It has been blessed and speeded on its way in the last few years by a number of books, for example Ardrey (1966); much of Carthy and Ebling (1964); Lorenz (1963); Morris (1967); and Storr (1968), some of which quickly became best sellers. The act of blessing has been performed not only in the protected gentility of academic discussions; it has burst through again and again to the public forum owing to serialization in newspapers, television appearances, and elsewhere. And so, suddenly, tentative views concerning a complex problem about which we know very little have become public property and are already being used here and there to buttress and justify certain political opinions and actions.

The relevance to this discussion of both the biological and the psycho-analytic points of view has been succinctly summarized by Lorenz (1964) in a recent symposium. He wrote:

There cannot be any doubt, in the opinion of any biologically-minded scientist that intraspecific aggression is, in Man, just as much of a spontaneous instinctive drive as in most other higher vertebrates. The beginning synthesis between the findings of ethology and psycho-analysis does not leave any doubt either, that what Sigmund Freud has called the 'death drive'; is nothing else but the mis-carrying of this instinct which, in itself, is as indispensable as any other (p. 49).

From the point of view of *any* scientist, the degree of certainty expressed in these assertions is breath-taking. As far as the present discussion is concerned, their major difficulties lie in the gaps which persist when the usual extrapolations are made from them to complex social behaviour in man. There is no doubt that under *some* conditions all men can and do display hostility towards groups other than their own, be they social, national, racial, religious, or any other. There is also no doubt, however, that under other conditions this hostility either does not appear or can be modified. The scientifically-minded biologist (as distinct from Lorenz's biologically-minded scientist) would have to specify for us in the case of human behaviour, as he does so often and so successfully for animal behaviour, the conditions under which social aggression in man does or does not appear; he would also have to provide criteria which enable him to distinguish aggression from other forms of behaviour. Unless this is done, statements such as that of Lorenz are just about as useful as would be attempts to explain the development of the rich variety of gastronomic traditions in terms of our undeniably innate need for food and drink, or as have been the attempts to reduce the complex forms of the use of language to a few basic laws of conditioning.

It is hardly startling to say that one of the best ways to predict whether a man will harbour hostile attitudes towards a particular group and what will be the content of these attitudes is to find out how he understands the intergroup situation. And it is hardly any more startling to say that this understanding will in turn affect his behaviour. This does not mean, of course, that emotional and motivational factors are unimportant. But it is just as true that the greatest adaptive advantage of man is his capacity to modify his behaviour as a function of the way in which he perceives and understands a situation. It is difficult to see why it should be assumed that he loses this capacity as soon as he confronts human groups other than his own, and that it is in these situations alone that most of his concepts, attitudes, beliefs and modes of thinking are no more than powerless and pale projections of instinctive or unconscious drives.

The purpose of this chapter is to present an outline of the cognitive factors in intergroup hostility. The principal argument will be clear from the preceding general considerations: it is that the psychology of intergroup relations cannot be properly understood without the help of an analysis of its cognitive aspects, and also that this analysis cannot be derived from statements about motivation and about instinctive behaviour. We live in a social environment which is in constant flux. Much of what happens to us is related to the activities of groups to which we do or do not belong; and the changing relations between these groups require constant readjustments of our understanding of what happens and constant causal attributions about the why and the how of the changing conditions of our life. These attributions are based on three processes which will be discussed in turn. They are the processes of categorization, of assimilation, and of the search for coherence.

Categorization

Much work has been done in social psychology on the so-called stereotypes. These can be defined as the attribution of general psychological characteristics to large human groups. There is no doubt that the content of various stereotypes has its origins in historical and cultural traditions. But what is perhaps more important is their general structure and function. As the late Gordon Allport (1954) and many others have pointed out, stereotypes arise from a process of categorization. They introduce simplicity and order where there is complexity and (often) nearly random variation. They can help us to cope only if fuzzy differences between groups are transmuted into clear ones, or new differences created where none exist. They represent, of course, tendencies towards simplification rather than sharp dichotomies; in other words, in each relevant situation we shall achieve as much stereotyped simplification as we can without doing too much violence to the facts. But there is good evidence that even when facts do turn against us and destroy the useful and comfortable distinctions, we still find ways to preserve the general content of our categories.

In a rather formal way, the problem of stereotypes is that of the relation between, on the one hand, a set of attributes which vary on continuous dimensions and, on the other, classifications which are discontinuous (Tajfel, 1959). For example, classifications into nationalities or racial groups are on the whole discontinuous; most people are clearly X or Y and rarely something rather indefinable in between. Height of people or colour of skin are continuous dimensions. If it were true that all the

Scandinavians were taller than all the Italians, we could predict the nationality of a man entirely from his height, and *vice versa*, despite the fact that these values were not the original criteria on which the classification was based. It will be obvious that, theoretically, the possible correlations of that nature may vary all the way from fully predictable relations to cases where there is no relationship at all; and that in the world of human groups there will be very many cases where there is no relationship, hardly any 'perfect' ones, and quite a number which show a strong positive correlation, such as, for example, some physical characteristics associated with race.

Three empirical statements need to be inserted at this point, all of which are based both on common experience and on a good deal of evidence from experimental work in social psychology. The first is that personal traits or characteristics can be treated as dimensions much in the same way as height and weight would be if we could conceive them only in comparative terms of 'more' and 'less', 'shorter' and 'longer', 'heavier' and 'lighter'. This is the kind of statement that I make if I say that someone is 'intelligent' or 'honest' or 'lazy'; these are essentially comparative judgements which could hardly be made in a vacuum of absolute assertions.

The second statement is that, through personal and cultural experience, dimensions such as 'intelligent', 'lazy', or 'honest' are subjectively associated with classifications of people into groups. As long as we have little specific knowledge about an individual, we will tend to ascribe to him the characteristics which we derive from our knowledge of his class membership, be it a class of trade unionists, undergraduates, animal lovers, or Patagonians. Two inferences follow directly: one is that, in many social situations which present notorious ambiguities of interpretation, it will always be easier to find supporting evidence for the assumed class characteristics of an individual than to find contradictory evidence. The second inference is perhaps socially more important: whenever we are confronted with the need to interpret the behaviour of the members of a particular group *en masse*, there is bound to be very little clear contradictory information following the ascription of this behaviour to the assumed class characteristics.

The third statement refers to two consequences of the tendency to simplify in order to cope. They are but two aspects of the same phenomenon and can be described as follows: when a classification is correlated with a continuous dimension, there will be a tendency to exaggerate the differences on *that* dimension between items which fall into distinct classes, and to minimize these differences within each of the classes. The results of an experiment conducted in Oxford in 1963 by Wilkes and myself can serve as an illustration.

Three groups of subjects were presented with a series of eight lines which differed in length from each other by a constant ratio. They were asked to estimate the length of each line in turn. For one group, the four shorter lines were labelled A, the four longer ones, B. (The possible effect of the labels A and B *per se* in the judgements of length was controlled.) For the second group, the labels A and B were attached each to half of the lines, but in a random relation to length. The third group had the lines without any labels. The series of eight lines was presented a number of times in successive random orders.

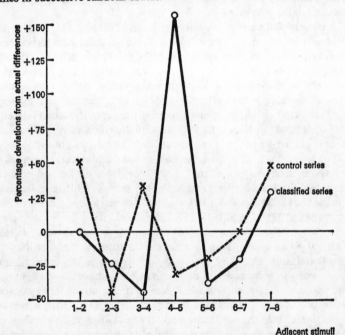

Figure 1 Comparison of actual and apparent differences between lines of adjacent length. (From Tajfel and Wilkes, 1963, p.111.)

Figure 1 presents the discrepancies shown by groups of subjects in the differences between their judgements of the lines after one fairly long experimental session. It will be seen that, at the point of break between the two classes (that is, between line 4 – the longest of the shorter class, and line 5 – the shortest of the longer class), the group which experienced a fully predictable relation between the labels A and B and the length of lines exaggerated the differences between the lines considerably more than did the other groups. None of the other differences between the judgements of the various groups reached the level of statistical significance. The phenomenon of subjective reduction of differences within each of the classes is also present, though much less noticeably.

Effects of this type can thus be obtained in simple judgements of length of lines. In a situation which lacked any 'social' or emotional relevance, the subjects reproduced the essential features of social stereotyping – the subjective accentuation of differences in *relevant dimensions* between classes of stimuli, and their subjective reduction within each class. It can therefore be assumed that the same features of the same categorizing process are responsible, in part at least, for biases found in judgements of individuals belonging to various human groups. In other words, if length of lines stood for personal characteristics subjectively correlated with a classification that is being used, and the classification itself would be in terms of racial, ethnic, national or other social criteria, we would have the full-blown stereotype. In addition, it can be shown that the more important a particular classification of people into groups is to an individual, the more likely he is to introduce sharp distinctiveness into his judgements of the characteristics of people who belong to the different groups.

These various biases of judgement have been demonstrated in a number of experiments (for a fuller review, see Tajfel, 1969). For example, Razran reported in 1950 on a study he had conducted several years earlier in which he presented to his subjects a series of thirty photographs of girls. 'The main basis for the selection of the photographs was a facial type that was ethnically non-specific and could readily fit most American white groupings' (p. 7). The subjects were asked to rate the photographs on various characteristics, such as likeability, beauty, intelligence and character. About two months later, the same thirty photographs (with the addition of fifteen new ones) were presented again to the same subjects – this time with surnames, some of which were typically Italian, Jewish and Irish (for example, D'Angelo, Rabinowitz, O'Shaughnessy), and some 'Old American' (for example, Adams, Clark etc.) 'chosen from the signers of the Declaration of Independence and the Social Register' (p. 8). The ratings of the minority group photographs shifted in accordance with the general stereotype of the ethnic group to which they were presumed to belong: for example, the 'Jewish' ones went down in likeability, beauty and character and up in ambition and intelligence; the 'Italian' and 'Irish' photographs shifted downwards (though much less than the 'Jewish' ones) in all these traits as well as in intelligence, but were also judged more ambitious than previously. Using photographs some of which were not clearly Negro or white, Secord, Bevan and Katz (1956) obtained data which were in principle similar to those of Razran. If a subject categorized a particular photograph as being that of a Negro, he tended to assign to it the characteristics of the Negro stereotype. The anti-Negro subjects tended to exaggerate more than the others the differences in the relevant stereotyped characteristics between the photographs they assigned to the categories of Negro and white – including the differences in physical characteristics, such as the colour of skin.

These effects of categorization can be shown to exist even when the stereotypes are not hostile and judgements are made in fairly 'natural' conditions. In an experiment conducted in Canada by Tajfel, Sheikh and Gardner (1964), students were asked to rate on a large number of characteristics two Indians (from India) who had just been interviewed in front of the class about their tastes in books, films, and so on. The stereotyped notions of Canadian students about Indians in general were elicited from another group of subjects. The former group judged the two Indians to be much more *alike* in those characteristics which were part of the general stereotype (for example, submissive, religious, family-oriented) than in those which were not (for example, confident, sociable, optimistic). Similar data were obtained when ratings of two Canadian students who were also interviewed in front of the class were related to the stereotype that the Canadian students held of themselves.

The function of categorization in the stereotyped judgements of people becomes clear when one considers the obvious differences between the judgements of lines in the experiments described above and the hostile stereotypes associated with prejudice. In the case of our lines, it would have been enough to present some form of reward to the subjects for accurate judgements and to penalize them for the inaccurate ones in order to eliminate quite rapidly the biases that were obtained. This is certainly not the case when hostile stereotypes are involved. Their rigidity and resistance to information which contradicts them is undoubtedly one of their most salient features.

This does not present, however, much of a mystery. In the first place, judgements of human characteristics in complex social situations are much more uncertain and ambiguous than judgements of lines in a laboratory setting. Contradictory information is therefore less clear and much easier to ignore. In the second place, and this is probably more important, the consequences of a mistake in judgement are radically different in the two situations.

If a man is hostile towards a group of people, he has an emotional investment in preserving the differentiations between his own group and the 'others'. Inaccurate judgements are not followed by the obvious dire consequences of inaccurate judgements about the physical properties of the environment. On the contrary, the preservation of these judgements is self-rewarding, and this is particularly so when prejudiced judgements are made in a social context which is strongly supportive of hostile attitudes towards a particular group. We are then confronted with a spiral effect in which the existence of prejudice at large not only provides additional support and rewards for hostile judgements; it also removes the possibility of a 'reality check' for these judgements which then feed upon each other and become more and more strongly entrenched in the form of powerful social myths.

Assimilation

The content of the categories to which people are assigned by reason of their social identity is generated over a long period of time within a culture; the origin and development of these ideas requires a discussion of their historical, economic and social background which is beyond the scope of this chapter (but see Banton, 1967). The task of the social psychologist is to discover how these images are transmitted to individual members of a society, and it is here that the second of the three processes previously mentioned, that of assimilation, comes into play.

Two points appear most directly relevant to the assimilation of ideas about one's own and other human groups. One concerns the learning of evaluations (or preferences); the other, the subtle interaction that occurs early in life between a child's identification with his own group and the influence of notions about various groups, his own and others, which are generally accepted in his society.

In his work on the development of moral judgement in the child, Piaget (1932) described the transition from the stage in which the value of pronouncements is judged by their source rather than by their content to a stage in which the child begins to interact and to co-operate with equals. At this point the child is beginning to learn to take the role of the other. This ability 'to see the same data from more than one point of view' (Holmes, 1965, p. 134) is not only the basis for the development of intellectual operations, but also for 'the emergence of a new morality', the progress from constraint to cooperation. According to Piaget, this progress cannot take place when the child is exposed to only one source of information and 'when it remains in awe of this source of truth' (Holmes, 1965, p. 135).

These tend to be precisely the conditions under which the child learns his socially sanctioned truths about a variety of human groups. It is not surprising, then, that later in life the ordinary categories of moral judgement, governed by the notion of reciprocity, apply with difficulty to individual members of some of these groups or to the groups as a whole. Thus, 'bad' or 'good', even 'liked' or disliked', become incontrovertible statements of fact not different in their mode of assimilation from, for example, 'large' or 'small'.

This can perhaps be illustrated from one of the studies (Tajfel and Jahoda, 1966) which we conducted as part of a wider research project on the development of national attitudes in children. In one of the tests, each child was presented with a number of black plastic squares varying in size. He was then asked to point to the squares which would represent the sizes of America, France, Germany and Russia if the square of the median size stood for his own country. In another test, his preferences for the same four countries were elicited through a series of paired comparisons.

One aspect of the results can be described as follows: at the ages of six and seven children in Britain agree rather more about which countries they like and dislike than about practically anything else concerning these countries. And this agreement on preferences still runs very closely to the agreement on factual items at the ages of ten and eleven. This can be put in a different way: at the age of six or seven, children in Britain agree rather more that they prefer America and France to Germany and Russia than that *both* America and Russia are larger in size than *both* France and Germany. There is no difference between the learning of these two kinds of 'fact'; the knowledge of 'facts' about preferences, about likes and dislikes, crystallizes at least as early as the corresponding knowledge of facts about size. Thus, the early formation of negative evaluations about outgroups does not present much of a mystery; and there is hardly any need to concoct magical brews made of 'territorial imperatives', 'instinctive' dislikes, blood bonds, and other such ingredients in order to account for these facts.

In the case of racial attitudes, as distinct from those which apply to national, ethnic or other outgroups, the learning and assimilation of socially sanctioned value judgements is made even easier through the existence of obvious visual cues which place each individual firmly and instantly in the category to which he belongs. This additional factor of 'visibility', combined with the rich linguistic associations of 'black' and 'white' (see Gergen, 1967, for a review) acts in several directions at once: it not only facilitates the placement of an individual in the appropriate category; at the same time, it helps in a more efficient 'filtering' of contradictory information, and thus provides a secure basis for jumping to conclusions about various characteristics of people who are instantly identified as one thing or another.

The same simplicity in attaching value judgements to crude and rudimentary categories applies to the formation of preferences for one's own racial, national or ethnic group. Children do develop these attitudes early in life, certainly well before they have any clear idea about the meaning of the categories to which they apply. In another study, also forming part of the research project mentioned above, children were presented with a series of twenty photographs of young men, and asked to put each photograph in one of four boxes which were labelled respectively: '*I like him very much*,' '*I like him a little*,' '*I dislike him a little*,' '*I dislike him very much*'. Several weeks later the same children were shown again the same photographs and told that some were of people who were English and some not English. Two boxes were provided, one labelled '*English*,' one '*not English*'. The children were asked to put in the appropriate box the photographs which, according to them, belonged to each of the two categories. One half of the children were tested in the order just described, the other half in the opposite order, starting with '*English*' – '*not English*' and having later the 'like-dislike' session.

One way to describe the results is in the form of a correlation in which one of the scores for each photograph consists of its average position in terms of 'liking' in the total group of children, and the other of the percentage of children who assigned that same photograph to the category 'English'. This correlation is very high (about 0·8); in other words, there is a great deal of consistency in the assignment of a photograph to the category 'English' on the one hand, and the degree of its liking on the other. The same photographs were used with roughly the same results in several other countries where, of course, the nationality categorization was in terms of Dutch-not Dutch, Belgian-not Belgian, Austrian-not Austrian, and so on.[2]

Data such as these do not, of course, *explain* anything. They only tell us that, with the help of devious stratagems, one can elicit from children a fairly objective index of high consensus in their preference for their own national group. But there are some situations which do enable us to assess indirectly the role that is played by social influences and by the social context in the development of children's preferences for their own national, ethnic or racial groups. There are many minority groups in the world today which stand low in the pecking order of human groups that each society constructs for itself. If it were true that the identification with one's own group is based on some kind of universal and 'self-generating' process, then the fact that a group is considered as inferior in the social order should not considerably affect the affiliation with it shown by its own young children. If, on the other hand, a system of preferences in the society at large does affect all of its members, then children of the groups assumed to be inferior should be exposed to a conflict in which the pro-

[2] Full reports of two of these studies are now available. They can be found in Jaspars, van de Geer, Tajfel and Johnson (1965), and Simon, Tajfel and Johnson (1967). See also Tajfel, Nemeth, Jahoda, Campbell and Johnson (1970).

gressive acquisition of their own group identity, and the formation of their own social self that goes with it, should clash with the ordering that is generally accepted and socially transmitted.

There are a few relevant studies in existence (and see also chapter 1). For example, Mary Goodman (1964), working in New England in the late 1940s, elicited by various means preferences for Negroes and whites in a group of nursery school children between the ages of three-and-a-half and five-and-a-half; 92 per cent of the white children expressed a preference for their own group – the corresponding figure for Negro children being 26 per cent. There is an earlier and famous study by Clark and Clark (1947) in which Negro nursery school children were shown a brown and a white doll and were asked which of the two they preferred and which of the two they thought they looked like. Sixty-six per cent of the children identified themselves with the brown doll; exactly the same proportion expressed a preference for the *white* one; in an answer to another question, 59 per cent declared that the brown doll 'looked bad'. We now have evidence that a similar conflict of preferences and identifications exists amongst children from coloured minority groups in Britain (see Milner, 1971; Jahoda, Thomson and Bhatt, 1972).

The sensitivity of children to the social context was particularly well brought out in a study conducted by Morland (1966). He worked with groups of nursery school children in Lynchburg, Virginia, and in Boston. Forty-six per cent of the Negro children expressed preference for their own group in Boston; only 22 per cent did so in Lynchburg. The trend was reversed for the white children's preferences for their own group: the figure was 68 per cent in Boston and 80 per cent in Lynchburg. Similar results were obtained in an interracial situation undoubtedly much less tense than in the United States. Vaughan (1964) found that, at the ages between four and eight, the proportion of Maori children in New Zealand expressing preference for their own group was about half of the corresponding proportion of the white children.

One further example from our own work will be provided. The study with photographs which has already been referred to was also conducted in Israel.[3] The Israeli Jewish population originates in part from Europe and in part from the Middle East and North Africa. According to recent figures, just over 60 per cent of the population is in the second category. Strains have developed, and there undoubtedly exists a correlation between socio-economic status and origin. The set of English photographs which served in several European countries was not used in the Israeli study. A

[3] This work was done in Haifa under the supervision of Dr Y. Rim of the Israel Institute of Technology. A full report is in press (H. Tajfel, G. Jahoda, C. Nemeth, Y. Rim and N. B. Johnson, 1972).

special set was prepared of which half were of Israelis of European origin and half of Israelis of Oriental origin. The subjects of the Oriental photographs could easily have been taken for southern, Mediterranean Europeans. Half of the children who made the judgements were of Oriental and half of European origin. There was again a very high overall correlation between the child's assignment of a photograph to his own national group and how much he liked it. But the most interesting results came in comparing the judgements made of the two categories of photographs.

Both groups of children, the Oriental and the European, expressed a greater overall preference for the European photographs, independently of their national assignments; both groups assigned a larger proportion of the European photographs than of the Oriental ones to the category Israeli. And there was an increase in both these trends for both groups as a function of age.

All this evidence points to the high sensitivity of children to the context of social influences in which they live – even when these influences are at cross-purposes with the powerful forces working towards an identification with the child's own racial or ethnic group. The enduring basis for future prejudices and conflicts is laid most crucially in childhood. And – as might be expected – the sensitivity to the social context continues throughout life. This was well brought out in a study by Pettigrew (1958) who worked in South Africa and in the United States.

In South Africa, he gave three attitude scales to his subjects who were white South Africans: an F-scale (measuring authoritarian attitudes) roughly comparable to the one used by Adorno, Frenkel-Brunswik, Levinson and Sanford (1950); a C- (conformity) scale and an A- (anti-African) scale. The C-scale was nearly as predictive of the attitudes towards the Africans as was the F-scale; students born in Africa were found to be more prejudiced, but not more authoritarian, than those not born in Africa; the same was true of students belonging to the Nationalist party as compared with others; the Afrikaners 'are both more anti-African and more authoritarian, and, when the F-scale differences are corrected for, they remain significantly more hostile to the Africans'. Results which point in the same direction were obtained by Pettigrew in a comparison of four small towns in Georgia and North Carolina with four similar locations in New England. He concluded that 'in areas with historically embedded traditions of racial intolerance, externalizing personality factors underlying prejudice remain important, but socio-cultural factors are unusually crucial and account for the heightened racial hostility'. To this it may be added that the scores on the F-scale which are designed to elicit the personality correlates of prejudice are themselves by no means free of conforming influences in societies which display a high incidence of one form or another of an authoritarian ideology. Thus, Pettigrew's conclusion can be viewed as a rather conservative estimate of the psychological importance in prejudice of 'socio-cultural factors'.

Search for coherence

The process of categorization provides the mould which gives shape to intergroup attitudes, and the assimilation of social values and norms provides their content. But this does not tell us very much about the manner in which individuals react to the specific inter-group situations which confront them, and about the way in which they try to come to terms with constant changes that occur in these situations. It is here that the consideration of the third process previously mentioned, the search for coherence, may be of some help.

An example can perhaps serve better to introduce this search for coherence than would a definition in general terms. One of the studies on the national attitudes in children, to which reference has already been made several times, was once piloted with a group of children in a primary school in a suburb of Vienna. A boy of about eleven was being interviewed and stated, like many others, his dislike for the Russians. He was then asked why he disliked the Russians. The answer was: 'because they occupied our country, and Hitler was their chief'.

If the individual is to adjust to the flux of social change, he must attempt to understand it; in other words, in order to deal with change he must construct for himself a system of causes which, according to him, determine the new course of events. The causal attributions must fulfil at least two criteria: they must equip him to deal with new situations in a manner which appears consistent to him; and they must do this in a way which will preserve, as far as possible, his self-image and his integrity. This need to preserve the integrity of the self-image is the only assumption of a 'motivational' nature that we need to make in order to understand the direction that the search for coherence will take.

One of the important categories of events contributing to the constant social change which affects all our lives is due directly to the fact that each individual is a member of numerous social groups which interact with other groups. Theoretically, two types of change (and consequently, of the need for adjustment to change) can be distinguished: intra-group and inter-group. The former consists of the individual's changing circumstances within the group or groups to which he belongs; the latter, of those aspects of the changing relations of his group with other groups which affect directly some important aspects of his life. In both cases, he needs to construct a 'theory' which will provide him with a satisfactory explanation of the causes of change. A 'satisfactory' explanation will manage to preserve personal integrity while at the same time – for reasons of cognitive economy – tending towards as much simplification as the situation allows for.

The effects of change – whether intra- or inter-group – on the manner in which an individual relates himself to his own group can only be of two kinds: an increase in the intensity of affiliation with the ingroup, or a decrease of it – that is, alienation from the group. In both cases, the changes of attitude need to be accounted for. In all cases in which this attribution is confined to social agents (as distinct from physical causes, such as natural catastrophes, and so on) it can go in two directions only: the causes of change may be attributed to some characteristics and actions of the individual himself and/or other individuals; or they may be attributed to the characteristics and actions of his own and/or of other groups.

It is this second category of causal attributions which is of interest here. Much that we know about causal attributions regarding social events points to the conclusion that, unless situational explanations are easily available (and often even when they are), actions of others tend to be explained in terms of their individual and fairly permanent characteristics (see, for example, Jones and Davis, 1965). In the case of individual attributions, this type of explanation provides obvious advantages in terms of simplification and of predictability of future events.

This need for simplification and for predictability is no less relevant in causal attributions to groups. There are, however, some important differences: the first is that explanations in terms of group characteristics obviously represent a considerably greater degree of simplification than is the case for individual characteristics; the second (already referred to) is that the feedback of causal attributions to group characteristics is much more complex, ambiguous, and difficult to interpret than in individual cases. It is therefore likely that the individual's needs, biases, interests and preconceived ideas will play a much greater part in the causal attributions to groups, and that for the same reason these attributions will be much more resistant to change than the individual ones.

The requirement of simplification also implies that large groups of people will be 'personalized' – that is, will be perceived as endowed with a set of characteristics that are usually attributed to an individual. If there is to be a satisfactory explanation of social events in terms of the characteristics of a group, these must be characteristics which are relevant to the situation and common to the group as a whole, with a corresponding neglect of individual differences between the members of the group. There is abundant evidence, both from psychological studies and from common experience, of this personalization of very large human groups.

Starting from this, some fairly general statements can be made:

1. Any change in the *status quo* between social groups imposes on the individuals involved a need to construct an explanation of the causes which account for the change. This explanation can be of two kinds: either (a) situational, or (b) referring to the characteristics of the groups.

2. Situational explanations are in terms of preceding events that do not originate in the groups involved (such as a natural catastrophe). When events of this nature are not concrete, clearcut and easily discernible, causes will tend to be attributed to the characteristics of the groups.

3. Causal attributions to group characteristics can be of two kinds; either referring to the non-psychological characteristics of a group (for example, its wealth or power, conditions in which it lives, its skin colour), or in terms of its psychological characteristics. This is, however, an uneasy distinction, since the non-psychological characteristics are often assumed to be related to, or to be the cause of, various psychological characteristics, and *vice versa*.

4. In view of this, a more useful distinction appears to be that between explanations in terms of group attributes which are assumed to be situational, transitional and flexible, and those which are assumed to be inherent and immutable.

5. Causal group attributions of complex social events must tend towards cognitive simplicity. Attributions in terms of 'inherent' group characteristics satisfy this requirement.

6. In their attribution of causality to inherent characteristics of groups, these 'ideologies' are also best fitted to shift the locus of responsibility for change either from the individual himself to a group, or from the ingroup to an outgroup. They will therefore be most likely to appear when other types of causal attributions either conflict with the prevailing values and beliefs, or represent a threat to the individual's self-image.

It follows therefore that not just *any* kind of inter-group conflict or competition should lead to the creation and spread of these attributes. But in actual fact most do; preventing popular interpretations of social conflict in terms of these inter-group ideologies would require careful social engineering which has rarely, if ever, been attempted. On the contrary, these simple notions are often created, encouraged and supported in conflicts between large groups. Any leader or politician knows intuitively that they help to maintain the internal cohesion of a group, that they can increase the influence of leadership, and that they are useful as a tool for furthering various social, political and economic interests. Most of all, they are a tool which – for reasons outlined above – is easily fashioned and highly effective in its use.

Summary and conclusion

The aim of this chapter is to stress the importance of the adaptive cognitive functioning of man in the causation of prejudice. I feel that this approach has the merits of economy, credibility and testability of explanation which are not always shared by views seeking the psychological roots of inter-group attitudes in the evolutionary past of the species or in unconscious motivation. Three cognitive processes have been considered from the point of view of their relevance to the genesis of prejudice in an individual: categorization, assimilation, and the search for conceptual coherence.

Though the chapter has not been concerned either with discussing ways to reduce prejudice or with outlining designs for future research, it is probable that the general approach adopted here has implications, both for social action and for research, which have not as yet been consistently and fully taken into account.

Inter-group conflict is a fact of life. It need not be determined by un-conscious motives or by aggressive instincts – but it does have psychological consequences such as were discussed in the previous sections of this chapter. And these consequences determine in turn a further intensification of conflicts and increased difficulties in reaching rational solutions. Is this vicious circle inevitable?

A change of beliefs and views that come about so easily and are so 'useful' to an individual's psychological well-being is an undertaking which is staggering in its difficulty. The first requirement for such changes is implicit in our discussion of the psychological need for coherence and understanding: as long as people interpret conflicts between large human groups in 'personal' terms, as long as they feel that their personal integrity and their image of themselves are involved, there is no way to break the fatal progression from objective conflict of interests to prejudice. And, therefore, short-cuts are not possible; the only chance we have is massive education in understanding that inter-group conflicts arise from objective and not from 'personal' reasons, planned against a background of social reform and of strong legislation preventing public forms of discrimination against minorities and other out groups.

Even then, all one can hope for is that the more vicious and inhuman forms of prejudice can be made less acute sooner or later. It is patently obvious that – despite the difficulties just mentioned – beliefs and views about causes of social events which are held by great masses of men are more easily accessible to change than their motives; and that there is at least a chance that a change of beliefs and views may affect in turn the management of conflicts, real or imaginary. It is therefore important *and useful*, for the purposes of science as well as for those of the society at large, that a consideration of prejudice as a phenomenon in the minds rather than in the guts of men should take precedence over views which are, on the whole, not only untestable but also useless in the planning of any form of relevant social change.

Even if it were possible to prove that inter-group hostility at large is due to unconscious motives or to an aggressive instinct, we still would be no further in knowing how to deal with the problem. Planning in terms of legal and social change combined with educational planning for attitudinal change has at least the merit of offering a glimmer of hope.

References

ADORNO, T. W., FRENKEL-BRUNSWIK, E., LEVINSON, D. J., and SANFORD, N. (1950), *The Authoritarian Personality*, Harper.

ALLPORT, G. W. (1954), *The Nature of Prejudice*, Addison-Wesley.

ARDREY, R. (1966), *The Territorial Imperative*, Atheneum.

BANTON, M. (1967), *Race Relations*, Tavistock.

BARTLETT, F. C. (1932), *Remembering: A Study in Experimental and Social Psychology*, Cambridge University Press.

CARTHY, J. D., and EBLING, F. J. (eds.) (1964), *The Natural History of Aggression*, Academic Press.

CLARK, K. B., and CLARK, M. P. (1947), 'Racial identification and preferences in negro children', in T. M. Newcomb and E. L. Hartley (eds.), *Readings in Social Psychology*, Holt.

GERGEN, K. J. (1967), 'The significance of skin colour in human relations', in 'Colour and Race', *Daedalus*, American Academy of Arts and Sciences.

GOODMAN, M. E. (1964), *Race Awareness in Young Children*, Collier, rev. edn.

HOLMES, R. (1965), 'Freud, Piaget and democratic leadership', *British Journal of Sociology*, vol. 16, pp. 123-39.

JAHODA, G., THOMSON, S. S., and BHATT, S. (1972), 'Ethnic identity and preferences among Asian immigrant children in Glasgow: a replicated study', *European Journal of Social Psychology*, in press.

JASPARS, J. M. F., VAN DE GEER, J. P., TAJFEL, H., and JOHNSON, N. (1965), *On the Development of National Attitudes*, Regent ESP no. 001-65, Psychological Institute, University of Leiden.

JONES, E. E., and DAVIS, K. E. (1965), 'From acts to dispositions: the attribution process in person perception', in L. Berkowitz (ed.), *Advances in Experimental Social Psychology*, Academic Press, vol. 2, pp. 219-66.

LÉVI-STRAUSS, C. (1966), *The Savage Mind*, University of Chicago Press.

LORENZ, K. (1963), *On Aggression*, Harcourt, Brace & World.

LORENZ, K. (1964), 'Ritualized fighting', in J. D. Carthy and F. J. Ebling (eds.), *The Natural History of Aggression*, Academic Press.

MILNER, D. (1971), 'Prejudice and the immigrant child', *New Society*, vol. 18, no. 469.

MORLAND, J. K. (1966), 'A comparison of race awareness in northern and southern children', *American Journal of Orthopsychiatry*, vol. 36, pp. 22-31.

MORRIS, D. (1967), *The Naked Ape*, Cape.

PETTIGREW, T. F. (1958), 'Personality and sociocultural factors in intergroup attitudes: a cross-national comparison', *Journal of Conflict Resolution*, vol. 2, pp. 29–42.

PIAGET, J. (1932), *The Moral Judgment of the Child*, Routledge & Kegan Paul.

RAZRAN, G. (1950), 'Ethnic dislikes and stereotypes: a laboratory study', *J. Abnorm. Social Psychol.*, vol. 45, pp. 7–27.

SECORD, P. F., BEVAN, W., and KATZ, B. (1956), 'The negro stereotype and perceptual accentuation', *Journal of Abnormal and Social Psychology*, vol. 53, pp. 78–83.

SIMON, M. D., TAJFEL, H., and JOHNSON, N. (1967), 'Wie erkennt man einen Österreicher', *Kölner Zeitschrift für Soziologie und Sozialpsychologie*, vol. 19, pp. 511–37.

STORR, A. (1968), *Human Aggression*, Allen Lane the Penguin Press.

TAJFEL, H. (1959), 'Quantitative judgment in social perception', *British Journal of Psychology*, vol. 50, pp. 16–29.

TAJFEL, H. (1969), 'Social and cultural factors in perception', in G. Lindzey and E. Aronson (eds.), *Handbook of Social Psychology*, Addison-Wesley.

TAJFEL, H., and JAHODA, G. (1966), 'Development in children of concepts and attitudes about their own and other countries: a cross-national study', Proceedings of the 18th International Congress of Psychology, Moscow, *Symposium, 36*, pp. 17–33.

TAJFEL, H., JAHODA, G., NEMETH, C., RIM, Y., and JOHNSON, N. (1972), 'Devaluation of children by their own national or ethnic group: two case studies', *British Journal of Social and Clinical Psychology*, vol. 11, part 3, pp. 235–43.

TAJFEL, H., NEMETH, C., JAHODA, G., CAMPBELL, J. D., and JOHNSON, N. (1970), 'The development of children's preferences for their own country: a cross-national study', *International Journal of Psychology*, vol. 5, pp. 245–53.

TAJFEL, H., SHEIKH, A. A., and GARDNER, R.C. (1964), 'Content of stereotypes and the inference of similarity between members of stereotyped groups', *Acta Psychologica*, vol. 22, pp. 191–201.

TAJFEL, H., and WILKES, A. L. (1963), 'Classification and quantitative judgment' *British Journal of Psychology*, vol. 54, pp. 101–14.

TINBERGEN, N. (1968), 'On war and peace in animals and man', *Science*, vol. 60, pp. 1411–18.

VAUGHAN, G. M. (1964), 'The development of ethnic attitudes in New Zealand school children', *Genetic Psychology Monograph*, vol. 70, pp. 135–75.

Chapter 5
Techniques for Reducing Prejudice: Changing the Prejudiced Person

J. Milton Yinger and George Eaton Simpson

J. Milton Yinger and George Eaton Simpson are the authors of the well-known textbook, *Racial and Cultural Minorities*, a psychological and sociological account of race relations from many viewpoints – the book now being in its fourth edition.

One of the most effective ways of learning about the nature of inter-group hostility is to study the techniques that are effective, and those that are ineffective, in reducing it; for such a study, to be valid, must be concerned with the causes and functions of that hostility.

Variables to consider in the development of strategies

Effective strategy is based on a precise knowledge of the goals one wants to achieve and on a thorough understanding of the obstacles in the way. We need to consider (a) the types of goals for which different groups are striving; (b) the types of persons to be affected, in terms of their relation to prejudice and discrimination; (c) the types of situations, in time and place, to which a strategy must adjust.

The strategies of a given period reflect assumptions about these issues, but the assumptions are often unexamined. The result is less effective action. We want to emphasize strongly, the *system* quality of prejudice and discrimination. They express cultural norms; they are embedded in institutional and interpersonal structures; they are related to the motives, needs and anxieties of majority- and minority-group members. Strategies, unhappily, often focus on one element only of the system. Perhaps we can illustrate this by a partially imaginary historical sequence, in which we will note major shifts in strategy.

The first stage in the break-up of patterns of dominance–submission is a slowly increasing readiness of dominants to admit some of those in the minority to relative equality of status if ... if, that is, they 'improve themselves', take on 'proper' attitudes and styles of behaviour, and the like. The underlying theory is: disprivilege is caused by the inadequacies of minorities. Hence sound strategy requires the removal of those inadequacies. There is often generous and well-meaning help from the dominants, in the form of educational support, for example. Considering the feedback mechanisms in complex social systems, this 'cause' should not be set aside; but it is a third-level cause, and becomes meaningful only when preceding 'causes' are recognized and acted upon.

The next stage of strategic effort, with its underlying theory, shifts major concern to the majority-group member: minority–majority relations are a problem because of the prejudices of those on top. A major campaign of education and persuasion must be mounted to help them see, and to set aside, their own prejudices and the culture on which they rest. This approach is also valuable; but insofar as it fails to see how prejudices are tied into the social system – in particular, into the system of discriminations which the dominant-group members participate in regularly – it cannot be very effective.

It is exactly this system of discriminations which is the focus of attention in the next stage. The institutions of a 'racist' society must be transformed, whether by organized legal and political action or by violent protest (the contrast, of course, is significant). According to those who take this approach, dominant-group prejudices are unimportant; at most they are reflections of the basic causes of injustice. And attention to the behaviour of the minority-group member is a travesty, for it seems to blame him for being victimized.

It is essential, of course, to deal with the structure of discrimination. If the reinforcements to that structure which come from culture and character are overlooked, however, gains that are won by costly effort may fade out, as the homeostatic forces in the total system bring it back to 'normal'.

In all of this, there is room for 'strategic specialists', who prefer to work on one part of the total system. There are times and places when one part of the system of discrimination is more vulnerable, suggesting that scarce resources should be expended there. There are no conditions, however, in which the several forces are not operative, a fact which a general theory adequate to strategic requirements must emphasize. And in the long run, structure, culture and character must all change.

Strategic disagreements sometimes rest on inadequate examination of conflicting goals, of variation among individuals in their readiness for change, and of differing situations. We must therefore look at the dilemmas and problems these circumstances present.

Types of goals

Those who are seeking to reduce prejudice and discrimination do not all agree on the immediate or long-run objectives. Some believe that peaceful coexistence is most desirable. Others are willing to accept and work for economic and political equality and integration but are opposed to 'social' equality (there is a vague and shifting line separating economic and political from social). Still others are working for complete integration, for a situation where each individual will be judged and treated as an individual and not in any way as a member of a *supposed* or functionless group. Functional group membership will continue to be important – it would be foolish to treat physicians as if they were engineers. Prejudice and discrimination, however, are characterized precisely by the fact that they disregard function; they treat the black physician and engineer and farm labourer and machine operator and teacher and unskilled worker as if they were all alike, although they share nothing in common *as Negroes* but a few traits – and these have a wide range of variation. That is why we call them a functionless group, just as 'white' people are.

We believe in the third goal mentioned above – complete equality and integration. This goal is harmonious with peaceful coexistence or pluralism, provided that the pluralism is chosen by individuals of the minority group as a matter of right and not enforced on them by the majority as a categorical requirement. Plural rights are limited, of course, by the legitimate needs for security and integration of the whole society. One of the great problems of modern society is the determination of differences that are allowable and are harmonious with the principle of the greatest good to the greatest number. We believe these differences can be very broad – broader than most societies, in this day of crisis, are permitting. Differences in language, in religion, in belief in the best methods for achieving life's values – these are not only permissible but necessary for a society that is eager to find better ways to solve its problems. *Active allegiance* to a system of law that opposes the democratic method for settling disputes is doubtless beyond the range of differences than an integrated society may permit. Advocacy of such a system is less dangerous to democracy than its suppression; but active programmes may well represent 'a clear and present danger'. Unfortunately, in the difficult and important task of separating advocacy from active programmes, a legitimate and necessary pluralism has been weakened.

In day-by-day moral decisions, one often has to decide between two values. Is it better to make the maximum number of public housing units available to disprivileged black families, or to promote housing integration even at the cost of turning away some of the families in greatest need? This raises the difficult question of quotas. Can they be 'benign', as Dodson (1960), Cohen (1960), and others have asked? That is, can they be designed to guarantee, in housing for example, that a neighbourhood that has become integrated racially will not rather quickly be resegregated? The word 'quota' has powerful associations with injustice to many people; and attaching the adjective 'benign' to it may not eliminate those associations, even if the goal is approved. The word 'quota' has recently been attached to another process, with equally praiseworthy goals, and communication has consequently been blocked by the connotations of 'quota'. Many colleges, for example, have been urged to increase the proportion of minority-group students, to set goals considerably above their present enrolment, to set a floor under which their level of participation will not be allowed to fall. Now the word 'quota' has traditionally meant a ceiling, not a floor; it has meant a barrier to fuller participation by a given group, rather than an active programme to encourage participation. So long as a word can be attached to two such different sets of activities, clarity of goals will be difficult.

In the early days of the desegregation movement in the United States, there was not a great deal of disagreement over goals, or over priorities because there was so much to do that any step seemed right. After a few' gains, however, value priorities begin to emerge, and serious dilemmas, within and between persons, are revealed. Is it better to promote justice, even at the cost of conflict; or to promote peace, even at the risk of some injustice: in political campaigns, should minority-group members emphasize welfare goals or status goals? The former are more immediately important to the least privileged, the latter to the middle-class minority-group members for whom bread-and-butter issues are less important, but prestige issues vital. As James Wilson (1960) has pointed out, the kinds of leaders and political arrangements needed to attain one of these goals are quite different from those required for the other; and if both are sought simultaneously, neither may be attained.

Is it liberty which is the primary goal – making certain that everybody has a fair start, that each has a choice among reasonable alternatives and the right to participate in decisions affecting his welfare, or, in a definition closer to John Stuart Mill, that every man is free from tyranny of leaders and from constraints by the majority when those constraints are unnecessary for the larger good? Liberty has perhaps been the first goal of liberal societies during the last two centuries. For others, however, the first goal is equality. They believe, with R. H. Tawney, that liberty is impossible without equality, that the democratic society, therefore, must strive to achieve a relative equality in the distribution of scarce goods. Some would say that this is so important that equality should be sought even at the sacrifice of some liberty.

It would take a long philosophical treatise to discuss the relationships among these goals. The French, and to an important degree the American, revolution assumed that they were not incompatible, but indeed mutually supportive. Many persons, however, would argue that they are mutually limiting; in the United States, for example, there has always been an underlying tension between the goals of liberty and of equality, with the former being more strongly supported, and fear being expressed that too much equality means the end of liberty. Today, the pluralism–integration question raises the issue of fraternity in a crucial way. The goal of sub-group fraternity is getting new emphasis, as for example in some phases of the Black Power movement.

Types of persons

Those who declare that *the* way to eliminate prejudice is 'education' or 'law' or 'more contact between peoples', or those who, against this, declare that prejudice cannot be eliminated because *the* prejudiced person is torn by a deep-seated anxiety that is basic to his ego, both make the mistake of failing to distinguish among the many different types of persons who show intergroup hostility. The reduction of prejudice and discrimination demands that we make such distinctions, for a different strategy will be effective for each of the different types of persons.

Robert Merton (1949) has devised a useful classification of four types of persons for each of whom a different group of strategies is appropriate.

1. The unprejudiced nondiscriminator, or all-weather liberal. Such a person must be the spearhead of any effective campaign to reduce prejudice and discrimination; but his force is reduced by several errors. There is the 'fallacy of group soliloquies'. 'Ethnic liberals are busily engaged in talking to themselves. Repeatedly, the same groups of like-minded liberals seek each other out, hold periodic meetings in which they engage in mutual exhortation, and thus lend social and psychological support to one another.' This activity does not appreciably spread the creed for which they are working. The fallacy of group soliloquies produces the illusion that there is consensus on the issues in the community at large and thus leads to the 'fallacy of unanimity'. His isolation from other points of view also produces the 'fallacy of privatized solutions'.

The ethnic liberal, precisely because he is at one with the American creed, may rest content with his own individual behaviour and thus see no need to do anything about the problem at large. Since his own spiritual house is in order, he is not motivated by guilt or shame to work on a collective problem. The very freedom of the liberal from guilt thus prompts him to secede from any *collective* effort to set the national house in order. He essays a *private* solution to a *social* problem.

These fallacies lead to the paradox of the passive liberal's contributing, to some degree, to the persistence of prejudice and discrimination by his very inaction (Pinkney, 1968).

2. The unprejudiced discriminator, or fair-weather liberal. This is the person who, despite his own lack of prejudice, supports discrimination if it is easier or profitable. He may show the expediency of silence or timidity, or discriminate to seize an advantage. He may refuse to hire Negroes because it 'might hurt business.' The fair-weather liberal suffers from some degree of guilt and is therefore a strategic person for the all-weather liberal to work on. The need is to bring him into groups of all-weather liberals, where he will find rewards for abiding by his own beliefs.

3. The prejudiced nondiscriminator, or fair-weather illiberal. This is the reluctant conformist, the employer who discriminates until a fair employment practices law puts the fear of punishment and loss into him, the trade-union official who, though prejudiced himself, abolishes Jim Crow because the rank and file of his membership demands it, the bigoted businessman who profits from the trade of minority-group members. Like the fair-weather liberal, he is a person of expediency, but this disguises a basic difference. Adequate strategy must recognize this difference. The fair-weather illiberal can be kept from discrimination only by an environment that makes discrimination costly and painful, not by appeal to his value creed. Legal controls, strictly administered, may at first increase his prejudice – or at least his verbalization of it – but they will reduce his discrimination.

4. The prejudiced discriminator, or all-weather illiberal. He is consistent in belief and practice. He believes that differential treatment of minority groups is not discrimination, but discriminating. Strategy in dealing with such persons must vary from region to region. In some subcultures of the United States the all-weather illiberal is a conformist, supported by the group norms; if he were to change, he would be alienated from the people important to him. In other subcultures he is isolated, and a change in his attitudes and behaviour would help to bring integration with people significant to him. He can be moved toward type three. Change of the illiberal who is supported by group norms requires legal and administrative controls and large-scale changes in the economic supports to prejudice.

It is important to understand the distribution of these various types and to realize the kinds of strategies that are effective with each. To try to appeal to all of them in the same way, or to assume that a given proportion of each type is found, when they are in fact very differently distributed, is to make serious strategic errors (Merton, 1949).

We need to note that such a classification has little reference to the intensity dimension; two all-weather illiberals, for example, may have very different patterns of behaviour because prejudice and discrimination occupy an important place in the personality organization of one and an unimportant place for the other. One cannot assume, moreover, that the same distribution would be true for each minority. In a given community one might find discrimination against both an Indian and a Negro group, but most of the white population may be fair-weather liberals toward the Indians and all-weather illiberals toward the Negroes.

The types are probably found everywhere, although certainly not in the same proportions.

Levinson draws a valuable distinction between the openly anti-democratic individual and the pseudo-democratic individual. The former is nearly the equivalent of Merton's all-weather illiberal, except that Levinson emphasizes the deep-seated irrational sources (a specialized causal explanation that Merton might not share entirely). The pseudo-democratic person is somewhat similar to the fair-weather liberal; but Levinson places a useful emphasis on the ambivalence of such a person's feelings: he discriminates but has some sense of guilt about it; he is prejudiced but also believes in democratic values. This is probably a widespread type of individual; hence development of an adequate strategy in reducing his prejudice and discrimination is an important task. Levinson notes the strategic importance of recognizing the ambivalence of the pseudo-democratic person. Such an individual is relatively unaffected by current literature which attacks prejudice as 'un-American' or 'un-Christian', for he has disguised his prejudice from himself by a group of rationalizations that seem to square his behaviour with his value creed. Strategy must find a way not simply of exposing his rationalizations (for the problem is not essentially a rational one with the individual), but of lowering the need for prejudice while strengthening the belief in democratic values.

Many of us are pseudo-democratic. Our actions may seem to others to be discriminatory, but if they tell us so, it is easy to say, 'Who, me? Why, I believe in democracy, an equal chance for everyone. But why should I pay those Mexicans higher wages to buy more liquor with? They're just as happy the way they are. Why should I put in a bathtub for my Negro tenants? They'd just fill it with coal.'

The human mind has an enormous capacity for holding mutually contradictory ideas without any feeling of discomfort. The pseudo-democratic individual will not become thoroughly democratic until the personal and group functions and the traditional supports of prejudice and discrimination are sharply reduced.

The strategic problem of distinguishing types of persons is also indirectly involved in Isidor Chein's (1946) discussion of 'dimensions of prejudice.' A person in whom one dimension is largest will respond to a different approach than the person in whom another dimension is largest.

There is the 'informational' dimension – for example, the holding of stereotyped beliefs – for which education is an important strategy. The 'conformity' dimension represents a need on the part of the prejudiced person to conform to the prevailing pattern. Legal measures proscribing discrimination will affect him. The 'status' dimension is the desire for ego satisfaction, for a position of superiority. Reduction of this factor in prejudice requires the equalization of opportunities and rights – giving ego motives less to thrive on. The 'emotional' dimension involves attitudes of actual hatred and hostility toward minorities. The need here is for the minimization of frustration (see also Katz, Sarnoff and McClintock, 1956).

A definitive classification of the types of persons involved in prejudice and discrimination would have to be far more complicated than those we have discussed. When so many variables are involved, a few types cannot cover the range of empirical combinations. Nevertheless, the distinctions drawn by Merton, Campbell, Levinson, and Chein can be of great value in strategic considerations.

Types of situations

When one has distinguished the types of goals and types of persons involved, one has a great deal of information about a situation in which prejudice and discrimination are found. But other factors must also be considered if strategy is to be effective. What is the legal pattern? Does it support discrimination or condemn it? Does the law condemn it ideologically but fail to provide enforcement techniques? To try the same strategy in a situation where one can count on legal support as one tries in a situation where the law is weak or actually supports discrimination is to be ineffective.

Is the situation one that requires immediate action, or is there time for more deliberate analysis?

Strategic errors have been made in both directions. In a time of critical hostility a community may 'appoint a committee' when what is most needed is training for their police in how to disperse a mob with the least violence. Or, oppositely, a group may 'call in the cops', may throw down the gauntlet to discriminators when what is most needed is the careful analysis of causes, the skilful rallying of allies, and the creation of a more favourable environment for change.

Is the discrimination supported mainly by lower-class members of the 'dominant' group, themselves insecure and hoping to climb a little higher on the backs of minority-group members? Or is the pattern primarily set by powerful groups who are exploiting prejudice to maintain their authority? Or, more accurately, how are those two supports interrelated? Associated with this is the question of power in a community. Who makes the key decisions; whose support is vital? Much strategic counsel is based on the assumption that major support for change must come from 'the conservative power elite'. McKee (1958–9) argues, however, that this leads to failure to create '. . . support for new policies by building a constituency in the community who have a genuine stake, personal or ideological, in effecting changes in the community's policies'. In some contexts, a coalition can be built up among organized Negro groups, an active liberal middle-class group, the Jewish community, some church groups and women's organizations. In many instances, when such a coalition is mobilized, such 'power elite' as there is may then find participation more desirable. Under other conditions, of course, this procedure may mobilize opposition. The need is for flexibility of judgement.

Is the strategy to be aimed at a large group of people or only a few? What will work for a small neighbourhood, with an intimacy factor involved, will be ineffective in a large city, a state, or a nation, either because the principles involved may be different or simply because what is feasible for a few may be impossible for many. Are the cultural differences between the majority and minority large or small? Migrants from peasant Mexican backgrounds, for example, with significantly different cultural values from those of an urban, industrial society (Kluckhohn, 1953) require different kinds of strategy to improve their situation than do those from highly literate, urban situations (e.g., many Japanese and Jews).

Many aspects of the society under study are important situational influences. What is the level of unemployment, the degree of tension and frustration, the extent of status dissatisfaction? What subtle cues are people receiving on issues wholly unrelated to intergroup relations that influence their readiness for various kinds of intergroup behaviour? In the United States, for example, the vast majority of motion pictures, TV shows, and advertisements show no Negroes or use them only in stereotyped roles. In the last few years, however, Negroes have appeared as parts of casual crowds, juries, or as professional men; a small but slightly increasing proportion of advertisements are 'integrated'. Were this trend to develop, what Americans come to look upon as 'normal' may be slightly affected (Elkins, 1959).

Basic institutional structure is a vital part of the situation within which strategy must be worked out. It is easy for Americans to view segregation as an individual, moral question (which it is, of course) and to disregard its institutional aspects. There continues to be regional isolation (northern liberal and Mississippi farmers live in significantly different cultural worlds). America has the beginnings of a national press, religious consensus, and university system; but compared with France or England these are weak. This is an important situational fact for the strategist.

Mapping out a programme

Having defined his goals and analysed the kinds of persons and situational factors to be dealt with, the strategist will be in a position to plan his anti-hostility programme. Unfortunately, planning and testing are not common.

Well-intentioned but unguided programmes can be useless or even harmful. When they fail, many people may conclude that intergroup hostility is inevitable. Others may decide that such hostility is so deeply embedded in our society that only revolutionary change can produce results. Assumptions of these kinds can be tested only by action that is guided by research.

One of the functions of research is to discover the points at which prejudice and discrimination can be attacked most successfully. Myrdal refers to the white man's 'rank order of discriminations' towards the Negro, with particular reference to the South. He believes the white man is most willing (although not necessarily very willing) to grant economic and political gains to Negroes and is least willing to grant what he calls 'social' equality. The Negro, on the other hand, is primarily concerned with just the 'concessions' the white man will make most readily. This seems to carry the obvious strategic implication that action programmes should centre upon economic and political discriminations. MacIver also states that the 'economic front' is a weak point in the defences of the discriminator. Advances in this area, it is argued, do not encounter the emotional blocks that guard questions of segregation in social contact.

Evidence on this question is not decisive, for there is variation in time and place. Behaviour may be different from the answer to interview questions (few Americans, for example, will verbally deny the right to freedom of economic activity, but their actions often speak louder); and rankings depend on what the actual situation is (if the right to vote has been won by Negroes, whites may not state high opposition to it even though they had earlier strongly supported the disfranchising situation.) (Myrdal, 1944; Edmunds, 1954; Killian and Grigg, 1961). It is also important to note, as Killian and Grigg do, that the rank order tells you nothing about the absolute level of a discriminatory tendency – which may be the more significant fact.

Empirical studies of the rank ordering hypothesis are not common. Williams and Wienir (1967) found, in a study of student attitudes at three universities, that there was a consistent ordering, but that it varied somewhat from the pattern described by Myrdal. Myrdal hypothesized (on the basis, as he noted, of observation, not controlled study) the following order, with the relationships on which the white man was least willing to yield given first: intermarriage, personal relations, public facilities (schools, churches, means of transportation), politics, legal and judicial activities, and economics. For the three student groups, the order was: intermarriage, personal relations, economics, public facilities, politics, and legal and judicial activities. The placement of economic privilege is undoubtedly crucial in understanding any given minority–majority situation.

Matthews and Prothro (1966) also throw doubt on the Myrdal thesis when it is observed from the Negro point of view. Recall that Myrdal's quite optimistic interpretation rested on the belief that the Negro rank order was just the reverse of the white. But Matthews and Prothro found that Negro political demands in the eleven southern states were sharply in opposition to what whites were willing to grant. They also added a time dimension, and found that Negroes were expecting extremely rapid progress, while whites were just beginning to get comfortable with the thought of glacial speed in changes of race relations. We should observe, however, that their study, done a decade ago, would not have served as a good basis for prediction of the actual speed of change in southern politics in the 1960s. National political factors, of course, were critical in effecting this change.

Despite these qualifications, knowledge of the strong and weak points of opposition is essential to sound strategy. This does not mean that weak points should always be attacked first, for greatest opposition may be found on issues of greatest importance, which therefore must be confronted in spite of the difficulty.

In addition to knowing the relative importance of various issues to the interacting individuals and groups, one needs to know, in mapping out a programme, how a given type of strategy will be viewed by all those involved. Do they regard it as a legitimate way to express a grievance or as deviation from the accepted standards? Or, as is commonly the case in societies under serious stress, is a given strategy accepted by some – whatever their views of the goals being sought – and rejected by others? In America today, various forms of public protest are applauded by some as necessary and right, while others see them as acts of rebellion against legitimate authority. Marvin Olsen (1968) has designed a scale to measure the extent to which respondents grant legitimacy to various acts and has tested it with a largely upper-middle class, urban white group. The questions form a Guttman scale:

If a group of people in this country strongly feels that the government is treating them unfairly, what kinds of actions do you think they have a right to take in order to try to change the situation? ... Which of these actions do you think groups have a right to take in our country?

1. Hold public meetings and rallies. (92 per cent)
2. March quietly and peacefully through town. (70 per cent)
3. Take indirect actions such as economic boycotts or picketing. (60 per cent)
4. Take direct actions such as strikes or sit-ins. (46 per cent)
5. Stage mass protest demonstrations. (41 per cent)

That 59 per cent of this highly educated group of respondents should oppose mass protest demonstrations is perhaps not so striking as the fact that 30 per cent oppose the right to 'march quietly and peacefully through town'. In any event, for those seeking change, it is necessary to know probable responses to various strategies.

Ralph Turner (1969) has extended our knowledge on this question by asking: under what conditions will acts of disruption and violence be viewed as forms of legitimate protest and when will they be considered crime and rebellion? He defines protest as an action with the following elements: it expresses a grievance, wrong or injustice; protesters are unable to correct the condition directly by their own efforts; they seek to call attention to the grievance, to provoke ameliorative steps by some target groups; and some combination of sympathy and fear is invoked. The same act can be defined in many different ways; and the subsequent course of events is strongly affected by the definition that emerges. Those who define a disorder as a protest, in Turner's use of the term, see it as a form of communication. If they define it as deviation, they see it as an individual criminal act. When it is called rebellion or revolution, the disorder is seen, not as an effort to communicate with others or to change the system, but to destroy it.

What conditions support these various definitions; in particular, when will a more-or-less legitimate protest definition emerge? Turner notes the following conditions: protesters must be seen as a major part of a group whose grievances are well known, who seem powerless to correct those grievances, and who seem deserving of support because they are customarily law-abiding and restrained in their methods. The appeal message must command attention, which requires a combination of threat and appeal. 'When the threat component falls below the optimal range, the most likely interpretation is deviance; above the optimal range, pre-occupation with threat makes rebellion the probable interpretation', (Turner, 1969). The conflict expressed by the disorder must elicit some expression of conciliation if it is to lead to a protest definition. This leads to the further question: when will those who are the targets of protest be inclined to prefer conciliation, in an effort to reduce the conflict potential? Turner suggests that this is likely to occur when there is risk of injury, to protesters and their targets, in a context in which norms against doing injury to others are strong; when the groups are interdependent in various ways; and when a conflict, rather than a protest, definition seems likely to entail greater commitment of activity and resources. The points of view of third parties are also important. If they are affected by the disorder, but likely to be injured in some way by taking a partisan position, they may think of it as protest. Finally, official actions are significant parts of the definitional process, it being generally realized that disturbances are acknowledged more now as legitimate protest.

Perhaps the more common error today among intellectuals is the belief that everything ought to be politicized, that there is little consensus to build on, and that therefore all issues should be made matters of public controversy.

Strategies with major emphasis on changing the personality

It has frequently been noted that attempts to reduce intergroup hostility can focus either on the prejudiced individual or on those aspects of the situation which allow and encourage discrimination. The former strategies try to change the values, the attitudes, the needs of individuals. They are sometimes based on the oversimplified theory that majority–minority conflict is 'fundamentally' based on personality factors. But they are sometimes consciously chosen specialties that are used in full awareness of the value and necessity of other approaches.

We shall describe and evaluate five kinds of approaches that emphasize the need for changing the persons who show prejudice and discrimination: exhortation, propaganda, contact, education, and personal therapy. These are not analytically precise and mutually exclusive categories, but one can draw useful distinctions among them. It is particularly difficult to distinguish clearly among the first four, because of differences in the use of terms.

We are describing 'pure types' that may never be found.

Exhortation

Exhortation is perhaps the most frequently used method in trying to reduce inter-group hostility. Appeal to men's better selves; revivify belief in their value creed; change their hearts and they will change their ways. Despite the frequency with which this approach is used, its value has not been tested in any way that permits one to speak with confidence about the degree of its effectiveness. Myrdal's famous work has brought a strong emphasis on the importance of the 'American creed' as an ideological weakness of the prejudiced person. There is a moral struggle going on *within* most Americans, says Myrdal, that prevents race relations from being worse than they are and makes an ideological approach to their improvement feasible. The strategy of exhortation tries to bring this contradiction to the forefront of our attention, to revitalize the creed.

Although exhortation sounds quite old-fashioned, it is essentially the strategy of many current activities, from demonstrations and rallies to 'guerrilla theatre'. In this last, the players attempt, by a surprise dramatic event, to call vivid attention to an issue and to persuade those who see (or experience) the 'play' that a given moral view is right. The theatre group may stage a severe interracial argument on a bus; then speak words of reconciliation.

Participants in these contemporary forms of exhortation doubtless feel quite secular in most instances. In many ways, however, such events are modernized versions of sermons, not lacking in surrogates for hell-fire and brimstone, followed by descriptions of the true road to salvation. As with all sermons, the central questions remain: are the sinners in the pews; are they listening?

In the context of other changes, exhortation may help to reduce prejudice – particularly by increasing the enthusiasm of those who are already convinced. It may also inhibit the discriminations, although it may not affect the prejudices, of many fair-weather illiberals who do not want to violate the community standards openly. It is easy, however, to exaggerate the influence of exhortation. As MacIver (1948) pointed out, the charge of inconsistency doesn't reach most men; they can easily get along on compromises. 'It is well to expose their rationalizations but nevertheless they have great capacity for finding new ones. They may have some uneasiness on this score, but often it is not potent enough to make them change their ways. This uneasiness, in fact, may lead to stronger intolerance, for it may raise one's guilt feelings, which are then allayed by a blinder defensiveness, by new discriminations which actually furnish new justifications for the prejudices.

The American creed, moreover, is not of equal importance among all individuals or in all times and places. And persons who deviate from the creed can justify their actions by declaring that they are conforming with the spirit of the creed, not with the 'sterile letter'. Beyond that, one must recognize a contrary creed – a moral code that justifies prejudice and discrimination.

Effective strategy seems to indicate that exhortation can play only a modest role in the total efforts to reduce prejudice and discrimination. The moral premises which it rests upon are not universally shared and are alloyed with countervalues; most of us are skilled at compartmentalizing our professions of belief and our other actions, overlooking any contradictions; and those who are most likely to show hostility to minority-group members are probably those who are least often reached by exhortation.

Propaganda

The 'propaganda menace' and the 'hidden persuader' have received so much attention in recent years that many people have come to regard them as almost all-powerful. The success of the mass campaigns of persuasion by modern nations and the skill with which commercial propaganda (advertising) has converted cigarettes and chewing gum into necessities make us believe that a tremendously powerful instrument for controlling human behaviour has been created. Why not turn this instrument to the purpose of reducing intergroup hostility?

Before examining attempts to use propaganda to control intergroup behaviour, it may be wise to state briefly the contemporary answer to the question: How effective is propaganda? As we have learned more and more about the problem, we have seen that there is no *general* answer. The question must be more complicated: how effective is a specific propaganda campaign with a stated group of people in a particular situation? Gradually it has become apparent that far more limits are imposed on the power of propaganda than was generally believed to be true a few years ago.

Modern societies, to be sure, are more susceptible to propaganda than stable 'sacred' societies.

Propaganda is limited, however, even under such favourable conditions. It is limited by knowledge of the facts on the part of propagandees; it is limited by a counter-propaganda; and above all, it is limited by the already existing values, needs, and hopes of the persons to whom it attempts to appeal. To put this point in another way: propaganda is most effective when it is dealing with a poorly informed public, when it has a monopoly in the field of communication (censorship), and when it either is working in an area in which the values and needs of the public are diffuse and poorly structured or ties its appeals closely to well-structured needs and values.

Propaganda may also have wholly unexpected and unintended effects, for ultimately it is interpreted by specific individuals whose own values and needs are brought to bear. Unintended or 'boomerang' effects of propaganda are particularly likely to occur when one tries to influence a heterogeneous group.

Propaganda to reduce intergroup hostility. On the basis of this brief discussion of some contemporary concepts employed by students of propaganda, we can perhaps evaluate more accurately the usefulness of propaganda as a strategy in the reduction of prejudice and discrimination. Literally millions of leaflets, pamphlets, cartoons, comic books, articles, and films have been issued in the struggle against intergroup hostility. How effective are they? Flowerman (in 1947) suggested that this question can be answered only when we have the following information: to what degree do pro-tolerance groups control the media of communication? What is the level of saturation – the proportion of a population who are reached by the appeals? What is the attention level? How do the propagandees reinterpret the message? Does the propaganda conform to group standards? (If it does not, it can have little effect. And those standards may include prejudice.) What is the sponsorship? Is it held in high esteem?[7]

The evidence seems to suggest that on many of these counts anti-prejudice propaganda has not been very effective. For the most part it reaches those who already agree with it. Radio programmes of 'inter-cultural education' that describe the culture and history of the Italians, Yugoslavs, and Greeks are listened to, respectively, by Italians, Yugoslavs, and Greeks. Each group may be made to feel better, more secure, more important, but they are scarcely informed about the others.

In some instances individuals have been confronted with anti-prejudice propaganda involuntarily. Some fight it, openly or covertly; a few may accept it; but many evade it by managing to misunderstand its message. A number of studies have been made of the effects of a 'Mr Biggott' series of cartoons, designed to show an absurd man exhibiting ridiculous prejudices. 'In each of them, Mr Biggott, the central character, is shown as a cantan-kerous and unattractive man of middle age and moderate income. In each of them he displays the anti-minority attitudes from which he earns his name' (Kendall and Wolf, 1949). Three cartoons are used in the last named study. One shows Mr Biggott glowering at an 'honour roll' billboard on which the community war heroes are listed. He says, 'Berkowitz, Fabrizio, Ginsberg, Kelly – disgraceful!' In another cartoon, Mr Biggott, lying sick in bed, says to a somewhat startled doctor, 'In case I should need a trans-fusion, doctor, I want to make certain I don't get anything but blue, sixth-generation American blood!' In an 'Indian' cartoon Mr Biggott says to a humble American Indian, 'I'm sorry, Mr Eaglefeather, but our company's policy is to employ 100 per cent Americans only.'

The assumption behind the cartoons was that the picture of an absurd man exhibiting absurd ideas would lead one to reject one's own prejudices. Cooper and Jahoda (1947) found, however, that prejudiced persons created many mechanisms of evasion. Understanding may be 'derailed' by avoiding identification with Mr Biggott (despite the sharing of prejudice). Mr X, on seeing the 'blood transfusion' cartoon, looked upon Mr Biggott as an inferior *parvenu*: 'I'm eighth generation myself ... He may not be the best blood either.' Then Mr X leads off into other subjects. Having understood the cartoon at first ('He don't want anything but sixth-generation

American blood! Ha! That's pretty good.'), he then felt it necessary to disidentify.

Because of the difficulties of reaching the audience for whom the propaganda would be most useful and because of the ease with which its points can be evaded, we cannot rely heavily on propaganda as a strategy. To be sure, a cartoon series is a brief stimulus. We do not know what the effects of an intensive, long-run propaganda campaign would be. A movie is a stronger stimulus, on which we have some information. There have been many studies to test the effects of movies on attitudes; and, partly on the basis of the results obtained, several movies (some propagandistically and others educationally inclined) have aimed at the reduction of prejudice. Our knowledge of the total long-run effects of movies, however, is still far from adequate because of several methodological weaknesses. Sampling problems have not been given much attention (school populations are so readily available to the researcher); the distortions in evidence produced by the 'before–after' type of experiment (the kind that has been most often used) have not been adequately explored; and the relation between pencil-and-paper responses and other kinds of behaviour has usually not been studied.

Despite these weaknesses it seems fair to say that many movies do have a measureable effect on attitudes as recorded in verbal tests. L. L. Thurstone and his associates made the first extensive studies in this field. For example, *The Birth of a Nation*, which pictured Negroes in a very unfavourable light, was shown to 434 students, grades six to twelve, in a small Illinois town containing no Negroes. The students were tested for their attitudes towards Negroes both before and after seeing the film. In the latter test they were, on the average, 1·48 scale points (on an eleven-point scale) more unfavourable to the Negro. After five months they were retested, and it was found that 62 per cent of the change that had been attributed to the film remained (Peterson and Thurstone, 1933. But Merton, 1940, has made a pointed criticism of the weakness of this kind of measurement). We do not know if the nonverbal behaviour of the children was affected, whether the new attitudes actually reshaped later experiences, whether giving them a test before the picture 'sensitized' them to prejudice so that the movie was a different experience from what it would have been had they not been pretested. We do not know if the test five months after the movie was a stimulus that renewed memory associations with the movie and the earlier test – and so was inevitably highly correlated with that test. Tentatively, however, we may say that movies do seem to influence prejudices.

Can motion pictures also reduce prejudice? 329 students at a southern state university were shown 'Gentleman's Agreement', a successful Hollywood picture which took a strong stand against anti-Semitism. They had first recorded their attitudes on a ten-item anti-Semitism and ten-item anti-Negro scale. After seeing the film they were again asked to record their attitudes and were compared with 116 students who had not seen the film. The results were as follows in Table 1.

Table 1

	Saw the film	Did not see the film
Lower anti-Semitism score	228 (69·3 per cent)	49 (42·2 per cent)
No change or higher anti-Semitism score	101 (30·7 per cent)	67 (57·8 per cent)

This difference is significant at the 0·001 level. Interestingly, anti-Negro scores also fell among those who saw the film ($p = 0.05$). The largest absolute gains were made by those whose anti-semitism scores were highest at the beginning (they had more room in which to change); but those whose original scores were low showed the largest change when it is calculated as a percentage of possible change. Those persons low in status concern also had significantly greater reductions in their scores (Middleton, 1960).

Within the limits set by the present evidence it seems unwise to say either that antiprejudice propaganda is powerless or that it can, by itself, effect extensive changes. Flowerman points out these minimum requirements if it is to have any influence: the propaganda must be received under favourable conditions, so that it will be looked at or heard; it must attract and hold the attention of the propagandee; it must be enjoyed, not bring pain; it must be understood, not evaded by misunderstanding. None of these is easy to accomplish. Propaganda is usually seen only by the already converted; if prejudiced persons happen to see it, they usually turn away; if they don't turn away, they often find it painful (because of guilt feelings or a sense of hostility); and if they don't find it painful, they frequently misunderstand its point. It is with the mildly prejudiced and the neutral, particularly with children, that these disadvantages are at a minimum.

Williams (1947) summarizes a number of principles that help one to understand the effectiveness of anti-prejudice propaganda:

In intergroup relations, as in many others, word-of-mouth propaganda, especially that which appears spontaneous and informal, is more effective than visual or formal propaganda in influencing attitudes and behaviour. . . .

In intergroup relations, as in many others, propaganda which makes an 'emotional' (value-oriented) appeal is likely to be more effective than that which is restricted to factual appeal.

But this plausible assertion may be countered with the view that such appeals arouse relatively uncontrolled emotions which are not likely to lead to tolerant or humane behaviour. It certainly appears that there are sufficient dangers in strongly emotional propaganda to warrant careful testing with different types of audiences. . . .

In intergroup relations, as in many others, the 'propaganda of the deed' is especially likely to have effects upon attitudes and behaviour. . . .

Propaganda which appeals to minority rights on the basis of the group's achievements tends beyond a certain point to arouse insecurity-hostility in the dominant group by stressing group differences and competitive success.

This hypothesis implies that appeals which suggest a status-threat to prejudiced groups are to be avoided. . . .

It is dangerous technique to employ mass propaganda emphasizing 'rising tides of prejudice' as a means intended to mobilize defenders of minority rights and good intergroup relations. Such propaganda is likely to have a boomerang effect upon slightly prejudiced or wavering elements: it creates the presumption of group support for hostile actions (pp. 66–7).

How should prejudiced propaganda be handled? Wise strategy needs to understand not only the possible uses of propaganda but also the techniques that are most effective in counteracting prejudiced propaganda. In recent years there has been a vigorous debate, and sharp differences in action, between those who believed that 'hatemongers' should be exposed, ridiculed, and made to stand in the glare of public attention and those who contended that they should be disregarded and offset by positive action. Experience with the problem of counteracting rumours during the Second World War added strength to the arguments of those who held that hate propaganda should often be ignored, so far as a direct response is concerned. By 'ignored' we do not mean 'overlooked'. One must pay careful attention to destructive rumours or propaganda against minorities; but they should usually be opposed indirectly, by positive action, not directly, by exposing them and pointing out their errors. If one tries to prove a rumour wrong by repeating it and then describing the truth, many listeners may hear only the rumour, if that is all they want to hear. Thus a person does the opposite of what one intends. If one ignores the rumour but supplies truthful information, those who have not heard the rumour may to some degree be 'vaccinated' against it.

There is, of course, a danger that proponents of the 'silent' treatment of hate propaganda will drift into a position of no treatment. If one ignores not only the hatemonger but the problem he represents, the silent strategy will fail completely.

Those who oppose giving publicity to the hatemonger and those who support it both give illustrations to demonstrate the effectiveness of their approach. The need is to see that there are very different ways of bringing public attention to an issue. Many 'professional haters' are sensationalists who thrive best on exposure if it brings them into a conflict situation where they can pose as martyrs and heroes to their followers and potential followers. Publicity for them is clearly unwise anti-prejudice strategy. Negative opposition that emphasizes a conflict situation and arouses emotions probably strengthens their appeal. Exposure of the hatemonger, however, need not be of this awkward variety. A competing programme that emphasizes positive goals deprives him of many of his arguments. McWilliams (1948) describes a Los Angeles rally called in opposition to a demonstration led by Gerald L. K. Smith, well-known anti-semite and racist. Smith's rally drew a small crowd and little attention, because the competing meeting did not interfere with him directly and did not make him the centre of attention. It publicized the problem but not the man; it did not confuse the issue by opposing his rights to speak. In this question of strategy, as in all others, a flexible policy is necessary. These rules may help to guide one's decisions:

1. Do not overlook the importance of hate propaganda.

2. Where possible, deal with it indirectly, by furnishing true information, by developing people immune to prejudice, not by direct attack.

3. Do not exaggerate the extent of the rabble-rouser's following or the strength of his influence.

4. Stress the injury his actions bring to the whole society, not to some 'poor, oppressed minority'.

Contact

It is often said, 'If there were only more contact, if people only knew each other better, there would be less prejudice.' Yet it is also known that prejudice frequently seems most intense in areas where there is most contact. How effective is contact with members of a minority group in changing attitudes and behaviour towards that group? This question requires careful study, for there are many factors that affect the results. It is related to broader questions of international relations, where it is also frequently assumed that contact *per se* will improve understanding.

In interviews with nineteen Indian and other Asian students in the United States, Lambert and Bressler (1955) discovered that contact – even when it was courteous and helpful – did not automatically create favourable attitudes. The effects depended not so much on the personalities of the individuals involved as on the total structure of the situation, especially the status conceptions of the two countries. Whenever the Indian students encountered certain 'sensitive areas' that involved implications of low status for their country – even if the Americans involved were disagreeing with the implications – they tended to respond negatively. Ideas that Indians are basically inferior, that India is an undesirable place to live, that India's social structure is undemocratic, inhumane, unenlightened, and the like, created negative responses when they were discussed.

Contact does not necessarily lead to improved understanding. The task is to discover the conditions under which attitude change does take place. Converging evidence from the sociology of knowledge and the psychology of perception shows that experience is situational: what we see or hear, what we believe, how we think are all dependent upon the total situation in which these actions occur and upon our total mental context. We never see an isolated unit of human behaviour; we see behaviour in a larger situation through the perspectives we have acquired. Most of us can look a 'fact' squarely in the face and, if we already have a frame of reference that involves it, turn it completely around. In a study of the rumour process, Allport and Postman described to various persons a picture containing a Negro and a white man with a razor in his hand. After the description, each person was asked to tell all he could about the picture to a third person, the third to a fourth, and the fourth to a fifth. In over half of the experiments, the razor was reported to be in the Negro's hand; and in several the Negro was threatening the white man with it (see Newcomb, Maccoby and Hartley, 1958).

The ambiguity of many aspects of human behaviour makes it possible to perceive that behaviour in a way which harmonizes with an already established belief.

A strong prejudice can have an almost paralysing effect on observation and rational judgement. Whatever the behaviour involved, it can be 'explained' by the prejudice. Even opposite kinds of behaviour are used as 'proof' of a supposed trait.

Contact with the members of a minority group can scarcely weaken a prejudice that is so impervious to experience. Behaviour that does not harmonize with the prejudice may not be seen at all; our perceptions are made selective and partial by the prejudice itself, which thus becomes self-confirmatory. Or if the behaviour is seen, it is treated as an 'exception': 'Some of my best friends are Jews, but – they're not typical'. Marrow and French (1945) showed that factory experience with 'old' (over 30!) women workers who showed high production records and low rates of absenteeism did not change the stereotypes of management and foreladies that the 'old' workers were liabilities. Human beings have an enormous ability to resist the meaning of facts that contradict their already established beliefs.

Contact with the members of a minority group may, of course, be of an unpleasant variety. This is sometimes held to be a cause of prejudice – the attitude is simply a generalization from a few unfortunate experiences. Unpleasant experience with individual members of a minority group, however, can scarcely be the cause of prejudice, because that experience would not be generalized to the whole minority group unless the prejudice were already there. Moreover, we cannot be certain that persons who report more unpleasant memories of contact with members of minority groups have actually had more such contacts. Memory is selective; they may remember (or invent) such contacts *because* they already have a stronger than average prejudice.

Thus we find that prejudice is sometimes explained as a result of the *lack* of contact with members of a minority group and sometimes explained as the result of the *presence* of such contact. Both theories explain only surface relationships.

Such observations do not mean, however, that one's experiences with individual members of a minority group have no effect on one's attitudes towards that group. Prejudice does not entirely precede and coerce the interpretation of experience. Unpleasant contacts probably increase the strength of prejudice. Oppositely, *certain kinds of contact* are effective in reducing the strength of a tradition of prejudice. We are learning to examine contact against a background of knowledge of the total personality of the individuals involved, the leadership, the power structure, the place of one attitude in a total value system (see Lippitt and Radke, 1946).

Allport has prepared a valuable outline of the variables that we must have in mind in any analysis of the effects of contact between members of different groups.

Quantitative aspects of contact:
1. Frequency
2. Duration
3. Number of persons involved
4. Variety
Status aspects of contact:
1. Minority member has inferior status.
2. Minority member has equal status.
3. Minority member has superior status.
4. Not only may the individuals encountered vary thus in status; but the group as a whole may have relatively high status (e.g. Jews) or relatively low status (e.g. Negroes).
Role aspects of contact:
1. Is the relationship one of competitive or cooperative activity?
2. Is there a superordinate or subordinate role relation involved; e.g., master-servant, employer-employee, teacher-pupil?

Social atmosphere surrounding the contact:
1. Is segregation prevalent, or is egalitarianism expected?
2. Is the contact voluntary or involuntary?
3. Is the contact 'real' or 'artificial'?
4. Is the contact perceived in terms of intergroup relations or not perceived as such?
5. Is the contact regarded as 'typical' or as 'exceptional'?
6. Is the contact regarded as important and intimate, or as trivial and transient?
Personality of the individual experiencing the contact:
1. Is his initial prejudice level high, low, medium?
2. Is his prejudice of a surface, conforming type, or is it deeply rooted in his character structure?
3. Has he basic security in his own life, or is he fearful and suspicious?
4. What is his previous experience with the group in question, and what is the strength of his present stereotypes?
5. What are his age and general education level?
6. Many other personality factors may influence the effect of contact.
Areas of contact:
1. Casual
2. Residential
3. Occupational
4. Recreational
5. Religious
6. Civic and fraternal
7. Political
8. Goodwill intergroup activities

Even this list of variables that enter into the problem of contact is not exhaustive. It does, however, indicate the complexity of the problem we face (Allport, 1954, pp. 262–3; and Amir, 1969 for a useful general statement). Because of the large number of variables affecting the influence of contact on interracial attitudes and behaviour, research conclusions are quite tentative. Yet certain principles are substantially supported. After one of the most intensive reviews of the effects of contact, Williams (1964) concludes that '... *in all the surveys in all communities and for all groups, majority and minorities, the greater the frequency of interaction, the lower the prevalence of ethnic prejudice.*' (Note that the same correlation can be stated: the less the frequency of ethnic prejudice, the more frequent is the interaction.). Williams does not stop with this statement of a simple correlation. By the introduction of several test variables, he is able to strengthen a causal inference: '*if* contacts can be established' – an interesting and important qualification – even quite marked prejudices cannot nullify the prejudice-reducing influence of interation.

Brief contacts, however, may not have a measurable impact. Trubowitz (1969) divided a group of grade school children into four categories, to participate in interracial contact through a three-day period. The categories were: joint trips and joint discussions; joint trips and separate discussions; separate trips and joint discussions; and separate trips and separate discussions. He hypothesized that planned interracial activity, particularly when heightened by discussion and trips, would produce positive attitude changes. He found, however, that little change occurred.

Nor is pleasurable association by itself adequate to reduce prejudice. What Sherif (1966) calls 'hedonistic associationism' – people like what is associated with their pleasures – overlooks the human skill in taking the pleasure and maintaining old attitudes. Sherif emphasized the impact of 'superordinate goals'. When individuals or groups are brought together within a situation which requires their active cooperation to achieve a mutually desired goal, stereotype and prejudice fade.

Selltiz and Cook (1962), in their study of foreign students in the United States, emphasized the importance of opportunities for intergroup contact, the 'acquaintance potential' of a situation. Those in smaller colleges, as compared with matched counterparts in intermediate and larger schools, had more personal contacts with Americans, contacts that were more than formal or official. Availability of contacts is not simply a matter of nearness. Interracial contact in the United States, for example, continues to be infrequent, despite the spread of the black population throughout the country. In his careful study of one American community, Molotch (1969) found that interracial contacts were infrequent in almost every activity, even in shopping, although there were some exceptions. It has often been remarked that 'eleven o'clock Sunday morning is the most segregated time of the week', but he found that eleven o'clock Saturday evening was even more segregated. In those few situations where interracial activity was quite common, as for example a city commission for civic activities, there were status contrasts and, within the commission, contrasts in power (for the blacks were chosen as 'representatives', not because of their personal expertise or influence). Such contacts are as likely to confirm stereotypes as they are to create greater sensitivity to members of another race.

The extent of black–white contact in the United States was recently recorded in a Harris survey. A representative cross-section of white people were asked: 'Would you say you have a great deal of contact with blacks, some contact, or almost no contact with blacks in the following areas?' (The results were published in the *Cleveland Plain Dealer*, 6 July 1970.)

Table 2 White contact with blacks

	Great deal (per cent)	Some contact (per cent)	Almost none (per cent)	Not sure (per cent)
Co-workers on the job	10	22	67	1
Someone who works for you	5	10	83	2
A friend you see socially	3	17	79	1
Supervises you at work	2	4	92	2
Neighbour	1	9	88	2
Shop where you shop	7	36	56	1

The Harris survey cross-tabulated these results by the expressed fear of violence. Those with least contact are more worried about racial trouble.

Table 3 Contact and fear

	High contact (per cent)	Medium contact (per cent)	Little contact (per cent)
Feel uneasy about violence	34	43	55
Don't feel uneasy	66	56	44
Not sure	—	1	1

The relationship between high contact and less fear of violence does not, of course, show the causal connections. It is perhaps significant, however, that those under 30 were more likely to say they were friendly with blacks and less likely to express fears of racial violence. More intensive community studies, moreover, allow us to speak somewhat more confidently of a causal connection. Warren has shown that suburban whites are not only individually isolated from Negroes, a situation which encourages race tension, but also share a community atmosphere which reinforces that isolation and tends to furnish a community response to the conflict situation. Primary lack of contact generates a secondary, community sustained lack of contact (see Warren, 1970). In another community study, Jeffries and Ransford (1969) applied controls for the effects of proximity to the Watts riot and prejudice. They found that contact with Negroes prior to the riot was an important determiner of white attitudes towards the disorder, to some degree independent of the control variables. 'Those lacking contact are more fearful of Negroes, cite more outside agitator explanations, evidence more feelings of increased social distance, and voice more punitive responses than those having contact.'

Effects of equal-status contact. The influence that has been most carefully explored in recent research is the degree of status equality or status difference among the participants in intergroup relations. In exploring this issue we must remember how resistant stereotypes are to evidence. Moreover, equal-status contacts are perhaps more likely to involve competition. In his study of an interracial adolescent group, Irwin Katz found that, despite its liberal and friendly atmosphere, there was the danger that competition for leadership and the other inevitable group tensions – having nothing to do with race – would be seen as racial in origin and meaning (Katz, 1955).

Nevertheless, there is good evidence that what might be called 'stereotype-breaking contacts' reduce prejudice. MacKenzie found that among university students, when several variables that might influence the results were controlled, knowing professional Negroes and having a variety of contacts with Negroes, produced statistically significantly more favourable attitudes (see MacKenzie, 1948). In a study which is in better control of the time dimension, Mann (1959) assigned seventy-eight graduate students at Teachers College, New York City, to six-person discussion groups. The groups, containing men and women, black and white, Southerners and Northerners, held four meetings a week for three weeks. At the beginning and at the end they were given sociometric tests and part of the Berkeley E-scale for measuring prejudice. Contact in the group significantly reduced both the E scores and the use of race as a friendship criterion.

A somewhat unusual kind of stereotype-breaking contact was experienced by many soldiers of the US Army in Europe during the winter and spring of 1945. In March and April, 1945, several Negro rifle platoons were attached to white companies. Two months later, the Information and Education Division of the Army Service Forces conducted a survey to discover the response of white officers and men to this change. Five trained interviewers asked all available white company grade officers and a representative sample of platoon sergeants in twenty-four companies that contained Negro platoons, 'Has your feeling changed since having served in the same unit with coloured soldiers?' The responses were as follows:

Table 4

	White officers (per cent)	White noncoms (per cent)
No, my feeling is the same	16	21
Yes, have become more favourable	77	77
No answer	7	2

Eighty-four per cent of the white officers and 81 per cent of the white noncoms answered 'Very well' (the most favourable answer on a four-point scale) to the question, 'How well did the coloured soldiers in this company perform in combat?'[1] Alongside these findings, however, it should be noted that in the last several years, contact in the American armed forces has been associated with extensive interracial conflict, indicating again the complexity of the issue with which we are dealing. Lacking formal study of the contemporary situation, we can only note the following variables as among those involved: (a) conflict is brought quickly to public attention, friendly contact is not; hence we do not know how sharply the present situation contrasts with the earlier one; (b) the Black Power separatist mood affects current contacts; (c) there is a high ratio of black noncommissioned officers now, thus the contact is not always equal status (and there are elements of status inconsistency for members of both races); (d) the current war situation (1971) creates more general frustration than the Second World War, because of motivational factors; (e) the ratio of black to white is much higher than it was in the period studied.

In many 'contact' studies, there are methodological problems of self-selection and limitation to verbal behaviour. Deutsch and Collins (1951) report the interesting results of different patterns of interracial housing in which these problems are minimal. In two housing projects Negro and white families were assigned to apartment buildings regardless of race (the integrated pattern); in two other projects different buildings or different parts of the project were used for Negroes and whites (the segregated biracial pattern). Interviews with the housewives in these situations revealed that the integrated pattern reduced prejudice much more sharply.

Table 5 Nature of housewives' relations with Negro people in housing projects

| | Integrated | | Segregated | |
	Koaltown (per cent)	Sacktown (per cent)	Bakerville (per cent)	Frankville (per cent)
Friendly relations	60	69	6	4
Accommodative relations	24	14	5	1
Mixed relations	7	11	2	3
No relations	5	0	87	88
Bad relations	4	6	0	4
Total cases	102	90	100	101

Source: Deutsch and Collins (1951).

1. 'Opinions about negro infantry platoons in white companies of seven divisions,' by the Information and Education Division, United States War Department, reprinted in Newcomb and Hartley (eds.), op. cit., pp. 542–6.

The effects of such types of contact would not be the same, of course, on persons whose prejudices were so strong that they would not join an interracial community; but among families who did accept housing on a biracial basis persons assigned (without regard to their original attitudes, for the type of arrangement was an administrative decision, not an individual choice) to integrated patterns discovered that their prejudices were very inadequate modes of adjustment. Those in the segregated projects had no such opportunity for revising their attitudes.

In a follow-up study of the effects of interracial housing, Wilner, Walkley and Cook (1955) derived evidence that supports many of the findings of Deutsch and Collins, but also introduces some qualifications. In interracial neighbourhoods, 'the assumption that segregation is right and inevitable is challenged' by the authority of the community project; and the white resident is confronted with the problem of reconciling the evidence concerning the behaviour of actual minority-group members with his stereotypes. Thus contact weakens the supports of prejudice. There are, however, a number of complicating factors:

The relation between *proximity and contact*, and the relation of each to attitude change; the influence of initial attitude on the outcome of the contact experience; the influence of social pressures – or social climate regarding intergroup association – on the outcome of the contact experience, and the ways in which the social climate is established and manifested; the effect that different proportions of minority group members have on the experience associated with proximity or contact; and the dimensions of attitude which undergo change.

The four housing projects studied by Wilner, Walkley, and Cook had a small proportion of Negro residents; none had more than 10 per cent. In all four projects, the extent of contact with Negroes was closely tied to proximity. The contacts that occurred were not simply unplanned conversation, but neighbourly activities of various kinds – borrowing and lending, helping during sickness, visiting. The white women who lived near Negroes perceived, more often than those living farther away, that the opinions of other white women in the project were favourable to interracial contact. They also held Negroes in higher esteem and were more likely to believe that the races were equal in such things as cleanliness, manners, intelligence, ambition. Although the attitudes towards Negroes which the white women had when they entered the project affected their responses, they were less important than proximity in the project.

Without discussing various refinements in the two studies of interracial housing, we can perhaps indicate their major finding.

One uncontrolled aspect of these, and most studies of contact, is the lack of any measures of selectivity of Negro participants. Are they more

Table 6 **Percentage sharing at least one kind of neighbourly activity**

	Per cent
Two integrated projects of the Deutsch and Collins study (192)	54
Integrated projects of the Wilner, Walkley and Cook study (91)	50
Two segregated projects of the Deutsch and Collins Study (201)	3
Segregated areas of the Wilner, Walkley and Cook study (234)	5

Source: Wilner, Walkley and Cook (1955, p. 143).

'contact prone'? Would the same results occur if a different pattern of selectivity prevailed? Some light on these questions may be thrown by a study in Los Angeles (although there are risks in making inferences through time and space back to the housing studies we have examined). Bonnie Bullough (1969) wondered why there had been a comparatively weak response to the growing opportunities for integrated housing among Negroes. Comparing two samples of Negroes in integrated neighbourhoods (n = 224) with one in a solidly Negro area (n = 106), she found that the latter were significantly higher in feelings of powerlessness and anomia. Without panel data, we cannot tell whether these feelings reflect or cause the housing patterns. From our interest here, however, they remind us of the need to take account of Negro as well as white attitudes in studies of the effects of contact.

Studies of the effects of contact among children are of great theoretical and strategic importance. It is often possible more nearly to approximate experimental conditions in working with children than with adults and the effects of intergroup contact on children compete with fewer other stimuli. In a valuable study of intergroup relations in a boys' camp, Muzafer Sherif (1961) and his associates (Sherif and Sherif, 1953) reveal the tension-building and stereotype-creating processes; and then indicate how harmony may be established or re-established. Although this research has no direct interest in majority-minority relations, it skilfully reveals more general principles of intergroup relations that are of wide applicability. The subjects were twenty-two eleven-year-old middle-class boys. There were no problem children among them; each had a good school record; and all were strangers to one another at the start. So far as possible they were matched into pairs on weight, height, skills, and previous camping experience and then assigned randomly into two groups. For a week the two groups lived separately at an isolated camping site. They were then brought into frequent competitive and often frustrating interaction. At the end of this second stage, there were strong reciprocal prejudices and stereotypes; members of the two groups did not want to associate; there was name-calling and conflict.

How could these expressions of tension and disharmony be reduced? One might make appeals to a common 'enemy', break up the groups by individual reward and rivalry, or shift attention to intergroup leaders. Sherif rejected these, however, in favour of an effort to reduce friction by introducing 'superordinate goals' – a series of tasks that required, for a mutually esteemed outcome, intergroup cooperation. These tasks were preceded by seven unstructured contact situations. By themselves, these contacts did little to break down the group lines, reduce stereotypy, or end the conflict. When the two groups had to work together, however, to raise enough money to bring a movie to camp or to get water flowing again (after the staff had devilishly disrupted the supply), group lines blurred, antipathies receded, and the differential rating of in-group and out-group disappeared.

Here is group-building and attitude-forming before our eyes. Undoubtedly, new variables are introduced when one deals with group identities that have lasted for years, not weeks. It is valuable, therefore, to follow Sherif's study with one that deals with an interracial camp. Marian Yarrow (1958) and her colleagues describe the interpersonal relationships that develop between Negro and white children during the 'equal status contact' of a two-week camping session. Two camps for low-income children had been run on a segregated basis. During the summer of this study, three sessions, the first six weeks, remained segregated, but the last two sessions were integrated. The staff was integrated in all sessions. Six to ten children, chosen to get age homogeneity and to avoid prior friendships, were assigned to a cabin. Out of thirty-two cabins, eight were studied intensively during each of the two integrated sessions.

At the beginning of each period, a racial status structure was apparent, with white children definitely holding the top positions – as determined by interviews with the campers – in nine cabins and a more mixed picture in the other seven. By the end of the two-week sessions, this status differential had lessened but not disappeared. In the segregated camps, 45 per cent of the children had formed themselves into mutual pairs – each choosing the other as best friend – by the time of the first interview. This had dropped to 35 per cent by the end of the period. Almost the same pattern was found in the desegregated groups (44 and 33 per cent), and 44 per cent of these pairs were interracial, despite the status differential. 'At the end of camp, in the eyes of the white children their Negro peers were significantly more desirable as friends than they had been earlier in the session. Indeed, at the end of camp, white and Negro campers were about equally desired as friends by the white children' (Yarrow, Campbell and Yarrow, 1958). There was also a significant growth in self-esteem among the Negro children and a reduction in the great sensitivity they showed at first to unfavourable behaviour on the part of other Negro children.

In the light of the fact that the situation for Negro girls is often noted to be more favourable than that for Negro boys, it is significant to observe that in a camping setting – and doubtless elsewhere – desegregation held greater initial hazards for Negro girls: they were more likely to internalize their feelings than were the boys; and important camp values – strength and athletic skill for the boys, physical beauty for the girls – put them, but not the Negro boys, at a disadvantage. Nevertheless, there were gains:

For the girls this experience of equal status contact results in a consistent change toward decreased self-rejection and a relaxation of tight control over their own behaviour. ... At the end of the camp the change is not complete (white girls, for example, still tend to stand as favoured ideals for their Negro cabin mates, and the Negro girls still channel most of their aggression towards members of their own race), yet necessary beginnings of change have occurred, particularly changes reflecting an enhancement of the Negro girls' self concept (Campbell and Yarrow, 1958).

Equal-status contact in a two-week camp cannot, of course, offset the influence of years of segregation. A far more important 'experiment' is taking place in recently desegregated schools, where hundreds of thousands of white and Negro children are seeing each other for the first time as fellow students. The results are exceedingly complex, varying with the attitudes of school and government officials, the responses of parents, the talents and tensions of the Negro and white children, the grade level, and many other factors. The transition from a segregated to an integrated school, as Robert Coles (1963) reported, is undoubtedly easier, from a personality standpoint, for first graders than for high school students.[2] Nevertheless, significant changes of attitude occurred even among many of the more segregationist-minded adolescents. Perhaps most important '. . . is the slow development of discretion and selection in the white child, the break-down of quick and total vision and the beginning of particular vision based on daily experience'. Negro children also begin to see whites as individuals, with their varying characteristics.

From the results of such studies as we have reported we cannot conclude that a decrease in prejudice is the inevitable result of equal-status contact. Ernest Campbell (1961) and Ray Schrader studied the attitudes of junior and senior high school students of Oak Ridge, Tennessee, before school integration and then again a year after desegregation. On four scales measuring anti-minority attitudes they found a significant shift in a negative direction. Prejudices had increased.

In the face of contradictory findings we must realize the need for a great

2. This is an intensive comparative study, by a child psychiatrist, concerned primarily with six- and seven-year-olds in New Orleans and sixteen- and seventeen-year-olds in Atlanta.

deal of research to explore the effects of specific conditions. For example, when are there too few members of the minority to break stereotypes (a few can be regarded as 'exceptions'), and when are there so many that a sense of threat to status develops?

What is the impact of personal insecurity in response to equal-status contact? In a study of 106 white boys from New York, most of them from the lower class, who attended a four-week interracial camp, Mussen found that twenty-eight boys became significantly less prejudiced against Negroes, but twenty-seven boys became signicantly more prejudiced. Those whose prejudice increased were those who had more aggressive feelings and needs and greater need to defy authority, felt themselves victims of aggression, felt that others were not kind and helpful, were more dissatisfied with the camp (see Mussen, 1950). The study points up clearly, however, the need for careful attention to the complexity of the results of equal-status contact.

One can perhaps sum up the present knowledge about the effects of contact on prejudice in these four related propositions:

1. Incidental, involuntary, tension-laden contact is likely to increase prejudice.

2. Pleasant, equal-status contact that makes it unnecessary for the individuals to cross barriers of class, occupational, and educational differences as well as differences in symbolic (nonfunctional) group membership represented by such symbols as 'race' is likely to reduce prejudice.

3. Stereotype-breaking contacts that show minority group members in roles not usually associated with them reduce prejudice. It must be added, however, that many people have little capacity for experiencing the members of minority groups as individuals; their stereotypes easily persist in the face of contrary evidence.

4. Contacts that bring people of minority and majority groups together in functionally important activities reduce prejudice. This is particularly true when those activities involve goals that cannot be achieved without the active cooperation of members of all the groups.

Do we want contact, equal status or otherwise? In recent years there has been some increase in separationist sentiments – in the United States most of all, some of it in the name of pluralism – both Negro and white – but much of it renewing established prejudices. In a valuable paper, Thomas Pettigrew (1969) summarizes the reasons often given by whites today to support racial separation: (a) each race feels awkward and uncomfortable in the presence of the other and benefits from separation; (b) since whites are superior, they will lose by integration (in schools, for example); (c) contact increases conflict. Black separationists have somewhat matching assumptions: (a) yes, each race does feel awkward and uncomfortable in the presence of the other; we're more comfortable by ourselves; (b) most whites *think* they are superior, so white liberals should spend their time working on white racists, not worrying over integration; (c) yes, contact does mean conflict, and it will continue to until after a period of autonomy, when blacks can enter into interaction on a fully equal basis.

We shall refer only briefly to Pettigrew's comments on each of these points. It is true, he notes, that some interracial contacts are awkward, that intraracial contacts may seem more comfortable. But, he asks, at what cost do we gain this comfort? Isolation leads to mutual misinformation and, more importantly, it promotes differences. There has been a reduction in racist beliefs in the United States during the last generation; wise policy should not be based on assumptions of its prevalence or increase. Contact does, under some conditions, increase conflict; but lack of conflict is no sign of progress. 'One of the quietest periods in American racial history, 1895–1915, for example, witnessed the construction of the massive system of institutional racism as it is known today . . .' (Pettigrew, 1969a).

Many people argue, Pettigrew notes, that 'in the long run' full integration may be desirable, but that for the immediate and foreseeable future, separation is necessary and wise. The 'white desegregationist', using some mixture of the three reasons given above, supports some public desegregation, but not extensive integration. This is basically a moderate version of the older segregationist view. Perhaps more interesting is the argument of some black leaders that autonomy must come first, then integration may be possible. The various positions are charted by Pettigrew in the following way in Figure 1:

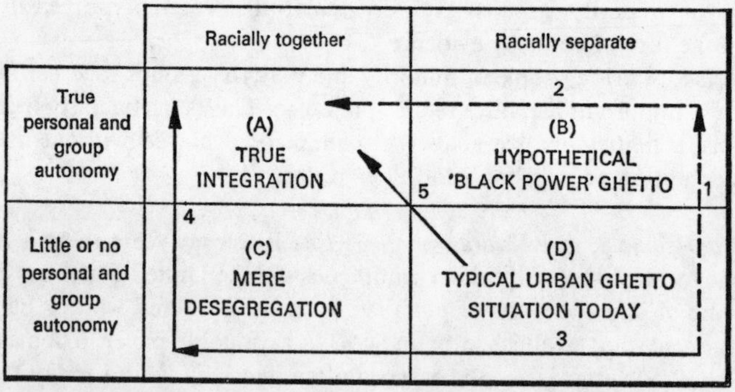

	Racially together	Racially separate
True personal and group autonomy	(A) TRUE INTEGRATION	2 (B) HYPOTHETICAL 'BLACK POWER' GHETTO
Little or no personal and group autonomy	4 (C) MERE DESEGREGATION	5 (D) TYPICAL URBAN GHETTO SITUATION TODAY 3

Figure 1 Schematic diagram of autonomy and contact-separation

Pettigrew marshals substantial evidence to support 'route 5'. With reference to the '3-1-2 route', for example, he writes:

The black separatist route has a surprising appeal for an untested theory; besides those whites who welcome any alternative to integration, it seems to appeal to cultural pluralists, white and black, to militant black leaders searching for a new direction to vent the ghetto's rage and despair, and to Negroes who just wish to withdraw as far away from whites as possible. Yet on reflection the argument involves the perverse notion that the way to bring two groups together is to separate them further. One is reminded of the detrimental consequences of isolation in economics, through 'closed markets', and in genetics, through 'genetic drift'. In social psychology, isolation between two contiguous groups generally leads to: (a) diverse value development, (b) reduced intergroup communication, (c) uncorrected perceptual distortions of each other, and (d) the growth of vested interests within both groups for continued separation. American race relations already suffer from each of these conditions; and the proposal for further separation even if the gilded ghetto were possible, aims to exacerbate them further (Pettigrew, 1969a).

Pettigrew may exaggerate the favourable outcomes of contact and overlook some of the costs (see also Eisenman, 1969 and Pettigrew, 1969b). But in our judgement he weighs the balance correctly.

Education

Most of us have a good deal of faith in the power of education (often accompanied by an anti-intellectualism that exalts the 'practical' man, the man of 'action', and disdains the expert and intellectual). It is frequently declared that education (shading off into programmes of contact, exhortation and propaganda) could reduce prejudice sharply.

This statement pays no attention to the obstacles in the way of getting an adequate programme of education in intergroup relations.

Effective strategy requires that we distinguish the following two problems in developing a programme of education to reduce prejudice and discrimination:

1. What are the barriers to setting up such a programme? Who will oppose it, and how may their opposition be reduced? Who will finance it?

2. After one has set up the programme, what techniques are most effective in changing the attitudes of different groups of people?

We perhaps know more about the second problem than about the first. One is justified in a modest optimism that when a programme has been set in motion, particularly with children, it can be fairly effective in preventing or reducing prejudices. But under what circumstances will an educational programme be set in motion? In March, 1971, the United States Department of Defence announced the creation of an institute to train, within a year, 1400 instructors to staff a programme in race relations. Classes will be required of every person who enters the service, with six-hour refresher courses each year thereafter. This ambitious programme to prevent racial conflict and unrest reflects deep concern over the serious racial tensions in the armed forces during the last few years.

It remains to be seen how effective the programme of the armed forces will be, although smaller scale efforts on some army bases have reduced conflicts. It is clear, however, that few institutions can match the armed forces in creating an extensive programme by a decision from the top. Yet the school system is also an area where some action is possible. Despite the close connection between formal education and the rest of society, there is a measure of autonomy in the school system. This autonomy is easy to exaggerate, but it is a strategic error to dismiss it too lightly. Those professionally connected with education, because of their functional role in society, are somewhat more concerned with the pursuit of truth. In our society they are also inclined to be somewhat more liberal than the average.

This modest resource has been only slightly used, although efforts to increase intergroup education have been greatly expanded in recent years. Educational institutions themselves still contain a great deal of discrimination. Few teachers are trained specifically in the analysis of majority-minority relations; seldom is a teacher chosen from a minority group (although the number of black teachers has recently increased); and few courses treat their material in a way designed to reduce prejudice.

In the last several years some labour unions have proved to be organizations in which the barriers to educational programmes concerned with reducing prejudice have not been too high.

What kind of education? The first job of strategy, in making use of education, is to determine the areas – such as schools and unions – where programmes are most likely to be adopted. But that is only half the job. Having cleared the ground, one must decide how to proceed. Is it a matter simply of transferring information, for knowledge leads to action? Or are the ways in which the knowledge is acquired, the total situation of learning, as crucial as the facts themselves? More and more we see that the latter is the case. How one learns an idea is important to one's mastery of it, to one's acceptance of the idea as valid, and to the likelihood of one acting upon it. The total personality is involved in the learning process.

Education and re-education must be guided by the fact that prejudice is frequently 'used' by the person; it is functional (not necessarily effective, be it noted). It will be 'unlearned' only when the entanglements with the total personality are loosened by the nature of the learning situation, by the reduction of tension and the elimination of any threats to one's ego. At the very least, when one gives up a prejudice one admits an error – and most of us are reluctant to do this. Fineberg (1949) illustrates the way in which sensitivity to the feelings of the prejudiced person contributes to re-education:

Mrs Tenney, a brilliant young woman active in community relations work, had remained silent at a dinner party when a woman whom she and her husband were meeting for the first time spoke of members of another race as mentally inferior to white people. It was an incidental remark. The conversation quickly drifted to something else.

Driving home, Mr Tenney said to his wife, 'I was watching you when Mrs Hammond put in that nasty crack about coloured people. Why didn't you speak up?'

'And spoil the chance of ever changing her mind?' asked Mrs Tenney. 'Had I spoken up, Mrs Hammond would have defended her opinion. If I had won the argument, it would have been to my satisfaction but not to hers. She would have disliked me for embarrassing her among her new acquaintances. She looks like a sincere, capable person. I think we can change her views on several things. When she made that quip about racial inferiority, I put it down in my little mental notebook. And what do you think I did while we were getting our wraps?'

Mr Tenney smiled. 'Knowing you as I do, I'd say you made a date with Mrs Hammond.'

'Right! When we know each other better, I'll introduce Mrs Hammond to Dr Sanford and to Mrs Taylor, who are as intelligent as any white person she ever met. One of these days Mrs Hammond will be working for our Interracial Commission. That's not a promise, John, but I'll try hard.'

In less than two months Mrs Hammond had abandoned the notion of racial inferiority without having been forced to recant, apologize, or even to recall the invidious remark. Her mentor, Mrs Tenney, is one of the few – there are altogether too few – who is concerned enough about racial and religious prejudice and astute enough to undertake the *re-education* of mildly prejudiced individuals.

Kurt Lewin was undoubtedly the leader in 'action research' – the analysis of the conditions under which change in human relations takes place and the study of the processes by which it occurs. Out of his studies has come the emphasis on the involvement of the total personality in the educative process. This has led to the development of several principles: Create an informal situation; see education as a group process, not simply an individual process; maximize the individual's sense of participation in getting new ideas (Lewin, 1948).

We are not expounding a general theory of education. We are concerned with the learning process in an area where emotional attitudes and stereotypes affect observation and the acceptance of evidence.

Intergroup education in the schools

With the great increase in public awareness of intergroup relations and tensions in the last two decades, schools at every level began to pay more

16. See Lewin (1948).

attention to interracial, intercultural, interfaith, and international questions. Specific courses have been introduced in a number of American cities, and teacher training programmes, literature designed for specific age levels, and some attention to intergroup relations in the total life of schools have increased.[3]

Several obstacles and weaknesses have become apparent in the short history of deliberately planned intergroup education. One fault on the part of many administrators is the segregation of teachers on racial or ethnic lines. Intergroup instruction is distorted if minority groups are not represented on the teaching staff. There have, however, been some notable changes in recent years. Thousands of Negro teachers are now assigned to interracial classes, in the North and in the South. Several hundred Negroes are members of formerly all-white faculties, and with the demand exceeding the supply, colleges and universities are now competing with one another in the effort to add black staff members. (Most of these teachers, of course, on all levels of education, teach subjects other than intergroup relations. Their influence on that topic is indirect and informal.)

A second type of difficulty in this new field lies in the attitudes of teachers. Intergroup education has no possibility of being effective unless those who are charged with carrying it out are competent and sympathetic. Routine performance of an assigned programme accomplishes little or nothing. Subtle or obviously prejudiced remarks or acts on the part of the teacher outside the programme itself may more than offset that which is included in formal instruction. Many pupils come from homes where prejudice is strong. If the teacher also harbours prejudice, the results of intergroup education are likely to be negligible.

Some school systems now include interest and skill in intergroup relations among the criteria used in the selection of new teachers.

Closely related to teachers' attitudes are school policies with regard to pupil assignment. In the matter of 'ability level', schools are confronted with a dilemma: in some ways it is more effective to teach relatively homogeneous groups, because methods and materials can be adapted to their particular needs. On the other hand grouping and tracking tend to create self-fulfilling prophecies, to create expectations in the minds of students and teachers alike about levels of performance. The result is that those in 'slow tracks' remain slow, those in 'fast tracks' are given further support and encouragement. Most of this is without any intent on the part of those making the assignments. Although there are problems of interpretation in their study, Rosenthal and Jacobson have demonstrated

3. For studies of the extent of some of the problems faced in intergroup relations teaching, see Subcommittee on Human Relations in the Classroom (1962; 1963). For helpful guides to intergroup teaching, see Noar (1963) and Briggs and Hummel (1962).

their major point that teacher expectations affect, not simply the grading of pupils, but their actual performances.

Recent studies indicate that the imparting of specific information about minority groups does not materially alter attitudes towards those groups. This is not to say that transmitting such information has no value, but simply that its usefulness in producing more favourable attitudes towards 'out-groups' is less great than many professional educators have believed.

In short, knowledge may be helpful but its acquisition does not automatically produce understanding and appreciation. For effective action the main attack must be made on basic and often emotionally held attitudes rather than on opinions.

The way in which minority groups are described – or entirely overlooked – in textbooks and other school materials significantly affects intergroup relations in school and the formation of attitudes. In 1949 the American Council on Education surveyed 315 published sources used in schools and found relatively little support for a democratic perspective. Neglect of minority groups on the one hand and stereotypy of a relatively moderate sort on the other characterized many of the textbooks and other writings (American Council on Education, 1949). Twelve years later, Lloyd Marcus (1961) found important changes in his analysis of forty-eight leading junior and senior high school textbooks in the area of social studies but a still inadequate coverage and treatment.

In a review of 'readers' used in elementary grades, Otto Klineberg (1963) finds an even less adequate picture.

The American people are almost exclusively white or Caucasian. The only exception discovered in the fifteen readers refers to a visit to a Western ranch, near which lived an American Indian family, who spent most of their time 'making beautiful things . . . to sell to the white people who came to the Indian country . . .' The Americans in these readers are almost exclusively North European in origin and appearance . . . the exceptions . . . are themselves significant. An organ grinder is given an appearance which is stereotypically Italian or Greek . . . Americans in these readers are predominantly, almost exclusively, blondes . . . There are occasional references to dark skin, but these usually relate to people far away. . . .

This was written in 1963. Since that time the situation has changed quite rapidly, particularly with reference to materials and courses dealing with Negro Americans, but in connection with other minorities as well.

The following bibliographies will give an indication of the range of materials available: Miles M. Jackson (ed.), A Bibliography of Negro History and Culture for Young Children, University of Pittsburgh Press, 1968; Minnie W. Koblitz, The Negro in Schoolroom Literature, Center for Urban Education, 1966; NAACP, Integrated School Books; A Descriptive Bibliography of 399 Pre-school and Elementary School Texts and Story Books, 1967; Doris White, Multi-ethnic Books for Head Start Children, Part I: Black and Integrated Literature; Part II: Other Minority Group Literature, National Laboratory on Early Childhood Education, Urbana, Illinois, 1969.

Some of the problems in intergroup education found on the primary and secondary levels also characterize college work. Many general college programmes are concerned with studying the democratic tradition and strengthening belief in the democratic heritage, but few have the specific aim of reducing prejudice, nor have they used techniques appropriate to that end. There are, of course, hundreds of courses in departments of sociology, anthropology, history and social psychology concerned with minorities and prejudice. These are usually elective courses, dealing with self-selected students; and they therefore face different problems in reducing prejudice. The changing of attitudes, if it is recognized at all, is only one aim, although that hope probably lies behind most of the courses. Since the reducing of prejudice is not explicitly sought – and methods appropriate to that aim are not adopted – one does not judge the effectiveness of a course by measuring changes in attitude. Nevertheless, many such measurements have been made, and they reveal that one of the results – perhaps a byproduct – of the study of minorities and prejudice may be an increase in tolerance. The results, however, are far from definite. About a third of the studies have found that the course of study produced no change of attitude (see Rose and Rose, 1948, for a summary of the results of many of these studies).

There is great need for research that will specify how different methods of teaching used with persons of different attitudes and tendencies will influence prejudice. Although they deal with only a brief 'educational' situation, Mittnick and McGinnies (1958) illustrate the value of such specification. Having classified students from two high schools into those low, middle, and high on a modified version of the California Ethnocentrism Scale, they randomly assigned persons of each category into six groups of nine members each. One month after this measurement, two groups from each category (six in all) saw a film 'High Wall' and then engaged in a half-hour, nondirected discussion. The film treated group prejudice as a disease, tracing its origins to family experience and community influence. Six additional groups saw the film but did not discuss it. Six groups served as controls. After seeing the film, the twelve experimental groups were given a thirty-three-item information test and all eighteen were again given the E-Scale test. One month later, both tests were readministered. Significant reductions in ethnocentrism occurred among both the film and the film-discussion groups. Among those whose initial scores were high in prejudice, however, the opportunity for discussion significantly reduced the gain, counteracting some of the effects of the film, while for the middle and low groups, discussion increased the gain. The measurement after one month showed that those who discussed the film significantly retained the lower ethnocentrism scores, while the film-alone groups regressed towards their original attitudes. Those with low scores and those who actively participated in the discussions learned more from the films.[4]

Not all of the educational needs *vis-à-vis* majority–minority relations are found among members of the majority. A significant recent development is the appearance of a black studies programme in many schools. This is being followed by demands for, and to some degree action on, Puerto Rican, Mexican, Indian and other programmes. Jewish studies have long been a part of traditional curricula, but are now being developed in some places somewhat more along the 'ethnic group' line of the newer programmes.

The implications of these developments for the topic of this chapter are not yet completely clear. Black students, for example, make up the vast majority of students in Black Studies programmes. They are presented with materials and educational philosophies ranging from scholarly emphasis on Negro history, literature, music, art (graphic and plastic) and experience to action programmes designed to speed the destruction of 'imperialistic societies'. With such contrasts in basic premises, inevitably there are sharp disputes among those who design and work in these programmes. Some see them as a necessary and appropriate way to emphasize black contributions to American culture and society; and others work to make the programmes agents of black separation.

We do not know of any systematic studies that evaluate the influence of Black Studies programmes on prejudice and discrimination, the topic with which we are concerned here. (In Britain, the Schools Council spent several thousand pounds in the late sixties and early seventies developing a race kit for teaching race in schools. And, though one study seemed to show that it *did* produce favourable attitudes, at the beginning of 1972, progress of the kit was still uncertain.) Effects will undoubtedly vary widely, depending upon the approach of the courses and the materials used, and on the students who participate. General theory leads us to two opposite predictions: courses that promote the growth of pride and the strengthening of self-identity may reduce prejudice. On the other hand, some of the materials and approaches seem likely to reduce the sense of common humanity, to promote stereotypes, and to create a world picture as inaccurately imaginary as the one white students have long suffered

4. For a study of the effects of attitude homogeneity among the members of an educational group, see Solomon (1963).

under. The balance, we suspect, will be determined, not only by struggles among the staffs and the schools where they work, but also by the total national setting. Slow progress in reducing discrimination and granting full rights to all citizens will support the chauvinistic elements in 'ethnic studies'. Rapid progress will support their broader humanistic potential, and thus help to break the vicious circle of majority–minority relations.[5]

Related to the question of the efficacy of intergroup education as such is the question of the general influence of education on anti-minority attitudes and behaviour. In a careful review of the poll data over a number of years, Stember (1961) concludes that education has important, but limited effects:

Yet, as we go up the educational ladder, old images of minorities are replaced by new ones, often no less harmful. Covert discrimination continues to be acceptable and most important perhaps, the desire to keep minorities at some social distance remains.

It would thus appear that the impact of education is limited. Its chief effect is to reduce traditional provincialism – to counteract the notion that members of minorities are strange creatures with exotic ways, and to diminish fear of casual personal contact. But the limits of acceptance are sharply drawn; while legal equality is supported, full social participation is not.

Not all prejudices, Stember notes, are affected in the same way by schooling. The more deeply rooted prejudices are affected only by a high level of training. Anti-Negro sentiments do not decline appreciably until one gets to the college level.

Personal therapy

If prejudice and discrimination are frequently manifestations of personal insecurities or of a basic personality instability, then an effective programme of strategy must be concerned with the reduction of emotional disturbances. The prevention and treatment of personality disorganization is a very large area which we can only touch upon; but we need to examine some of the general principles involved, as they refer to our problem. We need to avoid, as some specialists fail to do, exaggerating the effectiveness of personal therapy as a strategy. The authors of *The Authoritarian Personality* write, 'The major emphasis should be placed, it seems, not upon discrimination against particular groups, but upon such phenomena as stereotypy, emotional coldness, identification with power, and general destructiveness.' Such a statement is the result of an inadequate theory of the causes of prejudice and discrimination. We need to remember Robert Coles' (1967) word of caution, with reference to the world-saving value of therapy: 'If only more people could be analysed! . . . The same logic and

5. There has been a flood of materials on Black Studies. See, for example, Robinson, Foster and Oglivie (eds.) (1968); Rosovsky (1969) and Newsweek (1969).

reason that finally had glimpsed the workings of the unconscious mind would take control of the body politic; the same insight that at last had characterized and defined the shadowy, unmentionable forces at work in the family would now set straight man's racial, religious and national tensions'. But there are far too many feelings of rancour, prejudice and snobbery among the analysed – and even those who analyse – Coles notes, to allow any longer such an easy interpretation. There are some situations, in the view of the present authors, in which personality factors are relatively unimportant, others in which they loom large; but more often the several factors are closely interlocked, and none should be chosen for 'major emphasis'.

Personal therapy is frequently most effective when the reduction of prejudice is simply a by-product of the larger goal of a stable personality. In this field, as in so many others, prevention is far more effective than cure.

Even an extensive programme of prevention, however, would be inadequate. For a long time to come we need to be equally concerned with a programme of cure – of treatment for insecure persons who use prejudice and discrimination as modes of adjustment to their insecurities. Therapy may concentrate primarily on the tendencies of the individual or on the situations which are activating those tendencies. The latter approach is too often disregarded by psychiatrists and others concerned with personality reorganization; yet to treat 'society as the patient' is frequently a more effective approach than the intensive analysis of each individual (see Frank, 1948).

In the treatment of 'problem children' particularly – children who may exhibit prejudice among other manifestations of insecurity – a change in the situation around them is often far more effective than direct attention to their problems.

When personal insecurities are more deeply set, the situational approach is less likely to be effective. The responses of the individual may take on a rigidity that coerces the interpretation of every situation into the same mould. Alongside the therapeutic approaches that seek to modify the tension-laden situations, therefore, we need the direct treatment of unstable persons. This treatment can range from friendly counselling (simply listening, frequently) to intensive psychoanalysis.[6] Techniques that help an individual to face the causes of his hostility help to reduce its sharpness.

Public attention has been directed mainly to problems of therapy for dominant-group members. There is some tendency, in fact, to regard their

6. There is a vast literature on problems of therapy. See, for example, Redl and Wineman (1951), Bettelheim (1955) and Aronson (1969). It is unlikely that there are special principles that apply only to therapy dealing with prejudice. Processes that reduce hostility are likely also to reduce prejudice.

prejudices and hostilities as pathological, while those of minority-group members are normal responses to abuse. This may be good strategy at certain points in history, or a relatively harmless error in dealing with a thoroughly oppressed group. When a pattern of discrimination is breaking down, however, and anxieties and hatreds of the oppressed are being released from repression, we need a more tough-minded analysis of the therapeutic problems and possibilities among them.

We are not referring, of course, to more or less rationally chosen opposition to discrimination, but to the unconscious problems that express themselves in ways unlikely to affect social practices except negatively. Perhaps most important of these are the various paranoid symptoms. As Grier and Cobbs (1968) note:

For a black man survival in America depends in large measure on the development of a 'healthy' cultural paranoia. He must maintain a high degree of suspicion toward the motives of every white man and at the same time never allow this suspicion to impair his grasp of reality. It is a demanding requirement and not everyone can manage it with grace. . . . Of all the varieties of functional psychosis, those that include paranoid symptoms are significantly greater among mentally ill blacks than among mentally ill whites.

Since the anxieties of black men, in the psychiatric sense, have not yet been defined by most observers as one of the critical factors in the cycle of causes that sustain racial animosities, they have been studied less than they might otherwise have been (but see Chapter 21). In our judgement, however, direct and indirect methods of therapy to reduce those anxieties are a necessary part of a total strategic plan (for discussion of one critical issue, see Rubin, 1967).

Group therapy

Individual therapy is certainly a strategy that any complete programme must use, particularly in the treatment of persons with deep-seated prejudices. It suffers, however, from two disadvantages. It is costly in time and energy; and it is inadequate to cut the supports of prejudice that derive from groups.

Group therapy tries to overcome these disadvantages. It is an attempt to produce changes in the personality by using the knowledge of the effects of groups on attitudes and behaviour. The activities of therapeutic groups may range all the way from doing simple rhythmic actions together – a major step for some isolated schizophrenics – to enacting a plot that contains the anxiety-laden problem, to discussions in which fellow 'patients' get insight into their own problems by studying those of another. Group therapy has a long implicit history in religion, in drama, in other group practices; but as an explicit method of treatment for disorganized persons it is quite new, and as a strategy in the reduction of prejudice it is even newer.

The underlying theory is that the feeling of belongingness of group members breaks down their feelings of isolation, facilitates interaction among them, encourages role-taking and self-knowledge. The sharing of symptoms and problems with others brings a sense of security and a lowering of guilt tensions – 'I'm not the only one who faces this difficulty.' The therapist attempts to create a situation that is thoroughly permissive and informal. Individuals are allowed to express their feelings of hostility freely, for self-discovery can scarcely occur in situations that require inhibition and concealment.[7]

Ronald Lippitt and his associates, in a series of studies, compared the effects of democratic and autocratic leadership on the behaviour of ten- and eleven-year-old children. In the autocratic group, the children were told what to do, they were given no overall perspective of what they were doing (making masks), and the praise and criticism of the leader were given arbitrarily, with no objective reasons. In the democratic group all policies were determined by the members, the whole process was explained and technical help offered, alternatives were suggested, members chose freely what to do and with whom to work, praise and criticism were objective. These differences in group atmosphere had very different effects on the interaction of the chidren and on their relations with the adult leader. There was far more hostile domination of one child over another in the autocratic group, more demands for attention, more hostile criticism. On the other hand, the children were more submissive towards the leader in the autocratic group. Since there was no chance of becoming a leader, they expressed far less individuality. A scapegoat situation developed, in which the children, unable to resist the demands of the adult, attacked one of the other children (White and Lippitt, 1960).

Illness, of course, as well as therapy, has a group dimension. Treatment is ineffective if this is not understood. One aspect of the group dimension of illness is that societies and smaller groups have culturally defined 'sick roles', indicating how a person should (and may) behave when he is ill, and how he should be treated. The process of assignment of a person to the sick role, referring specifically now to mental illness, may begin when his behaviour deviations are minor. The assignment is part of the adjustment process of others who interact closely with him; it expresses efforts to handle their own anxieties and guilts, for example. The result may be to solidify the minor symptoms of the first person. In this sense, it is not the

7. Studies of group processes in the treatment of other problems are also of value to the student of prejudice. See, for example, Yablonsky (1965), Empey and Rabow (1961), and Volkman and Cressey (1963).

individual who is ill and needs treatment, but the group process, although individual differences in vulnerability are also involved, of course (see Scheff, 1966, Gove 1970 and also chapter 13. Gove's commentary is a valuable, but perhaps excessive qualification of Scheff). In the same way, prejudice is anchored in group processes and can be cured only by attention to group as well as individual factors.

The kind of principle of group process represented by such studies is basic to the atempts to reduce intergroup hostility by group therapy. Morris and Natalie Haimowitz report the effects of about thirty-five hours of group therapy in small groups with twenty-four persons. The individuals involved were from twenty-five to sixty years of age; they had a master's degree or its equivalent in psychology and three years of experience. Before and after the six-week period they were given the Bogardus social-distance test, the group being divided into 'friendly' and 'hostile' in their attitudes towards nineteen minorities on the basis of their willingness or unwillingness to admit members of the minorities to their clubs and neighbourhoods (steps two and three on the scale), even if not to marriage (step one). The scores after the group therapy were significantly different (at the 1 per cent level) from the scores before the therapy:

	Before	After
Friendly	7	13
Hostile	17	11

It is interesting to note that it was the mildly hostile, not the strongly hostile, who were most likely to change. Six of them moved into the friendly group, but only one strongly hostile person (out of nine) became mildly hostile. Four strongly hostile persons (and one mildly hostile) actually increased in prejudice during the sessions, apparently having been made more defensive about their attitudes by the experience.

One may wonder whether a social-distance scale is a valid measure of 'ethnic hostility' and whether the changes in attitude persisted, but the study suggests an approach that a complete strategic plan will contain.

In sum, as we examine the strategies that seek to reduce prejudice and discrimination primarily by changing attitudes, we find an increasingly effective approach which, in conjunction with other strategies, can help to reduce intergroup hostility.

References

ALLPORT, G. (1945), 'Catharsis and the reduction of prejudice', *Journal o Social Issues*, December, pp. 3–10.

ALLPORT, G. (1954), *The Nature of Prejudice*, Addison-Wesley.

AMERICAN COUNCIL ON EDUCATION (1949), *Intergroup Relations in Teaching Materials*, ACE.

AMIR, Y. (1969), 'Contact hypothesis in ethnic relations', *Psychological Bulletin*, May, pp. 319–42.

ARONSON, E. (1969), 'Threat and obedience', *Transaction*, March–April, pp 25–7.

AXLINE, V. M. (1948), 'Play therapy and race conflict in young children' *Journal of Abnormal and Social Psychology*, July, pp. 300–310.

BECK, D. F. (1958), 'The dynamics of group psychotherapy as seen by a sociologist', *Sociometry*, June, pp. 98–128, and September, pp. 180–97.

BETTELHEIM, B. (1955), *Truants from Life*, Free Press.

BRIGGS, W., and HUMMEL, D. (1962), *Counseling Minority Group Youth: Developing the Experience of Equality Through Education*, Ohio Civil Rights Commission.

BULLOUGH, B. (1969), *Social-Psychological Barriers to Housing Desegregation* University of California, Housing, Real Estate and Urban Land Studies Program and the Center for Real Estate and Urban Economics, Special Report, no. 2.

CAMPBELL, E. (1961), 'On desegregation and matters sociological', *Phylon*, Summer.

CAMPBELL, J., and YARROW, M. R. (1958), 'Personal and situational variables in adaptation to change' *Journal of Social Issues*, vol. 14.

CHEIN, I. (1946), 'Some considerations in combatting intergroup prejudice', *Journal of Educational Sociology*, March, pp. 412–19.

COHEN, O. (1960), 'The case for foreign quotas in housing', *Phylon*, Spring, pp. 20–29.

COLES, R. (1963), *The Desegregation of Southern Schools: A Psychiatric Study*, Anti-Defamation League of B'nai B'rith and Southern Regional Council.

COLES, R. (1967), *Children of Crisis,* Dell.

COOPER, E., and JAHODA, M. (1947), 'The evasion of propaganda: how prejudiced people respond to anti-prejudice propaganda', *Journal of Psychology*, January.

DEUTSCH, M., and COLLINS, M. E. (1951), *Interracial Housing*, University of Minnesota Press.

DODSON, D. (1960), 'Can intergroup quotas be benign?', *Journal of Intergroup Relations*, Autumn, pp. 12–17.

EDMUNDS, E. (1954), 'The Myrdalian thesis: rank order of discrimination', *Phylon*, 3rd quarter, pp 297–303.

EISENMAN, R. (1969), 'Comment on "Racially separate or together?"', *Journal of Social Issues*, Autumn.

ELKINS, S. (1959), *Slavery*, University of Chicago Press.

EMPEY, L., and RABOW, J. (1961), 'The provo experiment in delinquency rehabilitation', *American Sociological Review*, October, pp. 679–95.

FINEBERG, S. A. (1949), *Punishment Without Crime*, Doubleday.

FLOWERMAN, S. H. (1947), 'Mass propaganda in the war against bigotry', *Journal of Abnormal and Social Psychology*, October, pp. 429–33.

FRANK, L. K. (1948), *Society as the Patient*, Rutgers.

GRIER, W. H., and COBBS, P. M. (1968), *Black Rage*, Basic Books.

GOVE, W. R. (1970), 'Societal reaction as an explanation of mental illness: an evaluation', *American Sociological Review*, October, pp. 873–84.

JEFFRIES, V., and RANSFORD, H. E. (1969), 'Interracial social contact and middle-class white reactions to the Watts riot', *Social Problems*, Winter.

KATZ, I. (1955), *Conflict and Harmony in an Adolescent Interracial Group*, New York University Press.

KATZ, D., SARNOFF, I., and MCCLINTOCK, C. (1956), 'Ego defense and attitude change', *Human Relations*, vol. 9, pp. 27–45.

KENDALL P., and WOLF, K. (1949), in P. Lazarsfeld and F. Stanton (eds.), *Communications Research, 1948–49*, Harper & Row.

KILLIAN, L., and GRIGG, C. (1961), 'Rank orders of discrimination of Negroes and whites in a southern city', *Social Forces*, March, pp. 235–9.

KLINEBERG, O. (1963), 'Life is fun in a smiling, fair-skinned world', *Saturday Review*, 16 February.

KLUCKHOHN, F. (1953), 'Dominant and variant value orientation,' in C. Kluckhohn, H. Murray and D. Schneider (eds.), *Personality in Nature, Society and Culture*, 2nd edn, Knopf.

LAMBERT, R. D., and BRESSLER, M. (1955), 'The sensitive-area complex: a contribution to the theory of guided culture contact', *American Journal of Sociology*, May.

LEWIN, K. (1948), *Resolving Social Conflicts*, Harper & Row.

LIPPITT, R., and RADKE, M. (1946), 'New trends in the investigation of prejudice', *Annals*, March, pp. 167–76.

MACIVER, R. M. (1948), *The More Perfect Union*, Macmillan.

MACKENZIE, B. K. (1948), 'The importance of contact in determining attitudes toward Negroes', *Journal of Abnormal and Social Psychology*, October, pp. 417–41.

MANN, J. (1959), 'The effects of interracial contact on sociometric choices and perceptions', *Journal of Social Psychology*, August, pp. 143–52.

MARCUS, L. (1961), *The Treatment of Minorities in Secondary School Textbooks*, Anti-Defamation League of B'nai B'rith.

MARROW, A. J., and FRENCH, J. R. P. (1945), 'Changing a stereotype in industry', *Journal of Social Issues*, December, pp. 33–7.

MATTHEWS, D. R., and PROTHRO, J. W. (1966), *Negroes and the New Southern Politics*, Harcourt, Brace.

MCKEE, J. (1958–9), 'Community power and strategies in race relations', *Social Problems*, Winter.

MCWILLIAMS, C. (1948), *A Mask for Privilege: Anti-Semitism in America*, Little, Brown.

MERTON, R. K. (1940), 'Fact and factitiousness in ethnic opinionnaires', *American Sociological Review*, February, pp. 13–28.

MERTON, R. K. (1949), in R. M. MacIver (ed.), *Discrimination and National Welfare*, Institute for Religious and Social Studies.

MIDDLETON, R. (1960), 'Ethnic prejudice and susceptibility to persuasion', *American Sociological Review*, October, pp. 679–86.

MITTNICK, I., and MCGINNIES, E. (1958), 'Influencing ethnocentrism in small discussion groups through a film communication', *Journal of Abnormal and Social Psychology*, January, pp. 82–90.

MOLOTCH, H. (1969), 'Racial integration in a transition community', *American Sociological Review*, December, pp. 878–93.

MUSSON, P. (1950), 'Some personality and social factors related to changes in children's attitudes toward Negroes', *Journal of Abnormal and Social Psychology*, July, pp. 423–41.

MYRDAL, G. (1944), *An American Dilemma*, Harper & Row.

Newcomb, T. M., Maccoby, E., and Hartley, E. L. (eds.) (1958), *Readings in Social Psychology*, 3rd edn., Holt, Rinehart & Winston.

Newsweek (1969), 'Black mood on campus', 10 February, pp. 53–60.

Noar, G. (1963), *Teaching and Learning the Democratic Way*, Anti-Defamation League of B'nai B'rith.

Olsen, M. E. (1968), 'Perceived legitimacy of social protest actions', *Social Problems*, Winter.

Peterson, R. C., and Thurstone, L. L. (1933), *Motion Pictures and the Social Attitudes of Children*, Macmillan.

Pettigrew, T. (1969a), 'Racially separate or together?', *Journal of Social Issues*, January, pp. 43–69.

Pettigrew, T. (1969b), 'Rejoinder', *Journal of Social Issues*, Autumn.

Pinkney, A. (1968), *The Committed: White Activists in the Civil Rights Movement*, College and Universities Press.

Raths, L., and Trager, F. (1948), 'Public opinion and crossfire', *Journal of Educational Sociology*, February, pp. 345–68.

Redl, F., and Wineman, D. (1951), *Children who Hate*, Free Press.

Riddleberger, A., and Motz, A. (1957), 'Prejudice and perception', *American Journal of Sociology*, March, pp. 498–503.

Robinson A. L., Foster, C. C., and Ogilvie, D. H. (eds.) (1968), *Black Studies in the University*, Yale University Press.

Rose, A. M., and Rose, C. (1948), *America Divided: Minority Group Relations in the United States*, Knopf.

Rosenbaum, M., and Berger, M. (1963), *Group Psychotherapy and Group Function*, Basic Books.

Rosovsky, H. (1969), *Report of the Faculty Committee on African and Afro-American Studies*, Harvard University Press.

Rubin, I. M. (1967), 'Increase of self-acceptance: a means of reducing prejudice', *Journal of Personality and Social Psychology*, vol. 5, pp. 233–8.

Scheff, T. J. (1966), *Being Mentally Ill: A Sociological Theory*, Aldine.

Selltiz, C., and Cook, S. W. (1962), 'Factors influencing attitudes of foreign students toward their host countries', *Journal of Social Issues*, vol. 18, pp. 7–23.

Sherif, M. (1961), *Intergroup Conflict and Co-operation: The Robbers Cave Experiment*, University of Oklahoma Book Exchange.

Sherif, M. (1966), *In Common Predicament: Social Psychology of Intergroup Conflict and Cooperation*, Houghton Mifflin.

Sherif, M., and Sherif, C. (1953), *Groups in Harmony and Tension*, Harper & Row.

Slavson, S. R. (1943), *An Introduction to Group Therapy*, Commonwealth Fund.

Solomon, A. (1963), 'Authoritarian attitude changes and group homogeneity', *Journal of Social Psychology*, February, pp. 129–35.

Stember, C. H. (1961), *Education and Attitude Change: The Effect of Schooling on Prejudice Against Minority Groups*, Institute of Human Relations.

Subcommittee on Human Relations in the Classroom (1962), *Teacher Education for Human Relations in the Classroom*, Committee on Teacher Education, North Central Association of Colleges and Secondary Schools.

Subcommittee on Human Relations in the Classroom (1963), *Human Relations in the Classroom*, Committee on Teacher Education, North Central Association of Colleges and Secondary Schools.

Trubowitz, J. (1969), *Changing the Racial Attitudes of Children: The Effects of An Activity-Group Program in New York City Schools*, Praeger.

TURNER, R. (1969), 'The public perception of protest', *American Sociological Review*, December, pp. 815–31.

VOLKMAN, R., and CRESSEY, D. (1963), 'Differential association and the rehabilitation of drug addicts', *American Journal of Sociology*, September, pp. 129–42.

WARREN, D. I. (1970), 'Suburban isolation and racial tension: the Detroit case', *Social Problems*, Winter, pp. 324–39.

WHITE, R., and LIPPITT, R. (1960), *Autocracy and Democracy*, Harper & Row.

WILLIAMS J. A., and WIENIR, P. L. (1967), 'A re-examination of Myrdal's rank order of discriminations', *Social Problems*, Spring, pp. 443–54.

WILLIAMS, R. (1947), *The Reduction of Intergroup Tensions*, Social Science Research Council.

WILLIAMS, R. M. (1964), *Strangers Next Door*, Prentice-Hall.

WILNER, M., WALKLEY, R. P., and COOK, S. W. (1955), *Human Relations in Interracial Housing*, University of Minnesota Press.

WILSON, J. Q. (1960), *Negro Politics: The Search for Leadership*, Free Press.

YABLONSKY, L. (1965), *The Tunnel Back*, Macmillan.

YARROW, M. R. (1958), 'Interpersonal dynamics in a desegregation process', *Journal of Social Issues*, vol. 14.

YARROW, M. R., CAMPBELL, J., and YARROW, L. (1958), 'Acquisition of new norms: a study of racial desegregation', *Journal of Social Issues*, vol. 14.

Chapter 6
Techniques for Reducing Prejudice: Changing the Situation

George Eaton Simpson and J. Milton Yinger

Patterns of discrimination and segregation that lasted, in the United States, for three-quarters of a century after the abolition of slavery were as severe as anywhere in the world: yet they began to break up in the 1940s. This change is useful, therefore, for an analysis of the causes of change in prejudice and discrimination. These patterns of discrimination and segregation have become the target of a powerful movement, involving a larger share of Negroes than were ever before participants in active protests, a substantial number of whites, and more recently Chicanos, Puerto Ricans, American Indians, and others. The movement has evolved through several stages, with different strategies, different participants, and different kinds of conflict. Although there has been overlap and accumulation of strategies, rather than sharply divided periods, we might call 1944–54 the 'constitutional stage', marked at the beginning by the Supreme Court ruling against white primaries and at the end by the Court ruling against *de jure* school segregation.[1]

The next stage has two related but distinct parts. It is the period of nonviolent, but active protest against discrimination by private individuals and groups, but also of extensive statutory changes that register the same protest.

The third stage to which we shall refer also has various elements. We might call it the 'Black Power period', but with the involvement of numerous minorities it has become polychrome. We shall examine some aspects of this third stage below. In the light of past experience, it seems likely that it will not last more than a few years into the 1970s, and by the late 1970s the late 1960s may prove to have been the peak of conflict, to be followed by more constructive modes of change.

These three stages have in common a shift from primary interest in prejudice to major concern over discrimination. Some scholars, as well as action leaders, have taken the position that prejudice has little to do with intergroup relations, that these vary with the social structure, not with changes in individual attitudes.[2] We support this emphasis on sociological

1. This should not be read to mean that protests suddenly began in the 1940s. For comments on the immediately preceding period, see Dalfiume (1970).

2. See, for example, Blumer (1958), Rose (1956), Breed (1962), Sherif and Faris (1962), Reitzes (1959) and Rhyne (1962).

factors as a strategic matter, but would caution against swinging the pendulum too far in that direction. There are some situations in which attention to individual attitudes may be the most strategic approach. In general, these would be situations where the effort to improve the status of disprivileged persons has little community backing, where law, tradition, and the stratification patterns firmly support discrimination.

Nevertheless, the recent shift in emphasis is based on sound observation and theory. Many studies show that individual behaviour can be modified by changes in the situation, independently of personality structure. Or, to put this in terms that we believe are theoretically more adequate, a high proportion of persons have tendencies towards nondiscrimination that may be called out by strategic situational changes even though such tendencies normally are dormant.[3]

Compromise versus contention

Does this emphasis on discrimination mean that the extent of opposition is unimportant in strategic considerations? In our judgement it does not. It is an emphasis appropriate to the contemporary scene, but not necessarily to all other situations. In facing problems of discrimination against members of minority groups, the wise strategist will try to decide to what degree the practices should be opposed directly and immediately, and to what degree they should be attacked indirectly by eroding away their supports.

The strategist must decide not only the degree of contention and the degree of compromise that he will use, but also the way in which his programme will be carried on. It is usually necessary to secure the co-operation of the discriminator in changing an unhappy situation. This is not likely to be accomplished by exposing him to ridicule, attacking him as a person, and generally threatening his security. Opposition to discriminators is very different from opposition to discrimination.

The place of law and administration

In recent years there have been substantial efforts to reduce discrimination through the use of law and administrative decisions. These efforts are indications that many people – including most social scientists – now challenge an earlier belief that law was impotent to enforce interracial justice. In this challenge, there has sometimes been a failure to seek out the conditions under which law is most likely to be effective. Some observers, looking at the problem from the perspective of the United States today, a setting in which the legal approach is relatively effective, have simply

3. For a development of this point in general theoretical terms, see Yinger (1965, ch. 11).

reversed the earlier dogma to affirm that law is the crucial weapon in the fight to improve intergroup relations. The scientific task, however, is not to assert one position or the other, but is to analyse factors involved in the variation in the effectiveness of an approach through law. In our judgement it can best be described as a 'middle strategy'. It is unnecessary to wait until everybody in a society is ready for a change before it can be incorporated into law, as the extensive emphasis on the situational approach that we have given throughout this volume makes clear. On the other hand, to pass a law that has little support in other institutional patterns is a relatively ineffective move, although it may not be entirely meaningless. The fate of efforts in the United Nations to protect minorities shows that it is too early to hope to reduce discrimination substantially by international legal action. This does not mean that the efforts are not worth while; but it means that far more preparation by way of economic strength for minorities, shared values, the reduction of stereotypes and traditional prejudices, the relaxation of fear of war, and the like, is necessary before international legal action to protect minorities can be particularly helpful.[4]

Within the United States and many other societies, however, the necessary preparation for improving intergroup relations through the organized political community has been accomplished. Indeed, the analyses of social scientists concerning the nature and consequences of segregation are among the preparations.

With respect to the general strategic problem of compromise versus contention, in sum, we do not take an *a priori* position in favour of immediate legal and other forms of direct action or one that supports more indirect and long-run methods. What will be effective in one setting may fail in another; and in virtually every case a variety of approaches is required. An effort that might fail by itself can be a valuable element in a larger strategy. Education and conciliation, for example, may leave the tough institutional structure of discrimination undisturbed; but in a situation where vigorous direct action is also undertaken they may smooth the process of change. Legal action by itself may run into massive resistance or reluctant compliance that returns at once to the old patterns when surveillance is removed; but in a situation where educational and conciliatory processes have also been at work, gains won by legal coercion may gradually get the support of personal conviction and institutional practice.[5]

Underlying this statement on strategy is our belief that on the level of theory we also need a blend of separate, even superficially contradictory,

4. For several valuable papers dealing with law and conflict, see Danelski (1967).
5. For an interesting study of the effects of law in another area of interest, see Colombotos (1969).

views – a theory of conflict resolution, but also a theory of conflict. Neither is highly developed (see Simnel, 1955; Coser, 1956, 1967; and Fink 1968). In our view, the aim of policy should not be the elimination of conflict, but its redirection into constructive channels. The relatively open and public conflict of a strike may be preferable to the covert 'sabotage' and demoralization of workers who have no way of expressing their grievances. A massive assault on segregation barriers by freedom marchers and crowds may be preferable to the self-destructive bitterness and the lack of motivation of the dispossessed. What we need, therefore, is a complex theory both of conflict resolution and of the consequences of various forms of conflict.

Organizations opposing discrimination

One of the most significant developments in recent years has been the growth of the profession of intergroup relations and the increase in the number of organizations whose programmes, wholly or in part, are dedicated to the reduction of prejudice and discrimination. Two forces are involved in this development. Minority-group members have established a vast variety of organizations whose aim is the elimination of their own underprivileges and those of other minorities; and out of the total community have come other groups, public and private, concerned with the full realization of democratic values. These two sources are, of course, not distinct.

There are several hundred intergroup relations agencies, local, state, or national, with paid professional staffs in the United States. Doubtless there are at least as large a number working on a continuous basis with volunteer personnel, in addition to scores of temporary commissions and committees which have been formed in recent years.

As more and more people have been drawn into the field of intergroup relations as a full-time occupation, it has gone through the process of 'professionalization'. There have developed a body of principles to guide their work, a programme of training for staff members, coordinating organizations for the exchange of experience, and professional publications for research and information. This process is by no means complete. It will doubtless be some time before we have graduate schools of 'intergroup relations' to match our medical schools (or more probably, departments of inter-group relations in professional schools of 'social engineering'). But steps in this direction have been taken at several universities and it seems highly probable that further development along this line will take place.

A focal point of this professionalization is the National Association of Intergroup Relations Officials (NAIRO), an organization founded in 1947, with a membership (1970) of 1600 professional workers. NAIRO describes itself as follows:

... an organization of individuals concerned with advancing intergroup relations knowledge and skills, improving the standards of professional intergroup relations practice, and furthering acceptance of the goals and principles of inter-group relations work.

NAIRO seeks to further these purposes through: Exchange of experience and knowledge among professional workers and others concerned with racial, religious, and ethnic relationships.

Study, analysis, and research on problems and developments affecting inter-group relations.

Collection, compilation, and dissemination of information and ideas regarding programmes, methods, and techniques (*Journal of Intergroup Relations*, 1961, p. 291).

Alongside public and private nonprofit agencies there has developed a new kind of business firm specializing in race relations consulting, recruit-ment of personnel from minority groups, and helping to design govern-ment programmes. There are now perhaps 250 such firms in the USA and maybe two or three similar ones in Britain; most of the US ones are owned and operated by Negroes. Their primary aim is not to reduce discrimina-tion; they are businesses, not unlike white-operated agencies that specialize in consulting and employment services. Nevertheless, their work is partly motivated by the desire to change, and inevitably affects, patterns of discrimination. Faced with legal and public pressure to add black employ-ees, particularly on skilled and management levels, many companies have turned to these race-relations consultants for help. Wondering why (in the USA this) their sales are low among Negroes, or hoping to expand their markets, firms have sought guidance from Negro market specialists – often discovering in the process how poorly tuned they were to the sensi-tivities, styles, and tastes of blacks. This new occupation adds one more dimension to the intergroup relations profession (Friedman, 1970).

Public and quasi-public agencies in intergroup relations

We cannot begin even to list the numerous agencies and departments of various organizations now concerned with intergroup relations. Among public agencies there are the staffs of fair employment and fair educational practices commissions,[6] administrators of public housing, school officers, and advisers in various branches of the federal government and in the armed services. Although they often have legal powers to enforce their decisions, their emphasis is much more strongly on conciliation and

6. For a careful study of one state agency, see Mayhew (1968).

education. In only a small proportion of cases are the coercions of law employed.

Perhaps the most general of the agencies in the United States is the Civil Rights Commission. Its mandate is extremely broad, with its emphases changing from year to year as the national situation changes.

The US Commission on Civil Rights is a temporary, independent, bi-partisan agency established by Congress in 1957 and directed to: investigate complaints alleging that citizens are being deprived of their right to vote by reason of their race, colour, religion, or national origin, or by reason of fraudulent practices; study and collect information concerning legal developments constituting a denial of equal protection of the laws under the Constitution; appraise Federal laws and policies with respect to equal protection of the laws; serve as a national clearing-house for information in respect to denial of equal protection of the laws; and submit reports, findings, and recommendations to the President and the Congress.

In Britain there is a twin-headed organization, set up as part of race relations legislation. There is the Community Relations Commission, charged with encouraging harmonious relations between different groups in the community, and the Race Relations Board, whose job it is to enforce the Race Relations Act. The Home Office urban programme and the Education Priority Areas also feed money and expertise into areas with larger-than-average immigrant populations. On the local level there has been an extensive development of 'community relations boards' or 'mayor's committees', as they are frequently named in the USA. Some of these may be called quasi-public, for they are primarily advisory and have no official status. But many have been established by community ordinance and have professional staffs financed out of public funds.[7]

The municipal agencies have handicaps as forces in the movement to reduce discrimination, but they also have some significant strengths and accomplishments. They are often affected by the local political situation. This can be an advantage insofar as minority groups are in a balance-of-power position. More often, however, it is a disadvantage, because those seeking to hold or gain political power will give only token support to the agency if powerful interests in the community oppose the agency's recommendations on housing, recreation, or job opportunities.

Despite the obstacles faced by local civic unity groups, they have made important contributions to intergroup relations in many cities. They have countered violence and the threat of violence with firmness, with facts and open discussion. They have helped to reduce discrimination in city employment, particularly by increasing the employment of Negroes in police

7. For a discussion of the comparative effectiveness of private councils and public commissions, see Robbins (1961).

departments, schools, and public transportation. They have worked closely with city administrations, school officials, and fair employment practices commissions (which in some instances – Cleveland, Gary, Youngstown, Philadelphia – are part of the same agency). A few community relations boards have been assigned responsibilities in connection with public housing, and most of the boards are concerned with housing problems. There is little doubt that these agencies occupy a strategically important place in the efforts to reduce discrimination in American cities.

Private organizations in the field of racial and cultural relations

Complementing the official agencies concerned with intergroup relations are many private associations dedicated wholly or in part to the reduction of prejudice and discrimination and the enlargement of opportunities for minorities. They range from temporary local groups formed to try to solve a particular problem to permanent national groups with large professional staffs and annual budgets over a million dollars.[8] Some are concerned with civil rights generally, others with the special problems of particular racial or ethnic groups. Some emphasize education, others are involved in action programmes. We cannot describe fully even a small number of the American ones, but will mention a few here in order to note the range and importance of their programmes.

National Association for the Advancement of Colored People. The NAACP, founded in 1909, works for the elimination of segregation and discrimination against Negroes and other Americans. For the most part, it seeks its objectives through court and legislative action, although it has participated to some degree in the demonstrations and protest marches of the civil rights movement and has given legal and financial support to others in this movement. Campaigns for equality have been waged in the fields of housing, employment, education, recreation, law, travel, the armed forces, voting, and officeholding. Efforts have also been made to ban residential segregation, to secure passage of antilynching laws, and to bring about co-operation between religious organizations and the NAACP.

8. Figures for budgets, membership, and staff change from year to year. Those which we cite, for illustrative purposes, are mostly for the late 1960s or 1970. Those interested in the data for the current year may consult standard reference works and the official publications of the agencies themselves. In the material that follows we have drawn on the *Encyclopedia of Associations*, vol. 1, *National Organizations of the US* 6th ed., Gale Research Co., 1970; National Association of Intergroup Relations Officials, *Directory* of Intergroup Relations Agencies with Paid Professional Personnel, 1959; *American Jewish Yearbook*, vol. 71, Morris Fine and Milton Himmelfarb (eds.), American Jewish Committee and Jewish Publication Society of America, 1970. *The New York Times*, 5 July, 1970 and 28 June, 1970; and various official publications.

The Research Department has compiled a large quantity of material on race relations and civil rights, and the national office has published a monthly journal, *The Crisis*, since 1910.

The NAACP is a militant organization but one which operates within the framework of the democratic ideology and the democratic society. Before the 'Negro revolt' of the 1960s, it was regarded by many whites, especially in the South, and by some upper-class Negroes, as a radical organization; actually it had adopted at an early date various measures to exclude communists from its membership. And in the spectrum of current organizations in the civil rights field, the NAACP seems quite conservative.[9]

At the local level the NAACP serves as a legal aid society; but in fighting for the Negro's rights at the national level it selects cases for their strategic importance, and insofar as possible enters the courts only where there is good chance of success. Frequently it is expected that the decision will be adverse in the lower courts, but cases are prepared with extreme care so that they will stand up in the higher courts. The NAACP has won most of the several dozen cases it has argued before the Supreme Court.

The NAACP is an interracial organization, but its membership is preponderantly Negro. As its strength has grown and as the number of trained Negroes has increased, the influence of white members and officers has declined at the national level. It is doubtless more effective on the national than on the local level, but local activity has increased in recent years. There are about 1750 branches, youth councils, and college chapters, with a total membership of 462,000. The professional staff, headed by Roy Wilkins, totals about 150 persons; income in 1969 was nearly $4 million. In addition, there is the associated, but legally separate, NAACP Legal Defense and Education Fund, with a staff of twenty-five lawyers. It serves as the legal arm of the civil rights movement generally.

The NAACP has been the subject of rather continuous criticism, either for being too militant (as segregationists believe, of course, but as some 'moderates' – e.g., William Faulkner and Chet Huntley – also declare) or for being too conservative (as some participants in the current 'Negro revolt' believe). The result is that the NAACP, while it has expanded its National Board, to bring in a wider range of Negro views, has reduced the proportion of white Board members (from 22 per cent, 1963, to 12 per cent, 1969), has endorsed and to some degree participated in nonviolent action projects, and has severely criticized the administration of President

9. Not, however, to the Army. In a 1968 directive to its intelligence agents, released in 1971, the Army sought information on 'Aims and activities of groups attempting to create, prolong, or aggravate racial tensions'. NAACP, SCLC, CORE, and SNCC were among the groups listed (*Cleveland Plain Dealer*, 28 February, 1971, p. 1).

Nixon for its racial policies, nevertheless maintaining its essentially integrationist approach.

Southern Christian Leadership Conference. In 1955–56 the Montgomery Improvement Association, in Alabama successfully carried through a long and difficult boycott of city buses. The well-disciplined, nonviolent technique of the Negro group attracted national attention and brought its leader, the Reverend Martin Luther King, Jr, into the front ranks of the civil rights movement. To extend the use of nonviolent but direct resistance to segregation and discrimination, King and others formed the Southern Christian Leadership Conference. For two or three years SCLC was active in several local campaigns but not a major influence in the desegregation process. Then beginning with the sit-ins of 1960, the freedom-rides of 1961 and the crescendo of protests in 1963, SCLC leaped to prominence. King became, by almost any reckoning, the most influential Negro of the day.

Although King preached nonviolence throughout his career, which ended with his murder in 1968, he did adopt a more militant stance in the last two years. He spoke of civil disobedience to disrupt American society; urged black control and ownership of the ghettos; and used a rhetoric that was close to that of black power advocates. He continued to call for cooperation with whites, however, and for the attainment of an integrated society. In an article written shortly before he was killed, he opposed those who were suggesting that rioting was a necessary and valuable strategy.

Some observers, particularly those who take a radically militant point of view, believe that King's approach reached its peak in 1963 and was replaced by a non-integrationist black power strategy in the mid-1960s. The evidence does not support this belief. The new-breed radicals appeal to a minority of the American black population; their calls for drastic change and the elimination of discrimination, of course, are joined by the vast majority; but full equality within society achieved by forceful but nonviolent methods are the policies receiving most support. When the Harris poll, in 1970 (reported in Time, 6 April), asked a national sample of Negroes which leaders they thought 'very effective', the percentages were as in Table 1:

Table 1

	Per cent
Elected black officials	71
Civil rights leaders, such as the NAACP	67
Black ministers and religious leaders	56
Leaders of black militant groups	29

A *Newsweek* poll one year earlier showed that King remained a dominant figure. It is difficult to interpret these data.

It is not clear what the influence and direction of SCLC will be, whatever the continuing importance of militant, nonviolent integrationism may be. As with the other major organizations, the national setting, more than the individuals involved, will influence the direction of development of SCLC. It will fade out or change drastically if racial discrimination is not rapidly reduced. In a more favourable environment, it will evolve in ways consonant with the life and view of Martin Luther King.

Student Nonviolent Coordinating Committee. Following the dramatic and successful desegregation of lunch counters in Greensboro, North Carolina, in February, 1960, student groups throughout the South adopted the nonviolent method of seeking equal treatment in parks, restaurants, theatres, swimming pools, and other facilities. In April, Martin Luther King called together leaders of various student groups, meeting at Shaw University, Raleigh, North Carolina, and out of their conversations came the Student Nonviolent Coordinating Committee. Although intended, perhaps, as an arm of SCLC, SNCC soon broke away. By 1963 it had a staff of about seventy persons, headed by John Lewis, many of them drawing only subsistence pay, and a budget of $160,000. It was particularly effective in voter registration, often in the 'hard-core' areas least influenced by the integration movement.

Disagreements over strategy and goals became more severe within SNCC during the mid-1960s. It was caught up in the Black Power movement, Stokely Carmichael became its chairman in 1966, and the nonviolent philosophy was set aside. H. Rap Brown, Carmichael's successor as chairman, was even more vehement in his verbal attacks. The organization continued to support voter registration effectively, but began to organize all-Negro parties, as in Lowndes County, Alabama, under the 'Black Panther' emblem (Carmichael and Hamilton, 1967). In 1970 the name of the organization was changed to the Student National Coordination Committee; but by that time it had faded out as a major national organization, its new militant approach being taken up by CORE, and in a more extreme way by the Black Panthers.[10]

National Urban League. One of the oldest Negro organizations, the National Urban League, founded in 1910, has operated primarily as a social work agency. A large part of its work is devoted to the extension of

10. On the first several years of SNCC, see Howard Zinn (1966). For documents showing the changes in strategy, See Meier, Rudwick and Broderick (eds.) (1971), pp. 307–15, 352–60, 484–90. A book expressing the highly militant view of SNCC after 1966 is Julius Lester (1968). There are many references to SNCC in Harry Edwards (1970).

economic opportunities for Negroes in industry, business, and the professions and to improvement of housing. This objective is sought through discussions and conferences with business executives, industrialists, and labour union officials. Many Urban Leagues now provide clients with expert testing and counselling services in the professional, technical, clerical, skilled, and semi-skilled job categories. Other activities include providing information about Negroes, serving as adviser to governmental agencies and industry on health, welfare, and employment matters affecting Negroes, developing programmes to provide for the adjustment and social needs of in-migrant Negro workers, and assisting in the interracial planning of social services and community projects.

Although the League has taken little direct part in the protest demonstrations of the last several years, preferring to specialize in job training and placement and various social welfare programmes, it has recently taken a more militant stand. The late Whitney Young, Jr., for ten years executive director, proposed programmes for Negroes similar to veterans' benefits to compensate for the years of underprivilege, or a domestic 'Marshall plan' to guarantee a job for everyone willing and able to work and called for the building of a million low- and medium-income housing units a year to eliminate slums.

Young was fairly optimistic, for he could see changes, particularly in the job situation. He estimated, for example, that through the work of the National Urban League, 40,000 jobs were opened to Negroes in 1966, compared with 2000 in 1961.

Congress of Racial Equality. Founded in 1942, CORE had quietly applied the techniques of nonviolence and the sit-in, largely in the north, for many years before it was brought to prominent attention by the Negro revolt of the 1960s. CORE was established first as a committee of the pacifist Fellowship of Reconciliation in an effort to apply Gandhian techniques of vigorous, nonviolent resistance to American race relations. It has pioneered in the training of interracial groups for peaceful picketing, sit-ins, and negotiation. In recent years it has greatly expanded its activities and now has 70,000 members and a staff of seventy plus a number of 'subsistence workers'.

By 1964 CORE was a black nationalist, not an integrationist, organization. Its membership, which had been predominantly white, was by that time mainly black. Some whites remain, however, on the advisory committee. It is somewhat ironic to read that CORE, a pioneer in breaking down walls of segregation, in 1970 proposed separate schools for blacks and whites, with each race controlling its own. Innis said that CORE had talked with the Governors of Georgia, Alabama, Mississippi and Louisiana, and 'all conceded that the plane could fly, that their side could live with it' (Cleveland *Plain Dealer* 6 March 1970, p. 2A). Thus, for some, has the Civil Rights Movements come full circle.

There has not been extensive sociological study of private, voluntary race relations organizations that would help us to explain why one remains 'on course' while another changes its direction sharply or disappears.[11] Rudwick and Meier (1970) have raised that problem in a very helpful way by comparing the ways in which the NAACP and CORE responded to the sharply increased militancy of the black protest movement in the 1960s. It is tempting to explain the difference by individual, leadership factors, and these doubtless play some part. Rudwick and Meier wisely stress the structural differences between the two organizations. Following Sills, they note that the NAACP fits the 'corporate type' of formal organization quite closely. The national headquarters is strong and dominant, with legal control over the local branches, although in practice the local groups exercise considerable autonomy. CORE is a 'federated type' of organization. These differences partly reflect historical origins, with NAACP chartered under the laws of the state of New York, with a legally designated, self-perpetuating Board of Directors. CORE was founded by a more alienated group of pacifists, many of them theological students.

As a result of these and other differences, when the severe protests of the 1960s began to be felt by the major civil rights organizations, NAACP responded as corporately organized groups do: they took some of the opposition onto the Board, encouraged college and youth chapters in their direct action programmes, reduced even further the proportion of whites, and took a more critical stance with regard to the major issues of discrimination. But they did not drastically change their policies and goals. CORE, on the other hand, with its strong local autonomy, its longer history of direct action programmes, its rapid change of leadership, was much more strongly influenced by the changing mood of the 1960s.

The Black Panthers. The left-wing of the black protest movement has been occupied during the last five years by the Black Panthers. The organization was founded in Oakland, California, in 1966, in some ways a product of the split in strategy of SNCC, or at least illustrative of the radicalizing of one segment of the black nationalist movement in the mid-1960s. Although it has never been a large group, having reached a peak of about 5000 members in 1968, and dropping to perhaps 1000 by 1971, it has been the object of a great deal of attention and controversy. The aims of the Black

11. The literature on bureaucracy is a valuable source of theory on this question; studies of trade unions are useful, and we shall apply some theory derived from the latter below. Probably the most valuable direct study of a voluntary organization is Sills (1957).

Panthers are similar to those of other black nationalist groups, except perhaps for the violence of the verbal attack on the government, accompanied by affirmation of the sentiments of the Declaration of Independence, and demands that the government furnish jobs and decent income for all.

From the beginning there were differences over strategy and aims among the Black Panthers, as there are in any 'sectarian' group. These differences have become sharper, in the context of intense public opposition to the severity of Panther rhetoric and their violent stance. In his most recent remarks, the Chairman called for avoidance of confrontations with the police, increased church attendance, and greater effort to win support from the black community. From their self-imposed 'exile' locations in Algeria, however, Eldridge Cleaver and Mr and Mrs Michael Tabor call for intensified guerrilla attack on the United States. Stokely Carmichael broke with the black Panthers in 1969, presumably in opposition to their policy of direct confrontation with the police. By 1971 he believed they were 'practically finished', and called on black Americans to shift their attention to building 'mother Africa'. [12]

About one-quarter of America's black population, in the early 1970s, look with favour on the Black Panthers as a source of pride and for their efforts in favour of black control of their own communities. Their violence is written off as defence against police brutality. About another quarter are 'not sure' about Panther activities (it is difficult to separate the uncertain in this category from those who don't know about the Panthers; together they make up 34 per cent). Whites, on the other hand, are strongly in opposition. In April, 1970, the Harris poll asked respondents in a cross-section of American households: 'In general, do you feel the Black Panthers are a serious menace to this country, annoying but not very serious, or a force for good in the country?'

Table 2 **Attitudes (as a percentage of poll) toward the Black Panthers**

	Whites	Blacks
A serious menace	66	21
Annoying but not serious	24	19
Force for good	3	26
Not sure	7	34

12. The *New York Times*, February 6, 1971, p. 11; and March 21, 1971, p. 61. To get something of the underlying feelings and range of view of Black Panthers, as well as a picture of their organization and history, see Eldridge Cleaver (1968), Bobby Seale (1970), Earl Anthony (1970), a somewhat bitter attack by an ex-officer, indicating the sharp differences in view; Meier, Rudwick and Broderick (eds.) (1971), pp. 491–515; 'The Panthers: personal freedom *v.* public order', *Social Action*, whole issue, November, 1970.

National samples by the Gallup poll produce similar results. (These are not broken down by race, and presumably are mainly white respondents):

Table 3 **Attitudes (as a percentage of poll) toward the Black Panthers**

	Highly favourable	*Highly unfavourable*
College students (1971)	8	42
General public (1970)	2	75

In assessing the place of the Black Panthers in efforts to reduce discrimination, one of the most difficult questions has to do with the rhetoric and reality of their violent guerrilla activity, particularly in dealing with the police, and the degree to which the police tried to crush them. It is impossible to describe the Black Panther–police interaction 'in general'. The details of each encounter require examination. Perhaps this much, however, can be said to indicate our judgement about the context. In a day of sharp interracial conflicts, stereotypes have hardened on both sides. Police, seeing the Black Panthers through the prism of violent rhetoric and riots, have often acted first, and looked for specific law violations second or not at all. Members of the Black Panthers, seeing the world through years of discrimination, excessive use of police repression, and frustrated hopes, have talked hatred, gathered weapons, and in some instances, employed violence. They have also fed some hungry children. In the face of several court decisions in the Spring of 1971, finding Black Panthers innocent of charges or finding insufficient evidence even for an indictment, it seems clear that police actions during the preceding several years were much more repressive against the Panthers than was warranted or than the law allowed. The courts, on the other hand, in a somewhat calmer period, have recognized the right of Panthers to scream with pain and to demand change. They may also find, in some instances, that the rights of others, including police, have been violated. The basic question remains: have the Black Panthers helped to jolt the United States into action, or frightened it into retrenchment? The importance of this one organization should not be exaggerated; its approach and activity is more symbolic than causal. It is our judgement, however, that the 1968–69 confrontation period caused retrenchment rather than change, that it helped to elect reactionary politicians, slowed implementation of laws designed to achieve equality, and broke up essential alliances. It remains to be seen whether 'revolutionary intercommunalism' – self-selected segregation and community control – will have different results.

Black Power. Black Power, of course, is not an organization but a movement, or perhaps a style. Some see it as the successor to the civil rights movement; or it can be thought of as one of the forms which the rights movement took, beginning about 1964. Although as a movement it overlaps with the Black Panthers, CORE, and other organizations, it may be useful to comment briefly on it as a general approach to contemporary minority-majority relations. Black Power has a wide variety of meanings. 'The larger and more diverse a political movement's constituency, the more vague and imprecise its unifying symbols and rallying cries are likely to be. A slogan like black power has no sharply defined meaning; it may excite many different emotions and may motivate individuals to express their loyalty or take action for almost contradictory reasons' (Aberbach and Walker, 1970). Despite this range, we can identify Black Power as a movement that emphasizes confrontation strategies and 'nationalistic' (separatist) goals more strongly than most previous movements. 'We must fill ourselves with hate for all white things.' Such white things include the American political and economic system to some advocates of Black Power. 'We must destroy both racism and capitalism' (Huey Newton).

Since Black Power is an outlook, a point of view, more than a programme, we shall not examine the range of views further in this discussion of strategy. Indeed, it is not clear from such writings as Carmichael and Hamilton's *Black Power*, just what policies are called for. Nevertheless, the term designates a mood that is very important to understanding the contemporary scene.

Jewish organizations in the field of intergroup relations. There are dozens of Jewish organizations interested in intergroup relations, but perhaps the leading ones in this field are the American Jewish Congress, the Anti-Defamation League of B'nai B'rith, and the American Jewish Committee. The American Jewish Congress, founded in 1918, has a professional staff of 110: '. . . it is best known for activities designed to invoke legal sanctions against discrimination, including drafting legislation and participating in litigation affecting constitutional and legislative rights' (Robison, 1951). It is also interested in the investigation of intergroup tension and winning community support for its programme. The Anti-Defamation League, with a staff of 250, has a national office and twenty-five regional offices that work in co-ordination with other agencies on programmes to reduce discrimination in communities. On the national level the League has sponsored scores of workshops, published a great deal of anti-prejudice material, and developed an interest in most phases of intergroup relations. In 1959 it established a Department of Colleges and Universities to co-ordinate its work in institutions of higher education. The American Jewish Committee has emphasized educational work and is particularly prominent for its encouragement and sponsorship of research. Founded in 1906, it has the largest professional staff, 350, of the groups mentioned here.

A number of the Jewish agencies have joined together to form the National Community Relations Advisory Council in order better to co-ordinate their various programmes and to undertake some common projects. The Council is composed of the American Jewish Congress, the Jewish Labour Committee, the Jewish War Veterans, the Union of American Hebrew Congregations, the Union of Orthodox Hebrew Congregations, the United Synagogue of America, and thirty-five state and local organizations.

The National Conference of Christians and Jews. Although the National Conference of Christians and Jews has been, from its founding in 1928, primarily concerned with the promotion of harmonious relations among members of different religious faiths, it has also been interested in other aspects of intergroup relations. It has worked on the community level through its sixty-two regional offices, and on the national level by promoting seminars, providing advanced training in intergroup relations, sponsoring Brotherhood Week, and encouraging research. The Conference is strictly an interfaith agency, with the aim of developing understanding, tolerance, and co-operation, but with no desire to eliminate differences among the faiths.

Church organizations and intergroup relations. In addition to the Jewish agencies and the NCCJ, there are many organizations among Protestants and Catholics that are devoted primarily to the reduction of prejudice and discrimination. These are too numerous even to list.

The Negro revolution

Have these numerous protest organizations affected American society? Are the categorical lines of privilege and underprivilege that characterize a majority–minority stratification system being erased? We think that there is powerful evidence that this is happening – not, of course, without counter currents. Indeed, somewhat paradoxically, both the strength of the protest movement since the Second World War and the strength of the resistance are signs that significant change is taking place. To explore that paradox requires that we examine briefly the general theory of revolution.

America has been facing the classic revolutionary situation: the slowing down or reversal of a fairly long period of steady improvement. It is well established that revolutions do not occur among those who are most poorly off; nor do they occur among those who are well off and hopeful of the future. Typically there has been a long period of improvement, a sharp rise in aspiration and expectation – and then frustration.[13] It is clear that between about 1940 and 1955, Negroes in America had experienced the most rapid rate of improvement of occupational status and income they had ever known. But in the mid-1950s they hit a plateau. Much of the slowing down, it should be noted, was relative to new objectives and hopes, not to fixed standards (see Grindstaff, 1968).

It is significant that the levelling off of Negro gains in the mid-1950s did not hit their educational improvement. Thus their qualifications, expectations, and aspirations continued to increase while their opportunities ceased to improve. This is one of the major reasons why Negro students have taken such a vital role in the protest movement.

The growing number of Negro college students see a different world from that of their parents. Their hopes for full participation in American society have grown rapidly; they have no lack of knowledge of the opportunities in that society; yet they graduate, in a large proportion of cases, into segregated jobs, work at levels of skill and income far below those of their white contemporaries, and face a situation in which their training is partly irrelevant to their placement.

Varieties of 'sectarianism' among minority groups

With our brief comments we have only given examples of the hundreds of groups now concerned with intergroup relations and the general movement in which they participate. Perhaps we can draw these comments into focus by inquiring whether or not there is any pattern to the variety of minority-group organizations. We think there is such a pattern.

Minority-group protest organizations can helpfully be compared with religious sects (indeed, in many cases, they can well be regarded *as* religious sects). They exhibit the same three fundamental ways of responding to deprivation: one can say that the system within which the deprivation is felt needs drastic overhauling, but that it is capable of reform and contains some possible allies; one can see the system as fundamentally incapable of being remade – it must therefore be replaced; or one can see the system as so evil and resistant to change that the best choice is to withdraw from it. Seldom does any individual take one of these positions in a pure form; the purposes and strategies of groups also typically represent a blend. Yet various of the groups we have discussed approach more or less closely to one of the type positions. Their relationships can be described in the form of a triangle (see Figure 1), with the 'pure types' labelled at the angles, and illustrative guesses noted from among American Negro groups.

We lack systematic studies of the combinations of cultural, structural,

13. We cannot here develop this important branch of sociological theory. See Davies (1962), Edwards (1927), Brinton (1957) and Tanter and Midlarsky (1967).

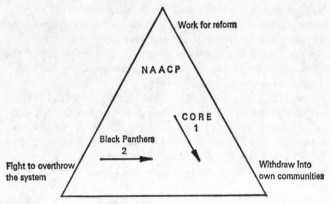

Figure 1 Strategic responses to discrimination

and characterological conditions that incline an individual or group towards one or another of these choices. The answers given to two critical questions reflect, in our judgement, cultural training, the structure of opportunities, and individual motives and experiences. They can be put into a Guttman scale:

Sources of 'sectarian' strategies

Probable strategy	Is the group optimistic about its own power to compete with the dominant group?	Is the group optimistic about the capacity of the prevailing system to change?
1. Fight for reform	yes	yes
2. Attack the system	yes	no
3. Work for separation	no	no

As one or another of the two variables change, the possibilities and the consequences of the various strategies change. Thus if one's sense of power goes up, as it has in the United States for many members of minority-groups, one moves along the plane from right to left in Figure 1. If perception of the capacity of the system to change goes up, one moves along the plane from bottom to top. (It should be noted that perception of the capacity to change is not identical with the actual capacity to change, although they are closely related. Their separation is a fundamental fact in any social system, whether it be as a result of the fact that minority-group members fail to perceive new opportunities, or believe in opportunities not there). If, after a period of rising hope, the sense of one's own power and of the system's change-capacity decline, there is a movement towards the lower-right corner. Arrow 1 may designate what happened to CORE after 1964; and arrow 2 what happened to the Black Panthers after 1970.

Some groups and leaders stand, or attempt to stand, equi-distant from the three angles. Or, more commonly, they take a non-doctrinaire position that says, in effect, that there is need for all three approaches.

The strategy of change

Thus a new context for intergroup relations has been created in the United States – and indeed throughout the world. We must be careful not to give our sole attention to the militant protest movements or the extensive legal changes, for they have been going on during a quiet revolution that has weakened the foundations of the earlier structures of relationship. The multiple forces at work – demographic, economic, international, religious, educational, and many others – have drastically been remaking views of the world held by minorities at the same time that they have significantly changed the structures within which intergroup relations occur.

With both hopes and power raised, it has been inevitable that minorities would protest the continuing patterns of discrimination and to seek to enlarge their gains. Much of the initiative has been shifted to the minorities. In discussing their differing levels of optimism, we noted the varying ways in which they bring pressure to bear on the discriminatory structure. It may be useful, however, to focus more directly on strategic questions, to try to discover the conditions that lead to one or another choice, and to estimate their consequences.

Nonviolent resistance

When Mrs Rosa Parks refused to give her seat to a white man on a Montgomery bus, she precipitated a series of events that have yet to run their course even now. In the months that followed, Negroes combined the strategy of economic boycott with a philosophy of nonviolent protest in a way that proved to be highly effective.

Under what conditions are such nonviolent protests likely to be effective? The most general factor is the extent to which potential opponents are divided or unified, both individually and collectively. If some are individually ambivalent, sharing values and goals with the protesters, while also holding contrary views, they are more likely to be persuaded by nonviolence. They may, indeed, not be ambivalent, but sympathize wholeheartedly with the protest, yet need an effective argument to disidentify with the dominant position of their own group.

It is a critical question, therefore, how members of a minority envisage the dominant group. If they see no moderates when in fact there are some, they are unlikely to act in such a way as to exploit the resources available to nonviolent protests. They may see no moderates, of course, because there are none. But there are other reasons. Those who themselves have been violent – on whatever side – are unlikely to recognize moderation on the other side because it makes their own actions seem less reasonable or civilized. A different series of interactions characterizes some white activists and intellectuals today, as during most times of crisis: for fear of being thought sentimental or unsympathetic to a just protest or insensitive to injustice, they describe a thoroughly racist society.

Applying this point of view to the Montgomery bus boycott as an illustration, we find several factors that contributed to its success. The supremacy of the constitution in the American legal system left no doubt what the ultimate court decision would be. The interdependent economy of the city meant that white supporters of desegregation were ambivalent. The bus company needed Negro riders; and white women, many of them working for $75 a week (these were 1955 dollars), needed their Negro maids, whom they paid $20. The quiet technique of the Reverend Martin Luther King and his co-workers was ideally suited to win the support of moderates and weaken the opposition, who were put in the position of extremists. In these circumstances, the restrained but insistent demand for equal services by the use of legal processes was effective.

What is the origin of this strategy of nonviolence? It has often been referred to as a Gandhian technique, and there is no doubt that the early leaders of CORE, SCLC, and others have been influenced by study of Gandhi and his work in South Africa and India (see Frazier, 1968). This is an inadequate explanation, however, particularly of the alacrity with which nonviolent resistance was adopted by thousands of Negroes, young and old, North and South, lower-class and middle-class, most of whom doubtless knew Gandhi only as a remote historical figure. The total explanation would certainly be complex, but these factors are probably involved: relatively powerless groups, who would inevitably be overcome in any open contest of force, have often found nonviolent resistance a way of maximizing their strength in dealing with an opponent who has some respect for law and a conscience. In a sense, this is a way of getting part of the dominant force over on the minority's side.[14]

To this perhaps humanwide source of nonviolent resistance one must add the Christian tradition. It comes as a natural part of the cultural training of most Negroes to believe that they can achieve through suffering, that they should turn the other cheek, that the enemy can better be overcome by love than by force. When Negroes were virtually powerless, this religious tradition led to otherworldliness, accommodative attitudes, and

14. For a discussion of its use in South Africa, see Kuper (1957).

repressed or deflected aggression. In the last decade, however, many Negroes have become militant. Vander Zanden (1963) suggests that the nonviolent resistance movement is an effort to mediate between the tradition of accommodation and the new militancy. The latter arouses guilt feelings which the nonviolent protests help to allay by their emphasis on suffering.

We shall not undertake to describe the wave of nonviolent protests that swept across the United States, particularly in the early years of the 1960s. There were thousands of boycotts, sit-ins, freedom rides, picketing, and mass rallies.[15] Some of these were designed to win a specific goal – to secure jobs or to open facilities from which non-whites had been barred – others were primarily symbolic affirmations of the need for an open society. Boycotts by a minority group become effective when their buying power, for the particular firms involved, represents the difference between economic health and bankruptcy. This requires, of course, that the group be sufficiently well organized to focus their opposition, and the absence of such focus on the part of groups who oppose the boycott.

Sit-ins and freedom rides involve a great deal of courage and self-discipline, for their purpose is to persuade people without violence to abide by a law that they have long been disregarding with support from the dominant community and the police. These protests started with restaurants and lunch counters, spreading out to parks, libraries, art galleries, swimming pools, churches, and transportation facilities, all of which were substantially segregated in the southern states in 1960. There were wade-ins, read-ins, ride-ins and pray-ins. Violence broke out in many cases, with many of the protesters being injured and thousands jailed. Several were killed. The total effect, nevertheless, was the desegregation of many public facilities, but more importantly, the dramatization of segregation and discrimination so vividly that they can never again be taken for granted in the United States.

Violent resistance

Almost everybody admires at least one revolution – usually one distant in time if the person is comfortable and a contemporary one if he is not. The staunchest defenders of law and order recognize the role of coercion in human affairs; but they want the use of violent coercion limited to the

15. These are not new strategies. Boycotts go back at least to the first decade of the century, and CORE began its sit-in movement in the early 1940s. But as a mass movement, such activities appeared only in the 1960s. For a sampling of studies, see Meier and Rudwick (1969), Eisenberg and Weisbrod (1963), Lees (1961), Proudfoot (1962), Lomax (1962), *New South* (1961), Lincoln (1961), Searles and Williams (1962), McGill (1963), Mitchell and Peace (eds.) (1961), King (1958), King (1963), *Newsweek* (1963), and Isaacs (1963).

official representatives of society. For those who deeply believe, however, that they suffer from that society – and at the hands of those representatives – such a restriction on the use of violence is unacceptable. Minorities in many places are saying: why should we simply capitulate to *their* violence? It is less moral than our own.

We cannot here undertake to discuss the conditions under which such loss of legitimacy is likely to occur. Briefly, it is the product of a cycle of causes, some of them psychological: rising aspirations and a sharply increased sense of relative deprivation on the part of minorities; pressure against the system; reaction by the dominant group, some of it violent (violence may actually decrease, but it is more visible, and probably more 'official', because the informal social control mechanisms prove to be inadequate); stronger pressure against the system, with supporting ideologies now justifying reciprocal violence (we are an internal colony, with every right to break free).

For the dominant group it is clear that violence is successful in maintaining allegiance only when it is minimally used. Greater use may maintain sullen and unwilling compliance, but not allegiance. A related principle applies to minorities: minimal violence used to underline a neglected legitimacy may get support, or not arouse major retaliation. When the conflict is heightened, counter-violence is increased and it becomes more difficult to maintain a publicly accepted definition that the minority violence was an understandable (if unfortunate) protest.

It is, of course, difficult to draw a line between violence and nonviolence. Is it violent to hurt a child personally, but nonviolent to support a system that causes the child to be malnourished as an infant, so that he does not fully develop, physically or mentally? Is it violent to smash the windows in a man's store and loot his shelves, but nonviolent to picket his business so that his economic loss is as great as it would have been had he been looted? Those who justify opposition to violence on moral grounds need to be certain they are not drawing a distinction without a difference.

Important as these moral questions are, the focus of our attention in this chapter is on strategy. In this light, a minority appropriately asks how the willingness or unwillingness to use violence increases the resources at its disposal and reduces the deficits. In a relatively open society the marshalling of resources is more dependent on the mutual trust within the minority than on their persuading or coercing the majority to make concessions. Effective action requires the *accumulation* of resources. Politically, this means the use of flexible and focused voting that can be brought to bear on particular issues and elections, rather than scattered and competitive politics that divides the minority vote. Economically, it means the building up, out of funds that are individually too small, of resources that jointly are adequate to accomplish a given purpose. Clifford Geertz (1962) describes the 'revolving credit associations' that exist in many villages and towns of southeast Asia and Africa. The associations are circles of friends and neighbours who make periodic contributions to a common fund. Each member, in an order determined by lot or by some prearranged method, has his turn in using the fund for some major purchase.

Similar arrangements are not uncommon among minority communities in the United States and elsewhere. Chinese, Japanese and Jews have been among those who have thus focused their resources. The Black Muslims accumulate collectively in a way that has permitted the founding of many businesses. Even the numbers racket can be looked upon as an incipient 'rotating credit association'; but as Coleman notes, the return is so small as a proportion of the 'investment' and the likelihood of winning so unpredictable, that the effect is to drain rather than aid the community.

What has this to do with the question of violence? Violence is an outward strategy. It is based on the assumption that coercing the majority is the primary need. Although it is sometimes justified as a source of minority community solidarity, it tends in fact to tear the fabric of trust on which community solidarity depends. Whenever a situation has developed in which discrimination by the majority has fallen off, and new procedures to take advantage of new openings are called for, violence deflects energy and wastes resources. It is one of the ironies of history that violence is most likely to erupt precisely when, and partly because, new opportunities are opening; and it may persist into the period when techniques for exploiting newly available opportunities are the chief need.

Interpretations of the impact of violence differ widely, not only because of differing moral premises, but also because the situation is extremely complex. One must be alert to long-run, and not only short-run, consequences, to all the unintended as well as to the intended effects. Among interpretations of the riots in American cities during the 1960s, for example, one finds such contrasting notions as these: riots increase hatred, confirm prejudices; action to remedy grievances must not follow them or it will appear that lawlessness and hostility are being rewarded. Yet others argue that desperately needed action seems to come only after a riot, which smashes complacency and exposes the problem as nothing else has been able to do. The assessment is difficult. It does seem clear that under some circumstances, riots are heard as a cry of pain. They may help to transform private trouble into a public issue, to use a theme developed by C. Wright Mills in another connection, by flooding the media of communication with the importance of the problem. Yet riots, in addition to the immediate losses and costs, tend to confirm mutual stereotypes, to increase segregation by speeding the flight of whites to the suburbs, and to give the participants a sense that they have struck a blow for freedom, when in fact they have only indicated the need for freedom, while leaving the basic difficulties intact.

We agree with B. L. R. Smith (1968) that extensive use of violence tends to spread through a society a 'revolutionary myth' that has serious unanticipated, long-run costs.

The costs are partly visible in such things as an increased sense of fear in the community shared by whites and blacks alike, the greater salience of politics for people's lives in a society which has usually resisted the encroachments of political attitudes into the sphere of basic human relationships, and the prospect that, since the stakes of politics are higher, ruling elites in the future may seek to manage conflict by excessive resort to force. Violence begets more violence and ultimately will leave deep scars on the nation's image of itself, profoundly alter life styles, and change the temper of the American mind.

Barrington Moore (1968) suggests that violence fails to work '. . . mainly when revolutionary rhetoric outruns the real possibilities inherent in a given historical situation', that is, when a group underestimates the opposition. We believe it also fails, in the sense that it entails great costs without concomitant gains, when it overestimates the opposition, when it fails to see possibilities that are available in a situation at much lower cost than that required by violence.

We are confronted, in the matter of violence, with an extremely sharp dilemma in any society that maintains serious barriers to full participation by some of its members. On the one hand, we are told by some that '. . . extremism on the left helps to undermine the democratic centre and prepare the way for a take-over by the right . . .'; but also that '. . . by following what they call moderate and responsible policies those devoted to liberalism may become the hostages, and even agents, of repressive and reactionary trends.'

A society cannot solve a dilemma of this kind. So long as the conditions that produce it exist, those seeking to reduce the deprivation and injustice suffered by minorities will be strategically split, with some sanctioning a mainly self-defeating violence and others accepting a mainly illiberal social system. The dilemma can be made to a greater or lesser degree irrelevant by undermining its causes, by using all the various strategies we have discussed to open up structures of opportunity. In our judgement, the level of violence is an index of relative success but is an inefficient strategy for bringing about that opening.

Changing the minority-group member

Our discussion of strategy has so far emphasized the task of removing special disprivileges faced by minority-group members. Where causes are cyclical, however, and mutually re-enforcing, this is not sufficient. Built into the personality systems and group structures of minorities are some of the consequences of *past* discrimination. These may persist into situations that are less discriminatory, preventing the reduction of prejudice and lowering the possibilities that present opportunities will be exploited. Thus the responses of minority-group members to prejudice and discrimination frequently lend support to further hostility. One line of approach that strategy may take, therefore, is to discover ways of changing some of the responses of the minorities. Let the Negro improve himself, they say, and prejudice will disappear. When the Jew stops being Jewish, there will be no discrimination against him. If the immigrant will adopt American (British, Australian) ways, no one will oppose him. This approach suffers from the double error of 'bootstrap' thinking (demanding that minorities change many characteristics that are the *results* of prejudice *before* the prejudice can be reduced). There is, however, a small way in which this approach is useful, as part of a total strategy. To the prejudiced person, the characteristics and the responses of minority-group members are part of the total situation that seems to him to justify his action. If they can be changed, or his conception of them changed, he will perceive the situation differently.

The emphasis on self-improvement is greeted with derision by some minority-group members because it seems to place the responsibility for prejudice on the oppressed people. In our view 'responsibility' for hostility, if one wants to use that term, must be located in the nature of man; but effective strategy may require attention to the best responses by members of the minorities.

There is great need for further study of the conditions which promote the perpetuation of minority subcultures and personality tendencies which prevent the entrance of minority-group members into the full range of community life even when barriers have been lowered. Perhaps recriminations can be avoided if one puts the issue, not in terms of a vocabulary of praise and blame, but in terms of cause and effect. One then asks a strategic question: to what degree is emphasis on changes in the motivation, values, behaviour, and group structures of minorities effective as a complement to changes in patterns of dominant-group discrimination and segregation, in the effort to remove inequities? Or, perhaps more adequately, under what conditions is emphasis on minority-group changes most effective?

Attention to minority tendencies is based on the interdependence of minority–majority patterns. The attainment of equality may demand not only the reduction of discrimination by those who are dominant, but a change in motivations by those who are suppressed. Minority-group norms and character structures are to some degree tuned to a discriminatory society; they reflect efforts to adjust to or deal with that society, for they are part of an interlocking system. When discrimination declines minority-group members may not be fully ready to seize new opportunities. Protected islands may be demanded, or built (and perhaps are needed during a period of transition) and the system may still be blamed. If, however, this blame is poorly placed, if it does not identify the true situation, it will be an expensive luxury.

Following this line of argument, we are led into one of the great issues of social change: what force is powerful enough to transform men, to create individuals ready and able to respond effectively to a new world? Some argue that violence can do this, that it is, to repeat Sartre's words, 'man recreating himself'. But this does not ask what he is recreating himself for. The Nazis were recreated and united 'by the terrorism around us,' just as Eldridge Cleaver remarked of 'the most beautiful sight ... leather jackets, black trousers ... and each with a gun'. Oppenheimer asks '... whether this therapeutic effect stems from violence or from the effect of struggling against oppression ...' And Fanon, even as he exalts violence, also notes its great psychic costs, for the individual, his family, and the total community.

Are there less costly ways to achieve necessary personal transformations? The power of some religious movements to 'revitalize' their adherents has often been studied. (This is not necessarily in contradistinction to violence, it should be noted, since violence may be heightened by the belief that one is fighting for a sacred cause.) One of the critical elements in Max Weber's analysis of *The Protestant Ethic and the Spirit of Capitalism* was his belief that Calvinism drastically reorganized the motivations and perceptions of its adherents. David McClelland, in *The Achieving Society*, traces the 'need for achievement' primarily to the family background wherein aspirations and values are taught. It has frequently been observed that the Black Muslims have a great power to reorganize the motives and goals of their members. Applying this thesis to race relations in the United States, at least, without specifically religious connotations, it may be '... that the real benefit of the civil rights movement is the psychological change it has produced and is producing in those Negroes who are active in it'. A more drastic interpretation of this thesis gives it a group dimension, and perhaps takes us back to the question of violence. As Coleman (1969) describes this point of view: 'Participation in revolutionary action transforms the previously apathetic masses by giving them a goal and the hope of achieving the goal'. Whatever one may regard as the most effective method for achieving this goal, it is clear thet some personality reorganization, not only of the majority-group member, but of the minority-group member as well, is necessary as part of the process whereby majority–minority systems are transformed.

Conclusion

The freedom movement of the last few decades has brought inescapably to the white man's attention the plight and the demands of non-white minorities. Probably more important, it has galvanized the minorities themselves into action; psychologically, it has increased their self-respect and the sense that they can struggle with their difficult conditions with some chance of success.

This does not mean that new patterns will emerge smoothly, automatically, peacefully. The speed of change, the degree of conflict which accompanies it, the extent to which attitudes change along with behaviour, depend upon the strategic skill of the contending groups and upon the way America deals with various problems before her that have nothing directly to do with majority–minority relations. Two of these problems are basic: international tensions and economic instability.

Throughout this analysis we have emphasized the interactive and cumulative nature of the forces influencing intergroup relations. For purposes of discussion it has frequently been necessary to isolate one aspect of the total pattern; but it would be a costly error to forget the total empirical scene, for that is what, in the last analysis, we want to understand and to control. The interlocking of the many factors that affect majority–minority relations greatly complicates the work of the student and of the social engineer.

The need for research

Only a small proportion of the time and energy spent in trying to improve intergroup relations is devoted to research – to analysis of the effectiveness of specific programmes and to the study of the total causal complex; hence much of the work may be inefficient or even harmful. In many areas of modern life, extensive research is considered indispensable. In industry, in medicine, in the development of military weapons, no important programme is adopted before vast sums have been spent to develop the most efficient means. This approach is only beginning to be used in the analysis and control of human behaviour. It is only in a partial sense that this is a 'scientific age'. A great many people, faced by the confusion and anxiety of modern life, have developed a prideful anti-scientism when it comes to understanding human beings.

But we firmly believe (this is a premise, not a conclusion) that the turning back to old formulas – traditional answers, unqualified nationalism, the seemingly self-confident declarations of the 'practical' man – can only deepen our problems. In the field with which we are concerned we must demand of every proposition its methodological credentials: what is the evidence? What variables are involved? How were they controlled? How does this harmonize with, or contradict, existing theoretical positions? It may seem like tedious business to some – to others it is exciting adventure – but there is no easier way to understanding and control.

Of the research that we do have in the area of intergroup relations a high proportion has been concerned with the causes of prejudice and discrimination, relatively little with strategies that are effective, in specific situations, in reducing them. There is great need for more of the latter.

References

ABERBACH, J. D., and WALKER, J. L. (1970), 'The meanings of Black Power: a comparison of white and black interpretations of a political slogan', *American Political Science Review*, June, p. 367.

ANTHONY, E. (1970), *Picking Up the Gun: A Report on the Black Panthers*, Dial.

BARRINGTON-MOORE, Jr (1968), 'Thoughts on violence and democracy', in R. Connery (ed.), *Urban Riots: Violence and Social Change*, Academy of Political Science.

BLUMER, H. (1958), 'Race prejudice as a sense of group position', *Pacific Sociological Review*, vol. 1, no. 1.

BREED, W. (1962), 'Group structure and resistance to desegregation in the deep South', *Social Problems*, Summer, pp. 34–94.

BRINTON, C. (1957), *Anatomy of Revolution*, Vintage Books.

CARMICHAEL, S., and HAMILTON, C. V. (1967), *Black Power*, Random House.

CLEAVER, E. (1968), *Soul on Ice*, Dell.

COLEMAN, J. S. (1969), 'Race relations and social change', in I. Katz and P. Gurin (eds.), *Race and the Social Sciences*, Basic Books.

COLOMBOTOS, J. (1969), 'Physicians and Medicare: a before–after study of the effects of legislation on attitudes', *American Sociological Review*, June, pp. 318–34.

COSER, L. (1956), *The Functions of Social Conflict*, Free Press.

COSER, L. (1967), *Continuities in the Study of Social Conflict*, Free Press.

DALFIUME, R. M. (1970), 'Stirrings of revolt', in A. Weinstein and F. O. Gatell (eds.), *The Segregation Era: 1863–1954*, Oxford University Press.

DANELSKI, J. (1967), 'Law and conflict resolution', *Journal of Conflict Resolution*, March, whole issue.

DAVIES, J. C. (1962), 'Toward a theory of revolution', *American Sociological Review*, February, pp. 5–19.

EDWARDS, H. (1970), *Black Students*, Free Press.

EDWARDS, L. P. (1927), *The Natural History of Revolution*, University of Chicago Press.

EISENBERG, W., and WEISBROD, M. (1963), 'Money talks in the City of Brotherly Love', *Progressive*, August, pp. 20–23.

FINK, C. F. (1968), 'Some conceptual difficulties in the theory of social conflict', *Journal of Conflict Resolution*, December, pp. 412–60.

FRAZIER, T. R. (1968), 'An analysis of nonviolent coercion as used by the Sit-In Movement', *Phylon*, Spring, pp. 27–40.

FRIEDMAN, S. (1970), 'Race relations is their business', *New York Times Magazine*, 25 October, pp. 44–69.

GEERTZ, C. (1962), 'The rotating credit association: a "middle rung" in development', *Economic Development and Cultural Change*, vol. 10, pp. 241–63.

GRINDSTAFF, C. F. (1968), 'The Negro, urbanization, and relative deprivation in the deep South', *Social Problems*, Winter, pp. 342–52.

ISAACS, H. (1963), *The World of Negro Americans*, John Day.

KING, M. L. (1958), *Stride Toward Freedom: The Montgomery Story*, Harper & Row.

KING, M. L. (1963), *Strength to Love*, Harper & Row.

KUPER, L. (1957), *Passive Resistance in South Africa*, Yale.

LEES, H.(1961), 'The not-buying power of Philadelphia's Negroes', *Reporter*, 11 May.

LESTER, J. (1968), *Look Out Whitey, Black Power's Gon' Get Your Mama*, Dial.

LINCOLN, C. E. (1961), 'The strategy of the sit-in', *Reporter*, 6 January, pp. 2–23.

LOMAX, L. (1962), *The Negro Revolt*, Harper & Row, chs. 10, 11.

MAYHEW, L. H. (1968), *Law and Equal Opportunity: A Study of the Massachusetts Commission Against Discrimination*, Harvard University Press.

McGILL, R. (1963), *The South and the Southerner*, Little, Brown.

MEIER, A., and RUDWICK, E. (1969), 'The boycott movement against Jim Crow streetcars in the South, 1900–1906', *Journal of American History*, March, pp. 756–75.

MEIER, A., RUDWICK, E., and BRODERICK, F. L. (eds.) (1971), *Black Protest Thought in the Twentieth Century*, 2nd edn. Bobbs-Merrill.

MITCHELL, G., and PEACE, W. (eds.) (1961), *The Angry Black South*, Corinth Books.

New South (1961), 'Freedom rides', July–August, whole issue.

Newsweek (1963), 'The Negro in America', 29 July, pp. 15–34.

PROUDFOOT, M. (1962), *Diary of a Sit-In*, University of North Carolina.

REITZES, D. (1959), 'Institutional structure and race relations', *Phylon*, Spring, pp. 48–66.

RHYNE, E. H. (1962), 'Racial prejudice and personality scales: an alternative approach', *Social Forces*, October, pp. 44–53.

ROBBINS, R. (1961), 'Local strategy in race relations: the Illinois experience with community human relations commissions and councils', *Journal of Intergroup Relations*, Autumn, pp. 311–24.

ROBISON, J. B. (1951), 'Organizations promoting civil rights and liberties', *Annals*, May.

ROSE, A. M. (1956), 'Intergroup relations *v.* prejudice', *Social Problems*, October pp. 173–6.

RUDWICK, E., and MEIER, A. (1970), 'Organizational structure and goal succession: a comparative analysis of the NAACP and CORE, 1964–1968', *Social Science Quarterly*, June, pp. 9–24.

SEALE, B. (1970), *Seize the Time: The Story of the Black Panther Party*, Random House.

SEARLES, R., and WILLIAMS, J. A. (1962), 'Negro college students' participation in sit-ins', *Social Forces*, March, pp. 215–20.

SHERIF, M., and FARIS, R. (1962), in M. Sherif (ed.), *Intergroup Relations and Leadership*, Wiley, pp. 3–45.

SILLS, D. (1957), *The Volunteers: Means and Ends in a National Organization*, Free Press.

SIMMEL, G. (1955), *Conflict*, Free Press, translated by Kurt Wolff.

SMITH, B. L. R. (1968), 'The politics of protest: how effective is violence?', in R. Connery (ed.), *Urban Riots: Violence and Social Change*, Academy of Political Science.

TANTER, R., and MIDLARSKY, M. (1967), 'A theory of revolution', *Journal of Conflict Resolution*, September, pp. 264–80.

UNITED STATES COMMISSION ON CIVIL RIGHTS (1969), *For All the People . . By All the People*, Govt. Printing Office.

VANDER ZANDEN, J. W. (1963), 'The non-violent resistance movement against segregation', *American Journal of Sociology*, March, pp. 544–50.

YINGER, J. M. (1965), *Toward A Field Theory of Behaviour*, McGraw-Hill.

ZINN. H. (1966), *SNCC: The New Abolitionists*, Beacon Press.

Section B
Focus on the Minority Group

This section deals with three common psychologically relevant variables that help determine the minority-group member's reaction to his situation. First, Harold Proshansky and Peggy Newton look at the particular significance of colour – its associations and the effect it can have on identity. Jack Mann adds the dimension of status – particularly where colour differences between majority and minority group members aren't present, showing how reactions may therefore differ. And Ronald Taft shows how the immigrants experience may add to one of the two aspects above, making still other reactions possible.

Chapter 7
Colour: The Nature and Meaning of Negro Self-Identity

Harold Proshansky and Peggy Newton

Harold Proshansky, as well as having a deep interest in the psychological development of minority groups, is also interested in the psychology of the environment generally. At the City University of New York, where he is the Provost and Dean of the Graduate School and University Center, he gives seminar courses in the relation of human behaviour and and experience to physical settings. He is also co-director of the Ph.D. programme in Environmental Psychology.

Peggy Newton was a research assistant to Martin Deutsch, director of the Institute for Developmental Studies at New York University, when this chapter was written. Since that time she has gone on to the University of Minnesota to do a Ph.D. in child development.

How does a Negro child learn about race? When does he learn that he is 'different' – that he is in a minority in a prejudiced white society? What does he feel about himself: who he is – what he can do?

In exploring these questions we find that there are no simple or definitive answers. The child learns about race both directly and indirectly: at home, at school, in the streets. Similarly, his feelings about himself grow out of a wide variety of personal experiences. In an absolute sense, each child's answers to the questions of race and identity are unique, yet we find certain attitudes, responses, and feelings which are shared by many Negroes. In some way, each Negro-American is forced to confront the question of 'who he is' in the prevailing white society.

Underlying our discussion of the Negro's self-concept is the reality of the discriminatory social caste-class system in America with its historic origins in the institution of slavery. We see this system as imposing a double burden on the Negro through severe social and economic inequalities and through the heavy psychological consequences suffered by the Negro who is forced to play an inferior role. There are obvious differences in schools, housing, employment, and income; less visible, but equally serious, are the heavy psychological costs of low self-esteem, feelings of helplessness, and basic identity conflict.

To understand some of the issues and problems of Negro identity – its unique features, as well as its white normative aspects – we must examine

Negro identity in relation to the norms and values of the dominant white society. The special properties of Negro identity reflect the idiosyncrasies of Negro institutional life as seen in family, school, church, recreational and employment settings. In turn, we see these distinctive features of institutions as arising in direct response to the discriminatory system imposed by a white society. These characteristics of institutions which are uniquely Negro serve to protect and preserve the Negro community – but not without cost to its members. The price for the adaptive nature of Negro institutional life is the maintenance and perpetuation of existing patterns of inequality.

In this chapter we shall consider several interrelated and significant questions concerning the self-concept of the Negro. First, we shall look at his self-identity from a developmental vantage point, examining research findings which describe the ways in which the young Negro child's beliefs and feelings about himself grow and change. These studies are primarily concerned with the *early* development of self-identity; unfortunately there is very little research on the development of Negro identity in adolescence and young adulthood. After having considered some of the developmental aspects of Negro identity, we shall then explore the consequences and the sources of conflict over Negro identity. In looking at the consequences of this conflict, we shall be primarily concerned with how conflict over racial identity directly or indirectly influences the behaviour of the Negro in culturally prescribed settings which demand specific motivation and particular motor and verbal skills. In a world that measures men not just in terms of what they want and *can* do, but more significantly in terms of what they actually *do*, the 'performance' of the Negro in school, at home, and on the job becomes a critical social issue.

Our discussion of the sources of conflict over Negro identity will emphasize the family, as we seek to understand *how* the young child learns about himself and his unique status as a Negro. Although we have described lower-class urban Negro family patterns, it is important to realize that not all Negro families are lower-class, nor do they fit the somewhat archetypal description presented. Our purpose is to show how the young child's negative feelings about himself may be reinforced and intensified in the home setting, particularly when the problems of poverty are added to the burden of being Negro. We shall also look at some of the characteristics of the schools which often provide additional conflict for the Negro child.

In the final section of the chapter, we shall examine some positive aspects of Negro identity and group resources for developing positive identification. We shall also consider very briefly the influence of the Civil Rights Movement and black nationalism on the young Negro's self-image and expectations.

Our discussion of the nature and meaning of Negro self-identity is necessarily limited by the state of research and theory in the field. While there has been considerable genuine concern about Negro identity, there has been little actual research on it. The research findings can only be described as incomplete, fragmentary, and at times contradictory. Hopefully, the present analysis should provide an inventory of the form and aspects of systematic research needed for understanding the development of the Negro's self-image.

In looking at the 'quality' or value of the existing research on Negro self-concept, we find that social scientists have been severely hampered by methodological problems. Techniques for measuring self-concept have often seemed artificial; reports have frequently been highly subjective, and the number of subjects have typically been small. Researchers interested in Negro identity have also tended to think only in 'black-white terms', ignoring important social-class variables. Simpson and Yinger (1965) point out the great pitfalls in drawing general conclusions from simple comparisons of Negro and white subjects, emphasizing the tremendous variability both in prejudice and its effects on minority group members. They suggest that the amount and type of prejudice and the form of reactions to prejudice depend on individual variables, such as age, education, occupation, temperament, and family training about the dominant group. Significant group factors include group cohesiveness, intergroup contact, colour variations within the group, surrounding group attitudes toward prejudice, and experience with other intergroup patterns.

Still another major problem in studies of Negro–white self-concepts, as well as in many other investigations making Negro–white comparisons, is the patent middle-class bias involved in most of the standard instruments used for measuring intelligence, achievement, and personality. Investigations of family structure, motivation, and occupational choices in Negroes have usually employed white middle-class standards as a basis for judgement. While to some extent such comparisons are inevitable, it is important to recognize their limitations and the form of inherent value judgement they impose on the Negro. In a discussion of personality differences, Georgene Seward (1956) cautions against judging the Negro by white norms. Not only is such a practice 'unfair' to the Negro, it also tends to obscure important dynamic factors, which have meaning only with reference to his subculture.

Unless an individual is viewed within his own frame of reference, his behaviour cannot be accurately assessed with regard to its normality or abnormality. . . . In the case of the Negro, to follow white norms may mean indicting an entire subculture for deviations forced upon it by exclusion from the main currents of the dominant culture.

When there are variations and difficulties in method and technique in studying the individual, we can expect to find corresponding differences and difficulties in concept and theory. This phenomenon is highly apparent in the field of self-concept research. The relevant literature contains a confusing assortment of terms which refer to the individual's beliefs and feelings about himself: 'self-concept', 'self-image', 'self-identity', 'self', and so on. While these differences in terminology reflect differences in theory and method, the differences are far from clear-cut. Furthermore, even when theorists or investigators actually employ the same term, they are by no means always in agreement as to its meaning.

In the present discussion, it is not our purpose to codify or integrate these various concepts to denote the individual's perception of himself as an object. We shall use the terms 'self', 'self-concept', and 'self-identity' interchangeably. As we have already indicated, the distinctions among the terms are difficult to maintain, and in the light of the methodological limitations imposed on existing data on the development of self, little is to be gained from attempting to maintain these distinctions in this discussion. Therefore, all of these concepts will be used to refer to that constellation of interrelated, conscious and unconscious beliefs and feelings which the individual has about himself.

Like any other attitudinal object or referent, the individual both 'identifies' and evaluates himself. Thus, he learns 'who he is' on dimensions such as appearance, group membership, achievement, and aspirations. This learning is never a neutral process, for the process of learning 'who one is' invariably carries with it value judgements, for example, 'good' or 'bad', 'desirable' or 'undesirable', 'worth much' or 'worth little'. In addition to the limited views of self, the individual also acquires a more general evaluative view of self which is usually called self-esteem or self-acceptance. In learning that he is 'black', 'dark', 'coloured', or 'Negro', the Negro child soon, if not simultaneously, learns the negative-value connotation placed on membership in his racial group. He learns that it is bad to be Negro, because he is not white.

The individual's existence is defined by many social groups or categories, so that he 'identifies' and evaluates himself along many basic dimensions. These dimensions differ in their importance to the individual and in their role in determining over-all feelings of self-esteem. The weight or importance of a dimension is determined by the dimension's normative value and the number of situations to which it applies, as well as by individual needs. For example, the concept 'Negro' has implications for a variety of personal characteristics, social settings, and institutional practices, while the concept 'Easterner' has far less significance in influencing the individual's self-identity.

When we consider the person's self-esteem, asking whether he generally sees himself positively or negatively, the importance of a preponderance of favourable judgements covering many dimensions of self for healthy personality development is almost axiomatic. Newcomb, Turner and Converse (1965) note, '. . . it seems quite clear that one of the individual's most basic and continuing needs is for a self-image that is essentially positive' (p. 141).

While Negro identity is the focus of the present description and analysis, many of the general findings and concepts to be presented clearly have relevance for other minority group members, for example, Puerto Ricans, Jews, Mexican-Americans, and lower-class whites. Our specific knowledge about development of self and its manifestations in individuals in particular social groups is limited. However, there is considerable evidence to support the assumption that there is a direct relationship between problems in emergence of *self* and the extent to which the child's ethnic or racial membership group is socially unacceptable and subject to conspicuous deprivation. This viewpoint is summarized eloquently by Negro psychiatrist and polemicist, Frantz Fanon: '. . . I begin to suffer from not being a white man to the degree that the white man imposes discrimination on me, makes me a colonized native, robs me of all worth, all individuality, tells me that I am a parasite on the world, that I must bring myself as quickly as possible into step with the white world . . .' (1967).

The development of self-identity in the Negro

Colour is an undeniable fact of the Negro's existence in a place like America. The inescapable reality of colour shades and shadows the Negro child's emerging sense of self, making the development of racial identification an integral part of his total development of self. As Seward suggests: '. . . colour is inherent in the concept of "self". As awareness of self emerges, it emerges in a race-conscious social context which assigns values to the perception of colour' (1956, p. 129).

The preschool and early elementary school years (approximately ages three to seven) are generally recognized as a crucial period in the growth and differentiation of the child's feelings about himself and his feelings towards others who are ethnically different (Allport, 1954; Proshansky, 1966). During this period the child becomes increasingly aware of racial differences and learns labels and emotional responses associated with various ethnic groups including his own (see Chapter 1).

While these studies (described in Chapter 1) have shown some variations in measurement techniques and in the age and geographical locus of the subjects sampled, their findings provide a relatively consistent picture of the development of racial identity in the Negro child.

We shall emphasize two basic processes involved in the development of racial identity. The first, *racial conception*, is concerned with when and how the child learns to make racial distinctions at a conceptual level. The second process, *racial evaluation*, deals with when and how the child evaluates his own racial group membership. For analytical purposes it is important to maintain this distinction between the two processes. However, in the actual development of the child, the processes by which he learns 'who he is' and the *value* of 'who he is' are inextricably linked.

Racial conceptions

The racial world for the Negro child is not only empirical but also conceptual. To be 'a Negro' establishes 'who he is' by relating him to all other individuals, known and unknown, who have the same defining features. In time, he must realize the *general* nature of his racial category because others label and identify him in these terms, making his racial group membership the nexus of his emerging self-identity. To achieve such understanding, the child must first learn to make racial distinctions: to recognize and be aware of the differences in skin colour and related characteristics between himself and others.

Many investigators have reported that the ability to make such racial distinctions first appears at roughly age three in both Negro and white children. This ability increases steadily with age until approximately six or seven, when all children are able to make these identifications accurately. Studies by Goodman (1952) and Morland (1958) reveal that it is during the fourth and fifth year that the greatest increase in racial awareness occurs.

It is important to note that the development of racial awareness in very young children is undoubtedly aided by the visibility factor inherent in skin colour distinctions. Although little research has been done on awareness of other types of ethnic distinctions among children of these ages, there is evidence that the development of such awareness roughly parallels that found for racial distinctions. Awareness of religious and national groups also emerges relatively early in the life of the child – although later than racial awareness – and also shows an increase with age (Hartley, Rosenbaum and Schwartz, 1948; Radke, Trager and Davis, 1949).

In the studies by Hartley *et al.* (1948) and Radke *et al.* (1949), there is evidence that membership in an ethnic minority may be a predisposing factor in the *early* development of ethnic awareness. In the latter investigation it was found that Jewish children between the ages of five and nine were more aware of their group membership (and more strongly identified with their own ethnic group) than were Catholic or Protestant children. However, the comparisons between Negro and white children in the studies previously cited have been inconclusive in determining which group first becomes aware of racial differences.

Several explanations have been offered for these contradictory findings. It is suggested that white children in the South, as compared with those in the North, are more sensitive to racial differences by virtue of the more explicit code in the area of Negro–white relationships. Or that Negro children in the South are less willing than Northern Negro children to put their knowledge of racial differences into words.

Racial awareness is a stage in the Negro child's achievement of a 'racial conception'. To attain a racial conception, the child must not only have the ability to make racial distinctions, but he must also be able to elevate these distinctions to the level of a general conception of the meaning of the terms, 'Negro' and 'white'. He must understand and be able to use terms to relate as well as distinguish among people.

Not only is the Negro child racially aware by the age of four or five, but he has already learned the relevant words, concepts, and phrases used to describe members of his own and other racial (and ethnic) groups. He uses these terms to describe himself and others; however, as we saw in chapter 1, there is evidence that until age eight or nine his racial conception is somewhat more apparent than real – that is, the child seems to have a 'verbal fluency' rather than a conceptual understanding of racial categories.

Racial evaluations

The Negro child does not learn about racial distinctions in an emotional vacuum as we have seen above, and in chapter 1. As we have previously noted, the young child acquires value-laden racial labels and fragments of popular stereotypes to describe his own and other racial and ethnic groups. Both Negro and white children learn to associate Negro with 'dirty', 'bad', and 'ugly', and white with 'clean', 'nice' and 'good'. For the Negro child, these emotionally charged descriptions and judgements operate to establish the white group as vastly superior to his own racial group.

The early presence of the emotional and evaluative aspects of racial learning is clearly demonstrated in a series of studies of young Negro and white children. Although different techniques have been used to measure racial evalution – for example, playmate selection, drawings, doll play and picture tests – the results of these studies have been consistent.

Does the Negro child like being a Negro? The empirical evidence suggests that for many childlren the answer to this question ranges from a qualified to an emphatic 'no'. Given a choice, a majority of both Negro and white children tend to choose a white doll in preference to a Negro one (Clark and Clark, 1947; Stevenson and Stewart, 1958; Radke and Trager, 1950; Goodman, 1952; Morland, 1962; Landreth and Johnson, 1953). In a recent study of 407 young children, Morland (1962) found that 60 per cent of the Negro children, but only 10 per cent of the white children, pre-ferred to play with children of the *other* race; in comparison, 18 per cent of the Negro children and 72 per cent of the white children preferred playmates of their *own* race.

The young Negro child does more than simply identify with the white society which surrounds him. His choices of dolls or playmates may be viewed not only as preferences for whites, but also as rejection of or hostility toward his own racial group.

The Negro child's rejection of his own racial group is well-founded. Quite early in life the child absorbs the cultural norms and judgements about his race, learning in a rudimentary way about his limited oppor-tunities and the prejudice against him. In a study of Negro children between the ages of three and seven, Stevenson and Stewart (1958) found that Negro children perceived children of their *own* race as aggressive, bad, and those 'whom other children fear', significantly more times than white subjects saw white children with these characteristics. In addition, both Negro and white subjects most frequently picked white children as 'winners in a game'.

The persistence and pervasiveness of these racial stereotypes have been clearly revealed in a study (Johnson, 1941) of Negro youth, between the ages of twelve and twenty, who lived in the rural South. Given a list of six possible racial categories or colours of people, these teenagers were asked to choose adjectives from the list, to describe people in thirty value-judgement situations. Johnson found that there was 'a decided tendency to classify as black a disproportionately large number of negative judge-ments'. For example, in the choice of the colour of the 'ugliest girl you know', approximately 40 per cent of 837 boys selected black, as compared with 11 per cent who chose yellow and 7 per cent who chose light brown. The results obtained for value judgements of behaviour were similar to those describing physical characteristics. Approximately 43 per cent of the boys and 23 per cent of the girls checked black as the colour of the 'mean-est boy (girl) you know'. Comments made during interviews with these subjects clearly suggest that their judgements were rooted in existing stereotypes and not in actual experience.

The young child's learning is not confined to behavioural stereotypes of Negroes. He also learns about the reality of the Negro's existence: his inferior housing, his limited opportunities for achievement, his low status, and his treatment from the larger society. When Radke and Trager (1950) asked five-to eight-year-old Negro and white children to choose either a 'good' or 'poor' house for white and Negro dolls, the researchers found that 82 per cent of the white children and 67 per cent of the Negro children gave the 'poor' house to the Negro doll. Conversely, 77 per cent of the white children and 60 per cent of the Negro children gave the 'good' house to the white doll. This finding has significance extending beyond the obvious conclusion that Negro and white children have learned that the two racial groups differ in their standards of living. Perceived differences in housing are associated with differences in economic dependence and in style of life; these differences are, in turn, linked with differences in social status, special privilege, and the ability to bring change. As Radke and Trager (1950) note,

For many of the children, concepts and feelings about race extend into adult world distinctions of status, ability, character, occupations, and economic circumstances. Social distinctions made by whites which put Negroes in an inferior status tend to be accepted as 'natural' or inevitable.

Drawing from his observations of and interviews with Negro children in the South, Coles (1967) describes how completely these children absorb the social system and comprehend how it affects them:

I have been continually astonished to discover just how intricately children come to examine the social system, the political and economic facts of our society . . . children . . . quickly learn to estimate who can vote, or who has money to frequent this kind of restaurant or that kind of theatre, or what groups of people contribute to our police force – and why. . . . I have been struck by how specifically aware they become of those forces in our society, which, reciprocally, are specifically sensitive to *them*. They remark on the scarcity of coloured faces on television, and I have heard them cheer the sight of a Negro on that screen.

The distinction between the Negro child's wish to be white and his knowledge of racial differences is clearly revealed in a study by the Clarks (1950). These investigators gave 160 Negro five-, six-, and seven-year-olds a colouring task in which the child was told, 'Colour this little boy (or girl) the colour you are'. In contrast with other measures of racial identity used in the studies previously described, the Clarks found far less evidence of identification with the white majority when using the colouring-task procedure. Even at age five, 80 per cent of the children correctly identified themselves on the basis of their own skin colour; at age six, 85 per cent of the children made the correct response, while at age seven, 97 per cent of the sample gave the appropriate identification. These results suggest that when given the highly concrete task of selecting a crayon and committing himself on paper, the child was forced to contend with the reality of 'who he was'.

The child's conflicts over his racial identification are highlighted when the results of the colouring task, discussed above, are compared with a second part of the same experiment in which the same subjects were asked

to colour the little boy (girl) 'the colour you like little boys (girls) to be'
In this situation only 48 per cent of the children coloured the child brown
or black, whereas 36 per cent coloured him white or yellow, and the
remaining subjects made irrelevant responses.

Numerous studies have shown that the tendency of the Negro child to
identify with the white majority and reject his own group decreases with
age (Clark and Clark, 1947; Radke and Trager, 1950; Morland, 1962).
This finding is to be expected for, as he grows older, the child is forced to
contend with the social reality of his colour and his consequent designation
by society. He must face the fact that he is a Negro and that he will be
treated as a Negro by members of his own group and, more significantly,
he will be treated as a Negro by the very persons he wishes to be: the
members of the white majority.

The Negro child is eventually forced to acknowledge and accept his
Negro identity; this acceptance of his race may decrease but it does not
eliminate the fundamental conflict involved in the development of his
self-identity. What he is and can ever hope to be, as a Negro, is somewhat
less than what he would be, or could ever hope to be, if he were white.
The child's awareness of this conflict may be conscious or unconscious;
however, the conflict itself tends to nourish feelings of self-doubt and a
sense of inadequacy, if not actual self-hatred. Given these circumstances,
we would expect the Negro child not only to be 'sensitive' to the question
of 'who he is', but also to characterize himself in unfavourable terms – that
is, to reveal a negative self-image.

Considering the importance and centrality of this basic conflict over
identity, it is not surprising that some of the Negro children in the studies
by the Clarks (1947) and Goodman (1952) were disturbed by the investigation, especially when they were required to make self-identifications.

The ambivalence, self-doubt, and lowered self-esteem of many Negro
children, resulting from their being Negro and not white, is seen in Coles's
descriptions of the drawings of Southern children involved in school
desegregation. Coles (1965) suggests that the drawings often indicated a
fear of white people and a feeling of 'lacking something' because they
were not white. Significant differences frequently appeared in the relative
size of the Negroes and whites drawn. In a number of instances Negroes
appeared as much smaller than whites and were drawn with missing or
mutilated body parts. Coles also noted an inconsistent use of colour. Some
children did not want to draw themselves as Negroes, while others 'compensated' by drawing whites a light shade of brown.

Where self-rejection occurs we are likely to find other psychological
consequences in terms of the behaviour, feelings, and sense of well-being
of the individual. In the next section, we shall consider these and other

consequences that follow from the racial identity conflict experienced by the Negro child.

Sources and consequences of conflict in Negro self-identity

In the previous section we had begun to consider the substantive nature of the Negro's self-identity, that is, what he thinks and feels about himself as a person. To expand and elaborate on this topic in this section, we shall consider both the conditions that foster a Negro self-identity and the consequences of this identity for the behaviour and experience of the individual. In undertaking such a discussion, it is necessary to specify its limitations, which are imposed by the type of available research on Negro self-identity.

The research on Negro self-identity has tended to be sporadic rather than systematic. Much has been written about the self-image of the Negro. Those writing in the field have generally agreed on the nature of the Negro's identity conflicts; however, the basis of their statements has usually been anecdotal evidence and general descriptions of the 'plight of the Negro' instead of carefully collected empirical data. To complicate the picture further, we find that most of the existing data focuses on the lower-class Negro; therefore, these findings cannot be generalized to apply to Negroes in other social class categories. In addition, most studies of the self-identity characteristics of lower-class Negroes have made comparisons with middle-class whites, thus making it virtually impossible to separate the race and social class factors.

The urban slum dweller, whether white or Negro, faces problems with self-image in a society which values individual initiative, success, and status. However, some properties of the self-identity of the lower-class Negro reflect his unique place in the social hierarchy.

We may ask about the self-image of Negroes who have achieved middle-class and upper-class status. There are undoubtedly significant class-associated differences in family structure and in attitudes towards the dominant white society, which influence the child's self-image and identification, his school achievement, and his eventual occupational status. Unfortunately the empirical research on these social class differences is extremely limited. On the basis of a comparison of intelligence test scores of Negro and white subjects from three social class levels, Deutsch and Brown (1964) suggest, '. . . the influence of racial membership tends to become increasingly manifest and crucial as the social class level increases'. They propose that lower-class status has a similar effect on Negroes and whites, but while higher status tends to bring the white increased 'participation in the cultural mainstream', the Negro of similar status is often denied such participation because of his race.

The concentration of research and theory on the lower-class urban Negro has perpetuated a narrow and limited view of Negro identity. Although research has usually been confined to the urban slum dweller, there has been a tendency to generalize these findings, applying them to all Negroes, regardless of social class or geographical location. We would expect that Negroes who had achieved occupational and economic success would be confronted by a different order of identity conflicts than the lower-class Negro. It would seem likely that the accomplishments and status of middle-class Negroes would merely redefine rather than eradicate the stigma of their racial group membership. Research on middle-class and upper-class Negroes is needed both to clarify these questions and to suggest the scope and complexity of the issue of Negro identity.

A further shortcoming of the existing research has been in its problem-centred approach. In dealing with a lower-class urban population, researchers have tended to look for 'problems', emphasizing negative elements of identity and seeing differences from white middle-class norms as 'problems'. As we shall point out in the final section of this chapter, there *are* positive and compensatory aspects of Negro identity. These positive elements of identity need to be given a larger place in research and theoretical formulations. In our concluding section, we shall consider those aspects and conditions of the Negro dilemma that strengthen rather than weaken his tie with his own racial group; we shall look at the potentially integrative rather than divisive forces in the development of Negro self-identity.

The Negro self-image: its effects on behaviour and experience

The Negro who feels disdain or hatred for his own racial group is expressing – at some level of awareness – disdain or hatred for himself. Where the self-image is rooted in and structured by this kind of self-rejection, we can expect negative effects on the behaviour and experience of the individual. In the discussion that follows, we shall look at some of the research which deals with the consequences of self-hatred and rejection. For the purpose of convenience, we shall consider the studies under two categories: 'personality adjustment' and 'achievement orientation'. By the term, 'personality adjustment', we mean how the Negro reacts to and copes with his underlying sense of inferiority or lack of self-esteem. Although the Negro's achievement orientation may also be seen as a mode of adjustment in response to a negative identity, we shall consider these topics separately.

Personality adjustment. Perhaps the 'real tragedy' for the American Negro lies less in the inferior, passive and servile role he is forced to play, and more in the fact that he comes to believe in this role. His self-image not only reflects this role structure but also confirms and supports it. As Pettigrew (1964b) points out, by judging himself the way others do, '... the Negro may grow into the servile role; in time the person and the role become indistinguishable'.

Many theorists have noted that the Negro does not find satisfaction in passive compliance with the demands of a white society. The Negro who conforms to these demands and consequently rejects himself pays a high price. A report by the 'Group for the Advancement of Psychiatry' (1957) suggests that beneath the Negro's mask of compliance lie anger, resentment, and fear. In hiding his feelings, the Negro may suffer serious psychological consequences, such as distorting his capacity for expressing his feelings or actually lowering his 'potential for affectivity' (Kardiner and Ovesey, 1962).

Kardiner and Ovesey, in fact, hypothesize that the Negro bears an inescapable 'mark of oppression', which reflects his strong identification with whites, who are simultaneously hated. This conflict leads to aggression which is channelled into compensatory defensive manoeuvres. In a study of the responses of 100 nine- to fourteen-year-old Negro and white boys on the Thematic Apperception Test (TAT), Mussen (1953) found that the Negro boys tended to perceive the world as hostile and threatening, while the white boys were more likely to view the world as a friendly place. Palermo (1959) found greater anxiety among Negro children in the fourth to sixth grade than he did among a corresponding group of white children. In their study of the Rorshach and TAT protocols of twenty-five adult Negroes, Kardiner and Ovesey reported that their respondents showed a strong need to avoid 'meeting reality head on' by denying, distorting, or simplifying provocative tension-producing situations.

The thread of consistency running through the studies cited above is sustained by Deutsch's extensive study of Negro and white lower-class children in grades four through six (1960). Deutsch found that the Negro children generally had more negative self-concepts, and were more passive, more morose, and more fearful than their white schoolmates. When the Negro child was aggressive, it was usually in some covert manner.

In the face of adversity, the Negro feels more than the frustration engendered by the caste system. His anger is intensified – particularly in the Negro male – by his sense of powerlessness (Drake, 1965). When hostility is expressed, it is often through indirect means. Among lower-class Negroes aggression is frequent, the chain of victimization is perpetuated, and the lower-class Negro is exploited by both whites and fellow Negroes. Other outlets for aggression are juvenile delinquency and crime, both of which provide means of 'striking back' at the white society.

Covert or indirect expressions of hostility are only one form of response to the frustration and sense of powerlessness experienced by the Negro. The need to escape is frequently manifested in the form of excessive use of alcohol, drugs, and gambling (Drake, 1965). A far more subtle form of escape embodies the old adage, 'If you can't beat them, join them'. Some Negroes, in effect, escape by 'turning white'.

In the case of the very light-skinned Negro, this desire may actually be accomplished by 'passing'. Other Negroes may attempt to 'look white' by using hair straighteners and skin bleaches. Drake (1965) suggests that this rejection of Negroid features reflects a reaction to the stereotype of the primitive and savage African. The preference for light skin also has traditional foundations in the USA. Since plantation days the light-skinned Negro has been favoured and granted special privileges, particularly in middle-class and upper-class society. We also find that parents tend to favour a light-skinned child (Coles, 1967; Grambs, 1964), and that dark-skinned men often try to marry wives of a lighter skin colour (Kardiner and Ovesey, 1962).

Psychologists have shown great interest in the defensive strategy of 'turning white' and in its implications for mental health and personality adjustment. Perhaps this interest stems in part from the fact that 'passing' represents a blatant expression of self-rejection and a denial of reality. Parker and Kleiner (1965) note a large body of research documenting the unhealthiness in aspiring to be white: 'Almost every clinical study of psychopathology among Negroes indicates that the Negro who is not identified with other members of his group, or who aspires to "be white", is relatively more prone to manifest various forms of mental ill health'.

In spite of some serious methodological problems, Parker and Kleiner's own research raises some important speculative questions about the dynamics of racial identification. As a measure of racial identification, Parker and Kleiner asked their Negro subjects how they would feel about a friend who tried to 'pass'. They found that Negroes in psychiatric hospitals tended to be strongly identified with Negroes or not identified with Negroes, while Negroes in the community tended to be ambivalent about their racial identification. On the basis of this finding, Parker and Kleiner suggest that ambivalence may be 'realistic and adaptive' for the Negro, but that extreme reactions or 'polarization of racial identification' are likely to be pathological, psychologically speaking. In their opinion '... the psychiatrically healthy Negro is an individual with conflicts about his racial identification. It is the mentally ill person who tends to remove this constant conflict from conscious awareness'. The logic implicit in this statement is that if the conflict about his racial identification becomes unbearable, the individual may deny the conflict entirely (either strongly identifying with or rejecting his racial group) and become mentally ill.

While it seems apparent that a denial of the conflict over identification is unhealthy, it cannot be assumed that conflict and ambivalence are healthy. Certainly, in light of the conditions that the Negro faces in America, such ambivalence is understandable. The crucial questions become: 'How severe is the conflict?' and 'How does the individual deal with this?'

It seems obvious that individual Negroes will find various means of dealing with this conflict. When faced with a severe form of it, not all individuals will become psychotic; some will resort to drugs, alcohol, violence, or other forms of escape. Many of these individuals, who certainly cannot be considered psychiatrically healthy, will remain in the community. Therefore, a judgement of mental health, based solely on whether or not an individual is in a psychiatric hospital, is open to serious question. We may also predict that some of the individuals in the community who are ambivalent about their racial identification may not be able to continue to function with this conflict and may later become psychotic or adopt another 'unhealthy' way of dealing with the conflict.

After examining the evidence available on the Negro and his conflicts over identification and also on the possibilities for positive identification, we would hypothesize that the psychiatrically healthy Negro is one who basically identifies with Negroes, but who is aware of and realistic about the problems facing him in a 'white man's' society. This form of identification with Negroes is to be distinguished from the extreme 'defensive' or reactive form of identification in which the individual denies that there are problems in being Negro. Unfortunately the Parker and Kleiner study does not distinguish between these two forms of identification with the Negro group and does not describe individuals in the community sample who have 'identified' with Negroes. It would be interesting to know if some of these individuals fit our description of a Negro who is positively identified with his race and yet realistic about his opportunities, as a Negro.

Achievement orientations. Human motivation involves a complex set of processes. Conceptually, an analysis of motivation includes analyses of the individual's end or goal, the strength of his desire, the value placed on the end, and his expectancy of achieving the end. In his consideration of achievement motivation in a modern industrial society, Rosen (1959) has suggested that achievement is dependent on three factors, which he labels collectively, the 'achievement syndrome'. The first factor is McClelland's 'achievement motive', which Rosen (1956) has defined as involving 'a personality characteristic . . . which provides an internal impetus to excel.' The second dimension, 'achievement-value orientations', involves a concern with social mobility and a development of patterns of behaviour, such as 'deferred gratification', which aid in the pursuit of long-term goals. The third dimension, 'educational and vocational aspirations' are the levels of academic and occupational achievements *desired* by parents for their children and desired by the children themselves. According to Rosen, high achievement depends on appropriate levels on all three of these dimensions.

Employing variations of Murray's TAT measure of *n* Achievement, investigators have found that Negro children are lower in achievement motivation than white children. Mussen (1953) found that Negro boys aged nine to fourteen, scored significantly below their white counterparts on *n* Achievement and also on *n* Understanding, a category which is intended to tap activities such as thinking, reflecting, and speculating. In measuring the achievement motivation of boys from six ethnic groups, Rosen (1959) reported that Negro boys were significantly lower in *n* Achievement than boys from four other ethnic groups: Jewish, white Protestant, Greek, and Italian.

Evidence suggests that *n* Achievement is related to social class as well as to ethnicity. In his study Rosen (1959) found that there were significant social-class differences among his subjects; he also discovered that social class was more strongly related to achievement motivation than was ethnicity. In addition, he found that Negro subjects in the top two social classes (I–II, according to a modified version of Hollingshead's Index of Social Position) were significantly higher in *n* Achievement than Class IV–V white Protestants. Rosen suggests that this relatively high Negro score may be indicative of the 'strong motivation necessary for a Negro to achieve middle class status in a hostile environment').

Rosen (1959) has explored 'achievement–value orientations' through the use of personal interviews with mothers who were asked to agree or disagree with items which reflected various orientations in child rearing: active versus passive, individual versus collective, and present versus future. It seems that the active, individual, and future orientations in child rearing are most conducive to the achievement of long-term goals. Rosen found that among the six ethnic groups that he studied, Negro mothers ranked fourth in 'achievement-value orientations'. This score was significantly lower than that of the Jewish mothers, who ranked highest in achievement values; however, the score of Jews was not significantly higher than the scores of Greeks and of Protestants, who were in the next two ranks.

Social class is also significantly related to achievement-value orientations. As might be expected, members of higher social classes tend to have high achievement-value orientations, and conversely, those in lower-class levels have relatively low scores on achievement-value orientation (Rosen, 1959).

Many investigators have explored the third dimension of Rosen's 'achievement syndrome': occupational and educational levels of aspiration. However, studies of the aspiration levels in Negro and white children and their parents have been inconsistent in their findings. In comparison with whites, Negroes have been shown to have high or low, and realistic or unrealistic, levels of aspiration.

For example, in a study of junior high school students in a small industrial town in Pennsylvania, Wylie (1963) found that Negro children generally had lower self-estimates or levels of aspiration for their schoolwork ability than did white children. However, when Negro and white subjects from lower socioeconomic levels were compared, there were no race differences. In contrast, in a somewhat similar but earlier study, Boyd (1952) reported very different results when he compared the aspiration levels of Negro and white students, matched for age, I Q, and socioeconomic status. He discovered that Negro children predicted relatively higher performances on arithmetic and target tests than did white children. Furthermore, in comparison with the white children, the Negro children had higher occupational ambitions, desired more foreign trips, and more frequently stated that they expected to be 'above average' students in high school. In discussing his results, Boyd suggests that Negro children may have higher aspiration levels because of insecure feelings or because they have developed better defence mechanisms than white children and are, therefore, able to tolerate a greater discrepancy between predicted and actual performance.

To confuse things further, Rosen found that Negro mothers had low occupational, but high educational, aspirations for their sons. When Rosen asked the mothers, 'How far do you *intend* your son to go in school?', 83 per cent of these mothers mentioned college. This percentage was not significantly different from those of the Jews, Greeks or white Protestants, but it was significantly higher than those of the Italians and French Canadians. However, when Negro mothers were given a list of occupations and were asked if they would 'be satisfied' if their sons were in these occupations, they expressed satisfaction with more low-status occupations than did any other group of mothers.

In some ways Rosen's measure of vocational aspiration is a negative one, since it seems to elicit the lower limit rather than the upper limit of aspiration. Because of the Negro's traditional lack of vocational opportunity, Negro mothers may be more accepting of low-status occupations than mothers from other ethnic groups. There may be a wide *range* between the vocation a Negro mother would most like her son to follow and a vocation with which she would be satisfied if her son actually did follow it. This possibility has been suggested by other studies, showing that Negro mothers and their sons have high vocational aspirations, although many researchers have labelled such aspirations as 'unrealistically high'.

In part, the contradictions in findings on the Negro's level of aspiration can be explained by differences in such factors as the samples studied, the indices used for measuring the level of aspiration, and the geographical setting. However, the studies are somewhat clarified, if we consider, whenever possible, the distinction between *desired* and *expected* occupational or educational attainment. The importance of these distinctions is illustrated in a study by Weiner and Murray (1963), who compared the educational aspiration levels of middle- and lower-class parents. Weiner and Murray point out that both middle-class and lower-class parents have high levels of aspiration for their children's education. However, the concept of education has a different meaning for each social class. The key difference in meaning lies in the realistic expectations of achieving the goal. Weiner and Murray note that if middle-class and lower-class parents are asked if they want their child to attend college, both groups of parents will answer 'yes'. However, the middle-class parent will answer 'yes' with the full expectation that his child will attend college, while the lower-class parent may hope that his child will go to college, but he may not actually expect it.

It is possible that in studies which have reported a high aspiration level for Negroes, researchers have been measuring what their subjects desire rather than what they expect. Perhaps measures of aspiration level which reflect what the subjects expect may yield lower levels of aspiration and may be more realistic. However, it is important to stress that even when a Negro's aspirations are based on his expectations, they may be distorted in light of his actual abilities and, more importantly, the opportunities available to him.

This situation is seen clearly in C. S. Johnson's (1941) study of rural Negro youth in the South. Johnson found that 58·8 per cent of the boys and 65·3 per cent of the girls preferred professional occupations. Of these youth, 26·4 per cent of the boys and 48·8 per cent of the girls actually *expected* to follow such occupations. In this case the subjects' expectations were not much more realistic than their desires. Johnson concluded: 'The gap between occupational expectation and reality is at present so great as to suggest that the expectation itself borders on fantasy'. Johnson also suggested that the desires and expectations for these occupations represented an attempt at escaping an unpleasant environment.

Ausubel and Ausubel (1958) have drawn similar conclusions about the aspiration levels of Negro children, basing their ideas on implications drawn from studies comparing lower- and middle-class children. They suggest that the lower-class child's expressed levels of vocational and academic aspiration do not necessarily reflect his 'real or functional levels of striving'.

His aspirations seem to show a lack of realistic judgement because of continued failure and low social status; therefore, a high level of aspiration is likely to represent an attempt to bolster self-esteem by presenting an image of 'aiming high' rather than actually striving for high educational or occupational goals. In the Ausubels' view, the conditions experienced by the lower-class child are intensified for the segregated Negro child. These interpretations are generally supported by Deutsch's (1960) study of the occupational aspirations of lower-class Negro and white fourth-, fifth-, and sixth-graders.

Deutsch (1960) found that *both* Negro and white boys tended to have unrealistic aspirations for high prestige occupations. Although it might be expected that Negro boys would be less realistic than white boys in these choices, only 26 per cent of the Negro boys, in contrast with 38 per cent of the white boys, expressed interest in high prestige professions. In comparison with the boys, the aspirations of the girls were much more realistic and the occupational desires of the Negro girls were significantly higher than those of the white girls. While 25 per cent of the Negro girls indicated a preference for white-collar jobs, such as secretary or bookkeeper, only 4 per cent of the white girls showed an interest in this type of job. However, the Negro girls were less interested than the white girls in the housewife-mother role and in the movie star-actress category.

In a study whose findings stand somewhat apart from those previously cited, Lott and Lott (1963) reported that Negro students had high but realistic levels of occupational aspiration. A comparison of Negro and white high school seniors in Kentucky showed significant differences in both occupational desires and expectations. The major differences between the occupational desires of the Negro and white boys were in 'glamour' jobs, such as pilot or politician, and in the clerical-sales-skilled-trade field of jobs. While 27 per cent of the white boys expressed interest in a 'glamour' job, only 12 per cent of the Negro boys did. While 18 per cent of the white students desired work in the clerical-sales-skilled-trade area, 39 per cent of the Negro students wanted a position in this field. An even sharper contrast was seen in the fact that 15 per cent of the whites versus 40 per cent of the Negroes expected to be in the clerical-sales-skilled-trade field ten years later.

The Negro boys showed somewhat exaggerated or unrealistic aspirations in their desires to enter professional or business fields; 41 per cent of the Negro boys and 46 per cent of the white boys wanted a professional or business career. However, only 30 per cent of the Negroes, in contrast with 41 per cent of the whites, actually expected to attain this type of job.

The occupational aspirations of the Negro girls described by Lott and Lott (1963) were consistent with those reported by Deutsch (1960) despite the age differences in the two samples. These findings suggest that the aspirations of these girls reflect their perceptions of their role as women – a role which places economic independence above the role of housewife and mother. In the Lott and Lott study (1963), 17 per cent of the white girls and none of the Negro girls wanted to assume the roles of wife and mother. Furthermore, 54 per cent of the Negro girls, but only 31 per cent of the white girls, wanted a professional job, such as teaching or social work.

Although Deutsch (1960) and Lott and Lott (1963) have reported similar findings about the aspirations of Negro girls, their results differ sharply from most of the other research in this field. Lott and Lott conclude that their Negro subjects' plans for the future were realistic in terms of available opportunities. They suggest that the difference in their findings may lie either in changing social conditions or in particular factors operating in the environment of a border community.

Another relevant factor in explaining differences in the 'realism' of the Negro's aspirations may be a 'knowledge of the means of achievement'. To understand how this factor might operate, we need to distinguish between dreams or desires and expectations. Dreams or desires, by definition, function to transcend reality; they are a source of hope and a salve against pain. In contrast, expectations are grounded in reality; they reflect the world 'as it is', not the world 'as it might be'. A problem arises when expectations become identified with dreams and a person expects what he has little or no possibility of achieving. We would hypothesize that this situation is likely to occur when a person has little 'knowledge of the means of achievement', that is, when he does not know how to achieve his goal, or when he does not recognize that his dream is unattainable. When the dream and expectation are not separated, the aspiration level is likely to be unrealistically high. The orientation towards the future would seem to reflect an emphasis on the goal, rather than on the 'means of achieving the goal.' Following this line of reasoning, we could infer that the Negro youth studied by Lott and Lott (1963) had a 'knowledge of means', which enabled them to have realistic expectations about their occupational futures.

The significance of a 'knowledge of means' is illustrated in a study of parents and their children in a suburb of New York City. The researchers Weiner and Graves (1960) found that parents and children from the lower socioeconomic status (SES) had occupational aspirations similar to those of parents and children from a middle socioeconomic level. In both SES groups most parents and children were interested in one of the professions. However, when the children from the lower SES group were asked how far they expected to go in school, 52 per cent expected to go through college and 33 per cent expected to finish only high school. Even more revealing was the fact that only 37 per cent of the lower *SES* subjects were enrolled in college preparatory courses. In contrast, 95 per cent of the middle *SES* students intended to go through college and 100 per cent of these students were taking the college preparatory curriculum.

In line with Weiner and Murray, Drake (1965) cites evidence suggesting that lower-class and lower-middle-class Negro parents often have high aspirations for their children but no clear idea of how to implement these plans. He proposes that Negro students in segregated high schools and colleges are often unaware of the opportunities and techniques for advancement.

Preliminary evidence indicates that many of these 'techniques for advancement' can be taught effectively in short periods of time. 'Cram' courses in how to pass qualifying exams and how to meet job requirements – for example, filling out applications, being interviewed, and so on – have succeeded in increasing the numbers of Negroes in several fields (National Urban League, 1966; Davis, 1967). The often dramatic success of short-term educational programmes supports the contention that many Negroes have high motivation for achievement but lack the more pragmatic, but also necessary, 'knowledge of the means of achievement'.

Sources of conflict

Our own discussion of the sources of Negro identity conflicts will consist primarily of a description of the family setting and some specific conditions within the home which seem to be related to problems with identification and self-esteem. While we recognize the family as a crucial source of self-attitudes and values, our emphasis on the family also reflects the focus of most of the existing research and theory. We also have included in our discussion a few suggestive findings about the Negro child in the school setting. Unfortunately, because of the previously mentioned limitations and inherent difficulties of research in these settings, most of our interpretations and hypotheses about the sources and transmission of identity conflicts will be highly speculative.

Family setting. Many of the child's earliest and most important feelings about himself are learned and nurtured in the family. Here the child receives his first impression about the world and about people and their worth. Often the teaching is indirect; feelings and attitudes are communicated through basic relationships and through the numerous interchanges and incidents which create the tone and texture of family life.

Several investigators have suggested that ethnic prejudice seems to be learned in the home. Trager and Yarrow (1952) comment on this process of learning: 'Parents' teaching of intergroup attitudes is frequently unconscious and is rarely direct or planned').

For the Negro child the home is usually the first place in which he learns about race and social discrimination, although his parents may avoid direct discussion of these topics. Georgene Seward (1956) observes, 'Before the child is conscious of being a Negro himself, he is affected by the tensions in his parents over *their* being Negro'. Elaborating on this point, Ausubel and Ausubel (1958) suggest that the parents' reaction to racial discrimination determines in part their basic attitude towards the child, whether they accept or reject him and if they use him for purposes of their own ego enhancement. In many cases the child's parents have suffered serious deprivations, both in their own emotional experiences and in their dealings with white society. Their feelings of anger, resentment, and hopelessness surround the child, making it very difficult for him to develop positive feelings about himself and his chances in the world. However, in spite of their own difficulties, some parents are able to provide a strong supportive atmosphere for their children, accepting them and fostering attitudes of self-worth. The Ausubels (1958) state '. . . the consequences of membership in a stigmatized minority group can be cushioned in part by a foundation of intrinsic self-esteem established in the home'. Pettigrew (1964b) comes to a similar conclusion, emphasizing the value of a warm, supportive, and stable home.

Until this point we have been discussing the family as a source of conflict in general terms. However, as we have noted previously, there are undoubtedly significant social-class-associated differences in family life and in attitudes towards the dominant white society which have differential consequences for the self-image of the Negro child. Rainwater (1966) labels the lower-class Negro family, the 'crucible of identity', focusing on the family's central role in transmitting values and attitudes towards society. The life patterns of the lower-class urban Negro form a distinctive subculture, which has arisen in response to the discriminatory system in America (Rainwater, 1966; Pettigrew, 1964b). The subculture is highly adaptive, fostering 'toughness' and self-sufficiency among its members, but ironically making it very difficult for its members ever to escape, to function in working- or middle-class worlds (Rainwater, 1966; Drake, 1965).

Frequently the parents of the lower-class child have been defeated and imprisoned by the dominant system. They are embittered and disillusioned and these attitudes are communicated to the child. Rainwater (1966) suggests that for most children growing up involves developing feelings of competency and mastery over the environment, but that for the slum child the process is reversed; he learns about what he cannot do, about blocks and barriers, about the futility of trying.

Harold Proshansky and Peggy Newton 197

The most salient feature of the lower-class Negro family life is its characteristic matriarchal pattern (Frazier, 1962; Drake and Cayton, 1962; Rainwater, 1966). With its origins in the plantation system and its perpetuation in unequal opportunities for employment, maternal dominance is encouraged and maintained. The problem is especially severe in Northern urban areas. Rainwater (1966) estimates that as many as two thirds of lower-class urban Negro children will not live in a family headed by a man and a woman during the first eighteen years of their lives (p. 181). The impact of this situation is heightened and intensified by the depressing effects of poverty. Not only may the father be absent, but the mother may be overburdened by many children, substandard living conditions, and her own need to work, so that she is unable to give adequate care to her children.

The attitude of the lower-class Negro mother towards her child may be one of ambivalence or indifference. Rainwater notes that there is '. . . little of the sense of the awesome responsibility of caring for children that is characteristic of the working and middle class' (1966). In the female-headed household the responsibility for child care is often turned over to the grandmother, female relatives, or older siblings. In general, there is less parent-child interaction than in working- and middle-class families. Discipline tends to be inconsistent, but the child is expected to meet high standards of behaviour and is severely punished when he fails to meet them (Kardiner and Ovesey, 1962). The emphasis is on obedience and responsibility, often encouraging the child to develop a 'precocious independence' (Ausubel and Ausubel, 1958).

In lower-class families, children are usually given more freedom outside the home and are likely to form important peer group contacts earlier than middle-class children (Ausubel and Ausubel, 1958). This situation has two specific related implications: first, it decreases the influence and significance of the parents; and second, it enhances the importance of the peer group. This transfer of the role of socialization from parents to peer group may be seen in part as a search for status and self-esteem.

Children from middle-class families derive status and a sense of importance from their parents' place and achievements in society. However, for the lower-class minority group child, the situation is reversed; his parents symbolize degradation and deprivation in the larger society. His relation to them is more likely a source of shame than one of pride.

The matriarchal character of the lower-class Negro family and its associated disorganized home life have important implications for the child's learning of sex attitudes and his attitudes towards marriage and child rearing. Parents who have had few experiences with family stability and adequacy are unlikely to be able to provide these experiences for their children. Similarly, because of their own feelings of self-doubt and self-hatred, parents may be unable to give their children needed affection and attention (Grambs, 1964).

These findings suggest that the lower-class Negro family pattern is likely to be perpetuated. A study by Pettigrew (1964a) lends weight to this idea. Studying twenty-one Negro working-class individuals who had grown up with a father during childhood, Pettigrew compared them with a matched group whose fathers had been absent during early childhood. The most dramatic difference between the goups was in the subjects' marital status. In the 'father-absent' group 33 per cent of the subjects were single or divorced, while only 4 per cent of the 'father-present' subjects were in this category. The 'father-absent' individuals also felt more victimized, 'less in control of the environment', and 'more distrustful of others' than men in the 'father-preseot' group (Pettigrew, 1964a). While the differences between the two groups were not statistically significant, the findings suggest the possible influence of father-absence in early childhood on personality development and marital adjustment.

The reversal of traditional sex roles has severe implications in a dominant culture which stresses male achievement. In spite of the distinctive Negro subculture and the reality of male-female differences in employment opportunities, the Negro male is still expected to be a responsible family provider. His failure in this role results in a serious loss of self-esteem and severe derision from the female members of the community. These factors serve to discourage him both from staying at home and from seeking and holding a job. His predicament may take the form of a 'self-fulfilling prophecy'. He is told that he is 'no good' and 'irresponsible' and to some extent he internalizes these judgements, which in turn influence his actions. When he fails, no one is surprised.

The issue of Negro male identity may be conceptualized as a twofold problem. The first is the Negro male's lack of status and economic and occupational achievement in the larger society. The second is the female's assumption of the dominant role and her critical, derogatory attitude towards males. While there has been an emphasis on the lack of adequate male models as an explanation for the Negro male's identity conflicts, we shall suggest that the female's attitudes serve to intensify the problem. We see these two factors as intimately related, feeding on each other to keep the Negro male in an inferior position. Erik Erikson (1966) has explored the consequences of the exploitation of the Negro male and the fact that the male is denied the status of 'responsible fatherhood'. He attaches particular significance to the imbalance in male and female roles and emphasizes that in a complex industrial setting, '. . . it may, indeed, become the gravest factor in personality disorganization'.

Surveying studies of the effects of father-absence, Pettigrew (1964b) suggests far-reaching implications for both personality and behaviour. He notes that boys raised without a father during early childhood were more immature, submissive, dependent, and effeminate than boys who had grown up with a father in the home. Father-absent children have also shown difficulty in differentiating masculine and feminine roles in comparison with father-present children. In the same line of evidence, Negro male and female high school students have reported a greater similarity of interests than their white counterparts; significantly, the interests of Negro girls were more masculine than those of white girls.

In a series of studies, Martin Deutsch and his associates have shown relationships among self-concept, family background variables, and academic performance. Comparing lower-class white and Negro children, Deutsch (1960) reported that 55 per cent of his Negro but only 9 per cent of his white subjects came from broken homes. He found that white subjects were superior in academic performance, had more positive self-images, and reported a more positive atmosphere than Negro children. A comparison of Negro subjects on the basis of their home status showed that subjects from intact homes exhibited significantly higher levels of academic performance than subjects from broken homes.

Studying the social influences on Negro and white intelligence differences, Deutsch and Brown (1964) found that for Negro subjects in the lower two SES categories, father-presence was significantly related to IQ. They also reported significant differences in IQ between Negro and white subjects at all three SES levels. The differences in IQ widened as social class increased. Deutsch and Brown observe that the Negro group shows greater deprivation on most social variables and '. . . whatever other measures and functions are sensitive to social effects will also reflect this deprivation' (1964, p. 34).

Other evidence suggests that the influence of father-absence on intellectual functioning may not be so important. Whitman and Deutsch found that father-absence was not significantly related to scores on the Gates Reading Test. The Coleman report (Coleman *et al*. 1966) showed that father-absence was one of the weakest home background factors in predicting school achievement for Negro pupils; however, father-absence was strongly related to academic achievement for the other minority groups surveyed. In a study of Negro boys, Robins, Jones and Murphy (1966) found that neither father-presence (nor absence) appeared to be related to the child's academic and behavioural problems.

Whitman and Deutsch have shown a relationship between SES and various home and family factors, many of which are, in turn, related to self-concept. In the lower SES homes there was greater crowding in the household and greater dilapidation in the neighbourhood surrounding the household than in higher *SES* homes. Lower *SES* parents tended to have both lower aspirations for their child's first job and lower educational aspirations than higher *SES* parents; in addition, lower *SES* children reported lower occupational aspirations than children from higher *SES* groups. As might be expected, *SES* was also significantly related to father-presence, with more fathers being present as *SES* increased.

In the same study, Whitman and Deutsch showed that deprivation, as measured by six environmental factors, was closely related to self-concept. They reported, 'As compared to the more advantaged children, about six times as many of the more deprived children fall into the least favourable self-concept category'.

The problem of male identification is not unique to members of the Negro lower class, but also seems to be characteristic of lower-class white males. In a study of high school senior boys, McKinley (1964) asked subjects from five social class levels, 'Whom do you most admire in your family or among relatives?' This question was intended to provide some measure of the boys' identification. In the upper class, all boys chose their father or a male relative as 'most admired', while in the working and lower classes only 58 per cent picked their father or a male relative; the others chose females.

Rainwater (1966) suggests that the problem of male identity is not necessarily due to the lack of a male figure, but rather to the type of male figure available as a model. He describes the succession of males – boyfriends, boarders, and so on – who may frequent the lower-class homes, noting that these men represent an affectional expressive role, but not that of a responsible provider.

The situation of the male may be seen in contrast with the Negro girl's learning of her sex role. She is encouraged to be independent and self-sufficient. She is also taught that males are an 'unworthy and unreliable lot' and not to expect much from them. In the home, the Negro girl tends to be favoured over her male siblings. Deutsch (1960) found that the Negro girl excels the Negro boy in academic performance and in personal and social adjustment. She shows a greater attention span, is more popular with classmates, and has a more positive self-concept than her male counterpart. The Ausubels (1963) view girls as 'less traumatized by the impact of racial discrimination', attributing this situation to the preferential treatment given to Negro females in the white American community. They suggest that Negro women have more continual contact with the white community and receive better treatment from white people than do Negro males.

In a provocative argument, Grambs (1964) questions the Ausubels' interpretation of male-female differences in school performance, as resulting from differential treatment in the community or from the lack of adequate male models. She hypothesizes that the impact of the discriminatory system is passed on to male children by their mothers, who are the prime sources of the child's self-concept.

Because of the direction and emphasis of the existing research, we have been concerned almost exclusively with lower-class family life. As we have suggested, there are important social-class differences in family patterns which we would expect to be reflected in differences in the form of identity conflicts. We also would expect that there would be important variations in family patterns within each social class. Jessie Bernard (1966) suggests that these differences within social classes are highly significant and she questions the validity of discussing Negro family patterns by social-class categories. She proposes a distinction between two strands or cultures, which she tentatively labels the 'acculturated' and the 'externally adapted'. In her view, these two strands run through all social-class levels and represent a dimension of internalization and acceptance (or lack thereof) of the values of the dominant society. She sees the difference between the two strands as one based on ethos, an acceptance of conventional standards or behaviour, particularly with respect to sex and work. She points out that discussions of social class family patterns obscure two important groups: low-income families with conventional family patterns and high-income families with unconventional family patterns. Of course, only a programme of systematic research on family patterns among Negroes in the various social classes can determine the validity of her analysis.

School setting. The 1954 Supreme Court decision which legally desegregated the public schools, augmented by the Civil Rights Movement and increased federal spending and legislation in education and civil rights, has greatly increased both the number and variety of people involved in and concerned with education, particularly education of the minority group child. Special attention has been concentrated on the urban lower-class Negro child, and numerous articles have been written on the special problems of the 'disadvantaged'. However, in spite of this display of great interest and outburst of publications, there has been relatively little research on the effects of school desegregation on Negro and white children (Proshansky, 1966; and Chapter 11 of this book).

Most theorists and researchers have assumed that segregation in the schools, whether *de facto* or legal, has devastating consequences for the Negro's development of a positive self-image (Clark and Clark, 1947; 1950). However, if we examine some of the possible sources of conflict for the Negro in the school, it becomes apparent that the issue is not a simple one: integration is not an automatic cure for the ills caused by segregated schools. Although the research in this area is limited, we shall attempt to specify some of the factors relevant to school desegregation.

One of the factors most frequently mentioned in studies of racially mixed schools is the attitude of white teachers toward their Negro pupils. If we assume that prejudice is a normative value, an assumption which is strongly supported by available evidence (Bettelheim and Janowitz, 1964), then we can expect the school teacher to express this prejudice in his or her treatment of the child – often in a variety of subtle ways. The issue gains increasing complexity when we realize that even a teacher who is relatively free of prejudice towards Negroes may react to class-associated differences between her own and her pupils' orientations toward learning, work and discipline. Furthermore, the middle-class or lower-middle-class teacher's reactions to his lower-class pupil's behaviour are likely to be interpreted by the child as further evidence of the general prejudice and discrimination that he experiences.

Even Negro teachers may be hostile and resentful towards lower-class Negro children. Frequently Negro teachers are from the lower middle class and have struggled to rise above their own backgrounds. They perceive lower-class children as a reminder of their past and a threat to their newly won security. In some cases, Negro middle-class teachers may displace their own self-hatred by expressing hostility towards lower-class Negro children (Grambs, 1964).

In examining the issue of teacher attitudes, it is important to recognize that the Negro pupil, as well as his teacher, brings preconceived ideas about racial differences into the classroom. The Negro child often comes bearing his parents' and his own justifiable resentment towards whites. The white teacher, in turn, reacts to this hostility, thus aggravating the conflict and prejudice in the classroom.

It also seems likely that Negro pupils who have low self-esteem or a negative self-image tend to perceive their teachers' behaviour as threatening, even if the teachers' actions are not discriminary. Bearing on this issue is a study by Brown (1967), comparing the self-perceptions of four-year-old Negro lower-class and white middle-class children. Brown asked his young subjects to look at pictures of themselves and to describe the child in the picture by choosing words from a list of bipolar adjectives, for example, happy–sad, good–bad, and the like. The child was asked to respond to the picture from four vantage points: his own, and those of his mother, his teacher, and his peers. On this basis, Brown derived a 'self as subject' and a 'self as object' measure.

One of Brown's most interesting findings was in the subjects' responses to how their teachers perceived them. Brown reported that the greatest difference between Negro and white subjects was on this part of the 'self as object' measure, and that a significantly greater number of Negro children than white children believed that their teachers saw them as sad (rather than happy), as frightened of a lot of things (versus not frightened of a lot of things), and as not having a nice face (versus having a nice face). Other suggestive findings, although not statistically significant, were on the items smart (versus stupid), healthy (versus sickly), liking to talk a lot (versus not liking to talk a lot), liking the way his clothes look (versus not liking the way his clothes look). On each of these characteristics the Negro children, more often than the white children, tended to believe that their teachers perceived them negatively.

Evidence of the importance of students' positive perceptions of teachers' feelings comes from a study by Davidson and Lang (1960). Using fourth-, fifth-, and sixth-graders in New York City as subjects (that is nine to eleven year olds), Davidson and Lang found that positive perceptions of teachers' feelings were significantly related to academic achievement and 'more desirable classroom behaviour', as rated by the teachers. The researchers also reported significant social-class differences in perceptions of teachers' feelings, with upper- and middle-class subjects feeling that their teachers perceived them more favourably than lower-class subjects felt that their teachers perceived them. As expected, social class was significantly related to school achievement. When controlling for social class, the authors found a significant correlation between favourable perception of teachers' feelings and academic achievement. They also reported that even under controlling for achievement, children's perceptions of their teachers' feelings were significantly related to social class.

The difference between the Negro and the white subjects' notions of how their teachers perceive them is a very important one. It is suggestive not only of the Negro children's insecure and uncomfortable feelings in school, but also of actual teachers' perceptions of their Negro students. Rosenthal and Jacobson provide evidence supporting the idea that self-fulfilling prophecies may be operating in the classroom. They found that in some classrooms students whom their teachers had expected to do well academically on the basis of fallacious test scores showed significantly greater achievement than students about whom the teachers did not have such high expectations. From these results we might also expect the converse to be true: teachers with low expectations of particular students will influence their performance in the direction of low achievement.

A Negro child may not only feel threatened by his teachers, but also by the school's curriculum, which may provide an additional source of conflict over his racial identity. The pervasiveness of white middle-class values in the schools has frequently been cited but has seldom been studied. The Negro child is reminded of his alien status in a white man's school through the books he reads, the language he hears, the behaviours that are stressed, the morals that are espoused and even probably by the food he receives as part of the 'hot lunch programme'. With the advent of the Civil Rights Movement and school desegregation, there has been increasing pressure on school boards, principals, and teachers to diversify the curriculum by teaching 'Negro culture' – its history, famous figures, and concerns – in the public school.

The effects of teaching 'Negro culture' on the child's self-image are largely unknown. It would seem reasonable to expect that its possible positive effects depend largely on how the subject is presented, the teachers' own attitudes, and the perceived purpose of the curriculum. It is possible that some methods of teaching Negro history may heighten competition, increase the child's sense of isolation, and intensify identity conflicts, instead of contributing to a positive self-image.

A final factor influencing and possibly threatening the Negro child in school may be termed the 'school ecology'. By 'school ecology' we are referring to the distribution of racial and ethnic groups within the school. With the increasing emphasis on school desegregation, this factor looms as an important consideration in examining and planning for the well-being of the Negro child. While the serious consequences of segregated schools cannot be denied, the racially mixed school also has its own special set of problems.

One of the most obvious factors contributing to possible disruption in the racially mixed school is the attitudes which Negro and white children have towards each other. The children come to school, bringing the attitudes about race which they have learned from parents and other adults in the community; these attitudes, in turn, have some influence over their behaviour towards children of the other racial group. In a very early study, Criswell (1939) found that Negro children in racially mixed classrooms accepted white prestige but increasingly withdrew into their own group as a response to white rejection. Many other studies support this finding (Horowitz, 1936; Radke *et al.*, 1950). In a trenchant analysis, Katz (see Chapter 11 of this book) describes some of the factors influencing performance of the Negro child who enters a racially mixed school or classroom; in some situations, social rejection and isolation may produce such effects as intellectual impairment and anxiety. It seems that the difficulties involved extend beyond simple 'mutual suspicion' and resentment between the two groups. In most cases, there are 'real' differences in the form of intellectual development and scholastic performance of the Negro student in comparison with his white classmate. Therefore, the Negro child in a racially mixed school is forced to cope with feelings of inferiority, which have some basis in reality, as well as those feelings induced by his status in and treatment by the dominant white society.

Harold Proshansky and Peggy Newton 205

Positive self-identity: some resources

Research and theory have tended to emphasize the negative aspects of Negro identity, ignoring or overshadowing its positive and compensatory features. The reader is sometimes left with the image of an entire race of psychologically crippled people, reduced to a level of minimal functioning and a state of precarious mental health. Given the 'Negro problem', and particularly its reflections in lower-class urban life, this emphasis on self-rejection, ambivalence, and extreme reactions to identity conflicts is understandable. However, just as the quiet child in the classroom often receives little attention from the teacher in comparison with the noisy, disruptive troublemaker, so the Negro who is positively identified with his group often escapes the notice of the researcher. As a corollary, it is also important to recognize that not all of the extreme reactions observed among Negroes, such as alcoholism, drug addition, and psychotic withdrawal, are mechanisms for coping with identity conflicts or feelings of self-hatred. These reactions may be in the service of other needs and conflicts.

Undoubtedly, many Negroes experience ambivalence about their racial identity, but its intensity, its 'history', and its ultimate effects on feelings and behaviour depend on a variety of conditional and individual factors. To enumerate a few of these individual variables, we find differences in innate potentials, such as intelligence and temperament, in addition to differences in experiences, such as socialization in the family, interracial contacts, and peer group reactions. These differences must necessarily create diversity among Negroes in response to their common 'self-dilemma'.

Researchers need to explore the full *range* of reactions to being Negro in order to understand how some Negroes feel little or no conflict about their identity while others are severely burdened and debilitated by conflict over their racial identity. They need to look at the Negro who accepts his group membership and who may frequently gain 'self-support' and 'self-enhancement' from it. In such studies there must be a search for both individual and group resources which aid in coping with severe privations and adversity.

It seems likely that how the Negro child reacts to discrimination and prejudice depends largely on his 'family resources'. As Pettigrew (1964b) points out, although the stress of the caste system may result in some self-hatred, given a stable and complete family the Negro may maintain '... his self-respect as a unique and worthwhile human being apart from the position of inferior being that the racists insist he assumes'.

For every stable, complete and supportive Negro home, there are many more that are ravaged by the economic and social effects of discrimination and prejudice. Therefore, our concern must extend beyond a simple query into the combination of unique circumstances which may lead to positive self-identity. We must look to the much larger question of the general resources available to any group – resources which strengthen group ties and feelings of group belongingness, particularly in the face of threat and frustration. The assumption implicit in our argument is that negative self-identity is frequently rooted in negative group identification. From this assumption, we would expect the converse to follow: that positive self-identity is dependent on positive group identification. Considerable evidence supports the idea that personal or self-pride is essentially the expression of group pride (Grossack, 1956; Noel, 1964; Lewin, 1948; Chein, 1948). Such group pride or belongingness is essential for individual growth and satisfaction; for, as Chein (1948) notes, adequate self-perceptions, individual security, and feelings of personal continuity are the major psychological functions of group belongingness for the person.

Group belongingness or positive group identification is not a problem for those groups that have status, power, and prestige in a society. The problems of group identification arise for those who are deprived of these benefits and who are often granted the unwelcome status of 'second-class citizenship'.

What are the conditions which foster positive group identification for these deprived citizens? It seems to us that there are at least three major resources for Negroes (and other minority groups) to establish strong group ties in the face of economic and social adversity.

The first resource we shall designate as *social insight*. By this concept, we suggest that the minority group member – child or adult – needs to understand the source of his group dilemma. If he is Negro, he needs to view the social system and the white man, not himself, as the source of his difficulties. We have previously indicated the danger that the Negro who is forced to play the 'servile inferior' may come to believe in that role and accept it as a measure of his own worth. It is very easy for the Negro to become somewhat fatalistic, to 'accept his lot', believing 'he is what he is, because that is just the way he is'.

The Negro does not need formal schooling to acquire such social insight, however desirable extended education might be for establishing his rightful place in American society. Social insight can probably best be fostered by and in the minority group itself. Grievances, problems, and injustices can be expressed and shared by group members, thus developing a 'heritage of understanding' and strengthening feelings of a 'common bond'. Prior to the Civil Rights Movement, which gained its momentum in the early 1960s, discussions of the Negro problem were largely confined to universities and a few select groups. Only recently has a continuing dialogue on race prejudice been achieved, and evidence indicates that the dialogue is spreading, involving more and more members of the Negro community, particularly the lower-class urban slum dweller. For some Negroes, the blame has finally been shifted from themselves to the social arrangements of the white society.

Insight without hope will not sustain the Negro in the midst of poverty and despair. The Negro must see possibilities for *action*. While he need not be involved in such action, he must feel that change is possible and that others, if not himself, are 'taking action'. Since the beginning of the Civil Rights Movement, these opportunities for action have greatly increased. There has been a dramatic rise since the Second World War in the number of local and national Negro, white, and mixed racial groups that have been formed to state and fight the case of the Negro.

At the present time, these groups vary both in their goals and the means they use (or plan to use) to achieve these goals. However, these variations are of little importance in terms of the Negro's feelings of positive identity; the crucial fact is the groups' existence. These groups represent hope and action; they are sources for group identification, even if the individual is not actually personally involved in group action. The presence of the groups also signifies a reversal of the Negro's traditional role; passive acceptance has been largely replaced by active rejection.

In this context it is necessary to examine very briefly some of the implications of the Civil Rights Movement. We view the achievements of the Civil Rights Movement as primarily symbolic, serving to raise hopes and establish status and token gains. The lower-class Negro has felt very little change in his daily life. The gap between 'what the white man says' and 'what the white man does' remains. Frustration seethes in the ghetto, as symbolized by increasing outbreaks of violence. Yet some of this frustration is being harnessed by a new and articulate black leadership, bringing together many otherwise alienated individuals of the slum community. The slogan is usually 'Black Power'; the emphasis is on 'separatism' – on black control of black communities. While the significance of ultimate effects of this new militancy is unknown, it is important to recognize that the tenor and rhetoric of the Negro's struggle have changed. The new young Negro is no longer willing to play the 'white man's game'.

The Negro's perception of the significance and historic weight of his struggle provide a further resource for feelings of self-worth. Isolated from and denied participation in the mainstream of American life for over one hundred years, the Negro has seemed to have no past, as well as no future. His forebears were vaguely defined 'blacks' from Africa, whose supposed primitive existence was used by whites to confirm the 'inferiority' of all Negroes. Unlike the Jews, American Negroes had no *apparent* heritage or tradition to give significance to their existence or to instil hope for their future. While they maintained and developed cultural expressions in music, art, literature, and language, these distinctive contributions were largely unrecognized, and Negroes remained isolated from other Americans and from black peoples in other parts of the world.

In the last decade, the American Negro's struggle has taken on a new, dramatic, world-wide significance. Spurred by the emergence of the African nations and the pervasive influence of the mass media, there has been a rediscovery of 'Black culture' and a growing bond uniting black peoples throughout the world. In his own battle, the American Negro is able to achieve a new sense of kinship and feeling of purpose – a new, larger, black identity. The struggle of black men has become symbolic of the struggle of all oppressed groups to achieve dignity and respect in the face of bigotry and discrimination.

References

ALLPORT, G. W. (1954), *The Nature of Prejudice*, Addison-Wesley.

AUSUBEL, D. P., and AUSUBEL, P. (1958), 'Ego development among segregated Negro children', *Mental Hygiene*, vol. 42, pp. 362–9; reprinted in A. H. Passow (ed.) (1963), *Education in Depressed Areas*, New York Teachers College, Columbia University, Bureau of Publications, pp. 109–31.

BERNARD, J. (1966), *Marriage and Family Among Negroes*, Prentice-Hall.

BETTELHEIM, B., and JANOWITZ, M. (1964), *Social Change and Prejudice*, Free Press.

BOYD, G. F. (1952), 'The levels of aspiration of white and Negro children in a non-segregated elementary school', *Journal of Social Psychology*, vol. 36, pp. 191–6.

BROWN, B. (1967), 'The assessment of self-concept among four-year-old Negro and white children: a comparative study using the Brown-IDS Self-Concept Referents Test', Institute for Developmental Studies (mimeo).

CHEIN, I. (1948) 'Group membership and group belonging', American Jewish Congress (mimeo).

CLARK, K. B., and CLARK, M. P. (1947), 'Racial identification and preference in Negro children', in T. M. Newcomb and E. L. Hartley (eds.), *Readings in Social Psychology*, Holt, Rinehart & Winston, pp. 169–78.

CLARK, K. B., and CLARK, M. P. (1950), 'Emotional factors in racial identification and preference in Negro children', *Journal of Negro Education*, vol. 19, pp. 341–50.

COLEMAN, J. S., *et al.* (1966), *Equality of Educational Opportunity*, US Government Printing Office.

COLES, R. (1965), 'It's the same, but it's different', *Daedalus*, vol. 94, pp. 1107–32; republished in T. Parsons and K. B. Clark (eds.) (1967), *The Negro American*, Beacon Press, pp. 254–79.

COLES, R. (1967), *Children of Crisis: A Study of Courage and Fear*, Atlantic-Little, Brown.

CRISWELL, J. H. (1939), 'Social structure revealed in a sociometric re-test', *Sociometry*, vol. 2, pp. 69–75.

DAVIDSON, H. H., and LANG, G. (1960), 'Children's perceptions of teachers' feelings toward them', *Journal of Experimental Education*, vol. 29, no. 2, pp. 107-18; reprinted in J. I. Roberts (ed.) (1967), *School Children in the Urban Slum*, Free Press, pp. 215-30.

DAVIS, C. H. (1967), Personal communication, November.

DEUTSCH, M. (1960), 'Minority group and class status as related to social and personality factors in scholastic achievement', Monograph no. 2, Society of Applied Anthropology.

DEUTSCH, M., and BROWN, B. (1964), 'Social influences in Negro–white intelligence differences', *Journal of Social Issues*, vol. 20, pp. 24-35.

DRAKE, ST. C. (1965), 'The social and economic status of the Negro in the United States', *Daedalus*, vol. 94, pp. 771-814; reprinted in T. Parsons and K. B. Clark (eds.) (1967), *The Negro American*, Beacon Press.

DRAKE, ST. C. and CAYTON, H. R. (1962), *Black Metropolis*, rev. edn., Harper & Row.

ERIKSON, E. H. (1966), 'The concept of identity in race relations: notes and queries', *Daedalus*, vol. 95, pp. 145-71; republished in T. Parsons and K. B. Clark (eds.) (1967), *The Negro American*, Beacon Press, pp. 227-53.

FANON, F. (1952), *Peau noire, masques blancs*, Editions de Seuil; reprinted in *Black Skins, White Masks*, Grove Press, 1967.

FRAZIER, E. F. (1962), *Black Bourgeoisie*, Collier.

GOODMAN, M. E. (1952), *Race Awareness in Young Children*, Addison-Wesley; Collier, 1964.

GRAMBS, J. D. (1964), 'The self-concept: basis for re-education of Negro youth', in W. C. Kvaraceus, J. S. Gibson, F. Patterson, B. Seasholes, and J. D. Grambs, *Negro Self-Concept: Implications for School and Citizenship*, McGraw-Hill, pp. 11-34.

GROSSACK, M. (1956), 'Group belongingness among Negroes', *Journal of Social Psychology*, vol. 43, pp. 167-80; republished in M. Grossack (ed.) (1963), *Mental Health and Segregation*, Springer, pp. 18-29.

GROUP FOR THE ADVANCEMENT OF PSYCHIATRY. Psychiatric aspects of school desegregation. New York: Group for Advancement of Psychiatry, 1957.

HARTLEY, E L., ROSENBAUM, M., and SCHWARTZ, S. (1948), 'Children's use of ethnic frames of reference: an exploratory study of children's conceptualizations of multiple ethnic group membership', *Journal of Psychology*, vol. 26, pp. 367-86.

HOROWITZ, E. L. (1936), 'The development of attitude toward the Negro', *Archives of Psychology*, no. 194.

JOHNSON, C. S. (1941), *Growing Up in the Black Belt*, American Council on Education; reprinted: Shocken, 1967.

KARDINER, A., and OVESEY, L. (1962), *The Mark of Oppression*, World.

LANDRETH, C., and JOHNSON, B. C. (1953), 'Young children's responses to a picture and inset test designed to reveal reactions to persons of different skin colour', *Child Development*, vol. 24, pp. 63-79.

LEWIN, K. (1948), *Resolving Social Conflicts*, Harper & Row.

LOTT, A. J., and LOTT, B. E. (1963), *Negro and White Youth*, Holt, Rinehart & Winston; reprinted as 'Negro and white children's plans for their futures', in J. I. Roberts (ed.) (1967), *School Children in the Urban Slum*, Free Press, pp. 347-61.

MCKINLEY, D. G. (1964), *Social Class and Family Life*, Free Press. pp. 152-66; reprinted as 'Status and the socialized son', in J. I. Roberts (ed.), 1967, *School Children in the Urban Slum*, Free Press, pp. 471-83.

MORLAND, J. K. (1958), 'Racial recognition by nursery school children in Lynchburg, Virginia', *Social Forces*, vol. 37, pp. 132–7.

MORLAND, J. K. (1962), 'Racial acceptance and preference of nursery school children in a southern city', *Merrill Palmer Quarterly*, vol. 8, pp. 271–80.

MUSSEN, P. H. (1953), 'Differences between the TAT responses of Negro and white boys', *Journal of Consulting Psychology*, vol. 17, pp. 373–6.

NATIONAL URBAN LEAGUE (1966), *Education and Race*, National Urban League.

NEUGARTEN, B. L. (1946), 'Social class and friendship among school children', *American Journal of Sociology*, vol. 51, pp. 305–13.

NEWCOMB, T. M., TURNER, R. H., and CONVERSE, P. E. (1965), *Social Psychology*, Holt, Rinehart & Winston.

NOEL, D. L. (1964), 'Group identification among Negroes: an empirical analysis', *Journal of Social Issues*, vol. 20, pp. 71–84.

PALERMO, D. S. (1959), 'Racial comparisons and additional normative data on the Children's Manifest Anxiety Scale', *Child Development*, vol. 30, pp. 53–7.

PARKER, S., and KLEINER, R. J. (1965), *Mental Illness in the Urban Negro Community*, Free Press.

PETTIGREW, T. F. (1964a), 'Father-absence and Negro adult personality: a research note', unpublished paper, cited by T. F. Pettigrew in *A Profile of the Negro American*, Van Nostrand, p. 20.

PETTIGREW, T. F. (1964b), *A Profile of the Negro American*, Van Nostrand.

PROSHANSKY, H. M. (1966), 'The development of inter-group attitudes', in L. W. Hoffman and M. L. Hoffman (eds.), *Review of Child Development Research*, Russell Sage Foundation, pp. 311–71.

RADKE, M., SUTHERLAND, J., and ROSENBERG, P. (1950), 'Racial attitudes of children', *Sociometry*, vol. 13, pp. 154–71.

RADKE, M., and TRAGER, H. G. (1950), 'Children's perceptions of the social roles of Negroes and whites', *Journal of Psychology*, vol. 29, pp. 3–33.

RADKE, M., TRAGER, H. G., and DAVIS, H. (1949), 'Social perceptions and attitudes of children', *Genetic Psychology Monographs*, vol. 40, pp. 327–447.

RAINWATER, L. (1966), 'Crucible of identity: the Negro lower-class family', *Daedalus*, vol. 95, pp. 172–217; reprinted in T. Parsons and K. B. Clark (eds.), 1967, *The Negro American*, Beacon Press. pp. 166–204.

ROBINS, L. N., JONES, R. S., and MURPHY, G. E. (1966), 'School milieu and school problems of Negro boys', *Social Problems*, vol. 13, p. 431; as cited in US Civil Rights Commission, *Racial Isolation in the Public Schools*, US Government Printing Office, vol. 2, p. 177.

ROSEN, B. C. (1956), 'The achievement syndrome: a psychocultural dimension of social stratification', *American Sociological Review*, vol. 21, pp. 203–11; republished in J. W. Atkinson (ed.) 1958, *Motives in Fantasy, Action and Society*, Van Nostrand, pp. 495–508.

ROSEN, B. C. (1959), 'Race, ethnicity and the achievement syndrome', *American Sociological Review*, vol. 24, pp. 47–60; republished in J. I. Roberts (ed.), 1966 *School Children in the Urban Slum*, Free Press, pp. 327–46.

SEWARD, G. (1956), *Psychotherapy and Culture Conflict*, Ronald Press.

SIMPSON, G. E., and YINGER, J. M. (1965), *Racial and Cultural Minorities*, 3rd edn, Harper & Row.

STEVENSON, H. W., and STEWART, E. C. (1958), 'A developmental study of race awareness in young children', *Child Development*, vol. 29, pp. 399–410.

TRAGER, H. G., and YARROW, M. R. (1952), *They Learn What They Live: Prejudice in Young Children*, Harper & Row.

WEINER, M., and GRAVES, M. (1960), 'A study of educational and vocational aspirations of junior high school pupils from two socioeconomic levels', dittoed paper, White Plains, N. Y., Board of Education; as cited by M. Weiner and W. Murray, 'Another look at the culturally deprived and their levels of aspiration', in J. I. Roberts (ed.), 1967, *School Children in the Urban Slum*, Free Press, p. 296.

WEINER, M., and MURRAY, W. (1963), 'Another look at the culturally deprived and their levels of aspiration', *Journal of Educational Sociology*, vol. 36, pp. 319–21; republished in J. I. Roberts (ed.) 1967, *School Children in the Urban Slum*, Free Press.

WHITMAN, M. and DEUTSCH, M. (1968), 'Social disadvantage as related to intellectual and language development', in M. Deutsch, I. Katz and A. Jensen (eds.), *Social Class, Race and Psychological Development*, Holt, Rinehart & Winston.

WYLIE, R. S. (1963), 'Children's estimates of their schoolwork ability as a function of sex, race and socioeconomic level', *Journal of Personality*, vol. 31, pp. 204–24.

Chapter 8
Status: The Marginal Reaction –
Mixed-Bloods and Jews

Jack Mann

Jack Mann has carried out many pieces of research on race relations in different parts of Africa, and has, with his colleague, Hamish Dickie-Clarke, devoted his time to understanding the psychological consequences of the South African situation.

What happens to the personality of someone who is tugged between the two sides in a racial situation? This is the problem of marginality, at least so far as race relations are concerned. At first sight marginality appears quite a simple issue to which a straightforward solution is readily available. However, on closer inspection the question is entangled in qualifications so important that the notion of marginality itself is jeopardized.

Park and Stonequist

Robert E. Park first wrote of 'the marginal man'. In a scattering of essays, he left behind a comprehensive theory of marginality; though he never sought to test his notions in a systematic manner and leaned heavily – perhaps too heavily – on impressions gained from his travels and on other writings that were themselves often impressionistic.

He viewed marginality in an historical perspective. The vast expansion of Europe over four centuries shifted people about and brought cultures together, but assimilation and amalgamation were not always immediate. Cultural conflict seems to accompany cultural assimilation; and, when cultures conflict, some individuals find themselves on the margin of these two cultures and neither fully nor permanently accommodated to either. These are the 'marginal men'. Cultural conflicts in them often lead to mental conflicts. (Park, 1928, 1931b, 1937).

The moral turmoil stemming from new cultural contacts shows itself most clearly in the mind of the marginal man. This is probably inevitable but for the marginal man it is likely to be relatively permanent, so that he becomes a personality type, characterized by instability, intensified self-consciousness, restlessness and *malaise* (Park, 1928). And because he lives simultaneously in two worlds, he is forced to become a cosmopolitan as well as a stranger to these worlds – the person with the relatively wider horizon.

Park attributed a number of other characteristics to the marginal man.

He claimed that mulattos, for example, are generally superior in achievement to Negroes of unmixed blood, take themselves more seriously, are more enterprising, aggressive, ambitious, tense and intelligent. They are generally more egocentric, often sensitive and sometimes obsessed with their anomalous situation. More and more they have made the Negro's cause their own and become the leaders, teachers, interpreters and perhaps even the emancipators of the Negro race, tending to gravitate to the cities where they can play the part of intermediary and interpreter between two races and cultures. (Park, 1931a, 1934).

Ordinarily, the marginal man is a mixed blood, like the mulatto, mestizo or Eurasian. Racial hybrids, however, are not the only marginal men. The emancipated Jew is 'historically and typically' the marginal man. In fact, Park (1928) claimed expansively, every immigrant probably goes through a temporary marginal phase.

Parks' conception of marginality was not entirely novel, though the term itself was fresh, picturesque and conveniently compact. The concept of a marginal area lying between two cultures had earlier been used in anthropology, although in only a territorial sense (Goldenweiser, 1925).

The theory was taken up and elaborated by Everett V. Stonequist, who began his work under the direct influence of Park himself. Although, like Park, Stonequist paid a good deal of attention to mixed bloods and to Jews, his category of marginal men was generously wide and embraced Europeanized Africans, westernized Orientals, denationalized Europeans, immigrants and their children, and American Negroes of both mixed and unmixed blood. He devoted a special section of his book to each of these racial or cultural 'hybrids', believing them to be particularly representative types of marginal men. Such types could also be detected, Stonequist thought, in the migrant from country to city, the *parvenu*, the *déclassé* and the career woman, though his eye was chiefly on people with conflicts he regarded as relatively severe (see Stonequist, 1937, 1939, 1942).

Characteristic features of personality could be shaped by the conflicts: Stonequist gave details of these features, giving more weight to the negative features and attempting a neater dovetailing of traits than did Park. The marginal man, according to Stonequist, sees himself from two conflicting points of view: those of the two groups between which he is poised; so that he experiences a divided loyalty and ambivalence. This ambivalence is at the root of the traits characterizing the marginal man and may well explain the apparently fluctuating, irrational, moody, temperamental conduct typical of him. Because his status is often called in question, he becomes excessively self-conscious and race-conscious. Made to feel unacceptable, he develops inferiority feelings for which he may compensate by becoming egocentric or pushing, or by rationalizing or day-dreaming.

Self-consciously seeing himself through the eyes of others, he tends towards hypersensitivity. Combining the knowledge of the insider with the sceptical attitude of the outsider, he may develop into an able critic of the dominant group and its culture. His perplexities are likely to make him a particularly reflective person, although the hyperactive thinking may be more conformist than creative because of his craving to fit himself to the ways approved by the dominant culture.

Such traits first appear at a particular stage of the marginal man's development. In outlining his life-cycle, Stonequist made an original contribution to theorizing about marginality. He noted three stages. The first is a preparatory one, in which (usually in childhood) the individual is being initiated into two cultures and experiences no inner conflict. It is at the second stage that the individual becomes marginal, when there is a crisis. The group conflict is experienced as a personal problem and the characteristic features of personality emerge. The third stage is marked by attempts to adjust to the crisis. Assimilation into the dominant group is one way of adjusting; assimilation into the subordinate group, another; and accommodation to an intermediate position between the two groups, a third. There are, of course, different degrees of adjustment. Some degree of personal maladjustment is inherent in the marginal situation. 'At a minimum it consists of an inner strain and *malaise*, a feeling of isolation or of not quite belonging.' At its most severe, it involves 'mental disorganization' and suicide (Stonequist, 1937).

Stonequist claimed that the concept of marginality has particular virtues. It brings together under one embracing concept several scattered terms referring to various kinds of people, and furthers identification of elements common to them all. It points to the 'key-personality' in culture contacts: the marginal man. 'It is in his mind that the cultures come together . . .' By trying to solve his own problem, he changes the situation (for instance, as a reformer); and so he promotes acculturation. Consequently, the best way of studying culture contact is to study marginal men.

Qualified though his claims were, Stonequist tendered evidence in support of them that was scarcely more substantial than that originally offered by Park. Two sets of data, apparently collected by Stonequist himself, did result from relatively direct and objective fact-finding. One set involved the analysis of responses given by between 270 and 278 American college students to two questions about race and nationality. The analysis suggests that a belief in a distinctive mission for the membership group was stronger amongst Negro students than amongst second-generation European or Jewish students. The other set derived from a study of 192 college students and employed an 'index of racial maladjustment' which unfortunately is not described in any detail. The index was particularly high for forty-five of the students who, because of physical appearance, were likely to be mistaken for members of the white, Indian or Mexican groups.

Objections and reformulations

The notion of a marginal man, then, has not wanted for acceptance. And sociological work on a variety of ethnic and other problems has been set quite cosily within the framework put together by Park and Stonequist.[1]

Nonetheless, used and accepted as it has been, the Park–Stonequist theory has had so many cogent objections levelled against it that nowadays it seems serviceable only in a drastically revised form.

One notable flaw found is of a descriptive kind. Unamplified, the term 'marginal man' may foster more confusion than illumination (Braithwaite, 1960). Is a marginal man someone on a particular margin or is he someone who is reacting in characteristic ways because he is on the margin? A way round the objection is to reformulate marginality by specifying different kinds. This is what Kerckhoff and McCormick (1955) and Cuber (1964) have done, by distinguishing between the marginal situation and the marginal personality, or by distinguishing between objective and subjective marginality. Turner (1964) has suggested that there are three ways of identifying marginality. By the objective criterion, someone is marginal because he is a member of two different groups, that place contradictory demands upon him and so put him in a marginal position. By the experiential criterion, someone is established as marginal because he experiences the conflicting demands of being in a marginal position. By the symptomatic criterion, someone is marginal because he possesses characteristic features of personality. A person could be in a marginal position without experiencing conflict; and he could have the symptomatic attributes without being otherwise marginal, seeing that circumstances other than marginal ones can bring out some of these attributes.

In spite of this, other features of the Park–Stonequist theory remain objectionable to some critics and are perhaps not remedied so simply.

Too many people have been labelled indiscriminately as marginal, according to one complaint (Golovensky, 1952). Certainly, more and more individuals and kinds of people have been brought forward to swell a throng that was already dense when Stonequist wrote his book. In the main their alleged marginality seems to be more of the social than of the racial or cultural type.[2]

1. Examples of the ethnic groups that have been dealt with in this fashion are: Hawaiian hybrids (Smith, 1934), Anglo-Indians (Cressey, 1935), Russian Creoles in Alaska (Wood, 1943), and the ancient Hebrew (Greifer, 1945). In race relations, the marginal man has been accepted as an important mediator in bringing about integration (Gordon, 1954; Frazier, 1957). In social research, he has been valued as a co-operative and highly qualified informant (Sjoberg, 1957).

The term, plainly, is conceived to be an accommodating one in its potential range, and it was partly because many or most Americans can be regarded as marginal in some sense that Golovensky (1952) argued strongly for a restriction in the range of the concept. Probably, too, the apparent prevalence of marginality is illusory. Close examination may show that only some of any sort called marginal are actually in a marginal situation. This is what Goldberg (1941) implied in discussing the Jews. Stonequist had viewed the modern Jew as a cultural hybrid, half derived from traditional Hebrew culture and half from western culture in one of its national forms. (A similar view is still encountered today: Krausz (1964), saw Jews in Leeds as pulled between Jewish and non-Jewish identifications.) However, Goldberg made out a strong case for the existence of a 'marginal culture' within which a Jew could function quite normally. Enclosed in a marginal culture of his own, a person would not be torn between two cultures; and second- or third-generation Jewish immigrants living in the United States have such a marginal culture (Goldberg, 1941) or set of integrated marginal sub-cultures.

Generally, any large in-between group could be a *shelter* from conflict. Riesman apparently believed this when he distinguished between open and secret marginality.

All the in-betweens may be in a marginal situation but only some to a more than mild degree. Thus, while Wirth and Goldhamer (1944) restricted marginal personality traits to a few types of American Negro (like those capable of passing and some intellectuals and artists), they also held that in a sense every Negro is a marginal man. On the other hand, Broom and Glenn (1965), described only well-educated Negroes as marginal. Probably, contemporary observers would agree that marked situational marginality is shown by certain kinds of Negro but would not agree on whether all Negroes are marginal.

From the foregoing, it seems that Stonequist and his followers sometimes took too simplified a view of the hierarchy and in doing so misplaced the margin. They tended to envisage two groups or cultures, arranged one above the other and with a single margin between them. At least occasionally, as with the Jews, a picture of more than two groups is more accurate. If three groups are pictured, with one between the others and overlapping slightly with each neighbour, only some of the people in the in-between group will be on either of the two margins. Furthermore, the two different

2. They include adolescents; people in developing countries; foremen; the Hebrew Christians; intellectuals; Afro-Asians studying in the West; working-class undergraduates; traders and other representatives of Western culture who work amongst Indians and Eskimos in northern Canada; women doing work normally done by men; the professional thief; Thorstein Veblen.

margins of the in-between group will involve different kinds of conflict, one margin entailing a conflict between intermediate and superordinal group and the other a conflict between intermediate group and subordinate group (Mann, 1965).

Wherever the margins are located there are so many of them in different hierarchies that one person could fall upon several. So marginality can be multiple. An example of this would be the European newcomer to the United States who teaches at a Negro college in the South, or the youngster who is marginal twice over, being in one marginal position that involves his Jewishness and in another that involves his adolescence (Radke Yarrow, 1958).

Fortunately, we can settle matters objectively. The psychological kinds of marginality which involve intangibles like inner experience, attitude and disposition, rely heavily on subjective evidence. The typical manner of fixing a *position* and/or *situation* as marginal, on the other hand, depends on features and events that are usually quite open to independent and impersonal observation. Someone deciding matters of marginal position notes, for example, whether someone has a white father and a Negro mother or is an immigrant who has left one nation for a very different one. A marginal situation can be defined as one in which there is any inconsistency in the rankings (Dickie-Clark, 1966).

Once a situation has been identified as marginal, a search can be made for whatever psychological conflicts may be related to it. The relationship is simple, according to Stonequist. The marginal man has personal experience of the conflict of cultures. they come together in his mind and there they conflict. But what marginality theory does seem to need is a bridging process that will link situation to psychological conflict.

A process of this kind was emphasized by Green (1947), whose work with second-generation Greeks and Poles in America convinced him that culture conflict is not enough to bring about the *experience* of that conflict. He found that, although both groups were culturally at an equal distance from the majority culture, they differed markedly in their identifications, with the result that only one group was racked by conflicts and developed the marginal-personality pattern. Identification and acceptance, Green suggested, are important intervening factors to take into account (see Chapter 9 of this book): the degree of identification that the individual experiences with each group on either side of him and the degree to which he is attracted by the group he is trying to leave and repulsed by the group he is trying to join. Green considered that someone trying to leave one group for another faces more of a problem in grudging, uncertain, unpredictable acceptance by the group he is trying to enter than in absolute rejection.

On the whole, the factors intervening between the marginal situation and the marginal personality will be of a psychological kind: motivational, attitudinal, perceptual, judgemental and experiential. Clearly, identification and the degree of acceptance experienced are important manifestations of these factors; but a full account of all the factors has yet to be given.

If Green is right, only some of those in marginal situations will be torn by conflicts. Antonovsky (1956) found, in fact, that no more than eight of his fifty-eight second-generation Jewish subjects were ambivalent in their identifications. They had a relationship with both Jewish and non-Jewish life that was unsatisfactory and full of conflict. The other subjects had 'come to terms' with their Jewishness in various ways, identifying strongly with the Jews being one of these ways. Does it follow that all of these had at one time or another experienced the plight of ambivalence but had subsequently, with the exception of the ambivalent eight, managed to resolve their conflicts? Stonequist implied that a typical marginal man would adjust to his difficulties (by, for example, identifying himself with the subordinate group) only after he had passed through a time of conflict; and the details Johnson (1957) collected about Negro youths suggest that usually a cycle of reaction has to be passed through before a final reactive stage is reached. All in all, it would probably be going too far to argue that everybody in a marginal situation must have experienced the conflicts of that situation; yet to ignore all except those with abiding conflicts would be to underestimate the pervasiveness of conflict, however temporary it might be,

There seem to be several ways in which the person who does have conflicts can resolve them. Assimilation into the dominant group and other kinds of adjustment listed originally by Stonequist seem to need renovation. In the main, the reactions to conflict that Stonequist and others thought of as modes of adjustment are not primarily subjective reactions. Reactions that are particularly subjective were treated separately as features of the marginal personality. In spite of this, the personality traits belong to the category of reactions to conflict; and for that matter they can be regarded also as forms of adjustment. Aggression, for example, is accommodating in that it serves to reduce the strain of marginality (Wardwell, 1955). At all events, because the marginal personality is one of the most conspicuous marks of the Park–Stonequist marginal man, it deserves a specially critical look.

Six questions about it seem worth asking. Firstly, just what does the marginal syndrome consist of and what major factors go to make it up? Given the final (lengthened) list of traits that can be shown to be found together, it should be possible to see how heavily the traits rest on only a few basic factors of personality. Turner (1964), distinguished two main sorts of marginal symptom: novel perspective; and a collection of mainly negative and emotional qualities. The composite sketch prepared by

Kerckhoff and McCormick (1955) groups traits together into four sets in which uncertainty, inadequacy, emotional turmoil and paranoid reactions are the chief ones. One factor analysis reduced a number of marginal traits to three chief factors, labelled insecurity feelings, self-pity and sensitivity (Mann, 1958). The factor analysis was based on responses to questionnaire items that were put to South African Coloureds. As will be seen below, several investigators have used this method to gather data about marginal traits.

A second question is closely related to the first. Do manifestations of the syndrome depend upon traits already existing in the individual? Before anything like the syndrome emerges there may have to be suitable pre-marginal traits or patterns in the individual for the conflicts of marginality to amplify and shape themselves. The third question is: assuming that a distinct syndrome can be detected, is it peculiar to the person caught up in the conflicts of a marginal situation? Park and Stonequist maintained that the marginal man's personality was typical and characteristic. Critics however, have wondered whether exactly the same traits may not be produced by conflicts that are in no way marginal (Mann, 1958; Turner, 1964; Vander Zanden, 1966). Fourthly, when non-marginal conflicts yield distinct traits of whatever kind, will these not overlay, distort and complicate the traits that are traceable to the marginal situation? (Watson, 1967).

Fifthly, is marginal conflict deep and enduring? Certainly, very profound disturbances of personality that are not easily shaken off have been attributed to marginal positions like those occupied by immigrants to Australia (Hammet, 1965; 1966). Nevertheless, instead of reshaping the whole personality, the marginal situation may merely bring about some fleeting changes in it; and it is to these perhaps that the psychologist should first address himself.

Sixthly, do different kinds of marginal situation yield different patterns of traits and transitory reactions? Different margins are the haunts of different conflicts (Mann, 1965). Perhaps the different conflicts make for different reactions. Indecision may characterize the man attracted by both his own group and one higher in the hierarchy that he has some chance of entering. It may not characterize the man attracted to his own group but repelled by a lower group into which he has some chance of falling. At the same time, and differences notwithstanding, there may be some traits, like insecurity, that are fostered by any kind of marginal conflict.

Past and future empirical research

Hard data providing basis for the answers to these questions come from recent studies of American Indians, South African Coloureds, and Jews. In all these studies, a questionnaire – though different in each study – served to measure features of the marginal personality. Only one study revealed a straightforward link between the marginal situation and the marginal personality. Chippewa schoolchildren were more likely to have much in the way of a marginal personality than white schoolchildren. On the other hand, no pertinent difference was found between Coloured and white schoolchildren or between Jewish and Presbyterian university students.

Physical appearance was an issue in the Chippewa and South African Coloured studies – remember, the ability to pass into a white group had been regarded by Stonequist as an important aspect of marginality. It turned out that a white-like appearance alone was not enough to bring forth relatively marked personality symptoms of marginality. There was no difference in the personality scores of two matched groups of adult and near-adult Coloureds. One group consisted of those able or nearly able to pass and the other of less passable Coloureds. Amongst Chippewa schoolchildren, appearance mattered only when there was a strong identification with the whites. Then the personality symptoms were particularly marked if appearance was Indian-like.

All the studies went into the relationships between subordinate group members and the dominant group. Evidently, certain subordinate-group features can be singled out as especially important in determining marginality. Amongst the Chippewa schoolchildren, those who were least Indian-like in appearance leaned most towards identifying with the whites. Amongst the Coloureds, the passables were not especially likely to prefer white attributes to coloured ones. However, they were especially likely to reject the barriers erected by whites against Coloureds. Amongst Jews, those adhering to conventional Jewish norms showed a preference for the Jewish group itself, while Jews deviating from the norms put Mediterraneans first. Jews of the latter kind, Lewit (1959) concluded, prefer the Mediterranean group because it is a more accepting group than the dominant north European group. By further analysis, Lewit found that the deviating Jews who preferred north Europeans to Mediterraneans were inclined to have less secure personalities than the deviating Jews who favoured Mediterraneans to a moderate degree.

Altogether, these examples of recent research shows how complicated issues of marginality can become once speculation gives way to testing. But they do suggest that groups that fall on the margin, objectively or subjectively, may yield quite definite answers to questions about marginality. Consequently they could be used in programmes to promote contact between different groups.

But one might also remember that not all outcomes of the marginal situation need be unfavourable. The marginal position need not be ordinarily distressing, and the conflicts of marginality need not always be painful. Conflicts can be bracing and challenging. Furthermore, while biculturality may torture, it may amount on the other hand to the best of two worlds.

Like other theories, the theory of marginality guides the researcher to particular problems which it throws into prominence. And at a time when racial differences, psychological as much as sociological or political, matter so much, the sensitivity to and study of certain individuals (like those with parents of different race) which this theory makes explicit use of, could be of real value, if systematically exploited.

References

ANTONOVSKY, A. (1956), 'Toward a refinement of the "marginal man" concept' Social Forces, vol. 35, pp. 57–62.

BRAITHWAITE, L. (1960), 'Social stratification and cultural pluralism', Annals of the New York Academy of Sciences, vol. 83, pp. 816–31.

BROOM, L., and GLENN, N. D. (1965), Transformation of the American Negro, Harper and Row.

BROWN, W. O. (1934), 'Culture contact and race conflict', in E. B. Reuter (ed.), Race and Culture Contacts, McGraw-Hill, pp. 34–7.

CRESSEY, P. F. (1935), 'The Anglo-Indians: a disorganized marginal group', Social Forces, vol. 14, pp. 263–8.

CUBER, J. F. (1964), Sociology, Vision Press.

DICKIE-CLARK, M. F. (1966), The Marginal Situation, Routledge & Kegan Paul.

GOLDBERG, M. M. (1941), 'A qualification of the marginal-man theory', American Sociological Review, vol. 6, pp. 52–8.

GOLDENWEISER, A. (1925), 'Cultural anthropology', in H. E. Barnes (ed.), The History and Prospects of the Social Sciences, Knopf, pp. 210–54.

GOLOVENSKY, D. I. (1952), 'The marginal-man concept: an analysis and critique' Social Forces, vol. 30, pp. 333–9.

GORDON, M. M. (1954), 'Social structure and goals in group relations', in M. Berger, T. Abel and C. M. Page (eds.), Freedom and Control in Modern Society, Van Nostrand.

GREEN, A. W. (1947), 'A re-examination of the marginal-man concept', Social Forces, vol. 26, pp. 167–71.

GREIFER, J. L. (1945), 'Attitudes to the stranger: a study of the attitudes of primitive society and early Hebrew culture', American Sociological Review, vol. 10, pp. 739–45.

HAMMETT, P. J. (1965) 'Marginality and mental health', Australian Journal of Social Issues, vol. 2, pp. 18–26.

HAMMETT, P. J. (1966), 'Identity under threat of marginality', paper presented at 4th World Congress of Psychiatry, Madrid, September, abstracted in Excerpta Medica, International Congress Series, no. 150, pt. 3, 1968, pp. 178–9.

HUGHES, E. C. (1949), 'Social change and status protest: an essay on the marginal man', Phylos, vol. 10, pp. 58–65.

JOHNSON, R. (1957), 'Negro reactions to minority group status', in M. L. Barron (ed.), American Minorities, Knopf, pp. 192–212.

KERCKHOFF, A. C., and McCORMICK, T. C. (1955), 'Marginal status and marginal personality', Social Forces, vol. 34, pp 48–55.

KRAUSZ, E. (1964), 'The Jewish dilemma', New Society, no. 71, pp. 15–16.

LEWIT, D. W. (1959), 'Minority group belonging, social preference, and the marginal personality', *Journal of Abnormal and Social Psychology*, vol. 59, pp. 357–62.

MANN, J. W. (1958), 'Group relations and the marginal personality', *Human Relations*, vol. 11, pp. 77–92.

MANN, J. W. (1965), 'Adolescent marginality', *Journal of Genetic Psychology*, vol. 106, pp. 221–35.

PARK, R. E. (1928), 'Human migration and the marginal man', *American Journal of Sociology*, vol. 33, pp. 881–93.

PARK, R. E. (1931a), 'Mentality of racial hybrids', *American Journal of Sociology*, vol. 36, pp. 534–51.

PARK, R. E. (1931b), 'Personality and culture conflict', *Publications of the American Sociological Society*, vol. 25, pp. 95–110.

PARK, R. E. (1934), 'Race relations and certain frontiers', in E. B. Reuter (ed.), *Race and Culture Contacts*, McGraw-Hill, pp. 57–85.

PARK, R. E. (1937), 'Introduction' to E. V. Stonequist, *The Marginal Man*, Scribner's, pp. 13–18.

RADKE YARROW, M. (1958), 'Personality development and minority group membership', in M. Sklare (ed.), *The Jews*, Free Press, pp. 451–74.

REID, I. DE A. (1957), 'Integration reconsidered', Harvard Educational Review, vol. 27, pp. 85–91.

RIESMAN, D. (1954), *Individualism reconsidered*, Free Press.

SEEMAN, M. (1956), 'Intellectual perspective and adjustment to minority status', *Social Problems*, vol. 3, pp. 142–53.

SJOBERG, G. (1957), 'The interviewee as a marginal man', *Southwestern Social Science Quarterly*, vol. 38, pp. 124–32.

SMITH, W. C. (1934), 'The hybrid in Hawaii as a marginal man', *American Journal of Sociology*, vol. 39, pp. 459–68.

STONEQUIST, E. V. (1935), 'The problem of the marginal man', *American Journal of Sociology*, vol. 41, pp. 1–12.

STONEQUIST, E. V. (1937), *The Marginal Man*, Scribner's; republished by Russell & Russell in 1961.

STONEQUIST, E. V. (1939), 'Race mixture and the mulatto', in E. T. Thompson (ed.), *Race Relations and the Race Problem*, Duke University Press, pp. 246–70.

STONEQUIST, E. V. (1942), 'The marginal character of the Jews', in I. Graeber and S. H. Britt (eds.), *Jews in a Gentile World*, Macmillan, pp 296–310.

TURNER, R. M. (1964), *The Social Context of Ambition*, Chandler.

VANDER ZANDEN, J. W. (1966), *American Minority Relations*, Ronald Press.

WARDWELL, W. I. (1955), 'The reduction of strain in a marginal social role' *American Journal of Sociology*, vol. 61, pp. 16–25.

WATSON, P. F. (1967), 'Marginality', *News Letter*, Institute of Race Relations, vol. 1, pp. 46–7.

WIRTH, L., and GOLDHAMER, H. (1944), 'The hybrid and the problem of miscegenation', in O. Klineberg (ed.), *Characteristics of the American Negro*, Harper, pp. 249–369.

WOOD, M. M. (1943), 'The Russian Creoles of Alaska as a marginal group', *Social Forces*, vol 22, pp. 204–8.

Chapter 9
Migration: Problems of Adjustment and Assimilation in Immigrants

Ronald Taft

Ronald Taft is the foremost Australian authority on immigration problems and has carried out three major studies of their modes of adjustment. His other interests include social psychology and educational psychology in general.

Socialization and resocialization

In the course of life we learn to live as a member of a community as well as a member of sub-communities within that community. When we move to a radically different type of community, as in the case of immigrants, or when going to boarding-school or entering the army, we have to adapt ourselves to the requirements of the new community.

The original learning to adapt to the communities of our childhood we call *socialization*,[1] and so the adjustment to the new community may be described as *resocialization*. This involves many of the same psychological problems and principles as the original socialization, but in some important ways it is different. In the course of socialization, for example, a child has to learn such universal social tasks as accepting adult responsibilities, learning to communicate with others verbally as well as in other ways, and behaving differently towards people according to their social status, like with parent and child. Having learned these tasks, as *general* principles, it is necessary for an immigrant only to learn them in the *particular* form in which they occur in the new society to which he is becoming resocialized.

Characteristic of any community are the prevailing values that enable its members to judge certain kinds of behaviour as more appropriate than others. These values supply the *social norms* – approved guide-lines for the behaviour of all members. These are mutually agreed – although usually not spelled out explicitly. How much a person accepts the social norms of a community as a guide for the evaluation of his own behaviour and that of others, reflects how much he uses it as his *reference group*. An

1. Socialization has been defined by Merton as 'the processes by which people selectively acquire the values and attitudes, the interests, skills and knowledge – in short, the culture – current in the groups of which they are, or seek to become, a member'. See Merton, Reader and Kendell (1957).

important aspect of socialization or resocialization to a community, is inducing the members of the community to accept it as their reference group. This implies conforming to what the culture prescribes and indentifying themselves with the community and its social norms.

Social norms are not the only aspects of the socialization process. A child also is taught social knowledge and beliefs. An example of social knowledge is knowledge of the norms and values held by society, and an example of social beliefs would be opinions held about the characteristics of persons who are members of particular groups, the so-called 'stereotypes'. Social skills also form a very important part of the socialization process. Language itself, which is central to becoming a member of society, is a social skill which usually has specific qualities relevant to the group of which the individual is becoming a member, such as dialects or jargon which mark a person out as a member of a sub-group within society at large.

Another social skill which is learnt by a child is the ability to manipulate people in his own environment. The child learns, for example, how to get attention from his parents and how to avoid punishment. Still another aspect of this process is the development of attitudes both pro and con some object. The child, in the course of socialization, learns that some states of affairs are to be preferred and others avoided; he learns feelings of prejudice towards some persons, ideas, or social institutions, for example against political dictatorship. These attitudes do not necessarily bring about particular forms of behaviour, like taking action against an object he is prejudiced against, but they are related to deep-lying reactions that play an important part in the adjustment of an individual to the world around him.

The provision of communication channels or social networks between individuals is another part of the socialization process. By means of this, the child develops relationships of varying degrees of intimacy with other people – a close emotional tie with the parents, siblings, and close friends for example (the *primary social groups*), and other more formal and ritualized ways of interacting with less important persons in the *secondary social network*.

In the course of socialization, some concept of identity is passed on to the person; a *social identity* is provided by the delineation of that person by his society in terms of the groups of which he is a member; for example, he may be a Dutchman, a Catholic, a citizen of Utrecht, a member of a particular family and of a particular social group. The individual himself may not adopt the complete social identity provided for him by society, but rather he may perceive himself as being more identified with groups other than the ones of which he is regarded by society as a member.

This raises the question of personality in the socialization process. Up to a point a person's personality is bestowed upon him by the training given him by his society which prepares him to perform in a defined way the social roles considered to be appropriate for him. But he also has an individuality which goes beyond these social pressures; he has, for example, his own peculiar pattern of abilities, temperament and individual goals, not to mention forms of self-expression. Where the pressures of his social environment run in the same direction as his individual dispositions he may be said to be adjusted, but where they do not he is (to that extent), maladjusted. Naturally, not all persons are fully adjusted to their society, and some, in fact, are quite alienated from it. Under certain circumstances, immigrants tend to be drawn disproportionately from those groups who are not well adjusted to their society. In a series of studies in Holland, comparing emigrants with a carefully matched group of non-emigrants, it was found that the emigrants had weaker ties than did the non-emigrants with both their primary and secondary groups in Holland as well as greater feelings of unease in Dutch society (Beijer et al., 1961).

What are the implications of the above analysis of the socialization process for the problem of immigrant adjustment and adaptation? All the ways of adapting to society which a person may learn are threatened when he moves from one society to another. Some of the social skills, knowledge, norms, attitudes etc., that he has learned in the course of socialization are not appropriate to the new society and changes are necessary. In the words of Eisenstadt, he has to be *desocialized* before he can be *resocialized*. (Incidentally, it should be pointed out that even among people who remain in their native community all their lives, there are periods in which some desocialization occurs; for example, when a young man joins the army.)

The processes of socialization and resocialization should be viewed somewhat differently in the case of immigrants who are still children. In their case, adaptation to the new community depends upon the influence that the latter has on their initial socialization, and the importance of desocialization and resocialization is diminished accordingly.[2]

The amount of resocialization required of an immigrant is, of course, partly a function of the differences between the society in which he was originally socialized and the new society to which he has moved, differences which may occur in any of the aspects of socialization that I described earlier. Not all immigrants will have the same motivation to change; some will be strongly motivated to adapt themselves – for example, if they anticipate permanent residence. Others, perhaps because they are unwilling

2. The special aspects of the adjustment and assimilation of immigrant children are discussed in Bhatnagar (1970) and Taft (1972).

refugees from their original society, may be reluctant to change. Again, in some cases, the new society may be more suited to an immigrant's temperament and goals than the old one was. And it should be remembered that adjustment is not equally easy or difficult in every respect for a given person; an immigrant may find, for example, that the new society offers plenty of opportunity for the pursuit of economic gain, but that there are anti-intellectual values which he finds frustrating in terms of his own values and abilities. This is a common viewpoint among highly educated immigrants in the USA and Australia (Kent, 1953; Taft and Doczy, 1961), and it leads to conflict and ambivalence on the part of certain immigrants who become integrated economically but remain 'Europeans at heart'.

Persons like this are resocialized only with respect to certain aspects of society; they develop certain social skills; for example, the ability to communicate in English and to perform social roles connected with the economic institutions – but their values concerning what is important in life may not change.

This analysis of socialization and resocialization provides a useful basis to consider the main aspects of the process of the adjustment and assimilation of immigrants.

Definition of terms

As we shall be using several terms that are related to the resocialization of immigrants, the main ones will be defined now.

Adjustment will refer to feelings of being in harmony with one's environment – although it does not necessarily imply that the outlook of the person and his social environment are identical. For example, an immigrant can be adjusted to his new country without necessarily changing his social norms or values.

Adaptation refers to changes made by the immigrant in order to fit in better with the environment and includes changes in attitudes as well as in behaviour.

Integration implies that the immigrant has to some extent become absorbed into the new community; for example, he has been accepted into certain social organizations or into informal friendship groups, or he feels emotionally that he is part of the new society. Integration may also refer to economic absorption in the sense that he has found a place in the economy.

Assimilation is the process whereby the immigrant and the native population become more alike as a result of social interaction. This does not imply that the immigrants assimilate completely to the 'host' population without the 'hosts' changing in any way, but under most conditions of actual assimilation it is the immigrants who do most of the adapting. Assimilation can refer to all aspects of the immigrant that are relevant to this adaptation; his appearance and style, his speech, his social behaviour, his beliefs, values and attitudes, and his integration with the society. Because of its generality, *assimilation* is the term that will normally be employed to describe these resocialization processes.

The considerations in this chapter of the psychological effects of immigration will be dealt with in turn under two major headings: problems of adjustment and problems of assimilation.

The adjustment of immigrants

In any society, the citizens differ in the degree to which they might be described as *adjusted*. In common usage this term often refers to emotional stability and freedom from internal conflicts and tensions – that is, freedom from psychoneuroses. In our treatment here we are more interested in a person's harmony or conflict with his external environment, although the degree of external adjustment will often be reflected in his emotional and personality adjustment. The external adjustment may reflect the internal state, and vice versa.

One of the most accessible indices of the external adjustment of a citizen to his society is his satisfaction with various aspects of his life, and this is the most common measure that is used to study adjustment in immigrants. While an immigrant's satisfaction is not a direct observation of the degree to which harmony exists with his environment, it can be assumed that it usually bears a close relationship to it. This is, however, not always the case. In a study of Hungarian 'intellectuals' in Australia, (Taft and Doczy, 1962) the criteria used to measure their adjustment were whether they held a job which was objectively of the same status as their pre-immigration occupation, and also whether they had any friends (irrespective of nationality).

These objective indices constituted a measure of 'occupational and social adjustment' which was different from and uncorrelated with the measure of satisfaction. An immigrant might, for example, have had no friends at all, but he could be quite satisfied with that state of affairs. It was, in fact, found that there was no relationship between the degree to which the respondents claimed to be satisfied with their jobs and the degree to which their occupational status had dropped since they had left Hungary. Despite such divergences as these between objective measures of adjustment and subjective feelings of satisfaction, the latter measure is the one that is usually preferred in studies of immigrant adjustment since it represents a more direct measure of it.

Satisfaction as an index of immigrant adjustment

The adjustment of an immigrant to his environment is very much a function of what he wants out of life, together with the capacity of his environment to satisfy him. These wants are usually referred to as *needs* and we should look briefly at the types of needs that should be taken into account in considering immigrant adjustment.

There are many needs common to all human beings, and there are some that are unique to each individual. These can be listed as:[3]

1. *Basic biological* needs: for example, eating, waste elimination, sex, physical activity, etc. While these needs are not all essential to life, failure to obtain gratification of them is, at the very least, severely frustrating.
2. *Social* needs: for example, the need for human contacts and communication; dependence on others; or the need to be helpful.
3. *Security* needs: the need to feel safe from physical and mental threats and to be free of painful anxieties and anguish emanating from feelings of guilt.
4. *Instrumental* needs: the need to attain goals that are instrumental to gaining more basic goals; for example, the need to earn money in order to obtain food, shelter, companionship, family life, etc. Instrumental goals often become autonomous, valued for themselves.
5. *Ego* needs: the need to be boosted and esteemed and the need for social status.
6. *Self-fulfilment* needs: for example, the need to utilize one's abilities and to develop them, artistic expression, the freedom to express one's own style of behaviour, to be able to act spontaneously, to enjoy emotional experiences and, possibly, to experience peak emotions such as awe and ecstasy.

Depending on the temperament and life experience of an immigrant, the relative importance of these needs will vary. For that reason, no general principles can be laid down *a priori* as to what satisfactions are needed in order for immigrants in general to be able to adjust to their new environment. It would be expected, for instance, that a small businessman who voluntarily left England for Australia to set up a new business would be more dependent on the satisfaction of his economic instrumental needs than would an intellectual. The satisfactions sought by immigrants, particularly intellectual ones, are often subtle and elusive; for example, the difficulty in expressing oneself freely in the vernacular language may constitute a major frustration in the life of an intellectual immigrant.

Because of these variations in the needs of immigrants it is important to

3. A useful classification and listing of needs has been made by Maslow (1954). The listing given here is similar, but not identical with that of Maslow.

take into account the type of immigrant when considering his problems of adjustment. Thus, a vast difference has been found between the level of satisfaction of highly educated immigrants in Australia and that of workers (Taft, 1966). Polish and Hungarian refugees who had undertaken some form of higher education before emigration were much less satisfied with their life in Australia than a comparable group of less well educated Polish refugees. From comments made by the intellectual immigrants in these studies, their sources of dissatisfaction seemed often to have included objections to the level of 'cultural' life in Australia, or to the professional opportunities. In either case, the problem seems to lie in the need for self-fulfilment.

While remembering the importance of self-fulfilling needs in the adjustment of intellectuals, the role played by these needs in the life of less well-educated immigrants should not be under-estimated. Thus, Beijer *et al.* (1961), refer to 'that unique cultural motive, whereby emigration is regarded as the liberation of an active personality from the shackles preventing its unrestricted development'. In his study of comparatively poorly educated Indonesians in Holland, Ex (1966) stressed the supreme importance of 'the freedom to do, or to leave undone' to their post-emigration adjustment.

Whether an immigrant will be satisfied or not in his new country is partly determined by the reasons for his decision to emigrate, partly by the circumstances of his actual immigration and partly by his experiences in his new country. The reasons for emigration will vary: an emigrant may move because his primary group – say, his family – is also emigrating, in which case he may have no individual motive at all. When this occurs, his satisfaction with his migration is likely, at least at first, to be a function of the 'success' of his family, and his continued relations with them. This is typically the case with wives and children. Richardson (1961), for example, found that British housewives in Australia were satisfied with their immigration if their husbands were pleased with their jobs.

Another reason for emigration is being forced to flee for political or personal reasons that make it intolerable or impossible to stay. In the case of such 'refugees' their motivation for emigration is self-preservation and, in the early stages, their satisfaction with the new country is virtually irrelevant to their behaviour, provided the atmosphere is not too oppressive.

The most common reason for voluntary emigration is that someone perceives that greater satisfaction could be obtained in the new country than in the old. This does not imply necessarily that the old country did not satisfy some of the person's needs, but only that the emigrant believes that the new country will provide relatively greater satisfaction. He will be prepared to emigrate from his original country if it seems to him that the *gain* in satisfaction is likely to be greater than the *cost* of making the move. This cost is difficult to estimate and it includes many intangibles that are not covered by financial considerations: for example, the discomfort of learning new ways and, perhaps, a new language; the loss of the pleasure associated with familiar social and environmental contacts; guilt feelings about abandoning aged parents; regrets at uprooting other members of the family who are reluctant to emigrate; and general anguish arising from fear of the unknown. Often, these cost considerations are not fully taken into account before the intending emigrant commits himself, but afterwards they may become augmented in retrospect, especially if the immigration goes badly.

An immigrant can partly rationalize his failure to find satisfaction in the new country by indicating that he needs to cut his continuing cost of emigration by returning home. On the other hand, when an emigrant pays a large cost for his emigration, in the sense described above, he is more apt to make a successful adjustment to his new country. In the above-mentioned study of British immigrants in Australia, Richardson found that the more satisfied ones had had more difficulty in arranging and undertaking their emigration. It seems that, having given a great deal of themselves in order to emigrate, their self-esteem required that they should make a success of their adjustment to the new country.[4]

As I have pointed out already, the success of the emigration may be judged by the balance between the gain in satisfaction and the cost of emigration. This means that if the emigration was forced by conditions at home, and the cost of emigration was comparatively low, a low level of satisfaction in the new country is sufficient to keep the balance. This is the case with political refugees such as Displaced Persons who emigrated from Europe after the Second World War. On the whole, it has been found in Australia that the degree of satisfaction with aspects of life in Australia is lower among refugees than among voluntary immigrants (see Taft, 1966).

Mental health of immigrants

So far we have been referring to what we have called the external adjustment of immigrants. We should also consider mental break-downs, which may be taken to represent signs of poor internal adjustment. Whether problems of adjustment to the new social environment play a part in the onset of the break-downs is difficult to establish (and see Chapter 22 of this book). Some mental health workers have claimed that emigration and the consequent problems play important roles as a precipitating cause.

As far back as 1932, it was demonstrated that there were high rates of

4. Theoretical support for such a psychological process is given by Festinger (1957) in his theory of cognitive dissonance.

schizophrenia among Norwegian immigrants in Minnesota (Ødergaard, 1932). It has also been argued that the stresses associated with acculturation to America are associated with certain types of psychosomatic illnesses (Ruesch and his fellow workers, 1948), and that there are higher rates of crime and juvenile delinquency among immigrants than among non-immigrants – at least in the US. The explanations offered for these inflated figures range from the strain of adjusting to a society that is different from the one in which the person was socialized, to conflicts and disintegration within the immigrant's primary group. For example, Krupinski and Stoller (in Stoller, 1966) attribute the high rate of alcoholism in single, male British immigrants in Australia to loneliness and difficulties in social adjustment. A high rate of schizophrenia and depressive states in older married women from southern and eastern Europe was also found, most of whom were completely unassimilated after *more than seven years* in Australia. Krupinski and Stoller attribute this break-down to the end of their usefulness in families in which the husband and the children have become assimilated and have left the mother in a state of isolation.

However, before fully accepting findings and explanations concerning break-downs in immigrants, it should be noted that there are many difficulties in trying to separate out the rates of mental illness that are due to national differences and those due to the strains of migration. An additional problem is that the migrants may have had a pre-disposition to mental illness before emigration, in which case a high incidence of break-downs among immigrants in a particular country might simply be due to a bias in the original selection. For whatever reason, it does seem, however, that migrants exhibit a higher than normal rate of mental disorder, and that particular groups according to age, sex, national origin and present conditions of life, are especially prone to suffer from particular disorders (but see Chapter 22 of this book).

The explanation for the mental pressures on an immigrant is usually given in terms of the stresses associated with the need to change. This explanation is supported by several studies that indicate that the best adjustment is achieved when the adaptations occur within a solid primary group; for preference, when the family adapts as a unit to the new country. This has been the finding of Kosa (1957), with Hungarians in Canada, Eisenstadt (1954), with Jewish immigrants in Israel stemming from various countries and Menges (1959) with Dutch migrants. These studies underline the importance for countries receiving immigrants not to try to expedite the acculturation process by disturbing family coherence, or by discouraging ethnic associations. The results of such efforts may be to upset the adjustment of the immigrants and to make the assimilation process more difficult.

The assimilation of immigrants

As we have already seen, the socialization process, and, by implication, the resocialization process, has many aspects. This is also true of the assimilation process (see Taft, 1966):

1. *Cultural knowledge and skills*
(a) *Ability to use the vernacular language colloquially, and the possession of other skills required for communication.* An example of the latter might be gestures (such as the appropriate use of the bow in Japan). Richardson (1961) has developed an interesting measure of knowledge of colloquial language for use with British immigrants in Australia. This consists of slang words that are known to nearly all Australians and to very few newly arrived immigrants.
(b) *Knowledge of the history and culture of the new group, its ideology, values, norms and social structure.* An immigrant cannot be considered to be fully assimilated until his knowledge of the new culture becomes equal at least to that of the indigenous citizen who holds a similar social position to himself. Very often the possession of the appropriate cultural knowledge and skills is taken by an observer to represent assimilation itself, so that an immigrant who is fully familiar with the new culture and is skilful in the use of the language is regarded as assimilated. This is actually only one aspect of the assimilation process, constituting an important part of what is usually called *acculturation* – that is, changes in cultural patterns brought about as a result of the interaction between the groups. Acculturation also implies what is covered in the aspect 5(a) below, the *adoption* of values and norms from the host group, as well as just *knowledge* of them. In a study of Hungarian refugees in the USA, Weinstock (1964) found that these two aspects of acculturation were sufficiently correlated to be added together to make an overall index.

2. *Social interaction*
(a) *Social acceptance.* That is, the degree to which there is an accepting attitude on the part of the host group to the members of the new group. This is equivalent to the absence of prejudice. Kosa (1957), in his study of Hungarians, found that immigrants who perceived little discrimination against their own nationality were more adapted to living in Canada. Similar results have been found in various studies in Australia (Taft, 1966), although the relationship is not a simple one, since many immigrants do not feel any prejudice against themselves until they have increased their social contacts with the host population to a sufficient degree to experience it personally.
(b) *Interpersonal contacts and relationships with members of the host group.* These contacts may vary in frequency and in the degree of intimacy and

may lead to the establishment of a new primary group for the immigrant, including close friendships and even a marital relationship with the host group.

3. *Membership identity and social integration*
(a) *Obtaining membership of the new society in a formal sense.* Typically, by becoming naturalized to the new citizenship, and in the case of sub-groups within that society, by obtaining formal membership. This is equivalent to secondary group acceptance rather than primary group, as in 2(b) above.
(b) *Integration into the new group.* This refers to filling a social position which is accepted by the host society as a legitimate one for the immigrant. He is permitted to carry out the roles and to receive the privileges and rights that go with the position. This facet differs from mere formal membership in that there is a social validation of the immigrant's new position. An example of this would be the economic integration, to which we already referred, in which the immigrant has a position in the economic structure of the new society. Like 2(b), this aspect also includes being accepted into marriage; that is, intermarriage with the host group in which the wife, at least, and possibly the family of the wife, accepts the immigrant in his formal marital position. The integration of an immigrant or group of immigrants may occur at different times with respect to different social institutions. Thus economic integration may precede integration into sporting organizations which, in turn, may precede being accepted into a position in a political or trade union organization. The order in which these various types of integration occur may reflect the characteristics of the receiving society, or of the immigrants or both.

4. *Social and emotional identification*
In the above description 3(b), we can assume that the immigrant is identified by society as a member of the new group, but this does not necessarily mean that he himself feels an allegiance to it or an affiliation with it. When he accepts the new group as his *own* reference group we may speak of his emotional identification with it.

5. *Conformity to group norms*
(a) The immigrant adopts the values, attitudes and expectations about people's behaviour that are held by the host society. For example, Bhatnagar (1964) found that Indian students in Britain held social values and attitudes that fell between those held by similar Indian students in India and British students in Britain. He drew the implication that the norms of the Indian students had started to converge towards those of the British, as a result of social and cultural contact. Religious values changed more than any other attitudes.

(b) He behaves in accordance with the norms set down for him by the new society.

(c) He conforms to the norms, not only in his behaviour but in his appearance and expressive behaviour. This last stage bears some affinity to 1(b) above since an immigrant must know the culture in order to be able to conform to it. Very often this change in appearance in order to look similar to the older members of the society is regarded, together with the language and cultural skills, as equivalent to assimilation. But these are not really sufficient to provide full assimilation; it is necessary also to consider the feelings of the immigrant, the attitudes of the host society, and the interaction between how the immigrant behaves and how he is accepted by the society.

Sometimes when the external conformity of an immigrant, or other ethnic minority member, reaches a certain level, he may merge into the society at large without a trace of his deviant origin; that is, he may 'pass'. Nevertheless, he may still have invisible memories, sentiments and even self-identifications which keep him in conflict about his true reference group. Such persons are said to suffer from problems of 'marginality', of 'living in two worlds' (see also Chapters 8 and 10 of this book).

Each of the above aspects of assimilation may be elaborated further by considering four aspects of their dynamics (Taft, 1966): (a) whether the immigrant is motivated to try to be assimilated with respect to that aspect ; (b) whether he makes any attempts to become assimilated to the aspect – for example, it does not necessarily follow that, because an immigrant believes that it would be good for him to learn the vernacular language, he will do anything about attempting to learn it; (c) whether he perceives that he has achieved assimilation with respect to the facet – for example, he may believe that he has acquired an intelligible knowledge of the English language, and (d) the actual level of assimilation achieved – for example, whether he actually has acquired a comprehensible use of the English language.

This complex analysis of the assimilation process reminds us that its course is an uneven one. Investigations into determining factors should analyse the different aspects individually.

The importance of social integration in the total assimilation process seems to be well established. In his studies of the 'absorption' of immigrants in Israel, Eisenstadt (1954) stresses the role of social integration and interpersonal contacts, and in various Australian studies (Taft, 1966), measures of informal social relations with Australians have also proved to be highly related to a number of other indications of assimilation, such as whether an immigrant feels himself to be 'Australian'. From the results of the study of Hungarian intellectuals, it seems that informal social relations with Australians play a more important role in assimilation in the earlier years after immigration than in the later. Studies of immigrant school children in Australia (Taft, 1966) and in Britain (Bhatnager, 1970) support the importance of social acceptance.

It is impossible to be dogmatic about the relative importance of the various aspects of assimilation, since it depends on the particular circumstances. In countries where ideology is centrally important to the culture the whole course of assimilation is dependent on this particular aspect of acculturation. In Israel, for example, assimilation is closely related to the immigrant's acceptance of the Zionist ideology (Eisenstadt, 1954; Shuval, 1963), and in Rhodesia, it is closely related to the acceptance of a hierarchical racial attitude (McEwan, 1964).

The relationships between the different aspects of assimilation

Some degree of order can be brought into all this by the use of statistical methods to determine which aspects tend to go together. Two different methods of doing this have led to similar results (Richmond, 1961; Taft, 1966). The indication is that there are two main groupings of assimilation trends: those related to 'primary assimilation' and those related to 'acculturation'. The former, which Richmond (1967a) divides into *satisfaction* and *identification* aspects, relate to such variables as being satisfied with life in the new country, feeling identified with it, feeling at home in the new country and desiring to stay there for the rest of one's life. The *acculturation* aspects refer to knowing and using the vernacular language, adoption of the prevailing values and social mixing with the host population, and includes both 'obligatory' and 'optional' aspects of social behaviour.

A rather similar division has been made by Ex (1966) in his study of Indonesian immigrants in Holland over a three year period. He distinguishes three stages of 'adjustment': the first, *habituation*, concerns the immigrants' perception of the new culture; the second, *assimilation*, refers to their behavioural changes; and the third, *acculturation*, reflects their emotional reaction to the culture. According to this schema, what Richardson has called 'acculturation' seems to precede 'identification' (called 'assimilation' by Ex). The Australian studies suggest that the more common sequence is that a degree of satisfaction with the new country must be experienced before the immigrant can become identified with it; and some degree of identification is needed before acculturation occurs. However, for any particular immigrant there may be an individually determined sequence of assimilation. Generalizations concerning sequences, at best, can only apply to limited groupings or 'types' of immigrants. Thus, intellectual immigrants who are unable to speak the vernacular, must usually overcome this handicap before any other aspects of assimilation can operate.

Another point is that set-backs and rejections often lead not just to hold-ups in the course of assimilation, but to actual regressions. These can easily occur in the satisfaction and internal adjustment of the immigrant and in his feelings of identification with his new country – that is, in his primary assimilation. But, regression can also occur in acculturation variables, so that a disappointed immigrant may even return to his native language and life values after having made considerable changes. On the other hand, Richmond (1967b) found immigrants in Canada who reacted to initial setbacks to their economic ambitions by lowering their aspirations to more realistic levels, thereby *increasing* their satisfaction with life. Obviously, differences in personality and circumstances make a difference to the course of regression. The return of an immigrant to his country of origin is often taken as an indication of regression, at least with respect to satisfaction, although studies of British immigrants returning from Canada (Richmond, 1967b) indicate that regression in this respect is not as common a cause as is often thought. He found that family ties played an important role in the return, and nearly one third of those who returned were planning to re-emigrate to Canada.

Richmond, the author of the Canadian study, also refers to a type of immigrant that he calls a 'transilient', someone who moves easily from one country to another according to occupational and family preferences without establishing deep ties. Such persons include not only intellectuals but also skilled and even unskilled workers. Their adaptation to their country of residence normally involves only limited assimilation, mainly in the area of cultural knowledge and skills, and models of the normal assimilation sequences do not apply to them.

Frames of reference in assimilation

One further point to note about the determinants of the course of assimilation is the orientation of both the immigrants and the host population towards the assimilation process itself. Gordon (1964) found three orientations in the USA: *Anglo-conformity, the melting-pot*, and *cultural pluralism*. According to the first, the immigrants are expected to conform to the prevailing culture; according to the second, a new amalgam culture will come out of the merging of the original and the immigrant cultures, and with the third, some of the separate ethnic traditions should be preserved side by side although the ethnic groups must assume certain national responsibilities that all Americans have in common, such as loyalty to the nation. Gordon points out that the current trend is for four communities – Protestants, Catholics, Jews and Intellectuals – to exist side by side in a pluralistic fashion, cutting across national boundaries within the American population. To these communities, Negroes could well be added as a fifth.

I have described these three assimilation orientations independently as *monism, interactionism* and *pluralism* respectively (Taft, 1963). My study of the frequency with which these orientations were espoused in Australia indicated that the preference of both Australians and immigrants was for *interactionism* and there was practically no support for *pluralism*. Australians tended to exaggerate the degree to which immigrants support *pluralism*, and the immigrants tended to exaggerate the degree to which Australians support *monism*.

Conclusion

The course of the mutual interaction of the immigrant and his new society, and the subsequent effects on both of them, are dependent on the demographic and psychological characteristics of immigrants, the reasons for the emigration, whether he emigrates with his family, the characteristics of his own ethnic group in the receiving country, other social and economic conditions in the latter country, and the prevailing frames of reference concerning the assimilation of immigrants. An understanding of these factors requires the combined resources of individual and social psychology, cultural anthropology, sociology and the social sciences, and is not to be easily achieved. A detached empirical approach based on a theory of how socialization and resocialization take place, utilizing an appropriate analytical model of all the important aspects, is the one that appears to have the best prospects for understanding the sequence of the process so that in those areas where it is a social problem, remedies can more rationally be worked out.

References

BEIJER, G., FRIJDA, N. H., HOFSTEDE, B. P., and WENTHOLT, R. (1961), *Characteristics of Overseas Migrants*, Govt Printing and Publicity Office, the Hague.

BHATNAGAR, J. K. (1964), 'A cross-cultural study of the interests and attitudes o Indian and British university students', unpublished M.A. thesis, University of London.

BHATNAGAR, J. K. (1970), *Immigrant Children*, Cornmarket Press.

EISENSTADT, S. N. (1954), *The Absorption of Immigrants*, Routledge & Kegan Paul.

EX, J. (1966), *Adjustment After Migration*, Martinus Nijhoff.

FESTINGER, L. (1957), *A Theory of Cognitive Dissonance*, Row, Paterson.

GORDON, M. M. (1964), *Assimilation in American Life*, Oxford University Press.

KENT, D. P. (1953), *The Refugee Intellectual*, Columbia University Press.

KOSA, J. (1957), *Land of Choice*, University of Toronto Press.

MASLOW, A. H. (1954), *Motivation and Personality*, Harper.

McEWAN, P. J. M. (1964), 'European assimilation in a non-European context' *International Migration Review*, vol. 2, pp. 107–27.

MENGES, L. J. (1959), *Geschiktheid Voor Emigratie*, Publikaties van de Rijks Psychologische Dienst, the Hague.

MERTON, R. K., READER, G. G., and KENDELL, P. L. (1957), *The Student Physician*, Harvard University Press.

ØDERGAARD, O. (1932), 'Emigration and insanity', *Acta Psychiatrica et Neuro Scand.* Supplement 4.

RICHARDSON, A. (1961), 'The assimilation of British immigrants in a Western Australian community', *REMP Bulletin*, vol. 9, nos. 1–2.

RICHMOND, A. H. (1967a), 'A theory and method for the psychological study of assimilation', *International Migration Review*, vol. 2, pp. 3–30.

RICHMOND, A. H. (1967b), *Post-War Immigrants in Canada*, University of Toronto Press.

RUESCH, J., JACOBSON, A., and LOEB, M. B. (1948), 'Acculturation and illness', *Psychological Monographs*, vol. 62, whole of no. 292.

SHUVAL, J. T. (1963), *Immigrants on the Threshold*, Prentice-Hall.

STOLLER, A. (1966), *New Faces: Immigration and Family Life in Australia*, Melbourne.

TAFT, R. (1963), 'The assimilation orientation of immigrants and Australians', *Human Relations*, vol. 16.

TAFT, R. (1966), *From Stranger to Citizen*, Tavistock Publications.

TAFT, R. (1972), 'Ethnic groups', in F. R. Hunt (ed.), *Socialization in Australia*, Angus and Robertson, ch. 4.

TAFT, R., and DOCZY, A. G. (1962), 'The assimilation of intellectual refugees in Western Australia', *REMP Bulletin*, vol. 9, no. 4, vol. 10, nos. 1–2.

WEINSTOCK, S. A. (1964), 'Some factors that retard or accelerate the rate of acculturation', *Human Relations*, vol. 17, pp. 321–40.

Section C
Focus on the Interaction

The four chapters in this section examine aspects of how the *individual* members of different races behave when they actually get together. Harry Triandis begins with an analysis of the way attitudes and behaviour are linked – the way someone of a particular race may not always behave in an interracial situation according to the way his attitudes or feelings tell him. Triandis does this mainly by reference to experimental studies. But Irwin Katz and Peter Watson look at two particular real-life situations – IQ testing and psychiatric treatment respectively – and they show how interracial contact may systematically affect these, hinting along the way that these two types of contact highlight what goes on in other situations in life, too. Anthony Richmond comes back to Professor Triandis's analysis but also on a real-life scale rather than a laboratory one, considering how interracial contact actually affects people – in housing, at work and so on. This chapter also acts as a convenient synthesis for this first part of the book.

Chapter 10
Interpersonal Attitudes and Behaviour in Race Relations

Harry Triandis

Harry Triandis completed his doctoral work at Cornell University in Ithaca, New York, moving immediately to the University of Illinois where he has been ever since except for a year at the Center for International Studies at Cornell University in 1968–9.

He is primarily concerned with the problem of interpersonal communication. His research has been concerned with the way culture influences how people perceive and think about their social environment. He is also concerned with the effect of difference in these individual perceptions on interpersonal communication and generally on interpersonal relations. He has conducted, in collaboration with others, empirical studies testing the effects of these relationships in Japan, India, Greece and Germany. He is the author of *Attitude and Attitude Change* and *The Analysis of Subjective Culture.*

When the people of one cultural group meet with those of another, each will bring to the relationship a number of attitudes and expectations, habits and values which are already established. As the relationship between these individuals develops some of these elements change and the behaviour which finally results will depend just as much on the context of the relationship (the situation) as on all these predispositions. The chapters by Katz and Watson, in this book, deal primarily with the effects of the situation on the interpersonal relationship, and so this chapter will deal mainly with the effects of these more 'internal' factors.

To begin with, let us look at the *sequence* of interpersonal behaviour between two people of different cultures. As an example I will use that of a European employer on a visit to the house of an employee of his belonging to the South Indian ethnic group called the Toda. What happens is that the Toda sees him coming, picks up his cooking utensils and leaves the house. How is this particular sequence of behaviour to be explained?

There is often a tendency to oversimplify explanations of the factors which determine sequences of behaviour such as the one just described. For example, one might say 'the Toda dislikes his boss' – but this does not explain why he took away his cooking utensils. And in fact, of course, the explanation of behaviour like this can be quite complex, and requires the use of several concepts. Psychology's contribution to ethnic or race relations consists of (a) the development of quantitative procedures for the measurement (so far as they apply to individuals) of many of these concepts, and (b) the development of a theory which shows not only how these concepts are related to each other, but also how they determine an individual's behaviour in an interpersonal situation.

This chapter starts with some definitions of the major concepts which are relevant to understanding the behaviour between individuals who are in ethnically heterogeneous situations. Then the relationships among these concepts is described. Finally, in the list of references, you will find details of publications which deal with the measurement of these concepts. Since the measurement aspect is technical it is unlikely to be of interest to the general reader, and so no further discussion of it is presented here.

Definitions

As this point some straightforward definitions may be useful. Firstly an *attitude*: this is an idea charged with emotion, predisposing an individual to action. The idea usually links two categories: for example, (my boss) is approaching (the house), in itself has no emotional implications, but some feeling is attached to each of the categories. In our example the Toda likes his boss, because the boss has always behaved well towards him. However, there is one thing about the boss which the Toda dislikes: the boss eats beef. This idea, which also involves the category 'boss' has a definite consequence in these particular circumstances – namely, the boss is not 'pure'. These circumstances and the overall culture from which they derive also provide a number of ideas about the transmission of purity and impurity, including the idea that impure cooking utensils transmit impurity. If the Toda were to eat with cooking utensils touched by the boss he would also become impure. So, the Toda is disposed in two ways towards his boss: on the one hand he would like to be with him; on the other, he does not want the boss to touch his cooking utensils.

In this example, the Toda's attitude or behavioural disposition towards his boss have been analysed, and we see several elements, not necessarily 'logically related'. The Toda feels ambivalent towards his boss. He feels good about the pay, and the fair and considerate treatment, but he feels bad about someone eating beef. In this particular case the net sum of all these emotions is positive, and the Toda likes his boss in spite of his eating habits. His attitude towards his boss, then, consists of three components: the *cognitive*, with all kinds of ideas involving the boss; the *affective*, which involves an emotion felt about the boss; and the *behavioural*, which involves a variety of ways of behaving towards the boss. Some of these elements are consistent among each other, but the total picture is complex and not entirely consistent.

The Toda's attitude towards his boss has just been described, but he also has *expectations* about interpersonal relations. These are ideas about behaviour and what the consequences of that behaviour might be. 'If I raise my voice, the boss will get mad', 'If I invite him into the house, he will come in'.

Another concept which has relevance for our analysis is *habit*. These are the bits of a particular individual's behaviour which recur. A person who usually takes off his hat when he sees an acquaintance does so not because he expects immediate rewards, or because he has particular attitudes, but out of habit, and probably without even thinking about his own behaviour.

Habits are closely related to *customs*, behaviour which is socially approved. *Norms* are beliefs that certain customs are desirable, or certain behaviour not desirable, and typically are stated in a 'should' or 'should not' form. They are closely related to *values*, states which we wish to achieve. In our Toda example, the value is purity. Purity is a state defined by the Toda culture as desirable, which has a variety of characteristics, tied by means of religious and other beliefs to other values. The culture also provides beliefs about impurity such as that it is caused by eating beef, and the relevant norm, then, is 'you must not eat beef'. This becomes a custom for a certain group so that most Todas do not eat beef, and it becomes a habit for the particular Toda in our example, so that he does not eat beef. We see, then, how a value is linked, through a network of beliefs, to norms, and how norms are represented in individuals as habits.

The final concept we need for our analysis of the interaction sequence between our Toda and our European is the concept of *role*. A role is a pattern of behaviour attached to a position in a social system. The employer–employee relationship, for example, includes a large number of appropriate ways of behaving, such as giving orders, paying and criticizing the work of the employee. The employee–employer relationship includes behaviour like asking for advice, obeying, receiving payment, accepting the criticism of the employer, and so on.

Returning now to the analysis of the interaction sequence. The Toda likes his boss, but does not like to have him touch his cooking utensils. He has long accepted the norm that he must not eat beef, but his boss breaks this norm and is therefore impure. The Toda does not want to be impure and if he removes his utensils from the house his boss will not be able to make him impure. The Toda knows of no custom concerning the visits of an employer to the house of an employee, only the role of employee, and that is to follow orders, to obey, to accept criticism, and so forth, but he does not know that this includes accepting a visit from his boss, although he is inclined to be friendly to him. His expectations, as well, incline him to be friendly, since this might determine whether or not he gets a raise and his solution is now predictable. Hastily, he removes the utensils, and hides them away from the house, and then quickly returns to greet his boss. In this way he has accomplished all that is consistent with his attitudes, norms, role, and expectations.

A more detailed analysis

While this explanation is adequate, it is in itself an oversimplification. To analyse social behaviour more completely we must consider not only how attitudes, norms, roles and values determine behaviour but also how these concepts are related to each other.

The European has a large number of visible characteristics – clothes, accent, rate and level of speech, type of hair, colour, and a large number of behaviour patterns (eating beef). A Toda will attend only to a fraction of all possible characteristics, but *infers* higher order characteristics (such as purity) from lower order characteristics (such as eating beef). People pay attention to those characteristics which are most uncommon, or most unusual and for the Toda, who is a non-beef eater, the European's eating behaviour is striking, different, noticeable. The higher order characteristics are organized into an 'implicit personality theory' that conforms to the theories of personality held by the Toda community. For example, being impure has implications about other kinds of higher order inferred characteristics.

The Toda also has some notion of what the average human and the ideal employer are like. His liking for the European depends on the extent to which he is similar to the average human and to the ideal employer. Naturally, the concept of the average human is greatly influenced by Toda culture. In fact, most people the Toda knows are other Todas, and he is quite likely to place his self concept rather near the concept of the average human. The result is that any deviation between the Toda's perception of the European and his perception of himself is a deviation between the perception of the European and his perception of the 'average human'. When the deviation is large the European will be seen as inhuman, sub-human, and consequently very 'bad'. Notice then, that *the perceived similarity between the Toda and the European is important in determining the Toda's liking of the European.*

The more the characteristics of the European differ from those of the average Toda the more the Toda's stereotype of the European reflects these characteristics (Campbell, 1967). In other words, the relationship between the perceived and inferred characteristics of the European *and* the Toda determine the cognitive and the affective component of the Toda's attitudes towards the European. What about the behavioural aspect of these attitudes? In part this is dependent on the other aspects of attitude, and in part on the Toda's norms and role perceptions. Clearly, his desire to avoid exposing the cooking utensils is related to his norms. Similarly, his willingness to obey the European, a behavioural predisposition, depends on his employee–employer role perceptions. Finally, the behavioural disposition to be friendly is in part dependent upon his expectations.

The Toda's behaviour towards the European is determined by all these influences. Specifically, we can predict his behaviour from his behavioural dispositions, habits, and expectations. We have then a network of influences on behaviour, which is represented in Figure 1.

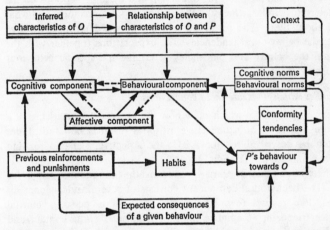

Figure 1 Hypothesized relationships between the variables discussed in this chapter

Current research has as yet not advanced enough to permit specification of the relative importance of each of these influences. However, the existing studies suggest that this framework adequately accounts for most observations. Research does suggest, however, that the relative importance of norms, habits, roles and attitudes depends on the situation, the particular behaviour and the personality of the individual. For example, norms determine behaviour in church much more than at a party; norms are more important for behaviours in formal settings than for other settings; they are more important for a behaviour such as *to marry* than for a behaviour such as *to admire the ideas of*; and some personality types, called authoritarian, give greater weight to norms than do other people.

One of the important points made by this diagram is that the social situation (the context) has a direct influence on the behavioural norms, and hence on the behavioural dispositions and the behaviour itself. The situation's influence on the behaviour is more direct than its influence on the cognitive and affective component of attitudes.

Summary of the relationships among the concepts

Each person has a large number of characteristics. Only a sample of these is perceived by others – those relevant to the cultures from which they come. Once the characteristics are perceived they become inferences about higher order traits (such as purity) and are organized into an implicit personality theory. The similarity between the perceiver's view of what is average and what is ideal, on the one hand, and these perceptions on the other, determines in large measure the way he understands them and what he feels about them. The roles and relevant norms determine, in large measure, the behavioural tendencies. The expectations together with the habits and the behavioural tendencies determine the specific behaviour that is observed.

Some studies which illustrate these connections

First we examine studies which show how the various characteristics of a person are related to someone else's attitudes towards him – attitudes which can be described by our ABC: the Affective, Behavioural and Cognitive components (Triandis, 1964).

The affective component primarily concerns the liking of one person for another. The behavioural component consists of several independent dimensions, like respect (e.g. admire the ideas of a person), marital acceptance, friendship acceptance, rejection from equal status contact, and superordination (e.g. criticize) vs subordination (e.g. obey). The cognitive component is the most complex: it involves a large number of personal characteristics.

Reviewing the responses of college students from several parts of the world (Triandis, 1967) it can be seen that *interpersonal liking* is most closely related to similarity in beliefs, high levels of linguistic skills (fluency) and grammatical accuracy. Similarity in race, religion and a high-level occupation are of lesser importance.

On the other hand, *marital acceptance* is much more strongly determined by similarity in race, age and religion, than by fluency, or a higher occupational level. *Friendship acceptance* is determined much like marital acceptance, but in some samples race and religion become less important in determining this acceptance. Rejection from contact with equals occurs in many parts of the world when the other person is of a different race or religion. Other factors, such as differences in beliefs, lack of fluency, and ungrammatical speech, may also contribute to this, but they are less important.

Turning now to the cognitive component, people see others as *strong*, *big* and *heavy* when those others are male, young, and have the same religion and occupational level as the person who is making the judgements. Similarly, people are seen as more *active* when they are young, male, and of high prestige than when they have the opposite attributes. However, in Japan there is an exception: there, high activity was related to low level occupations. It appears that the Japanese expect high status persons to move slowly and with 'appropriate dignity'.

There are, however, some studies which show different results for particular people. For example, similarity in race is very important in determining the marital acceptance of American white males and females, as well as for black females, but it is much less important for black males. The same religion is important for marital acceptance for American and Indian students, but of little consequence for Japanese students. A high level occupation is exceptionally important and leads to high acceptance for American black and for Japanese college females, but is less important for white American females.

These studies show that the interpersonal attitudes of different samples are dependent on different characteristics and reflect different emphases on these characteristics. For example, while for American students similarity in race and belief is emphasized when choosing friends, Greek students emphasize similarity in religion and occupational level, and German students similarity in occupational level. Japanese students emphasize both similarity in occupational level and race.

Finally, there is an abundance of studies which shows that sub-groups of people agree among themselves in attributing characteristics to members of different groups. For example, white American college students ascribe the characteristics 'slow-moving', 'athletic' and 'musical' more to blacks than to whites, and the characteristics 'political', 'self-satisfied', 'thrifty', 'nationalistic', 'conservative' and 'unreligious' more frequently to whites. High status persons are seen as having more of the characteristics of the white stereotype and low status persons more of the characteristics of the black stereotype. These results correctly describe *both* prejudiced and unprejudiced white students.

Similarity and interpersonal attitudes

One of the frequent results in the above-mentioned studies is the relevance of similarity in interpersonal perception. Some people – Rokeach is one – have argued that similarity in beliefs is most important in determining interpersonal attraction, and dissimilarity in beliefs the major factor in prejudice. This view is clearly inconsistent with 'common sense' notions, which, for example, hold that prejudice is due to a difference in race. Extensive tests of Rokeach's views have resulted in partial support for his views. These studies indicate that for extremely intimate behaviour, for which there are clear norms and a person can expect to receive pressure from others, the fact that a person has similar beliefs, though he is different in race, does not substantially reduce his rejection by prejudiced persons. On the other hand, for formal behaviour, such as inviting someone to dinner, similarity of beliefs is an important determining influence overriding race-based prejudice.

An illustrative experiment is one from a series done by Rokeach and Mezei (1966). The basic design involved a naïve person placed in a situation in which he interacted with four stooges (experimental confederates). Two of the stooges (one white, one black) agreed with the person and two (again one white, one black) disagreed. In one study the naïve person was asked to select two persons with whom to go to coffee, while the experimenter supposedly interviewed the other two. In another study, the naïve persons were applicants for various jobs in two mental hospitals. The stooges engaged them in a 'spontaneous' discussion that was arranged so that two (one white, one black) agreed and two (one white, one black) disagreed with them. After about ten minutes the experimenter returned and asked the applicants to write down the names of the two persons in the group with whom they would most prefer to work. In both types of study, Rokeach and Mezei found that the naïve persons chose the white and black stooges who agreed with them over all other possible combinations. In other words, there was no tendency to choose the two white stooges, but rather the choice was on the basis of similarity of beliefs. Of course, the kind of behaviour involved here is superficial and non-intimate, and therefore falls well within the generalizations that I set out in the previous paragraph.

While similarity in belief leads to attraction, similarity in status also leads to friendship. It has been shown (Triandis et al., 1966) that the greater the similarity in the status of two persons the more likely it is that they will want to develop a friendship. On the other hand, when it comes to respect, one study (of Greeks) found that the greater the status of the other person, the greater the respect, and the lesser the status of the person making the judgement the larger the respect. In other words, when low status persons make these judgements, the greater the dissimilarity in the status the greater the respect.

Attitude and behaviour

The theoretical system presented earlier suggests under what conditions attitudes will be related to behaviour; specifically, if the norms, habits and expectations are inconsistent with the attitudes, behaviour will not be related to attitudes. On the other hand when the norms, habits and expectations are experimentally controlled then attitudes will be related to behaviour. In some studies (e.g. Davis and Triandis, 1971) where such controls were possible, attitudes were, in fact, found to be correlated with behaviour. When there was inconsistency between attitudes and norms then behaviour was much more likely to be consistent with the norms than with the attitudes.

A study by Linn (1964–65) illustrates the latter point. He asked female students to respond, but only verbally, to a questionnaire which inquired about their readiness to pose with a black of the opposite sex for pictures that were to be used for different purposes, ranging from laboratory work to a nation-wide campaign for racial integration. Four weeks later the students were asked by a fictitious psychological testing company to volunteer to help develop a semi-projective personality test. During an interview with the representatives of this company the subjects were asked to pose for pictures with a black. Now the subjects actually had to *do* something. Linn found 50 per cent of his subjects gave verbal responses indicating extreme willingness to pose with a black, but when confronted with the actual possibility of doing this, only 24 per cent actually agreed to do so. After the experiment the students were asked to explain this discrepancy. Many indicated that they intellectually approved of the idea of posing with blacks but were concerned about the effects of this action on their parents, home-town friends and 'other people' in general. In other words, when attitudes and norms are inconsistent, behaviour tends to conform to norm prescriptions. These subjects had certain expectations about the consequences of their behaviour which were inconsistent with their attitudes, hence, the expectations controlled behaviour much more powerfully than the attitudes.

The theoretical framework set out in Figure 1 also reveals the importance of roles in determining behaviour. Roles are part of the social situation. The situation controls behaviour more definitely than it controls attitudes. In fact, attitudes often change to become consistent with the behaviour which has just taken place. In other words, attitudes are often caused by behaviour, rather than the other way around. This is a factor often used in law – race relations law included – and is particularly clear in studies by Marian Radke Yarrow (1958) in which several hundred pre-adolescents were assigned to cabins in a summer camp that were either racially integrated or segregated. Their behaviour showed very little difference in what they did in these two kinds of cabins. The summer camp *situation* determined most of the behaviour, and the interactions among the children were quite similar regardless of the nature of the camp. On the other hand, there was greater evidence of tension, such as attempts to leave the camp reported by both white and black youngsters in the integrated cabins than in the segregated cabins. The authors concluded that behaviour is more susceptible to situational influences than are cognitive or affective responses; and that the latter are more complexly determined. When placed in a situation having specific norms (set up by the management of the camp) the children behaved in a stable, unambiguous way and showed little confusion. But at the subjective level they appeared 'unsettled' by the new experience. Such observations are quite consistent with the framework which is summarized in Figure 1.

Individual differences in interpersonal attitudes

This framework, however complex, is oversimplified in that it does not incorporate any of the factors which separate prejudiced from unprejudiced individuals. It must be viewed as a general framework which is appropriate for most humans in most cultures. Before we complete this chapter then, we will take a brief look at the problem of individual differences in social perception, with particular reference to prejudice.

There is considerable evidence that certain kinds of child-rearing practices develop personalities which are more likely to show prejudiced behaviour (see Chapter 3 of this book). There is some evidence that fathers who are aloof, stern, and punitive, who administer physical punishment, and insist on a hierarchical family structure have children who are more likely to be prejudiced. These children tend to avoid introspection, reflection, and imaginative fantasy and are prone to believe in mystical determinants of an individual's fate. They tend to adopt extreme social attitudes not only with respect to minority groups, but also with respect to political parties, religious systems, and so on.

Important relationships between child-rearing patterns and different ideas of the nature of interpersonal relationships have also been found. Children reared in punitive, coercive families tend to think that behaving like this is the most effective way of regulating their interpersonal relationships. Bossy parents create an unpredictable world for their children, since the explanation of why something is good or bad lies within the parent rather than in external, analysable events. Such child-rearing leads to insecurity and anxiety so that under certain conditions the highly insecure are also most prejudiced.

When we look at the places around the world where there is much prejudice, we note that there is usually some advantage to be had by being prejudiced. For example, when one group exploits another, it can 'justify' its economic advantage by regarding the exploited group as inferior. 'These people cannot take care of themselves; I must lead them and charge a fee' being a typical view. Generally, the exploiting group develops strong norms that require all members of that group to conform to an appropriate pattern of behaviour and to adopt appropriate stereotypes which will justify the exploitation and minimize the contact between the two groups and the blurring of the distinctiveness of each group.

Insecure persons are particularly likely to conform to group norms, since rejection of such norms increases their insecurity. When norms of prejudice exist such people are most likely to conform. Of course, insecurity is not necessarily due to child-rearing practices. It might be the result of the influence of other factors, such as change in social class, which may result in unfamiliarity with and uneasiness in a new social environment. Or it might be caused by being at the bottom of a social hierarchy with no one to look down upon, a position which is also likely to be extremely frustrating, and hence lead, under certain conditions, to some aggression. If aggression against the sources of frustration is too costly (e.g. it may lead to severe punishment) the person might redirect his aggression to safer targets. One theory of prejudice holds that frustrated individuals, unable to aggress against their oppressors, direct their aggression to minority groups in the form of prejudice and rejection.

There is much experimental evidence to support some of these relationships. For example, the theory of authoritarianism developed by Adorno and his collaborators in the early 1950s has generated a vast volume of research demonstrating the kinds of relationships described above that are obtained between child-training and interpersonal attitudes. Much of this work can be criticized for a variety of technical reasons, but a balanced evaluation of it, such as that provided by Kirscht and Dillehay (1967), is on the whole favourable so far as the major arguments of the theory are concerned.

The economic determination of prejudice can be substantiated by looking at hard facts, such as Noel and Pinkney's (1964) study of prejudice in the American South. Their conclusion that 'the greater the probability of outgroup economic competition, the greater the probability of outgroup prejudice', seems well supported by their data.

Social structural determinants of interpersonal attitudes

This brief sketch of what determines interpersonal attitudes would be distorted without some reference to broader kinds of influences, such as the group's social structure. Most individuals belong to many groups, and feel loyalties to several. Anthropologists have described two kinds of structure where loyalty is concerned: the pyramidal-segmental and the cross-cutting (Le Vine, 1965). In the first, the individual belongs to different 'alliances' depending on the 'level of conflict'. For example, in Bedouin society conflict may exist between brothers who would, however, combine to fight against cousins who would in turn combine against more distant relatives, and so on. The larger the scale of conflict, the larger the size of the alliance, so that the conflict occurs between groups of approximately equal power. This is an example of the pyramidal-segmental type of social organization.

The cross-cutting type of organization is characteristic of those societies in which a person has loyalties to relatives who are dispersed throughout the society. For example, among some African tribes, such as the Kipsigis, this is the typical organization. The interpersonal attitudes of people in these two kinds of societies are quite different. In the first kind they see outgroups as hostile, threatening, powerful and they tend to act defensively and cautiously. There is much internal fighting, suspicion, and interpersonal hostility within the tribe. In the second type there is little internal fighting, people are sociable, cooperative and show little aggression within the tribe, but in war they are offensive. The second type of social organization apparently leads to a view of outgroups as weak, inferior, dishonourable, and inviting plunder. In other words, the type of social organization determines the perspective of individuals with regard to outgroups and the nature of their interpersonal attitudes with people from other ethnic groups.

General overview

This chapter began with an example of an interpersonal encounter involving people from two cultures. This showed that a complete understanding of an episode like that requires some knowledge of three aspects of interpersonal attitudes – cognitive, affective and behavioural – as well as an understanding of the expectations, habits, norms, roles and values of the two individuals involved. The way some of these variables are related to each other was also shown and how jointly they determine interpersonal behaviour. Figure 1 depicted some of these relationships diagrammatically.

The sketch did emphasize the importance of cultural similarity as a determinant of interpersonal liking. It also showed how various beliefs are related to norms, how norms are related to customs, how customs are related to habits, and how all of these are related to values.

A small sample of empirical studies was then reviewed. This sample showed that certain personal characteristics elicit particular attitudes but there are many exceptions to the stated generalizations. The problem of the relationship of attitude and behaviour was discussed at some length, and studies which clarify this relationship were reviewed. Child-training and societal influences upon interpersonal attitudes were then illustrated with a few studies.

The network of relationships shown in Figure 1 is by no means complete. For example, the 'context' of behaviour exerts a large influence on interpersonal attitudes and has not yet been discussed.

The interpersonal attitudes of a particular individual will reflect also his childhood experiences, what he heard from the mass media, what he was told by his ingroup, and what he experienced in face-to-face encounters with members of other groups. Perhaps the most important force is one of conformity to the views of his own ingroup.

An analysis of a riot

Another example of the interrelations of the framework presented so far will be useful here now that the framework has been described.

The context: a policeman killed a black youth who was looting a store, in a black American ghetto (see Bloombaum, 1968). The black youths of the neighbourhood perceived the event as follows: 'here is somebody who is very different from me, killing somebody very much like me'. The inferred characteristics of the aggressor can only be extremely unfavourable, while those of the victim are distorted so that the looting behaviour is seen as a 'background' and the good characteristics of the victim, true or hypothesized, are seen as the 'figure'. At this point, the cognitive component with respect to the police is most unfavourable, and this generalizes to all those who are like a policeman, for example, white, and all those who like and help policemen, in this case, for example black merchants in the particular neighbourhood. The affective component is intensely negative, both because of its consistency to the cognitive and because the negative affect is generated by fear that something similar will happen to oneself. The behavioural component is under the influence of several kinds of norms: the person's immediate ingroup is ready for blood; the more remote ingroup, the black community, is vaguely sympathetic, and the norms related to revenge are extremely appealing. However, previous reinforcements and punishments suggest caution. Perhaps it is possible to live with the system, perhaps the system is not all bad. Furthermore, previous habits militate against action – one has little experience with riots. Moreover, the expected consequences of the behaviour are clearly going to be unpleasant – perhaps death. The system then is now in tension. The behavioural component of attitudes predisposes an explosion; the habits, and expected consequences of the behaviour inhibit this explosion. At this point some member of the gang acts. Our hero is now confronted with a different context. His conformity tendencies accentuate his willingness to yield to the group's behavioural norms. Furthermore, he is under the influence of other norms which state that 'you must help your ingroup in reaching its goals'. Finally, as tension increases his cognitive field is constricted, and his habits and the expected consequences become less important and his own attitude more significant. So the youth makes a bomb and throws it at his neighbourhood store (owned by a black merchant).

The action is symbolic, in part, of his hatred for the whole 'system', which did much to make him the way he is. By segregating him from the major segment of society it created a consciousness of ingroup; by exploiting him economically, and by refusing to give him dignity it has fostered a self-image which is compatible with that of the bomb-thrower. The system did not reinforce behaviour incompatible with bomb-throwing, such as constructive participation in the building of a better environment. Nor did the system make the expected consequences of the behaviour completely unthinkable – i.e. death was relatively remote.

This is a barely adequate description of a very complex human encounter. But it illustrates how the variables of Figure 1 operate. It also tells us something about what we can do, as citizens, to change the conditions that lead to such events. The choice is between changing the conditions that lead to the interpersonal attitudes of the blacks or creating a different society where the habits and consequences of behaviour can be different. For example, a repressive society which makes the consequences of the behaviour very serious, e.g. certain death, might avoid such behaviour. But at what price?

References

ADORNO, T. W., FRENKEL-BRUNSWIK, E., LEVINSON, D. J., and SANFORD, R. N. (1950), *The Authoritarian Personality*, Harper & Row.

BLOOMBAUM, M. (1968), 'The conditions underlying race riots as portrayed by multidimensional scalogram analysis: a re-analysis of Lieberson and Silverman's data', *American Sociological Review*, vol. 33, pp. 76–91.

CAMPBELL, D. T. (1967), 'Stereotypes and the perception of group differences', *American Psychologist*, vol. 22, pp. 817–29.

DAVIS, E. E. and TRIANDIS, H. C. (1971), 'An experimental study of black-white negotiations', *Journal of Applied Social Psychology*, vol. 1, pp. 240–62.

EDWARDS, A. L. (1957), *Techniques of Attitude-Scale Construction*, Appleton-Century-Crofts.

KIRSCHT, J. P., and DILLEHAY, R. C. (1967), *Dimensions of Authoritarianism*, University of Kentucky Press.

LE VINE, R. A. (1965), 'Socialization, social structure and inter-societal images', in H. Kelman (ed.), *International Behaviour: A Social Psychological Analysis*, Holt, Rinehart & Winston, pp. 66–126.

LINN, L. S. (1964–65), 'Verbal attitudes and overt behaviour: a study of racial discrimination', *Social Forces*, vol. 43, pp. 353–64.

NOEL, D. L., and PINKNEY, A. (1964), 'Correlates of prejudice: some racial differences & similarities', *American Journal of Sociology*, vol. 69, pp. 609–22.

ROKEACH, M., and MEZEI, L. (1966), 'Race and shared belief as factors in social choice', *Science*, vol. 151, pp. 167–72.

TRIANDIS, H. C. (1964), 'Exploratory factor analysis of the behavioural component of social attitudes', *Journal of Abnormal and Social Psychology*, vol. 68, pp. 420–30.

TRIANDIS, H. C. (1967), 'Towards an analysis of the components of interpersonal attitudes', in C. W. Sherif and M. Sherif (eds.), *Attitudes, Ego-Involvement and Change*, Wiley, pp. 227–70.

TRIANDIS, H. C., VASSILIOU, V., and NASSIAKOU, M. (1968), 'Three cross-cultural studies of subjective culture', *Journal of Personality and Social Psychology*, vol. 8, no. 4, part 2, pp. 1–42.

TRIANDIS, H. C., VASSILIOU, V., and THOMANEK, E. K. (1966), 'Social status as a determinant of social acceptance and friendship acceptance', *Sociometry*, vol. 29, pp. 396–405.

YARROW, M. R. (1958), 'Interpersonal dynamics in a desegregation process', *Journal of Social Issues*, vol. 14, pp. 1–63.

Chapter 11
Negro Performance in Interracial Situations

Irwin Katz

Irwin Katz is the author of over fifty articles and reviews on social psychology and race relations. He has been a consultant to the United States Commission on Civil Rights and the United States Office of Education. His publications include, *Social Class, Race and Psychological Development* and *Race and the Social Sciences.* Prior to his present job at the City University of New York he was a professor of psychology and a research psychologist of the Center for Research on Conflict Resolution at the University of Michigan.

Interracial situations

Despite strong resistance by whites to Negro demands for equal rights, it is clear that the basic trend in (American) race relations is towards the elimination of discriminatory practices. Employment opportunities for nonwhite minority groups will no doubt continue to expand in commerce, industry, and the professions, as well as in government service. However, as Negroes are integrated into the American system they will increasingly have to perform complex tasks in situations of face-to-face interaction, and comparison, with whites. To a significant extent, the upward mobility of blacks will depend upon their ability to function effectively in these racially mixed settings. This is important because of the strong influence, both favourable and detrimental, that such face-to-face situations have been shown to have on Negro performance. In the field of education, for example, recent research suggests that Negro pupils learn better, on the whole, when a majority of their classmates is white rather than black, (Coleman *et al.*, 1966), though the achievement of Negroes shows more variability in the predominantly white classroom. When different desegregated schools are compared, the academic achievement of black pupils is found to be related to what has been called the *quality of the interracial social climate*, as indicated by teachers' reports of interracial tension. In schools where most teachers report no tension, Negro students are more proficient, more interested in attending college, and more optimistic about being rewarded for their efforts to learn.

Such results, being merely correlational, do not really demonstrate causal relationships between particular types of biracial situation and

Negro performance. But they do indicate the desirability of studying in greater detail the psychological processes that operate in these situations. Useful information can be obtained from studies of a person's reactions under controlled, laboratory-like conditions.

Psychological analysis of interracial performance settings

In order to clarify the effects upon behaviour of various types of interracial achievement situation, some colleagues and I began several years ago a programme of research that is still in progress. Most of the research has been done on male college students, but the main findings do have implications for other age groups as well.

Factors which may have a detrimental effect

The first discovery was that situations in which Negroes and whites came face to face can have detrimental effects upon the intellectual performance of Negro youths. For example, in two early studies conducted at an urban university in the north, various mental and physical tasks were allocated to work groups made up of two black and two white students all of whom initially were total strangers. (Katz *et al.* 1958; Katz *et al.*, 1960). In general, Negroes displayed marked social inhibition and subordination to their white partners. When groups were engaged in problem solving which necessitated cooperation between all the members for success the Negroes made fewer proposals than did whites, and tended to accept the whites' contributions uncritically. On all the tasks blacks made fewer remarks than did whites, and spoke more to whites, than they did to one another. The whites, on the other hand, spoke more to one another, than they did to the Negroes. This behaviour occurred even when group members could expect a financial bonus for good teamwork, and were informed that their abilities were higher than those of people in other groups.

In the second experiment, special efforts were made to increase the self-confidence of the Negroes. Black and white team-mates were matched on intelligence by means of individual testing beforehand and then were told that they had ability equal to that of their partners. In addition, they were 'made' to display apparently equal ability on certain mental tasks that were given in the group situation, through secret manipulation. Despite these procedures the Negro subjects later still revealed feelings of inferiority and anxiety. On a questionnaire given afterwards they ascribed higher ability to whites on the very tasks that had been rigged to ensure equal performance and expressed relatively low satisfaction with the group experience.

That this type of face-to-face racial situation produced genuine impairment of intellectual functioning in the Negro students, rather than just an inhibition of outward high visible behaviour, is apparent from another study carried out at the same college, (Katz and Cohen, 1962). This time, pairs of subjects composed of one Negro and one white were given a series of mental problems to solve cooperatively. However, before discussing each problem the men had to record privately their individual solutions. *Negroes made more errors than they had made on the same problems at a prior, individual testing session. White subjects, on the other hand, made fewer private errors than they had made previously.*

In another study, conducted in the South, individual black students from a predominantly Negro college were told that they would receive a painful stimulus (electric shock) while working on a task in which they had to learn a code (Katz and Greenbaum, 1963). The performance of those who worked in the presence of a white experimenter and a white 'fellow subject' was more adversely affected by the shock instructions than was the performance of those who worked in the presence of a black experimenter and a black 'fellow subject'. Apparently, feelings of insecurity at being alone in a strange white environment made the Negro students highly vulnerable to the additional stress presented by the threats of electric shock (which in fact was never given).

These experiments suggest three factors that may affect Negro students in a way which hampers their performance when they are face-to-face with whites. First, it can be assumed that novel types of contact with white strangers possess a *social threat* component. Negroes may be fearful of arousing white hostility by being assertive or displaying intellectual competence. The amount of social threat should be a direct function of (a) the amount of evidence of hostility from whites (or the extent to which evidence of white friendliness is lacking) and (b) the amount of power possessed by whites in the actual confrontation, as stemming, for example, from numerical predominance, control of authority positions, and so on. Note that in all of the experiments described (except the one that used electric shock instructions), white subjects tended to ignore their Negro partners, the institutional setting was a predominantly white college, and the experimenters were white faculty members.

It seems likely that Negroes would be under some degree of social threat in a school or job which has just been integrated – or made multiracial. Cold indifference on the part of white school or work mates could frustrate their needs for companionship and approval, which would result in lowered self-esteem and a wish to escape from an unpleasant environment. In this way a Negro pupil or worker would be distracted from the task he was supposed to do, and this would adversely affect his performance.

An example of how the presence of white adult strangers can seriously disrupt verbal learning in young Negro children is provided by an experiment carried out in a Negro area of a large city (Katz *et al.*, 1968). Negro boys of average age eight were tested individually by either Negro or white adult males. Their task was to learn a list of paired words – that is, to learn which word of one list went with that of the other list. Irrespective of how well they actually did on the task, half of them periodically were told they were doing well and the other half just as often were told they were not. The results were clear-cut: for each type of examiner, approval – being told they were doing well – produced better learning than disapproval, but regardless of type of feedback – approval or disapproval – children learned better when tested by Negroes than by whites. The poorest learners were boys with a high need for approval, as measured by a personality test, and who were told by the white tester that they weren't doing well. In short, the white adults' expressions of approval had relatively little effect on the boys' performance whereas their disapproval was sometimes highly disruptive.

Apparently, black pupils in segregated schools seem to react anxiously to white strangers who are seen as figures of authority. However, it is entirely possible that a relatively brief period of friendly acquaintance would dispel these apprehensions of the Negro pupil. The previous experiment did not explore that possibility. It is also noteworthy that the adults in the experiment were male. When a similar study (as yet unpublished) was carried out with female examiners, there were no differences in learning due to the race of the adults. That white males had an adverse effect, but non white females, can perhaps be explained in terms of relative strangeness – the children who were tested had had one or more white female teachers but no white male teachers and so were less familiar with the latter.

Another factor that could detrimentally affect black students' performance in face-to-face racial situations is low *expectancy of success* in competition with white standards. The Negroes in our studies may have lacked motivation to engage in the experimental tasks for this reason. The experiments indicate that the Negro's low expectancy of success may result from feelings of inferiority that have no basis in reality, but probably reflect an emotional reaction to the demeaning role in American society that has been imposed upon his racial group by the dominant white majority. However, because of the lower achievement standards and inferior educational services that often mark the predominantly Negro school, low expectations of success on the part of recently desegregated minority group pupils may well be quite realistic. When the black transferee enters a school that has substantially higher standards than he knew previously he may become discouraged and therefore not try to succeed. The same process could operate with Negro adults who enter integrated job settings for the first time.

As a third type of detrimental influence, the Negro college students in our experiments may have anxiously anticipated disapproval, disparagement or rejection by their white partners and the white experimenter as a consequence of poor performance. This factor can be called *failure threat*. A high expectation of failure at a task does not by itself constitute failure threat – it is necessary also that the failure have a social meaning which is harmful: for example, academic failure, at whatever stage in school, often results in strong disapproval by parents, teachers and perhaps classmates.

To diminish the adverse influence of the three factors that have been mentioned – social threat, low expectation of success and failure threat – Negroes should, at least in fields of life which are important from a career point of view, participate in integrated situations – schools, jobs and so on – as early in life as possible. This conclusion is supported by findings in studies of desegregated schools: the earlier the age at which Negro pupils first enter racially mixed classes, the better their academic achievement, irrespective of their ability (Coleman, *et al.*, 1966).

Returning to the experiments mentioned previously, it follows from the foregoing analysis that if Negroes could be made to perceive intellectual competition with whites as neither threatening socially nor hopelessly difficult, their performance should improve markedly. To test this proposition, Negro undergraduates were placed in another problem-solving situation which was secretly controlled (Katz and Cohen, 1962). They were given instructions which, in effect, *forced them to disagree openly* with a white partner while at the same time showing ability equal to that of the partner. As a result of this experience, the black students were able to function more effectively and autonomously when they later worked on another, unrigged task with the same white person. This study demonstrated that in face-to-face interracial situations, Negro inhibition could be removed quite readily through an appropriate type of training.

Factors which improve Negro performance

More important, in a later phase of the research programme it was found that, under certain conditions, face-to-face racial situations can actually have a beneficial effect upon black intellectual achievement. It was discovered that *with factors which aroused anxiety minimized by experimental manipulation, Negroes performed better when anticipating comparison with whites, or evaluation by white authorities, than they performed in settings which were all Negro.*

Four types of experiment have thus far been done. In the first type the anxiety of Negroes was diminished by presenting a 'code' task with instructions that emphasized its lack of real-life significance. Two such experiments were carried out at a Negro college known for its high academic quality. The first used instructions which stated: 'This is not a test of any kind. Your scores will not be shown to anyone at your college, and you will not be compared with other students'. Subjects worked at the task in two racial settings. One featured another Negro who posed as a second subject, and a Negro experimenter who introduced himself as a psychologist. In the other condition these two roles were filled by whites. In white company, it was found, there were higher scores on the 'code' task (Katz and Greenbaum, 1963). The second study was similar to the one just described, except that subjects worked individually with no other subject present. Again, coding performance was higher with a white tester than it was with a Negro tester (Katz *et al.*, 1965).

To account for this beneficial effect of the white adult, it was assumed that he was perceived by black subjects as a more powerful and prestigious figure than the Negro examiner. (Whites, after all, are the economic gate-keepers in American society). Therefore, the prospect of getting approval from whites had *high positive incentive value*, while the prospect of getting disapproval from whites had *high negative incentive value*. Since the task was explicitly defined as not being important academically, etc, the subjects were not unduly fearful of doing poorly, and could therefore strive to make a favourable impression on the white authority figure. That Negro students view white experimenters as more powerful evaluators than Negro experimenters was confirmed in a subsequent (unpublished) study elsewhere in which subjects rated the white experimenters as being not only more competent but more important too.

In another type of experiment, such tasks as code, arithmetic and scrambled words were presented to students (at predominantly Negro colleges) as tests of intelligence. The instructions typically read: 'This test is part of a new scholastic aptitude examination that all students will take. It will be used to evaluate your intellectual ability. Your score will be used in advising you about your academic and professional potentialities . . .' In addition, subjects were informed either that their scores would be compared with norms for students at their own, predominantly Negro college (Negro comparison), or with norms for all college students throughout the state (white comparison). Finally, to allay anxiety the tester was always a Negro.

Five experiments of this type were done, involving four colleges. Two of these were in the Deep South and at the time of testing had relatively low standards. Subjects at these colleges achieved higher scores when, because of the instructions they were given, they expected to be compared with other Negroes (Katz *et al.*, 1964). The three other experiments used one of the same Deep South colleges after a new, selective admissions policy had been introduced, as well as two non-selective, state-supported institutions in the Upper South and North respectively. Better performance was obtained with these students when they were told they were being compared with predominantly white groups. In sum, when tested by a Negro, and not placed in face-to-face confrontation with whites, students in Negro colleges of moderate academic quality were favourably motivated by the challenge of comparison with whites, whereas students in institutions of relatively low quality worked better in competition with Negro norms (Epps *et al.*, 1971; Katz *et al.*, 1972).

My interpretation of the foregoing results is that, except in the most depressed types of segregated learning environment, such as in Deep South non-selective colleges, the opportunity for comparison with whites is highly stimulating, since it provides the Negro with more useful information for self-evaluation than does comparison with other Negroes. This is so because, in general, white intellectual standards are more relevant to future career prospects. *We can say then that comparisons with white norms are beneficial because of their better informational value.* By using only Negro testers in these experiments this effect was not offset by subjects' fears of eliciting white disapproval if they failed to meet what was for them a difficult standard.

The outcome of the comparison experiments is all the more remarkable when one notes that most of the subjects, being southern, had never sat in a classroom in which there were both Negroes and whites throughout more than twelve years of schooling. The beneficial effect of crossracial comparison should, if anything, be even greater for younger Negroes who are probably aware of the significance of white achievement standards, but have had less time to fall behind them (due to the social factors associated with segregated schools). This generalization is consistent with what is known about the superior attainment of Negro pupils who enter desegregated classes at an early age.

Consider now a third type of experimental demonstration of the beneficial effect of face-to-face racial confrontations upon the achievement of Negroes. Again, simple mental tasks requiring speed and accuracy were used in conjunction with intelligence-test instructions. But now, the race of the tester was varied, while the race of ostensible comparisons was either varied or held constant by means of suitable instructions. To maximize the social effect of the experimenter, the subjects in their first year of university were told that immediately after completion of the testing the experimenter would see each of them privately, score his work, and explain what the score meant with regard to prospects of future academic and vocational success.

As the theory would predict, in the presence of a white examiner the subjects performed better than in the presence of a Negro examiner when they were being compared with Negroes (that is, a relatively easy standard);

and they performed better with the Negro examiner than with the white examiner when told they were being compared with whites (that is, a relatively hard standard). *The poorest performance was obtained by a combination of Negro tester and instructions indicating comparison with other Negroes.* To review the principles upheld by the results: when there was no anxious anticipation of possible face-to-face criticism by a white authority figure, the riskier but also more informative white comparison standard was preferred by the Negro subjects. On the other hand, when white evaluation *was* expected, the less informative but also less risky Negro-peer comparison standard was preferred (Katz *et al.*, 1972).

It would of course be fallacious to make a literal application of these findings to the desegregated classroom – that is, to conclude that Negro pupils should not have both white teachers and predominantly white classmates at the same time. What the study suggests, though, is that even when performance possesses strong evalutive significance both crossracial comparisons and crossracial evaluations can improve Negro motivation, *provided that threatening features of the situation are kept at a minimum.* Here emotional supportiveness on the part of teachers would be of critical importance, both in its direct significance to Negro children, and in its influence upon the social reactions of their classmates.

The findings of another experiment of the type just described are relevant here, too. This differed from its predecessor, however, in two ways: it was conducted at a Negro college with relatively high standards of admission, and all subjects were told they would be evaluated against the norms of white contemporaries. Now, even though only the crossracial comparison was used, higher test scores were attained with a white examiner than with a black examiner. Apparently, for the *able* Negro students who had been accepted into this college, meeting a white standard of competence did not seem so difficult as to dampen their desire for evaluation by a white authority figure (Katz *et al.*, 1970).

Finally a fourth type of research was done on the factors that produce optimal achievement in face-to-face racial situations. Its special feature is the experimental manipulation of subjects' expectations of success on a test of intellectual ability, accomplished by giving them different types of information – ostensibly based upon their scores from prior administration of the same test. Three groups of subjects at a non-selective black college were told, respectively, that they had little chance, a moderately good chance, or a very good chance of equalling the norms for their age groups. It was found that with white-norm instructions, low expectancy of success was highly detrimental to performance, while with Negro-norm instructions the low-probability feedback did not impair motivation. Both norm groups had sharply higher test scores, and the difference between them tended to disappear, when expectancy of success was high. *The results suggest that in interracial competition, Negroes can be readily discouraged by unfavourable feedback, but can also be highly responsive to favourable prospects for success* (Katz *et al.*, 1972).

Summary – Five-factor model

To recapitulate, research on minority group youths and children is on the whole consistent with a five-factor model of Negro achievement in interracial educational settings. On the negative side of the ledger are the following:

Social threat. Given the prestige and power of the white majority group, rejection of Negroes by white contemporaries or authorities should tend to elicit emotional responses (fear, anger and humiliation) that are detrimental to intellectual functioning.

Low probability of success. Where there is marked discrepancy in the performance standards of Negro and white schools or job situations, or where feelings of inferiority are acquired by Negroes outside the school or job, minority-group newcomers in integrated environments are likely to have a low expectancy of success; consequently their motivation to do well should be low.

Failure threat. When failure entails disapproval by significant others, low expectancy of success should elicit emotional responses that are detrimental to performance.

On the positive side are these factors:
In an atmosphere of social acceptance Negroes will desire to compare their own ability with that of whites because of the *high informational value* of such interracial comparisons for self-evaluation, and the *high incentive value* of receiving favourable evaluation from whites. The experiments indicate that *provided* the strength of the negative factors is kept low, Negro achievement on simple cognitive tasks is better in racially-mixed situations than in all-black situations.

The low-achieving Negro student

One might be tempted to conclude from the evidence just presented that school desegregation benefits only the more capable Negro. But according to an analysis by the United States Commission on Civil Rights the apparent gain in achievement-test scores associated with racially balanced schooling is roughly as large for Negroes of low ability as for those of medium and high ability. Why is it that low ability children give no indication of being demoralized by the large achievement gap between themselves and their white classmates? The answer to the question is perhaps suggested by the results of research recently conducted by some colleagues and myself in an all-Negro elementary school in the North (Katz *et al.*, 1968). Boys of mediocre ability (and this included most of the boys in the school) tended to be unduly self-critical of their work, even when they were not being observed by teachers. In contrast, the superior students were more readily satisfied by their private efforts. The low-achieving students were also highly anxious about their school work in general. It was as though these overly self-critical, segregated children had accepted a grossly exaggerated conception of their inferiority as Negroes (and see Chapter 7 of this book).

The commission's data on achievement suggest that having an opportunity to compare themselves with white peers would have a corrective influence on the self-evaluations of these Negro children, thereby improving their will to learn. Acquiring relatively realistic perceptions of his own ability relative to classmates of high proficiency need not produce discouragement in the disadvantaged pupil – indeed, it may have the opposite effect – *provided* the child has a secure awareness of opportunities for social and material reward commensurate with his own efforts and capabilities.

References

COLEMAN, J. S., *et al.* (1966), *Equality of Educational Opportunity*, United States Department of Health, Education and Welfare, US Government Printing Office.

EPPS, E. G., KATZ, I., PERRY, A., and RUNYON, E. (1971), 'Effect of race of comparision referent and motives on Negro cognitive performance', *Journal of Educational Psychology*, vol. 2, pp. 201–8.

KATZ, I. (1964), 'Review of evidence relating to effects of desegregation on the intellectual performance of Negroes', *American Psychologist*, vol. 19, pp. 381–99.

KATZ, I., GOLDSTON, J., and BENJAMIN, L. (1958), 'Behavior and productivity in biracial work groups', *Human Relations*, vol. 11, pp. 123–41.

KATZ, I., and BENJAMIN, L. (1960), 'Effects of white authoritarianism in biracial work groups', *Journal of Abnormal and Social Psychology*, vol. 61, pp. 448–56.

KATZ, I., and COHEN, M. (1962), 'Effects of variations in assertiveness of Negroes on interaction with whites', *Journal of Abnormal and Social Psychology*, vol. 64, pp. 319–25.

KATZ, I., and GREENBAUM, C. (1963), 'Effects of anxiety, threat, and racial environment on task performance of Negro college students', *Journal of Abnormal and Social Psychology*, vol. 66, pp. 562–7.

KATZ, I., HENCHY, T., and ALLEN, H. (1968), 'Effects of race of tester, approval–disapproval, and need on Negro children's learning', *Journal of Personality and Social Psychology*, vol. 8, pp. 38–42.

KATZ, I., EPPS, E. G., and AXELSON, L. J. (1964), 'Effects upon Negro digitsymbol performance of anticipated comparison with whites and with other Negroes', *Journal of Abnormal and Social Psychology*, vol. 69, pp. 77–83.

KATZ, I., ROBERTS, S. O., and ROBINSON, J. M. (1965), 'Effects of task difficulty, race of administrator, and instructions on digit-symbol performance of Negroes', *Journal of Personality and Social Psychology*, vol. 2, pp. 53–9.

KATZ, I., ATCHISON, C. O., EPPS, E. G., and ROBERTS, S. O. (1972), 'Race of evaluator, race of norm, and expectancy as determinants of black performance', *Journal of Experimental Social Psychology*, vol. 8, pp. 1–15.

KATZ, I., ATCHISON, C. O., EPPS, E. G., and PERRY, A. (1970), 'Factors affecting response to white intellectual standards at two Negro colleges,' *Psychological Reports*, vol. 27, pp. 995–1003.

KATZ, I. (1967), 'The socialization of academic motivation in minority group children', in D. Levine (ed.), *Nebraska Symposium on Motivation*, Lincoln, Nebraska, University of Nebraska Press, pp. 133–91.

UNITED STATES COMMISSION ON CIVIL RIGHTS (1967), *Racial Isolation in the Public Schools*, vols. 1 and 2, US Government Printing Office.

Chapter 12
Some Mechanics of Racial Etiquette

Peter Watson

Peter Watson is twenty-nine and was educated at the universities of
Durham, London and Rome. After postgraduate work, he was a member
of the clinical staff at the Tavistock Clinic before going to the Institute of
Race Relations to carry out research into the intellectual development of
immigrant children and to found and edit the institute's monthly, *Race
Today*. He then joined *New Society* where he became Associate Editor. He
now writes on the social services for the London *Sunday Times*, but still
finds time to carry out a certain amount of psychological research.

Negro lawyers in the United States sometimes get white clients – when
those clients are entangled in proceedings which they feel might shame
them in front of a white lawyer. Also in America, in some southern
states, whites will be addressed by Negroes using their first names – just so
long as no other white is around; when whites return, so does the 'mister-
ing' (Goffman, 1968). Latin Americans, who customarily talk to each
other with their heads only a few inches apart, have been known to climb
over chairs, typewriters and the office flowers to speak in this way to the
American or British businessman firmly barricaded behind his desk.

Anecdotes like these, of what could be called racial etiquette, often show
a psychological sensitivity that more rigorous and formal studies cannot
match. No one has tried to organize them into a complete picture and no
overall theories as yet exist (and insofar as part of their impact comes from
their idiosyncratic nature they may be better left without a theoretical
basis.) They do, however, serve to highlight fresh areas of study and, in
some cases where professional 'etiquette' is concerned, it may indeed be
possible to piece the details together into a plausible theory that has practical implications.

That such details can be important at least one government has no
doubt. The US Foreign Service, a few years ago, enlisted the expertise of
social psychologists and anthropologists as aides to help people going
abroad in the Service to better understand the different manners in different cultures, the unconscious ways in which people of different backgrounds may offend one another. These aides would teach the different
conceptions of courtesy in, say, the Middle East, India or Latin America:

they would show, for example, how – to an Arab – fifteen minutes is roughly the psychological equivalent of five minutes to an American, so that for an Arab to turn up twenty-five minutes late for an appointment is not insulting: in his time scale the Arab will be the equivalent of what to the Westerner is just under ten minutes late.

Now, with different races in the same country these matters can be more important because less allowance for them is usually made, the offences occurring more unconsciously and so possibly, in the long run, more hurtful because of that.

Remembering that such behaviour can be more or less conscious, it can also be divided into that which occurs in the 'private' world of one group and that which either occurs in the 'public' world of in interaction or is changed by the presence of someone from a different race. As we shall see, these two may interact themselves in some professional situations at least, setting up a vicious circle.

Let's start with jokes: not only because they're funny but because they fall into both categories, public and private. Everyone knows racial jokes – normally they are within-group phenomena: occasionally, however, they cross the races, like the coloured comedians in the north of England, who perform mainly in front of white audiences, often exploiting their colour in the manner of the black Bradfordian who cautions his audience that unless they laugh at his jokes he'll come up and move in next door.

The reaction of a racial group to jokes disparaging of itself has been found to vary from group to group – between, for example, Jews and Negroes. Wolff *et al.* (1934) found that Jews and Gentiles both thought anti-semitic jokes less funny than a sample of non-racial jokes, but Jews were less favourable than Gentiles to the anti-semitic jokes. That you might expect – except that Middleton and Molard (1959a and b) found the opposite with Negroes and whites in a similar experiment. At least some of the Negroes reacted *more* favourably to anti-Negro jokes than whites, presumably, as he said, due to guilt among the whites. So jokes are probably better as a barometer of interracial feeling – showing what things are currently seen, by both groups, as personally important – than as a specific technique in reducing racial conflict as Burma (1946) maintains.

Outside jokes, language can be equally revealing, as we must all be aware. How many times, almost without thinking, for example, do whites slide in and out of the words 'Negro' and 'nigger', according to circumstance? Similarly with the Negro's use of 'ofay'. But more revealing is the various private languages that some groups make use of. Clarence Major analyses, in his book *Black Slang*, a host of words and phrases of the American Negro – words like, 'attic' for head, 'bubble dancing' for washing up, or 'Brown Abe' for a penny. The world they reveal cannot, of course, be summed up entirely in sociologese, but taking the whole dictionary, Major says that what they most describe is a 'sinner-man-black' syndrome, the 'Br'er rabbit' reaction. (Br'er rabbit, a central figure in African folk tales, is a trickster always able to survive the threats of far larger animals.)

Hartman (1971), too, has shown how language, for some Negroes, may change as the interracial climate changes. Not only is there the slang I've just mentioned but private meanings are also given to 'white' words, even by educated Negroes. 'Boss' may mean employer to the whites – but almost the opposite to Negroes – 'wonderful'. Hawk is a bird to whites, to blacks 'cold, windy weather'. But for some educational progress may mean adopting idiosyncratic word usage – the verbal equivalent of 'passing' – someway between Negro dialect and white; this may occasionally creep over into language problems even connected with speech or clumsy sentence constructions.

Beyond this, Levitt and Abner (1971) showed that there are, in any case, more idiosyncratic differences with ordinary words between races than you might think. Using the semantic differential technique, they found that, surprisingly, words like 'money' or 'work' did not differ between races but that 'father', 'TV', 'police', and 'next year' did. It was also interesting to see that blacks could understand other blacks' concepts less well than whites could understand other whites'; on the other hand, blacks understood whites' concepts better than whites understood blacks'.

Consumption behaviour is a newish field of study, one yet to be developed in studying interracial behaviour. But buying patterns of racial products, for example, racial cosmetics, skin whitener or hair straightener, would speak louder than any questionnaire. So does the Negro version of that consumption boom, Christmas – a black Christmas, of course, with a 'St Trick' in place of St Nick. (And, in 1969, when St Trick was given most publicity, it was followed at New Year with the equivalent for that time – black astrology.)

Other studies, like Cox (1969) show different aspects. He looked at differences in advertisements in using Negroes between 1950 and 1968. He found that the biggest change was not so much in the amount of Negroes, though that did change, but in the number of highly qualified jobs with status that they modelled.

But perhaps the most practical are those anecdotes and studies which show how the races change their behaviour, consciously or unconsciously, in the presence of someone from a different race. Erving Goffman has described the way Chinese salesmen change the price of their goods according to the look of the foreigner in the store and this is a fruitful line of research. Davis and Triandis (1971), in experimenting with interracial negotiations, have, for example, been able to develop a screening question-naire to spot which people will 'get on' with those of another race.

But for the most systematic, as well as potentially the most useful picture of racial etiquette, we have to turn to the professional situation where you have psychologist/interviewer/psychiatrist, on the one side, and subject/interviewee/patient, on the other. This is because it is usually easy to measure the effects of varying race on behaviour since some aspect of behaviour measurement is the object of these encounters anyway. More-over, it is precisely because they *are* assessment situations that makes them most important. These situations are, in fact, more susceptible to this sort of social influence than we might think.

Examiner effects

Hill and Stevenson (1965), for example, working with adolescent, institu-tionalized delinquent girls, found that on a simple sorting task there was a significant interaction between the *sex* of the experimenter and perform-ance when certain reinforcements were used. When a 'social' (supportive) reinforcement was given subjects performed better if the tester was a member of the opposite sex. The authors reanalysed the data from three earlier studies and found a consistent reproduction of this pattern.

Young (1959) studied the effect on test results of experimenters' and subjects' *personalities*. On a digit span test he found that subjects with 'poorly adjusted' experimenters did better than subjects with 'well ad-justed' experimenters.

Cantril (1944) compared the results obtained by *middle-class* and *working-class* interviewers to questions concerning union members' views on strikes. There was a significant difference in the percentage of respon-dents favouring or opposing 'sit-down' strike action related to the class of the interviewer. (In general less people said they wanted unofficial strike action and more opposed it when interviewed by a working-class interviewer.)

Sarason (1954) has noted the importance of the *age* of the experimenter or clinician. He quotes two examples both of which suggest that anxiety in the subject or patient was related to the age of the clinician or examiner. In general, the younger person appeared to have been seen by the subjects as less prestigious. In Sarason's clinical example the patient's anxiety in-creased when the clinician was younger although in the other situation – an intelligence test – the general effect was for anxiety to be reduced with the younger tester. In both cases, though, the effect was marked, though obviously the direction of its operation varied.

Results can also be affected by the examiner's *behaviour* – either during the test administration or before it. Exner (1966) and Sack (1952) have described studies showing differences in intelligence test performance as a result either of a 'warm' versus 'cold' interpersonal relationship between examiner and subjects or a rigid versus a more natural way of behaving on the examiner's part.

Finally, Masling (1960), and Rosenthal and Jacobson (1966 and 1968) have all shown how an experimenter's expectations may also influence test results. In Masling's paper he reports an experiment in which student volunteers gave projective tests to other subjects. Half of the student volunteers were told that 'experienced testers' of the Rorschach (the ink-blot test being used) elicited more human than animal responses from subjects, and the other half were told the reverse. The two groups of 'examiners' obtained very different ratios of human to animal responses from their subjects.

Rosenthal's (1968a) *Pygmalion in the Classroom* study is by now well known. In this study class teachers were told that certain children in their classes had been identified (by tests) as scholastic 'spurters' – that is, they could be expected to 'develop' academically. These children had in fact been selected at random from a list of pupils so that both 'spurter' and the other control groups were of equivalent ability. After four months and eight months the 'spurter' group of children showed larger rises in I Q than did the other (control) children not so identified. Expectations aroused in the minds of the teachers appeared to be 'fulfilled' in the pupils – a phenomenon which will recur later in the discussion.

Influences upon test results have been shown to be exerted, therefore, by the age of the examiner, the sex, social class, appearance, the examiner's expectations and other aspects of his or her behaviour.

Now, in the last chapter of his book, *Identity: Youth and Crisis*, Erik Erikson (1968) makes the point that the whole test event itself 'underlies a certain historical and social relativity'. It would appear, from the experimental results already described, that the kinds of examiner characteristics which have been found to affect test results are those which do provide the examiner–testee relationship with a significance reflecting and symbolizing the social and/or historical relativity of certain groups within society. Given a way of looking at psychological testing as Erikson has suggested, and in view of the kinds of examiner influences already found to be evident and of the anecdotes mentioned at the beginning of this chapter, to find that the race of the examiner affects test results also should come as no surprise.

By many psychologists, however, this has been looked upon as a mere methodological problem (see for example Shuey, 1966, and Dreger and Miller, 1968). But is this in fact so? Is there a case for arguing that the extent and nature of this effect is such that it is of more than mere methodological significance? Combined with those from other studies, some drawn from psychiatry, but all of an essentially similar nature, the results of investigations which do reveal this effect would appear to support such a conclusion. In order to be able to assess any such wider significance of this effect, however, its extent and the nature of its operation must first be described.

The interaction of examiner's race and test results

To begin with, of all those studies so far carried out the overwhelming majority have been concerned with the effect of the examiner's race upon the performance of minority group members (mainly, but not exclusively, the American Negro) rather than the effect of race of tester upon majority group subjects or patients (although, as will be seen, in one or two cases this has been carried out).

For clarity these studies can be organized into a handful of groups, the first of which includes the basic aspects of response.

Fundamental aspects of test responses such as their number and strength have been found to vary as a function of the race of the experimenter. Pasamanick and Knobloch (1955) studied forty 2-year-old Negro children and found that they responded with restricted verbal behaviour on the Gesell Development Examination (which measures motor as well as language development) when tested by a white experimenter.

Rankin and Campbell (1955) had forty white male subjects participate in what was nominally a word-association test but in which their Galvanic Skin Response (GSR) was recorded also. Readjustments (simulated) of the apparatus on one of the subject's wrists was made by either a white or a Negro experimenter while the apparatus on the other wrist continued in operation. 'A highly significant difference in GSR response to the two experimenters was found' – and the greater response was made to the Negro.

Opinions and attitudes. Another important way in which the race of the experimenter may exert an influence is in the measurement of certain attitudes. Whittaker *et al.* (1952) working with Negro subjects found that when they were presented with words derogatory to Negroes (e.g. 'nigger', 'coon') on a tachistoscope the recognition of the words, whether because of perceptual defence or response suppression, was affected by the race of the experimenter. Word recognition for these items occurred earlier and more easily when the tester was a Negro.

In New Zealand, G. M. Vaughan (1964) gave 240 Maori and pakeha (white) children tests of ethnic awareness and attitudes. Half the children of each ethnic group were tested by a Maori experimenter and the other half by a white. On the awareness tests the experimenter variable did not affect the children's performance. On the attitude tests, however, there was what Vaughan described as a defensive reaction by older Maori children who showed more favour for pakeha figures (on picture-preference and doll-preference tests) when tested by a pakeha experimenter than by a Maori.

Negroes in America were also shown, by Cantril (1944), to respond differently (some would say more frankly) when interviewed by a Negro as compared to being interviewed by a white. Interviewed by Negroes, for example, Negro respondents were more likely to say that they thought members of their race would be treated better in America if the USA were to be conquered by another country, in this case either Japan or the Nazis. In similar fashion Price and Searles (1961) reported that Negroes, when questioned by a Negro interviwer, gave higher educational aspirations for their children, agreed that more changes should be made in the way the country was being run, and were more sympathetic with the student sit-in protest demonstrations and with school desegregation than they were when interviewed by a white.

Not surprisingly, the other side of the coin has also been empirically verified. Summers (1966), using white and Negro interviewers who administered an (anonymous) questionnaire on racial attitudes, found that white students were more likely to give 'socially acceptable' (non-prejudiced) answers when the interviewer was a Negro.

Pettigrew's (1964) studies add further weight in this direction. He had interviewers of different races ask Negroes whether they agreed with a number of statements such as:

'The trouble with most white people is that they think they are better than other people'.
'I have been a victim of group discrimination'.
'I sometimes feel that prejudice has hurt me personally'.

In all these, and other cases, greater agreement was registered by more respondents when that respondent was interviewed by a Negro.

Oriental and white or Negro and white interviewers were used in two experiments by Athey, Coleman et al. (1960) in which questionnaires were given in a house-to-house survey. The questions dealt with interracial situations such as interracial neighbourhoods, marriage, medical consultation and so on. In all cases significantly more 'socially acceptable' answers were given by the white (middle-class) respondents to Oriental or Negro interviewers than were given to white interviewers.

Another interesting interaction effect due to race has been shown by Freedman (1967). He had subjects listen to an appeal to volunteer for a special course in preparation for teaching in a 'tough' mixed school. One group of subjects heard the appeal made by a Negro and a second heard an identical appeal delivered by a white. Both groups were then asked to respond to three questions relating to their evaluation of the idea and their willingness to participate in the special programme. The white 'appellant' received a higher ranking than the Negro in terms of his personal characteristics, but the latter had more success in eliciting willingness to participate.

As well as sheer differences which are obtained with opinion and attitudes related to the race of the interviewer Price and Searles (1961) also showed that Negroes tended to be more *correct* in the answers they gave when questioned by another Negro. Studies of this sort lead naturally to those carried out in the educational and intellectual field, in which the effects of the race of the tester (or teacher) have again been demonstrated.

Education and intelligence. It will be recalled that when discussing the basic aspects of test responses it was noted that Negro children were more verbally inhibited when tested by someone who was white. On this basis it would appear likely that on tests involving verbal responses, the performance of Negroes (and perhaps of minority groups in general) would be affected by the race or ethnic group of the tester.

In fact quite a number of early writers felt the race of the tester to be an important variable in intelligence test administration. The first empirical study was carried out by Canady and published in 1936. He had Negro and white experimenters give an early version of the Stanford-Binet intelligence test to both Negro and white subjects. When the test was administered by a tester belonging to the same race as the subject the latter's performance was several points higher than when he was tested by someone of a different race.

Both Price and Searles (1961) and Pettigrew (1964) found that Negroes answered survey questions and intelligence tests more correctly when interviewed or tested by Negroes. And also using the Stanford–Binet test La-Crosse (1964) and Forrester and Klaus (0964) reported that the performance of Negroes was superior when tested by a Negro – though in some cases the significance was not great.

Kennedy and Vega (1965) found that a white examiner's influence on Negro subjects was detrimental to their performance only when the reinforcement given by the (white) examiner was negative in nature. Otherwise the interaction effect was not maintained.

This more analytical approach to interracial interaction in the testing situation has been most fully described by Professor Irwin Katz. His work has shown that under some circumstances Negroes may actually score better when tested by a white examiner (see Chapter 10).

Personality. The effect of the tester's race in the administration of personality tests is far less clear than in the types of study so far discussed. Riess, Schwartz and Cottingham (1960) studied the responses of Negro and white subjects to Negro and white stimulus figures on TAT cards administered by a Negro or white examiner. They concluded that skin colour of the examiner did not affect the length of the stories produced by the subjects. Sarason (1954) has maintained that with projective personality tests such as the Rorschach, test behaviour (and/or interpretation) can vary according to the characteristics of the examiner, although race specifically was not mentioned. However, in a study published in 1967 Baratz gave to a group of 120 Negroes the Test Anxiety Questionnaire. It was found that Negroes tested by another Negro reported less anxiety than those tested by a white examiner. Using a verbal projective test Katz (1962) found that Negro boys showed *less hostility* when the test was administered by a white person and when the test was introduced as an intelligence test. He interpreted these results as showing that Negro boys *suppressed* hostility when tested by whites. In a similar study in a suburb of London Watson gave almost the same test with similar instructions to West Indian and Asian children (Watson, 1970). Again less hostility was reported with the white tester but this effect was obtained only with the West Indian children and not with the Indians and Pakistanis.

In some of the studies showing race of examiner effects which have just been outlined it has to be said there were methodological shortcomings. However, although removal of these shortcomings would perhaps have reduced such effects as were found it is doubtful if they would have eliminated them entirely. Inasmuch as the central point under discussion is not the extent of this effect but the significance of the fact that it operates at all these drawbacks due to methodology are of reduced importance.

Relevant psychiatric studies. Before proceeding to a discussion of these results and their significance it can also be noted that an effect, apparently similar in nature, appears to operate in certain psychiatric studies too. But though similar, its operation can, in a sense, be said to be the reverse of the studies previously mentioned. For whereas in psychological testing the behaviour of the respondent has been shown to vary according to the race of the tester, in the psychiatric studies it is the behaviour of the psychiatrist which has been shown to vary according to the race of the patient.

Peter Watson 275

Ari Kiev has described how there are different forces operating upon minority groups (see Chapter 21) which would certainly seem to account for some of the differences in incidence of mental illness found between some ethnic groups. In turn these differences in incidence of some illnesses would account for at least some of the differences also observed in the treatment of mental illness for some groups. But in fact recent studies have indicated that even when these 'forces' *have* been allowed for, differences in the treatment given to different ethnic groups *still* persist.

Singer (1967) for example, in a study of 320 schizophrenics admitted to a Philadelphia hospital and of whom fifty per cent were Negroes, found that the latter group were more likely to receive less intensive treatment and to be discharged sooner than were the white group. Furthermore, whereas with white patients the treatment given was likely to be 'tailored' – related to certain characteristics of the individuals seen, such as the amount of education they had received – this was not the case with Negroes who, as a group, received far more homogenous treatment. A number of other studies such as Hollingshead and Redlich (1958), Maas (1967), Karno (1966) and Yamamoto *et al.* (1967) have confirmed this result although the Singer study shows best how the treatment behaviour of the psychiatrist varies according to the race of the patient *per se* and *not* just because of social differences (e.g. in class or income) arising from but separate to the factor of race.

Such results as these enable a theoretical link to be made between the studies in which they were obtained and those showing examiner effects in testing. It would appear that in some clinical situations at least the behaviour of one of the participants can vary as a function of the race of the other.[1]

Some preliminary implications

In spite of the fact that further extrapolation of these results is necessary before a full assessment of their significance can be attempted, on a careful reading some implications will already be evident.

Intelligence tests

Firstly, and most obviously, it can be maintained that the clinical picture obtained by the professional worker who is a member of one ethnic group about a subject or patient from another ethnic group is, because of interaction effects based upon their race, susceptible to inaccuracies and is

1. The possibility that *both* participants are affected, the psychologist or psychiatrist and the patient, is not, of course, ruled out. In fact it is highly likely that this happens – but no studies exist to support such an assertion. However, a discussion of the ways in which this might operate is included later in the chapter.

therefore, of diminished reliability. An assessment of the *extent* of this (distorting) effect is not really possible. In any case the prevailing flavour of race relations which this effect will tend to reflect, will always be changing and so such an assessment may be neither practicable nor desirable.

Remember, however, that the *extent* of this effect in any particular case is not to be confused with the *significance* of the fact that it happens at all. (It is not maintained, for example, that *all* the difference in IQ between certain ethnic groups is due to the fact that minority group members usually have their IQs tested by a psychologist from the majority group; this would be too much to claim. But the significance of the fact that the race of the tester can make a difference to test performance may stretch beyond just accounting for IQ differences and will be discussed more fully a little later.)

Another important implication from the results presented so far, and one that is somewhat less obvious, is that in the *usual* clinical situation in which the participants are of different races, not only is the ethnic factor interfering as suggested but *neither* of the participants themselves is usually or necessarily aware that this is so. (This is clear from the evidence on testing and support for the fact that it happens in the psychiatric situation will be presented shortly.)

In its turn this has a number of implications.

For his part the respondent (patient) may accept that the assessment or diagnosis which he receives (from a clinician who belongs to another ethnic group) is, within the usual bounds of reliability attributable to such procedures, accurate and objective. As a consequence, this 'objective' part-description or measurement about himself is likely to be incorporated as part of *his* ideas about himself – to become, in other words, part of his identity (and also thereby contributing to ideas about his group's identity). It is in the extent to which self-concepts affect an individual's *subsequent* behaviour or performance (whether consciously or unconsciously) that the importance of the biasing interaction operating in an interracial clinical situation lies. Two examples will be described in order to suggest the ramifications possible from such a bias: again in intelligence testing, and in psychiatric treatment.

The effect of an individual's ideas about his (or his group's) intellectual ability upon his performance on subsequent occasions has been investigated by various writers. Among others, Professor Irwin Katz has noted strong evidence that Negro students have feelings of intellectual inferiority compared with white students. (As he himself points out, this arose no doubt from an awareness of actual differences in racial achievement.)

Any particular aspect of an individual's self-concept, such as feelings of intellectual inferiority compared with members of another race, can be brought into salience for that individual if, when he is given an intellectual task to do, he is told in the instructions given before the test, that his results will be compared with those of members of that other racial group. (By such a method the normal competitive examination can be simulated in controlled investigation.) Katz *et al.* (1964) did this with two groups of Negro students. Both were of equal intellectual ability – but the individuals of one group were told that their results would be compared with those for whites, whereas those in the other group were told that their results would be compared with those for other Negroes. Remember, the groups were of equal ability and doing an identical task – yet the Negro students who thought they were being compared with whites did less well on the test than those in the other group who thought they were being compared with Negroes. The former group, 'invited' to compare themselves with whites, 'expected' their chances of (relative) success to be reduced – and this is exactly what happened.

The other group, without such expectations, did better. This is an experiment which neatly demonstrates, in Erikson's words, the social and historical relativity of the test situation, brought out by the test instructions, as well as the effect of the Negro students' ideas of their (relative) ability upon their actual performance subsequently.

Other studies, some reported by Katz but also in Coleman *et al.* (1966), indicate that in a variety of studies performance has been shown to be related to expectancy and where this is in comparison with whites this expectancy – and hence performance – is usually lowered. (It should be said that in some cases in which Negroes performed in biracial environments their performance was better. These, however, were cases where tension was eliminated from the situation or nearly so – situations, in other words, probably rare in number in real life.)

An understanding is needed at this point of the nature of this process which can be seen revealed as a circular one. Tested by a white tester, the Negro respondent, because of the social history of race relations, has a lowered expectancy of success. As a consequence of this he does do less well than he otherwise might and this enhances any feeling of (intellectual) inferiority that he may already have had and increases the likelihood that on subsequent occasions his expectancies will again be further lowered.[2] The fact that this process can go unrecognised by *either* participant is of no less importance and the implications of this will be discussed later.

2. Another point here concerns evidence which appears to suggest that Negroes (and perhaps other minority groups) are more dependent on reinforcement from other people than 'internal' reinforcement or 'satisfaction', compared with whites. This increases the importance of the group to the individual so that to the minority group member the 'image' of his group has even more effect on his behaviour than does the group image of the majority group on its members.

Mental illness. Some similarities with this 'circulatory' process can also be seen in studies carried out in the field of mental illness. Although pieces of the mechanism vary, the process would appear to be substantially similar – and the resultant effect also. It was mentioned earlier that a number of studies have shown how members of minority groups receive different treatment to that for majority groups – how treatment was invariably less intensive and either shorter or quickly deteriorated into long-term and merely custodial care. These differences, it was noted, were in addition to the differences to be expected from those social differences (such as in education and income) also found between ethnic groups.

Some writers have implied that these results were due to a conscious decision on the part of the psychiatric staff to discriminate against minority groups in their treatment procedure (Maas, 1967). Others have put it down to a 'sociological realism' on the part of the psychiatrist (Singer, 1967). On this explanation the psychiatrist is said to take the view that the minority group patient is a social victim as much as a psychiatric problem since his world clearly is more likely to have aspects which provoke objective – as opposed to neurotic – anxiety. As a consequence the psychiatrist treats the minority group patient as less ill than he would if he was a majority group patient presenting similar symptoms. It is this, Singer says, which accounts for the shorter and less intensive treatment which minority group patients get. They are, given equal symptoms to whites, looked upon as less ill.

To some extent both of these accounts provide explanations for differences found. Each has, however, the same methodological failing in not controlling for differences in treatment procedure of individual psychiatrists. In a recent study without these failings, Yamamoto *et al.* (1967) suggest that neither of these explanations can provide a complete answer.

As with others, the authors report white psychiatrists administering differential treatment to white, Mexican-American, and Negro patients. What they also found, however, was that there were large individual differences between psychiatrists in the extent to which differential treatment was given and that this behaviour was not related *either* to the psychiatrists' views on whether cultural and environmental influences were relevant to the therapeutic procedure, or to whether oppression or discrimination had any psychological effects, *or* to any *conscious* preferences in the treatment situation for patients of any ethnic group. In effect, just as earlier it was shown that minority group subjects were unaware that they were performing 'differently' on psychological tests when tested by whites

3. Remember, it is not maintained that this happened with all of the psychiatrists – since the study did reveal and stress individual differences as already noted. (Differences in treatment procedure were related to 'social distance' as felt by the psychiatrists between them and other groups – but this does not really affect the argument.)

so were the psychiatrists unaware that they were giving different treatment according to the race of their patients.[3] The effects of this differential treatment for these reasons now need to be considered.

In the first place the inferior treatment which minority groups receive means that on their return to society their mental fitness must be less than it could be were they to receive their 'due' amount of treatment and less than that of majority group members. Derived from this are two possibilities both of which appear to be supported by empirical evidence. Since minority groups will have had less acquaintance with treatment procedure, then combined with other social differences characteristic of their groups, they will have relatively less familiarity with mental health concepts. Added to this is the fact that if they do not realize that they are receiving inferior treatment, as is implied in the evidence, then the condition in which they return to society may well affect their conceptions as to what the 'norm' is for their (ethnic) group. A study by Maas (1967) appears to confirm the first of these points for he showed that Negroes did have less understanding of mental illness; and studies by Caldwell (1959) and Hokansen and Calden (1969) have shown a greater tendency among 'normal' Negroes to report psychiatric symptoms on personality tests compared with equivalent white populations.

Given this state of affairs a further prediction that might be made would be that minority groups would seek psychiatric treatment less readily than majority groups because they understand the problems less; and moreover, when they do arrive in the clinic they may well be more severely ill. The evidence on this is not plentiful but what there is does offer support (Hollingshead and Redlich, 1958, Vitols, 1963 and Singer, 1967).

The action and interaction of many of the points made above no doubt stem in part from social factors which apply almost equally well to lower class whites too. But insofar as differential treatment can be and is based on colour alone, as already noted, variations in aspects of the general psychiatric picture for Negroes can also be put down, if only in part, to these treatment differentials, or their consequences.

The end result of the picture pieced together above is that Negroes might seek treatment after a longer period than whites and also be more severely ill (perhaps also as a consequence of this longer period in seeking treatment). From this it follows that, if anything, the treatment they should *then* receive ought to be more intensive compared with that for whites, as a group. Any repetition of the treatment differentials described previously would then only aggravate the position more, giving the vicious circle another twist.

The relationships described here, although complex, are of sufficient importance to merit such detailed treatment. For it would appear that in two aspects of psychology at least, vicious circles are operating in which biases, artificially introduced as a result of interaction effects based upon the race of the participants and the social and historical relativity of the relations between the races, become exaggerated. (And it cannot be said often enough that the operation of these vicious circles may go unnoticed by either participant.)[4]

Just as the views or self-concepts of the subject or patient will be affected by the feedback which he receives from the clinical encounter so will the clinician's ideas about his subject or patient (and possibly the subject's group) be affected. This is, of course, natural, but it was mentioned earlier that the ideas which a teacher has about the abilities of his pupils can affect their performance subsequently. It may then follow that in so far as psychologists or psychiatrists have 'ideas' about differences between racial groups which are based upon these biasing effects then it is possible that these ideas will give rise to expectations (perhaps implicit) about the intellectual ability or mental health – or something else – of individuals belonging to these groups, that these expectations themselves may be biased and, perhaps, that these will, in turn, be fulfilled.

Here, therefore, a way (though it has to be admitted not a very clear way) is open for another weighting to be given to the self-fulfilling process, other aspects of which have already been discussed.

A wider issue?

Before returning to the initial question of whether the results and processes described here can be said to have any wider significance, a brief summary of the argument will help:

1. In at least two clinical situations, intelligence testing and treatment for (certain) mental illnesses, interaction effects inherent in the situation due to the fact that the participants are of different races influence the behaviour of either, or of both of these participants.

2. One or both of the participants may be unaware of the operation of this effect.

3. The minority group respondent incorporates these (biased) pictures of him into aspects of his self-concept.

4. The psychologist or psychiatrist may incorporate these (biased) evaluations into his ideas of the subject or patient (and may generalize to members of his patient's group).

4. In his book, *A Profile of the Negro American*, T. F. Pettigrew (1964) has discussed other results which suggest that similar 'circular' mechanisms may operate in other areas of psychology – in aspects of personality and in crime.

5. Thus a biasing effect is introduced of which neither participant is necessarily or usually aware.

6. Its nature, as discussed, may affect subsequent behaviour, especially of the minority group member so exaggerating any bias.

7. Differences due to this biasing effect, because participants *are* unaware of the reasons for them, may come to be regarded as real – by both participants.

One important general point raised by these studies concerns the interpretation of the fact that one or both of the participants in the situation may be unaware of the interaction effects operating and therefore oblivious to their implications.

Looking at the whole process it can be seen that in both cases which were discussed in detail the results of the bias were such that minority group members were presented in a light more unfavourable than would have been the case had no such biasing effect been operating. Another way of saying the same thing is that in the whole process the outcome was 'discriminatory', although no such eventuality was necessarily intended.

That discrimination is possible without the awareness of the individual performing the discriminatory act is likely to be almost a contradiction in terms to many, an argument uncomfortable to some, suspect to most and almost impossible to prove. Nonetheless the empirical studies reviewed here would appear to support such an assertion. Obviously a lot more work needs to be done in order to verify the results of some of the work that has been reported and the arguments are by no means well established. But precisely because of the importance of such a concept, the fact that it is unestablished combined with psychology's definitive relevance to a person's identity, all those situations in which stereotypes come into play (for that is, in a sense, what generalized self-concepts and expectations are – stereotypes) in all those situations, individuals may be affected in ways similar to the clinical ones described.

One final point. Erikson (1968) has noted that minority group authors have often written of their inaudibility (DuBois), invisibility (Ellison) and their namelessness (Baldwin). He interprets this as a 'powerful demand to be heard, seen and recognized and faced as an *individual with a choice*' rather than as men marked by what is all too superficially visible. They are, he says, involved in a battle to reconquer a 'surrendered identity'.

Although less eloquent, the studies described here, in revealing the mechanics of what goes on in interaction, ought to be able to make a contribution. The perceptive black man understands what goes on in this situation. Neither the ordinary black man nor most whites do. For some

time yet the books which come from black men will meet that blindness
that has been discussed here in the eyes and ears of the whites. Never was
empirical data more necessary to overcome such a fundamental misunderstanding.

References

ATHEY, K. R., COLEMAN, C. E., REITMAN, A. P., and TANG, J. (1960), 'Two
experiments showing the effect of the interviewer's racial background on response
to questionnaires concerning social issues', *Journal of Applied Psychology*,
vol. 44, pp. 224–46.

BARATZ, S. S. (1967), 'Effect of race of experimenter, instructions and comparison
population upon level of reported anxiety in Negro subjects', *Journal of
Personality and Social Psychology*, vol. 7, pp. 194–6.

BURMA, J. H. (1946), 'Humour as a technique in race conflict', *American
Sociological Review*, vol. 2, pp. 710–15.

CANADY, H. G. (1936), 'The effect of "rapport" on the IQ: a new approach to
the problem of racial psychology', *Journal of Negro Education*, vol. 5, pp. 209–19.

CANTRIL, H. (ed.) (1944), *Gauging Public Opinion*, Princeton University Press.

CALDWELL, M. G. (1959), 'Personality trends in the youthful male offender',
Journal of Criminal Law, Criminology, and Police Science, vol. 49, pp. 405–16.

COLEMAN, J. S., *et al.* (1966), *Equality of Educational Opportunity*, US Dept. of
Health, Education and Welfare.

COX, K. (1971), 'Social effects of integrated advertising,' *Journal of Advertising
Research*, vol. 10, pp. 41–4.

DAVIS, E. E., and TRIANDIS, H. C. (1971), 'An experimental study of black–
white negotiations', *Journal of Applied Social Psychology*, vol 1, no. 3, pp. 240–62.

DREGER, R. M., and MILLER, K. S. (1968), 'Comparative psychological studies of
Negroes and whites in the United States: 1959–1965', *Psychological Bulletin
Monograph Supplement*, no. 70.

ERIKSON, E. (1968), *Identity: Youth and Crisis*, Faber & Faber.

EXNER, J. E. (1966), 'Variations in WISC performances as influenced by differences
in pretest rapport', *Journal of General Psychology*, vol. 74, pp. 299–306.

FORRESTER, B. J., and KLAUS, R. A. (1964), 'The effect of race of examiner in
intelligence-test scores of Negro kindergarten children', paper presented at the
meeting of the *Southeastern Psychological Association*, April.

FREEDMAN, P. I. (1967), 'Race as a factor in persuasion', *Journal of
Experimental Education*, vol. 35, pp. 48–51.

GOFFMAN, E. (1956), *The Presentation of Self in Everyday Life*, Free Press.

GOFFMAN, E. (1963), *Behaviour in Public Places*, Free Press.

GOFFMAN, E. (1968), *Stigma*, Penguin Books.

HARTMAN, A. (1971), 'Psychological conflict in negro American language behaviour',
Amer. J. Orthographic History, vol. 41, pp. 627–35.

HILL, K. T., and STEVENSON, H. W. (1965), 'The effects of social reinforcement *v.*
non-reinforcement and sex of E on the performance of adolescent girls', *Journal
of Personality*, vol. 33, pp. 30–36.

HOKANSEN, J. E. and CALDEN, G. (1960), 'Negro-white differences on the MMPI,
Journal of Clinical Psychology, vol. 16, pp. 32–3.

HOLLINGSHEAD, A. B., and REDLICH, F. C. (1958), *Social Class and Mental
Illness: A Community Study*, Wiley.

KARNO, M. (1966), 'The enigma of ethnicity in a psychiatric clinic', *Archives of General Psychiatry*, vol. 14.

KATZ, I., and BENJAMIN, L. (1960), 'Effects of white authoritarianism in bi-racial work groups', *Journal of Abnormal and Social Psychology*, vol. 61, pp. 448–56.

KATZ, I., EPPS, E. G., and AXELSON, L. J. (1964), 'Effect upon Negro digit-symbol performance of anticipated comparison with whites and with other Negroes', *Journal of Abnormal and Social Psychology*, vol. 69. pp. 77–83.

KENNEDY, W. A. and VEGA, M. (1965), 'Negro children's performance on a discrimination task as a function of examiner, race and verbal incentive', *Journal of Personality and Social Psychology*, vol. 2, pp. 839–43.

LaCROSSE, L. (1965), 'Race of examiner: effects on the Stanford–Binet with adolescents', *Journal of Social Psychology*, vol. 64.

LEVITT, D. W. and ABNER, E. V. (1971), 'Black-white semantic differences and inter-racial communication', *Journal of Applied Social Psychology*, vol. 3. pp. 263–77.

MAAS, J. (1967), 'Incidence and treatment variations between Negroes and Caucasians in mental illness', *Community Mental Health Journal*, vol. 3.

MASLING, J (1960), 'The influence of situational and interpersonal variables in projective testing', *Psychological Bulletin*, vol. 56.

MIDDLETON, R. and MOLARD, J. (1959a), 'Humour in negro and white subcultures: a study of jokes among university students', *American Sociological Review*, vol. 24, pp. 61–9.

MIDDLETON, R. and MOLARD, J. (1959b), 'Negro and white reactions to racial humour', *Sociometry*, vol. 22, pp. 710–15.

PASAMANICK, B., and KNOBLOCH, H. (1955), 'Early language behaviour in Negro children and the testing of intelligence', *Journal of Abnormal and Social Psychology*, vol. 50, pp. 401–2.

PETTIGREW, T. F. (1964), *A Profile of the Negro American*, Van Nostrand.

PRICE, D. O., and SEARLES, R. (1961), 'Some effects of interviewer–respondent interaction on responses in a survey situation', paper presented at the *Annual Meeting of the American Statistical Association*, December.

RANKIN, E., and CAMPBELL, J. (1955), 'Galvanic skin responses to Negro and white experimenters', *Journal of Abnormal and Social Psychology*, vol. 51.

RIESS, A. R., SCHWARZ, S.. *et al.* (1960), 'TAT responses of Negro and white subjects to Negro and white examiners', *Journal of Abnormal and Social Psychology*, vol. 56.

ROSENTHAL, R. (1964), 'The effect of the expert on the results of psychological research' in B. A. Maler (ed.), *Experimental Personality Research*, vol. 1, Academic Press, pp. 79–114.

ROSENTHAL, R., and JACOBSON, L. (1966), 'Teachers' expectancies: determinants of pupils' IQ gains', *Psychological Reports*, vol. 19, pp. 115–18.

ROSENTHAL, R. and JACOBSON, L, (1968a), *Pgymalion in the Classroom*, Holt, Rinehart & Winston.

ROSENTHAL, R., and JACOBSON, L. (1968b), 'Self-fulfilling prophecies in the classroom: teachers' expectations as unintended determinants of pupils' intellectual competence', in M. Deutsch, I. Katz and A. R. Jensen (eds.), *Social Class, Race and Psychological Development*, Holt, Rinehart & Winston, ch. 6.

SACK, E. L. (1952), 'Intelligence scores as a function of experimentally established social relationships between the child and the examiner', *Journal of Abnormal and Social Psychology*, vol. 47, pp. 354–8.

SARASON, S. (1954), *The Clinical Interaction: With Special Reference to the Rorschach*, Holt, Rinehart & Winston.

SHUEY, A. M. (1966), *The Testing of Negro Intelligence*, 2nd edn, Social Science Press.

SINGER, B. (1967), 'Some implications of differential psychiatric treatment of Negro and white patients', *Social Science and Medicine*, vol. 1, pp 77–83.

SUMMERS, G. F. and HAMMOND, A. D. (1966), 'Effect of racial characteristics of investigator on self-enumerated responses to a negro-prejudice scale', *Social Forces*, vol. 44, pp. 515–18.

VAUGHAN, G. M. (1964), 'Effect of ethnic grouping of experimenter upon children's responses to tests of an ethnic nature', *British Journal of Social and Clinical Psychology*, vol. 3.

VITOLE, M. M., et al. (1963), 'Delusions and hallucinations in white and Negro schizophrenics', *American Journal of Psychiatry*, vol. 120.

WATSON, P. (1970), 'How race affects IQ', *New Society*, July 16.

WHITTAKER, E. M., GILCHRIST, J., and FISCHER, J. J. (1952), 'Perceptual defence or response suppression?', *Journal of Abnormal and Social Psychology*, vol. 47, pp. 732–3.

WOLFF, H. A., SMITH, C. E., and MURRAY, H. A. (1934), 'The psychology of humour: I, a study of responses to race-disparagement jokes', *Journal of Abnormal and Social Psychology*, vol. 28, pp. 341–65.

YAMAMOTO, J., JAMES, J. C., BLOOMBAUM, M., and HATTEM, J. (1967), 'Racial factors in patient selection', *American Journal of Psychiatry*, vol. 124, pp. 630–36.

YOUNG, J. (1959), 'Test performance and examiner's personality', *Journal of Personality*, vol. 25.

Chapter 13
Race Relations and Behaviour in Reality

Anthony H. Richmond

Anthony H. Richmond is Professor of Sociology and Coordinator of the
Ethnic Research Programme at the Institute for Behavioural Research,
York University, Toronto. His previous academic appointments were at the
Universities of Liverpool, Edinburgh, British Columbia and Bristol College of
Science and Technology. His many publications include, *Colour Prejudice in
Britain*, *The Colour Problem* and *Post-War Immigrants in Canada*.

Innumerable studies of racism have shown that it is associated with
personality factors such as authoritarianism, alienation, status consciousness, rigidity (for a review see Blalock, 1967). However, these personality
variables and their associated attitudes are merely predisposing influences
upon behaviour. How people actually behave in situations of inter-group
contact will depend upon a variety of other historical, cultural and
situational determinants. Race relations in reality are more complex than
psychological studies alone would suggest. Van den Berghe (1967) distinguishes between *paternalistic* and *competitive* types of race relations.
Paternalistic systems are characteristic of agricultural and pastoral
societies or plantation economies. Such societies are rigidly stratified on an
ethnic basis and everyone knows 'his place' in the system which operates
as a benevolent despotism. In contrast, competitive systems of race relations are characteristic of large-scale industrial societies. There is more
mobility, both geographical and social, and race relations are characterized
by a competitiveness that generates suspicion and hatred. Under these
circumstances, there is a greater 'need' for prejudice on the part of the
competing groups, both of whom may exhibit aggressive behaviour towards each other. Van den Berghe's distinction is somewhat oversimplified
but it draws attention to the structural and cultural variables that must be
taken into account.

Situational determinants include the numerical ratios of the groups concerned, the relative distribution of economic and political power and the
influence of third parties who have a constraining effect, or align themselves
with one side or the other.

Competition is only one form of conflict in industrial societies that may manifest itself in race relations. Even where there is consensus concerning the ultimate goals of racial integration and equality there may be conflict concerning the means of achieving and the speed of movement towards these goals. Contradictory values concerning the ultimate 'assimilation' of racial minorities may coexist with beliefs in the importance of maintaining ethnic identity and 'race pride'. Racial conflict may also arise from fundamental opposition between incompatible religious and political beliefs or when racial differences coincide with a rising tide of 'nationalist' sentiment which reinforces competition or a struggle for power (Richmond, 1972).

Blumer (1958) has suggested that out of the conditions of initial contact between ethnic groups there emerges a 'sense of group position', which is largely independent of individual personality characteristics. The sense of group position includes not only the vertical dimension of social relations, but also the appropriateness of certain patterns of residence and other aspects of social behaviour. Once established, a sense of group position may give rise to attitudes of sympathy, condescension and tolerance, as well as antipathy and extreme prejudice. Behaviour in situations of contact with members of another racial or ethnic group may be determined by the institutional structure of the society, the legal and customary sanctions that may be brought to bear upon the persons concerned and the specific situational factors, such as the presence or absence of third parties, who may exercise an influence over the actions and reactions occurring.

The situation in the United States, particularly the North, may be contrasted with that in the Republic of South Africa and with the emerging patterns of race relations in Great Britain. In the United States, the white population is a numerical majority but the Negro population is a substantial minority whose position in the system of ethnic stratification is still an inferior one, in which a great deal of discrimination occurs. However, legal sanctions are being used increasingly to ensure equal treatment for Negroes in employment, housing and public accommodation. In contrast, law is used as an instrument for enforcing the policy of *apartheid* in South Africa with severe penalties being used against anyone, regardless of race, who fails to conform to a rigid pattern of discrimination and segregation in all spheres of life. The fact that the African population is a numerical majority in South Africa clearly generates more severe feelings of insecurity among the dominant white population which has enjoyed a privileged social status over a long period. The situation in Great Britain contrasts with that in the United States and in the Republic of South Africa in so far as there has been no previous history of racial contact. As a consequence, no clearly defined 'sense of group position' existed to pattern the relations between coloured immigrants and the native population. The essentially unstructured situation of racial contact that has arisen in the last two decades in Britain has resulted in ambiguity and uncertainty as far as social policy and everyday behaviour are concerned.

Several studies have drawn attention to the inconsistency between attitudes and overt behaviour and the effects of relatively structured and unstructured situations upon behaviour in situations of interracial contact. In unstructured situations the relationship between personality factors, expressed attitudes and overt behaviour is a complex one. For example, in endeavouring to explain the differential probability of a white person talking to or eating with a coloured immigrant in an English city it was found that sex, age and economic status were more important than various indices of racial prejudice but that, of the attitudinal items, a measure of 'cosmopolitanism' did correlate positively with the frequency of interracial contact (Richmond, 1973).

Merton (1949) distinguished between four categories: (a) prejudiced discriminators; (b) unprejudiced discriminators; (c) prejudiced non-discriminators; and (d) unprejudiced non-discriminators (see also Chapter 5 of this book). He suggested that the degree of consistency between attitudes and behaviour would depend upon the sanctions brought to bear upon the individual to conform to the expectations of others in the situation in question. A classical study by La Piere (1934) showed that the proprietors of hotels, motels and restaurants were more likely to accept non-white clients when faced with the reality situation than if asked by letter to indicate whether they would admit such persons. A later study by Kutner, Wilkins and Yarrow (1952) substantiated the earlier findings. Two white women and one Negro woman entered eleven restaurants in a fashionable locality and were served in a normal manner. Later, letters were sent to each establishment inquiring about reservations for a social affair at which some coloured persons would be present. In the majority of cases the requests for reservations were ignored or refused. In these cases, the discrepancy between attitudes and behaviour was in a *positive* direction in the sense that behaviour was more liberal than the attitudes expressed.

A carefully controlled experiment by Linn (1965) has shown that under certain circumstances the opposite may occur. When asked if they would be willing to pose for a photograph with a Negro of the opposite sex, a sample of females enrolled in introductory sociology courses showed a greater willingness to do so when asked hypothetically than when faced with the reality situation. The discrepancies in this case were in a negative direction and clearly aroused a great deal of anxiety in the respondents. They were aware of the differential pressure brought to bear upon them in the college situation where the norm of behaviour was a liberal one, and in their own family and community where different expectations prevailed. The possibility that the photograph might be seen by people outside of the college meant that many of the girls were unwilling to go through with the proposal to have their photograph taken with a Negro of the opposite sex. Reviewing the evidence from his own and other studies, Linn came to the conclusion that discrepant behaviour in a *negative* direction was more likely to occur in situations where the respondent lacked actual experience and where the level of social involvement with the member of another racial group was high. Discrepant behaviour in a *positive* direction will increase if the level of social involvement is low, and if the prejudiced attitudes have not been overtly tested.

Williams (1964) also demonstrated the importance of structured and unstructured situations in determining whether discrimination will take place. He showed that in public places such as restaurants and hotels the manager or his representative frequently does not know whether or not he will act in a discriminatory way. Faced with an actual situation, he seeks clues from his white customers to indicate whether or not they will object to his serving Negro patrons. The first overt act by any white customer may be the most important influence on the manager's reactions. Direct intervention by a white customer on behalf of a Negro almost always brought service for the Negro concerned. Williams concluded that in stable, recurring intergroup situations well defined and mutually understood patterns of behaviour become institutionalized. However, in unstructured situations, such as those frequently found in the northern states of the United States and in Britain, new patterns of either discriminatory or non-discriminatory behaviour may emerge. They become the focal points for change in inter-group relations. Such incidental factors as pressure of time, spatial arrangements, initial conduct and self-confidence of minority group persons concerned and expectations as to whether the situation will set a precedent may all be important. Williams emphasizes that any unpatterned situation is potentially a generator of change.

The relationship between social change and prejudice was studied by Bettelheim and Janowitz (1964). They draw attention to the gradual amelioration of attitudes and behaviour in the United States, as far as the relations between majority and minority group members were concerned. They attributed this to changes in age structure, education, and above all the effects of legislation and judicial decisions in changing the institutional structure of American society. They also referred to evidence from their own and other studies which suggested that, in advanced industrial societies, downward social mobility is associated with ethnic intolerance. The authors attributed this to the insecurity and loss of personal and social controls consequent upon the status dislocation. More recently, Hodge and Treiman (1966) questioned the evidence for the association between downward mobility and prejudice. A representative national sample of the adult white population in the United States showed that, although downward mobility was associated with unfavourable attitudes towards integration, this could be explained without assuming that mobility *per se* was a source of prejudice. Given that there was less pro-integration sentiment in the lower levels of occupational status, the findings could be explained in terms of a tendency to express views that were a compromise between those prevailing in the former level of occupational status and those characteristic of others at the new level of occupational status.

Various studies have demonstrated the association between low education, income and socio-economic status and the tendency to express prejudice and to support discriminatory behaviour. However, there are exceptions to this rule and, whether or not high status persons appear to be more tolerant depends partly on the dimension of prejudice under consideration and the particular group against whom it is expressed. Williams has shown that better educated people may be less likely to subscribe to stereotypes, but more likely to reject intimate relations with members of certain minority groups, particularly Jews (Williams, 1964). He suggests that prejudice reflects a sense of threat and that white Gentiles in the upper socio-economic strata are likely to be less prejudiced against Negroes and more prejudiced against Jews than their fellows in the less affluent and poorer educated strata, for whom the Negro population is a more immediate source of competition.

The importance of perceived competition and the size of the minority group has been explored by Blalock (1967). He suggests that the greater the average gap between the dominant and minority groups, the less is the perceived threat to the former group and the less the need for additional discriminatory practices in order to limit the competitive position of the minority. As the relative size of the minority group increases, so does the incidence of discriminatory behaviour. However, assuming that discrimination actually results in handicaps for the subordinated group as the minority percentage increases the individual becomes less of a competitive threat owing to the greater handicap imposed on him. This line of reasoning leads one to expect a positive relationship between the size of the minority group and the incidence of discrimination but the relationship would be non-linear. Represented diagrammatically, the association between discrimination and minority percentage would show an upward curve with decreasing slope.

A distinction must be made between the competition that a minority group may represent for the dominant group, and the extent to which it represents a power threat. The power threat posed by a numerically large minority group will also be related to the motivation to discriminate. Blalock suggests that this will also exhibit a non-linear relationship but one with an increasing, rather than a decreasing, slope.

This analysis illustrates the problem facing minority group leaders. They may become more militant in an attempt to remove discrimination in areas where competition is felt, but they cannot do so beyond a certain point without the white population seeing them as a power threat and retaliating with more severe discriminatory measures. Minority group leaders must exert sufficient pressure to obtain their short-term objective, while at the same time forming coalitions with members of the majority group in those situations where the minority is not perceived as a real threat.[1]

Experimental studies conducted by Muzafar Sherif (1966) have shown how inter-group conflict can be generated when two groups come into contact in pursuit of urgently desired goals which can only be obtained at the expense of the other group. Such competitive interaction generates unfavourable attitudes and stereotyped images of the out group. Conflict between the two groups produces an increase in solidarity within each group and may result in other forms of social reorganization, including changes of leadership. Sherif also demonstrates that when conflicting groups come into contact in situations that compel cooperation towards a superordinate goal their previous hostility towards each other may be reduced. The superordinate goal may involve action against a third group, perceived as a common enemy, or cooperative activity towards the achievement of sufficiently compelling goals which could not be achieved by a single group through its own efforts and resources. Sherif concludes that when groups are motivated by the pursuit of common ends, exposed to common dangers, or recognize a common predicament, they tend to band together. He considers that this tendency is facilitated by advances in technology and means of communication. However, the effects of industrialization upon systems of race relations do not appear to be wholly consistent in this respect.

Industrialization and discrimination in employment

Blumer (1965) has pointed out that logically one would expect the process of industrialization to undermine any system of rigid ethnic or racial stratification. Industrialization as a social process normally implies a commitment to a rational and secular outlook, an emphasis upon contractual relations in place of status relations, the introductions of an impersonal market system, together with the promotion of the physical and social mobility of the population. All these factors tend to undermine traditional social orders, throw individuals into new situations and give rise to a reorganization of society at a new level of economic development. Theoretically, the preservation of a system of racial relations, which allocates people to social positions other than in terms of their qualifications and

1. The way in which the NAACP worked with and through the Federal District Courts in the south to obtain school desegregation orders exemplifies this process.

abilities appears to be incompatible with a rational economic order in an advanced industrial society.

However, Blumer shows that, in fact, during the early stages of industrialization in the southern states of the United States and in South Africa, where the system of racial stratification was deeply entrenched before industrialization, the changes in the economic system did not undermine the established system of race relations but merely adapted to it. In fact, the rational operation of a commercial or industrial firm introduced into a racially stratified society may involve the maintenance of conventional patterns of racial discrimination. Blumer goes on to show that members of dominant and subordinate racial groups are not necessarily thrown into a competitive relationship as a consequence of industrialization. This may occur in certain cases where a firmly established racial order does not exist or where the latter is definitely undergoing disintegration. In other cases, legal and customary sanctions effectively reduce the points of contact and competition. Therefore, the basic framework of relations between the dominant and subordinate groups is not necessarily modified by the industrialization process.

Far from dissolving the significance of race, Blumer suggests that in practice considerations of economic rationality are subordinated to those of preserving the superordinate status of the dominant racial group. The evidence led him overwhelmingly to the conclusion that changes that arise in the relations between different races in an industrial society do not occur from any considerations of industrial efficiency. They are the product of outside political pressures.

Blumer shows that, in the American South, managerial policy supported and maintained racial alignment and discriminatory practices for three-quarters of a century. Changes are only just beginning to appear and these have not risen indigenously in southern industry but as a result of federal government and other outside pressures. He considers that South Africa further confirms his thesis in so far as industrialization definitely followed the racial divisions in the society and reflected the social position of whites, Africans, Coloured and Indians. Recent changes have sharpened and intensified racial lines. This was not an indigenous development within industry but arose from the policies of *apartheid*, enforced by the nationalist government.

Discrimination in employment undoubtedly persists in South Africa, the United States and in Britain. In South Africa it has the full support of the Government and is enforced by law. Early legislation included the Mines and Works Act, 1911, the Apprenticeship Act, 1922, the Industrial Conciliation Act, 1924, and the Wage Act, 1925. These Acts effectively prevented Africans from becoming artisans in the skilled trades (except for a limited extent in the non-white areas), and also from forming a common front with other workers in union negotiations. Opportunities for non-whites to obtain higher education or professional employment are severely limited and competition with whites at these levels is effectively prevented by law. Although economic pressures and shortages of white skilled labour have led to some modification of the job reservation system, wage differences between races for the same work remain very large. Furthermore, political pressures brought to bear through the *Terrorism Act* and other legislation have made any criticism of or opposition to *apartheid* increasingly hazardous, even to white liberals. Economic needs are also forcing South Africa to make concessions to businessmen and diplomatic visitors, from other African and Asian countries, that are not made to the indigenous populations of non-white origin. However, internal and external threats to white supremacy tend to produce even more oppressive 'police state' measures in defence of the *status quo* (Adam, 1971).

In the United States the law is used to combat racial discrimination, but has not succeeded in eliminating it nor in removing the many obstacles to equality of opportunity for Negroes in the economic sphere. Fair employment practice legislation, special educational training and vocational rehabilitation schemes, and the policies of non-discrimination upheld by the AFL–CIO[2] at the national level have failed to remove the many sources of discrimination against Negroes in American industry locally. Unemployment rates among Negroes are double those of the white populations and the majority of Negroes are in low status and low paying jobs. Low income and education create a vicious circle of poverty and cultural deprivation that persists from one generation to another.

Recently, Blau and Duncan (1967) have shown that Negroes are not *only* handicapped by having poor parents, less education and inferior early career experiences. Even when these handicaps have been overcome, and Negroes with similar education and the same first jobs as whites are considered, the ultimate occupational status and income of the former is less than that of comparable whites. Even college educated Negroes do not manage to achieve an income or occupational level comparable to that of similarly educated whites. The former even fail to rise as far above their lower social origin as college educated whites rise above their higher ones. There can be no doubt that racial discrimination plays an important part in creating these discrepancies. Blau and Duncan suggest that the fact that Negroes obtain fewer rewards than whites for their educational investments may explain why many Negroes exhibit little interest in pursuing higher education. It is significant that other ethnic minorities in the United

2. American Federation of Labour and Council of Industrial Organizations – the governing body of American labour unions.

States, particularly those of immigrant origin, have not suffered the same handicaps as Negroes, and when educational handicaps are removed, their achievements are similar to native whites of native parentage.

Blau and Duncan note that the highly educated Negro suffers more from occupational discrimination than the less educated Negro. A similar conclusion was reached in a carefully controlled study of racial discrimination in Britain. The study, carried out by Political and Economic Planning (1966), showed that the higher the qualification of a coloured immigrant, the more frequently he experienced discrimination. Discrimination was experienced by 70 per cent of the coloured immigrants with English trade qualifications, by 44 per cent of those having an English school-leaving certificate and by 36 per cent of those with no qualifications. Similarly, claims of discrimination were high among people with formal qualifications obtained before coming to Britain. Immigrants with the highest qualifications and general ability, including knowledge of English and familiarity with British life and customs, were the ones who experienced most discrimination. Situation tests were conducted in which an Englishman, a Hungarian and a coloured immigrant with comparable qualifications and experience were sent to apply for job vacancies: the coloured tester was rejected twenty-seven out of thirty times, the Hungarian thirteen out of thirty times and the English tester not at all. The attitude of these particular employers was that they would only take coloured immigrants for particular menial tasks or if the labour shortage became exceptionally acute. The report also notes that the experience of coloured school leavers, whose education has been mainly in Britain, tends also to be unfavourable, suggesting that the basis of the discrimination is racial and not cultural.

Many employers in Britain adopt a quota system, limiting the number of coloured immigrants that they will employ, and few will promote coloured workers to supervisory positions. The majority of employers will not accept coloured office staff, irrespective of qualifications. In the absence of legislation governing employment, the situation in Britain has been essentially unpatterned. As a result, coloured workers have been unable to predict when they are likely to experience discrimination and have had no redress when this has occurred. The Race Relations Act of 1968 made it unlawful for an employer, or anyone concerned with employment, to discriminate on grounds of race. However, certain types of employers have at least temporary exemption from the provisions of the Act. These include establishments employing not more than ten people and those whose main business is conducted outside the United Kingdom.

The Act also gives explicit approval to the concept of a 'benign quota'. Discrimination in employment is allowed 'if the act is done in good faith for the purpose of securing or preserving a balance of persons of different racial groups employed in the undertaking'. The difficulty likely to be incurred in administering such a system means that there may be many loopholes open to an employer who does not wish to employ coloured workers in other than menial positions (Hepple, 1970).

American experience supports the view that when Negroes and whites work alongside each other there are fewer problems than employers anticipated. Integration is now the official policy of the armed forces of the United States and has been successfully implemented without more than the odd disturbing incident. White soldiers in integrated army units exhibit less prejudice and learn to accept Negro officers. Studies in factories have shown that Negro and white workers entering into informal work relationships with each other change their conventional stereotypes and work effectively together. Hope (1952) reported that the International Harvester Company with the support of the Labour Union had succeeded in promoting Negroes to positions over white workers in several of its southern plants. Other studies have shown that a clear and forceful managerial policy against discrimination is effective in achieving satisfactory work relations between whites and Negroes.

Experience in Britain confirms that, once immigrants are employed in a firm, the problems previously anticipated by managers and white workers rarely materialize. In 1954 I showed that West Indian workers employed in factories during the Second World War were initially rejected by employers and fellow workers but that they gradually became accepted as part of the natural order of things (Richmond, 1954). While not completely incorporated into the life of the factory, they were at any rate tolerated and respected individually, according to their merits. Very similar conclusions were reached by Peter Wright (1968) in his study of coloured workers in British industry. Although coloured workers were usually only employed because of a lack of alternative source of labour and were often in unskilled dead-end jobs, they achieved a limited degree of social integration in employment. However, coloured workers tended to maintain some measure of social separation from other workers and this was most marked in the case of Asian immigrants, where linguistic and religious differences were significant. Sheila Patterson's (1968) comparative study of West Indian, Irish and Polish workers in Croydon also led to the conclusion that colour was usually less important than education, skill, adaptability and knowledge of English in achieving effective integration at work.

However, these studies were undertaken at a time when employment opportunities were expanding and the numbers of coloured workers comparatively small. Public opinion generally had not hardened against nonwhite immigration into Britain during the 1950s and early 1960s as it has since. A more recent study by Sheila Allen (1971) rejects the view that coloured immigrants will inevitably move from initial conflict, through various accommodative and adaptive responses to eventual assimilation. She argues that processes of absorption may be reversible and that conflicts of interest between natives and immigrants and coloured and white workers may re-emerge under certain conditions. Her investigation of Pakistani workers in Bradford, England, suggests that coloured immigrants have been more readily absorbed into industries with weakly organized unions. Sometimes the interests of the coloured workers may be served by the creation of separate organizations or sections of unions rather than integration into the existing labour unions, which may discriminate against them.

Segregation and discrimination in housing

Voluntary social separation, whether in the context of industrial employment, religion and recreational activities or housing does not necessarily involve discrimination. Members of religious minorities, particularly, are inclined to choose their place of residence and select their friends and marital partners from their own religious group. When race and language are superimposed upon religion as bases of social differentiation this reinforces the tendency towards voluntary social segregation. However, in practice, residential segregation and other forms of social separation are frequently imposed upon a minority or subordinate group by the dominant group in the interests of maintaining the latter's superior status position.

This is particularly evident in the case of racial segregation in the United States, where differences of religion, language or culture cannot explain the formation and preservation of racially segregated ghettos. Although successive waves of European immigrants have passed through the 'zones of transition' in American cities to be subsequently dispersed throughout the urban and suburban areas, American Negroes have exhibited an increasing tendency towards segregation. Taueber and Taueber (1964) have noted that the historical trend towards improving socio-economic status of immigrant groups has resulted in decreasing segregation for them, but that Negro residential segregation has increased steadily, despite advances in the socio-economic status of Negroes. Negroes in Chicago in 1950 had a segregation index of 79 and by 1960 this had risen to 83.[3] Comparable indices for foreign-born groups were Germany: 19; Italy: 32; USSR: 44; Mexico: 54; and Puerto Rico: 67.

Residential segregation is partly a function of income, but this explains only a small proportion of the non-white segregation in Chicago in 1960.

3. The segregation index measures the percentage of any given group that would have to move from its present location in order to be distributed throughout the city in the same proportion as other groups with which the comparison is made.

Using a technique of indirect standardization, Taueber and Taueber showed that only 12 per cent of the racial segregation was attributable to income differentials.

Even when Negroes succeed in moving out of the ghettos in the central city areas, they tend to be concentrated in certain outer urban areas where only a small proportion of the white population resides. A pattern of 'invasion and succession' has been established in most American cities. This appears to be the result of a severe shortage of housing for middle-class Negroes on the one hand and, on the other, the persistent belief that Negroes, irrespective of their income or occupational status, are a threat to the social status of a residential area. As Mayer (1957) has pointed out, when the status of a neighbourhood is threatened by a few Negro families moving in the inhabitants take measures to combat this threat, either by fleeing the neighbourhood or by violence against the newcomers. The belief that the invasion of an area by Negroes will reduce property values is widespread and tends to be encouraged by real estate salesmen. Evidence suggests that depreciation in property values need not necessarily take place under these conditions and the reverse may sometimes occur. However, the *belief* that property values and social status are threatened, is sufficient to make the flight of the white inhabitants appear rational under the circumstances. Among the other factors influencing the behaviour of white residents in these circumstances is the belief that educational standards in the local public schools will be affected by the increasing number of Negro children. The fact that the latter may have received inferior education in their former locality lends some reality to this fear.

Meanwhile, the large majority of American Negroes live in ghettoes in the city centres. The city ghettos have grown as a result of the rapid rate of natural increase of the Negro population and the continuous flow of Negroes from southern rural areas to the cities of the North and West. Simultaneously, the white population has tended to move away from the central areas of cities to the suburbs. Within the ghettos poor housing conditions, poverty, unemployment and family disorganization have given rise to high incidence of ill-health and of crime. Even though some Negroes have improved their income and occupational status, their success is less visible than that of the immigrants who preceded them, because residential segregation and discrimination have forced the Negro to remain in the ghetto with little hope of escape for himself or his children.

McEntire (1960) has drawn attention to some of the mechanisms of imposed segregation. These include race restrictive covenants which were promoted by property owner associations, real estate boards and even the Federal Housing administration. Differential criteria for the granting of mortgages, the 'block-busting' tactics of real estate salesmen, aiming ot promote an 'invasion-succession' cycle, together with a variety of social pressures upon white people not to sell or rent to Negroes, have been largely responsible. The use of violence to deter potential Negro residents in an all-white area is not unknown.

Despite the general tendency towards residential segregation, there are some examples of both privately developed and public interracial housing in the United States. Private developers of interracial housing, since they are contravening established custom, are generally faced with special problems in the acquisition of land, financing and marketing. The Federal Housing administration and mortgage granting institutions have been reluctant to invest in racially mixed housing. There has been some change in this policy over the last decade and McEntire concludes that lack of mortgage financing is no longer a major obstacle to open occupancy housing. Largely because of the extreme shortage of housing for Negroes, projects that begin as interracial housing on an open occupancy basis frequently become all-Negro housing projects unless 'benign quotas' are deliberately imposed. Somewhat similar conclusions arise from an examination of low rental public housing in the United States. Because of their low economic status and extreme housing needs, Negroes tend to have a proportionately higher share in public housing. Public housing is not popular in the United States and, compared with Britain, only a small proportion of the population is accommodated in this way. Tenants are selected according to need with priority for families displaced by slum clearance. Tenants must not have more than a certain income; if their income rises above the limit, they must leave the housing project. The Federal administration of public housing left the question of segregation or integration to be determined by the local authorities. After the Second World War an increasing proportion of public housing was on an open occupancy basis, although this did not necessarily mean complete integration. In some cases, an integrated project included segregated apartment blocks in a 'checkerboard' pattern, rather than complete integration within particular buildings.

Jahoda and West (1951) studied the relations between Negro and white tenants in one public housing project. They showed that 35 per cent of the whites and 23 per cent of the Negroes anticipated some problems before moving in, but in fact 80 per cent of the whites and 97 per cent of the Negroes reported that they got on well together. Some experience of interracial contact prior to moving into the public housing project led to more realistic expectations. It was also found that the more integrated occupancy patterns, compared with the area segregated pattern, gave rise to more favourable attitudes towards the interracial project. However, this could have been due to some self-selection on the part of those who lived in the more integrated units. Even in the public housing project, there was some fear of 'invasion', giving rise to a tendency for white tenants to move out when they were free to do so. Rosenthal and his colleagues (1967) studied the interaction between Negro and white children in an integrated housing project, where 10 per cent of the families were Negro. Detailed observations of the children over a period of a year by a number of observers who watched the children coming and going to school and playing in the locality led to the conclusion that parental anxiety on the part of the Negro families led to more restrictions upon the activities of the coloured children. Other than when they were going to and from school, Negro children made fewer unaccompanied appearances outside the apartment and were more frequently supervised in their activities by their parents. It seems that the Negro parents were anxious to avoid any incidents that might provoke hostility on the part of their white neighbours.

Harvey Molotch (1969) studied racial integration in an American 'transition community' in which Negroes were moving into a hitherto all-white area. Theoretically, this could have led to smaller zones of ecological segregation and little interaction, or to ecological integration and overt conflict, or to 'transracial solidarity' in which whites and blacks interacted freely and without constraint. In fact, it appeared that integration occurred in retail shops, some churches and formal organizations, when measured in terms of numerical use and attendance. However, this was not accompanied by interaction at the primary group level, or any evidence of emerging solidarity. Exceptions were found in certain 'deviant' groups such as the 'Veterans for Peace in Vietnam' and the local 'Organization for Human Rights', where ideological considerations appeared to override racial differences and provide a basis for transracial solidarity. Only a small minority of both races were actively involved in such organizations and social life in the area remained largely segregated.

Studies of housing in Britain suggest that, although coloured immigrants represent a much smaller proportion of the population than Negroes in the United States, they experience similar difficulties in obtaining housing. Although the majority of immigrants do not expose themselves to possible discrimination by looking for accommodation on the open housing market, when they do so they experience substantial discrimination. Much property on the private letting market in England explicitly precludes coloured people when advertised. However, the P.E.P. study (1966) showed that even when advertisements not specifically excluding coloured applicants were followed up 75 per cent actually resulted in discrimination against a coloured applicant. Situation tests showed that fourteen out of eighteen accommodation bureaux and twenty out of thirty estate agents rejected coloured applicants. In the field of house purchase similar levels of discrimination were found. Coloured immigrants enquiring about house purchase were given no addresses or fewer addresses of property for sale and were frequently advised that it would be difficult or impossible to obtain a mortgage. It was emphasized that regular building societies were reluctant to give coloured immigrants mortgages with the result that they usually had to borrow money from less scrupulous agencies who demanded larger initial deposits and higher interest rates.

Public or 'council' housing constitutes a much larger proportion of the market in Britain than in the United States. Elizabeth Burney (1967) showed that the policies of local authorities tended, intentionally or unintentionally, to discriminate against coloured immigrants. In particular, the stipulations that a person housed by the local authority must have been resident in the area for a given period tended to place any newcomer to the area in a disadvantageous position. This view was also confirmed by the findings of Rex and Moore (1967) in their study in Sparkbrook. This emphasized the extent to which immigrants were forced to seek alternative ways of meeting their housing needs (for example, by the multiple occupation of lodging houses), which were likely to evoke the disapproval of their neighbours and of the municipal authorities. Attempts to limit the zones in which multiple occupation was permitted led to the further segregation of immigrants.

In a study in Bristol, England, which I conducted, it was found that even when allowance was made for such factors as age, sex, marital status, occupational status and length of residence, coloured immigrants were more likely to be living in overcrowded conditions, without exclusive use of such amenities as baths and toilets than were white migrants to the city (Richmond, 1973). Although comparatively few coloured immigrants were living in local authority housing estates in Bristol, where numbers were small and families were dispersed, the social integration of West Indian families on the estates was comparatively high. The P.E.P. study concluded that the types of accommodation occupied by the majority of coloured immigrants would eventually become due for slum clearance and that this would involve local authorities in providing council housing. Furthermore, those immigrants who had put their names on waiting lists would eventually qualify and as more immigrants actually obtained council housing this would encourage others, who had not previously considered doing so, to seek this type of accommodation. As a consequence, they anticipated a substantial increase in demand for public housing on the part of coloured immigrants. Whether the white residents in existing housing projects would be willing to accept larger numbers as readily as those on the Bristol estates accepted small numbers, is open to question.

Segregation which, elsewhere, has come about as a result of competition, self-selection and only incidentally as a result of public policies is maintained with the full force of the law in the Republic of South Africa. Swanson (1968) has pointed out that the origins of *apartheid* in South Africa go back to the pastoral communities of the Boer republics and the traditional African tribal societies. However, they were also established in the urban areas at a very early stage. The Native (Urban Areas) Act of 1923 was one of the earliest attempts to ensure the effective separation of the white and African population in the urban areas. This Act was subject to various amendments and its purposes further reinforced by the Group Areas Act of 1950. The terms of this Act ensure the effective residential segregation of Europeans, Africans, Coloured and Asians. Furthermore, it provided for the forcible relocation of individuals and families who were then located in an area designated for another racial group. The relocation programme particularly discriminated against Asians who had depended upon the businesses they had established in African and other areas and whose property and businesses were lost as a result. Van der Horst (1965) has pointed out that the separation of African 'locations' or dormitory suburbs and the central areas occupied by the white population has increased as a consequence of the growth of the towns. As the latter have increased in size, so the older locations have been moved further out. New townships still further away from the white towns have been created. As a consequence, cities like Johannesburg have vast sprawling African suburbs, largely of the 'shanty town' type, stretching fifteen to twenty-five miles from the centre of the city and housing numerous industrial, commercial and domestic workers. The ecological distribution is almost the reverse of that of American cities where the ghettos are centrally located. Nevertheless, social separation is even greater and is enforced by law.

Education, public accommodation and voting

In South Africa, the non-white population has been gradually deprived of the limited franchise that some had achieved before the Nationalist government came into power in 1948. Subsequently, even indirect representation in Parliament was gradually whittled away, leaving Africans with no representation in urban areas at all and only a limited voice in the government of the 'Bantustans' or former African reserves.

In the United States, the opposite process has taken place. The Supreme Court did not affirm the legal right of the Negro to vote in the South until 1944, but in many States steps were taken to ensure that in practice Negroes did not qualify. The 'segregation-law package' denied the vote to recipients of welfare assistance, parties to a common law marriage, anyone guilty of a variety of minor offences (excluding traffic and game laws), and in many localities there was little hesitation in using coercive measures to

Anthony H. Richmond 301

discourage voter registration among Negroes. Subsequent federal legislation and voter registration campaigns increased the representation of
Negroes, although there are still many denied the vote today. In Britain,
coloured immigrants who have British or Commonwealth citizenship may
exercise the franchise without restriction. However, their numbers are
still so small that it is unlikely that they have any significant influence upon
the outcome of elections, except in certain wards where the proportion
may be somewhat above average.

The relative concentration of minorities in particular areas raises a
dilemma with regard to voting. Geographical dispersion means the dissipa-
tion of any effective political power. At the same time, concentration in
particular localities may enable the minority group to influence the outcome of an election and even return a representative to the municipal or
other government body concerned. However, this very fact increases the
incentive on the part of the majority group to impose restrictions upon the
opportunity to vote.

Discrimination in places of public resort such as bars, restaurants,
hotels and business or public offices, together with various forms of transportation, is found in Britain, the United States and South Africa. Only in
the latter country is it enforced by law. At one time the myth of 'separate
but equal' facilities was maintained as an ideal by the South African
courts, but new legislation introduced by the Nationalist government
removed any obligation to ensure that separate facilities were equal in
quantity or quality. In the United States laws against discrimination in
public places have been in existence in some States since the nineteenth
century, but in others discrimination and segregation was enforced by
law. The US Civil Rights Act of 1964, which was a federal enactment,
made it illegal to discriminate in places of business involving inter-State
commerce and transport. All the States outside the South have some kind
of legislation on the subject but, in many cases, it is dependent upon the
institution of court action by the victim and has little effect. In twenty-one
states anti-discrimination agencies have been established with administrative powers of enforcement. A systematic study of anti-discrimination
legislation in the United States led Lockard (1968) to conclude that public
accommodation laws were probably more successful than those on employment and housing. For example, he found that two-thirds of the complaints concerning public accommodation were successfully settled, compared with only one-third of the cases of employment or housing discrimination brought to the attention of agencies. In Britain, the P.E.P. study
showed that despite legislation that had been introduced twelve months before the study was conducted there was still some residual discrimination
against coloured immigrants particularly with regard to holiday resorts.

American experience has shown that anti-discrimination legislation benefits the middle-class Negro who has sufficient education to qualify for employment above the level of an unskilled worker and whose income renders him otherwise eligible for housing or amenities that would be too expensive for the majority of Negroes. It is sometimes suggested that anti-discrimination laws cannot change the attitudes of the white population, although in the long run, they may succeed in doing just that. What is more certain is that the laws cannot by themselves eliminate poverty and overcome the inequality of educational opportunity which is holding back the potential achievement of the majority of the Negro population. Although anti-discrimination legislation assists middle-class Negroes more than others, it is, nevertheless, valuable and will become increasingly important as more Negroes obtain higher education and better employment.

In the United States, the main turning point in education was the decision of the Supreme Court in 1954 that any segregation in public schools was unconstitutional. School districts were ordered to integrate their schools 'with all deliberate speed'. A decade later less than half the segregated schools had been integrated and in the South less than 10 per cent of Negro children were in schools with white children. The majority of these were in the border area. In the urban areas of the northern states, desegregation of schools has been rendered difficult by the extent of residential segregation. As a consequence, the extensive use of special transportation to take children away from their neighbourhood to more distant schools has been used as a means of reducing *de facto* school segregation. In England, similar problems have arisen due to the residential concentration of coloured immigrants. The Department of Education has recommended a maximum of 20 per cent of coloured immigrant children in any one school, but this has been difficult to enforce. In South Africa, segregation in schools and universities has been enforced by law. Since 1954, when the majority of schools formerly administered by churches were taken over by the government, there has been an increase in the number of African children receiving elementary education, but emphasis has been placed upon the use of the vernacular language in the schools and, indirectly, they have become a means of indoctrinating the children into an acceptance of their separate and inferior status within the society. A small minority of Africans receive secondary and higher education, but they are limited to employment in the service of their own communities.

Various studies have shown that an awareness of racial differences is not found among very small children but, when parents are acutely aware of racial identity, may emerge as early as two or two and one half years. By the age of four, nearly all normal children will be at least minimally and occasionally aware of the physical differences of race, and in communities where prejudice and discrimination are found, may well have developed incipient ingroup/outgroup orientations. Fully fledged racial attitudes may be formed in the early years at school (but see, of course, Chapter 1 of this book). Teachers and peer groups at school may play an important part in reinforcing racial consciousness and prejudice. By the same token, they may be important influences in diminishing antipathetic attitudes towards racial minorities. There may be initial resistance by parents, teachers and pupils to the admission of coloured children to a previously all-white school. However, once racial integration has been achieved there is little evidence of any serious difficulties in the classroom, apart from those arising from the educational level of the minority group and the language and cultural barriers that sometimes exist in the case of immigrant children. When the initial educational level of the first generation immigrants is low, the cultural handicap may persist in subsequent generations, but the evidence from Blau and Duncan (1967) suggests that this is less important than the restrictions on social mobility and occupational achievement resulting from racial discrimination.

Although teachers may refuse to countenance racial prejudice or discrimination in the school, these attitudes are not necessarily carried over into the community. Studies in Britain have shown that a complete absence of racial discrimination in choice of friends and contacts at school may be entirely compatible with segregation in leisure-time pursuits and other activities outside the school. The long-term effects of school integration are difficult to predict. When school integration is achieved by transporting children from one part of the city to another it may have the effect of heightening frustration, generating unrealizable aspirations on the part of minority groups, enhancing bitterness and alienation. Young people who have never known life outside the ghetto may passively accept their position. In contrast, those who, through personal experience or through the vicarious stimulation of the mass media of communication, have had their horizons widened may be more disposed to violent protest.

Racial violence

Violence as a characteristic of race relations takes a variety of forms. It is important to distinguish the use of violence by a dominant group to maintain its position and to repress any incipient tendencies towards revolution from the organized violence used by subversive groups as a means of protest and the spontaneous outbursts of violence exhibited by minority groups in riot situations (see Chapter 6).

Violence is an everyday occurrence in South Africa, where the police use coercive and brutal measures in dealing with the African population, enforcing pass laws and other regulations with little respect for human dignity. Occasionally, as at Sharpeville in 1960, police may use armed force to combat peaceful protests by the African population. Furthermore, law and order are hard to maintain in the 'shanty towns' and violent crime is common. However, punitive measures against those who are critical of the South African regime, including the use of detention measures against both white and non-white opponents of *apartheid*, ensure that organized protest of a violent nature is comparatively rare. However, the cumulative frustration of the African population may occasionally express itself in violence directed against each other or the Asian population, who are more immediate and less threatening targets than the white population.

In Britain, violence has occurred from time to time and appears to have been associated particularly with periods of actual or potential economic recession, when unemployment among certain sections of the white population gave rise to hostility against coloured immigrants. The earliest examples were disturbances that broke out in the dockland areas of Cardiff and Liverpool after the First World War. Somewhat similar events occurred in Liverpool in 1948. The best known examples of violence in Britain occurred in Nottingham and the North Kensington area of London in 1958. It has been shown that, although the precipitating causes of these disturbances were often of a minor nature and their repetition over a period of several weeks may have been aggravated by the publicity given to them by the mass media, the underlying causes were associated with a sudden increase in unemployment among juvenile male white workers (Richmond, 1961). The distinction between underlying and precipitating causes has been emphasized in studies of race riots in the United States. Grimshaw (1960) has distinguished between 'classic' race rioting, such as occurred after the First World War, which appeared to reflect the social composition of, and deprivations experienced in, particular localities and the riots which have occurred since the Second World War, which appear to have involved a wider cross-section of the population. Recent disorders indicate the emergence of a new militancy on the part of some sections of the Negro population. However, Lieberson (1965) has shown that race riots in the United States are less a function of increased numbers, high unemployment rates and poor housing than of a breakdown in the political process and the absence of effective channels for legitimate protest on the part of the Negro population. Cities in which Negroes were members of the police force, where they were represented on municipal governing bodies and where there were effective channels of communication with the administration, were less likely to experience riots than those areas where no such representation existed.[4]

4. In an article in the Nebraska Symposium on Motivation (1967) T. F. Pettigrew presents a substantially similar analysis of violence but from a different theoretical standpoint.

A study of racial attitudes in fifteen American cities, conducted in 1968, threw some light on the factors associated with the extensive disorders that have occurred in the USA in recent years (Campbell, 1968). Advocacy of violence by Negro respondents was associated with a variety of grievances and ideological beliefs. There was no simple correlation with education but it was most frequent among young males. The same applied to whites who approved of counter-violence against Negroes. The percentage of whites who said that they would engage in vigilante activity was nearly as great (5 per cent) as the percentage of Negroes who said they would join a riot (8 per cent). In both cases it appeared to be associated with the desire to exhibit manly daring. At the same time, almost the entire Negro population defined riots as genuine protests against real grievances and tended to sympathize with others who became more actively involved in violent protest.

Another survey, conducted shortly after the assassination of Dr Martin Luther King, obtained information from a sample that was representative of Negroes and whites in the country as a whole, rather than confined to the cities (Opinion Research Corporation, 1965). Only 6 per cent of Negroes and 2 per cent of whites in this sample said that demonstrations that might lead to violence were a good way of achieving equal rights for Negroes. Only half of these said that they personally would get involved in such violent activities. However, when white respondents were asked, 'If you were a Negro, and you thought that rioting was a way to help get action on the Negro's problems, do you think that you probably would or probably would not join in a riot or a violent demonstration', 15 per cent said they probably would. It is indicative of the extensive fear and potentially explosive situation that 31 per cent of the Negro households and 46 per cent of the white households sampled, possessed a gun (see also Chapter 6 of this book).

Although changes in the United States have been in the direction of increasing Negro participation in the political and social system, the incidence of violence has been increasing, and is probably even greater than in South Africa. The US National Advisory Commission on Civil Disorders, 1967, noted that Negroes firmly believe that police brutality and harassment occur frequently in Negro neighbourhoods and this belief was unquestionably one of the major reasons for intense Negro resentment against the police. Although they concluded that the incidence of physical abuse or harassment was probably exaggerated, they considered that police misconduct should not be tolerated, even if it was infrequent. The Commission's extensive studies of the disorders that occurred in 1967 led it to conclude that none of the city riots was 'typical' in all respects. While the disorders were racial, they were not interracial in character. They involved violent action within Negro neighbourhoods against the symbols of white American society – authority and property – rather than against white persons. The typical rioter was not a hoodlum, habitual criminal or a completely uneducated person. Most often he was a teenager or young adult, a lifelong resident of the city in which he rioted and somewhat better educated than his Negro neighbour. He was proud of his race, extremely hostile to both whites and middle-class Negroes and critical of the political system and its leaders.

One of the Commission's most important findings would be true of Britain, South Africa or any country where racial minorities are subject to discrimination and segregation. Segregation and poverty created the racial ghetto, a destructive environment totally unknown to most white people, but 'white institutions created it, white institutions maintain it and white society condones it'.

References

ADAM, H. (ed.) (1971), *South Africa: Sociological Perspectives*, Oxford University Press.

ALLEN, S. (1971), *New Minorities, Old Conflicts: Asian and West Indian Migrants in Britain*, Random House.

BETTELHEIM, B., and JANOWITZ, M. (1964), *Social Change and Prejudice*, Free Press.

BLALOCK, H. M. (1967), *Toward a Theory of Minority Group Relations*, Wiley.

BLAU. P., and DUNCAN, O. D. (1967), *The American Occupational Structure*, Wiley.

BLUMER, H. (1958), 'Race prejudice as a sense of group position', *Pacific Sociological Review*, vol. 1, no. 1, Spring, pp. 3–7.

BLUMER, H. (1965), 'Industrialization and race relations', in G. Hunter (ed.), *Industrialization and Race Relations*, Oxford University Press.

BURNEY, E. (1967), *Housing on Trial: A Study of Immigrants and Local Government*, Oxford University Press.

CAMPBELL, A., and SCHUMAN, H. (1968), *Racial Attitudes in Fifteen American Cities*, Survey Research Centre, University of Michigan.

GRIMSHAW, A. D. (1960), 'Urban racial violence in the United States: changing ecological considerations', *American Journal of Sociology*, vol. 66, no. 2, pp. 109–19.

HEPPLE, B. (1970), *Race, Jobs and the Law in Britain*, 2nd edn, Penguin.

HODGE, R. W., and TREIMAN, D. J. (1966). 'Occupational mobility and attitudes towards Negroes', *American Sociological Review*, vol. 31, no. 1. pp. 93–102.

HOPE, J. (1952), 'Industrial intergration of Negroes: the upgrading process', *Human Organization*, vol. 2, pp. 5–14.

JAHODA, M., and WEST, P. S. (1951), 'Race relations in public housing' *Journal of Social Issues*, vol. 7, nos. 1 and 2, pp. 132–9.

KUTNER, B., WILKINS, C., and YARROW, P. (1952), 'Verbal attitudes and overt behaviour involving racial prejudice', *Journal of Abnormal and Social Psychology*, vol. 47, pp. 649–52.

LA PIERE, R. (1934), 'Attitude versus action', *Social Forces*, vol. 13, December, pp. 230–37.

LIEBERSON, S., and SILVERMAN, A. R. (1965), 'The precipitants and underlying conditions of race riots', *American Sociological Review*, vol. 30, no. 6, pp. 887–98.

LINN, L. S. (1965), 'Verbal attitudes and overt behaviour; a study of racial discrimination', *Social Forces*, vol. 43, no. 3, pp. 353–64.

LOCKARD, D. (1968), *Toward Equal Opportunity*, Macmillan.

MAYER, A. J. (1957), 'Race and private housing', *Journal of Social Issues*, vol. 13, no. 4, pp. 3–6.

MCENTIRE, D. (1960), *Residence and Race*, University of California Press.

MERTON, R. K. (1949), 'Discrimination and the American Creed', in R. M. MacIver (ed.), *Discrimination and National Welfare*, Harper & Row.

MOLOTCH, H. (1969), 'Racial integration in a transition community', *American Sociological Review*, vol. 34, no. 6.

OPINION RESEARCH CORPORATION (1968), *White and Negro Attitudes Towards Race-Related Issues and Activities*, a CBS News Public Opinion Survey.

PATTERSON, S. (1968), *Immigrants in Industry*, Oxford University Press for the London Institute of Race Relations.

PETTIGREW, T. F. (1967), 'Social evaluation theory: convergencies and applications', Nebraska Symposium on Motivation, p. 241–318.

POLITICAL AND ECONOMIC PLANNING (1966), *Racial Discrimination*, P.E.P.

Report of the National Advisory Commission on Civil Disorders, Bantam Books, 1968.

REX, J., and MOORE, R. (1967), *Race, Community and Conflict: A Study of Sparkbrook*, Oxford University Press.

RICHMOND, A. H. (1954), *Colour Prejudice in Britain*, Routledge & Kegan Paul; reprinted, Negro Universities Press, Westport, 1971.

RICHMOND, A. H. (1960), 'Applied sociology and public policy concerning racial relations in Britain', *Race*, vol. 1, no. 2, pp. 14–26.

RICHMOND, A. H. (1961), *The Colour Problem*, revised edn. Penguin Books.

RICHMOND, A. H. (ed.) (1971), *Readings in Race and Ethnic Relations*, Pergamon Press, pp. 20–25.

RICHMOND, A. H. (1972), *Migration and Race Relations in an English City: A Study in Bristol*, Oxford University Press for the Institute of Race Relations.

ROSENTHAL, B. G., MILLER, D., and TERYENY, F. (1967), 'The measurement of social interaction among Negro and white children in a housing community', *Journal of Social Psychology*, vol. 71, pp. 27–37.

SHERIF, M. (1966), *Group Conflict and Corporation: Their Social Psychology*, Routledge & Kegan Paul.

SWANSON, M. W. (1968), 'Urban origins of separate development' *Race*, vol. 10, no. 1, pp. 31–40.

TAUEBER, K. E., and TAUEBER, A. F. (1964), 'The Negro as an immigrant group; recent trends in racial and ethnic segregation in Chicago', *American Journal of Sociology*, vol. 69, no. 4, pp. 374–82.

VAN DEN BERGHE, P. L. (1967), *Race and Racism: A Comparative Perspective*, Wiley.

VAN DER HORST, S. T. L. (1965), 'The effects of industrialization on race relations in South Africa' in G. Hunter (ed.), *Industrialization and Race Relations* Oxford University Press.

WILLIAMS, R. M. (1964), *Strangers Next Door: Ethnic Relations in American Communities*, Prentice-Hall.

WRIGHT, P. L. (1968), *The Coloured Worker in British Industry*, Oxford University Press.

Part Two
The Race Variable and Key Issues in Psychology

Race affects as many issues as does psychology – or almost. This half of the book gets away from an analysis of the interracial interaction as such and looks instead at those areas of life where race is relevant and where psychology can help in an understanding of the situation. Education, language, crime, mental illness: in all these race is now an 'issue' and in all there is a sizeable body of relevant psychological research not available elsewhere between the covers of just one book. At appropriate points cross-references are made to Part One.

Section D
The Interaction of Personality and Culture

James Ritchie goes on from where Anthony Richmond left off. He examines why it is that some cultures have more prejudice than others and tries to define the characteristics that account for this. Oscar Ferron looks explicitly at those cultural differences between people which have the most profound psychological consequences and which therefore may be expected to influence relations between people of different backgrounds.

Chapter 14
Culture, Personality and Prejudice

James E. Ritchie

James Ritchie's research and major interest is in the area of ethno-psychology, especially in the cross-cultural study of child rearing. He has published many articles on the contemporary Maori in New Zealand. He is a Fellow of the American Anthropological Association and of the British and the New Zealand Psychological Societies. Though he trained and has taught in New Zealand universities his background includes periods of study at the London School of Economics and at various American universities including Harvard, Columbia and teaching at the University of California, at Santa Cruz. He has recently been involved in the development of a social science curriculum for high schools in the Territory of Papua and New Guinea.

Not every society is equally ethnocentric. The potentiality for prejudice is not evenly spread in individuals or in societies, and is even less evenly demonstrated in overt acts of discrimination, repression or savagery. Why do some individuals show more prejudice than others? Why do some cultures seem to be more 'prejudice-prone'? These are questions about the very nature of the relationship between social character and surrounding, supporting culture. Why do some cultures build into individuals more need for prejudice than others? How and why do societies provide 'suitable' target groups for the expression of prejudice? Why are the target groups so often the same (darker-skinned people, Jews or other religiously defined out-groups, foreigners)? Why are the attributes ascribed to them so often the same? (Katz and Braly, 1933). What can be learned from those cases where they are not the same? What permits and gives power to the force and frequency of overt discriminatory acts? We know a little about the personality development of at least one category of very common prejudiced belief from the work of Adorno *et al.* (1950) in *The Authoritarian Personality*, but why is this so common a form in Western societies? Is it universal?

Not all of these questions can be adequately answered. We are only beginning the task of pulling psychology out of its own ethnocentric quagmire, and cross-cultural research raises a host of methodological problems and conceptual and communication difficulties. To continue this task the psychologist needs a concept of culture, either his own or someone else's, because without it the supports to prejudice cannot be understood and its genesis remains obscure.

What is ethnocentrism?

Much of the confusion in social science about ethnocentrism stems from treating it as a single variable. It is, in fact, a constellation of attitudes, a syndrome, drawing its strength and content from sources in the culture, the social system, and from the incidents of living.

The syndrome always includes a belief that one's own standards are universal, or true, and one's own group strong (it is still more extreme if the target group really is weak in relation to one's own). The target group is defined as exploitable, to be hated, a traditional enemy, or available to be plundered and not infrequently reacts in a prejudiced way to the dominant one. The ethnocentric society is frequently preoccupied with keeping social distance, both within itself and without. Its structure divides labour and distributes resources in such a way that a few have and most have not. Slavery in some form is usually present if only in the sense that some individuals are, because of their low status, considered to have fewer social and political rights. Marcuse (1964) argues that this is increasingly likely to occur where the distinction between work and play is sharply drawn; where leisure is differentially allocated and many individuals are virtually extensions of the machines they operate. In such circumstances, those tyrannized by industrial society may not themselves show greater ethnocentricity but their reduced level of total human satisfactions may increase the ethnocentric tendency of the social system of which they are part. The fewer the common goals shared in a society, the higher the competition for its goods and resources, the greater is the tendency for the generation of ethnocentric attitudes. When 'The Good' is considered to be finite, limited and hard to attain, the tendency is increased.

Societies that are highly ethnocentric have sharp definitions of membership, well-defined social boundaries, a high degree of status mobility and insecurity and frequently strongly delineated economic, religious or political ideologies. These are frequently policed by a central authority (collective or personalized) which demands obedience, and feels justified in using force to achieve cooperation. There is a preoccupation with order which is itself defined as difficult to maintain, not as something natural and emergent. This authority is usually associated with a marked emphasis on male virility and vigour, with sharp sex role definitions and anxiety about their maintenance. With the emphasis on male assertiveness and power goes an ultimate willingness to die to protect the in-group or oppose the out-group. Often necrophilic altruism, self-sacrifice to preserve the group, is valued positively as noble rather than stupid. Group or individual failure may be externalized with safety onto out-group members who are also used as bogey-men for threats in child training. Child rearing is characterized by punishment, threat and deprivation.

This is a fair stereotype of the ethnocentric syndrome, though any one society will not contain all features or any to the same degree as another. The perpetuation of this syndrome depends on child training which teaches a social character that will carry it. It depends, too, on the persistence of the components of social structure involved in its maintenance. But it depends, most of all, on cultural assumptions about the moral order, the natural order and the relationship of man to both.

Culture and ethnocentrism

To say we learn from others, that prejudice is learned, that it has historical, or sociological explanations is true enough, if somewhat unhelpful. But why does what we learn perpetuate a pattern? Without some supra-individual system how is it that so many people learn the same things? And what is it that makes one system flagrantly ethnocentric and another only mildly or passively so?

Philip Mason (1961), discussing the reasons for prejudice, gives three basic answers to the general question of the origins of prejudice. He invokes the psychoanalytic explanation that rigidity of standards (super-ego forces) lowers self regard (ego) and that to resolve the conflict the individual externalizes, or projects negatively valued desires or fears (id) onto a convenient and socially approved object. He also recognizes that black as a concept is associated with evil, the devil, dirt, defecation, the libido, and the long dark nights of the northern winter. Finally, some contribution comes from a competitive society that sets man against man. Things are undoubtedly more complex than this yet you can find lots of such comment. Always there is implicit in such explanations a concept of culture mediating and conserving patterns by which super-egos are furnished with content, symbolic systems perpetuated and competitive or other social modalities preserved, but rarely is the content of the culture made explicit. This is, perhaps, due to the lack of adequate theoretical language with which to deal with cultural analysis.

Even the concept of culture itself causes difficulty. In its widest sense culture can be thought of as the equivalent of a programme in computing; a code or set of instructions that an individual builds up for organizing the reception of sense data, for referring it to his store of past associations, ideas and knowledge, and of reacting to it. Many writers have emphasized the implicit nature of the cultural process, its ubiquity in behaviour and the way in which it patterns consciousness and unconscious processes alike.

In the sense of something experienced, culture is personal to the members of a group who, growing up together, learned the code together. Culture is the implicit patterning of behaviour in a group: the same set of meta-messages which patterns the transmission of behaviour from parent to child maintains and supports the structure of, and between, social institutions. You can begin its analysis anywhere. Marcuse (1965) suggests you start by asking 'How are the literature, arts, philosophy, science, religion of a society related to its actual behaviour?'.

You can begin by looking at the messages in childrearing, as I have done in most of my research. Or you can study national or group self-images or their images of specific or generalized others.

Culture as values

This concept may seem so semantically slippery that there is little chance of using it confidently either in an empirical or theoretical manner. Systematic ideas, such as those in Talcott Parsons' general theory of action (Parsons and Shils *et al.*, 1951), provide a framework in which we can begin to think of a culture as essentially offering some patterning of preferred alternatives or value orientations.

The pattern variables of Parsons' theory (1951) are one set of possible analytic tools. There are five sets of alternatives, dichotomous choices implicit in the decision to perform any action. One may attend to the immediacy of gratification or have regard for later consequences (affectivity – affective neutrality); one may act in self-interest or on collective considerations (self-orientation – collectivity orientation); one may evaluate the action in general terms or rules or act merely in terms of specific situational considerations (universalism – particularism); one may view the situation in terms of what qualities are ascribed to it or what things can be achieved (ascription – achievement); finally one must 'decide' on the scope of significance of the situation and the act whether to react to many aspects of the situation (diffuseness) or simply to one (specificity). As operational concepts the pattern variables have not proved easy to use. No one yet, as far as I know, has attempted to apply them to the cross-national study of ethnocentrism. This remains an interesting prospect. It seems likely that some patterns of choice will be more highly related to, or predisposed towards, prejudice than others will be.

Other analytic schemes of values and value orientations have been proposed. Aberle's list (1950) of the functional pre-requisites of a society is one such, though for our purposes it barely gets us far beyond Sumner's basic idea of dislike of the unlike (Sumner, 1906). Florence Kluckhohn (1950, 1961) sees value orientations as organized in dominant and substitute profiles on five basic dimensions – the view of man's essential nature (evil, mixed or good), his relation to nature (subservient, in partnership, dominant), orientation in time (past, present or future), engaged in a mode of activity (being; being-in-becoming; becoming), a relationship orientation (lineal, colateral, individualistic).

Clyde Kluckhohn (1954) presented a more extensive discussion of universal values. His list of universals includes the belief that social life shall be ordered, that the behaviour of members shall be predictable in terms of the premises of the culture. Accordingly people should act in terms of the moral system of their society and show conformity rather than nonconformity. All societies, therefore, have a definition of normality and, on the other hand, some standards for the recognition of abnormal behaviour. All cultures believe that society has the right to exercise some restraint over its members; all place some limitations on the free choice of those members; all believe that an individual's needs must be tempered in terms of the needs of other members. In no known society is incest freely permitted; deference to one's parents and basic reciprocity or compensation of one's kin for services which they may give are universally recognized. As a general rule, no society tolerates a state of war, each against all, and in general, it is deemed good to preserve human life at least within the kin group. Human suffering is never a matter of no concern and in general it must be avoided or alleviated. Indiscriminate lying or cheating is negatively sanctioned, though it may be permitted in certain areas and relationships within the social structure. All societies make use of common psychological means for the release of tension and stress and in particular all provide for positively valued expression through fantasy, though there may be difference in the degree of permission in this respect.

These are content universals. Ethnocentrism is clearly linked, if indirectly, to many of them. Beyond these universal values Kluckhohn (1956) postulated a set of cultural alternatives, more complex than the pattern variables. Human behaviour, he says, is based on 'anthropocentric two-valued logic', binary choices between this and that. These choices cluster into values which are organized as orientations. Orientations themselves show this binary form. Three orientations seem predominant – the relation of man to nature, the relation of man to man, and the relationship towards man and nature together.

As a man stands in relation to nature he may take three kinds of orientations, each of which offers two choices. He may view his relationship as determinate, that he has a place in the order of things, and can, by playing along with natural objects and tendencies, achieve a relationship which is orderly, lawful and progressive. Or he may regard the universe as indeterminate and accept his place in things, or not, as the case may be. An indeterminate belief assumes the world to be disorderly or chaotic but does not preclude the attempt to force order onto it. The second orientation is that of unitary belief as against pluralistic conception. Here the essential choice is between a world view based on the assumption that the natural universe is locked into a single overall system and one which views natural events as the outcome of plural forces, as a product of oppositions. Finally, the world may be viewed as basically positive, sympathetic and supportive or as hostile, bad and destructive.

In relationship to other men there are eight basic orientation alternatives. A value system may place pre-eminent value on individual effort or on the products of group living. A culture may emphasize egoism or altruism. It may regard either autonomy or dependence as of greater importance. Activity and striving may be valued over passivity and acceptance, or vice-versa. Some cultures regard discipline as more desirable than fulfilment, a distinction in which safety, control and thrift contrast with adventure, expansion and consumption. Either the physical or the mental aspects of life may be valued. Tension or relaxation may prevail over most activities. Present time may be the preoccupation or the society may elaborate dimensional time – that is to say, a man may see his relations to other men as sequentially bound in cause and effect in time or not.

Two value orientations seem to apply to man's performance both in respect to the world and to other men. These are the alternatives of quality versus quantity and the dichotomy between regarding each experience as unique or the search for experience that has a general quality.

On an *a priori* basis it seems likely that some profiles on such a conception of cultural value orientation would be more likely to permit the development of ethnocentric attitudes and discriminatory action. Take, for example (on the Clyde Kluckhohn formulation), this profile:

Determinate – unitary – evil – individual – egocentric – autonomous – active – fulfilment – physical – tense – present time – quality – general.

A culture with these orientations would very likely display what we more ordinarily call an authoritarian totalitarian ideology and exhibit the nastier features of what we ethnocentrically call the protestant ethic. A little reflection on the central ideas in the policy of *apartheid* and the prevailing culture in the Union of South Africa which makes the policy possible supports this proposition.

Kluckhohn's intention is, of course, to find a set of descriptive categories that are ahistorical and non-ethnocentric. If he has succeeded then we should be able to find associations between them and ethnocentricity free from the biases arising from particular historical traditions or concentration on particular kinds of political processes – imperialism for example.

Configurationist theory of this type has been in eclipse for the last decade yet we clearly have need of formulations of this kind to supplement the more sociologically and psychologically oriented explanations of the phenomena of ethnic relations. Kecskemeti (1954), for example, concludes that descent from an hierarchically low status group is one of the main causes of discrimination. Whether he is right or not he is postulating an ordering of man's relation to man unthinkable for, to take only one case, a Hopi Indian. The ethnocentricism which is universal does not necessarily lead to prejudiced discrimination. This arises when more specific values are present, when they become matters of focal concern and when the society becomes mobilized, or individuals mobilized in defence of their peculiarity. Beyond culture, then, we must seek explanation in social process as well as in symbolic process.

The strain towards consistency

Rather more attention has been focused recently on a variety of formulations in social psychology collectively termed consistency or congruity theories and summarized very well by Brown (1965). These include the 'dissonance theory' of Leon Festinger (1957), various conceptions of 'balance theory' (Heider, 1958, Newcomb, 1959, 1961; Harary, Norman and Cartwright, 1965) and the congruity theory of Osgood and his associates (1955). Basic to all these is the postulate that inconsistency in attitudes or beliefs is psychologically intolerable or basically abhorrent. But implicit in all is the likelihood that some situations, or cultures, exacerbate the condition of strain by exposing the individual to inconsistencies.

The strain of inconsistency arises when, in the mind of an individual, he sees his own attitude (A) and that of another person (B) as discrepant towards some object (X) which may be a thing, a person, a belief, a practice, or a group. Basically, the strain arises because of imbalance of liking or disliking. Thus things are in balance when:

Both A and B like X and like each other
Both A and B dislike X and like each other
A likes X but dislikes B who dislikes X
A dislikes X but dislikes B who likes X
Strain occurs when:
A likes B but their attitudes to X conflict
A dislikes B but their attitudes to X are in agreement

When, for a group, one aggregates the balance state of individuals towards some out-group then there is less strain when the out-group is similar to the in-group or when all members of the group agree to dislike the other. In a similar way Rokeach (1960) postulates that prejudice is due more to perceived differences in value or belief than to perceptions of different 'race' or 'colour'. Perceived similarity of beliefs, correspondingly, should be associated with lower prejudice levels. His research procedures establish these hypotheses but the idea seems to me implausible. It can't, for example, account for the following bit of Negro doggerel:

She's got to be *white*, Jack –
'Cause white is right
Both day and night!
She's got to be *old* and white
'Cause if she's old
She's been white longer!
She's got to be *big* and white
'Cause if she's big
She's much *more* white!
But listen, Jack –
If she can't be white
Then let her be real light brown!
(Quoted by Lincoln, 1967)

Black power is about the state of being black. Colour is the cue to the imputing of beliefs which then must hang like an albatross around the necks of Negroes. But Rokeach does focus our attention on one strong cultural fact. If you want to understand the cultural sources of ethnocentrism look closely at the symbol systems of core beliefs – especially religion and myth – and this applies as much to Christianity as to Black Muslims or Ras Tafaris.

Nevertheless, consistency theory (though not strictly cultural in kind) has much to offer. The technicalities are formidable (and so, often, is the language) but in sophisticated hands (for an example see Campbell and Le Vine, 1968) these theories can lead to derivation of testable hypotheses. For example, here are some: the more similar the out-group the less likely is prejudice; the greater the in-group liking the higher the degree of ethnocentricism; the most dissimilar of any of a set of in-groups will show the greatest hostility towards out-groups. One can generate hypotheses very freely from consistency theory.

Campbell and Le Vine regard these as hypotheses yet to be tested through experimental social research. They lie, however, very close to the level of commonsense and one would be somewhat surprised to find them not confirmed.

This kind of conception of culture as a recipe for consistency and of ethnocentricism as an epiphenomenon of inter-group strain has been a major focus in an extensive programme of cross-cultural research on ethnocentrism, located at Northwestern University (Campbell and Le Vine, 1961). The directors of this study have devised a field manual by which a large number of cooperating ethnographers can report broadly comparable data from a wide range of societies (Le Vine and Campbell, 1965). Conclusions from this project have yet to appear, but two interim statements (Campbell and Le Vine, 1965, 1968) show the order of information and theorizing which may result. Already, the brief set of generalizations with which this chapter opened could be greatly extended through their work. The project is, however, both too extensive and, at this stage, tentative, to be easily summarized or usefully employed for present purposes. But, as a sample, here are twelve testable propositions arising from their work.

The more ethnocentric the society:

1. The more authoritarian in family (or domestic group) structure, community structure, supra-community structure (i.e., the greater the command power of leaders, the more total is loyalty, deference, and obedience to them).

2. The more severe the sanctions against those who defy authority or violate cultural prohibitions and taboos of any kind.

3. The more persons in it tend to believe that deviance is widespread and anarchy an imminent possibility if autocratic leaders are absent.

4. The more fragile is integration at the societal level (as evidenced by outbreaks of internecine warfare).

5. The more persons in it indulge in malicious gossip and witchcraft and sorcery accusations against each other, i.e., against those of the same status as themselves.

6. The more its culture involves belief in supernatural powers controlling individual fate rather than mastery by the individual himself over his environment.

7. The fewer the cultural categories for natural and social events, the more rigid adherence to previously held categories in the face of novel facts or situations, and the greater the reluctance of informants to admit that anything is indeterminate, unknowable, or complicated.

8. The more punitive are fathers (or other primary male authority figures) to their pre-adolescent sons, and the more are sons afraid of their fathers.

9. The greater the emphasis on obedience to authority as a prime value to be inculcated in children.

10. The greater the reliance on physical punishment in child training practices.

11. The greater the emphasis on subordination of wives to husbands, children to parents, junior siblings to senior siblings, in family groups.

12. The greater the emphasis on the subordination of women in the society and the greater the hostility to male homosexuals or any male manifesting behaviour labelled as 'effeminate'.

The effects of ethnocentrism

The effect of prejudice on individuals is covered in a literature almost impossibly wide to be easily summarized. The condition of the American

Negro (Pettigrew, 1964, 1965; Graubard, 1965) is the most widely documented record. The Kerner Report (1968) on the riots of 1966–67 concentrates on white prejudice as the source of the tragedy but does not examine what it is in American culture that makes prejudice functional. Time is possibly shorter than most people think for the industrial North of the United States. By the 1980s black votes will be near to control of city government in many, if not most, northern urban centres. This is the reality behind 'Black Power' which makes it far more than a futile gesture of anti-racist racism. Black poverty, the shattered structure of roles in the black family, the concentration camp atmosphere of the ghettos, welfare dependency, suppressive and often vicious policing, drugs and the marketing of bodies, an environment of deprivation and decay, all these and more have an impact on the culture of the target group but do not constitute the *content* of that culture which is something else again.

A parallel set of phenomena are widely associated with poverty alone, so much so that, on the basis of study of the poor in India and Mexico, Oscar Lewis (1960) speaks of the culture of poverty. His accounts of what the culture of poverty is like (1959, 1964, 1966) have a passive depressed quality that Eric Fromm calls necrophilic–displaying a tendency towards decay, decline and death. Why is it, though, that a Mexican peasant accepts as fate what a Black Muslim or Black Panther in Chicago or San Francisco clearly is no longer willing to accept or take?

The peasant can conceive of no other culture than what he has – his state is not clearly the result of the actions or attitudes of an out-group. The Negro activist lives in a sub-culture permeated at almost every point by the dominant conceptions of the American value system. He reacts as a black *American*, in consonance with the dominant values of activity, effort and hope, a radical belief that the system can be changed, that personal and social perfection be attained, that you need to be aggressive to get ahead, and so on.

The current aims of the Negro reform and protests are for nothing short of full access to constitutional and civil liberties, now. The watch cries are 'Freedom' and 'Equal Opportunity' and there is no doubt that they are uttered in the sense in which all Americans can understand them. When Kenneth Clark urges that the walls of the black ghettos be breached rather than built higher to make a separate but equal black nation (as some would urge), the means he involves to do this are not only by appeal to agencies of the Federal Government but also to white commerce. He can think in terms of mobilizing all the resources of American society because he thinks in common cultural terms with the members of that society. Business is so central a part of American life that its means can be used, by threat or appeal, to change the existing situation (Graubard, 1965). Nothing of this kind is available to the Mexican peasant, and if it were his dominant value orientations would lead to its automatic rejection. The culture of the Negro American is American but it is also distinct and changing. The situation where white Americans and black Americans have conflicting attitudes towards Negro identity is balanced while there is mutual hostility between white and black, but not if Negroes and Americans try to keep up a pretence of approval each for the other. Negroes can maintain a positive identity with less strain if it is clear that they are negatively valued in the wider society.

Similarly, while race relations in New Zealand stand in good repute it is remarkable that, as something close to educational parity between races is attained, young Maoris are emphasizing positive aspects of Maori identity and castigating white New Zealanders for continuing to accept, as reality, an imperfect state of affairs. The wider society often offers no other identity than a negative one – membership in a 'problem' minority, ignoring that others, non-members of the minority, have similar problems. No one *wants* to be reduced to being someone else's problem, but in a passive-dependent situation this can be forced upon the oppressed as a self-definition.

In terms of the balance model, if the surrounding society is perceived as negatively evaluating the minority group any member of that group will experience strain unless he can positively evalute himself in terms of minority membership. Black Americans and minorities in similar situations are starting to realize this to an increasing degree and build a basis to strengthen positive identity. The risk of increasing the wider society's negative evaluations ('the natives are getting too big for their boots') is well worth taking because it brings into the open attitudes that might otherwise be smothered up in social candy-floss ('our natives really are not as bad as theirs' and similar remarks).

In conditions of strain there has been a shift in Negro American values. The 'slave mentality', the mother-centred family, the rejection of achievement, all that 'Uncle Tom' implies, now lies outside the self-image of an increasing number of Negroes. They no longer accept the way the wider culture says that Negro identity should be defined. The most significant factors in this shift have not been the migration North out of the caste system of the deep South, nor the enactment of urban renewal, welfare or other Negro aid measures, but nothing less than a twin and complementary set of revolutionary processes. Negroes have rejected the slave identity and with it the cultural premises on which it rested; secondly, their revolutionary urge has been matched by a similar spirit of rejection and revolt in young Americans more generally. In the 1960s the freedom rides of white activists to join with their Negro counterparts in desegregating services and voter registration brought the two together – and freedom was the issue for both. Gunnar Myrdal said that the answer to the American dilemma lay in the heart of white America and there, in a sense he never suspected, the answer really does lie. Socio-economic change has been the predominant process in culture change in America generally, for at least forty years. By some cultural dynamic the forefront is now where it was during the great melting-pot period. Generational change, which is far more sweeping and extensive than any other kind, is now appearing as the chief mode of cultural change in America.

Margaret Mead (1964) has argued that the basic mode of change in America during the 'melting-pot' period, involved a three generation process. As each successive wave of migrants arrived, the parental generation suffered cultural dislocation. Their descendants tried to become as American as they could as soon as they were able, thrusting their parental origins as far behind as possible. The third generation, less assertively, live with greater comfort in their culture, which is no longer new, strange, or something to be attained by effort. I suspect that this process has been of less importance during the last three decades, than change arising from increased industrial employment, adaptation to urban living and a technocratic society. But in the current emergence of the 'new young' it is possible that we are seeing the generational model reasserting itself (see also Chapter 9 of this book). Is young America shouldering aside its parental generation as did the children of the immigrants who fled to America after the Irish potato famine, the Russian pogroms or the Nazi oppression? Are they similarly out to break the old mould and make a new one in the shape of the ideals of Thoreau and the founding fathers? Indeed Mead (1968) later postulates that social change is now so rapid that elders must develop the methods and means to learn from young people who are the only ones who really know the directions in which cultural growth is heading.

It could be argued that this is a return to a condition of cultural normalcy in American social change; that given the profile of American cultural values, the psycho-dynamics of its kind of family, the openness of its institutions, the prevailing change process is not mediated by wealth, power, status, technology, or through political or social institutions, but by the generational discrepancy in a society that sees itself and human nature as perfectable.

The growth of affluence and suburbia, as a phase in cultural history for that society, subverted this process but has not destroyed its potent myths nor its underlying symbolism. Edward Albee's play, *The American Dream*, is a negative Horatio Alger story. The real American dream does not always require violent rejection of parents by children but does place the individual central to processes of social change, even if arrayed against him are entrenched concentrations of massive social power (Domhoff, 1967). Thus, each generation is implicitly trained to reject and remake. Both for white and black individuals recent social history has turned this destructive potential back into the family thereby increasing the change potential in the society.

There is a strong possibility that for the Negro group the evolution of what have seemed to be destructive family and social dynamics has reached a threshold where the society is producing in ever increasing numbers people capable of destruction of the system itself; a process not unfamiliar to students of culture change, or of revolutions. Lee Rainwater (1966) argues this case effectively. In the process of fashioning a sub-culture in which to survive, the Negro has had to accept a situation where 'whites, by their greater power, create situations in which Negroes do the dirty work of caste victimization for them . . . they are constrained to behave in ways that inflict a great deal of suffering on those with whom they make their lives . . . by the immediate necessity to suffer . . . or to make others suffer'. He analyses the Negro family, matri-focal, ambivalent about marriage, acceptant of illegitimacy, inclusive of other relatives, evocative, responsive, but unstable, closely linked with the neighbourhood and with the Negro world. As he indicates, there is, within the system, tolerance of violent expression and open directness. 'Tell it like it is' is first of all a tenet of family interaction; so, too, is active and immediate conflict resolution, the avoidance of, or reaction against, psycho-social 'castration', the lessons of collective strength. The identity switch from being depressed and put upon to assertion, is a change of reference frame – from accepting white-defined identity to black-defined identity – but it builds on the strengths of the culture of the Negro family, community, or Negro national segment.

Along the way the concept of Negritude, of an African identity, has been a mediating support, a clear use of a pseudo-culture for reasons of re-integration of real culture. From a non-identity as descendant of slaves, the progression has led to an identity as far distant as possible in psychological space from the real world of white oppression, then back again to confrontation of that world. The autobiography of Malcolm X (1966) documents the process vividly. Through his career he moved from an assimilationist identity which reflected ghetto experience, to very active membership then leadership in the Black Muslim movement but finally transcended even this to become a man speaking for his people – for them all. It was from this non-sectional stance that he spoke, until his death, and it was this that earned the respect of black and white alike. The transitions he made seemed disruptive because there were few models to follow; the route had to be forged. But others followed more easily, though with no less a revolutionary intent. In terms of institutions, art or literature, Negro culture has little to show, but as experience there is far, far more than white America knows or would be willing to accept or admit.

Ethnocentricism in America is leading to this ultimate point; Marcuse calls it generally the 'Great Refusal'; and it is happening elsewhere, indeed everywhere. It is a refusal to accept an ego-alien identity. As a Maori once said to me, 'Who wants to work for a bloke who won't employ you'. In effect, since prejudice inhibits or prevents the evolution of a common cultural identity and common social structure, there is ultimately no alternative but to be revolutionary in attitude if not in action towards the culture that supports prejudice. Most black Americans cannot 'pass' because of their colour; they will not accept 'passing' because of their identity. Most Maoris could 'pass' but they reject 'passing' for the same reasons. We are emerging from a phase in history that was essentially destructive of cultural differences, national, ethnic, regional or otherwise. The denial of differences, as an overstated and over-anxious reaction to the need to stress similarities, has become disfunctional in a world where ego loss and alienation are the now universal threat. To meet that threat individuals ask 'In what ways can I demonstrate that I am me?' They may seek the support of groups to answer this question (witness the hippies and other identity cults), but when they do so they are likely to become bound up in the same processes in groups that require out-group hate and the other universal supports of ethnocentricism.

We need to understand how group culture and personal identity can interact to counter this process. To say that ethnocentrism is universal is not to endorse its acceptance.

Culture and identity

White writers, even in the social sciences, frequently speak of minority groups in ways that reveal their own scientific ethnocentricity. The use of terms like 'absent father', 'castrating mother', 'negative identity', and 'culturally deprived' implies that minority experience is negative, ego-alien and mutilating or mutilated. But is this so?

When we first began work on the relationship between Maori personality and culture we similarly slipped all too easily into a language derived from a pathology model of human behaviour and oriented our research towards the evidence of pathology. Fortunately, the evidence for the contrary view was so forceful that during fieldwork itself we had to change orientation. The contrast between the Rorschach-derived description of Maori individuals and the life-history material (Ritchie, 1963) demonstrates this very clearly. (The Rorschach personality tests uses ambiguous ink blots as stimuli into which subjects – or patients – 'project' their own stories, revealing, according to psychoanalytic theory, the main aspects of their personality).

The Rorschach records were severely limited, constricted and indeed if ordinarily interpreted, indicative of guardedness, anxiety, vigilance, impoverished mental life and the usual psychological characteristics we associate with cultural deprivation. The life-history data, and Thematic Apperception Test, another 'projective' test, records show a contrasting liveliness, a social responsiveness, a willingness to accept and respond to a culturally defined set of imaginative challenges and good general psychological adjustment at least for the business of living with and for their own kind. Using a pathology model one sees pathology: given an adjustment and growth model, provided you know what to look for, one sees psychological health.

It is certainly possible that some (sick) individuals amongst the minority may see themselves as victims and introject a negative identity but, even for them, more important than the perception is the response to it. Identity, as Erikson (1966) points out, is something chosen, assertive, and it contains both positive and negative components. There is also a time, in individual terms developmentally, and in group terms historically, when episodes of identity confusion are more prevalent, more likely and more frequent. From such times, if choice is denied and growth prevented, a passive dependent orientation may emerge for many or even most members of a minority or (as in South Africa) amongst a suppressed majority.

The cultural variable of greatest significance, therefore, is the degree of choice allowed to the individual in the formulation of his own 'identity'. The white 'honkey' in the US who fails to 'see' black people around him is (whatever else of damaging nature he may do) providing the black individual with the right and opportunity to assert his own identity. Oppression may do the same thing provided that the culture of the oppressed contains the identity message – 'be yourself' – and some group or other can support the individual in doing so.

I no longer believe that any but a very small part of all the research we have done on the personality effects of minority status is of any but historical value. I am more inclined, instead, to look for insight into the interpretive accounts by artists who write of black experience not only for what they say but for what they signify. No one who ever listened to Mahalia Jackson, who *really* listened, could then write of the castrating female in Negro slum families. If I offer you a choice of the stereotypes of the black Momma, the American Mom, or whatever it is the British have, which you choose depends on what kind of maternal experience you would like to claim as your personal past *and* on what is available from your memory for you to claim or reject. What a Negro claims, or any other minority group, or any individual anywhere, is what he or she needs to feel complete, to be free to grow. This growth goes on even in the most unpromising of environments.

Within any society there is a range of options available, however small.

From a social point of view this may be of minor significance – roles are the focus of attention. But from the personal point of view the optative is the locus of self-esteem, even if the choice is limited to acceptance or rejection of socially prescribed roles. Whatever liberty or privilege a dominant society withdraws or withholds from a minority, however its laws or the ethnocentric attitudes of its members deprive or injure them, it cannot deprive them of their identity and the inner strength and comfort this can bring. But what ethnocentricism frequently does is cause the minority to mask their real identity so that it is enjoyed only at the fantasy level or in activities like religious cults, 'rapping' sessions, alcoholic euphoria or moody togetherness, blues music, in humour, and in the limited world where the minority culture can for a brief time restore a sense of both its validity and the identity its members derive from it.

Identity is the key to understanding the culture and the personality of those who suffer discrimination, the impregnable stronghold of cultural continuity surviving long after custom, language and tradition depart, surviving appalling oppression and attack – the phoenix from the ashes last time, this time and next time.

By way of summary

Culture supports ethnocentricism to some degree for all human groups, but the excesses of prejudice are probably associated with particular value-profiles within culture as well as with non-cultural variables, like pressure on the land and demography generally. The highly ethnocentric culture requires for its transmission a particular set of child-rearing practices of which those described in studies of the authoritarian personality are a common form but possibly not the only set. The presence of cultural prescriptions of an ethnocentric kind provide continuing support and maintenance for a social structure that provides a 'place' for discriminated minorities. Cognitive strain increases the identification of target groups, emphasizes their dissimilar features over the similarities and reduction of strain provides reinforcement for discriminatory practices.

Social science has focused attention on the social problems produced in the minority groups by ethnocentricism. A more objective focus looks not merely at these destructive processes or damaged products but at the reactions in terms of identity of those whom the prejudiced victimize. In this view the right to define oneself and one's destiny remains psychologically inalienable. The one response to which the ethnocentric has no answer is the statement 'I am not really the way *you* think I am but the way *I* think I am'.

Psychology has been preoccupied with the appearance of things in the confrontation between the prejudiced person and his victim. It has been preoccupied with the sources of prejudice in white society and the observable and measurable effects of it. Research of this kind has merit but needs to be supplemented by more sophisticated and subtle inquiry into and understanding of response, of the victim as a person, and of the culture of his kind. The research record bears the stamp of over-concern with pathology. Even in the oppression of South Africa blacks are 'making it'. On what terms do they do so? In the last analysis; on their own.

A case in point

Over the last fifteen years we have been working towards an understanding of the New Zealand Maori and of ethnic relations in these terms (Ritchie, 1960, 1963, 1964; Beaglehole and Ritchie, 1958; Westra and Ritchie, 1967).

Value analysis of myth and of ethnography (Ritchie, 1960) reveals a culture which at contact had many similarities to the western pattern. This provided a basis for an early working together but the high levels of ethnocentricism in both cultures brought confrontation in the mid-nineteenth century. Competition for similarly valued resources was the obvious factor in this clash but no less potent were conceptions of ideal character which made the European intrusion psychologically so dissonant that violent opposition resulted.

The continuing strength of Maori culture threw up a continuous sequence of revitalization movements, some aggressive and built around the institution of warfare, some religious and centring on ethical and moral expression of the cultural core. In this century, as in most such situations, the strength shows in renewed political vitality, in a variety of voluntary associations, in reintegration of the family, and more recently still in the arts borrowing the forms of western expression for the statement of messages of what it means to be Maori in the present time.

What is most spectacular about this sequence is not the absence of prejudice (as New Zealanders so often falsely claim), but that the existence of a high level of white ethnocentricism has not prevented a prevailing ethos of integration and good relations being maintained. Maoris, of course, are not black, but they are the darkest target around, so lightness of colour alone cannot explain the low level of discrimination. What can account for it is the changing, adapting and viable identity to which Maoris have always had access; their continuing concern to maintain a changing and demonstrably viable culture in which to anchor their identity. Indeed, there are now a number of identities or identity components associated with variants of this culture. There is a future in any one of several different ways of being Maori even in spite of white denial of the authenticity of Maori cultural experience (Ritchie, 1964).

In some ways a Maori can be more Maori now than a generation ago;

he can join a dance group, relearn his language, engage in Maori politics, still retain a sense of contact with central institutions of the tribal gathering or death ceremonial, enjoy Maori family experience and cultural sentiment, join a very wide array of voluntary associations. White New Zealanders might hope that ultimately Maoris and Maori culture will just fade away, but the authentic contact with culture is strong enough for enough Maoris to resist this ethnocentric attitude. So long as they do, it does not matter with what ignorance white society greets them.

References

ADORNO, T. W. et al. (1950), The Authoritarian Personality: Studies in Prejudice, Harper.

ABERLE, D. F. et al. (1950), 'The functional prerequisites of society', Ethics, vol. 60, no. 2, pp. 100–11.

BEAGLEHOLE, E., and RITCHIE, J. E. (1961), 'The Rakau studies' in B. Kaplan (ed.), Studying Personality Cross-Culturally, Row Peterson.

BROWN, R. (1965), Social Psychology, Free Press.

CAMPBELL, D. T., and LE VINE, R. A. (1965), Propositions about Ethnocentricism from Social Science Theories, mimeo, Northwestern University.

CAMPBELL, D. T., and LE VINE, R. A. (1961), 'A proposal for co-operative cross-cultural research on ethnocentrism', Journal of Conflict Resolution, vol. 5 pp. 82–108.

CAMPBELL, D. T., and LE VINE, R. A. (1968), 'Ethnocentrism and intergroup relations', in R. P. Abelson et al. (eds.), Cognitive Congruity Theories, Rand McNally.

DOMHOFF, G. W. (1967), Who Rules America, Prentice-Hall.

ERIKSON, E. H. (1966), 'The concept of identity in race relations', Daedalus, Winter, pp. 145–71.

FESTINGER, L. (1957), A Theory of Cognitive Dissonance, Row Peterson.

GRAUBARD, S. G. (ed.) (1965), 'The Negro American', Daedalus, Winter and Fall.

HARARY, F., NORMAN, R., and CARTWRIGHT, D. (1965), Structural Models, Wiley.

HEIDER, F. (1958), The Psychology of Interpersonal Relations, Wiley.

KATZ, D. and BRALY, K. W. (1933), 'Racial stereotypes of 100 college students' Journal of Abnormal and Social Psychology, vol. 28, pp. 280–90.

KECSKEMETI, P. (1954), 'The psychological theory of prejudice', Commentary vol. 18.

KERNER, O. (1968), Report of the National Advisory Commission on Civil Disorders, Dutton.

KLUCKHOHN, C. (1954), 'Culture and behaviour', in Gardner Linzey (ed.), Handbook of Social Psychology, Addison Wesley.

KLUCKHOHN, C. (1956), 'Towards a comparison of value emphases in different cultures', in Leslie White (ed.), The State of the Social Sciences, University of Chicago Press.

KLUCKHOHN, F. R. (1950), 'Dominant and substitute profiles of cultural orientations', Social Forces, vol. 28, pp. 376–93.

KLUCKHOHN, F. R., STRODBECK, F., et al. (1961), Variations in Value Orientations, Row Peterson.

KROEBER, A. L., and KLUCKHOHN, C. (1952), 'Culture: a critical review of concepts and definitions', *Papers of the Peabody Museum*, vol. 47, no. 1a.

LE VINE, R. A., and CAMPBELL, D. T. (1965), *Ethnocentricism Field Manual*, mimeo, Northwestern University.

LEWIS, O. (1959), *Five Families*, New American Library.

LEWIS, O. (1960), 'The culture of poverty in Mexico City', *Economic Weekly*, June, pp. 965–72.

LEWIS, O. (1964), *Children of Sanchez*, Penguin.

LEWIS, O. (1966), *La Vida*, Random House.

LINCOLN, C. E. (1967), 'Colour and group identity' in 'Colour and Race', *Daedalus*, Spring, pp. 527–41.

MALCOLM, X. (1966), *Autobiography*, Grove Press.

MARCUSE, H. (1965), 'Remarks on a redefinition of culture', *Daedalus*, Winter, pp. 190–207.

MARCUSE, H. (1964), *One Dimensional Man*, Basic Books.

MASON, P. (1961), *Commonsense About Race*, Gollancz.

MEAD, M. (1964), *Continuities in Cultural Evolution*, Yale University Press.

MEAD, M. (1968), 'Problems and progress in the study of personality', in Norbeck, Price-Williams and McCord (eds.), *The Study of Personality: An Interdisciplinary Appraisal*, Holt, Rinehart & Winston.

MORRIS, C. (1942), *Paths of Life*, Harper & Row.

MORRIS, C. (1956), *Varieties of Human Value*, University of Chicago Press.

NEWCOMB, T. (1959), 'Individual systems of orientation' in S. Koch (ed.), *Psychology: A Study of a Science*, vol. 3, McGraw-Hill.

NEWCOMB, T. (1961) *The Acquaintance Process*, Holt, Rinehart & Winston.

OSGOOD, C. E., and TANNENBAUM, P. H. (1955), 'The principle of congruity in the prediction of attitude change', *Psychological Review*, vol. 62, pp. 42–55.

PARSONS, T., SHILS, E. *et al.* (1951), *Towards a General Theory of Action*, Harvard University Press.

PETTIGREW, T. (1964), *A Profile of the Negro American*, Van Nostrand.

PETTIGREW, T (1965), 'Complexity and change in American racial patterns: a social psychological view', *Daedalus*, Fall, pp. 974–1008.

RAINWATER, L. (1966), 'The crucible of identity: the Negro lower-class family', *Daedalus*, Winter, pp. 172–216.

RITCHIE, J. E. (1960), *Values in Personal and Social Change*, unpublished thesis, Library, Victoria University, Wellington.

RITCHIE, J. E. (1963), *The Making of a Maori*, A. H. & A. W. Reed, Wellington.

RITCHIE, J. E. (1964), 'The future of being Maori', in Lloyd-Pritchard (ed.), *The Future of New Zealand*, Whitcombe & Tombs, Christchurch.

ROKEACH, M. (1960), *The Open and Closed Mind*, Basic Books.

SUMNER, W. G. (1906), *Folkways*, Ginn & Co.

WESTRA, A., and RITCHIE, J. E. (1967), *Maori*, A. H. & A. W. Reed, Wellington.

Chapter 15
Family, Marital and Child-Rearing Patterns in Different Ethnic Groups

Oscar Ferron

Oscar Ferron was born in Calcutta. He was educated by the Irish Christian Brothers in two of their public schools and later at the Madras University by the French Jesuits. He served in World War II and emigrated to Britain in 1948 where he obtained the post-graduate Teachers' Diploma of London University in 1950. While serving as a teacher at the Ambrose Fleming Grammar Technical School, Enfield, he obtained an M.A. degree in Education at London University in 1957. In 1959 he was appointed Lecturer in Education at the University College of Sierra Leone, and in 1963 he joined the staff of the Ahmadu Bello University, northern Nigeria. In 1964 he was awarded a London Ph.D for his work on 'The Tested Intelligence of West African Children'. After further service in England, and as head of the department of teacher education at Njala University College, Sierra Leone, he is now professor of education in the University of Guyana.

The purpose of this chapter is to try to understand the way of life in the home country of four groups of coloured immigrants in Britain: Africans, West Indians, Indians, and Pakistanis. This is a convenient example of the psychological differences possible between European and non-European groups – and hopefully lessons learnt can be generalized to, say immigrant groups in the USA, Canada, Israel and Australia. The greater one's understanding of the patterns of culture of coloured people – particularly intimate patterns with long-term psychological effects on the people concerned – the more adequate the provisions which can be made for the stranger, the assumption being that under favourable conditions culture contact must result in gains for both host and immigrant communities.

Africans

According to an estimate made in 1968, it would appear that there are now something over 88,000 Africans resident in the United Kingdom. Although Africans who are permanently resident in Britain constitute a small proportion of the total coloured population, an understanding of the basic framework of African culture is a necessary prerequisite for an appreciation of the origin and evolution of the culture of Negroid peoples all over the world. Negroes from the Caribbean often resent being lumped together with Africans, whom they consider to be very different, but it is also probably true to say that this attitude is characteristic of the Africans themselves who, until recently, have tended to despise their own culture as a result of varying degrees of westernization.

In most African societies religion represents a whole way of life, and religious life and social life for the African are often coterminous. Every experience from birth through to initiation rites, sowing, reaping, marriage and death, are all part of a single religious phenomenon. What we in the West would regard as superstition, is to the average African a meaningful response to the natural and supernatural influences that surround him, and as they have been interpreted for him by his culture. The African's view of life may in a somewhat over-simplified way be stated thus: the individual is a member of an extended family group, and of a community consisting of the living and the dead, which is linked together by the communal possession of land. The land is the preserver of life in a subsistence economy, the repository of the dead, the venue and abode of spirits. It can be polluted by sexual intercourse out of doors, and purified by receiving the blood of animals and other human beings in propitiatory sacrifices to the gods in the spirit world.

Nothing in the African's world happens by chance. Every occurrence that threatens his existence has a cause and can be explained. He is not concerned so much with how things happen as why afflictions befall him, and his energies are directed towards forestalling them and ridding himself of their menace. In such a conception of the world, magical beliefs are inevitable, and those who specialize in magical practices wield an influence over the community comparable to that of the Ministry in the early Christian Church. In most former British Colonial territories in East, West and Central Africa, and in South Africa, African populations are made up, in the main, of three religious elements: Christianity, Islam and Paganism. The Christian missionaries offered the Africans a new ethic, which in many ways was in direct conflict with the everyday lives of practising Christians. Their religious teaching struck at the very heart of African social life and the basic assumptions of its conceptual world. They condemned idolatory, superstition and polygamy from which accrued so many social and economic benefits. They tried to break the link between the living and the dead, and they disapproved of the Africans' existing educational system: the secret societies which hitherto had enshrined the basic virtues of tribal life. There was no compromise, and no adequate psychological substitute was provided. True, they built churches and schools, and often made provision for the material needs of their congregations, but the language and ethical difficulties were such that all that happened was that the Africans replaced black man's magic by white man's magic.

After centuries of tradition the African was not in a position to comprehend: (a) the distinction between religious life and social life; and (b) an ethic based on individualism which was so foreign to his thinking. The concepts expressed by what we refer to as 'sin' and 'individual conscience' are difficult for the average rural African to grasp. An act is not sinful unless it is discovered, and when it is, it becomes a communal rather than an individual responsibility, for which the gods must be propitiated by sacrifice on a communal basis. There is nothing sinful in an African having sexual intercourse with a woman, providing it is in no way damaging to society, and even adultery with another man's wife may be duly condoned by the payment of a fine for 'woman damage'. The rationale for severe corporal punishment is that the evil spirit within a child must be beaten out of him, since it is the devil in him, not the child himself, who is responsible for his delinquent behaviour. It is therefore possible that African children do not perceive corporal punishment as an indication of parental rejection in the way that European children may do. In any case, according to the African's conception, parents cannot sin against their children. It involves changing a whole way of life, with a complete overhaul of his conceptual framework, for the average African to accept the western version of Christianity in its entirety.

Islam, on the other hand, did not strike at the core of the African's beliefs, or of his way of life. For the Moslem, too, social and religious life are one, and he does not disapprove of polygamy. But above all Islam has a capacity for absorbing elements of the indigenous culture of its adherents, in whatever part of the world it may happen to be practised. However, Islam, like Roman Catholicism, is relatively impervious to modern influences, and child-rearing practices do not readily change within its context. Moreover, it is not as powerful a status symbol in African society as is Christianity, and despite their inheritance of centuries of culture, African Muslims tend to be less advanced in the western sense than their Christian compatriots.

It would thus appear that for a complex of reasons – religious, social, conceptual, psychological and educational – the dominating influences in the life of the average African child are the beliefs and ways of thinking of his ancestors. The child's nurturing and disciplining is mainly in the hands of the illiterate mother and her co-wives and female relatives. In African society, the father plays little or no part in the upbringing of his children, until perhaps the boys are old and strong enough to help him on the farm. Moreover, a child belongs to the community and every member of the community has a right to discipline him. Within the family unit itself, other female members, like co-wives with vested interests in relation to their own natural-born children, and aunts and grandmothers, may singly or conjointly play a more significant part in the nurturing process than the mother herself. Apart from the mother's own idiosyncrasies of behaviour, in a system such as this, there can be no consistency of discipline, and the child's main orientation in life, which is reinforced by religious beliefs, will be towards developing skill in avoiding punishment by making sure that he is not caught. On the other hand, the system has its advantages in that the child's emotional security is not dependent on the mutual adjustment of a man and a woman in the marital situation, as in western society. In fact, many African parents send or give their children away to friends and relatives, for fear of 'spoiling' them, and in order to give them a good start in life.

Beginning with the traumatic experiences of childbirth, made much more severe for the African than the European child by primitive midwifery practices, going on to similar traumatic experiences such as those involved in smoking out a room in which the child is born, to ascertain whether or not he has come to stay, or pinching his nose and forcing pap down his mouth with his head dangling over his mother's knees, and perhaps ending with what must appear to the child a complete rejection on the birth of a new baby, as a result of forced and abrupt weaning, it is rather surprising that, generally speaking, most Africans appear stable, relaxed and cheerful, with an amazing capacity to withstand frustration.

This may be due partly to the fact that most African cultures absolve their members from personal responsibility, but it may be too that African babies enjoy a very secure life in close proximity to the mother, and later maternal deprivation is amply compensated for by other adults, particularly the grandmother. The grandparents occupy a very special position in relation to the child in most African societies. In certain East African societies the grandfather may endearingly refer to his grand-daughter as 'my bride', the grandmother to her grandson as 'my husband', and the relationship between grandparents and grandchildren is essentially one of equality. In the cultural context, grandchildren are perceived as being sent to replace the grandparents, who can now retire with a certain peace of mind to the spirit world knowing that their mission in life has been successfully completed.

Another major difference between African and European child-rearing practices is the emphasis that the African places on the well-being of tribe and community to the comparative neglect of the needs of the individual child. Of course, the African's fondness for children is commonplace, and there is no doubt that from birth to the time of weaning the African child enjoys a princely, highly stimulating life compared with that of his European counterpart; but it would appear that children in Africa may not always be desired for themselves. The birth of a child is sometimes looked upon as evidence of the father's virility and the mother's fertility. These are two very important aspects of African life, and while the lack of virility may have similar effects on the male in any culture, for an African woman to be barren is a positive disgrace. A man's status in the African rural subsistence economy is determined not only by the number of his wives, but also by the number of children he can produce by those wives. Children provide labour on the farm and their services are greatly valued. Until comparatively recently the only children who were sent to school were the lazy, troublesome ones who did their parents no credit, and even today female education may be neglected because some mothers are reluctant to release their daughters from home duties. By the time an African girl is nine or ten years old she can perform practically any household chore, including the preparation of meals, which an adult woman can, and of course her services as a nanny are much in demand. Boys, too, render invaluable service on the farm and around the house.

This attitude to child labour, so typical of western societies a century ago, colours the African's attitude to play and the use of toys. Play in childhood is sometimes frowned upon, and children may be punished for playing when they should be attending to their duties.

Finally, many illiterate Africans desire children because they are an insurance against unemployment and old age. Children are brought up to respect their parents and elders and to feel a sense of gratitude to the mother particularly for bringing them into the world. Unquestioning obedience is considered to be the highest virtue, and rebellion is universally condemned. My experience of African children is that they are the most polite, affectionate and grateful children I have ever encountered in all my travels, but unfortunately the growing child's obligations are not restricted to the natural parents, but may extend to relatives as well, and in fact in varying degrees to all members of the tribe who are older than himself. The result is that the successful African is usually weighed down by a financial and social burden of familial and tribal obligations which he can never completely discharge. This sacrificing of the younger generation to maintain the older is in direct contrast with the current norms of western society which are probably more forward looking, although the ideal is probably a balance on the basis of mutual rights and obligations. Of course, the child-rearing practices suggested here are neither static nor universal to every community, to every stratum of society, or indeed to every natural family unit within any given stratum.

It is in the area of the realization of *individual* potentiality and the development of intellectual capacity that the ill-effects of African child-rearing practices are perhaps most pronounced. In an investigation conducted in East Africa, it was found that, using the Gesell Schedules, African children up to about the age of two to three years were well in advance of American norms, and developmental quotients as high as 360 were reported (the theoretical overall average being 100). After that age there was a steady deterioration, and at five to six years of age American norms had greatly surpassed those of the Africans. The finding was confirmed in an investigation conducted under the auspices of the University of Sierra Leone. A group of pre-school children belonging to the community of Freetown Creoles, one of the most educationally advanced communities in Africa south of the Sahara, was compared with a control group of British children by means of a pre-school performance scale of twenty-five items, specially designed for the purpose. The test was divided into five sub-tests designated: perception, muscular co-ordination, drawing and writing skills, and language items. The performance of the British children on all five sub-tests was found to be superior to that of the Africans.

This investigation, which lasted from 1960 to 1964, was followed by another started in September 1965, in which after a pilot experiment lasting one year, an experimental group of children entering the University Experimental School at Njala, Sierra Leone, was compared with four control groups of African children in other parts of the country. The teacher in the experimental group was specially selected and his teaching skill was assessed as being superior by any standards. The group in question was provided with as stimulating a classroom environment as one could devise. Time samplings were taken, and there were frequent discussions between the investigator and the experimental teacher to ensure that the apparatus and material, either in its original or in a modified form, was put to the most effective use. At the end of the school year the experimental and control groups were compared. There were no significant differences in either language or number, except that the experimental group was found to have made certain gains in language, but not in number, over *one* of the control groups. The crippling effect of the tribal environment as far as the development of certain scholastic skills in a western type of school is concerned, would appear to be obvious.

West Indians

Let us now consider the second group of coloured immigrants in Britain: the West Indians who form the largest single group of coloured people in the country. Most of them come from Jamaica, Trinidad, Barbados and Grenada, with the majority of these from Jamaica.

Although the Caribbean is an area of considerable cultural diversity, the present social structure in the various islands is the result of an interaction between the basic Negro culture which the slaves brought with them from Africa, and the dominant European culture as interpreted by the white planters. Most West Indians in Britain originally belonged to the lower classes in their respective homelands, but even among the lower classes there are variations from community to community and from family to family, so that generalizations about the resultant personality are very difficult to make.

Clearly, in any culture-contact process there will be a general tendency to adhere to elements of the original culture which do not clash head-on with major aspects of life represented by the demands of the dominant culture; and there can be no doubt that many of the beliefs and practices widely followed in the West Indies are of African origin, not only because they maintained the *status quo*, but also because over the years they have continued to satisfy the psychological and social needs of the slaves, as well as those entailed by the structure of society after emancipation. This would suggest that in an entirely new set-up represented by life in Britain, one could not expect a complete passive acceptance of the norms of British society, but rather a modification of the norms of West Indian society to meet the realities of the present situation. This is precisely what appears to be happening.

For example, marriage has always been the ideal in Jamaican society, but because of economic conditions it has been an ideal which is unattainable for many people. However, with changed economic conditions in Britain, and the need to satisfy other dominant needs in an unfamiliar environment, concubinage, far from having been abandoned overnight, still represents a stage in a process, the only difference being that the next stage – i.e. marriage – is reached in a matter of months, according to West Indian norms in British society, while in Jamaica it could take from a few years to a lifetime, and in many cases may never be achieved at all.

From the point of view of childhood patterns of training, the essential difference between West Indian and West African norms is that, among West Indians to a greater extent than among Africans, the child may be subjected to a bossy, aggressive, demanding mother who has to wrest a living from a harsh environment, often without any financial support from a parturient male, who gives his name to the child, but little else, and who, for the most part remains an absent father figure.

Otherwise, a desire for, and attitudes towards, children in both types of society are basically similar. Very often we find almost identical child-rearing practices, with an orientation towards child labour, corporal punishment, lack of sufficient opportunity for play and mixing with other children, an insistence on gratitude and care of the mother in her old age, and a somewhat inconsistent discipline. The greater ambiguity resulting from a clash of European and African norms is partly offset by a higher degree of literacy, but as Madeleine Kerr (1952) points out, the nature of the education process is such that children who are potentially creative are prevented from realizing and utilizing their gifts. On the other hand, the cooperativeness of West African society, with its emphasis on interpersonal relationships, is modified to the extent that while there is a time and a place for cooperation and good neighbourliness under certain circumstances, for the most part West Indian culture tends to be competitive and secretive, sometimes seeking advantage and redress through such practices as Obeah.

Field work among West Indians suggests that two main types of personality develop as a result of this interaction. On the one hand, those who withdraw from the competitive struggle of making a living against overwhelming odds may appear to be 'accommodating, deferential, dependent, individual, happy, irresponsible, apathetic and childlike', whereas those who are not prepared to accept defeat so easily may appear overtly or covertly aggressive with the characteristic 'chip on the shoulder'. These types represent two theoretical extremes, so that in real life one finds many combinations and variations of behaviour. Changed economic conditions and a higher standard of living *per se* will not change the personality pattern. In fact, to what extent the average West Indian will achieve a higher degree of personality integration than was possible at home, will depend upon the family patterns that emerge in course of time, and his reactions to the attitudes of the host community.

Perhaps the one factor in the culture pattern of certain West Indian islands that has had the most far-reaching consequences for personality development, was the fact that the Negroes themselves internalized the British norm of colour prejudice so that 'white' came to be associated in their minds with what was good, pure and superior, and 'black', especially in relation to skin pigmentation, came to be regarded as something of which to be ashamed. So clearly delineated was this dichotomy that until recently it was possible to speak of a fair upper class, a brown middle class and a black lower class. The significance of this curious phenomenon is that the West Indian ideal, which is essentially a European one, cannot be anything more than sheer fantasy, and since he has renounced his African inheritance, the Negro in the Caribbean seems to have developed a deep-seated belief in his inability to produce a culture of his own.

But in Britain, it is possible that within a favourable social climate the deadlock may be resolved. Through education, West Indian child-rearing patterns will gradually approximate to those of the host community.

Finally, as in the case of Africans, religion is an important element in the training of all West Indian children, and although the white planters put every obstacle in the way of their slaves being converted to Christianity, this is now the most widely prevalent form of religious expression in the area. But it is a Christianity with a strong Old Testament flavour which fits in well with the extra punitiveness of the society. The average person is not greatly disturbed by the contradiction in religious observances and superstitious practices, nor by the inconsistency of a discipline which disapproves of stealing and lying in one context, but applauds and encourages it in another. Thus a child may be punished for lying to its mother and also for not lying to the landlord who comes to collect the rent.

As in many parts of Africa, Church membership tends to be a status symbol and the Church becomes an avenue of social mobility. Religion serves many psychological functions for the Negro, the most important being that of wish fulfilment, since in the eyes of God all men are equal and everybody has an equal chance of getting to heaven. It also serves as an emotional outlet and provides opportunities for leadership, recreation and social intercourse. But it is rather curious that despite its importance in everyday life at home, there has been a marked falling off of church attendance among West Indians in Britain. This may be due to such factors as climate and prejudice, but it has been suggested that for Negroes all over the world, revivalist forms of Christianity with their concomitants of music, dance and trance, are the only forms that provide a large measure of psychological satisfaction, especially for the poor and deprived.

Indians and Pakistanis

A few words now about the Indians and Pakistanis in Britain, who together outnumber the West Indians. In some respects they may be considered to be similar because they all come from a sub-continent that was once India. On the other hand, they represent two different oriental ideologies and it was a clash of these basic idealogies that caused India to be partitioned.

But, India and Pakistan are vast countries and there are many regional differences. Thus the militant Pathans in Pakistan are very different from the more peaceable Bengalis in Bangladesh. The emergence of the new state of Bangladesh was in itself the result, partly, of the differences in basic culture patterns. We must therefore appreciate that, as in the case of the Africans and the West Indians, generalizations are both impossible and dangerous, especially when we are dealing with cultural groups which are confronted with the overwhelming problems of culture contact and culture conflict. Our main concern, however, is with the ways in which the general outlook of these peoples have an effect on the upbringing and education of their children in Britain.

A noticeable feature of the Hindu way of life in India is the rigid caste system, which is one of the most effective devices yet produced by man for ensuring that those located low down on the social scale do not entertain ideas of moving upwards. But confronted with prejudice against themselves, Hindus become very sensitive about their caste system, and often in Indian communities settled abroad, Hindus of different castes live, eat and work together, although social distance is maintained in all kinds of subtle ways, and almost invariably the marriage taboos are enforced to ensure the perpetuation of caste. These attitudes have to be transmitted to children, and the resultant personality is very often a curious mixture of superiority, cliquishness and secretiveness on the one hand, or servility and latent hostility on the other, which affect interpersonal relationships with members of out-groups. The Sikhs, who broke away from the Hindu caste system, have a tendency towards community pride and overt aggressiveness.

As with Africans and West Indians, so also with Indians and Pakistanis, religious life and social life are one, so that religious considerations normally play a very important part in the upbringing of their children. Hindus believe in one 'Supreme Being', the initial creator of the universe, who, for the most part, remains unknown and undefinable. Below this supreme being there is a trinity of gods: (a) Brahma, the Creator, (b) Vishnu, the Preserver and (c) Shiva, the Destroyer. Below the trinity are a number of demi-gods and goddesses, who, in a sense, correspond to patron saints among the Roman Catholics.

A Hindu home, like a Catholic home, is likely to have pictures and statues of the favourite gods and goddesses of the family, who are supposed to take a special interest in human affairs, and who, it is believed, will intercede for persons who are devoted to them. The twin pillars of the Hindu faith are Karma and Dharma – that is, salvation and duty. Hindus believe in the transmigration of the soul, and they maintain that one's present status in life depends upon the kind of life that one led previously. For salvation, Hindus need to rely on a number of gods whom they must placate and supplicate, and if their astrologers can give them a little glimpse into the future they can not only adjust their lives accordingly, but also have the necessary time interval during which to resign themselves to their fate. The psychological significance of this for child-rearing is that the individual has a built-in device for striving to achieve what is written in the stars, but equally, he may tend to become a fatalist and give up the struggle if he feels the odds are against him. In fact without authoritative guidance he is nothing, and very early in their lives this lesson is driven home to Hindu children. Dependence, superstition, fatalism and moral rectitude, therefore, form the bases of the Hindu way of life. On the other hand, provided he believes in a Supreme Being, in theory, the Hindu is free to believe anything he likes, and his tolerance of other religions lies in the fact that most educated Hindus can see that there is some truth in all religions. Thus a child's over-dependence in a British school can be partly compensated for by the fact that however authoritarian child-rearing patterns in the home may have been, there will be little opposition to the teaching and experiencing of universal truths.

Although there are many points of contact between Islam, Judaism and Christianity, Moslem discipline in the home appears to be more rigid and authoritarian than one tends to find in Hindu homes, where children are often reasoned with and made to see the folly of their ways. Muslims all over the world tend to regard themselves as a closed brotherhood with God as their father, and Islam lays down a detailed code of conduct and behaviour for its adherents, which has changed little, if at all, over the centuries. God is God and Mohammed is His prophet. But Allah, the same God whom the Jews and Christians worship, is for the Moslems a severe God. He made the world. It is His. Therefore, He can do with it what He likes. The faithful who adhere strictly to the teachings of the Koran can merely hope for a little consideration. Deviants and infidels will be destroyed by the wrath of God. However, although authoritarian, the Moslem way of life and style of thinking is based on a Judaic–Christian ideology. We usually find, therefore, that except for certain taboos regarding pork and alcohol, and their attitudes towards women, educated Muslims seem to be able to assimilate western norms much more easily than Hindus.

Another feature of both Hindu and Moslem society that has some significance for childrearing in western countries is the status of women in these two societies. For one thing, the illiteracy and semi-illiteracy of most wives must inevitably have serious repercussions for both the intellectual and emotional development of children, since they must 'return' to India or Pakistan every night and are forced to oscillate between two different worlds. These parents sometimes have objections to extra-curricular activities after school, and seem to have no qualms about using their children as personal interpreters during school hours. It is difficult to say whether or not marriages in these cultures can give a sense of satisfaction and fulfilment to women, who tend to be regarded as mere child producing machines. In the course of certain field investigations it has been observed that Hindu mothers particularly, may suckle children up to the age of five or six years, and one observer noted how a Hindu mother fed her adolescent son hand to mouth.

In Hindu homes, the father usually takes an active part in the upbringing of his sons, but he may often be a stern and socially distant father figure who is admired but feared. There are age status norms and there is considerable sex differentiation from an early age, so that the warmest relationships tend to be between mother and son, and perhaps between mother and daughter. On the whole, children tend to have an emotionally secure childhood, but training in independence and initiative is not usually emphasized. Family relationships are characterized by subservience on the part of the females, and duty on the part of the males.

The attitudes towards corporal punishment and play are not as severe as among Africans and West Indians, but rote learning of prayers and passages from the scriptures is introduced early in life, and can become the characteristic way of learning. In the Moslem household, as the boy is removed from the influence of his mother at a relatively early age, and since his father takes it upon himself to instruct him in his religion, there tends to be a closer relationship between father and son, but the discipline is for the most part authoritarian.

I have tried to give a bird's eye view of the underlying ideologies that are but contributory factors to child-rearing patterns in a continent, a subcontinent, and in a culturally diverse group of islands in the Caribbean sea. Many Africans, West Indians, Indians and Pakistanis, among them my friends, as well as students and colleagues, past and present, may become agitated at what I have written. As an immigrant myself, I can appreciate how emotionally disturbed one can get when outsiders criticize, or appear to criticize, our cultures, and especially when they make reference to the most intimate relationships of cradle, home and nuptial bed. Many Europeans and Americans who do not possess the qualification of in-group membership have made similar courageous attempts. Inevitably, there have been many inaccuracies, and this chapter is no exception. The state of our knowledge in these areas is still very imperfect – partly because educated Westernized natives are too inhibited to volunteer information.

Reference

KERR, M. (1952), *Personality and Conflict in Jamaica*, Liverpool University Press.

Section E
Education

Education is possibly the most important area where there are race
differences. This has been the centre of much controversy lately and this
section tries to put the professional disagreements into perspective.
Ronald Goldman emphasizes how the long-term consequences of multiracial schools are more subtle and perhaps also more important than we
might think. Peter Watson puts the Race and IQ debate into historical
context and Irwin Katz reports on new research developments that are
beginning to change the conventional wisdom about how disadvantaged
children can or cannot be boosted to achieve equality of opportunity.

Chapter 16
Education and Immigrants

Ronald Goldman

Professor Ronald Goldman, now Dean of the School of Education, at La
Trobe University, Melbourne, Australia, has worked in several countries
involved in educational provision for racially or ethnically 'different'
immigrants. Principally, his work has been in the USA and the UK at
Reading and Manchester. He is currently working in the Centre for Urban
Education, on migrants in Australia.

Problems and opportunities

Immigrants in any society present many educational problems to the host
community, especially if they arrive in considerable numbers. Adults have
to be inducted into a society strange to them, a new language may have to
be acquired, new habits of dress, hygiene, feeding and living will be demanded. Socialization, normally taking a period of twenty years for
indigenous citizens, has to be engaged upon quickly and painfully by the
newcomers (see Chapter 9). This may entail the learning of entirely new
social systems, as many studies in the USA and Australia indicate. Spanish-
speaking Puerto Ricans settling in New York, Surinamese in the Hague,
Pakistanis in Bradford, England, and Indians in Fiji experience similar
problems, although the geographical settings are vastly different.

The children of immigrants face similar adjustments to that of their
parents but without the stability which comes from experience and matur-
ity. Indigenous children have been socialized to their own society from
birth and where an educational system is competitive, newcomers are
obviously at a disadvantage. Indeed, the deficiences are numerous and may
be classified in terms of social, cultural, educational and even racial disadvantage (Bloom *et al.*, 1965).[1] Invisible immigrant groups – those without
marked physical differences – such as the Southern Irish in England, or
Barbadons in Jamaica, have many problems, but because they do not
stand out as visible minorities, they are not subjected to such a complex
series of difficulties (Le Page, 1955).

For the host community the adjustments which have to be made

1. See Kiev (chapter 21), who would not agree wholeheartedly with this concept of
'invariable disadvantage' – for example, concerning mental illness.

are considerable. When small numbers are involved educational institutions can cope but where there are neighbourhood schools and immigrants settle together in a district the pressure upon teachers to produce a suitable socialization programme is considerable (Passow, 1963).

But in analysing problems it is easy to overlook the fact that immigrants also provide opportunities and benefits, not only to society but to schools and other educational institutions. Culture is enriched by the introduction of new elements of music, art, and literature. History, geography and world religions often studied remotely through textbooks can be seen at first-hand through the experience of immigrants in the school. As communication and travel speeds up we are conscious that we are one world and immigrants may save us from a too narrow and too parochial introspection. One long-term benefit to education, seen by too few educators, is that immigrants cause us to re-examine the validity of the traditional curriculum and textbooks, school structure and organization and such matters as selection processes. In Britain, immigrants settling in the inner city areas are producing concern, long overdue, for the education of slum children and the large proportion of children not destined for higher education. Social class and educational opportunity, social mobility, technical education, are all interwoven with questions of how best to induct immigrants into our society. The truth is that many societies have not been very successful in inducting a sizeable proportion of their indigenous children into their own way of life, especially from lower socio-economic groups. Education and the class structure has recently been the subject of many investigations in Britain.

Education and cultural shock

Psychologists define culture as the total assumptions of a society about itself – and it is evident that immigrants experience cultural shock when they settle in a different society. For some this is traumatic, and with children certainly, a bewildering if not a hurtful experience. The Pakistani child, perhaps within forty-eight hours of leaving his small village, may be attending a British primary school. The cultural shock is considerable and the adjustments required are complex and numerous, from learning how to use a school lavatory to learning a new language.

Little is known of the expectations of immigrants of the host community, but it is known that the motivation for immigration is not only economic (see Chapter 9). Where the move occurs from a less developed to a more developed society one expectation is for the better education for their children which the host society can offer (Goldman, 1969b). It comes, therefore, as a shock when their children, because of linguistic and other disadvantages, do not appear to make immediate educational progress, and may even be labelled as 'backward' (Goldman, 1966). The shock is not confined to education but involves other institutions, such as the church.

Cultural shock is also experienced by the host community; this can be seen in schools, although there is a distinction between schools which have only one or two ethnically different children and those which have an increasing and sizeable number. In the first immigrants may be regarded as interesting additions to the school, but in the second may be thought of as a growing nuisance, if not a menace to standards, by making undue demands upon the school's resources (Kawwa, 1965).

Adaptations required by educational systems

It will be seen that where immigrants settle in concentrated groups, and the pattern is a common one in the inner city ring of large conurbations, the educational system has to be adapted to the new demands made upon it. More teachers, specially qualified teachers, a different approach to the curriculum, language teaching equipment and other aids may have to be provided. Most educational administrations react slowly and cautiously to the new situation created by immigrants, in some cases wisely because they need to know the dimension and nature of the educational problems to be solved. In some cases, however, the reaction is slow because of hostility to an alien group, reluctance to spend public money on them or a fear of public opinion.

The adaptations required may be analysed in two ways, one revealing the immediate stresses experienced by schools and the other revealing the long-term educational requirements a multiracial society has to face.

Immediate schooling requirements. In societies with well developed educational systems neighbourhood schools tend to be the pattern, having an intake of children from the immediate area in which the school is placed. Primary schools have an intake from the immediately adjacent streets, whereas secondary schools tend to take from a somewhat larger area. Immigrants, particularly in the first phases of immigration, tend to concentrate in areas which offer employment and where friends and relatives have settled previously. Schoolchildren from immigrant populations, therefore, are usually not spread thinly over a nation's schools, but tend to be concentrated in certain heavy industrial areas and only in certain schools of the larger cities.

In England, for example, at a time when the child immigrant population of school age was less than 2 per cent of the overall school population, Birmingham, the country's second largest city, had an average proportion of 5 per cent of immigrant children in its maintained schools. Even so, there were twenty-two primary schools with between 16 and 70 per cent coloured immigrant children. This pattern may also be seen in Birmingham's secondary school system, and is reported in England's larger conurbations, Manchester, West Riding, and London. It can be seen more dramatically in the USA.[2] in areas such as Harlem in New York City, southern Chicago, or large industrial cities such as Cleveland, Cincinatti and Pittsburgh. The implications of this *de facto* segregation – not enforced by law, but decided by economic pressures, availability of housing and other factors – can be seen most dramatically in a school system report on Washington D.C. (Passow, 1967).

Legislative attempts are often made to 'spread' the immigrant intake over schools more evenly; in England the famous Department of Education and Science Circular 7/65 suggested the intake of immigrants in any one school should not exceed 30 per cent of that school's population. Schemes to bus children, re-zone areas and other plans have developed in America, where *de facto* segregated schools are resisted by some administrators as contrary to America's stated ideals; but as long as neighbourhood schools exist the only key to avoiding ghetto schools is to abolish the ghetto itself, by a deliberate policy of balanced desegregated housing schemes. Such schemes have been successful in Holland, Brazil and Israel. The implications of this policy for education will be discussed later.

In less developed countries, where school systems are not yet established for all children, segregation in educational systems exists for varied reasons. In Fiji, for example, the indigenous inhabitants of Polynesian and Melanesian descent number about 200,000, but the Indians migrating gradually since the end of the last century, initially to supply labour for the sugar plantations, now outnumber the Fijians with a population of about 220,000. Physically and culturally the two peoples are very different and the original Fijians fear the dominance of the immigrants, who have a faster birthrate. The two peoples have settled separately, established their own schools and there is very little mixing among the young, so that interracial understanding is limited and friction between them is considerable. This is an example of two peoples of equal status and rights sustaining parallel school systems which do not appear to contribute to suitable socialization for a duoracial society (Goldman, 1966).

Some societies try to absorb immigrant children into their school systems with as little adjustment as possible. Others set up reception centres or reception classes in certain schools to aid the process of induction. Where

2. For the purposes of this chapter, I define American Negro migrants, who have moved from the deep South to northern cities in increasing numbers since the Second World War, as immigrants. They are as validly categorized so, as are Puerto Ricans and Mexicans, in New York and California, respectively.

the teaching of social habits and remedial linguistic teaching is needed this has certain educational advantages, but surveys made in England indicate that if too many children of the same ethnic group are kept together for remedial purposes they make less progress than if placed in classes with indigenous children (Goldman and Taylor, 1966).

Concentration initially tends to be on language teaching, despite all the evidence to show that children do not need to be 'taught' a language if they live and talk with peers who do so. The obsession with language teaching may be more a desire to do something tangible in terms of a clearly categorized subject in schools, rather than the less tangible and, some believe, the more important educational tasks of changing attitudes, creating good relationships and appreciating the culture of the immigrant. Most school systems in adapting to the immigrant appear to assume that the host community must educate, but that there is little the host community has to learn from immigrants.

Several specific and immediate problems must be faced by teachers and educational administrators when immigrant families send their children into the school system. One is the immediate difficulty of assessing the ability level of immigrant children for the purpose of placing them in appropriate school 'streams' or subject 'sets'. Many investigations have shown clearly that all tests for diagnosing educational potential are weighted in favour of those familiar with certain cultural ideas and a particular form of visual ability associated with higher socio-economic levels. Attempts have been made to construct 'culture free' or at least 'culture fair' tests, but these are on the whole regarded as unsatisfactory. The linguistic impediments of most immigrants are obvious when facing, for example, an English intelligence test. Even if the test is of the non-visual kind (the instructions are read aloud by the teacher and call for no reading facility by the pupil) the instructions may be only partially understood and the test results therefore invalidated (see Chapter 18).

Professional educators are somewhat worried to find an unduly large proportion of immigrant children labelled backward or even ESN (Educationally Sub-Normal), largely because of cultural and linguistic differences (Coard, 1971). The misconception that to be different is to be inferior is a dangerous assumption, frequently made in education, particularly in relation to immigrant populations. The hypothesis has been advanced that although school performance by immigrants is poor the same children are above average when compared with their peers in the country of origin, simply because immigrant parents possess the economic means and the initiative to emigrate. Vernon, among others, has shown that there are nine major environmental handicaps to mental development (and consequently suitable school performance) which are important in gauging educational potential. He argues that those who come from non-Western rural societies must produce more individuals with Western-type mental skills (Vernon, 1965), and this is to some extent supported by the observed fact that test scores and school performance improve with the length of stay of immigrant children (Saint, 1963).

However, against this must be weighted the evidence that the IQ and other test scores are very faulty devices for assessing the ability of indigenous children, particularly from lower socio-economic levels. Studies in England of canal children, gypsies and more recently those in city slum areas, indicate that many complex factors are involved (Wiseman, 1964). Similar results are found in investigations in Sweden with Lapp children and in other countries with small but constant migrant populations.

Linked with 'culturally induced backwardness' are linguistic problems, immediately evident to any school receiving immigrant children. Language is vital for communication and so for education; linguistic limitations, therefore, are the first and most tangible indications of where intensive teaching or remedial work is initially most required. Three categories of defect appear to cover the difficulties of immigrant children.

Total language deficiency exists where not only is the host language not spoken, but sometimes the written script is alien. The younger the child the easier it is for him to learn a new language, not formally, but by 'the direct method', that is in conversation with his peers. This kind of immigrant is perforce bilingual. Studies show that bilingualism tends to lower capacity for learning generally, especially where children are not fully involved in the host society life and culture. Native bilinguals (speaking English and Welsh, or American and Spanish) do not have this impediment as compared with foreign bilinguals. The greatest danger is when an immigrant child learns the language for a certain segment of the environment in which he operates – for example, the school – and another language for other specific situations – in the family or religious grouping (Alleyne, 1965).

Partial language deficiency where some, but very little vernacular of the host society is spoken in the home, or the child has acquired some host language from a longer residence in the host society. He may find the host script alien, but has a basic familiarity with it from public signs, newspapers and magazines, television and other sources. Here there exists a foundation to be built upon by teachers.

Dialect or sub-language impediments. Some immigrant children may speak the host language well but dialect may make it difficult to communicate. This may be not so much a dialect as a sub-language such as 'pidgin' English, which when mixed with Creole in the West Indian, becomes almost another language. The problem is intensified among such groups who believe they are speaking English, when it is not a recognizable language to the indigenous English. Evidence indicates that it is far more effective to teach a new language to immigrants who know they cannot speak the language of the host community than to provide a remedial language programme for those who believe their language requires little improvement. Thus, Puerto Ricans, whose vernacular is Spanish, and Asians, whose vernacular is perhaps Urdu, appear to have less difficulties educationally than southern Negroes settling in northern USA and West Indians settling in England.[3]

Long-term educational requirements. The immediate problems of educational institutions must be seen in the long-term planning of a society as it looks to its future. Some societies deliberately seek to discourage immigrants as permanent residents and regard them as seasonal citizens – Mexicans moving into California, New Mexico and Texas for the harvest – or on limited work permits for a certain period. If they bring children no major adjustment to the educational system is necessary, other than temporary summer or 'seasonal' schools. Some societies, notably South Africa, plan for educational segregation under the seldom realized slogan 'separate but equal'. The South African native is technically not an immigrant but it is apparent that there is in South Africa a self-conscious role-reversal, in that the immigrant Europeans behave as the major occupants and the numerous indigenous Africans suffer all the disadvantages and impediments, certainly in education, of immigrants elsewhere.

In societies which believe in equality of opportunity, which inevitably means equality of educational opportunity, 'separate but equal' schools are vaguely recognized as contrary to their major egalitarian assumptions (Floud *et al.* 1956). There are groups in all societies which claim the right to have separate schools to protect the rights of the minorities, even to help minorities retain their sense of identity and separateness. The Roman Catholic church throughout the world has an established system of schools, colleges and universities outside state systems, where the state allows it. Jewish groups, political groups and others sometimes contract out of state school systems. But it is one thing to contract out from personal conviction and another to be forced out into an alleged 'separate but equal' system.

Studies in motivation and in particular into the self-image of different

3. Lederman (1969) reports that West Indian boys in English secondary schools were less intelligible and therefore less socially acceptable to English boys than Asian boys who originally spoke no English.

ethnic groups reveal that such separateness is regarded as inferior with a subsequent lowering of motivation and a poorer self-image (Katz and Pettigrew, 1967). Some of Katz's work and that of others may on the surface appear to run contrary to these conclusions in that in certain American situations Negro students in segregated institutions appear to have more confidence and fewer insecurities than Negro students in unsegregated institutions. But this may be one of the natural results of more than a century of non-competition with white Americans in education (Katz, 1967).

Certainly, the attitudes of teachers and educational administrators are important formative influences on how the ethnically different child generates his self-image. If the teacher does not value the immigrant child, deplores poor performances and indicates his poor expectation of the immigrant child's future performances, the child will form a poor self-image. Practised over whole generations of schoolchildren in relation to a particular coloured, ethnic or religious group, the whole group-image will tend to be poor (Rowley, 1968; Zahran, 1967).

An ingenious experiment of this situation in reverse in a South San Francisco grade school illustrates the point well. The experimenters informed the teachers that a new test could predict which slow learning students were likely to be late developers of an unusual kind. The test was given and teachers were then told which students had displayed this high potential for improvement. The students named were actually taken at random out of a hat. When tested later there were marked gains in the scores of students in the lower grades but all students designated as 'late developers' made significant improvements. One young Mexican American classified previously as mentally retarded with an IQ of 61, scored 106 after selection as a late developer. The experimenters note that 'teachers' expectations of their pupils' performance may serve as self-fulfilling prophecies'. As Eliza Doolittle says in Shaw's *Pygmalion* 'The difference between a lady and a flower-girl is not how she behaves, but how she's treated' (Rosenthal, 1968).

The poor self-image and motivation regarding school work and achievement appears to be related also to opportunities open to the pupil when he leaves school. The high rate of unemployment among immigrant school-leavers in certain countries discourages hard work at school as preparation for a career, if discriminatory practices in employment are known to exist. Job expectations exert a considerable influence upon the attitude to school and what hard work will produce. This would seem to be particularly true of groups which for generations have been conditioned 'to know their place'. In a study in Georgia, USA, the investigators found that Negro boys stated their job expectations to be in teaching, semi-skilled work or only in those jobs where they knew Negroes had succeeded, such as sport or show business. The girls similarly sought teaching, nursing and hair-dressing jobs, all based upon a realistic expectation of what society would allow. Limits were clearly recognized. These pupils did not aim as high as matched white students in suburban northern schools, nor were their achievements, creativity scores as high or approach to work as flexible (Goldman and Torrance, 1967).

It will be seen that long-term planning for a multiracial society, by the use of educational institutions, is dependent upon what kind of society it aims to be and whether the implications of full human rights for immigrants are seen and accepted. An educational system can be used to further the aim of integration and, either deliberately or by default, further the contrary aim of educational segregation. Even if integration is accepted as the major aim, the amount of integration of immigrants is a complex matter. Complete assimilation of a minority by inter-marriage, steady absorption of its values and way of life, is often thought of as the logical conclusion of an integration policy, but this may be strongly resisted by the immigrants who wish to retain their own customs of courtship and marriage, dress, religious and other practices. This is a legitimate exercise of human rights long fought for by minority groups in most countries in the world. It is a major issue which also affects education and which education itself influences. For example, a Pakistani family, because of its Moslem tradition of protecting the girl, will insist upon certain behaviour of the daughter in relation to boys at school and in dress requirements. Evidence indicates that the girls obey their parents in a limited way, having secret dates with non-Pakistani, non-Moslem boys, and even changing their traditional clothes to more acceptable school clothes in a friend's house, on the way to and from school (Shakoor, 1969). First generation immigrants are more resistant to these subtle assimilative pressures than later generations.

As noted previously, housing policy is the key to a satisfactory integrative educational system, if a society decides integration is necessary (Goldman, 1968a). In terms of educational resources and the beneficial effects upon the ability and performance of immigrants, segregation appears to produce wasteful results, leading to tensions, self-destructive frustration and poor educational performances by immigrants. Frustration and aggression are closely related as the 'Black Power' movement indicates. The presence of unfulfilled, bitter and frustrated minorities who possess a poor self-image in which schooling and teachers have been an obvious instrument of perpetuating inferiority, is a picture few societies would contemplate, but one which nevertheless results when aims are unclear and policy is confused.

Studies have established that Negroes in the USA are not genetically less capable of learning and that lower intelligence test scores are probably due to environmental differences. Many deduce that apart from inferior status originating from the days of slavery, inferior education has compelled poor performance and the one immediate remedy is quality education (see Klineberg, 1963, and Chapter 18). This can in the main only be achieved by integrated institutions. Yet the situation contains a paradox, and to some extent, an irreversible trend in that the host community fears that the poor performance of immigrant groups will affect the quality of their own children's performance. Thus, as schools have become partially integrated indigenous children have been withdrawn for one reason or another from urban school systems into wealthier suburban schools on the periphery of the cities. This process can be observed in northern USA where, in Cleveland 58 per cent, in Philadelphia over 50 per cent, in Manhattan 73 per cent, and in Washington D.C. over 80 per cent of the city schools are virtually segregated institutions (Goldman and Taylor, 1966).

Few societies such as Holland see the issues clearly enough to devise an integrated housing policy, thereby producing an integrated social as well as a school community; most allow the housing patterns to develop on random lines, which predictably lead to concentrated ghetto areas, as in the USA and then seek to remedy the situation later (see Passow, 1969).

Administratively, four types of schemes are advanced in an attempt to reverse the situation for a more meaningful mixing in schools in the USA.

There is the *Princeton Plan* which attempts to pair adjacent racially imbalanced schools. This appears to be more suitable for small communities than large cities – because the large city tends to produce by its sheer size and complexity a difficult pattern for this kind of pairing. There is *open-enrolment* which allows pupils to transfer from overcrowded segregated schools to other schools in the city. It has had very restricted success largely because of the high costs of transportation where complete open-enrolment is allowed. A further factor is that those in poor schools tend to wish to enrol in better schools with the result that poor schools become seriously under-used while the better class suburban schools risk becoming seriously overcrowded.

The *Educational Complex* in New York City is a plan to build a group of schools together not in 'white' or 'black' areas but at intermediate points and to bring together elementary and high schools, with pupils, teachers and parents in close association. The *Educational Park* scheme aims to accommodate all school populations of 10,000 on a single site providing, because of this huge concentration, unparalled resources of swimming pools and other community amenities which make all citizens in adjacent areas wish to send their children to school there. These schemes have been evaluated by several investigators (see Fischer, 1966; Jacobson, 1964).

There are further remedial, often called compensatory, measures of a long-term nature which are used to counteract or reverse the educational deprivations of immigrant children. The most arresting and successful are the compensatory programmes for Eastern Jewish groups in Israel. These are regarded as disadvantaged children from a largely Arab rural and tribal background, having previously had no urban experience or formalized education, who have been incorporated into an Israeli system with a largely westernized European educational system (Smilansky, 1964).

Other measures which have proved most successful involve concentrated attention to the pre-school education or first school years of the ethnically different child (Deutsch, 1967). Smaller classes are arranged and structured enrichment programmes are designed to sharpen children's perception, develop a more extended and accurate language, generate an enthusiasm for learning, develop purposive concentration and ability to listen for longer periods of time, and through all these build up a positive, confident, strong self-image. Many educators maintain that these programmes and intentions could well be applied to the indigenous disadvantaged school population of any country and could revolutionize educational systems if applied intelligently. Such compensatory programmes do, however, help to reverse the disadvantages and are tokens of society's intention to provide greater opportunity for education. But unless there are accompanying supports from the community in more positive attitudes towards racially different minorities, a diminution of discriminatory practices and a welcoming acceptance of other groups for what the minority groups can offer, most of what these school compensatory programmes can achieve will be dissipated.

Social education in a multiracial society

The problems so far analysed have focused upon how to educate children, and through them, immigrant parents. We have noted the importance of the host community's attitudes to the newcomers, especially expressed by teachers, but we should also note the importance of attitudes of peers in school and neighbourhood, educational advisers, inspectors and administrators, policemen, shopkeepers and all the population who often indirectly transmit values and assumptions, sometimes of a negative and discriminatory kind. The immigrant child is not protected, even in school, from racism and from the expression and practice of prejudice.

The host community therefore requires some social education on two matters: who are the newcomers and what they can contribute, and what are the implications of living in a multiracial society? This would be simple if it were merely a matter of conveying information, but education for tolerance, or acceptance, of alien groups is more in the realm of educating the emotions, a much more complex and difficult task. Educational planners and reformers tend to have spent a long time in higher education and are thoroughly indoctrinated to the importance of the education of the intellect. Only more recently has motivation and the feeling element in what makes individuals behave become the focus of attention. It is this area which needs exploration, particularly in the demanding field of social education (see, for example, Burgin and Edson, 1966).

Studies in prejudice reveal that the young assimilate attitudes very effectively from their elders. In my view these analyses convincingly demonstrate the complex causes of prejudice, such as economic rivalry, sexual and social fears of inferiority, natural suspicion of the stranger and a reluctance to change a well established way of life to accommodate strange groups. Yet, although the younger generations tend to absorb and acquire the attitudes of an older generation, their primitive and basic fears of the strange tend to be minimized. The young are not naturally tolerant of peers who are different and sometimes actively persecute the physically and mentally abnormal (Goldman, 1968b). But because the young show more plasticity in their early years, education of a positive kind towards tolerance is more fruitful for them than for adults.

The social education of the young

Schools could more self-consciously analyse their aims, as distinct from increasing performance in literacy, numeracy and other subject tasks, particularly in the field of social education.

There are various methods by which these aims can be implemented but they will have little effect if the whole school ethos, and particularly the attitudes of the teaching staff, are not consistent with these goals. Domnitz (1965) reports the recommendations of a UNESCO conference on educational techniques for positive social education. Some of these recommendations are already being applied in some countries:

1. Teachers and student teachers are regarded as key people in such programmes and therefore the provision of pre-service and in-service courses should make teachers more aware of the problems and research in this field. Acquaintance with techniques of role playing, socio-drama and sympathetic social studies, together with a knowledge of good class materials to use with children would create more positive potential in schools.

2. Teachers should help to develop more critical thinking habits in the young, to guard against poor generalizations and stereotyped assumptions about human groups. Evidence indicates that convergent, rather than divergent, thinking of a conventional kind is too widely practised in schools (see Torrance, 1962).

3. Curriculum reform would help, particularly in such social subjects as history, geography, social studies and religion, so that stress is made upon human similarities and the varied contributions offered by all nations to society and civilization. In Britain the Schools Council produced a race pack – yet got cold feet about its release in 1972.

4. Alongside this the provision of textbooks and classroom materials – pictures, films, filmstrips – is required to make curriculum reform effective. Too many textbooks contain omissions, distortions and inaccurate assumptions concerning nationality and race (Lauwerys, 1953).

5. School norms need to be established where interracial and other mixed groups exist. The 'different' groups need sympathetic presentation to the receiving group, including a clear appreciation of their language and culture (UNESCO, 1959).

6. For older pupils in secondary schools overt examination of interpersonal relations and group processes will aid attitudes of a positive kind. This provides them also with the opportunity to examine discrepancies of attitudes and opinions between the school and other social groups, such as the family, the neighbourhood or mass media.

Social and remedial education for adults

Where adults are concerned the educational work to prepare them for acceptance of a multiracial society will tend to be more remedial, that is corrective rather than formative. It is well to recognize, as all investigations indicate, that the older the person is the more difficult it is to effect attitude change; that prejudices develop in clusters, feeding and supporting each other, serving simultaneously the same emotional insecurities; and that prejudices only continue with adequate social support and with some measure of social approval. Since emotional insecurities and frustration are endemic in human nature, it is impossible to eliminate these emotional problems and it may be that some emotional outlets, more creative and positive than expressions of hostility to scapegoat minorities, would lead to better mental health.

It is simpler to analyse causes than to suggest remedies and the field of empirical studies is noticeably weak in this respect. Some suggestions, however, have come from investigators (see Fusco, 1964):

1. The involvement of parents in their children's social education – by observing the children and their teachers at work, by discussing with teachers their children's psychological and emotional needs, by including in PTA programmes discussion of other social and racial groups.

2. Group therapy with adult groups, meeting as parental or community groups, tends to be more effective in changing group attitudes than traditional lecture-discussion methods (Tausch, 1961).

3. A method of making a community[4] aware of discrimination and its effect in their own area is the 'community self-survey' technique. Prominent citizens are asked to gather facts and prepare a report on the community. Prejudiced individuals who cannot deny facts collected by their own group and particularly its most popular and respected members, are then likely to derive in-group support when they change their ideas and feelings.

4. Inter-group contacts, where members rely upon each other's skills and work, on the basis of equal status requiring cooperative effort, may lead to attitude change, as in task forces in the army and housewives in integrated municipal housing projects.

5. Mass media may be a powerful instrument in attitude change if respected and successful figures in politics, sport, commerce, show business, convey tolerant and accepting attitudes towards minorities. Theoretically this should provide the social support an attitude change requires by demonstrating that 'top' people find acceptance the norm. Many societies' radio and television services include other racial and ethnic group numbers in their programmes. The mass media techniques mentioned above have not as yet been adequately assessed.

Conclusion

This chapter has attempted to describe the varied ways in which education, both as a process and an institutional system, is involved in any society faced with an inflow of immigrants. All societies face the task of socializing their citizens; this process begins at birth and continues later through formal schooling. Immigrants add a new dimension to the task of socialization, presenting many strains upon education systems and yet provide many opportunities to re-examine the social purpose of particular educational institutions.

The investigations discussed in relation to the varied problems of cultural shock, immediate and long term adaptations of the educational system and the task of social education in a multiracial society, are largely psychological in nature and cover a wide field. Description has necessarily been limited to the normal school age range, although pre-school programmes and after-school employment have been touched upon. The

4. A fuller discussion of the issues referred to here is given by the Director of the London Educational Priority Area Project – see Betty (1969).

field of higher education has been largely ignored, not because it is unimportant, but because of lack of space. Studies in multiracial societies all over the world, but particularly from the United States, indicate that the disadvantages experienced by children throughout the school system are also experienced by racially different groups in higher education. But the proportions of those proceeding to higher education from these racially disadvantaged groups are significantly less than those from the indigenous groups. In Britain no evidence has accumulated since the immigrant populations have not yet gone into the sector of higher education in substantial numbers. Indications are that Asian Sixth Formers have succeeded in gaining proportionately more places in Technical Colleges and University places for Applied Sciences than in the Arts. There appear to be better opportunities for those mathematically and scientifically inclined, but the factors here are difficult to analyse or even identify clearly.[5]

Obviously it is difficult to distinguish between the objective findings of many researches and the interpretation of their meanings for education, but several points stand out and their implications are far-reaching.

Certain societies have clear integrative or segregative aims in education when dealing with immigrants of different ethnic, racial, religious and cultural groups to the host community. These societies are few. Most tend to be confused and uncoordinated, *to make ad hoc educational assumptions and adjustments* which are not always consistent and frequently devised in haste. In the realm of social planning, school systems are subject to strain by the growth of ghetto concentrations of immigrant populations. Where wedded to a neighbourhood school system vast sums of finance may have to be expended to create a non-segregated school system, which a carefully planned housing policy could avoid.

Educators discover that some immigrant children suffer from various disadvantages not dissimilar to those of their own indigenous children in city slums, but in addition they suffer from cultural and racial disadvantages, being members of a visible minority. The lack of adequate educational and ability diagnostic tests is evident, and techniques for teaching the language of the host community take some time to develop. But emphasis upon language teaching tends to obscure the more far-reaching adaptations demanded by the presence of immigrants: to face the complex and difficult task of positive social education in the young and attitude-change in adults.

5. Dr Goldman's own project – the Didsbury Compensatory Education Project – is a good case on point. The project publishes its own 'occasional papers' and interested readers are referred to them for more information. However, a short description of the project and its aims can be found in the I R R *Newsletter* October 1968. See also Goldman (1969b) [ed.].

References

ALLEYNE, M. H. (1965), 'Research on the effects of bilingualism on education', in J. Jones (ed.), *Linguistics and Language in a Multilingual Society*, Unwin.

BETTY, C. (1969), 'Race, community and schools', *Race Today*, June.

BLOOM, B., DAVIS, A., and HESS. R: (1966), *Compensatory Education for Cultural Deprivation*, Holt, Rinehart & Winston.

BURGIN, T., and EDSON, P. (1966). *Spring Grove: An Experiment in the Education of Immigrant Children*, Oxford University Press.

COARD, B. (1971), *How the West Indian Child is Made ESN by the British School Systems*, New Beacon Books.

DEUTSCH, M. (1967), *The Disadvantaged Child*, Basic Books.

DOMNITZ, M. (1965), *Unesco Report*, Institute for Education.

DOUGLAS, J. W. B. (1967), *The Home and the School*, Panther Books.

FISCHER, J. (1966), 'Race and reconciliation: the role of the school', *Daedalus*, Winter.

FLOUD, J. E., HALSEY, A. H., and MARTIN, F. M. (1956), *Social Class and Educational Opportunity*, Heinemann.

FUSCO, G. (1964), *School–Home Partnership in Depressed Urban Neighbourhoods*, US Dept of Health, Education and Welfare.

GOLDMAN, R. (1966), *Education and Race*, paper prepared for the Social Science Research Council.

GOLDMAN, R. (1968a), *Breakthrough: Autobiographical Accounts of the Education of Some Socially Disadvantaged Children*, Routledge & Kegan Paul.

GOLDMAN, R. (1968b), 'Social education for a multi-racial society', *Technical Education*, December.

GOLDMAN, R. (1969c), 'Immigrant children and cultural shock', occasional paper, *Didsbury Compensatory Education Project*.

GOLDMAN, R., and TAYLOR, F. M. (1966), 'Coloured immigrant children: a survey of research, studies and literature on their educational problems and potential (1) in Britain, (2) in the USA', *Educational Research*, vol. 8, no. 3 and vol. 9, no. 4, June and November.

GOLDMAN, R., and TORRANCE, E. P. (1967), 'Creative development in a segregated Negro school in the south', *Georgia Studies of Creative Behaviour*, December.

JACOBSON, N. (ed.) (1964), *An Exploration of the Educational Park Concept*, Board of Education, New York.

KATZ, I. (1967), 'Some motivational determinants of racial differences in intellectual achievement', *International Journal of Psychology*, vol. 2, no. 1.

KATZ, I., and PETTIGREW, T. F. (1967), *Contributions to the Nebraska Symposium on Motivation*, University of Nebraska Press.

KAWWA, T. (1965), 'A study of the interaction between native and immigrant children in English schools', unpublished Ph.D. thesis, University of London

KLINEBERG, O. (1963), 'Negro–white differences in intelligence test performance' *American Psychologist*, vol 18.

LAUWERYS, A. J. (1953), *History, Textbooks and International Understanding*, UNESCO.

LEDERMAN, S. (1969), 'The social acceptance of immigrants', *Race Today*, vol. 1, no. 2.

LE PAGE, R. B. (1955), 'The language problem in the British Caribbean', *Caribbean Quarterly*, vol. 4. no. 1.

MONSERRAT, J. (1964), 'School integration: a Puerto Rican view', in M. Weinberg (ed.), *Learning Together*, Integrated Education Associates, Chicago.

PASSOW, A. H. (1963), *Education in Depressed Areas*, Teachers' College Press, Columbia University.

PASSOW, A. H. (1967), *Towards Creating a Model Urban School System: A Study of Washington D.C. Public Schools*, Teachers' College Press, Columbia University.

PASSOW, A. H. (1969), *Deprivation and Disadvantage*, UNESCO Institute for Education.

ROSENTHAL, R., and JACOBSON, L. (1968), *Pygmalion in the Classroom*, Holt, Rinehart & Winston.

ROWLEY, K. G. (1968), 'Social relations between British and immigrant children' *Educational Research*, January.

SAINT, C. K. (1963), 'Scholastic and sociological adjustment problems of the Punjabi-speaking children in Smethwick', unpublished M. Ed. dissertation, University of Birmingham.

SHAKOOR, A. (1969), 'The Pakistani child immigrant and cultural shock', occasional paper, *Didsbury Compensatory Educational Project*.

SMILANSKY, S. (1964), *Progress Report 1964*, Henrietta Srole Institute, Jerusalem.

TAUSCH, A. (1961), 'Experimentelle untersuchungen über Art und Ausmass', *14th International Congress of Applied Psychology*, Copenhagen.

TORRANCE, E. P. (1962), *Guiding Creative Talent*, Prentice-Hall.

UNESCO (1959), *Education for International Understanding: Examples and Suggestions for Classroom Use*, UNESCO, Paris.

VERNON, P. E. (1965), 'Ability factors and environmental influences', *American Psychologist*, vol. 20, no. 9.

WARNER, W. L., and SROLE, L. (1945), *The Social Systems of American Ethnic Groups*, Yale University Press.

WISEMAN, S. (1964), *Education and Environment*, Manchester University Press.

ZAHRAN, M. A. S. (1967), 'The self concept in the psychological guidance of adolescents', *British Journal of Educational Psychology*, June.

Chapter 17
Race and Intelligence through the Looking Glass

Peter Watson

Humpty Dumpty would have made the ideal psychologist. Besides being good at sitting on the fence, he was, as he admitted, a master in the ways of using words to mean just what he chose them to mean – 'neither more nor less'.

He, like a great many psychologists after him, would have had a field day with the words: *race* and *intelligence*. True, these words are vaguer than many others and consequently leave more room for disagreement: but, in recent years, there has been at times an almost wilful misunderstanding between psychologists, biologists, anthropologists and educationists over the use to which they have been put – something which has hardly helped the understanding of the relation between the two.

The modern technical bases of the words' usage are not difficult to grasp, but an understanding of them *is* needed if such unnecessary disagreement is to be avoided.

To be sure, anthropologists have often criticized each other's use of the term race; for a long while, classification by type of hair or skin colour gave a rather subjective and therefore unreliable guide. In 1775, for instance, Blumenbach distinguished people by their colour into Caucasians (white), Mongolians (yellow), Malayans (brown), Ethiopians (black) and Americans (red). The difficulty, of course, is that since races are interfertile, crossbreeds occur which render the idea of pure races, as time goes on, less and less plausible. But even here the essential modern idea of race is to be found: this is that races are *breeding populations*, whose members breed more often with other members than with non-members. This has proved a particularly practical definition in the sense that one consequence of such breeding patterns is 'genetic drift' – the accumulation of certain genetic characteristics in a certain *breeding population* (not individuals) which can be used to distinguish it from other populations. Advances in recent years in serological genetics mean that we can now recognize certain genes by their chemical reactions with the components of human blood. This is what enables breeding populations to be distinguished and, possibly, the reasons for the differences to be better understood in an evolutionary sense. Boyd, for example, one of the first to define races in this way, refined Blumenbach's understanding by replacing the Caucasian race with a 'European' one on the basis of such serological techniques. Other biologists and anthropologists, however, though they have used these serological techniques, have also used recent anthropological thinking and recognized between thirty and thirty-four races – reintroducing what might look like the old confusions.

Irving Gottesman (1968) has put an acceptable order into this, though, by suggesting that the discrepancies can be resolved if we understand the term 'race' at three levels. First, he says, we should think of *geographical race*. By this is usually meant those groups of populations previously confined together by what were in earlier times insurmountable physical barriers like oceans, deserts and mountains. The example Gottesman himself uses is the American Indians who range from Alaska to Tierra del Fuego. They show a variety of different appearances but all have a low incidence of the genes for type B blood and Rh-negative blood. There are about ten of these geographical races.

Next comes *local race*. The breeding groups within geographical races comprise the local races – among Amerindians the Navajos or Eskimos would be examples. There are hundreds of local races: sometimes they are separated by physical barriers but they may also be separated by social ones.

Finally, there is *micro race*. Within local races, mating may concentrate along certain lines owing to a wide variety of reasons (for example, one might be linked to transport: over time, people may mate with others who are more easily accessible). This can produce a concentration of minor forms of genetic variation in relatively small localities (a well-known example is the variation of blood groups in Wales).

But what the serological technique most has to offer, now, is a perspective on race. It rubs in the fact that, in a very practical sense, the term 'race' applies best to populations, rather than to individuals. It shows that any race classification must have a sizeable element of the arbitrary and that, therefore, rather than waste a disproportionate amount of time on classification, we should instead try to understand the significance of the major *differences* between populations. The serological approach also underlines the fact that differences between races are quantitative, not qualitative, since the evidence suggests that all genes are found in all races.

We have to break here for a purely technical point – but an important one. Strictly speaking, the discussion of race and intelligence ought to be about *all* breeding populations on earth. In fact, most of the discussion has compared American Negroes and American whites. The reasons for this lie in the fact that the experimental evidence, genetic *and* psychological, is most complete for these groups and, in recent years, because the US Negro's civil rights struggle anyway has been the most bitterly fought 'racial' issue. It follows that though the type of studies carried out in the US may be expected to be repeated in other situations in the future outside that country, the results obtained there may not.

If aspects of any race definition are arbitrary, as biologists and anthropologists concede, the same is true, many people feel, of the definition of intelligence (and that includes some psychologists). Yet this sort of criticism – easy to understand though it is – is by no means always true. Psychologists' understanding of intelligence has been shown to be *inadequate* at times in the past, and revised according to scientifically obtained results, but that's a better word – inadequate – than arbitrary.

For example, the new British IQ test, at present in its last stages of development, incorporates the latest research ideas into its structure (Watson, 1970). It gives a profile of abilities rather than a single IQ figure because this, in the past, appears to have attracted to itself a greater significance than the evidence would justify. And the new test has incorporated evidence which suggests that there may be equivalent forms of ability, for example, one which shows itself in the talent to spot relations between objects (convergent thought), and the other in the talent to generate new ideas (divergent thought).

These kinds of revisions are more important than criticisms that tests use questions that require specialized knowledge rather than some more general culture free ability. This sort of criticism neglects the research on which the tests are based. The research is quite straightforward: Charles Spearman said that intelligence was the ability to 'educe relations and correlates' a definition many psychologists would agree with (Eysenck, 1971). The tests they have devised are aimed at estimating just this – getting over environmental effects. So various tasks have been thought up which involve doing things *not* normally encountered anywhere – school, work or home. Others involve words, numbers and spaces. What has been found is that people who do well on one kind of test tend to do well (sometimes better, sometimes worse) on others. This has given rise to the idea that there is a basic general intelligence factor, called *g*, with a number of 'sub-abilities' such as number ability, spatial ability or perceptual ability. Intelligence tests are groups of tasks measuring all these abilities that have been given to large numbers of people from very different backgrounds and which are selected because they are relatively little influenced by those backgrounds.

In other words, if you agree that intelligence *is* the ability to 'educe relations and correlates', then IQ tests are the best tools we have for measuring intelligence and are not as arbitrary as they look. If you don't agree, you have to have something additional or alternative. Only the idea of divergent and convergent thinking has modified Spearman's definition so far, but this is important in the context of the present chapter because few studies have been carried out to show how different breeding populations differ on this ability.

So you can see why, when it comes down to it, the race and intelligence debate has been about the performance of American white and Negroes on IQ tests. In what follows I shall refer to other breeding groups only when a point can be made by doing so.

One might begin by saying that, in fact, a variety of factors have been found to correlate with IQ – metabolic rate, weight, height, a certain kind of electrical activity in the brain, degree of anoxia at birth, anxiety level, a person's mother's concern for his or her language development, someone's father's occupation and years of schooling, and many, many others (Gottesman, 1968). This is no final validation of IQ, of course, but it does confirm that the intelligence concept, as used by psychologists, is not as nonsensical as some critics maintain.

But that doesn't mean that the average results of psychological studies on the differences between races need be taken at anything like their face value. The average result that counts, a crude one all sides admit, is that the US Negro scores somewhere between ten and fifteen points below his white counterpart. There are variations – occasionally some groups of Negroes outstrip whites – and as we shall see these can be very enlightening; but, taken region by region, whites come out on top. What we need to understand, therefore, is three things: why the gap is the size it is; why it is in the direction it is; and why it varies as it does.

This gap of about fifteen IQ points is, in fact, about as far as the agreement goes on this subject. What you will find, if you examine the published research is that many results obtained over the last thirty or forty years are, incredibly, *still* not regarded as substantiated and that the interpretation of others varies widely. For example, the average difference in IQ between whites and Negroes from the north has been found in some studies to be ten points, that between certain southern Negroes and whites twenty points. Two interpretations (at least) are given as to what this might mean. On the one hand it could show that even in the north – with more equal opportunities – Negroes still fall below whites. On the other, it might be interpreted as showing that if the differences in environment between north and south can change the interrace gap in IQ by ten points, then this and environmental differences can produce changes in IQ of the order of magnitude normally found between races.

Similar sorts of conflict have arisen over the interpretation of twin studies (important in this field because their genetic variation is strictly controlled and, in monozygotic twins, is identical, so enabling us to study the uncontaminated effects of environment). Gottesman, on the one hand, quotes studies of the differences in IQ *within* pairs of identical twins – studies which show an average difference of six points and which range from 0 to 20, even when reared together. Reared apart, the average difference between identical twins was eight points in one study and fourteen in another. Because of this sort of difference, with genetic equality we *are* sure of, Gottesman concludes that race differences in IQ which are of much the same order of magnitude, can result from environmental differences.

Arthur Jensen (1969), on the other hand, quotes studies showing the correlation of the IQ of one identical twin with another – an average of 0·87 – one of the factors which led him to his conclusion that heredity outweighs environment by four to one.

One could go on almost endlessly giving ostensibly contradictory results like this, getting nowhere. But notice that these claims, though they may be designed to seem contradictory, may not in fact be so. Put simply, for example, the Gottesman and the Jensen points could be added together to read: heredity outweighs environment by four to one, but the twenty per cent of variation produced by the environment could account for that fifteen point difference in IQ between races.

This is an important point in the history of this particular scientific row. For not only have psychologists been Humpty Dumpties, they've shown symptoms of Mad Hatterism – a rudeness in not listening to other people's arguments – too. And they have not only been insensitive to each other, but to the sensibilities of blacks: I shall show later on how crude has been the understanding by many white psychologists (who should surely know better, if anyone does) of what factors could conceivably look differently to the black, compared with the white. (It is this insensitivity, I would argue, rather than the actual nature of the results, that forces some blacks – including black psychologists – to label intelligence as a white man's concept).

This general insensitivity is one of the reasons why Jensen's 1969 article created such a controversy. In the years previously, the genetic evidence had been underplayed in contrast to the environmental side which had been over-interpreted. But this over-interpretation was itself a reaction, to the even earlier underplaying of environmental influences as, for example, in Audrey Shuey's book, *The Testing of Negro Intelligence*. This, in 1956, had left out some twenty or so studies of major importance which disagreed with her conclusions. But Shuey's book came after the United Nations had made an unsupported claim, in 1950, that intelligence was wholly environmentally determined . . .

To start with, one thing we can try to do is put back some perspective and sensitivity to psychologists' arguments and to black feelings.

What you find, if you go back as far as the Second World War, is that even then the interaction theory, of heredity *v.* environment, made sense to most people familiar with the evidence. In fact, ideas were sophisticated enough for Cooper and Zubeck (1958), in the middle fifties, to carry out the following ingenious experiment, demonstrating the heredity *times* environment interaction.

They used two strains of rat, genetically distinct, which had previously been bred for thirteen generations as either 'bright' or 'dull'. After weaning, groups of the two strains were put, separately, into three kinds of environment: a restricted kind, containing a box for food, a pan for water and nothing else; the 'natural' kind – the usual lot of the lab rat; and an enriched kind, with ramps, swings, balls, tunnels, slides, patterned walls and such like. After a while in these, the rats then had to learn to run mazes, and the errors they made doing this were recorded. What was found was that the restricted environment did not affect the performance of the dull rats, but brought the performance of the bright rats down to the dull level. And in the enriched environment it was found that the performance of the bright rats was not improved, but that the performance of the dull rats was raised till it was nearly as good as that of the bright ones.

The right kind of environment, then, could, with rats at least, compensate for genetic differences. That heredity had some influence over intelligence was never in doubt, in these earlier years. What psychologists were interested in at this time, was how the manipulation of the environment could alter intellectual performance. It was in the race to discover this that the genetic side started to slide out of view.

This was helped by the publication, in 1951, of a book by J. McV. Hunt, called *Intelligence and Experience*. To Hunt we owe much of the idea that a person's intellectual capacity is in large part determined by his or her early experiences in childhood. As Thomas Pettigrew (1964) has pointed out, in his book *A Profile of the Negro American*, this influenced the spread of the twin ideas that intelligence need not be fixed throughout life and that someone's ability may not necessarily develop to the full, irrespective of the consequences or conditions in his life.

You can see how misunderstanding might have arisen: this coterie of ideas spread together, based originally on animal studies but soon seemingly confirmed by studies on children. Kirk, for example, showed in 1958 that early educational action could often bring about startling increases in the intellectual functioning of mentally retarded children – even, on occasions, among those who had been diagnosed as organically impaired. At least four other studies, dealing with black and with white normal children, showed that nursery or other pre-school training could raise children's IQs.

So with that fifteen point gap in IQ between the races in the back of psychologists' minds, research on the environmental correlates of low IQ expanded. Studies such as that showing gypsies to have a lower intelligence than ordinary English people, and for this to decline as they grow older, or that children in orphanages have lower IQs than those brought up at home, grew in number and were also taken as support for a purely environmental explanation of the differences in IQ between both individuals and groups.

In this way there began an era of research into what Pettigrew later called the 'mediators of intellectual underdevelopment'.

There are four of these: physiological, economical, psychological and educational. The second and fourth of these were the main preoccupation of the sociologists – sociologists who, as we shall see, were later shown to have been mainly responsible for underplaying the statistical data through which genetic arguments about race differences in intelligence were represented. Here again we see that blindness or insensitivity to *all* the aspects of the situation.

But first let's look at the physiological mediators of intellectual underdevelopment. These operate through the mother onto the fetus. A pregnant mother's diet that was poor in vitamins was shown by R. F. Harrell and colleagues (1956) to affect the intelligence of the child to which she gave birth. A sample of mothers was chosen from the lowest socio-economic level – 80 per cent were Negroes: one group was fortified with iron and vitamin B complex during pregnancy, the other group wasn't. The children of the fortified group, at three years of age, were, on average, five IQ points ahead of the children of the non-fortified group. And a year later they were eight points ahead. Interestingly, Harrell and his colleagues repeated their experiment later with an all-white group of mothers in another rural part of America – but failed to show the same effect. So it would seem that it is not until the worst poverty and stress is reached that there is any effect due to diet – but that then there is a marked effect.

Economic difficulties may affect intelligence, too. This is because poor economic conditions may influence the number of premature births. Whatever their race, premature babies contain a higher percentage of mental defectives, have a greater susceptibility to disease and greater abnormality associated with the nervous system. And insofar as premature births are likely to be more hazardous there is the added risk of brain damage associated with that. And indeed, what you find is that among Negroes – over-represented among the poorer segments – all these risks are greater and the incidence of all the abnormalities is higher.

When we come to the relation between the Negro's personality and his intellectual functioning we are on the ground that is the psychologists' very own and which, therefore, you would expect to be the strongest: yet for some it has proved the one in which they have been more insensitive than anywhere else. Harold Proshansky's chapter, earlier in this book, shows well how varied and worrying some of these effects on personality may be. But on top of this there is a solid body of research evidence exploring how these personality changes affect IQ,

In an article in the *Journal of Abnormal and Social Psychology* in 1951, Elizabeth Weisskopf reported on 'Intellectual malfunctioning and personality' in which she showed how a child may do badly at school due either to conscious or to unconscious reasons: these vary from the child's wish to avoid testing his own worth, to punishing his parents – or even himself. S. R. Roen compared a group of Negro soldiers with a group of white ones (in 1960). He made sure they were equated on background variables and then investigated how their performance on personality tests varied according to how well they did on intelligence tests. He found a high correlation for Negroes but not for whites. And he particularly singled out the fact that Negro soldiers who had low intelligence scores rated 'especially' low on his self-confidence questionnaire.

Marian Radke Yarrow (1958) studied Negro and white children at a summer camp and found that the races differed in their reactions to the interracial experience. Whites were more likely to be openly aggressive, fighting, shouting, dashing around, and so on. The black children, on the other hand, she said, seemed to turn all their feelings 'inward': they became anxious, couldn't sleep, had nightmares, wet the bed. Now, psychological theories about stress predict that individuals, whatever colour they are, who are anxious, who turn their feelings inward, do indeed perform poorly on IQ tests – it's as if they're too busy dealing with their feelings to do the test properly.

Living in a white dominated world would seem to be one major source of Negro anxiety and lack of self-confidence. Irwin Katz and his colleagues (1964) gained experimental support for this when they gave a certain task to Negro students in a southern state of the US with one of two sets of instructions (and see also Chapters 12 and 17 of this book). One set was worded so as to induce the Negro students to anticipate that their performance would be judged on an essentially black standard – with the other Negroes in their college; the other was phrased to induce an anticipated comparison with a white standard – the whole white population throughout the rest of the US. Although the two groups of Negro subjects were equated for ability, those who anticipated comparison with whites did worse on the task than those who anticipated comparison with blacks. They were also more concerned about their performance.

Pettigrew (1964) also says that the 'role' of Negro is a critical factor. In the US, he says, the Negro is not expected to be bright, for this may seem 'uppity' to the white. He may, therefore, 'grow' into the role of stupid as a self-fulfilling prophecy begins to operate. A consequence of this, Pettigrew says, is that he will, more and more, feel threatened in the white intellectual world. Though there is no direct evidence to support these two contentions there is some fairly strong indirect evidence suggesting they are not just thin theoretical webs.

Rosenthal and Jacobson's work with the overall title of *Pygmalion in the Classroom* (1968) is well-known now as evidence that self-fulfilling prophecies can occur. And Irwin Katz has shown convincingly that the performance of Negro children on IQ tests given under different instructions varies in accordance with a theory which says they see tests given by white people as very stressful (in one case, a test was experimentally shown as an equivalent force in provoking stress in a Negro as the threat of an electric shock).

Still other personality factors may be significant for intellectual functioning. These, too, depend on how the Negro reacts to being a Negro in a white world. One way he may do this is the way of passivity and lack of ambition. The interesting thing about this is that it may be more crucial at some stages of development than in others. Jerome Kagan and colleagues (1958), for example, found these personality variables to be crucial in white children: lack of passivity and ambition divided those children whose IQ scores improved between the ages of six and ten and those whose didn't.

Two other factors are slowness and impulsivity. Negro children are more likely to be at the extremes of either end on this. Slowness is obviously important as many IQ tests involve items that are timed. K. S. Davidson and colleagues (1950) noticed with one group of Negro and white children that much of the difference in IQ between them were due to the time taken to make the response – in other words, it wasn't that they made errors but that they took longer to get things right.

Other more recent research has shown, perhaps surprisingly, that the extreme opposite may be just as damaging. Persons who react impulsively on IQ tests, as poorer whites and Negroes tend to, make more mistakes, research shows. In fact, it is now almost an accepted axiom to try to get children *not* to rush their answers on tests – answers which, on reflection, they may regret.

Finally, mention must be made of a series of experiments over the years which follow naturally on from the ones just discussed but the significance of which may only now be being realized. Brief mention has already been made of a couple of them: the series, carried out by half a dozen different experimenters, is one which shows that Negroes may perform differently on intellectual tasks according to whether the tester is white or Negro. Professor Irwin Katz discusses a lot of his own work on this subject elsewhere in this book, and all that needs to be pointed out in this chapter is that the effect was first noted in 1936, has continued to be noticed and, very recently, has been instrumental in suggesting a new theory to account for racial differences in IQ; I shall return to this at the relevant point in the chronology.

These personality factors were the third in Pettigrew's mediators of intellectual underdevelopment. In many ways they consitute some of the best controlled studies to date in this field and it is significant that in the later onslaught on environmentalism which was to follow, the points raised in these studies have never been properly countered. This is another reason why they have given rise to a new theory accounting for intellectual differences between races.

The same cannot be said for the more sociological mediators – which have become the central area for disagreement.

Perhaps the underlying reason for this has been one of methodology: in the first place, it would seem that many studies (of attempts to boost IQ, for example) have not been followed through over time, leading to too hasty conclusions; and, secondly, by using the method of *correlation* – noting that, say, low performance is associated with a particular variable like not having a father in the home – a causal relationship has been inferred – for example, that the absence of a father *causes* poor intellectual development. But logically, of course, this is not necessarily so. And given that the genetic evidence lay fallow, unused, notions about the relation of environment to performance became over-simplified.

On its own, of course, the evidence was fairly convincing. For example, a collection of different studies showed that there was no difference in IQ between whites and Negroes in infancy but that one developed later on. Both R. T. Osborn and H. Tomlinson, in separate studies (see Pettigrew, 1964) found that it was only after a few years that a difference in IQ between children of different races occurred. Some of this deficit has been put down to the greater use of verbal skills that are made by intelligence tests at later age levels – skills which Pettigrew says are particularly affected by the restricted environment the Negro is more likely to encounter.

Other important evidence was the fact that good correlations were found between Negro social class and IQ, the known tendency for Negro families to be more likely to lack a father (father absence, as I have already noted, being associated with lower IQ). These details, together with three studies showing that once class factors were rigorously controlled, Negro–white differences virtually disappeared, the recognized inequalities between schools of different areas and, finally, with Cooper and Zubeck's rat experiment in mind, showing what could be done with varying environments, the concept of compensatory education grew up.

And, of course, once studies which showed that enriched environments did improve performance were published, the environmentalist argument seemed home and dry. One snag in this, though, again underplayed at the time but which bounced back later, was that many of the studies undoubtedly showing that enriched environments do bring improvement in IQ were done not with US Negroes but with various other groups, like Indians, soldiers, or the inhabitants of Honolulu. The Osage Indians, for example, had a piece of luck not given to other Indians – oil was discovered on their land – and prosperity, material and educational, resulted. Following this, the performance of Osage Indians on IQ tests eventually rose from its initial level below that of Negroes to be equal to that of the whites in the area.

L. R. Wheeler found that in east Tennessee, over a ten-year period which had seen wide economic, social and educational advance, the average IQ of the (white) children in the area had lifted by eleven points.

The evidence that the same happened with Negroes was not, in fact, as extensive as was assumed. There was some, though: Otto Klineberg, working in Harlem, found that the IQs of Negroes there was strongly correlated with the time they had lived in the north – a (relatively) enriched environment educationally, compared to the south (see Pettigrew, 1964).

But various enrichment programmes did, between about 1958 and 1962–3, improve the IQs of Negroes. Or at least they *appeared* to for, as we shall see, the results themselves were later challenged directly.

New York City's 'Higher Horizons' project, for example, was early on reported to be successful. The project catered for a mostly Negro (but selected) group of children and saturated them with specialist treatment – remedial-reading teachers, social workers, psychologists and the like. In the first year, the project cut 8–9 year olds' backwardness in reading to one month from six. Another scheme, Washington's 'talent search', started in 1959, was designed to boost some 200 12–13 year olds, nine tenths of whom were Negro. This, too, reduced the failure rate in the schools and produced 'notable instances' of IQ gains. St Louis's 'Banneker Group' is probably the best known of the projects – certainly it was to begin with. Sixteen thousand children, in twenty three schools, made up the Banneker Group, 19 out of 20 children there being black. This project lacked the resources of specialists that other schemes had: the approach involved elements of self-help, parent–school participation, intragroup competition, and community work. In the first four years of the project, the median IQ of the children increased by 10 points from 85 or so to 95 or so and the percentage of Banneker children going on to high schools tripled.

In the mid-1960s, then, this was where the conventional wisdom stood. With the benefit of hindsight, I have tried to show where the main weaknesses of this position were located – because, in the late 1960s, one by one those weaknesses were exploited.

In the winter of 1969, Californian psychologist, Professor Arthur Jensen, published his article, 'How much can we boost IQ and scholastic achievement?' in the *Harvard Educational Review*. Quite possibly, this became one of the most controversial papers ever published in psychology. The article was a wide-ranging review of various topics centring around the title – though, as we shall see, it had some curious (but all-important) gaps.

Jensen's article ranged far wider than race differences in IQ but so far as the present chapter is concerned he did three things: first, he rebutted, or tried to rebut, many of the environmentalists' results – the sort of result I have just outlined above. Second, he presented, as a cogent whole, genetic evidence on IQ which had till then gone by default, and which showed, he claimed, that heredity accounts for four-fifths of the variation between people and groups in IQ. And third, he gathered evidence which, he thought, showed that there are two kinds of intellectual ability, abstract reasoning – the general deduction of relations – and associative learning (including abilities like rote memory). To many in the watching world this was new – and its significance was not properly appreciated: we shall return to it in a moment.

Jensen's article consists of 117 pages of text and nearly six of references so I can do no more than list its main relevant points here. First, there were a number of specific counter-attacks on certain studies. For example, unlike the studies mentioned earlier, Jensen claims that even when socio-economic and status differences between blacks and whites *are* controlled there is still a gap in IQ between them of eleven points. He also argued that father-absence does not have the effect that the sociologists and psychologists had previously said. And, he said, there *are* differences in the early development of Negro and white children. Specifically, he argued that compensatory education projects (he specifically mentioned the 'Higher Horizons' and 'Banneker' projects) did not improve the IQs of the children taking part as earlier investigators had said. In a later paper, published in the winter of 1971 in Britain, he also said that schools do not cheat minority group children – that is, they do not discriminate against them in the educational service they offer and also, in contrast to Osborn and Tomlinson's studies, that the IQ gap between races does *not* grow larger – that is, there is no cumulative development of an IQ deficit due to a progressively poorer environment.

In other words, Jensen put back the genetic side of the argument onto the centre of the stage and severely knocked some environmental notions. Now, some readers may have noticed that in this subject the nature of the argument is such that points are either made that are flatly contradictory or the opposing arguments avoid answering each other direct. In the first case, for example, it is either said that booster education does or does not lift IQ period. In the second case, as the example I gave earlier demonstrates, one side will say IQ is determined mainly hereditarily, the other that races differences in IQ are solely due to environment. Neither of these approaches is exactly helpful if you are trying to pick your way through the evidence to a conclusion that accounts for the facts – all or most of them, including the seemingly contradictory ones.

It seems to be one of those arguments in which your current view is affected more by the latest result you have heard than the overall perspective of years of study. But, now nearing the end of this chapter, we are in a position to put that perspective into the results, Professor Jensen's included. And this does, I think, lead us to a sensible theoretical conclusion, one that not only makes sense of the results but also allows future experiment to test the theory's full validity and its implications.

Many people seem to have agreed that where Jensen has gone flatly against the environmentalists his results are either more recent or obtained with a better method and are therefore more reliable. What we can see, though, after this chronological perspective, is that there are many results which Jensen did not even attempt to answer. In doing this, Jensen and his followers have been as guilty of insensitivity to inconvenient results as earlier psychologists and sociologists were. And it is, significantly, the results to which Jensen has published no answer that suggest a new theory which may bring together apparently irreconcilable results.

No reply, or alternative interpretation, for instance, was given by Jensen or his main followers, to at least two studies showing that Negro children in the US south suffered a breakdown of spatial ability – a breakdown described as similar to those suffered by people who have gone through periods of sensory deprivation. Neither has an answer been given to the additional studies showing that this disability could be corrected and that Negroes benefited more from the correctional procedure than whites. No reply either has been forthcoming on the results of physiological damage to the Negro fetus and its consequences. But most of all no real reply has been offered to the evidence regarding the intellectual consequences of the Negroes personality reactions due to living in a predominantly white society.

I took great care to describe these in some detail to show that this point is not, as some of Jensen's followers have maintained, a minor quibble. These would amount to a major obstacle to any predominantly genetic theory of race differences in IQ even if they did not suggest a credible alternative account of such differences themselves. But they do.

Post-Jensen, we can see that the more sociological mediators of intellectual underdevelopment are of less importance in accounting for race differences than previously allowed; but that pushes our gaze on to psychological mediators every bit as much as genetic ones.

Take as our starting point for this final aspect of the discussion, Jensen's own acknowledgement of Audrey Shuey's conclusion that, with socioeconomic status controlled, the IQ difference between US whites and Negroes narrows from fifteen points to eleven points. What needs explaining is (a) the size of this gap and (b) the direction. Eleven points is suspiciously close to the average difference – nine points – found by James Shields (1962) in his study of the within pair IQ differences of monozygotic, or identical, twins – twins whose environments, however different they were, were very unlikely to be as different as blacks' is from whites'.

A colleague of Shields's, Elliot Slater, for a long time editor of the *British Journal of Psychiatry*, and a man with a great interest in and knowledge of genetics, found in his studies of identical twins (Slater, 1953) that small differences 'in energy' between them could produce large differences in personality over time. He never applied this idea to variation in IQ but, given the relation of personality to intelligence, the idea that IQ differences could be due to 'energy' differences is a hypothesis well worth testing.

This sort of evidence – genetic evidence – suggests, first, that the sort of difference observed between the IQ of whites and Negroes could occur due to environmental differences. It also suggests that small differences between people or groups can produce larger differences in psychological characteristics. What next needs explaining, then, is why this difference takes the direction it does.

Here we return to the studies of several investigators, including myself, showing the interaction of Negro personality with performance. The burden of the research – some of which is reported in greater detail by Irwin Katz in an accompanying chapter – is that friction between whites and blacks, in which blacks very nearly always come off worse due to being in a minority, causes a drop in intellectual functioning. A good way of conceptualizing this is to see the Negro as chronically in a condition of stress.

Such an idea has been in existence for a long time – though it is only very recently that the full significance has been grasped. As early as 1936, for example, H. G. Canady (1936) reported that when black and white students were tested by black or white testers, they scored several points higher when tested by someone from their own race.

The one interpretation that we need to make in all this is that the test situation in which a black person is tested by a white, represents to the black something of the friction-ridden atmosphere of the wider society outside.

This effect of the race of the tester was shown again in 1955 when Pasamick and Knobloch (see Pettigrew, 1964) noted that two year old Negro children were more verbally inhibited when tested by a white than when tested by another Negro. And both Pettigrew and Price and Searles (later still, in 1961) showed that Negroes did better on questionnaires and intelligence tests when the tests were given by Negroes.

Katz's own work has been the most systematic of all in this field. He has shown, over the last ten years, that the race of the tester, whether a test is seen as a test or not; which race is to be used as the standard for comparison; all these interact in such a way as to suggest that, for a black living in a white society, that white society *can* be more rewarding for him, provided he feels secure, but that in the natural course of events this is not usually so. Whites can offer the black, if you like, more of the keys to success. (Experimentally, when blacks were manipulated to feel more secure they performed better when tested by whites. On the other hand, experiments also show that the *natural* state of affairs is for Negroes to feel anything but secure in the presence of whites and that in this case Negroes did worse when tested by a white. In one experiment it was actually shown that for a Negro who has to take an IQ test anyway, being tested by a white is as much a threat as the fear of an electric shock.) So threat or stress are not unnecessarily strong words in this context.

Evidence is building up that this stress is an important factor in explaining the *direction* of race differences in IQ (recently, for example, I got results that would suggest a 'Katz effect' with West Indians in London schools).

There is also a certain amount of corroborative evidence. Jensen claimed that Negroes showed more associative learning ability – rote memory, for example – than whites and less abstract reasoning ability. He had no explanation of this except to infer a genetic one. Yet what is known about the effects of stress on intellectual performance would predict this. For, under stress, performance on associative learning abilities, like rote memory, gets relatively better, whereas abstract reasoning gets worse. A look, too, at the usual curves showing the distribution of IQ between races is instructive. Usually they are shown as below in Figure 1:

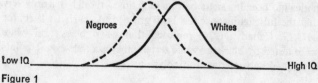

Figure 1

that is, they are identical curves separated by a few IQ points. But in fact, if you look closely, at least some studies differ from this. With these a more accurate picture would be, as Figure 2 shows:

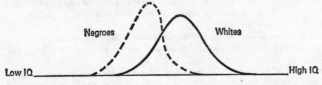

Figure 2

This time the distribution of the Negro curve is skewed: Negroes, in other words, are disproportionately more likely to get a score of around 90 – to complete those bits of I.Q. tests which make use of associative learning abilities, and less well on abstract reasoning rather than equally poorly all the way through. Again, then, stress theory is supported by these curves rather than a genetic difference.

Finally, we may recall Marian Radke Yarrow's (1958) experiment with black and white schoolchildren at a summer camp. Remember that the Negroes reacted by turning their feelings aroused by the interracial interaction inward, in the form of nightmares, bed-wetting and anxiety. White children, remember, turned theirs outwards, in fighting, shouting, dashing around. It is another aspect of stress theory that individuals who respond to stress by turning their feelings in, suffer more intellectually than those who turn them out.

Much more research along these lines needs to be done. But this line is, I would argue, more sensitive to the position of the black than much previous research. (Yet it is also fair to point out that no one has yet shown the race of the tester to make as much as eleven points difference. The assumption is made that one test is only a microcosm of the wider picture and that an eleven point difference is the result of a lifetime of living in stressful conditions. But experimental ways to test this will have to be found).

It is only fair to conclude that there are far more loose ends on all sides of this debate, far more, as I have tried to show, than many of the protagonists like to acknowledge.

Not only that – but there are fragments of evidence suggesting theories well away from the traditional ones (for example, some of the physical differences found between Negro and white babies in some studies have prompted one or two people to ponder the evolutionary significance of this). To say that is not sitting on the fence (though that habit did Humpty Dumpty far more good than coming off it): it is merely exercising scientific caution – the lack of which seems to have dogged this particular subject more than most.

Peter Watson 375

References

CANADY, H. G. (1936), 'The effect of "rapport" on the IQ: a new approach to the problem of social psychology', *Journal of Negro Education*, vol. 5, pp. 209–19.

COOPER, R. M., and ZUBECK, J. M. (1958), 'Effects of enriched and constricted early environments on the learning ability of bright and dull rats', *Canadian Journal of Psychology*, vol. 12.

DAVIDSON, K. S., *et al.* (1950), 'A preliminary study of Negro and white differences in Form 1 of the Wechsler–Bellevue Scale', *Journal of Consulting Psychology*, vol. 14.

EYSENCK, H. J. (1971), *Race, Intelligence and Education*, Maurice Temple Smith.

GOTTESMAN. I. (1968), 'Biogenetics of race and class', in M. Deutsch, I. Katz and A. Jensen (eds.), *Social Class, Race and Psychological Development*, Holt, Rinehart & Winston.

HARRELL, R. F., *et al.* (1956), 'Influence of vitamin supplementation of diets of pregnant and lactating women on intelligence of their offspring', *Metabolism*, vol. 5.

HUNT, J. McV. (1951), *Intelligence and Experience*, Ronald Press.

JENSEN, A. (1969), 'How much can we boost IQ and scholastic achievement?', *Harvard Educational Review*, vol. 39, no. 1.

KAGAN, J., *et al.* (1958), 'Personality and IQ change', *Journal of Abnormal and Social Psychology*, vol. 56, pp. 261–6.

KATZ, I., *et al.* (1964), 'Effect upon Negro digit – symbol performance of anticipated comparison with whites and with other Negroes', *Journal of Abnormal and Social Psychology*, vol. 69, pp. 77–83.

KIRK, S. A. (1958), *Early Education and the Mentally Retarded*, University of Illinois Press.

PETTIGREW, T. F. (1964), *A Profile of the Negro American*, Van Nostrand.

PRICE, D. O. and SEARLES, R. (1961), 'Some effects of interviewer – respondent interaction on responses in a survey situation', paper presented at the Annual meeting of the American Statistical Association, December.

ROSENTHAL, R. and JACOBSON, L. (1968), *Pygmalion in the Classroom*, Holt, Rinehart & Winston.

SHIELDS, J. (1967), *Monozygotic Twins Brought up Together and Apart*, Oxford University Press.

SHUEY, A. (1956), *The Testing of Negro Intelligence*, Social Science Press.

SLATER, E. (1953), 'Psychotic and neurotic illness in twins' *Medical Research Council Special Research Series*, no. 278, HMSO. (Assistance of J. Shields)

WATSON, P. (1970), 'The new IQ test', *New Society*, 22nd January.

WATSON, P. (1970), 'How race affects IQ', *New Society*, 16 July.

WATSON, P. (1972), 'Can racial discrimination affect IQ?' in Richardson, K., Spears, D., and Richard, M., *Race, Culture, and Intelligence*, Penguin.

WEISSKOPF, E. (1951) 'Intellectual malfunctioning and personality', *Journal of Abnormal and Social Psychology*.

YARROW M. R. (1958), 'Interpersonal dynamics in a desegregation process', *Journal of Social Issues*, vol. 14.

Chapter 18
Alternatives to a Personality-Deficit Interpretation of Negro Under-Achievement[1]

Irwin Katz

A major barrier to the reduction of racial inequalities of opportunity in the United States is the low academic achievement of most Negro youths. The racial gap in school performance was recently documented by a national survey which found that about 85 per cent of all Negro American students in elementary schools and high schools score below the average of their white contemporaries on tests of basic knowledge and skills (Coleman *et al.*, 1966). Psychologists and educators who are familiar with this problem generally assume that the black pupil's learning difficulties are largely motivational in nature. Given the extensive experimental evidence of the crucial role of motivation in learning, and a strong consensus among teachers that most lower-class Negro children are not sufficiently interested in schoolwork, this assumption seems reasonable.

Little is known, however, about the *causes* of low motivation in these pupils. Of the various explanations that have been proposed, the ones that have perhaps had the most influence are those that emphasize the damaging effects of various personality traits acquired in early childhood. These 'personality deficit' approaches to the problem of low academic achievement amongst Negroes have hitherto not been critically examined against the available evidence. This I will now attempt to do. Alternative hypotheses will then be described, and suggestions made about new directions for research.

Personality-deficit hypotheses about Negro under-achievement

Writers who stress the influence of personality factors on racial differences in academic achievement tend to attribute the non-white student's apparent inadequacies to a basic failure of the socialization process in the home. According to these authors, early childhood experiences in poverty environments create enduring personality formations that are inimical to effective achievement striving not only in the classroom but, indeed, in virtually all areas of life. Ausubel and Ausubel (1963) stress two features of

---

1. Some of the material in this chapter was originally prepared for the National Institute of Child Health and Human Development, United States Department of Health, Education and Welfare.

child rearing which they claim to be typical of low-income Negro families. Firstly, harsh authoritarianism on the part of parents, who control their children mainly by means of punishment and place considerable social and emotional distance between themselves and their children. Secondly, early relaxation of close parental supervision, which makes the child precociously independent of adult influence but exposes him to the exaggerated socializing influence of his own contemporaries. They maintain that these two features, combined with the child's growing awareness of the stigma attached to being black in a white-dominated society, create a personality marked by feelings of unworthiness, lack of self-control, and hostile rejection of adult values.

Similarly, Bettelheim (1964) believes that 'human personality is shaped in infancy, and that the early characteristics are extremely resistant to change'. He claims that the Negro child's earliest experiences of life often produce 'a life-long distrust of others (including one's teachers and what they teach) and of oneself'. Mistrust, shame and doubt become the dominant characteristics in children from economically deprived homes. He concludes that the black pupil is predestined to failure even before he enters kindergarten or first grade.

Another writer who stresses the role of early socialization in Negro homes is McClelland (1961). Negroes as a group, he maintains, lack the achievement motive (n Achievement) because of the matricentric structure of their families, and the persistence of child-rearing practices that originated in slavery. He takes for granted that strong mother dependency weakens the development of n Achievement in sons. Moreover, 'Negro slaves . . . developed child-rearing practices calculated to produce obedience and responsibility, not n Achievement, and their descendants, while free, should still show the effects of such training in lower n Achievement – which in fact is exactly the case'.

Family structure is emphasized by Pettigrew (1964), Bronfenbrenner (1967), Moynihan (1965) and others, who claim that the relatively high incidence of father absence in lower-class families is a major cause of academic disinterest and failure on the part of children, especially males. Presumably, father-deprived boys lack a masculine model with which to identify, and develop personalities marked by impulsivity, effeminacy and immature dependency.

In evaluating the evidence relating to these explanations of lower-class under-achievement in terms of early-acquired personality deficits, one must ask not only (a) whether specific personality differences have been found between children from backgrounds of poverty and backgrounds of affluence, but also (b) whether demonstrated personality differences have been related to differences in school achievement. If empirical findings indicate that the disadvantaged pupil does tend to possess traits that are academically detrimental, it should then be asked (c) whether the traits have been shown to be products of early family influences, and (d) whether the traits, once they are formed, appear to be relatively unmodifiable. *Measured by these criteria, research findings provide little in the way of support for a personality-centred viewpoint, despite its wide acceptance in the clinical literature on race and poverty.* In the brief survey of research that follows, Negro children (usually lower-class) are generally compared with age peers of higher status (usually middle-class whites).

Evidence relating to personality-deficit hypotheses

Much of the empirical work on Negro personality has been stimulated by the notion that members of this group still bear a 'mark of oppression' that represents the emotional wound of living in a white world of prejudice and discrimination. Thus a frequently studied characteristic of Negro children is their inclination towards hostile rejection of their own race and identification with the white majority. This conflict of identity has been found repeatedly in both the North and South of the United States, a variety of projective techniques being used to measure the racial evaluations of whites and Negroes (see Chapter 7 of this book). Derogation of their own race appears in children from minority groups as early as age three, remaining strong until later childhood when it tends to become less apparent (being perhaps still present, but concealed). Hence the development of this characteristic cannot be attributed to school influences alone. On the other hand, it has not yet been related to social class or family factors. At the present time virtually nothing definite is known about its effect on school performance.

If a child believes he belongs to an intellectually inferior group, he might be expected to lack the confidence to strive for success in the classroom. However, most of the studies on racial identity have dealt with children's evaluations of their group's moral, social and physical-appearance characteristics, and not with evaluations of its intellectual attributes. Theoretically, there is no compelling reason why attitudes about non-intellectual traits should be closely tied to scholastic motivation. Smith (1968) makes this point in a recent paper on the socialization of personal competence. Where academic self-esteem has been investigated in Negro and white young people, the findings on race differences have been equivocal, as will be shown later.

Another characteristic that is supposed to be associated with the 'mark of oppression' is chronic diffuse hostility and distrust. Using projective tests, Hammer (1953) and Mussen (1953) found differences in the amount of fantasy aggression expressed by Negro and white children. Projective data gathered by Karon (1958) suggest that adult and adolescent Negroes, particularly in the South, have a tendency towards extreme repression of aggressive impulses. But the specific sources of aggressive impulses in Negro children, their stability over time, and their possible relationship to academic failure, have not been adequately investigated. It is interesting to note, however, that Sarason and his associates (1960) have concluded from their research on white children that fear and hostility towards adults are important elements in the development of school anxiety, a characteristic to be discussed later.

A considerable amount of research has been done on children's need for achievement, this being measured mainly by means of their fantasies. There are a good many difficulties with the concept of a global achievement motive as embodied in the fantasy-based measure, which have recently been reviewed by Smith (1968). He writes:

There are questions about its generality . . . its openness to influences that contaminate its value as a measure of motivation. The findings in regard to its relationship to achievement-oriented behavior have been ambiguous . . . Given this less than encouraging record, one suspects that there has been slippage between the theoretical definition of the motive and what has actually been captured in the measurements (p. 307).

The problem of the generality of the achievement motive is especially relevant to the study of class and cultural differences in academic performance. For example, the lower-class Negro pupil's lack of interest in classroom learning may not mean that he lacks the achievement motive, but simply that it is directed towards non-intellectual pursuits. In comparing the behaviour of individuals from different social backgrounds, it may be necessary to abandon entirely the concept of a single global achievement motive in favour of a notion of many relatively independent achievement motives specific to particular areas of competition.

I have proposed a new methodology for studying children's achievement motivation on individual activities. This attempts to elicit from children their own feelings about this performance on specific tasks, and then measures the emotional effects on them (self-reinforcement properties) of either favourable or unfavourable self-appraisal (Katz, 1967). Results recently obtained with this technique will be discussed later.

A predisposition which is strongly associated with scholastic achievement, though the nature of the casual relationship has not yet been empirically unravelled, is Rotter's (1962) *sense of personal control of the environment*. People differ in the extent to which they feel that they can extract material and social benefits from their environment through their own efforts. In its broadest sense, this construct refers to the degree to which people have a sense of being able to accomplish what they set out to achieve and accept personal responsibility for what happens to them. Crandall *et al.* (1965) have applied it more specifically to the intellectual achievement of children. They devised a questionnaire which assesses the extent to which favourable reactions from parents, teachers and peers are believed by the child to depend *either* upon the quality of his own efforts *or* upon extraneous factors, such as luck, or the personal bias or whim of the evaluator. The sense of internal control has been found to be stronger in white children and adults than in Negroes, and stronger in the middle class than in the working class (see Battle *et al.*, 1963).

A child's feelings about whether his own efforts determine his external rewards should clearly affect his expectancy of success, and thus his willingness to strive. His level of performance should in turn affect the rate at which he is encouraged and rewarded by those around him, and therefore his sense of control over his environment. Crandall *et al.* (1962) found that white grade-school boys who felt that they themselves controlled their own successes got high scores on intellectual tests and engaged in much intellectual activity in their own spare time. Similarly, in their large-scale survey of American public-school students, Coleman and his co-workers found that a sense of personal control was closely related to academic achievement in both whites and Negroes.

The Coleman team measured three types of student attitude relevant to academic motivation: interest in school work, academic self-confidence and a sense of personal control over rewards. For Negro students, sense of control was clearly the most important, contributing at different grades from two to several times as much of the accounted-for variance of verbal achievement as either of the former. Moreover, the relation of Negroes' sense of control seemed far more closely related to achievement than any family-background factors. Finally, a comparison of the races revealed that among older children this sense of fate control accounted for about three times as much test variance among Negroes as whites (a result which the Coleman Report points out is not attributable to racial differences in variability of fate control scores).

Since the Coleman findings represent merely empirical correlations, the causal connection between a sense of internal control and other variables can only be surmised. Nonetheless, there are strong suggestions in the data regarding the relative importance of home and school determinants. For Negroes, sense of control was little influenced by home factors or objective school characteristics, but one circumstance apparently affected it strongly: as the proportion of white students in schools increased, so the Negroes' sense of personal control – 'internality' – grew stronger.

Thus internality appears to be a personality factor of considerable im-

portance in academic motivation, and one which is relatively lacking in Negro children. However, it is not closely related to particular characteristics of the Negro home; rather, it seems to be very much dependent on the social environment (specifically, the racial composition) of the classroom.

Turning to another characteristic, Feld and Lewis (1967) have found that black pupils in racially isolated as opposed to racially mixed schools have inordinately high levels of anxiety. They gave the Test Anxiety Scale for Children to the entire second-grade population of a large school system in the eastern part of the United States. Negroes had substantially higher anxiety scores than whites, not only on the total scale but also on each of four sub-scales derived by means of factor analysis: test anxiety, remote school concern (e.g., 'When you are in bed at night, do you sometimes worry about how you are going to do in class the next day?'), poor self-evaluation, and somatic signs of anxiety. It is noteworthy that Negro children from racially mixed schools showed less anxiety on the questionnaire than did those who were racially isolated. However, the meaning of this comparison is not entirely clear, since the Negro children in desegregated schools came from homes of relatively high socio-economic status, a factor found to be associated with low anxiety. There were sex differences between white pupils – white boys obtaining lower anxiety scores than white girls – but none for Negroes.

Anxiety about school in Negro boys and girls was closely related to the mother's educational level when other home factors were controlled, a finding that is consistent with research on white children by Sarason *et al.* (1960), and Hill and Sarason (1966). These investigators found that parents have a key effect on school anxiety. In another relevant study, I analysed the role of parental behaviour and attitudes by means of a Reinforcement History Questionnaire that asked children about characteristic reactions of their parents in a variety of situations (Katz, 1967). In a sample of northern Negro boys, children who were anxious about school were also inclined to denigrate their own performance; and these two characteristics were both related to largely negative behaviour on the part of parents – who were reported to be unaccepting and punitive. Moreover, the variables of anxiety, self devaluation and parental punitiveness were all related to school achievement. These data extend to Negro boys one of the main findings of Hill and Sarason, namely that there is a substantial link between school anxiety and academic failure; the data also shed light on the kinds of social set-up at home that give rise to school anxiety.

If inadequate support in the home is in fact one of the most important causes of emotional blocks to learning in lower-class Negro children, it would be useful to know a great deal more than we do at present about the child-rearing values, attitudes and practices of Negro parents. The most relevant recent studies have compared mother-child relationships in Negro families of different classes – using direct observations of behaviour. Kamii (1965) looked at the behaviour of lower-class and middle-class mothers towards their four-year-old children in a midwestern community. The two groups differed considerably: middle-class mothers satisfied their children's need for affection and security, encouraged and rewarded them for verbal efforts, and generally reinforced 'desirable' behaviour more significantly than did lower-class mothers. In another investigation in the north, Hess and associates (1965) sampled a wide spectrum of Negro families, taking groups of mothers and their four-year-old children from four different classes. In general, the class differences observed in maternal attitudes and behaviour were consistent with those reported by Kamii: upper-middle-class mothers praised their children's efforts more than the others did, and were anxious to give their children emotional support rather than demand unquestioning obedience to their injunctions and commands.

The observations of Kamii and of Hess and his colleagues are consistent with general sociological findings: in crowded lower-class homes, where mothers are often away at work during the day, and both parents lack intellectual sophistication, the child's early efforts at speech and general understanding are less likely to be encouraged than in middle-class homes, with the result that he tends to expect less reward for intellectual effort. This, combined with his relatively high expectation of punishment for failure to meet adult demands, probably lays the basis for later school anxiety.

Thus school anxiety would seem to be (a) especially characteristic of lower-class children, (b) related to academic performance, and (c) an outcome of early home experiences. *However, there is reason to believe that conditions in the school can greatly modify this characteristic.* In their longitudinal study of white pupils, Hill and Sarason found that there was little relationship between anxiety scores obtained before and after a four-year interval. Moreover, these changes were associated with changes in academic achievement. *One can only presume that the changes are to some extent a reflection of different types of experience in the classroom, and in the total school culture.*

In this review of research on personality, early socialization and school achievement, reference should be made to families without fathers, since a number of writers have asserted that the absence of fathers amongst children from lower-class homes is a major cause of academic failure. While it is a reasonable assumption that a child's development can be affected by the absence of his father, there is no evidence that this affects school motivation and achievement. Deutsch and Brown (1964) reported lower IQ scores for Negro children from broken than from intact homes, but a more comprehensive follow-up study by Whitman and Deutsch (1968) found no such relationship; and in recent well-controlled, large-sample surveys – notably the Coleman survey and Wilson's (1967) California study – the presence or absence of a father has not been found to influence the scholastic attitudes or achievement of lower-class Negro or white students. Moreover, Feld and Lewis (1967) found virtually no relationship between family intactness and school anxiety.

To sum up: two characteristics of deprived children stemming from their early home experiences have been found to be related to school performance – sense of personal control over environment, and school anxiety. Research on children's self-evaluation and on the behaviour of parents has given some strong indications of the kind of parent-child interactions that are involved. *However, there is reason to believe that both a sense of personal control and anxiety are greatly modifiable through later school experiences.*

Cultural conflict hypothesis

In contradistinction to the various notions of cultural *deprivation* that were reviewed above, is the concept of cultural *conflict*. Inkeles (1966), Riessman (1962), Cloward and Jones (1963) and others have pointed out that minority groups have distinctive systems of values and goals that are not taken into account by the schools their children attend.

The lower-class Negro child may acquire the kind of competencies – motives, attitudes and skills – that are needed for optimal adjustment to the conditions of life he is likely to encounter. The skills that are valued in his own culture may be intrinsically difficult and require for their mastery a good deal of effort and persistence, yet they may be totally ignored by the educational establishment. Thus the low academic motivation of the Negro pupil may be a reflection of the lack of relevance of the competence goals of the school to the competence goals towards which the child has been socialized by the transmitting agents of his own culture.

The concept of a distinctive lower-class culture, or life-style, involves several complex issues which will not be discussed here. What will be considered is the question of group differences in achievement orientation. An extensive literature on educational and job aspirations and expectations has been ably reviewed by Proshansky and Newton (see Chapter 7). Studies of Negro and white children and their parents generally show only small differences when social class is controlled. Comparing classes, aspirations of high- and low-income adults and children are consistently reported as high – most individuals at both economic levels desire college attendance and professional or white-collar occupations. Thus as regards expressed achievement goals, the 'culture conflict' hypotheses would seem to be in error. However, when realistic expectations of achieving the goals are measured, stable class differences appear: these more *functionally relevant* goal levels are lower among low-income students and parents. (Though even statements of 'realistic' expectation from the poor are often unrealistically high, when measured against the objective availability of the stated goals or against actual striving behaviour.)

Thus it seems that the main difference between the achievement orientations of the poor and the affluent lies not in the choice of goals, but in their expectations of attaining them. This conclusion calls for a refinement of the 'culture conflict' hypotheses, if it is to be useful in stimulating research on academic motivation.

Educational deprivation hypothesis

Clark (1965) places responsibility for the massive academic failure of ghetto school children directly with teachers and administrators of ghetto schools. To him, every one of the assumptions associated with the terms 'cultural deprivation' and 'cultural difference' is 'primarily an alibi for educational neglect, and in no way a reflection of the nature of the educational process'. He believes that a key component of the deprivation which afflicts ghetto children is that generally their teachers do not expect them to learn, and think of their function as being one simply of custodial care and discipline. He concludes that the motivational problems of these children will be solved when teachers can be motivated to teach effectively – that is, to set high standards of scholastic performance, and to provide good instruction, combined with emotional acceptance and support. Clark's position represents a radical recasting of the whole issue of pupil motivation. In effect, he is asserting that there really is no problem of Negro motivation, only a problem of the willingness of teachers to teach effectively – that the apparent indifference of their pupils is merely a reflection of their lack of interest.

Clark's contention brings to mind the striking *Pygmalion in the Classroom* experiment of Rosenthal and Jacobson, in which manipulation of the teachers' expectations had a marked influence on the intellectual growth of their pupils in the early grades. While the experiment had somewhat equivocal results, it suggests a possibly fruitful approach to Clark's hypotheses. For example, by elaborating the basic paradigm of manipulating teachers' expectations as regards their pupils' effects both on teachers' behaviour and on their pupils' motivation and performance could be measured separately. But with the possible exception of this one experiment, there is little factual evidence to show that favourable changes in the attitudes of ghetto school teachers can, *per se*, greatly improve the academic motivation of their pupils. Certainly, the results to date of the many recent teacher-training efforts in urban school systems are not encouraging.

Many social scientists have argued that *de facto* segregation is inherently deprivational. Among them, Pettigrew (1969) has most fully elaborated the motivational side, drawing his evidence mainly from the two recent federal reports by Coleman (1966) and the US Commission on Civil Rights (1967).

The Coleman findings (cross-sectional correlations) indicated that as the proportion of whites in a school increased, Negro achievement seemed to rise, and that this apparent effect was cumulative. The relationship held good even when family characteristics of the Negro students were taken into account. A more intensive analysis of Coleman's data by the Civil Rights Commission revealed that the apparent benefits to Negroes of sitting in racially balanced classrooms persisted even when the following factors were controlled by means of cross-tabulations: (a) the quality of educational services available; (b) academic ability and social background of classmates; and (c) academic ability and home backgrounds of Negro students. Reanalysis of the Coleman data by McPartland (1969) has shown that it is desegregation in the classroom rather than in the school that has the most critical effects.

Pettigrew concludes that the reason why Negroes do relatively well in predominantly white classes is that they are better motivated to succeed in this setting – where academic success seems more attractive – and there are increased opportunities for crossracial social comparisons. He discusses the conditions under which crossracial comparison would arouse anxious expectations of failure and feelings of social threat in Negro students, but points out that on balance the consequences of such comparison appear to be beneficial.

Directions for future research

Self-evaluation of performance

I have developed an experimental technique for studying children's covert evaluations of their own performance. An exploratory study was carried out in a northern all-Negro elementary school (Katz, 1967). Fourth- to sixth-grade children were taken individually from their classrooms for testing by a white male adult. During a phase of the experiment that elicited their opinions of their own work, a series of simple tasks (picture assembly, or construction of four-letter words) was presented to each child, who was seated alone at a table, surrounded by partitions. Near the child on the table was a metal box with three buttons which activated small light bulbs of different colours labelled 'Good', 'Poor', and 'Don't Know'.

The instructions were in part as follows: 'We think you will enjoy doing these things more if you can tell yourself how nice a job you think you did. So after you finish each one you can press the button which shows how you feel about the kind of job you did . . . No one will know which button you pressed'. The experimenter left the room after explaining the procedure. Hence, the self-evaluations were ostensibly private, unobserved, and for the child's own amusement. But the set-up was deceptive; the button pressings were mechanically recorded by counters concealed in the box.

In another phase of the testing, the extent to which the subject's self-evaluations had emotional consequences was investigated by ascertaining whether the coloured lights used in the self-evaluation box had acquired positive or negative incentive value by virtue of being associated with self-criticism or self-approval. All subjects coloured a simple line drawing with crayons, both before and after the self-evaluation phase of the experiment. Three crayons corresponded in colour to the three light bulbs on the metal box, and there were also two crayons of different colours. During the crayon colouring task, the metal box was not on the table, and could not be seen.

The drawings were scored on the basis of amount of pre-post change in the use of crayons. Greater or less use of a particular crayon was assumed to be indicative of positive or negative change, respectively, in the affective value of the colour.

In the first study, seventy-nine Negro children were tested. Two types of subjects were used: those whom teachers regarded as good students and those regarded as poor. Of the total sample, only ten were girls. Among the girls there was little difference between the self-evaluations of good and poor students; so they were temporarily dropped from the research. Among boys, poor students were more self-critical and had overall less confidence in themselves than the good students. That the differences between groups were not created by a few extreme scores is evident from the data on thirty-six boys who evaluated their performance on the picture assembly tasks: only three out of seventeen good students, but fully sixteen out of nineteen poor students, used the 'Poor' button at least once out of a total of six self-evaluations. Another male sample of roughly equal size that evaluated their constructions of simple words showed similar differences between high and low academic achievers.

As a check on the possibility that the students' opinions of their capabilities were reasonably accurate appraisals of their actual performance, judges unacquainted with the experimental procedures were asked to rate the subjects' work. They detected no differences in quality of performance associated with academic achievement or self-assessment.

With respect to the emotional consequences of self-evaluation, there was a tendency (not statistically significant) for boys who had been highly self-critical to avoid use of the crayon whose colour had previously been associated with the label 'Poor'.

These results suggest that among northern Negro American children academic failure is not necessarily associated with low or unstable standards of self-evaluation. The standards of the low-achieving Negro boys, as inferred from their predisposition towards self-criticism, were *unrealistically high*. They seem to have internalized a mechanism for imposing failure experience upon themselves, *even when their actual performance did not warrant it*. This was particularly true in the case of students who had a personal history of frequent punishment and infrequent rewards for achievement efforts. The home experiences of students were investigated by means of a 'Reinforcement History Questionnaire' devised by Baron. It contained twenty-one items dealing with characteristic reactions of the father or mother to the child in a variety of situations. It was found that both low academic achievement and self-criticism were particularly prevalent in children who felt their parents gave them little encouragement and were more than usually punitive. Baron's questionnaire has been expanded to include items on how children felt about their teachers' behaviour, for use in future studies.

Expectancy

This term refers to a person's estimate of the probability that a given situation will have a favourable or unfavourable outcome for him. When applied to achievement situations, the person would seem to be estimating two probabilities: (a) what the likelihood is of attaining a certain standard of performance, and (b) having attained that standard, how he will be rewarded. Other things being equal, the higher his estimated probability of reaching his goal, or of receiving a reward, the higher should be his motivation. Presumably, Rotter's concept of internal control refers to a generalized feeling that favourable outcomes will be achieved in a wide range of situations. For the student, a sense of personal control over events probably involves feelings of intellectual competence, and trust in the fairness and responsiveness of his general social environment.

Negroes, it was noted earlier, score lower on questionnaires testing their sense of personal control than do whites. In the Coleman survey, however, Negro students had appreciably higher scores in desegregated schools than in schools with a majority of Negro pupils, and in all schools this was more closely related to academic performance of Negroes than any other variable measured. Further research on this sense of 'efficacy' in Negro students could take a variety of directions. Firstly, the nature of the causal link between this efficacy and academic achievement, which is not ascertainable from Coleman's correlational analysis, needs to be investigated in depth. Longitudinal studies of this sort could be conducted on deprived students, measuring their sense of control prior to various transitional points in their academic careers. Secondly, research should be done on the problem of how new 'expectancies' are learned (or old ones changed). Thirdly, the measurement of the sense of environmental control in lower-class children requires methodological changes and refinements. Present scales do not distinguish between the two types of expectancy that seem to influence Negro academic achievement: one being based on how they judge and estimate their intellectual ability, and the other reflecting their confidence in the systematic responsiveness of their general social environment. In addition, present scales do not distinguish clearly between whether environments are seen as simply capricious or indifferent, or whether they are actually felt to be biased, discriminatory and malevolent.

Incentive value

A well-known method for studying learning motivation in different classes and races is one which compares the effectiveness of different types of rewards, such as tangible *versus* symbolic and person-centred *versus* response-centred.

Zigler and Kanzer (1962) have accounted for various findings by suggesting that socially deprived children develop more slowly than their middle-class contemporaries. They have proposed a developmental hierarchy of reinforcers needed for learning throughout childhood, according to which early dependency on primary need gratification diminishes as several reinforcers (expressions of affection, attention, praise) become increasingly effective. Later, the social reinforcers in turn become less important motivationally than mere information that one's responses are correct. Thus in the final stage the child is more concerned with being right for right's sake, than in receiving adult approval. According to Zigler and Kanzer, this process is central to the child's progress from infantile dependence to autonomy.

Experiments that have compared responsiveness to verbal reinforcement in different groups of children – whether the reinforcers emphasized praise, correctness, or both – do not consistently support this developmental view. What we need now are more refined procedures to find out what particular relevant characteristics in a child respond to reinforcement from what kind of adult. For example, Katz, Henchy and Allen (1968) found that the verbal learning of young Negro boys was affected by an interaction of three variables: the child's need for approval, the race of the experimenter, and the type of evaluation given by the experimenter (praise as opposed to criticism). Further studies should also be done in which the sex, class, race and other characteristics of the adult model are varied, as well as the characteristics of the child, the kind of social reinforcement, and the nature of the child–adult relationship.

The foregoing seem to be some of the more promising directions for experimental research on motivational processes in achievement situations. The enumeration is not intended to be exhaustive. It does not, of course, include more global approaches to family and school influences on academic motivation.

References

AUSUBEL, D. P., and AUSUBEL, P. (1963), 'Ego development among segregated Negro children', in A. H. Passow (ed.), *Education in Depressed Areas*, Teachers' College, Columbia University.

BATTLE, E., and ROTTER, J. (1963), 'Children's feelings of personal control as related to social class and ethnic group', *Journal of Personality*, vol. 31, pp. 482–90.

BETTELHEIM, B. (1964), 'Review of B. S. Bloom's *Stability and Change in Human Characteristics*', *New York Review of Books*, 10 September, pp. 1–4.

BRONFENBRENNER, U. (1967), Paper read at the Conference on Poverty, University of Wisconsin.

CLARK, K. B. (1965), *Dark Ghetto*, Harper & Row.

CLOWARD, R. A., and JONES, J. A. (1963), 'Social class: educational attitudes and participation', in A. H. Passow (ed.), *Education in Depressed Areas*, Teachers' College, Columbia University.

COLEMAN, J. S., *et al.* (1966), *Equality of Educational Opportunity*, US Dept of Health, Education and Welfare.

CRANDALL, V. C., KATKOVSKY, W., and CRANDALL, V. J. (1965), 'Children's beliefs in their own control of reinforcements in intellectual–academic achievement situations', *Child Development*, vol. 36, pp. 91–109.

CRANDALL, V. J., KATKOVSKY, W., and PRESTON, A. (1962), 'Motivation and ability determinants of young children's intellectual achievement behaviours', *Child Development*, vol. 33, pp. 643–61.

DEUTSCH, M., and BROWN, B. (1964), 'Social influences in Negro–white intelligence differences', *Journal of Social Issues*, vol. 20, pp. 24–35.

FELD, S., and LEWIS, J. (1967), 'The assessment of achievement anxieties in children', Mental Health Study Center, *National Institute of Mental Health*, multilith.

HAMMER, E. F. (1953), 'Frustration–aggression hypothesis extended to socio-racial areas', *Psychiatric Quarterly*, vol. 27, pp. 597–607.

HESS, R. D., JACKSON, V., and JACKSON, D. (1965), 'Early experience and the socialization of cognitive modes in children', *Child Development*, vol. 36, pp. 869–86.

HILL, K. T., and SARASON, S. B. (1966), 'The relation of test anxiety and defensiveness to test and school performance over the elementary school years: a further longitudinal study', *Monograph of the Society for Research*, *Child Development*, vol. 31, whole of no. 2.

INKELES, A. (1966), 'A note on social structure and the socialization of competence', *Harvard Educational Review*, vol. 36, pp. 265–83.

KAMII, C. K. (1965), 'Socio-economic class differences in the pre-school socialization practices of Negro mothers', unpublished Ph.D. dissertation, University of Michigan.

KARON, B. P. (1958), *The Negro Personality*, Springer.

KATZ, I. (1967), 'The socialization of academic motivation in minority-group children', in D. Levine (ed.), *Nebraska Symposium on Motivation*, University of Nebraska Press.

KATZ, I., HENCHY, T., and ALLEN, H. (1968), 'Effect of race of tester, approval-disapproval and need on learning in Negro boys', *Journal of Personality and Social Psychology*, vol. 8, pp. 38–42.

MCCLELLAND, D. C. (1961), *The Achieving Society*, Van Nostrand.

MCPARTLAND, J. (1969), 'The relative influence of school and of classroom desegregation on the academic achievement of ninth-grade Negro students', *Journal of Social Issues*, vol. 3, no. 3, pp. 93–102.

MOYNIHAN, T. P. (1965), *The Negro Family*, US Dept of Labor.

MUSSEN, P. H. (1953), 'Differences between the TAT responses of Negro and white boys', *Journal of Consulting Psychology*, vol. 17, pp. 373–6.

PETTIGREW, T. F. (1964), *A Profile of the Negro American*, Van Nostrand.

PETTIGREW, T. F. (1969), 'The Negro and education', in I. Katz and P. Gurin (eds.), *Race and the Social Sciences*, Basic Books.

RIESSMAN, F. (1962), *The Culturally Deprived Child*, Harper.

ROSENTHAL, R., and JACOBSON, L. (1968), 'Self-fulfilling prophecies in the classroom', in M. Deutsch, I. Katz and A. Jensen (eds.), *Social Class, Race and Psychological Development*, Holt, Rinehart & Winston.

ROTTER, J., SEEMAN, M., and LIVERANT, S. (1962), 'Internal *v.* external control of reinforcement: a major variable in behaviour theory'. in N. F. Washburne (ed.), *Decisions, Values and Groups*, vol. 2, Pergamon Press.

SARASON, S. B., DAVIDSON, K. S., LIGHTHALL, F. F., WAITE, R. R., and RUEBUSH, B. K. (1960), *Anxiety in Elementary School Children*, Wiley.

SMITH, M. B. (1968), 'Competence and socialization', in J. A. Clausen (ed.), *Socialization and Society*, Little Brown.

WHITMAN, M., and DEUTSCH, M. (1968), 'Some effects of social class and race on children's language and intellectual abilities', in M. Deutsch, I. Katz and A. Jensen (eds.), *Social Class, Race and Psychological Development*, Holt, Rinehart & Winston.

WILSON, A. B. (1967), 'Educational consequences of segregation in a California community', in US Commission on Civil Rights, *Racial Isolation in the Public Schools*, US Govt. Printing Office.

ZIGLER, E., and KANZER, P. (1962), 'The effectiveness of two classes of verbal reinforcers on the performance of middle-class and lower-class children', *Journal of Personality*. vol. 30, pp. 157–63.

Section F
Language

Language has been under-played in some general books on race relations though it is more important in some situations than others. But the deceptive problems of learning a new language when, say, one is an immigrant in a new country, are probably harder than most of us think – and John Macnamara's chapter explains why this should be. He also explains the relation of learning, or not learning, foreign languages on international attitudes. The interrelation of the media and technology with language and the effect that this has on the way we speak and on our own self-conscious and national or international sentiments is a new field of study, potentially very important in race relations; it is introduced here by Joshua Fishman.

Chapter 19
Learning Each Other's Languages

John Macnamara

John Macnamara is a graduate of University College, Dublin, and
of the University of Edinburgh (M.Ed. and Ph.D). From 1960 to 1968 he was
lecturer in educational psychology at St Patrick's College, Dublin; for 1968–69
he was research fellow at the Educational Research Centre, St Patrick's
College; in September 1969 he took up a post as Associate Professor at the
Department of Psychology, McGill University, Montreal.

In summer 1965 he was a fellow at a Research Conference on Learning and the
Educational Process conducted by Professor Lee Cronbach at Stanford
University. He was a visiting scholar at the Department of Psychology,
McGill in 1966–67 on a Canada Council post-doctoral fellowship.

His publications include *Bilingualism in primary education: A survey of
Irish experience*, Edinburgh University Press, and he edited a special issue of
the *Journal of Social Issues on Problems in Bilingualism,* 1967.

Contemporary work on the psychology of language can be arranged under
three main headings: psycholinguistics, sociolinguistics and applied
psychology.

Psycholinguistics is the most theoretically oriented of these three, being
concerned with the psychological processes which underlie the ability to
communicate in language (see Miller, 1965). One of its main interests is the
description of those characteristics which enable a human being to learn a
language and the way in which he learns it. Sociolinguistics is mainly concerned with the varieties of language within a community, in other words,
who uses which variety when speaking to whom about what (see Fishman,
1971). This aspect of the field is also concerned with the reasons why
people switch from one variety to another, and why some languages die
while others live. The interest of applied psychology in language is as
varied as applied psychology itself. However, the two fields in which
interest is greatest are clinical and educational psychology. This chapter is
about the contribution of applied psychology to the solution of linguistic
problems associated with race relations.

The task of overcoming barriers to communication between societies
which speak different languages usually falls on schools. One has only to
reflect for a moment on the number of school hours devoted to language

throughout the world, not to mention the serious attention it receives from educators and politicians, to appreciate the size of this task. Societies look to education to break down barriers and prejudices among peoples. Language teaching, which is usually regarded as the heavy artillery of the campaign, is where the educational psychologist with an interest in language plays his part. He has hitherto received little help from psycholinguistics, which is still far too new and too absorbed with fundamental theoretical issues to be able to guide the practitioner in the school (see Chomsky, 1966). Recent work in linguistics and psycholinguistics has nevertheless revealed to the educational psychologist the complexities of language learning and cautioned him against over-simplifications. In fact, owing to the work of the linguist Noam Chomsky, and the psychologist George Miller, as well as their associates, the 'traditional' learning theories of psychology – classical and operant conditioning – have been largely abandoned as explanatory models of any but the most peripheral aspects of language learning.[1] As a result, psychology is without a model of learning which can be applied to language with any confidence. To lack a good theory is, however, better than to adhere to a bad one, and the whole debate has, I believe, revealed to psychologists depths in the nature of language and of the language user which previously they had hardly suspected.

Sociolinguistics, though as new as psycholinguistics, has an immediate relevance to language teaching and has already begun to make an impact on applied psychology. Its importance is that it has drawn attention to the many varieties of language, apart from the standard form, and to the rules for their usage which are found in every speech community of even moderate complexity. For example, in informal male company men are permitted to use language which is rarely appropriate (even for men) in mixed company; the language of informal chats is not considered appropriate for a lecturer; and even a lecturer's language is not that of formal prayer.

This has obvious implications for language teaching which has hitherto been almost exclusively confined to standard forms of language. Already the work of sociolinguists such as Basil Bernstein (1961a;1961b) has had an important influence on educational programmes for disadvantaged children – who in the US are frequently coloured children (see Bereiter and Englemann, 1966). Sociolinguists, too, play an increasing part in the development of national plans for the teaching of language in countries the populations of which consist of numerous ethnic and linguistic groups (UNESCO, 1953; 1963; Ramos, Aguilar and Sibayan, 1967.) Even so, it seems to me that sociolinguistics is only beginning to make its presence felt

1. See Chomsky (1964), Chomsky and Hampshire (1968), Fodor (1965), Miller, Galanter and Pribram (1960), and Smith and Miller (eds.) (1968).

and that it has yet to make its full contribution to the teaching of language throughout the western world.

For the most part educational psychologists have confined their work on the linguistic aspects of race relations to evaluation, since so far their main concern has been to evaluate the effects of language programmes in schools. Some might well argue that the principal contribution of educational psychology in the whole area is a rigorous procedure for separating the effects of these programmes from the effects of other factors such as social class, teaching ability and students' aptitudes, factors which if ignored would have obscured the effects of language programmes. Educational psychologists have also been responsible for the development of numerous tests with which to evaluate the effects of these programmes.

The bulk of the work so far points to the conclusion that bilinguals, in comparison with monolinguals, are somewhat retarded in linguistic attainments, but not in non-linguistic ones.[2] Further, there are several studies which suggest that when bilingual students are taught mathematics through the medium of their weaker language, the result is some retardation in the subject *without* a compensating improvement in language skills (see Macnamara, 1966; also 1967). These are, of course, merely the overall trends in the findings; there are numerous exceptions to the general rule.[3]

This set of findings ought to be squarely contrasted with the whole tradition of 'elitist' bilingualism, but so far as I am aware has not been (see however, Fishman, 1965). Throughout the ages a knowledge of languages other than the mother-tongue has been one of the hallmarks of an educated man. Educated Romans in the early Christian era were expected to know Greek; scholars in the middle ages could not have got on without Latin; from the Renaissance almost to our own day scholars all over Europe were expected to know Greek and Latin which they often cultivated to the neglect of their mother-tongues; Russian aristocrats at the court of Catherine the Great were expected to know French; educated persons of the last century in many parts of the Austro-Hungarian Empire, particularly in Bohemia, Hungary, Croatia and Slovenia were expected to know German; these are but a few of the more obvious examples drawn from Europe. Further examples can easily be found among the Arab and Indian peoples.

2. For reviews of the literature on the effects of bilingualism on 'intelligence', see Darcy (1953 and 1963). For a review of the effects of bilingualism on language and other school attainments, see Macnamara (1966).

3. See particularly Peal and Lambert (1962). The findings of this interesting study run counter to the general findings about both intelligence and attainment. It seems likely that at least some of the exceptions, of which Peal and Lambert's findings form one, are due to the fact that the settings in which they were obtained differed from the settings in which the majority of the studies were conducted; see, e.g. Malherbe (1946).

When confronted with the pyschological findings I have outlined above, the question which most educators raise is – has education through the ages been wrong? Has it not been an advantage to scholars to learn languages other than the mother-tongue? Any answer to such questions must be tentative, but this is no reason to turn one's back on them.

School language programmes in the past were intended to put students in touch with a wider circle of people either through literature or through conversation (or both), as well as to give them access to ideas which could not be found in their own language. These are still the main reasons for learning languages. Yet the psychological studies to which reference has been made did not attempt to assess the efficacy of programmes in achieving these objectives, leaving themselves open to the criticism that they missed the main point of the whole exercise. One might expect future studies to look at the extent to which students use their knowledge of languages to communicate with speakers of those languages, the extent to which they read the literature of those languages, and the extent to which their languages help them further their education. Judged by these criteria many of the present day programmes for teaching foreign languages to post-graduate students might be considered a failure; whereas many of the language programmes in developing countries – in Africa, for example – might be considered an enormous success. Moreover, it is important to inquire whether or not such programmes have had favourable effects on students' attitudes to the peoples whose languages they have learned. In this connection several studies by Wallace Lambert and his associates are an important beginning (1961, 1963, 1967). They have sought to determine the effects of varying attitudes on progress in language learning and of language learning on attitudes both towards the people who speak the foreign language and towards the learner's own people.

A further point to note about school language programmes in the past is that they were intended for the culturally elite. In contrast, education today is for the masses, and most psychological studies of bilingualism have been carried out on working-class immigrants in the United States. Many of these studies failed to take account of the socio-economic status of the persons who were studied; even those studies which did control for it over-generalized their findings, and failed to recognize that they might not apply to middle-class families which have traditionally paid meticulous attention to the standard varieties of the languages they used. Furthermore, the tests which psychologists have used to measure either linguistic or other attainments were themselves expressed in the standard variety of the languages which were involved and most of them were written tests. We do not yet know how effectively bilinguals are able to communicate in the non-standard varieties of their languages, or in various settings for various purposes. In other words, the studies carried out by educational psychologists have, until now, lacked a sociolinguistic perspective.

My reason for contrasting the findings of psychological studies with the experience of European educators is to place both in perspective. The reasons for language learning and language teaching are more compelling today than they have ever been in the past. This is particularly true of developing countries, such as most African ones, not merely because many of them have adopted English or French as a *lingua franca* among peoples who collectively speak a large number of indigenous languages, but also because the native languages have not developed a vocabulary suited to the expression of certain concepts which are required in education, especially in the technological subjects. Furthermore, suitable literature in the native languages is either insufficient or non-existent.[4] The value of the psychological findings to hand is not to discourage bilingualism – it is, after all, an obvious necessity for innumerable students. No, it is instead to warn that students who must conduct their studies in a language other than their mother-tongue are likely to encounter serious difficulties in their education owing to insufficient mastery of the language of instruction. The value of educational experience throughout the ages has been to encourage among all who are engaged in education the hope that with sympathy, thought and effort these difficulties can be overcome.

In order better to understand the nature of the difficulties encountered by students who have to study in a second language, my colleagues and I have conducted a series of studies in Ireland and in Montreal (see Kellaghan and Macnamara, 1967). These first revealed that deficiencies in a second language are not confined to ignorance of vocabulary, phraseology or syntax. Fewer bilingual students solved problems expressed in their second language *even* when it has been ascertained that they understood every word, idiom and syntactic structure used in expressing the problems (see Macnamara, 1967, and Macnamara *et al.*, 1968). This finding led us to pursue an analysis of reading in two languages in order to discover where *precisely* bilinguals encountered relative difficulties in reading their weaker one (Macnamara, 1970). For the purpose we chose bilinguals who were clearly strong in one language and weak in another. The materials we used to test them consisted of extremely common words and rather simple syntactic structures. To sum up the results, we found significant differences in favour of the stronger language between the speeds at which the bilinguals interpreted the meanings of individual words and the meanings of sentences; in the speed at which they could pronounce the individual words they were required to read; and in ability to anticipate the sequence of words in

4. For a bird's-eye view of the problems which many countries face, see Kloss (1967). For the educational difficulties, see Bull (1964).

continuous prose (see Miller, 1956). The overall result for the persons we studied was that not only reading, but understanding what was being read, took much longer in the second language than in the mother-tongue.

Now, does it matter that a person reads French, for example, more slowly than he reads English? It would be quite outside the scope of our work to attempt a complete answer to this question as it might relate to reading for pleasure or to the creative response of a person reading a literary work. The answer must instead be confined to reading for understanding, and here, unless I am greatly mistaken, speed of reading has an importance all its own.

I assume that educated persons generally read at a rate which enables them to digest comfortably what they read, a rate that will vary with topic and circumstances. However, I assume that if a person is set a written problem in a relaxed manner and without an explicit time limit he will read it at a rate close to that which is optimal for his purposes. This is because human nature places certain limits on all human performance, among them the span of short-term memory. This span is not more than a few seconds and can embrace no more than about seven to nine separate units (Millar, 1965). If a person is to function within these limits and solve the problem, he has to reduce all the incoming information to manageable proportions and hold it firmly in that little span of awareness which we call short-term memory. If he reads too quickly he may miss some relevant points of information; if he reads too slowly and does not employ the extra time for processing the information – they may slip his mind. An optimal rate would lie somewhere between the two. Now we have seen that if a person is to read the problem in a weaker language, he will probably have to read it more slowly. It would appear that the slower rate in the weaker language does not allow him any added leisure for thinking about what he reads – the extra time being fully employed on the task of decoding the language. Consequently, some important points may slip the mind and in practice he may have added difficulty in determining what is important, since to do so presupposes some idea of the problem as a whole. As a result, the difficulty of the problem is multiplied and if it is a difficult one to begin with a man is more likely to fail. I have a suspicion that the increase in difficulty of which I speak is even more likely to upset primary school children, many of whom convey the impression that they give up and consider themselves lost if after one or two readings they have not discovered what the whole thing is about. Although there is a good deal of speculation in this reasoning, it does tie all the findings together and would explain why problems presented in the weaker language are more difficult to solve.

A second series of studies has been conducted by Professor Wallace

Lambert and his associates at McGill University, Canada (Lambert, 1963; 1967; Lambert, Gardner, Olton and Turnstall, 1961). In several North American settings they have found a marked relationship between motivation and attainment: for primary school, secondary school and college students the stronger the pupil's motivation for learning a language, the better the attainment in it. Further, in several, but not all, groups they found that the best progress was likely to be made by these students whose motives to learn the language were based on the desire to know and understand speakers of the language rather than on the desire to better themselves materially or academically. Finally, they found that primary school children who had become bilingual were more favourably disposed to the nature group which spoke the language they had learned than were those who had not become bilingual.

In all these studies, of course, there is the problem of determining whether or not there is a causal relationship between motivation and attainment, and if there is, in which direction it operates. The evidence suggests that motivation does have an effect on attainment (see Chapters 12, 13, 18 and 19 of the present book), and indeed that a student's motivation to learn a language can frequently be traced to his home. There are, however, indications also that attainment has an effect on motivation and on attitudes. As some people get better at a second language they seem to feel uncertain about their identity and constrained to re-establish themselves in their mother-tongue group. These findings, already impressive, suggest that the area of attitudes and motivation is an important one for research into the psychology of bilingualism in race relations.

The two series of studies which have just been described indicate that learning a second language and studying through the medium of a second language may give rise to complications which have hitherto not been fully appreciated. Only if such studies are carried much further and expanded to cover the whole range of linguistic skills in two languages (that is, reading, writing, listening and speaking), the range of linguistic styles (for example formal and informal speech), as well as a wide variety of linguistic settings, only then will we be in a position to understand the vast numbers of students who have no option but to be bilingual. Some of these seem to carry bilingualism as an added grace, others are torn by their loyalties to two communities. Some gain intellectual strength from access to a second community and a second literature; others are made to appear stupid in school, particularly if their accent is good enough to conceal deeper linguistic deficiencies.

What can be done at present to help lessen the burden of learning a second language? Many, under the influence of high-pressure sales talk, seem to expect miracles. They believe that with modern methods and teaching devices, like 'language laboratories', you can pour languages into children's heads as you pour tea into cups – something which is far from the truth. There are some indications of advantages to be gained by the use of modern methods and devices, but in general progress has been slight.[5] The learning of language is still a long and arduous task; and it is not a service to students to pretend otherwise. Recent studies by Carroll (1966, 1967) and his associates (Davis, 1967) single out only two variables over which the educator has control and which have a substantial effect on level of attainment: these are the number of years during which students have pursued their study of a language and whether or not they have spent some time among native speakers of that language. However, Lambert, in some of the studies to which reference has already been made, observed that an unfavourable attitude could counteract the advantages of years of study and of opportunities of meeting native-speakers of the language which students were learning in school. Several groups of Montreal high-school students who had studied French in a largely French-speaking city for periods of up to seven years obtained marks in standard tests of French achievement *no higher* than those obtained by high-school students in Connecticut who had studied French in an English-speaking environment for only two or three years.

Of course, the years have brought certain changes in language teaching, the main one being a shift of emphasis from the study of literature to the development of oral skill. But the general effect of this shift has been to change what students learn, not to revolutionize the learning process.

Ultimately, we must look to psycholinguistics with its concentration on these processes to suggest radical revisions of teaching methods. In the meantime the wisest course for educational psychologists to follow is to broaden the basis of their evaluation of language programmes, to learn from sociolinguistics the varieties of language which can most profitably be taught to various types of students, to analyse the difficulties which such students encounter whether in their intellectual work or in their personal adjustment, and to suggest remedies aimed at overcoming these particular difficulties. Such a policy would afford to educational psychology its best chance of being able to make a significant contribution to the solution of the very real problems associated with language learning, and may yet prove to be one of the most effective methods of improving relations between the races.

5. There are two excellent reviews of the literature: see Carroll (1963; 1966a). See also, however, the interesting studies of Asher (1968).

References

ASHER, J. J. (1968), 'The total physical response method for second-language learning', San Jose State College, mimeo.

BEREITER, C., and ENGLEMANN, S. (1966), *Teaching Disadvantaged Children in the Schoolroom*, Prentice-Hall.

BERNSTEIN, B. (1961a), 'Social class and linguistic development: a theory of social learning', in A. H. Halsey, J. Floud and C. A. Anderson (eds.), *Education, Economy and Society*, Free Press.

BERNSTEIN, B. (1961b), 'Social structure, language and learning', *Educational Research*, vol. 3, pp. 163–76.

BULL, W. E. (1964), 'The use of vernacular languages in education', in D. H. Hymes (ed.), *Language in Culture and Society*, Harper & Row, pp. 527–33.

CARROLL, J. B. (1963), 'Research on teaching foreign languages', in N. L. Gage (ed.), *Handbook of Research on Teaching*, Rand McNally.

CARROLL, J. B. (1966a), 'Research in foreign-language teaching: the last five years', *Northeast Conference, Working Committee Reports*, pp. 12–42.

CARROLL, J. B. (1966b), *A Parametric Study of Language Training in the Peace Corps*, Graduate School of Education, Harvard University.

CARROLL, J. B. (1967), *The Foreign-Language Attainments of Language Majors in the Senior Year: A Survey Conducted in US Colleges and Universities*, Graduate School of Education, Harvard University.

CHOMSKY, N. (1964), 'A review of B. F. Skinner's *Verbal Behaviour*', in J. A. Fodor and J. J. Katz (eds.), *The Structure of Language*, Prentice-Hall, pp. 547–78.

CHOMSKY, N. (1966), 'Linguistic theory', *Northeast Conference on the Teaching of Foreign Languages*, pp. 43–9.

CHOMSKY, N., and HAMPSHIRE, S. (1968), 'The study of language', *Listener*, vol. 79, pp. 687–91.

DARCY, N. (1953), 'A review of the literature on the effects of bilingualism upon the measurement of intelligence', *Journal of Genetic Psychology*, vol. 82, pp. 21–58.

DARCY, N. (1963), 'Bilingualism and the measurement of intelligence: review of a decade of research', *Journal of Genetic Psychology*, vol. 103, pp. 259–82.

DAVIS, F. B. (1967), *Philippine Language Teaching Experiments*, Alemar-Phoenix, Philippines.

FISHMAN, A. (1971), 'Sociolinguistics', in K. W. Back (ed.), *Social Psychology*, Wiley.

FISHMAN, J. A. (1968), 'Sociolinguistic perspective on the study of bilingualism', in J. A. Fishman, R. L. Cooper, R. Ma *et al.*, *Bilingualism in the Barrio*, US Dept. of Health, Education and Welfare, Office of Education, vol. 2, pp. 952–99.

FODOR, J. A. (1965), 'Could meaning be an r_m?', *Journal of Verbal Learning and Verbal Behaviour*, vol. 4, pp. 73–81.

KELLAGHAN, T., and MACNAMARA, J. (1967), 'Reading in a second language' in M. D. Jenkinson (ed.), *Reading Instruction: An International Forum*, International Reading Association, pp. 231–40.

KLOSS, H. (1967), 'Bilingualism and nationalism', *Journal of Social Issues*, vol. 23 pp. 39–47.

LAMBERT, W. E. (1963), 'Psychological approaches to the study of language', pts 1 and 2, *Modern Language Journal*, vol. 47, pp. 51–61 and 114–21.

LAMBERT, W. E. (1967), 'A social psychology of bilingualism', *Journal of Social Issues*, vol. 23 pp. 91–109.

LAMBERT, W. E., GARDNER, R. C., OLTON, R., and TUNSTALL, K. (1961), 'A study of the role of attitudes and motivation in second-language learning' McGill University, mimeo.

MACNAMARA, J. (1966), *Bilingualism and Primary Education*, Edinburgh University Press.

MACNAMARA, J. (1967), 'The effects of instruction in a weaker language', *Journal of Social Issues*, vol. 23, pp. 121–35.

MACNAMARA, J. (1970), 'Comparative studies of reading in two languages', TESOL Quarterly, pp. 107–16.

MACNAMARA, J., *et al.* (1968), 'An analytic comparison of reading in two languages', *Irish Journal of Education*, vol. 2, pp. 41–53.

MALHERBE, E. G. (1946), *The Bilingual School*, Longman Green.

MILLER, G. A. (1956), 'The magical number seven, plus or minus two: some limitations on our capacity for processing information', *Psychological Review*, vol. 63, pp. 81–97.

MILLER, G. A. (1965), 'The psycholinguists', in C. E. Osgood and T. A. Sebeok (eds.), *Psycholinguistics: A Survey of Theory and Research Problems*, Indiana University Press, pp. 293–307.

MILLER, G. A., GALANTER, E., and PRIBRAM, K. H. (1960), *Plans and the Structure of Behaviour*, Henry Holt.

PEAL, E., and LAMBERT, W. E. (1962), 'The relation of bilingualism to intelligence', *Psychological Monographs, General and Applied*, vol. 76, no. 546.

RAMOS, M., AGUILAR, J. V., and SIBAYAN, B. P. (1967), *The Determination and Implementation of Language Policy*, Alemar-Phoenix, Philippines.

SMITH, F., and MILLER, G. A. (eds.) (1968), *The Genesis of Language*, MIT Press.

UNESCO (1953), *The Use of Vernacular Languages in Education*, Paris.

UNESCO (1963), *Foreign Languages in Primary Education*, Institute for Education, Hamburg.

Chapter 20
The Sociolinguistics of Nationalism

Joshua Fishman

Joshua Fishman has taught linguistics at many universities in the United States prior to his present post at the East–West Centre in Hawaii. His books include *Language Problems of Developing Nations* and *Bilingualism in the Barrio*. He is a consultant to the American College for the Uses of Sociology.

What is nationalism and when does it arise?

Nationalism may be defined as the heightened ethnic beliefs, attitudes and behaviour of societies mobilized on behalf of their acknowledged self-interest. In order for such activity to occur it is first necessary for a population to become convinced that it possesses common socio-cultural characteristics and that these similarities are important. Neither of these traits – recognition of common socio-cultural characteristics and conviction with respect to their overriding importance – is part of man's biological make-up and neither exists in all human populations at all times. Therefore, this inquiry can begin with a brief look at the circumstances that tend to heighten or to dampen this recognition and these convictions.[1]

Beliefs, attitudes and behaviour about belonging are sharply circumscribed in populations that are not exposed to messages or visitors from outside their immediate environment. Most non-industrial, non-urban, non-literate populations have exhibited very local or 'primordial' attachments to near kin, immediate territory, and the experienced customs and social structures related to them. Broader ties or allegiance among these populations are normally restricted to their political, religious or cultural

---

1. The literature on nationalism abounds in definitions of this phenomenon as well as in typologies pertaining to various kinds of nationalism. For a review of several definitional attempts, both recent and classical, see Znaniecki (1952). Typologies of nationalism have thus far been of doubtful value since they tend to do little more than characterize or catalogue the problems faced by nationalities *vis-à-vis* their neighbours at various points in history. While it would be foolish to lump all manifestations of nationalisms together, thus overlooking differences in intensity or in focus that differentiate between them, it seems to me that these are better understood as stages, capable of regression or of further development, depending on the degree of external opposition encountered, rather than as distinct or discontinuous types. In this connection, see Fishman (1972).

elites (nobility, clergy and literati) who have had the opportunity to become aware of more extended ideas related to wider groups as well as the chance, by reading or by travel, to verify those ideas.[2]

Broader unity

A basic feature of nationalism is the way the characteristics of a culture which are seen as common widen far beyond their original primordial bounds. Nationality thus represents an expansion of beliefs, attitudes and behaviour about belonging to more distant – sometimes only heard-about – kin, to more distant territory and to more dissimilar socio-cultural set-ups than those that govern the lion's share of any individual's own behaviour. He comes to recognize his relationship and his interdependence with a human population most of whose members he has never met, and to believe this relationship and interdependence to be quite naturally rooted in the socio-cultural similarities that they share.

Stressed authenticity

Small societies enforce fidelity to local custom by means of face-to-face interaction. Larger societies enforce fidelity to larger scale unity by means of mass institutions – governments, organizations, communications media, schools. These institutions both formalize and stress authenticity of culture, since face-to-face sanctions implemented via social structure are inadequate for either the attainment or the preservation of broader unity in large and impersonal social units. This stress on authenticity-oriented belief, attitude and behaviour is crucial in order to reach, influence and activate large numbers of individuals who may actually lead quite different daily lives and who interact with only a small proportion of the total community throughout their entire lifetime.[3]

2. The contrast between traditional, transitional and modern populations is convincingly presented in Lerner (1958). Such contrasts are inherent in much of the modern social psychological and sociological literature on modernization of the developing nations. In this connection, see *Journal of Social Issues* (1968).

3. Nationalist movements view broader unity and stressed authenticity as means of reconstituting the natural and spontaneous unity and authenticity that purportedly existed in their origins as small and emotionally satisfying communities. Both unity and authenticity are purported to have existed prior to the predominance of the division of labour and experience that results from large and impersonal societies. Thus, nationalism seeks to reverse the balance between mechanical and organic unity, between *gemeinschaft* and *gesellschaft*, between the sacred and the secular, in order thereby to release for current purposes the dormant genius and strength of populations which would otherwise be fractionated and de-ethnicized by current adversaries, both human and technical. For this view of nationalism as a rediscovery and reformation of the past in order to control the present and plan the future of larger ethnic communities, see Gellner (1964).

Social change

Nationalism provides a redefinition of personal and group identity, purpose and possibilities. Such a redefinition becomes attractive or is desired when prior, more traditional definitions, are rendered inoperative or non-productive as a result of social change. Throughout human history populations have become more conscious of and more concerned with their ethnicity when it has been impressed upon them that they could expect certain benefits – or that they were denied certain benefits – as a result of it. In modern days such impressions have most frequently spread at the same time as basic economic changes such as those accompanying the growth of commerce and industry.

Early industrialism was particularly dependent upon the proximity of natural resources that could be exploited given the current level of technology, and human populations that could provide the necessary productive manpower for this exploitation. However, the co-occurrence of newly valuable natural and human resources has become operative in different parts of the world at widely differing times in history. On such occasions the political and social integration that developed tended to favour those populations that controlled the (then necessary) resources and (that tended) to exploit or submerge those about them that did not. Populations that control valuable resources in common also tend to develop further whatever socio-cultural similarities they already possessed and to attribute their more fortunate economic circumstances to the seeming superiority of their social and cultural institutions.

Nationalistic movements have commonly spread as newly favoured populations (given whatever economically based changes were then uppermost) sought to protect themselves from the claims and controls of less favoured but previously established socio-political units. Similarly, nationalistic movements have spread as hitherto backward groups, formerly under the sway of regions that had already experienced social change and social advantage, began to savour or even only to anticipate their own day in the sun, i.e. their own growing correspondence between precious but localized natural and human resources.[4]

New elites

In addition to charting the successive appearance of industrialization in various parts of the globe, it is common to begin the study of the attain-

4. While Gellner provides a very brief and convincing presentation of how successive waves of economic change are basic to the rise of successive nationalisms, a more quantitative (but nevertheless still programmatic) presentation of this view is found in Deutsch (1953). Economic development is also stressed and specifically related to language and political integration by Inglehart and Woodward (1967).

ment of broader unity and stress on authenticity in populations not hitherto marked by such emphasis with the crystallization of new proto-elites. Regardless of how such proto-elites come into being – e.g. with changes in markets, new methods of production, the discovery of newly functional natural resources, the perfection of new methods of transportation, and so on – they consist of individuals whose own life styles, self-awareness, and power potentials are changing and, therefore, of individuals who are interested in fostering social change that will ally with them numerically significant populations. Since the existing institutions of power – secular and religious – are still closed to them, they seek to reorganize society in order to attain control of reorganized institutions of power. Ideologies of broader authenticity are evolved, paralleling the lines of socio-cultural similarities recognized as manageable by new proto-elites, in order to organize large populations in the direction of socio-political changes favourable to the new proto-elites. Nationalist movements initially seek to indoctrinate discrete populations with the awareness of broader socio-cultural unity that new proto-elites have already attained. New proto-elites have usually included men of letters as well as economic, political and military men, i.e. individuals who could manipulate symbols as well as individuals who could manipulate resources on behalf of desired socio-political regrouping.[5]

The city

The city has played a triply important role in the spread of nationalistic beliefs, attitudes and behaviours. First of all, it has been both the product and the centre of social economic change *per se*. As a result new proto-elites tend to congregate in cities since it is there that the changes that have already influenced them, and that tend to increase their influence over others, are concentrated. Secondly, hitherto traditional populations from the countryside flock to the city in times of social change and dislocation in order to recapture there some semblance of the security which their old way of life once gave them. Their need for new self-definition and reference-group affiliation makes them particularly susceptible to the communications on the very matters sponsored by the new proto-elites. Last of all, the city facilitates communication from elites to masses in view of its higher

5. Among the foremost students of the contributions of elites and their ideologies to the formation of nationalisms one certainly can count Kohn (1961), Kedourie (1961), and Minogue (1967). In general, this has been the basic approach to nationalism among historians and philosophers, schooled as they are in the textual analysis of the writings of great men, even when they have been aware that societal circumstances favourable to the elites under study were also necessary. For a more judicious recognition of the role of elites, one that relates them to social and economic changes affecting the masses, see Friederich (1963).

density of interaction networks, communication channels and communication occasions. As a result of all of these co-occurrences city folk have always more quickly accepted and implemented the broader unity and the intensified authenticity components of nationalism.[6]

Integration and differentiation

Broader unity and intensified authenticity commonly utilize those building blocks that already exist in terms of socio-cultural integration in the ethnic domain. However, they aim beyond that which already exists in two important ways. First of all they consciously seek greater within-group uniformity and saliency of history, heroes, holidays, customs, values and mission. Thus nationalism not only aims beyond current local diversity and patterned non-observance, but also, not infrequently, seeks to counteract them. It aims at a more unified and authentic *future* by discovering and hallowing a highly unified and authentic *past*. Secondly, nationalism formalizes the limits of permissible unity by authoritatively contrasting insiders with outsiders. Just as integration is in part pre-existing and in part cultivated, so differentiation from outsiders also contains these two components. The 'natural distribution' of socio-cultural integration and differentiation is either too gradual, too inconsistent or too non-salient for the purposes of effective mass organization of human and physical resources. Nationalism intensifies and restructures both the integration of those *within* the fold and their differentiation from those *without* it.[7]

Those ethnic groups that define themselves in terms of consciously intensified and structured integration of their 'own' consciously intensified and structured differentiation from 'outsiders' are termed nationalities or nationality societies. Nationalism is their system of belief, attitude and behaviour for integration, differentiation, and other goal-directed activity. The territory they control (if indeed they control a territory) is their nation.

Possible transformations

All of the above observations have been taken from the point of view of the *appearance* of nationalism among hitherto traditional populations organ-

6. So crucial is urbanization to the spread of modern nationalism that many investigators, e.g. Lerner and Deutsch, have effectively used indices of urbanization in lieu of indices of industrialization, mobilization or modernization that are so much more difficult to obtain. The continued role of religion in nationalism – indeed, the constant interpenetration of the two in ancient, medieval and modern days – is painstakingly documented by Baron (1947), thus demonstrating the co-occurrence of universal and particularistic features in both.

7. The heightening of both in-group similarities and out-group differences are movingly related in many accounts of localized nationalistic movements. For a retrospective account of particular poignancy, see Chaudhuri (1951).

ized in societies at a smaller scale than that normally attained by the nation-state. However, nationalism usually continues to function beyond the stage of intial mobilization, although there is nothing inevitable about its stages or their sequencing. Subsequent to their initial appearance socio-politically successful nationalisms often pass through a stage of consolidation in which their emphasis turns to modernization rather than to cultural unity or authenticity *per se*. The very socio-economic opportunities and potentials that initially stimulated the formulation of nationalistic ideologies are directly exploited or developed by newly empowered elites. Cultural symbols, values and loyalties are utilized, however, to motivate, organize and move populations toward more advanced socio-economic goals (in education, industry, commerce, agriculture, consumption habits, etc.)[8]

Further socio-political expansion is also a possible subsequent stage of nationalism. Even broader cultural unities and more abstract authenticities are recognized which indirectly confirm the arbitrariness of the boundaries set at previous stages of nationalism. These broader aspirations may claim *irridentas* not previously liberated or united during earlier integrative efforts or they may point to *similarities* with neighbours that are now viewed as more basic and as stemming from a still earlier and even more authentic cultural era than that responsible for the dissimilarities formerly noted. Such broader nationalisms are frequently referred to as pan-movements. They are rightfully considered within the cycle of nationalism as long as they are primarily rationalized in terms of broader ethnic similarities derived from reconstructions of authenticity rather than primarily in terms of economic need or messianic mission.[9]

Unsuccessful nationalism too must be recognized as a possible outcome of attempts at socio-political mobilization and integration. This occurs where potential changes in the allocation of resources do not materialize or are reversed, when proto-elites do not succeed in mobilizing populations toward a certain definition of unity and authenticity, or when a competing proto-elite and the particular underlying socio-economic changes and over-arching symbolism with which it is associated succeeds in attracting population to a greater extent than do its rivals.

8. The insufficiency of nationalism *per se* for the solution of post-integrational or post-independence problems has been documented by many students of developing societies. As a result, the original nationality-forming elite is often removed in favour of a more technologically and economically oriented nation-building elite. See Hopkins and Wallerstein (1967), and, in greater depth, Apter (1965).

9. For an interesting comparison between several successful and unsuccessful pan-movements, see Deutsch, *et al*. (1957). Other interesting materials on pan-nationalisms are available in Kohn (1961) and in Karemzadeh (1968).

Language as the medium of nationalism

Since language is fundamental to human society and culture it must also be fundamental to any attempt, such as nationalism, to reorganize society and culture. Nationalism, however, contrasts with most other affiliative and reformational movements in its greater use of vernaculars for the purposes of carrying ts message to the masses that it seeks to unify and activate. How else but through the vernacular could proto-elites hope to easily communicate with recently urbanized but still predominantly illiterate populations? How else could they hope to quickly convince them as well as activate them on behalf of the steps needed in order to *attain* broader unity and to *safeguard* cultural authenticity? Mass political participation, mass military activity, mass modernization of economic pursuits – these too call for a high flow of communication from elites to followers, particularly if these goals are to be accomplished quickly and in the face of competition from other elites, both traditional and modern. It is not surprising then that nationalisms focus upon vernaculars as their media of communication, in contrast to the languages of avowedly more 'universalistic' religions and empires.[10]

Language as the message of nationalism

However, the vernacular is much more than a medium or mechanism of nationalism. It is also one of its most common messages or drives. The vernacular of the masses is at once an instrument and a symbol of their broader unity. It is at once both the means of attaining as well as itself an aspect of the cultural authenticity that they pursue. Indeed, it is not merely their vernacular but, very quickly, also their *national language*, the badge of their nationality and of their nationhood. It once united their ancestors as it now reunites them. In it their forefathers expressed the wisdom, the beauty and the individuality of the culture which now they seek to recapture and reactivate.

Through nationalism masses of people attain a new sense of identity and purpose. Their new (or old-new) songs, poems, slogans and proverbs, the moving phrases of their leaders and teachers, their rediscovered national

10. The objectively functional role of language in the re-organization of the economic and of the political system is another major programmatic focus of Deutsch's *Social Communication and Nationalism* (1953). His many indices of mobilization all have in common the fact that they highlight exposure to vernacular communication from elitist groups attempting the activation of populations in specific directions. A more recent attempt to indicate the indispensability of the vernacular in national and regional modernization – as well as the problems of larger scale political integration – likely to flow therefrom – may be found in Myrdal (1968, pp. 81–9, 1639–40) as well as elsewhere.

epics and their newly launched national literatures are part and parcel of a sense of awakening or rebirth. But a rebirth requires a mother and in the case of nationalism this is the mother-tongue without whose tender care and endless bounties it is felt that neither songs, nor poems, nor slogans, nor proverbs, nor speeches, nor epics, nor nationality, nor nation would have come into being, and, in a sense, this is so.[11]

Some language problems of nationalism

However, the vernacular of the people is not an entirely unmixed blessing for any newly developing nationalism. To begin with the vernacular itself is not nearly as unitary nor as widely shared as nationalist ideology implies. Language variations are distributed quite as continuously over space as are ethnic variations themselves, although, to make matters even more difficult, the two are not necessarily jointly distributed. Thus, instead of a single vernacular, traditional rural populations, because of their natural isolation, more frequently display dialects that differ in varying degrees and in varying ways. In addition, it is not at all uncommon for populations that differ little in terms of ethnic behaviours to differ substantially in language and *vice versa*.

Thus, nationalist movements must not only fashion a unified and unifying nationality out of countless manifest differences in daily ethnic routines and beliefs; they must also fashion an equally unified and unifying language out of a manifest diversity of phonological, lexical, grammatical and semantic systems. Nationalisms undertake to produce standard languages, consciously employed and conscientiously espoused, where previously there existed only regional dialects unthinkingly employed and unemotionally abandoned: e.g., Macedonian, Malaysian, Indonesian, Hindi, Afrikaans, and so on.

However, the newly reborn national tongues must not only be standardized, they must also be enriched. The more successful a nationalist movement, the more likely that its national language will come to be used for many additional and for higher functions than those with which its dialectal varieties were associated. The lexical needs of urban and urbane society extend to governmental operations, scientific technology, abstract philosophical systems and the concerns of higher education more generally. Even earlier, the national language must carry the novel but crucial messages of national unity, authenticity and activism. Language scholars,

11. There are few studies that focus on vernacular national language as substantive (rather than procedural) aspects of nationalism. Among the first detailed studies of this type was Clough (1930). Also of interest in this connection are Pidal (1945), and Vossler (1932). No detailed comparative or theoretical analyses are, as yet, available, but a general, comparative framework is provided in Fishman (1972).

writers, journalists and teachers are among the most frequent contributors
to the urgent lexical expansion of new national languages along lines that
strike a responsive chord among users who must be made to feel that this
new variety is really theirs, even though it may obviously differ in so many
ways from the varieties they have hitherto used for informal interactions
and traditional pursuits.[12]

Both standardization (codification) and lexical expansion (elaboration)
meet a common barrier in the realm of implementation: the fact that
traditional populations have become accustomed to associating a language
other than their vernacular with the higher realms of intellectual, ethical
and aesthetic concern. Sacred languages, languages of supra-ethnic
eurrency in trade, governmental administration and learning, languages of
long established standardization, elaboration and implementation – these
are among the hallmarks of pre-national elites. These elites may or may
not also utilize local vernaculars, depending on the degree of their direct
interaction with local and more traditional populations. Nationalist
movements have usually not only *used* the vernaculars for purposes of
mobilization, but they have *championed* them as means of removing previously established elites (e.g., English elites in Ireland, German elites
in Hungary, Hungarian elites in Slovakia, Polish elites in the Ukraine)
and as symbols of completely indigenous authenticity. To the extent that
nationalisms disrupt long-established diglossias they may also disrupt
long-established religious, intellectual and esthetic traditions (e.g. the
French culture vogue in Germany and Russia, the Danish culture vogue
in Scandinavia). Thus, via its link to the vernacular, nationalism is not
merely the pursuit of new economic and political opportunities under the
guise of newly broadened and authenticated ethnic ties; it is also a profound revolution with frequent and fargoing intellectual, religious and
esthetic consequences.[13]

Some nationalistic problems of language planning

Just as nationalist movements are encumbered by language (at the same
time that they promote languages to the position of national symbols), so
language planning itself is encumbered by nationalism – at the same time

12. The language trials and tribulations of nationalist movements remain to be
carefully documented. In addition to Clough's study, much information and many
valuable concepts in this connection can be gleaned from Haugen's (1966) work.
Another important reference in this connection is the volume edited by Fishman,
Ferguson and Das Gupta (1968).

13. The pioneer paper on diglossia is that by Ferguson (1959). The distinction
between diglossia and bilingualism, as well as the relationship between these two
concepts, is developed by Fishman (1967).

that it seeks to serve the new nationality and its nation. Every incipient nationalism must fight a two-front war: against the existing social and political elite on the one hand, and against contending regionalisms on the other. Both of these struggles have very definite consequences for the planning of the national languages that correspond to nationalist movements.

The boundary-defining and contrast-heightening that nationalisms engage in (in their pursuit of broader unity and unsullied authenticity) is reflected in language planning by emphases on historical reconstruction and purification. The same enemies that are opposed in the struggle for national identity and autonomy are also opposed in the quest for linguistic identity and autonomy. The cleansing of the body politic and the ridding of the culture of particular foreign elites, customs and symbols has its very definite counterpart in the cleansing of the language of those features that can be identified or associated with those very same opponents.

However, the process of maximizing divergence relative to a particular foe is complicated not only in relation to the extent to which the foreign ingredients have infected the indigenous, but also to the extent to which there is or is not an appreciable inherent difference between the foreign and the indigenous to begin with. Thus, just as nationalist movements struggling to unify and to authenticate populations that shared many cultural similarities with their no-longer-acceptable overlords had to search more deeply and more painfully for unity and authenticity via scrupulous divergence, so did their language planning have to struggle most ceaselessly to build up the initially meagre differences between their neonate national language and the contaminating language of the foreign oppressor. The best examples of planned nationalities and consciously diverged languages (*ausbau* languages) are derived from those nationalist movements that were faced by initially few and seemingly slight structural differences between themselves and those from whom they sought to diverge, (e.g., Yiddish from German, Macedonian from Bulgarian, Ukrainian from Russian, Malaysian from Indonesian).[14]

A similar parallelism between general social and more narrowly linguistic challenges to broader unity and indigenous authenticity has obtained in coping with interregional variation. Nationalist movements blessed with only one centre of more promising economic and intellectual development more easily settled on the major locus and source of their broader unity and authenticity. In their case regional divergences – in custom and in language – were more easily counteracted by the newly unified attitudes, beliefs and behaviours, or were reduced to the level of localistic sentiment

14. The pioneer treatment of *ausbau* languages is contained in Kloss (1952). A brief summary and extension of his concepts in English is available in Kloss (1967).

unrelated to national roles or political goals. However, nationalistic movements faced by several centres with nearly equal claims either required compromise solutions which fully gratified none of them, or compromises which gratified one over the others. In either of these latter cases seeds remained, often lying dormant for generations, that might at some future time blossom forth into yet newer nationalist movements. In the absence of active supra-ethnic ties and opportunities, marked unevenesses in economic and social development and the phaselike nature with which new stages of development arrive in various regions of a polity are likely to set off new nationalist awakenings in areas where they have not existed for some time before.[15]

Concluding sentiments

Nationalism has far from run its course in human history for, true to its phaselike nature from its very earliest manifestations, it is still a young and robust sentiment in those many parts of the world where it has more recently flowered, just as it appears to have at least temporarily spent itself in those parts where it has functioned longest. Like all pervasive human quests (the quest to transcend life on earth, the quest to improve the material comforts of life on earth), the quest for broader ethnic unity and greater ethnic authenticity has produced both pain and pleasure, creativity and absurdity. It should probably not be approached from the point of view of predicting its ultimate demise, but rather, from the point of view of predicting its better control.

Mankind has learned to control family loyalties without rejecting such loyalties completely. Similarly, mankind has learned to control religious loyalties without rejecting them completely. Indeed, we have reached a stage in our development when politics are expected to be religiously neutral, at least in their inter-policy dealings. At this time when dozens of new nationalities have recently appeared on the scene and when dozens of others are recognizably struggling for appearance (or reappearance) we cannot realistically or ethically pray that ethnicity and nationalism will soon disappear. We can only pray to learn to control it better, to balance it off with still broader loyalties, so that its creative potential will remain while its destructive features are lessened.

15. Thus far there has not yet been a comparative study of language planning processes as these are encumbered by nationalist demands. Some attention to this problem is found in Haugen's work cited earlier. Additional examples can be found in Heyd (1954), and Rosario (1968). For an example of how an unrecognized centre subsequently sponsored a nationalism and a national language of its own, the reader should examine Lunt (1959). Additional comparative details are provided in Rubin and Jernudd (1971) and in Fishman (1972).

References

APTER, D. E. (1965), *The Politics of Modernization*, University of Chicago Press.

BARON, S. W. (1947), *Modern Nationalism and Religion*, Harper & Row.

CHAUDHURI, N. C. (1951), *The Autobiography of an Unknown Indian*, Macmillan.

CLOUGH, S. B. (1930), *A History of the Flemish Movement in Belgium*, Smith.

DEUTSCH, K. W. (1953), *Social Communication and Nationalism*, MIT Press; 2nd edn, 1965.

DEUTSCH, K. W., *et al.* (1957), *Political Community in the North Atlantic*, Princeton University Press.

FERGUSON, C. A. (1959), 'Diglossia', *Word*, vol. 15, pp. 325–40.

FISHMAN, J. A. (1967), 'Bilingualism with and without diglossia; diglossia with and without bilingualism', *Journal of Social Issues*, vol. 23, no. 2, pp. 29–38.

FISHMAN, J. (1972), *Language and Nationalism*, Rowley.

FISHMAN, J. A., FERGUSON, C. A., and DAS GUPTA, J. (eds.) (1968), *Language Problems of the Developing Nations*, Wiley.

FRIEDERICH, C. J. (1963), *Man and His Government: An Empirical Theory of Politics*, McGraw-Hill.

GELLNER, E. (1964), *Thought and Change*, University of Chicago Press.

HAUGEN, E. (1966), *Language Conflict and Language Planning: The Case of Modern Norwegian*, Harvard University Press.

HEYD, U. (1954), *Language Reform in Modern Turkey*, Israel Orienta' Society, Jerusalem.

HOPKINS, T. K. and WALLERSTEIN, I. (1967), 'The comparative study of national societies', *Social Science Information*, vol. 6, pp. 25–58.

INGLEHART, R. F., and WOODWARD, M. (1967), 'Language conflicts and political integration', *Comparative Studies in Society and History*, vol. 10, pp. 27–45.

KAREMZADEH, F. (1968), 'Pan movements', *International Encyclopedia of the Social Sciences*, vol. 11, pp. 365–70.

KEDOURIE, E. (1961), *Nationalism*, Praeger; revised.

KLOSS, H. (1952), *Die Entwicklung Neuer Germanischer Kultursprachen*, Pohl.

KLOSS, H. (1967), '*Abstand* languages and *ausbau* languages', *Anthropological Linguistics*, vol. 9, no. 7, pp. 29–41.

KOHN, H. (1961), *The Age of Nationalism*, Praeger.

LERNER, D. (1958), *The Passing of Traditional Society*, Free Press.

LUNT, H. G. (1959), 'The creation of standard Macedonian: some facts and attitudes', *Anthropological Lingustics*, vol. 1, no. 5 pp. 19–26.

MINOGUE, K. R. (1967), *Nationalism*, Basic Books.

MYRDAL, G. (1968), *Asian Drama*, Pantheon.

PIDAL, R. M. (1945), *Castilla, La Tradicion, El Idioma*, Espasa Calpe, Buenos Aires.

ROSARIO, G. DEL (1968), 'A modernization-standardization plan for the Austronesian-derived national languages of southeast Asia', *Asian Studies*, vol. 6, no. 1, pp. 1–18.

RUBIN, J., and JERNUDD, B. (1971), *Can Language Be Planned?*, East-West Center, University of Hawaii Press.

VOSSLER, K. (1932), *The Spirit of Language in Civilization*, Routledge & Kegan Paul.

ZNANIECKI, F. (1952), *Modern Nationalities*, University of Illinois Press.

Section G
A Miscellany of Other Key Issues

The three areas of interest and relevance considered in this final
section – mental illness, crime and work – are grouped together for
convenience since they naturally fall under no other heading.

Chapter 21
Psychiatric Disorders in Minority Groups

Ari Kiev

Ari Kiev's main interest is in the practice of psychiatry in different parts of the world. He has written books on transcultural psychiatry, Mexican-American folk healing and edited several works on the links between primitive magic and medicine and on psychiatry in communist countries. In New York City, he directs a suicide prevention clinic at New York Hospital and is Chief Psychiatric Consultant to several drug abuse rehabilitation centres.

Introduction

Social psychiatry is concerned with the effect of the sociocultural environment on the underlying conflict, the clinical syndromes, the distribution, frequency, treatment and management of psychiatric disorders among different populations and sub-groups within populations. (And it is part of the conventional wisdom that heredity, physiology and psychodynamics contribute significantly to the personality and psychopathology of the individual.) Minority groups are of special interest to social psychiatry because of their unique social and cultural experiences of social change, and reduced opportunities, which may increase or decrease the risk that an individual will develop psychiatric disorder.

Studies of the psychiatric disturbances among minorities have tended to focus theoretically on just one of several ways of organizing the social experiences of the minority group. Broad factors have been studied, such as social change in general – or more specific aspects of it such as modernization, acculturation, migration or discrimination. While these same categories are used in this chapter, it needs emphasizing that they are not mutually exclusive and are in fact likely to be experienced simultaneously by minority group members in an undifferentiated way.

Social change

There is an extensive literature relating increases in the rates of psychiatric disorder to social change and other socio-cultural factors, though this sort of conclusion is by no means universally accepted.

But rapid change can be very disruptive, even though changes towards socio-cultural integration, by contrast, may be beneficial. For example, one group of Eskimos (from Barter Island) are known because they place greater value on adaptability than on conformity and so have voluntarily chosen to change large segments of their society to fit a Western model (Chance, Hsien and Hung-Ming, 1967). Because they were carried through by the group as a whole, inter-generational conflicts were kept to a minimum and a balance between the old and new successfully maintained.

Social change may lead to conflicts between new and traditional ways of organizing our values: cultural versus material goals, the group or the individual, new leaders or traditional leaders, secularization or traditional religion. In his study of acculturation among Ojibwa Indians, Hallowell noted that the substitution of the old system for a new system of beliefs derived from Western values had serious consequences for some individuals. In so far as their psychological equilibrium was supported by motivations, aspirations and values that were tied to the old system of beliefs, the consequences of losing the whole system were shown in the form of apathy, alcoholism, overt hostility, crime and a generally juvenile way of behaving.

The disruption of extended kin groups may also be important. Individuals have to contend with traditional difficulties without being able to fall back on traditional solutions, since these may not be available any more. The solution to psychological conflicts acquired early on by means of the adoption or achievement of an acceptable adult role is not often available in the transition situation. And to this must be added new conflicts for which there has usually been no preparation. People from villages may not be able to cope with the competition, isolation and lack of emotional support in the urban setting. Erna Hoch noted that the joint-family system in village India, for example, does not prepare individuals for the emotional differentiation so necessary in an urban industrial society.

This phenomenon, which is found in other societies in transition from the traditional to the modern, refers mainly to the shifts in expectations which people must undergo. They can no longer expect others to gratify their dependency needs or provide jobs for them merely because of family ties. On the other hand, they cannot assume responsibility for groups larger than their immediate families if they are to prosper in the modern urban setting. Both these shifts mean that a more specific outline of their obligations and expectancies is needed in the new situations where achievement and function are more important than status or role due simply to birth or kinship. In addition, the persistent need for security that was provided in the joint family cannot be satisfied in the city.

As an example, take Tunisia, where a variety of social changes have occurred since independence in 1957. These include a reduction in traditional religious practices, the emancipation of women, urbanization, increased social security, the elimination of private property and the abolition of nomadism. According to one investigator, these changes have occurred simultaneously with the reduced use of various ecstatic ceremonial trances which were beneficial in providing release for sexual guilt and tension for those suffering from milder psychiatric disorders (Sleim, 1964). The ceremonies have been replaced by collective anxiety neuroses which spread by contagion, an increase in egotistical materialism and individualistic self-seeking and a reduced consideration for the welfare of the group.

Modernization

There is also considerable evidence that in developing countries rural migrants are ill-equipped to cope with urban living. In Africa, for example, prior to westernization, life was highly organized and regulated by the tribal group. The new increase in movement to and from towns has been associated with disruption of the supports which traditional patterns and rules of behaviour normally give (Hoselitz, 1966; United Nations, 1963). In the city the family is weakened by occupational, social and geographical conflicts, by the reduced impact of traditional authority and the break-up of extended families. The primary family has become the focus of security, and must cope with numerous ambiguities in the norms governing relationships, since traditional norms no longer apply in the urban setting. It cannot control the courtship and marriage choice of the more independent young people. While this may be all to the good since the new criteria for choosing marriage partners tend to make more sense than traditional ones, it does weaken the control of adults over the younger generation. Women gain authority through economic independence, responsibility for the household, and the unavailability of the male parent. This is followed in turn by a loss of authority for the men because of their reduced status within the social system.[1]

New jobs and relationships at work also create tension in the urban setting. The shift from ascriptive to achievement criteria brings together co-workers from different backgrounds. Personal and tribal ties lose their economic significance and often become a source of friction if preferences are shown to one particular ethnic group. The absence of community organization reduces opportunities for progress in several ways: the psychological support which comes from community organization and which enables people to overcome obstacles is missing so that people may readily

1. Implicit in the generally accepted view noted above is the assumption that the traditional family was free of tension and conflict. This is not always so. Conformity to tradition may have been due to apathy and resignation. Tensions are rife in many pre-industrial societies and are channelled into witchcraft, ritual rebellion and various institutional activities. Furthermore, change in the urban family and even high rates of divorce and marital instability are not always indicative of a change for the worse, but may be representative of changes in the nature of interpersonal relationships brought about by different social and economic requirements of urban living.

drift into apathy; informal networks for helping people, advising about jobs, and lending emotional support also have little opportunity to develop when there are no formal community organizations.

Opportunities for social deviance are abundant in urban areas, particularly where primary social controls in the form of internalized (super-ego) standards cannot be introduced or maintained (Moore, 1966). Ambiguous and conflicting standards add to the difficulty of establishing stable patterns of conduct.

Inter-generational conflict is particularly great between the second and third generation offspring of immigrants. This is because the third generation usually has less tradition to draw upon as well as more exposure to the new situation. A similar kind of gap is increasingly being created in modern industrial societies between generations who, because of incredibly rapid and vast social changes, are unlikely to be socialized in similar worlds or to find old techniques useful in adaptation. The lack of common language and the impersonal relationship of the work situation also generate insecurity and low morale. State or government involvement in the life of the individual and family may foster antagonism.

The life of the detribalized, semi-educated and marginal African who is a member of a partially urbanized (and westernized) society is particularly stressful. Renouncing his old culture but failing to assimilate the new, he becomes particularly prone to psychiatric disturbance. In many places, there has been a higher incidence of behaviour disturbance, such as drug addiction, abnormal sexuality, and delinquency. An increase in psychiatric disorders in Africa has been attributed to detribalization (Carothers, 1953) in Kenya, alphabetization and industrialization (Field, 1960) in Ghana, rapid economic development and urbanization (Boroffka and Marinho, 1955–7) in Lagos, and culture change (Leighton *et al.*, 1963) in Nigeria.

Migration

Does migration increase the risk of developing psychiatric disorder? Ødegaard (1932) has suggested that psychiatric disturbances may in fact *lead* people to migrate and that therefore the high rate of psychiatric disorder among Norwegian–Americans which he found in his study was due to the high rate of disturbances in this group prior to their migration.

Still others have shown that migration itself is asociated with an increased risk of psychological and physical illness. Andean Indians suffer from a variety of psychosomatic disorders when they settle in the coastal regions, not only because of cultural differences (custom, language, dress) but because their characteristically high haemoglobin levels, so necessary for adaptation to the low-oxygen levels of the Andes, are physiologically maladaptive for the lower altitudes of the coast (Seguin, 1956).

Others have found that migration from an intolerable to a tolerable situation can have beneficial effects on the mental health of groups of people and can reduce the rate of psychiatric disorders. A number of studies have also reported lower rates of mental hospitalization among immigrants than the native-born. In an unpublished study, Murphy found that the ratio of immigrants to native-born in first admissions to mental hospital was lower than the ratio which had been projected from the census or similar sources. When the probable distribution of different age groups within the population was taken into consideration, native rates exceeded immigrant ones at most ages. In Texas, Jaco (1959) found that the rates of psychiatric illness for Hispano-Americans were lower than for Anglo-Americans and in Cape Province, South Africa, the mental hospitalization rates for the Cape Coloured have been found to be lower than for the local whites (Chance, Hsien and Hung-Ming, 1967).

Only in the study of groups settling in Western societies has the evidence tended regularly to support the theory that migration is significant in producing mental illness. Incidence rates of psychiatric disorders have invariably been reported as higher among westernized portions of specific cultural groups. Okinawans in Okinawa had less than the average rate of psychosis, while Okinawans in Hawaii had a high rate of hospitalization. Western trained Javanese doctors have higher psychosis rates than the Javanese in the army. English trained Chinese males, in the 29–49 age range have a much greater hospitalization rate for all disorders than do Chinese educated males at the same age in another study. Similar observations have been made about acculturating Indian groups, as Hallowell's study of Ojibwa.

Discrimination

There is considerable evidence that many groups in different countries suffer from psychiatric disturbances because of their experiences of discrimination. Where minority-group status is based on ethnic or religious traditions, those able to adhere to traditional patterns have less difficulty than those who like alcoholic agringade, in Mexican America, attempt to acculturate, only to encounter discrimination and limited opportunities (Kiev, 1964b, 1968a).

These subtle psychological dimensions of status emerge most clearly in clinical accounts of psychotherapy of minority group members. In a study of Negro boys, Brody (1964) found that many Negro mothers denied the real significance of colour in their own lives at the same time as displaying morbid sensitivity to any issue concerning race in general. This sensitivity and denial caused communication difficulties between them and their sons.

A number of different adaptive patterns have been described as a consequence of such identity confusion, including identification with white people as a defence against aggression, denial of colour, accepting whites as superior, hostility and anti-social behaviour and the development of hypertension and other psychosomatic illnesses.

Barriers to therapy have been described in Negro patients who have difficulty in differentiating between primary self-concept derived from their family experiences and their secondary self-concept derived from their encounters with discrimination which affect their self-image and their views of the therapists (Karne, 1966). While passivity and dependency often mask hostility, they also reflect traditional views of appropriate behaviour in the patient role and a reluctance to communicate real feeling (Heine, 1950). Racial conflicts are also often used as unconscious defences or rationalizations to conceal more basic universal conflicts (Adams, 1950).

These issues are highlighted by a study of the anachronistic and restrictive Indian Reservations in the United States. The Apache child is exposed to sexuality, brutality with alcoholic adults, and has little opportunity, according to Boyer (1966), for healthy psychological growth. The absence of a suitable adult model to emulate, contributes to confusion in identity and drunkenness becomes an approved outlet of poorly integrated sexual and aggressive energies. The dependency patterns and neurotic conflicts which develop from failure of adequate 'ego–id' integration in childhood are reinforced by the subtle discouragement of independence and individualism on the reservation, by problems in adapting to the larger society and by the absence of traditional outlets. The Indian is likely to become passive, dependent, lazy, shiftless and drunken, in accord with the expectations of reservation authorities and other Indians. The Navaho no longer rely on the extended family and traditional healers and so experience increasing difficulty in coping with culture-bound problems as well as the problems of discrimination. The traditional religious and spiritualistic values of an agricultural society conflict with the values of industrial society. The Navaho have less time for traditional singing, participate less in their rituals and learn fewer versions of their numerous songs. Alcoholism and self-destruction have become modern-day counterparts of the traditional patterns of bravery and courage for many Navaho (Kaplan and Johnson, 1966). Opler (1967) has described a dramatic and violent form of suicide by the inhalation of fire among the Apache which has emerged in the context of cultural breakdown along with rising rates of alcoholism, mental illness and demoralization. Suicide occurs most often among Apaches, who are most likely to be caught in the conflict of two cultures with little opportunity to turn to older cultural traditions and little security in the inter-generational hierarchy.

The culture of poverty

Slum dwellers in Latin America and other developing areas are exposed to special stresses and strains by virtue of the social distances between the 'culture of poverty' and the dominant institutions in their societies. According to Lewis (1961), the 'culture of poverty' does not refer to backward, isolated, integrated, self-sufficient primitive people such as the peasantry, the working class or the proletariat. Rather, it covers 'the poorest peasants, plantation labourers, and the large heterogenous mass of small artisans and tradesmen, usually referred to as the lumpen proletariat'. These marginal, unskilled, illiterate people, uninvolved in political, labour, social welfare or cultural activities, are often unemployed and frequently in debt. They are viewed with apathy, suspicion or fear and are in contact with few social institutions other than the jails, the army and the public relief systems.

These people know the middle-class values, but do not live by them. They do not marry although they recognize marriage and the church. They have fewer resources to maintain the stability of the family, and there is a minimum of organization beyond the level of the nuclear and extended family. Such a low level of organization contributes to their marginality in complex, specialized, organized societies. They have little knowledge of the ways to acquire skills and lack courage to participate in the community. According to Lewis, the social and psychological characteristics of the culture of poverty include crowded quarters, inadequate privacy, gregariousness, alcoholism, violence, wife-beating, and physical force in child training; early initiation to sex, free unions or consensual marriages, and a high incidence of abandonment of mothers and children; present-time orientation, the inability to defer gratification and plan for the future, a sense of resignation and fatalism, and a belief in male superiority; a martyr complex among women, a high tolerance of psychological pathology, a propensity towards feelings of marginality, helplessness, dependency and inferiority; oral fixations, weak ego structures, confused sexual indentification, and lack of impulse control. All these characterize the people of the slum, reflecting their alienation from the values and institutions of the larger society.

Psychiatric disorders

Much of the literature on psychiatric disorders in minority groups has focused on the etiological role of acculturation, social change, migration and discrimination in the development of fundamental psychotic disorders (Kiev, 1963, 1964a). Evidence from other studies (for example, clinical, experimental and psychological) does not firmly prove the psychological or sociological etiology of these conditions, and in so far as the evidence increasingly points to the fundamental biological basis for these disorders, it is useful to consider other ways of conceptualizing the evidence at hand. Social change, migration, discrimination, acculturation and other stressful experiences of minority groups may be significant in the development of psychotic disorders when they are associated with the loss of social traditions/systems such as the extended kin group and folk medical customs which are a psychological support to disturbed individuals. Thus some individuals suffering from schizophrenia may not be identified in traditional settings. The kinds of social isolation to which the schizophrenic may be most vulnerable is particularly common in shanty towns, crowded slums and urban ghettos. The town may bring about chronic social breakdown rather than lead to underlying disorders, i.e. states of non-functioning superimposed on underlying disorders. Recent studies suggest that many of the most visible symptoms of schizophrenia are, in fact, secondary patterns from specific cultural or situational factors and should be distinguished from the fundamental disorder itself. When these manifestations appear in the setting of the city, patients may be identified as new cases rather than old cases, thus falsely influencing the comparative urban–rural rates.

It is important to recognize that psychiatric problems may not show up immediately upon exposure to stress. In the first several months after migration, for example, excitement, enthusiasm and anxiety are generated by the new environment, especially if the individual is not prepared, does not speak the language and is unemployed. In the next four or five months, problems associated with the absence of a defined social structure may appear as the impetus of initial enthusiasm declines. In the second half-year new conflicts associated with real problems in adjustment to the new situation and problems in giving up old habits and patterns begin to develop. It is not uncommon at this time for individuals to question the meaningfulness and validity of their new life.

Our knowledge of the psycho-social etiology of the psycho-neuroses, psychosomatic disorders and behaviour disorders is considerably firmer than is the case with the more severe psychotic disorders (Kiev, 1965). Indeed, much of the effect of the various stressful experiences described above are applicable to the less severe disorders, although large-scale and systematic epidemiological data on these conditions have been less accessible than have data on cases in need of hospitalization. In societies with few facilities, their needs have been viewed as less urgent and they have received lower priorities than the psychotic disorders (Kiev (ed.), 1964). In addition, such conditions have often been viewed as matters for judicial and police measures. Nevertheless, the data that have been collected has shown that both neurotic and behavioural disorders increase with the social stresses experienced by minority groups.

A theoretical rationale for treatment, prevention and research

Psychological stability requires that an individual receives a certain amount of intellectual support from his fellows, a stabilized world-view which explains the mysteries of birth and death and an illusory security in the face of an uncertain world. A system of rules and expectations for dealing with the daily anxieties of inter-personal relationships and environmental challenges also seem essential for psychological comfort. Certain stressful and emotionally arousing experiences undermine security and confidence in accustomed ways of coping with life, increase self-consciousness, bodily reactions and behaviour and alertness to environmental cues. The conscious attempt to adjust habitual responses to assumed environmental expectations produces generally increased insecurity, dependency and susceptibility to environmental influences. Sudden or even gradual exposure to the unfamiliar is unsettling. This holds for the disaster victim who can no longer recognize the familiar as well as for the immigrant exposed to new sights, sounds, smells, and customs.

Immigrants with satisfactory prior experiences in adapting may fare better than those from the 'culture of poverty' who have been irreversibly impaired by deprivation in their early life. The consequences of poor prenatal and obstetrical care, malnutrition and mental deprivation include high rates of infant mortality, epilepsy, mental retardation, functional mental retardation and emotional immaturity. The latter may later manifest itself in terms of low frustration tolerance, problems in controlling sexual and aggressive drives, delinquency, alcoholism, crime and chronic withdrawal and apathy states.

Unequal access to opportunities within the social system at different stages may have different effects. A Negro in a northern city may not encounter discrimination until he enters the occupational system. This will have a different effect than early exposure to it, say in education; while the individual may acquire adaptive skills for dealing with discrimination, he may also incorporate various negative stereotypes into his sense of identity with all this implies in terms of suppression and repression of drives toward self-realization. Discrimination and prejudice produce sensitivity and self-consciousness which in turn impair emotional stability and performance, thereby confirming the self-fulfilling negative expectations of the prejudiced.

Discrimination increases the risk of psychological difficulties for those who are vulnerable – i.e. those sensitive to the attitudes and expectations of others. Those content with their own group probably are strengthened by discrimination save in those situations where they are forced into second-class citizenship. Where discrimination is subtle and insidious, it offers illusions of opportunity and makes available education for goals that cannot be reached because of social obstacles. In such situations, individuals may develop needs that cannot be gratified. The development of disorder later on may be less severe, however, in view of the early opportunities to develop strengths.

Thus difficulties can be avoided by the individual who does not unnecessarily depend on others for his self-definition but instead relies on traditional support from his group. Further, it is extremely important to carefully assess the natural history of a minority group's special experiences as well as the individual's psychiatric disturbances. Individuals are exposed to different stresses at different critical periods of life when vulnerabilities differ. Exposure to stress, the duration and frequency of exposure and preparation for it are crucial variables in determining individual risk. The extent of cushioning elements in the culture or in geographically accessible home towns must be considered.

Still others, in a state of tension, anxiety and uncertainty because of their heightened suggestibility, are influenced by political and religious groups which espouse social revolution or the millenium. While these people may fail to adapt to the larger society, they may find a meaningful world-view and activity which may resolve their psychological distress. The continued use of folk medicine in Africa and the development of voluntary societies modelled after the tribal societies is an example of the adaptive significance of such customs.

This theory emphasizes that preventable difficulties result from the environment's effect on the individual's own pattern of behaviour. An individual's responses of over-reaction, over-dependency, hyper-suggestibility and difficulty in mastering anxiety produce much of the problem.

Prevention and treatment

This theory has implications for research treatment and preventive programmes. In a plural society, individuals must be helped to acquire skills for harnessing anxiety to learning about the relationship between their previous and present world. The adaptive and maladaptive values of tradition in urban industrial society, differences between ascriptive and achievement values, universalistic and particularistic criteria must be understood. Preventive programmes must directly assist the potentially vulnerable individual to recognize his strengths, to identify with successful members of his sub-culture, and see that expectations fostered in one cultural setting do not apply universally.

Most important, this theory distinguishes between the basic and the secondary manifestations of psychiatric disorders. In our work in the Cornell Programme in Social Psychiatry, we have come to distinguish between the fundamental symptoms of psychiatric disorders and the symptoms and the behaviour patterns superimposed on the fundamental disorders by the reaction of both the patient and significant others (Kiev, 1968a). It is in this reaction and its effects that cultural and social factors can be seen to play their most significant role. It is likely that the basic symptoms of schizophrenia and the depressive disorders are the same universally and that what differs from patient to patient and culture to culture are the explanations and reactions to them which serve to complicate or to smooth the clinical course. This is illustrated by reference to our current investigation of the social world of patients who have made serious suicide attempts. Most patients were found to be suffering from clinically identifiable psychiatric disorders which had gone unrecognized for considerable periods of time prior to the suicide attempts. The non-recognition of these disorders was often due to ideas about illness and symptoms which were decidedly influenced by socio-cultural factors. Patients frequently felt that their symptoms were reasonable in the face of environmental stresses of personal inadequacies, and as such did not recognize the pressure of illness justifying their entry into the sick role, with all that that implies in terms of non-responsibility for their illness and the necessity to seek professional help. Cultural factors strongly determine the criteria for entry into the sick role. To the extent that the patient's symptoms are defined as reasonable responses to environmental stresses or as purposeful manifestations of deviant behaviour, the patient may not enter the sick role and secondary reactions of guilt, desperation, hopelessness and suicidal behaviour may develop because of the non-identification of an illness pattern. Thus, patients may feel excessively guilty about a reduction in performance resulting from reduced energy, insomnia, weakness or weight loss or they may be subjected to pressure and criticisms by others who may try to talk them out of a depressed mood by arguing that they have no reason to feel that way (Parsons, 1951). Thus cultural definitions and non-definitions of illness may serve to intensify and complicate a basic underlying disorder (see also Chapter 13 of this book). Minority-group experience is significant in influencing not only the recognition of symptoms and the criteria for entry into treatment, but attitudes and expectations regarding treatment.

In the treatment of patients in our programme, we distinguish between the basic symptoms of the depressive disorders – e.g. insomnia, loss of appetite, loss of energy, depressive mood – which are treated along medical lines with psychopharmaceuticals, particularly the antidepressants, and the life difficulties of the patients which are treated with a variety of techniques including environmental manipulation, supportive psychotherapy and family counselling. We stress the view that symptoms and difficulties may not be causally related, but that rapid reduction of symptoms will assist in coping with the environment. Exploration of the purposeful elements and dynamic meaning of depression is assiduously avoided, greatest attention being focused on the support of ego functions and the development of better interpersonal skills when that is indicated. This approach, which is more closely modelled on the traditional doctor–patient relationship rather than the psychotherapeutic model, is particularly useful for members of minority groups who are accustomed to depending on the doctor rather than on themselves and for whom this approach is more comfortable.

In addition, by not focusing responsibility for the illness or treatment on them but rather on symptom relief, the doctor retains considerable leverage to influence the patient in other areas of his life. This, I believe, is less rapidly done when the patient is confronted head-on with responsibility. We distinguish between the subjective distress and psychological abnormalities and the associated environmental factors or social experiences which may be causes, complications or consequences of the disorder, and which are often used to rationalize non-entry into the sick role, or non-acceptance of treatment.

Priority is given to the relief of symptoms through the use of active psychopharmaceutical agents. It is often best to wait until the patient has clinically improved to determine social problem areas which are often temporary responses to the patient's disturbance or magnified by the misperception of a schizophrenic thought disorder or depressive mood. Supportive psychotherapy during this phase of treatment focuses on symptom response to medication, the non-responsibility of the patient for his symptoms and the encouragement of a supportive and helpful role on the part of significant others all of which reduce guilt and anxiety, the secondary complications of the underlying condition.

Dynamic interpretations of the patient's symptoms and interpersonal relationships are assiduously avoided until symptomatic relief has been achieved. At this point, a more traditional psychotherapeutic model is followed, the main focus being to help the patient to understand how his own patterns of behaviour, attitudes and expectations of others may lead to unfavourable responses and disruptive secondary responses on his part. Knowledge of the patient's cultural background and how it contrasts or conflicts with his present environment is especially useful here in facilitating the progress of treatment. Knowledge of the patient's culture enables the psychiatrist to differentiate basic psychopathological patterns from social problems common to members of the immigrant group, thereby allowing the psychiatrist to focus his efforts on those areas he can most affect.

Research

Research efforts must also carefully attend to the distinction between psychological and social phenomena. To adequately understand the psychiatric experiences of particular groups, it would be useful to know their pre-minority-group patterns and experiences as well as the nature of the social world to which they must accommodate. Have they always been a minority group? Have they coped with diverse situations in the past? Have they adapted well to modern urban society or only to primitive tribal or rural agrarian societies? Have their family patterns, marital customs, values, religious customs, attitudes towards education and other cultural patterns been obstacles to coping with change and with modern industrial societies irrespective of the attitudes of the majority group? Do they share economic activities with the majority group, or are they in need of exploiting the majority group or being exploited by it? Do the traditions of the minority discourage independence, learning, education and mobility? Are they secure in their own traditions in a pluralistic sense or eager to extend their effect in a military way? Such information has rarely been obtained. The evidence available has suffered from the methodological weakness of the difficulty of specifying valid and reliable empirical measures of important social parameters – e.g. the speed of social change, the magnitude of social stress and the extent of social integration.

The complexity of studying the frequency and distribution of psychiatric disorders in different minority groups has been considerable also. Most studies have been inconclusive because of lack of information about hospital patterns, available beds, community attitudes and alternative treatment methods. The actual number of cases in a given time period (incidence) cannot be firmly determined from hospital data alone. Hospital studies do not measure potential cases, spontaneously recovered cases or all relevant deaths. Prospective and longitudinal studies which might assess incidence, spontaneous recovery, individual risk, and the lag between the start and recognition of an illness, have been limited by different methods of investigation, diagnosis, case identification and accessibility of patients.

Deciding on what constitutes a case is often a difficult matter. If only illnesses with conspicuous clinical manifestations are counted, many cases are lost, as for example simple schizophrenia. Since such cases often occur in families with high frequencies of the same disorders, the actual number of cases lost is sometimes even greater than can be explained by not counting cases with conspicuous clinical manipulations. Further problems arise when one has to decide which cases to include on the basis of time of occurrence of the symptoms – i.e. whether to count people who have improved or recovered.

Diagnostic factors obviously loom large in making for difficulty in comparing studies: psychiatrists don't always agree on diagnoses, or on the criteria of diagnosis. The clinical diagnosis is therefore unreliable and will continue to be so until some objective diagnostic methods are developed. The data in most studies focus on incidence of hospitalization, not on incidence of disorder in the community. Such data are fine to plan services, but to determine the frequency of occurrence of cases being produced in order to determine (a) the extent of the public health problems, and (b) any clues to the etiology of psychiatric disorders, it is necessary to have data on the incidence of all disorders.[2]

Even when some of these matters are worked out, the complexities are tremendous. Thus if social change leads to an increase in mental illness and one does not see an increase, it doesn't necessarily mean there isn't one. Similarly, an increase can be attributed to the change in the manifestations of the disorders because new conditions reward a different kind of behaviour, suppress it or punish it. With social change, the so-called exotic disorders, e.g. Koro (Yap, 1965), susto (Kiev, 1968b), spirit possession (Kiev, 1961), windigo psychosis (Cooper, 1934) may manifest themselves as typical psychiatric disorders seeking the assistance of modern rather than native healers, leading to a false increase in the number of cases counted. This is seen in the case of '*buffee delirante aigu*' in Haiti, an exotic condition which ultimately leads to schizophrenia in a great number of instances (Sanseigne *et al.*, 1961). An increased number of counted cases without increase in the amount of the disease present, may be due to new diagnostic techniques, new treatments and improved case-finding methods. When the population increases in size, there may be an increased number of cases although rates may remain unchanged. It is also possible to get an increased prevalence rate without an increased incidence rate when better treatment methods increase the number of survivors.

Other methodological weaknesses of previous studies are the absence of good information about the population at risk, which is crucial for determining accurate incidence or prevalence rates. Most studies have had difficulty ascertaining the size and the age and sex characteristics of the population. Without such census information the actual rates cannot be determined.

Finally, it should be noted that few studies have adequately controlled for the numerous factors which might have contributed to psychiatric

2. While it is possible to transform prevalence data gathered in community surveys to incidence estimates by Weinberg's (1949) correction for mortality, this method has many limitations, especially since the estimated length of illness is not certain.

disorder in addition to the variable under study. Many studies have concerned themselves with whether or not minority groups had more illness than other groups in the same community. A more useful question would be whether or not they had more disorder than those of the same group who in another social setting were not a minority. By controlling minority-group membership in this way, one controls for race, ethnicity, social change, and migrant status, studying only minority-group status. There are other ways for controlling relevant variables. This should always be considered at the same time that one must try to determine how these various factors contribute to the development of disorder.

Despite the methodological problems noted above, which limit the strength of the scientific conclusions which can be drawn, there has been an abundance and variety of consistent and pertinent data collected which underlines the nature and magnitude of the psychiatric problems of minority groups and suggests the directions which must be taken in further research, treatment, and prevention.

References

ADAMS, W. (1950), 'The Negro patient in psychiatric treatment', *American Journal of Orthopsychiatry*, p. 305.

BOROFFKA, A., and MARINHO, A. A. (1955–57), 'A preliminary survey of the in-patient population of the mental hospital in Lagos-Yuba', in *Conference Report*, edited by T. A. Lambo, First Pan-African Psychiatric Conference, Abeokuta, Nigeria, Ibadan Govt. Printer.

BOYER, L. B. (1966), 'Folk psychiatry of the Apaches of the Mescalero Indian reservation', in A. Kiev (ed.), *Magic, Faith and Healing: Studies in Primitive Psychiatry Today*, Free Press, pp. 284–414.

BRODY, E. (1964), 'Colour and identity conflict in young boys', *Archives of General Psychiatry*, vol. 10, p. 354.

CAROTHERS, J. C. (1953), *The African Mind in Health and Disease*, WHO Monograph Series, no. 17.

CHANCE, N., HSIEN, R., and HUNG-MING, C. (1967), 'Modernization, value identification and mental health: a cultural study', *Transcultural Psychiatric Research Review and Newsletter*, vol. 4, October, pp. 108–10.

COOPER, J. M. (1934), 'Mental disease situations in certain cultures', *Journal of Abnormal and Social Psychology*, vol. 29, pp. 10–17.

FIELD, M. J. (1960), *Search for Security: An Ethnopsychiatric Study of Rural Ghana*, Northwestern University Press.

HEINE, R. W. (1950), 'The Negro patients in psychotherapy', *Journal of Clinical Psychology*, vol. 6, p. 393.

HOCH, ERNA, personal communication.

HOSELITZ, B. (1966), 'Main concepts in the analysis of the social implications of technological change' in B. Hoselitz and W. E. Moore, *Industrialization and Society*, UNESCO.

JACO, E. G. (1959), 'Mental health of the Spanish-American in Texas', in M. K. Opler (ed.), *Culture and Mental Health*, Macmillan.

KAPLAN, B., and JOHNSON, D. (1966), 'The social meaning of Navaho psychopathology and psychotherapy', in A. Kiev (ed.), *Magic, Faith and Healing: Studies in Primitive Psychiatry Today*, Free Press, pp. 203–29.

KARNE, G. (1966), 'The enigma of ethnicity in a psychiatric clinic', *Archives of General Psychiatry*, vol. 14. p. 516.

KIEV, A. (1961), 'Spirit possession in Haiti', *American Journal of Psychiatry*, vol. 118, pp. 133–8.

KIEV, A. (1963), 'Beliefs and delusions of West Indian immigrants to London' *British Journal of Psychiatry*, vol. 109, pp. 356–63.

KIEV, A. (ed.) (1964), *Magic, Faith and Healing: Studies in Primitive Psychiatry Today*, Free Press.

KIEV, A. (1964a), 'Psychiatric illness among West Indians in London', *Race*, vol. 5, January.

KIEV, A. (1964b), 'Psychotherapeutic aspects of Pentecostal sects among West Indians in London', *British Journal of Sociology*, vol. 15, pp. 129–38.

KIEV, A. (1965), 'Psychiatric morbidity of West Indian immigrants in an urban group-practice in London', *British Journal of Psychiatry*, vol. 111, pp. 51–116.

KIEV, A. (1968a), *Curanderismo: Mexican-American Folk Psychiatry*, Free Press.

KIEV, A. (1968b), 'Suicide prevention', *Cornell Alumni Bulletin*, Winter.

LEIGHTON, A. H., LAMBO, T. A., HUGHES, C. C., LEIGHTON, D. C., MURPHY J. M., and MACKLIN, D. B. (1963), *Psychiatric Disorder Among the Yoruba*, Cornell.

LEWIS, O. (1961), *Children of Sanchez*, Random House.

MOORE, W. E. (1966), 'Industrialization and social change', in B. Hoselitz and W. E. Moore, *Industralization and Society*, UNESCO.

MURPHY, H. B. M. (1959), 'Social change and mental health in causes of mental disorders', *A Review of Epidemiological Knowledge*, Millbank Memorial Fund unpublished. pp. 280–329.

ØDEGAARD, O. (1932), 'Emigration and insanity: study of mental disease among Norwegian-born populations of Minnesota', *Acta Psychiatrica et Neurologica*, supplement 4, pp. 1–206.

OPLER, M. K. (1967), *Culture, Psychiatry and Human Values*, Atherton.

PARSONS, T. (1951), *The Social System*, Free Press.

SANSEIGNE, A., and DESROSIERS, M. (1961), 'The evaluation of psychopharmaceuticals in underdeveloped countries', in *Psychiatry in the Underdeveloped Countries*, American Psychiatric Association, pp. 52–8.

SEGUIN, A. (1956), 'Migration and psychosomatic disadaption', *Psychosomatic Medicine*, vol. 18, pp. 404–9.

SLEIM, A. (1964), 'Disorders in Tunisian society: their evolution and frequency as a foundation of socio-economic and cultural changes since independence', *La Tunisie Medicale*, January-February, pp. 37–53.

UNITED NATIONS (1963), *Report on the World Social Situation*, UN.

WEINBERG, A. A. (1949), 'Psychosociology of the immigrant: an investigation into the problems of adjustment of Jewish immigrants into Palestine', *Social Studies 2*, Israel Institute of Folklore and Ethnology.

YAP, P. M. (1965). 'Koro – a culture-bound depersonalization syndrome', *British Journal of Psychiatry*, vol. 3 no. 170, January.

Chapter 22
Crime and Delinquency in Immigrant and Minority Groups

Anthony Bottoms

A. E. Bottoms was born in India, where his father was a medical missionary. He graduated in law at Oxford University, and then went to Cambridge as a member of the first postgraduate course at the Institute of Criminology. After a short period as a Probation Officer in Essex, he returned to Cambridge to join the research staff of the Institute. In 1968 he moved to Sheffield University, where he is Senior Lecturer in Criminology.

Psychological studies have shown that people who have strongly punitive views about the treatment of criminals often also have very hostile feelings towards members of ethnic minority groups. In dealing with the subject of crime and delinquency among immigrant and minority groups we are, therefore, treading on ground in which emotions are likely to be easily aroused, and there is a particular need to keep the analysis as dispassionate as possible.

The desirability of a cool approach is emphasized by the number of times that assumptions in this area have been proved wrong. Thus, in the United States 'during the years when immigration was at its height, it was generally believed that there was an undue amount of crime among the foreign born . . . [but] such statistics as are available indicate that [their] crime rate . . . is less than that of native whites with the same age, sex and rural–urban distribution' (Cressey, 1964). In 1964 the number of foreign workers in Switzerland reached a high level, and 'several xenophobic statements appeared in the daily press . . . claiming an imminent danger from the high level of criminality', which was subsequently shown to be largely unfounded (Ferracuti, 1968). And in 1902 a member of the British Parliament, seeking the strict control of alien immigration, asserted that 'among the thousands who come here there is a considerable proportion of bad characters', but the Royal Commission on the Aliens Question, which reported the following year, found this to be untrue.

A first task, then, seems to be to appraise the facts. Unfortunately, these are extremely elusive, partly because of limitations inherent in all criminal statistics, and partly due to technical difficulties in comparing criminal statistics with population statistics. The discussion which follows is therefore not a straightforward one, but it could not be simplified without serious risk of distortion.

Statistics on offenders need to be treated with great caution. They usually adopt as their basic unit of measurement either *convictions* (as in Britain) or *arrests* (as in the USA). But either of these indices may give us a seriously inaccurate picture of the actual crime rates of different social groups. For example, in England and Wales in 1967, 208,935 males were convicted of indictable offences, as against 33,935 females, a ratio of over six to one. But, in the same year, there were almost half-a-million crimes which were reported to the police but not detected. Suppose all these had been committed by women – this would completely destroy the six to one ratio. And in addition to this there are many crimes which are never reported to the police at all, for a variety of reasons such as the triviality of the loss or a view that it is a private and not a police matter. So it is clear that those who are convicted are but a minority of offenders, and the problem for criminologists is to determine to what extent they are a *representative* minority.

There is at present no firm answer to this problem. Some research has been carried out, comparing official records of crime with what people in the general population are prepared to report of their past misdeeds. These studies – which have become known as 'hidden delinquency' studies – tend to indicate that those who actually appear in court generally admit more crime than others, and hence that the official statistics give fair (though exaggerated) indications of the main social characteristics of at least the more serious and persistent offenders. But, as we shall see, in relation to ethnic groups the results are anything but conclusive; so as a preliminary we are driven back to the customary expedient of using figures on *recorded* offenders, but with a constant implicit acknowledgement that these are subject to important limitations – and to save intolerable tediousness the reader will have to make these for himself.

With this *caveat* let us look, country by country, at what we know of crime among minority groups.

The United States

Precise figures for the crime rates of different racial groups are impossible to obtain. The FBI's annual *Uniform Crime Reports* do not cover the whole of the United States because they depend for their completeness on voluntary returns which are not always forthcoming from all areas of the country. One is forced to assume that the two-thirds coverage achieved by the UCR tables on race accurately reflects the overall national picture. A further problem relates to the data on race in the *general* population, for the Bureau of the Census has noted that, in its figures, 'the nonwhite and Negro estimates ... are considerably understated because of under-enumeration in the [1960] Census' (on which subsequent population estimates throughout the 1960s were based). And clearly, comparing crime rates against an under-enumerated population leads to an overstatement of the true level of crime.

Hence the following table has to be very cautiously interpreted:

Table 1 Major[1] crime rates in USA, 1967

Race	Proportion of total major arrests (per cent)	Proportion of estimated national population (per cent)
Whites	63·3	87·9
Negroes	34·9	11·0
Others, including not known	1·8	1·1
Total	100·0	100·0

Negroes

It can be seen that, in this crude comparison, Negroes are arrested for major offences three times more often than would be expected from their proportion in the United States population. But further qualifications need to be made in interpreting such a finding, notably the possibility of a differential operation of the famous four consistent variables of crime – that is, everywhere the young, the male, the urban dweller and the lower-class person is over-represented in the official records of crime (Cressey, 1964). The sex ratio of Negroes and whites, and the proportion of each in the crime-prone ages, is very similar, but census data show that Negroes tend to live proportionately much more in the central city areas than do whites, and it is in precisely these areas that crime is always highest, regardless of the cultural origin of the residents. Moreover, the average social-class position of the Negro is well below that of the white: in 1965 the median family income for whites was $7170 and for Negroes $3874, and it has been calculated mathematically that, even in a totally non-discriminating society, it would take the Negro as much as sixty to eighty years to achieve occupational parity, starting from the present position.

In addition to this we have to consider whether part of the differential might be due to discrimination in police practice. Professor Wolfgang (1964) notes in his authoritative study that 'the assertion may well be true, but despite the many documented individual cases of such discrimination there is practically no verified, methodologically adequate, scientific research to prove that this kind of bias actually causes the disparity in

1. The *Uniform Crime Reports* divide crimes into two basic categories. The rate given here is from the total of the first (main) category. The crimes comprised within the category are listed in full in Table 2.

rates'. But even if we take the line of extreme caution and interpret the figures leaving aside such a possible bias, the factors of census under-enumeration and of urban–rural and social-class differentiation still indicate that the gross figure of a Negro crime rate three times that of the white population is a considerable exaggeration of the true position when like is being compared with like. However, if such a comparison were possible on a national scale it remains possible that the Negro rate would still be somewhat higher than that of the whites, and this was indeed found in carefully controlled studies in Baltimore in 1947 (Moses, 1947) and more recently in New Jersey (Stephenson and Scarpitti, 1968). Over forty years ago, Professor Sellin (1928) wrote: 'Nothing ... points to a conclusion that the Negro's real criminality is lower or as low as the white's', and until the recent availability of the results of certain hidden delinquency studies, this still seemed to be the case. Nor need this necessarily be surprising, in view of the way the Negro group has been consistently ostracized and subordinated by discriminatory social practice.

The proportion of Negroes arrested varies quite widely with different kinds of offence, as shown in Table 2 below:

Table 2 **Proportion of Negroes arrested for different major offences, 1967**

Offence	Negroes among all arrests (per cent)	Offence	Negroes (per cent)
Robbery	60·8	Burglary	32·5
Murder	59·4	Auto theft	31·0
Aggravated assault	49·1	Larceny	30·5
Rape	47·5	Negligent manslaughter	21·8

Thus the offences in which Negroes especially predominate are those of personal violence[2] – there is quite a marked difference between these offences and the numerically much greater offences against property, a point of some importance for theoretical discussion. However, we should not infer from this that white people must be unusually careful in their dealings with Negroes for fear of violence. On the contrary, although there are no national statistics on this point, research studies in homicide and rape show unequivocally that violence against a member of a different racial group is very rare, and, if anything, commoner among whites than among Negro offenders – for a summary of the evidence see Wolfgang (1964).

2. The offence of 'robbery' in legal usage is restricted to theft accompanied by personal violence or threats of violence.

Other races (including immigrants)

The relevant figures for coloured races other than Negroes have been shown in Table 1. Bearing in mind census under-enumeration and the inclusion of 'race unknown' among this category, the rate of crime is clearly not excessive even before correcting for social class and so on. However, the category is a heterogeneous one, including, for example, both American Indians, with their relatively high rates, and the Japanese Americans who have very little known crime – a fact usually attributed to the high degree of social control in their communities.

The considerable disquiet about immigrant crime prior to the United States anti-immigration legislation has already been quoted. Studies at the time showed marked variations in the crime rates of different national groups but overall they had relatively low rates. One writer showed, however, that this overall rate masked an interesting age-differential – those who were under thirty having noticeably higher rates (Van Vechten 1941). A further finding of especial interest was that those immigrants who stayed together in special 'colonies' tended to have lower rates than groups more widely dispersed (Beynon, 1935), from which, paradoxically, it seems that a group seeking close assimilation with the host society may, by that very seeking, acquire high crime rates which may then hinder assimilation. Another crucial point to emerge from these American studies was that in most situations the second generation have higher rates than their fathers, a finding which should alert those responsible for prevention programmes in Britain and elsewhere.

Although, however, general immigrant crime rates in America have been low, there is evidence that some immigrants have in the past played an extremely important part in *organized* crime there. Thus Professor Bell, in his important paper of 1953, noted that 'men of Italian origin appeared in most of the leading roles in the high drama of gambling and mobs, just as twenty years ago the children of East European Jews were the most prominent figures in organized crime, and before that individuals of Irish descent were similarly prominent', attributing this to specific conditions of American politics and the American economy interacting with the immigrant group (Bell, 1953).

Great Britain

The situation in Britain is complicated because the official statistics on crime do not contain any figures on the race or nationality of offenders, although it has been recommended by an official committee that in future this information should be presented (Home Office, 1967). Our present knowledge is thus restricted to research studies, notably the important surveys by McClintock (1961; 1963)[3] of robbery and crimes of violence in Greater London, and Lambert's (1970) detailed study of crime and policing in one division of Birmingham. For other parts of the country our knowledge is very scanty, but overall a reasonably consistent picture does seem to be emerging, which can be summarized as follows (see Bottoms, 1967).

The Irish

Irish immigrants appear to have relatively high gross rates for most offences in relation to their proportion in the population. Thus in McClintock's studies, the gross figures showed them to be over-represented by six times among robbers – although this finding is based on small numbers – and by four times amongst violent offenders. However, here again – as with the American Negroes – there are many qualifications to be made of the data, for example social class, area of London (Irishmen live proportionately less in the suburbs where crime rates are lower), and age (we can expect many immigrants to be young men). There is limited data available from McClintock's further national study of recidivists – persons convicted on at least two separate occasions – which suggests that, taking age into account, there is still an over representation (except perhaps among children), but that it is much less strong. Since most recidivists commit property crimes, this also suggests a high rate of Irish involvement in theft and similar offences, a point confirmed from Lambert's study for most types of theft (but not shoplifting). Lambert's work also offers support for the view that children of Irish-born parents were probably not over-represented in figures of juvenile delinquency. Additional supporting evidence of the comparatively high adult Irish rate, on crude data, is found in other small-scale studies, for example a recent book on the population of Birmingham Prison (Sparks, 1971). But a study of married adult prisoners found no over-representation (Morris, 1965), thus tending to confirm the view that the Irish who do commit crime in England are the more rootless single men.

There is evidence from Lambert's study and elsewhere that Irishmen are particularly over-represented in crimes of drunkenness and other associated crimes such as assaults in and around public houses, and wilful damage. This is consistent with findings by Bagley (1968a) of an excess of alcoholics among Irish immigrant patients in Camberwell; other studies among the Irish elsewhere have produced similar results. The reasons for this are obscure and complex.[4]

3. These surveys include data only up to 1960. McClintock is currently conducting research which will update the information to 1970: this work will be available in 1973.

4. Possible factors of importance here are (a) evidence that resort to spirits is an institutionalized trait in Irish culture, (b) Bagley's suggestion that in his sample

It is uncertain whether the apparently high Irish crime rate would remain if one carried out a fully controlled study taking into account all relevant social factors. But even if Irish crime in England is no greater in quantity than that of the native English, this is still substantially higher than the extremely low crime rate in Ireland itself. Clearly, then, the fact of migration itself, often coupled with the move from a semi-rural to an urban environment, is of some importance in this connection; but no full study has yet been carried out of this problem.

Coloured immigrants

Immigrants from the British Commonwealth – notably India, Pakistan and the West Indies – were shown in McClintock's study of crimes of violence to be over-represented in the crude figures in London in 1960 by approximately three times. To this figure one needs to apply the usual qualifications. They tend to live in the more central areas of London where, the study showed, by far the most violence is committed, and indeed if one takes the population of the old County of London as a guide, instead of the Greater London figure, the over-representation of coloured immigrants decreases from three to two, and that of the Irish from four to three times. Then there are the usual qualifications for age and social class; and also for census under-enumeration which has been found to operate for coloured immigrants in Britain as for Negroes in the United States of America, although in this particular case (comparison of 1960 crime with 1961 census) this may be offset by the rapid rate of coloured immigration at that particular time.

McClintock also showed that as much as 60 per cent of the violent crimes of Commonwealth immigrants in 1960 came into the category of 'domestic disputes', i.e. disputes arising in the home, or with a neighbour or fellow-employee.[5] Indeed, if one analyses for that year the cases *other than* domestic disputes, and compares them with the County of London population, there is virtually no over-representation even without considering the relevant social factors.

---

alcoholism might perhaps have masked schizophrenia in a number of patients, and (c) Gibbens and Ahrenfeldt's (1966) discussion of Irish immigrant delinquency in terms of absence of controls. But this is largely speculative in the present stage of research.

5. The corresponding figure for those born in the United Kingdom was just under 30 per cent. No comparable figures for the generality of assaults exist for the United States; but for homicide, where it is commoner for offender and victim to be well known to each other, Wolfgang (1958) found in his Philadelphia study that 66 per cent of the Negro victims were killed by persons with whom they had a 'primary contact', i.e. close friend, family member, paramour or homosexual partner, as against 56 per cent of white victims.

All these points should make it clear that Sir Ronald Howe, a former senior police officer in London, was irresponsibly over-simplifying the position when he said in 1968 that 'violence is increasing in Britain because so many coloured people are being admitted'.

Violent crime is, of course, only a small part even of more serious crime, the vast mass of which is made up of theft and of offences of breaking and entering property. At the time of my 1966 survey (see Bottoms, 1967), there was little evidence about the rate of property crime among coloured immigrants, but such limited data as there were indicated that this rate was probably lower than that for the native English population. If this were the case it would tend to result in a low overall crime rate for coloured immigrants, in view of the numerical predominance of property crime.

Confirmation of this, at least in one area, came from Lambert's subsequent research in Birmingham. West Indians, who constituted 4 per cent of the population of the police division studied, were responsible for 3 per cent of known property offences; the corresponding figures for Pakistanis were 2·3 and 0·7 per cent. These are crude figures uncorrected for other social factors: as Lambert (1970) comments, 'the finding is the more striking bearing in mind that there is more crime committed in areas where immigrants live than in other areas within the division'.

Lambert noted that, in his area, coloured immigrants were only importantly over-represented among drug offenders.[6] National figures published in an official report on cannabis confirm that in 1967 coloured offenders were responsible for an undue share, 27 per cent, of all convictions relating to that drug, but, not surprisingly in view of the great increase in drug use in Britain recently, the report also shows that the proportion of coloured immigrants among cannabis offenders had shown a steady decline since 1963, when the figure was 55 per cent (Advisory Committee on Drug Dependence, 1968). There are, however, no reliable figures relating to the involvement of coloured offenders in offences relating to other types of drug such as heroin, cocaine, or the amphetamine group. Most researchers suggest that drug offences among coloured immigrants can be explained partly as a vestigial continuation of activities which were acceptable in the country of origin, and partly in terms of a response to a situation of social disorganization. This is also probably true of offences of living on immoral earnings, in which Commonwealth immigrants are over-represented, at least in the London area. Both kinds of offence may be partly organized, but no evidence either way has yet emerged on this point; and it certainly seems clear that neither Commonwealth nor Irish

6. An additional finding of some interest was that Asians, but not West Indians, were over-represented among 'administrative' motoring offenders, i.e. those prosecuted for failure to tax, insure or license themselves or their vehicles.

immigrants in Britain have developed organized or syndicated crime in the way that immigrants did in the United States of America.

In the late 1960s the Inland Revenue carried out a pilot survey of one thousand randomly selected Indian and Pakistani immigrants to check on the validity of claims for tax relief for dependent relatives overseas. Just over half of the tested claims were found to be fraudulent, suggesting an overall tax loss of £5 to £7 million per annum (House of Commons, 1968). Criminologically, this is extremely difficult to interpret since we have no comparable data about Englishmen, who certainly often defraud the revenue but not usually by claiming for dependents living abroad.[7] However, even if one argues that the rates are high,[8] it should be noted that the Indian and Pakistani rates are not high for *all* fraudulent offences: a study by Dr Hadden of more 'direct' frauds in London in 1963 showed them to have a very low rates in comparison with the English (see Bottoms, 1967, Table 5).

Apart from these figures for fraud, and Lambert's geographically limited study, we have almost no data at present which differentiate between the various nationalities involved in the Commonwealth migration. Yet West Indians, Pakistanis, Indians and Cypriots are very different cultural groups, and their crime patterns may well be different. Furthermore, with the growing up of the second generation, and various changes in the host–minority relationships, it is by no means clear that the situation outlined above will remain for the future. This emphasizes the general need for further studies on the pattern of crime among minority groups over a number of years.

Israel

Israel is a country which is demographically unique, virtually the entire Jewish population having immigrated since the beginning of this century. However, the rate of immigration greatly accelerated after the establishment of the State of Israel in 1948, and by 1957 the 'old' (pre-Israeli) population constituted only 42 per cent of the nation. When one calculates the comparative rates of crime of the Israeli Arabs and the pre- and post-1948 Jewish settlers, the former have much the highest rates, but it is also

7. On the same page of the *Civil Appropriation Accounts* which reports the Indo-Pakistani study, it is shown, that, in cases detected by the Inland Revenue *without special surveys*, some £10 million taxes are annually found underpaid due to fraud and evasion. In the light of this the fuss created about the Asian immigrants seems distinctly excessive.

8. West Indian rates for the same type of claims were not found to be as excessive; the contrast with Asians corresponds to the difference found by Lambert in respect of administrative motoring offences, and probably reflects different cultural traditions about the role of and attitudes towards Government bureaucracy.

clear that the new immigrants have had a consistently higher rate of crime than the older settlers, even when controlled for age (Schmelz, 1969). There are, however, marked differences in the rates of crime among the new immigrants from different continents: thus in 1957 those from Africa had a rate of thirteen serious offences per thousand immigrants, while those from Asia had ten and those from Europe and America only five (Shoham, 1962). Of course, these immigrants were Jewish and not necessarily typical of the continents which they came from–it is known, for example, that the Jewish community in Britain produces exceptionally few delinquents.[1]

Dr Shlomo Shoham and his colleagues have carried out research into the social aspects of crime in Israel, with special reference to the conflict of conduct norms as between the seventy different ethnic groups in the country (Shoham, ed., 1970). In our context, their most important study was a survey of post-1948 Jewish immigrants in the Sharon – an area stretching right across the pre-1967 Israeli boundaries, just north of Tel-Aviv (Shoham *et al.*, 1966). Here, four social variables were especially studied, namely (a) degree of urbanization, (b) length of stay in the country, (c) ethnicity (European or non-European), and (d) degree of cultural heterogeneity in a district – that is, the extent of the cultural gap between the immigrants and the receiving community. It was found that these four variables were all associated with juvenile delinquency among the second generation; and the rank order of the degree of association was in descending order of the variables as listed above. Of special interest was the high rate of delinquency among the children of the Yemeni immigrants, as this group is, effectively speaking, treated as 'lower class' by other groups. It was generally noticeable that the age of onset of delinquency among the immigrant juvenile delinquents was lower than among those born in Israel, though on the whole their offences were less serious. It is clear that the Israeli experience, although unique, is of importance for criminological understanding, and that there is a more general need to examine social variables in the sophisticated way that has here been pioneered.

Europe

On the continent of Europe and in Scandinavia there is relatively little permanent migration, and minority groups are mostly groups of foreign workers temporarily in another country. Professor Ferracuti (1968) carried out an extremely thorough review of existing studies and his overall con-

9. This point cannot be demonstrated statistically, but is based on the universal experience of penal administrators in Britain. Recently, for example, an approved school set up specifically for Jewish boys, but also admitting Gentiles, found itself with no Jews at all in its population.

clusion was that: 'Crime among European migrant workers is... not such as to cause alarm... although isolated areas of concern exist, the "dangers" claimed by some sections of the public have not materialized'.

There are, however, some interesting differences shown in the various studies so summarized. A study by Zimmermann showed that Italians, Spaniards, Greeks and Turks in Germany each had overall crime rates lower than the host population, with Spaniards and Italians especially low. Except among the Spaniards, however, crimes against the person were high for all immigrant groups, though, as with Negroes in the United States and Commonwealth immigrants in Britain, much of this was intragroup violence. A contrasting picture was found in Sweden, where Hungarians, Yugoslavs and Poles were shown, in research by Sveri, to have higher crime rates than the native population, though Italian and Austrian immigrants had low rates.

But although Poles have relatively high rates in Sweden, they seem to have low rates in France. This emerges from a report by M. Philippe Robert which forms an Annexe to the Council of Europe version of Ferracuti's paper. Robert shows that Italians, Spaniards and Poles have low crime rates, Belgians have rates approximating to the native French rates, and North African immigrants have high rates. Looking at the various crimes in more detail, an interesting contrast emerges between two immigrant groups, for the Belgians have low rates for intentional violence but high rates for unintentional violence (especially negligent injuries resulting from traffic accidents), while for North Africans the converse is true.

This bald summary of the European situation is based on crude figures only. But it does draw attention forcibly to what is perhaps the principal point to emerge from this rapid survey of the available data – namely, the great diversity of criminal patterns of minority groups in the various different countries. The complexity of the task of adequate explanation is clearly apparent.

Hidden delinquency studies

Before turning to the problem of explanation a word must be said on the relationship of the results of the 'hidden delinquency' studies to the picture derived from figures of *recorded* crime. We have already indicated that very few such studies have compared different cultural groups. One which did was carried out by Epps (1967). He administered 'self-report questionnaires' anonymously to high-school boys in Seattle, and found no significant differences in delinquency level between his Negro and white subjects, but a significantly lower level among the Orientals. If the Oriental result confirms the official statistics, that for Negroes clearly does not, and seems to suggest that a seriously misleading picture is given by the official data in the Uniform Crime Reports.[10]

But the matter is not as simple as that. One of the most interesting methodological problems in criminological research is that self-report *questionnaires* have usually yielded results showing a lack of the expected correlation between low social class and delinquency, yet *interview* studies of various types have contradicted this, and suggested that there are real differences in crime rates between social classes, even though these are exaggerated if only recorded crime is studied. In view of the low social-class position of Negroes relative to whites in the United States, it is clear that Epps's results have to be interpreted within the context of this problem, about which criminologists do not agree. Since my own inclination is to support those who suggest that the interview is the more valid instrument, it follows that I would want further evidence before rejecting the broad conclusions of the data from official statistics. As it happens, such data have recently become available in an interview study by Martin Gold (1970) of juvenile delinquency in Flint, Ohio: 'Negro youngsters confessed to no more delinquent behaviour than white youngsters, and the validation data testify that they were equally honest. This is not to say that Negro teenagers did not score higher on both the frequency and seriousness of their delinquency, for they did: but this is wholly accounted for by social status differences'. Although the study relates only to *juvenile* delinquency in one town, it clearly raises very important issues, and further replication of it elsewhere must be regarded as a research priority.

In Britain the first hidden delinquency study to include data on nationality was published by Dr Belson in 1968. Using a new 'anonymous interview' technique he found that boys born outside the United Kingdom have a lower rate of theft than others and also that coloured boys have relatively low, and Jews very low, rates. Again, these findings are based on small numbers and the categories are rather broad, but the results are similar to those obtained from research on recorded crime in Britain, especially if, as was tentatively suggested earlier, Irish-born children have official rates lower than their parents. It is also worth noting that Dr Belson found very little difference between the groups in their likelihood of being caught by the police. If one accepts the validity of his interview method, these data go some way towards validating my own earlier speculation that 'within broad limits, conviction statistics can be relied upon as an indicator of the extent of immigrant crime in Britain' (Bottoms, 1968), but clearly it would be unwise to generalize from this to the situation in other

10. For a later questionnaire study giving very similar results see Chambliss and Nagasawa (1969).

countries, in view of differences in police practice, and in the social perception of different minority groups.

The problem of explanation

It should be clear by now that the first task of anyone trying to explain differential crime rates in different cultural groups is to ensure that they are truly differential rates, and are not explicable in terms of other social factors such as age and social class. One clear need which has emerged from this survey is for much more information, both in official statistics and from research, to make this possible.

Let us assume, however, that one has 'matched' in this way and, say, American Negro rates in a particular area are still definitely higher than those for whites. What kind of explanation can one seek?

Heredity

One possible answer is a genetic one. If we could show that crime was in no way hereditarily determined, this could be ruled out at once, and this approach is taken by some leading American textbooks. However, there is evidence from studies which compare the 'concordance rate' of identical and fraternal twins, that there may be partial hereditary determination of at least some crime. One of the leading British criminological textbooks regards this evidence as 'strong but not conclusive' (Walker, 1968). If this is correct, then we shall have to look further. Professor Eysenck has rightly pointed out that one of the major difficulties of asserting that a criminal tendency is inherited is its very implausibility – how can one inherit a tendency to break into houses? But he and others have in recent years put forward a psychological theory of crime which purports to explain it (Eysenck, 1964) and is in fact the only modern theory so far advanced to include the hereditary element. Crudely summarized, the theory is that crime is the result of a failure of social learning. The average child is essentially delinquent (predatory, aggressive, etc.) and has to be socialized out of these natural selfish drives. There are two essential elements in determining whether he becomes adequately socialized – the efficiency of the social training he receives, and his inherent conditionability. One's eye can often be conditioned to blink at the sight of a stimulus if previously that stimulus has been shown simultaneously with a puff of air blown into the eye. And there is a correlation between ease of 'eye-blink conditionability' and the personality trait of introversion/extroversion – extroverts are more difficult to condition. Moreover, there is strong evidence that extroversion has an important hereditary component (Shields, 1962). Since conditionability can be partly inherited, so the argument runs, crime is in part hereditary.

Not even its advocates would regard this theory as fully proved; and indeed Eysenck himself has recently been obliged to make some modifications in it (Eysenck and Eysenck, 1970; 1971). However, even assuming its correctness, it still does not follow that differences in crime rates between racial groups are the result of hereditary forces. Even if groups differ as to extroversion (and not all do), this could well be the result of environment rather than heredity, since no one suggests that extroversion is entirely hereditarily determined. Research in this area is still very tentative. Although standard personality inventories measuring extroversion have been shown to be valid when used cross-culturally, there are still certain technical problems which effect the interpretation of the scales. (See generally Kline, 1967, and Tsujioka and Cattell, 1965). But even accepting the scores at their face value, the differences which emerge are not confined to groups of different skin-colour – thus Indian students are more extraverted than their English counterparts (Rao, 1966), but so are white Americans (Cattell and Warburton, 1961). So the existing evidence does not support any general genetic view of differences in the crime rates of different racial groups; and one is left with environmental explanations, mainly of a socio-psychological kind.

Socio-psychological explanations

Perhaps at least some of the crime among minority groups can be explained in the same way as similar crimes in the majority group. For example, census data show that Negroes in the United States have a higher proportion of families with an absent father (through death or desertion) than do whites, even when the social-class variable is controlled; hence, if one accepts the importance of the broken home and other family disorganization as of aetiological significance with regard to crime – a widely held view, but not one shared by all criminologists – it is clear that here lies part of the explanation of differential rates, even if these are accentuated by other aspects of the minority group's social situation.

But here we are more concerned with the special experiences of minority groups, and their importance in relation to crime. Three matters call for particular attention – namely, cultural background, the effects of migration, and interaction with the majority group.

Cultural background. One of the clearest examples of the importance of cultural background was seen among Hungarian immigrants in Detroit in the 1930s. The Hungarian peasant had a traditional right to 'steal' wood from his lord's estate for fuel, and in their new cultural environment the immigrants transmuted this norm by deeming it permissible to steal coal from trucks standing on the railway (Beynon, 1935).

Cultural background can, of course, also be important in a much more generalized way. The traditional strong bonds within the Jewish community, and the strongly Christian cultural background of West Indian immigrants in Britain, may well be of importance in explaining low theft rates.[11] Or again, Oscar Lewis (1967) has argued that persons living in great poverty develop, the world over, a distinctive social life-style, which includes ready resort to violence and theft, and he suggests that this 'culture of poverty' will very likely remain as a 'received' culture pattern from parents to children unless some action is taken to alter it. This theory is clearly of relevance to Negroes, Puerto Ricans and others in the United States. It is important to recognize, however, that such differences are not genetic, any more than is the difference between the divergent cultures of the middle and working classes.

Effects of immigration. An Englishman who moves from London to Yorkshire has to make adjustments to his new cultural setting, which is subtly different from that of the capital. Clearly, then, immigrants will usually face important difficulties and uncertainties through the very fact of immigration, perhaps especially if there are language problems in the new society, or if the move is from a rural to an urban environment. Their children may very well find crucial problems of cultural adjustment arising from their situation of living with the differing cultures of their parents and their schoolfriends. These problems may affect also the structure of the family – if, for example, the children perceive their parents as less omnipotent, or as playing a different social role in the new culture than in the accustomed one. Clearly, points such as these are especially crucial to the problem of the usually higher criminality of the second generation of immigrants, on the assumption that the child's solution to these adjustment problems will often be a delinquent response. (Though it remains an important question why a delinquent response, rather than, say, a relapse into mental illness, results from the problem of adjustment – see Chapter 20 of this book).

Interaction with the majority group. One must also see the crime of minority groups in the context of their relationships with the majority group. The importance of perceiving these relationships as a process of dynamic interaction was convincingly demonstrated in John Rex and Robert Moore's (1967) study of Sparkbrook, Birmingham, where the authors

11. This is consistent with a widely held view that the level of crime in an area is inversely correlated with the degree of social cohesion. There are a number of studies which tend to support such a view – see for example Maccoby *et al.* (1958) and Shoham *et al.* (1966).

stress in particular the crucial effect which housing policies may have in creating within a community stereotyped views of the behaviour of a minority group. And once such views are established, they become themselves an important element in the way in which various members of the groups perceive each other, and hence the general race-relations situation. Clearly, an analysis of this kind is of great relevance to crime in a number of ways – for example, in showing how different types of police–minority group relations, or differential levels of discrimination against the minority group, may emerge, which in turn may have effects upon the crime rate.

These points are very fully discussed in Lambert's subsequent study of the same part of Birmingham, where he concentrated particularly upon the police role, and concluded that 'the police are not alone in being challenged by the changing demands of a multiracial society, but the consequences of the police not responding to that challenge are uniquely serious'. Few who have studied the recent American literature on 'race riots' and collective violence (Masotti and Bowen, 1968) will disagree with Lambert's emphasis on the importance of majority group response, or of the special importance of the police response within that sphere (see Chapter 6 of this book). Of particular importance is the Kerner Report of 1968, the conclusions of a committee with a not particularly radical membership which was set up to investigate the 1967 racial disorders. Their massive report was a major indictment of many aspects of American society, and it pulled no punches:

The causes of the recent racial disorders are embedded in a tangle of issues and circumstances – social, economic and psychological – which arise out of the historic pattern of Negro-white relations in America.

The abrasive relation between the police and the minority communities has been a major – and explosive – source of grievance, tension and disorder. The blame must be shared by the total society.

In the United Kingdom, also, a strikingly similar official analysis of the early stages of the Northern Ireland disturbances placed the blame largely on an unthinking and discriminating majority response (see Northern Ireland Government, 1969).

The suggestion that crime rates will increase if there is a negative or discriminatory stance by the majority to the minority group has traditionally invoked R. K. Merton's (1957) use of the concept of 'anomie'. Anomie arises in Merton's view where, in societies with agreed culturally prescribed goals, there is a high aspiration to the goals but a socially structured blocking of approved means of achieving the goals. There are, he suggests, various possible responses to such a situation, one of which is the attempt to achieve the goals by illegitimate means, i.e. crime. This analysis is clearly relevant to the situation of minority groups, if the essential assumption of agreed societal goals exists. However, in recent years when a consensual model of society has seemed less appropriate, especially in America, a number of writers have suggested a need to move beyond anomie theory. Some influential voices have proposed instead the Marxist concept of alienation (see Horton, 1964, and Taylor, 1968), provided that this is understood in a fully human sense, i.e. suggesting that the subject is capable of meaningful choice and intentions, and is not simply propelled by external constraints, yet is unable to achieve this true humanity in his situation of separation from the sources of power in the society. Perhaps only this kind of analysis can make sense of the increase in explicitly political deviance among minority groups, especially in the USA (see Horowitz and Liebowitz, 1968): and this increased political articulation is in turn both based upon and helping to engender a realization that the laws of a community themselves sometimes simply reflect the sectarian interests of past or present ruling groups. The adoption or rejection of such a stance has, however, theoretical implications extending well beyond the question of crime in minority groups, and the issues raised cannot be fully explored here.

Future developments

It seems clear that the three suggested features of the experience of minority groups – cultural background, the effects of immigration, and interaction with the majority group – will be of varying importance in explaining the criminality of different groups in different countries, or of the same group at different points in time. We cannot expect to develop a single neat explanation for all groups, simply because we must see each group in relation to the majority group, and different countries have different and changing social structures which will create different patterns of interaction between the majority and minority groups. Thus, while Wolfgang (1964) and most others stress discrimination, rejection and lack of integration as prime determinants of the crime rates of American Negroes, other points seem more relevant at present to the explanation of immigrant crime in Britain.

The way forward seems to be to develop theories which attempt to explain the particular levels and types of crime within selected minority groups. This we are hardly yet in a position to attempt, other than speculatively for most minority groups, because of the need for greater information, in particular about the detailed aspects of the criminal behaviour of each group, and how they and their neighbours perceive it. For, in my view, the absurd but infectious habit of treating criminal behaviour as a homogeneous entity must stop, and we must begin to ask questions such as why, in Britain, domestic disputes are apparently so common among Asian immigrants, while housebreaking seems to be very rare in the same group. But to do this, we must make a detailed assessment of such incidents and then spend time in participant observation in various areas, talking to families and social groups of the immigrant and the host communities, and obtaining research information about their attitudes to the race relations situation, to the police, to the general problems of migration and to various kinds of criminal behaviour, while not forgetting to relate such data to analyses of social processes in the wider society. This approach seems to offer the greatest hope of specificity of theoretical explanation in the future.

The future contribution of psychology

Compared with some of the other aspects of race relations covered in this book, the psychological contribution in this chapter is more implicit than explicit: motives and reactions are hidden among statistical rates and a sociological framework. But there are perhaps two ways in which within this framework, psychologists could contribute far more explicitly in the future.

Personality and attitude studies

Despite the potential importance of personality and attitude studies, rather little attention has been paid to them in this context. Bagley (1968b) has concluded that earlier suggestions that persons of schizoid personality may be particularly likely to emigrate are unfounded, but fuller personality studies of emigrants are needed. Another important possibility is that personality and social attitudes are differentially connected with delinquency in different cultural groups, and this has been studied in a cross-cultural research project on Japanese and American boys (Mizushima and De Vos, 1967). Very similar results, including divergence between delinquent and non-delinquent subjects, were found when the California Personality Inventory was applied to the two groups, but cultural differences are emerging between the two delinquent groups as to perception of social roles and concern with violence. More recently, a study of black and white delinquent boys in the USA has suggested that the blacks have shorter time perspectives, and are less interpersonally mature as well as more 'externally oriented': these differences are attributed to the culturally repressed situation of the blacks (Cross and Tracy, 1971).

Learning and controls

A further important psychological contribution seems likely to come from analyses of learning and controls. This can be shown by a theory put forward by Gibbens and Ahrenfedlt (1966) about Irish crime in England. In effect, this theory uses the first two, but not the third, of the special experiences of minority groups which I mentioned earlier – but discusses cultural background and the effects of migration in psychological terms. The authors suggest that Irishmen are brought up in a society with strong external controls (the Catholic Church; the Irish mother), which are internalized by the young. On coming to England the external controls are removed and crime often results, although the internal controls remain strong enough to cause considerable guilt, sometimes expressed in heavy drinking.[12] There seem to be some deficiencies in this theory, for it does not appear to explain why the internal controls themselves are insufficient to prevent crime, nor does it adequately explain differences between those who do and do not commit crime. Moreover, it needs to be refined and expanded to take account of sociological aspects such as the move from a rural to an urban society, and reactions of English society to Irish migrants. But the theory is nevertheless important and suggestive, and should certainly be among the hypotheses tested in any full study of Irish crime in England which may be undertaken along the lines suggested in the previous section.

12. The work of Julian Rotter (1966) is of relevance to the concepts employed in this theory, and could possibly be of use in its refinement. Interestingly, as Taylor (1968) has shown, Rotter's work is also relevant in relation to the concept of alienation.

References

ADVISORY COMMITTEE on DRUG DEPENDENCE (1968), *Cannabis*, HMSO.

BAGLEY, C. (1968a), 'A comparative study of mental illness among immigrant groups in Britain', unpublished.

BAGLEY, C. (1968b) 'Migration, race and mental health', *Race*, vol. 9, pp. 343–56.

BELL, D. (1953), 'Crime as an American way of life', *Antioch Review*, vol. 13, pp. 131–54; reprinted in M. E. Wolfgang *et al.* (eds.) (1970), *The Sociology of Crime and Delinquency*, second edn, Wiley.

BELSON, W. A. (1968), 'The extent of stealing by London boys', *Advancement of Science*, vol. 25, pp. 171–84.

BEYNON, E. D. (1935), 'Crimes and customs of the Hungarians in Detroit', *Journal of Criminal Law, Criminology and Police Science*, vol. 32, pp. 139–47.

BOTTOMS, A. E. (1967), 'Delinquency amongst immigrants', *Race*, vol. 8, pp. 357–83.

BOTTOMS, A. E. (1968), 'Delinquency amongst immigrants – a further note', *Race*, vol. 9, pp. 250–51.

CATTELL, R. B., and WARBURTON, F. W. (1961), 'A cross-cultural comparison of patterns of extraversion and anxiety', *British Journal of Psychology*, vol. 52, pp. 3–16.

CHAMBLISS, W. J., and NAGASAWA, R. H. (1969), 'On the validity of official statistics: a comparative study of white, black and Japanese high-school boys', *Journal of Research in Crime and Delinquency*, vol. 6, pp. 71–7.

CRESSEY, D. R. (1964), *Delinquency, Crime and Differential Association*, Nijhoff, The Hague.

CROSS, H. J., and TRACY, J. J. (1971), 'Personality factors in delinquent boys: differences between blacks and whites', *Journal of Research in Crime and Delinquency*, vol. 8, pp. 10–22.

EPPS, E. G. (1967), 'Socio-economic status, race, level of aspiration and juvenile delinquency', *Phylon*, vol 28, pp. 16–27.

EYSENCK, H. J. (1964), *Crime and Personality*, Routledge & Kegan Paul.

EYSENCK, S. B. G., and EYSENCK, H. J. (1970), 'Crime and personality: an empirical study of the three-factor theory', *British Journal of Criminology*, vol. 10, pp. 225–39.

EYSENCK, S. B. G., and EYSENCK, H. J. (1971), 'Crime and personality: item analysis of questionnaire responses', *British Journal of Criminology*, vol. 11, pp. 49–62.

FERRACUTI, F. (1968), 'European migration and crime', in M. E. Wolfgang (ed.), *Crime and Culture*, Wiley, pp. 189–219; also available as 'Criminality and migrant workers', *Report of Fifth European Conference of Directors of Criminological Research Institutes*, vol. 1, Council of Europe, 1968.

GIBBENS, T. C. N., and AHRENFELDT, R. H. (eds.) (1966), *Cultural Factors in Delinquency*, Tavistock.

GOLD, M. (1970), *Delinquent Behaviour in an American City*, Brooks Cole.

HOME OFFICE (1967), *Report of the Departmental Committee on the Criminal Statistics*, Cmnd. 3448.

HORTON, J. (1964), 'The dehumanization of anomie and alienation', *British Journal of Sociology*, vol. 15, pp. 283–300.

HOROWITZ, I. L., and LIEBOWITZ, M. (1968), 'Social deviance and political marginality', *Social Problems*, vol. 15, pp. 280–96.

HOUSE OF COMMONS (1968), *First, Second and Third Reports from the Committee of Public Accounts, Session 1967–68*, pp. xiii-xˈv and 313–21, commenting on *Civil Appropriation Accounts (Classes I-V), 1966–67*, paras. 26–30.

KERNER (1968), *Report of National Advisory Commission on Civil Disorders*, Bantam Books.

KLINE, P. (1967), 'The use of the Cattell 16 PF Test and Eysenck's EPI with a literate population in Ghana', *British Journal of Social and Clinical Psychology*, vol. 6, pp. 97–107.

LAMBERT, J. (1970), *Crime, Police and Race Relations*, Oxford University Press.

LEWIS, O. (1967), *La Vida*, Secker & Warburg.

MACCOBY, E., *et al.* (1958), 'Community integration and the social control of juvenile delinquency', *Journal of Social Issues*, vol. 14, pp. 38–51.

MASOTTI, L. H., and BOWEN, D. R. (1968), *Riots and Rebellion: Civil Violence in the Urban Community*, Russell Sage.

McCLINTOCK, F. H., and GIBSON, E. (1961), *Robbery in London*, Macmillan.

McCLINTOCK, F. H. (1963), *Crimes of Violence*, Macmillan.

MERTON, R. K. (1957), *Social Theory and Social Structure*, Free Press, revised edn.

MIZUSHIMA, K., and DE VOS, G. (1967), 'The application of the California Personality Inventory in a study of Japanese delinquency', *Journal of Social Psychology*, vol. 71, pp. 45–51.

MORRIS, P. (1965), *Prisoners and their Families*, Allen & Unwin.

MOSES, E. R. (1947), 'Differentials in crime rates between Negroes and whites', *American Sociological Review*, vol. 12, pp. 411–20; reprinted in M. E. Wolfgang *et al.* (eds.) (1970), *The Sociology of Crime and Delinquency*, second edn, Wiley.

NORTHERN IRELAND GOVERNMENT (1969), *Disturbances in Northern Ireland*, Report of the Commission Appointed by the Governor, Cmnd. 532.

RAO, S. (1966), 'A note on the investigation of the MPI with different occupational groups in India', *British Journal of Social and Clinical Psychology*, vol. 5, pp. 274–5.

REX, J., and MOORE, R. (1967), *Race, Community and Conflict*, Oxford University Press.

ROTTER, J. (1966), 'Generalized expectancies for internal versus external control of reinforcement', *Psychological Monographs*, vol. 80, pp. 1–28.

SCHMELZ, U. O. (1969), 'Differentials in criminality rates between various groups in Israel's population', *Scripta Hierosolymitana*, vol. 21, 'Studies in criminology', pp. 264–319.

SELLIN, T. (1928), 'The Negro criminal', *Annals of the American Academy of Political and Social Science*, vol. 140, pp. 52–64.

SHIELDS, J. (1962), *Monozygotic Twins*, Oxford University Press.

SHOHAM, S. (1962), 'The application of the culture-conflict hypothesis to the criminality of immigrants in Israel', *Journal of Criminal Law, Criminology and Police Science*, vol. 53, pp. 207–14.

SHOHAM. S. (ed.) (1970), 'Research in criminology in a country of social change', *Israel Studies in Criminology*, vol. 1, pp. 9–34, Gomeh.

SHOHAM, S., *et al.* (1966), 'Immigration, ethnicity and ecology as related to juvenile delinquency in Israel', *British Journal of Criminology*, vol. 6, pp. 391–409.

SPARKS, R. F. (1971), *Local Prisons: The Crisis in the English Penal System*, Heinemann Educational Books.

STEPHENSON, R. M., and SCARPITTI, F. R. (1968), 'Negro–white differentials and delinquency', *Journal of Research in Crime and Delinquency*, vol. 5, pp. 122–33.

TAYLOR, L. J. (1968), 'Alienation, anomie and delinquency theory', *British Journal of Social and Clinical Psychology*, vol. 7, pp. 93–105.

TSUJIOKA, B., and CATTELL, R. B. (1965), 'Application of the 16 PF Test in America and Japan', *British Journal of Social and Clinical Psychology*, vol. 4, 287–97.

VAN VECHTEN, C. C. (1941), 'The criminality of the foreign born', *Journal of Criminal Law, Criminology and Police Science*, vol. 32, pp. 139–47.

WALKER, N. (1968), *Crime and Punishment in Britain*, Edinburgh, revised edn.

WOLFGANG, M. E. (1958), *Patterns in Criminal Homicide*, Wiley.

WOLFGANG, M. E. (1964), *Crime and Race*, Institute of Human Relations Press; shortened version published in England as 'Race and crime', in H. J. Klare (ed.) (1966), *Changing Concepts of Crime and Its Treatment*, Pergamon.

Chapter 23
Tests as Inadvertent Sources of Discrimination in Personnel Decisions[1]

Sidney Irvine

Sidney Irvine is forty-nine and has worked on aspects of psychology and race in universities in England, Africa and now Canada. His main interests are in the way culture affects thought and in personnel selection techniques. He has contributed many articles to British and American psychological journals. When he was in Africa he helped both governments and international firms produce selection tests for local workers.

R. M. Guion (1966) has stated that discrimination in hiring practices exists whenever persons with an equal probability of success on the job have unequal probabilities of being hired for it. In multi-racial work situations, the use of objective tests as screening devices for applicants may be advanced by equal-opportunity employers as arguments for their well-intentioned lack of bias in hiring and in promotion procedures. However, recent work underlines the fact that the use of objective tests and other scientifically controlled devices in selecting effective workers from a multi-racial work pool is no guarantee of lack of bias in personnel selection.

Even the best-intentioned of employment policies can come apart through the use of tests that are apparently arbiters of potential when the tests themselves, unknown to their users, reduce the probability of hiring men who might well succeed, given the opportunity. If the tests behave abnormally, the employer who uses them may inadvertently discriminate against those whom it is his policy to hire.

The purpose of this chapter is to make known to a general audience some of the recent findings from the application of tests across cultures so that institutions using selection devices may evaluate their own procedures in the light of recent scientific advances. Briefly, common fallacies about the culture content of tests are examined first. Then certain logical fal-

1. This paper was first prepared while I was employed at the University of Western Ontario. I am glad to acknowledge financial help from that institution and the inspiration of my colleagues Dr James Sanders and Dr Art Blue. The Canada Council also supported this research in part from 1968 to 1971. For discussions past and present, Professor Alec Rodger and Dr Lee J. Cronbach must take credit for sharing several ideas with me, but responsibility for any faults in argument and any errors is undeniably mine.

lacies in the use of wrong answers, averages and cut-off points. The problem of the psychological equivalence of test scores in non-western cultures is also given detailed attention. The criterion problem is pointed out and, finally, positive recommendations are made for using tests to reduce the probability of inadvertent discrimination.

Fallacies about test content
Implicit versus explicit content

Serious students of the use of tests across cultures have for some time realized that, almost without exception, tests constructed and standardized in one culture have built-in potential sources of bias when they are used to evaluate the performance of people from other cultures. Here one might benefit, in a discussion of culture-bias, from a conceptualization that distinguishes a test's *explicit* and *overt* content from its *implicit* or *covert* content. Explicit content includes such aspects as the language the test is printed in; its modality (that is, whether it uses figures, symbols or words); its declared sampling of the abilities or skills measured by the test; its format (whether it is multiple-choice or open-ended). In short, any aspect of the test that is observable and subject to experimental control. One example of the thinking of psychologists about the relation of explicit test content to performance is that of the verbal–non-verbal distinction in group tests of reasoning. When it was brought to the attention of psychologists that verbal reasoning tests *implicitly* favoured subjects from higher socio-economic backgrounds, some considered that the tests would be more fair if only the verbal or language barrier could be removed. This omission was judged sufficient to eliminate social-class differences in skills with words. Tests with low verbal content were thought to get nearer to potential ability. Here was an argument, then, for sampling the domain of skills more effectively or 'fairly' by using a figural mode of testing reasoning. The assumption was that by altering the explicit content of reasoning tests, a fairer estimate of ability would result through changing the implicit relationship of the test to a socio-economic factor. This meant that whereas social-class differences in language skills had previously been only implicit in test content, it was hoped these would vanish through explicitly changing the test itself. The supposition was that the ability tested was the same in both verbal and in non-verbal test formats. However, recent research has shown that when the modality of the tests is changed then what is tested by the test alters also. This, though, is the benefit of hindsight.

Figural, spatial and mechanical tests, relying heavily on pictorial or diagrammatic symbols, are as susceptible to *implicit* content restraints as are verbal tests. Far from offering a culturally neutral milieu, for example, they present a test environment that is a function of, among other influences, the carpentered and angular world of Western industrial societies the ideas – maybe only half-admitted – of the original test constructor, the logic implicit in the language he used, and the affective climate – perhaps modally reinforced by the indigenous school system – necessary for the completion of the test within prescribed time limits. Hence the giving of a test where no words are used is no guarantee of the fairness of that test. The test merely becomes more difficult to label because the meaning of the test score for an individual from another culture can not be easily made *explicit*. For example, results from using *Raven's Progressive Matrices*, a hardy annual in the cultivation of 'culture-fair' reasoning tests (Irvine, 1969a), show that in African samples average scores can change appreciably with different methods of test presentation and that the items are perceived differently by different ethnic groups.

Cultural influences as implicit content

It could be said that all cultural influences on test performance are initially *implicit* in that they are covert until some happy accident, insight, or, devoutly to be wished, empirical evidence, changes their status and makes them explicit enough to be mentioned in the test manual. Some glimmer of understanding of the complexity and pervasiveness of cultural factors influencing test scores in general, however, can be gained when one realizes that, at the end of primary schooling, in Africa and other developing countries, simple tests of arithmetic processes show much less variation between ethnic groups, either in range of scores or averages, than other tests. The reason is relatively simple. When arithmetic is socially valued, has been overlearned, or drilled consistently, until number bonds are second nature, and a premium is placed on speed as well as accuracy, then environmental influences (outside the classroom environment, that is), are greatly reduced. What is left are individual differences in ability to count quickly and accurately.

Verbal, spatial, mechanical and dexterity tests do not present situations where skills have had either equal reinforcement or equal value placed on them in non-Western cultures. The major fallacy in our thinking about 'culture-fair' testing is the implicit assumption that when words have been removed from tests they, the tests, can be treated as if their skills had been overlearned. And this is simply not so. Well-meaning personnel and student selection programmes seeking to be fair by using 'non-verbal' tests may not be as fair as they think they are.

Finally, anyone observing people doing 'non-verbal' tests will see considerable lip-movement when hard problems are being worked through. If the test is standardized on an English-speaking group, the tacit assumption in the standardization is that English (and the logic implied by the use of

English) will be used *internally* to seek solutions to problems. We do not yet know what happens when Urdu, Jamaica dialect or Swahili is the subvocal language. We know, however, that many languages do not have specific equivalents for either directional prepositions or such words as 'square', 'triangle', 'fulcrum' or 'junction box'. This covert assumption that verbalization will take place in English is built into test standardization, and is an example of the superordinate social value control system that regulates *implicit* culture-content in testing. By ignoring the implications of such sources of culture-content one commits just as great a fallacy as when one ignores *explicit* examples of culture-content in tests, shown in questions involving, for example, knowledge of seasons, snow, English idiom or rules of the road.

Fallacies in using test scores cross-culturally

We turn now from test content to test use. Assuming one knows what one has when a test has been applied, the question remains as to how to use it. Briefly, my discussion on content looks first at the case of the wrong answer; then at the use of cut-offs and averages. Finally, I raise the problem of test content again in another guise, the spectre on this occasion being the unresolved issue of psychological *equivalence* of test scores.

The wrong answer

All cognitive tests of a 'closed' nature have right and wrong answers. The rightness of a response is usually decided technically by its closeness of agreement with the overall test score itself – an internal criterion – or by its agreement with a score from another independent measure with which one wishes to compare a single sample or item. Classical test theory has taught us to reject, in the first try-out of any test, those items that do not meet established test criteria either internal or external. Our experience with wrong answers (see especially Irvine, 1969b, and Schwarz, 1963) indicates to us that the use of tests across cultures in industrial situations is liable to call not for a rejection out of hand of wrong answers, but a re-examination of answers in case the 'wrong' answer has an equal or better correlation for a different culture with the test score than what is considered to be the correct answer. For a little-publicized but highly appropriate study, in which the virtues of the term 'stencil' (referring to the use of a hand-scoring key) answer may be seen over the use of the term 'correct' answer, McElwaine's (1963) report to the International Labour Office is mandatory reading. The evidence is so strong that a principle may be stated. *When tests are being used with members of an ethnic minority group, the first protocols should be subjected to rigorous scrutiny, involving a re-standardiza-*

tion if necessary. This seems to be a basic principle that emerges logically from the evidence accumulated over the past twenty years. And this principle takes precedence over the seven other principles of test administration listed below. In summary, a 'wrong' answer may certainly indicate a cultural difference from the original test standardization. That evidence, however, may or may not relate to the abilities sampled in the test. The test user must prove that the responses (particularly in multiple-choice questions) give no additional information than would be given by simply recording a 'wrong answer'. Otherwise, he may inadvertently discard information that could, in industry and commerce specifically, lead to a correct hiring decision.

Cut-offs and averages

The major problem of interpreting test results from minority or alien ethnic groups takes the discussion one step further. Personnel selection can be unfair if persons administering the tests assume that such results can be interpreted *as if* they came from the parent culture. The *use* of the test score is, in effect, an extension of the content-meaning problem. One is assuming that high or low test scores in one culture have the same relationship to job performance as high or low test scores in another culture, *for whatever reason*. There is, of course, some justification for the argument that as long as a selection device does its job in relation to work performance then the ethnic identity of the applicant is irrelevant. When the ethnic identity of the applicant itself gives grounds for believing that the test-criterion relationship will change, however, the argument falls away. Perhaps it is better to check that the selection devices do operate in the same way from culture to culture.

For example, most screening devices operate on a cut-off basis. If the relation between ultimate performance and the selection device is such that high scorers do well on the job and low scorers do poorly, then low scorers have a low probability of success and are rejected. But if the situation were reversed and low scorers on the selection battery did well on the job, then low scorers would be employed. The point is that low scores *per se* are no justification for rejection. Only if the relationship between the selection device and the criterion justifies rejection on a low score does the low score have meaning.

It has often been said that immigrant groups, *on the average*, perform less well than British groups on standardized tests. Some reasons for this have already been hinted at. But one has seldom seen the piece of evidence that would *logically* (defined as inference from current test theory) allow a low score from an immigrant to be interpreted as evidence of unsuitability for employment. Such evidence would have to be that the scores of immigrant groups on a selection battery bear the same relation to their performance scores as British scores do. And the literature does contain evidence to show that different relationships among selection tests and between those tests and the later job performance exists. Lopez (1966), for example, shows that in applying tests to Negro and white toll collectors, the correlation was $+0.39$ with criterion performance for Negroes and -0.24 for whites. In other words, a high score on the screening battery would mean acceptance of Negroes but rejection of whites. This is an extreme example, but the onus on firms and institutions using selection devices is to show that they operate in exactly the same way for immigrants and minorities as they do for the native work population. Otherwise, they may inadvertently be discriminating in their hiring practices, whatever their declared policy, simply through not verifying their assumptions.

The 'same score'

Let us consider another aspect of interpreting test scores. What guarantee is there that the 'same score' on the same test *means* the same for persons from different ethnic groups? Take, for example, the score from an omnibus test of non-verbal intelligence, or a reading comprehension test. In the previous section it was shown that the same score could have different meaning in relation to a particular criterion. Suppose, however, we examine the problem of psychological equivalence. For a much fuller discussion of this issue see Irvine (1970), and Irvine and Sanders (1971).

A simple illustration, from recent work in Africa, points out how easy it is for test items to alter their meaning when applied in another culture. One of the important criteria for test construction is that the relative difficulty of items in a test should be constant across different random or representative samples from the same population. One can test this by inter-correlating the item difficulties for a single test from a number of sub-samples. Table 1 below shows the results of correlating item difficulties on a fifty-item reading comprehension test. The difficulties were derived from the required minimum of two American groups of first and second grade children (ages 6 and 7) and two Nigerian groups of grade five (10 years old) children.

Table 1 **Intercorrelation matrix of item difficulties** (N $=$ 50)

	White 1	White 2	Black 1	Black 2
White 1	—	98	54	60
White 2		—	59	65
Black 1			—	96
Black 2				—

The results show that agreement between the order of item difficulties is almost perfect – as one would expect of a well-constructed test – within the two white groups and also within the two black groups. But between the pairs of ethnic groups the order of item difficulties changes substantially. Further, the *average* scores of the black and white groups were found to be very close. But this did not mean that the scores of Nigerian children were made up from the same set of easy or difficult items as the American children. Nigerian children, on the whole, found the same items as easy or difficult as other Nigerians. American children likewise tended to pass or fail a particular set of items for any given score. But the probability of the same score, particularly around the average, being made up from the same set of items in *both* cultures was much more remote. The reason was presumably that children from the two different cultures perceived them differently and reacted to them in different ways.

Intelligence tests and reading tests usually sample a number of psychological processes. Mechanical information and dexterity tests are likewise complex. The more heterogeneous a test is in its demands on processes, the more liable it is to change its meaning in other cultures. By this we mean that the mental processes that the logic of constructs compels us to assume to be necessary for problem-solving in any one culture may indeed be identical for any other. On the other hand, they may be different for any one problem, depending, for individuals, on the nature and rate of conceptual development: and for groups, on the common directing influence of the socially inherited value system. The dilemma facing the well-meaning industrial user of tests is fairly evident. Even if he derives two identical scores from members of different ethnic groups, he has little guarantee that they are psychologically equivalent. For some extremely sensitive group situations, or highly technical man–machine interaction systems, psychological equivalence may be a *sine qua non*. Although our technology cannot guarantee equivalence, at least we are able to minimize gross non-equivalence through controlling more strictly group testing conditions. Some advice on how to do this is given later on in this chapter.

Perhaps also it is time that we actively considered verbalization of test protocols with at least *some* applicants as the closest we can get to verifying the processes they use to arrive at answers. It is at present the best because it is the only one known to us that we have.

The criterion problem

If tests are used in industry and commerce, it is because they have something in common with work performance. They function as screening devices that will either (a) indicate aptitude for training, or (b) aptitude for the job where no training is necessary or possible. If, for any reason, the meaning of the test changes or, alternatively, the meaning of job performance changes, e.g. by the introduction of a new production layout or a new supervisor with a different approach to man management, or both test and criteria change in an unrelated fashion, then the selection of personnel by tests becomes, at best, an uncontrolled hazard. Criterion stability becomes as important an issue as test stability, if one wants any man, irrespective of social or cultural origins, to have an equal probability of success on the job. And this is the second essential for fair industrial practice.

When one looks closely at assessment of competence on the job, there appear to be output or production criteria that can be assessed on an assembly line. Output on a given machine over a given period seems as objective a criterion as one could wish for. It assumes, however, a one-to-one relationship between the product and man–machine interaction. When assembly lines are team operations and the production of one man is either a function of a team acting in concert with him at the same time or of the production of someone who feeds him components which are then refined, adjusted or fitted, then the problem becomes more difficult. In such situations, where ethnic groups are homogeneous, output can, and often does, become a function of likes and dislikes, harmony or conflict. If a production line or office environment is ethnically diverse, then the possibility of criterion measures being invalidated by covert psychological factors, not directly measured by the production criterion, is increased.

If the criterion is a graduated scale of assessment by supervisors, then similarly one would have to be certain that the criterion gave equal probability of success to anyone in an inter-cultural environment. One would have to make sure that assessments of efficiency were not a function of ethnocentrism on the one hand or, just as important, the conversion of unconscious prejudice into over-compensation in the assessment of people from ethnic or cultural minorities.

The research, in this delicate area, is more lacking than evident. However, two examples from Africa may be helpful. In a Central African survey of educational aptitude (Irvine, 1964), some primary schools and most secondary schools had both African and European teachers teaching the same groups of African students. When teachers' estimates were asked for as a criterion with which to relate experimental tests, we found that African teachers consistently over-estimated potential, and European teachers were much less generous in their assessments. Nevertheless, scaling the estimates removed the inherent mean differences between teachers. The study showed that both European and African teachers *ordered* the students on a set of criteria in a valid way. In this sense, the students themselves represented a kind of scale – top to bottom – that was more absolute than relative within the closed circuit of the classroom.

Experienced African and European teachers could point out individual differences accurately. However, when a numerical value was placed on the performance of each individual within the wider context of potential for long-term success, the measures took on an unreliability that reduced their effectiveness. This unreliability lay not in the ordering of individuals, but in assessing a numerical value for each. Once again, the numerical value, or grade – A, B, C, etc. – would have been misleading. But the judgements of rank order were stable and worthwhile measures over the long term.

On the other hand, industry and commerce seldom present the closed, 'captive' environment of the school. Because of this, criterion specification becomes much more crucial. In a national survey of the use of aptitude tests in pre-independent Zambia (Irvine, McArthur and Brimble, 1964), the criterion problem in cross-ethnic comparisons in both the mining industry and in the public service was acute. Criteria were inadequate and the paper and pencil aptitude tests as a consequence showed little promise in such situations at that time. Although the assessments were usually those of white supervisors, they also included reports from Africans in supervisory roles. There was nothing to suggest that the assessments were any worse, or any better, for being given either within ethnic groups or across ethnic groups.

To sum up, there are just as many pitfalls in the criterion situation as there are in the tests themselves. The opportunities for inadvertent discrimination in assessing work performance are perhaps even greater. Personnel selection cannot take place without giving as careful study to criteria as is normally given to tests. And one cannot blame tests for not relating effectively to faulty criteria.

Some positive safeguards
Group test administration

One might consider, in the light of the material presented above, that personnel selection in industry and commerce presents, when the cultural background of applicants is a significant variable, a pessimistic prospect. And indeed, without the knowledge at our disposal, urging restraint and further work, it is pessimistic. Yet, just as there is research that has cautioned against unguarded uses of tests in other cultures, so there is a significant body of work that, in the last decade, has indicated how to overcome some of the difficulties associated with their use.

It is indeed true to say that the last ten years of psychological research in developing countries has shown significant advances in the use and development of tests in non-Western cultures. The lessons that have been learned in those cultures can with profit be used in modern industrial and commercial settings where a significant number of applicants have diverse ethnic backgrounds. Although in my view the state of the science is not even near a theory of abilities that would help us solve many of our testing problems, the major technological difficulties that stand in the way of useful empirical research are slowly being removed, so that advances are being logged with increasing experience in the field.

Briefly, the basic research has shown that, when Western criteria of performance are applied, tests can be adopted and constructed for cultural groups in such a way that their results will not be distorted and that, *within each cultural group*, good validities with the criterion can result. The key to the solution of many problems lies, for the most part, in communicating to the people taking the test the nature and purpose of the test. Test format and test presentation are crucial.

A number of researchers, notably Schwarz (1963), Silvey (1963), Irvine (1966) and Vernon (1969) have demonstrated or synthesized sets of principles for test presentation that are necessary safeguards in personnel selection. Some of these principles are produced here as aids to the construction of tests for use in intercultural settings.

1. Every test response must be learned. No assumption should be made about a person's ability to respond in the manner required by the test. Both test materials and methods of recording answers must be fully understood.

2. Often, in other cultures, the instruction not to turn back to previous tests is bewildering and distressing to the people taking the test. Hence, omnibus test booklets are undesirable. Each test should be separate from every other and should be accompanied by its own instructions.

3. Instructions should be oral, not written, since the ability to read instructions is not part of the test situation. Flexible visual aids should demonstrate each type of test item and response, preferably by building up the components through the use of plastigraph or flannelgraph – techniques that allow cut-outs to be stuck to boards so that a large class can see.

4. If translations for test instructions are necessary, these should not be literal. They should be idiomatic expressions of the intent of the test demonstrator, who ideally should be from the same ethnic group as those taking the test. This will reduce the possibility of extraneous motivational influences on test scores.

5. Supervised practice for each test is essential to make certain that test instructions have been understood.

6. Familiar test material should be given first, so that early attempts at recording answers in a certain way are the only unfamiliar element. As recording answers becomes more automatic, unusual or abstract materials can be presented.

7. The climate of testing must be as convivial and dramatic and enjoyable as possible. Fully trained testers should employ every strategy to make the situation positively reinforcing and cheerful.

These seven principles are important because they try to ensure that the test will measure what it is supposed to measure, and not the ability of the person taking the test to obey a number of complex, written instructions that are characteristic of modern group tests. If these rules are not applied, then other sources of variance will most probably confound the test score with adverse results generally, but especially when a narrow spectrum test of a specific skill is involved, as indeed is often the case in industrial and commercial settings.

Before I proceed to the next section on individual and performance tests, it is perhaps appropriate to draw the reader's attention to the most significant of recent reviews of the state of personnel selection in developing countries – the paper by Ord (1971b). Reading of it is recommended in order to put the suggestions that have been listed into their proper technical context in a depth that is not possible here.

Critical incidents and individual tests

A second aspect of testing might very well concern the use of individual performance tests. Macdonald (1944–45), and Biesheuvel (1952), were pioneers in the development of performance tests across cultures. Further more recent advances in performance tests have come out of Australia and New Guinea and the South Pacific (see Ord, 1971a). The pioneers and the recent workers in this field found that, just as in group tests, the problem was to tell or communicate to the applicant what it was that he had to do. Understandably, their early work was largely concerned with untrained and relatively unskilled labour. If skilled labour applies for employment, there seems to be some justification for employing the 'critical incident' technique to construct meaningful performance tests.

This technique is based on finding from a large range of behaviours in a complex task a much smaller number (one, ideally) of tasks that will sample that range of behaviour effectively. It is perhaps best represented by the statement, 'It is difficult to conceive of a man as an x unless he can do y'. For example, a man could hardly say he was a plumber unless he could joint and seal copper tubing. Similarly, a man who says he is an electrician might be of no use to an employer unless he could decode coloured wiring diagrams and link up terminals effectively. In both cases a 'critical incident' would be that which effectively sampled the range of behaviours required on the job. Such an incident would be the basis of first screening or selection. This is not the omnibus 'trade-test'. It is a carefully derived and scientifically controlled sampling of the skills likely to be used on the job.

Clearly, this approach seems to be very promising when applicants from other countries apply for employment. Critical incidents may be derived from any number of careful job analyses. Performance of them, overseen by testers proficient in the language of the job applicant would at least establish the basic qualifications of the applicant. The reader will note that language is here considered a separate issue – and this can be considered next.

Problems of communication on the shop floor are not new; they are only made worse when there is more than one language to be contended with. Employing the 'critical incident' technique once more, it seems that communicating and using effectively the language of the work environment are crucial for the supervisor or team leader. When work groups are mixed, and the language used is either not English, or an abbreviated form of English, then all workers should be able to comprehend, or learn through listening to it, that work language. But the *use* of that language may not present a critical criterion for employment except in the very important intercalary positions between management and worker. I am reminded of a story by a colleague who witnessed work in a Boston bakery. The languages of the workers employed in the bakery were so diverse that none of the workers could talk to any other worker but the bakery was efficient because of an empathy built up through detailed knowledge of the job requirements, the relatively small number of components in the final product, and the simplicity of the process. Verbal communication was unnecessary. Interpersonal communication by gesture, expression, demonstration and eye contact was, however, manifest. Although this example reminds us of the kind of situation in which the lack of language should not be mistaken for lack of effective communication, it must be admitted that for most workers, the ability to understand and act on the *oral* instructions given in the working situation is necessary.

Taped tests of listening comprehension may be helpful diagnostic devices in allocation to special training programmes – either for the native-born worker who is required to work in a foreign language or dialect environment or the immigrant who has to work in an English-speaking group. Industry and commerce has, on the whole, tended to test recruits in written and reading comprehension while little attempt has been made to analyse the oral language through which instructions are passed on. Tests of listening comprehension are much more realistic, and, applied to all workers, more fair than language usage tests. They tacitly recognize that a man's passive vocabulary is much more extensive and relevant to the work situation than his active vocabulary.

Perhaps it is now time for personnel selection to recognize this well-known psychological phenomenon operationally in inter-ethnic work situations, by devising appropriate screening devices.

Finally, the employer has to decide whether, for any man, the technical skills are more important, equally important or less important in any one job than communication skills. If they are more important, then alterations in language environment may be necessary to accommodate those skills if they come from overseas. If equally important, training programmes to eradicate language problems are needed so that technical skills may not be diluted. If less important, then some sacrifice in technical efficiency will have to be tolerated if language is crucial. I cannot prescribe here, but decision theory may help to find the correct answers to a local problem. Selection tests themselves will not provide an answer.

Conclusions

This brief, and, in retrospect, general essay into the problem of testing in industrial settings where ethnicity is a factor, shows that solutions can be found. They will not be found without investment and skilled personnel and the wish on the part of the employer to adopt a non-restrictive policy. However, tests are only as good as their users. In the hands of even well-intentioned users they may accidentally exclude workers on account of their cultural backgrounds. Recent research indicates how complex the problem is and, indeed, how well worth while, socially, the unravelling of these complexities may be in a world where ethno-homogeneity is seldom a viable assumption of the work situation.

References

BIESHEUVEL, S. (1952). 'Personnel selection tests for Africans', *South African Journal of Science*, vol. 49, pp. 3–12.

GUION. R. M. (1966) 'Employment tests and discriminatory hiring', *Industrial Relations*, vol. 5, pp. 20–37.

IRVINE, S. H. (1964), 'Selection of Africans for post-primary education in Southern Rhodesia: pilot survey', *Bulletin of the Inter-African Labour Institute*, vol. 11. pp. 69–93.

IRVINE, S. H. (1966), 'Towards a rationale for testing attainments and abilities in Africa', *British Journal of Educational Psychology*, vol. 36, pp. 24–32.

IRVINE, S. H. (1969a), 'Figural tests of reasoning in Africa', *International Journal of Psychology*, vol. 4, pp. 217–28.

IRVINE, S. H. (1969b), 'Culture and mental ability', *New Scientist*, vol. 42, pp. 230–31.

IRVINE, S. H. (1970), 'Affect and construct: a cross-cultural check on theories of intelligence', *Journal of Social Psychology*, vol. 80, pp. 23–80.

IRVINE, S. H., MCARTHUR. R. S., and BRIMBLE, A. R. (1964), *The Northern Rhodesia Mental Ability Survey*, Institute for Social Research, Zambia.

IRVINE, S. H., and SANDERS, J. T. (1971), 'Logic, language and method in construct identification across cultures', paper delivered at the *NATO Scientific Conference on Cross-Cultural Testing*, Istanbul, Turkey.

LOPEZ, F. M. (1966), 'Current problems in test performance of job applicants: 1', *Personnel Psychology*, vol. 19, pp. 139–51.

MACDONALD, A. (1944–45), *Selection of African Personnel*, Reports of the work of the Personnel, Technical and Research Unit, Middle East Force, Ministry of Defence Archives, London.

MCELWAINE, D. G. (1963), *Report to the Government of India on an Aptitude Testing Programme for the Selection of Trainees for Industrial Training Institutes*, International Labour Organization Geneva, no. S.F. 0/33/B.

ORD, I. G. (1971a), *Mental Tests for Pre-Literates*, Ginn & Co.

ORD, I. G. (1971b), 'Educational and occupational selection in developing countries: a review', working paper for Symposium 22 of the 17th International Congress of Applied Psychology, Liege, 25–30 July, *University of Waikato*.

SCHWARZ, P. A. (1963), 'Adapting tests to the cultural setting', *Educational and Psychological Measurement*, vol. 23, pp. 673–86.

SILVEY, J. (1963), 'Aptitude testing and educational selection in Africa' *Rhodes Livingstone Journal*, vol. 34, pp. 9–22.

VERNON, P. E. (1969), *Intelligence and Cultural Environment*, Methuen.

Acknowledgements

Permission to reproduce the following readings in this volume is
acknowledged to the following sources:

5 Harper & Row Inc.
6 Harper & Row Inc.
7 Holt, Rinehart & Winston Inc.

Author Index

Aberbach, J. D., 159
Aberle, D. F., 314
Abner, E. V., 269
Abrams, M., 48
Adam, H., 293
Adams, W., 421
Adorno, T. W., 38, 59, 62, 65, 89, 251, 311
Aguilar, J. V., 394
Ahrenfeldt, R. H., 438, 449
Albee, E., 322
Alger, H., 322
Allen, H., 258, 389
Allen, S., 295-6
Alleyne, M. H., 348
Allport, G. W., 23, 36, 37, 39, 46, 48, 80, 116, 117, 118, 140, 180
Amir, Y., 118
Anthony, E., 157
Antonovsky, A., 219
Apter, D. E., 408
Ardrey, R., 78
Arendt, H., 71
Aronson, E., 137
Asher, J. J., 400
Atchison, C. O., 262, 263, 264
Athey, K. R., 273
Ausubel, D. P., 193, 197, 198, 201, 377-8
Ausubel, P., 193, 197, 198, 201, 377-8
Axelson, L. J., 261
Axline, V. M., 140

Bagley, C., 437-8, 449
Baldwin, J., 282
Banton, M., 85
Baratz, S. S., 275
Baron, H., 388
Baron, S. W., 407
Bartlett, F. C., 77
Battle, E., 381
Baumrind, D., 68
Beaglehole, E., 327
Beck, D. F., 140
Beijer, G., 226, 230
Bell, D., 436

Belson, W. A., 443
Benjamin, L., 257
Bennis, W., 73
Bereiter, C., 394
Berger, M., 140
Berghe, P. L. van den see Van den Berghe, P. L.
Bernard, J., 202
Bernstein, B., 394
Bettelheim, B., 48, 137, 203, 289, 378
Betty, C., 356
Bevan, W., 83
Beynon, E. D., 436, 445
Bhatnagar, J. K., 226, 234, 236
Bhatt, S., 88
Biesheuvel, S., 468
Bird, C., 38
Blake, R., 34
Blalock, H. M., 286, 290
Blau, P., 293-4, 304
Bloom, B., 343
Bloombaum, M., 253, 276, 279
Blumenbach, H., 360
Blumer, H., 145, 291-2
Bogardus, E., 51
Boroffka, A., 419
Bottoms, A. E., 432, 437, 439, 440
Bowen, D. R., 447
Boyd, G. F., 192, 360
Boyer, L. B., 421
Braly, K. W., 311
Breed, W., 145
Bressler, M., 115
Briggs, W., 132
Brimble, A. R., 461
Brinton, C., 161
Broderick, F. L., 154, 157
Brody, E., 420
Bronfenbrenner, U., 378
Broom, L., 217
Brown, B., 186, 200, 203-4, 383-4
Brown, R., 59, 63, 317
Brunswik, E. Frenkel see Frenkel-Brunswik, E.
Bull, W. E., 396
Bullough, B., 124

Burdick, H., 38
Burgin, T., 354
Burma, J. H., 268
Burney, E., 300

Calden, G., 280
Caldwell, M. G., 280
Campbell, A., 306
Campbell, D. T., 244, 318–19
Campbell, E., 103, 126
Campbell, J., 87, 125, 126, 272
Canady, H. G., 274, 372
Cantril, H., 270, 273
Carmichael, S., 154, 157, 159
Carothers, J. C., 419
Carroll, J. B., 400
Carthy, J. D., 78
Cartwright, D., 317
Cattell, R. B., 445
Cayton, H. R., 198
Chambliss, W. J., 443
Chance, N., 417, 420
Chattergee, B. B., 62
Chaudhuri, N. C., 407
Chein, I., 102, 103, 207
Chethick, M., 28
Chomsky, N., 394
Churchman, C. W., 44
Clark, K. B., 24, 26, 27, 29, 40, 88, 182, 184, 185, 202, 320, 385
Clark, M. P., 24, 26, 27, 29, 88, 182, 184, 185, 202
Cleaver, E., 157, 170
Clough, S. B., 410
Cloward, R. A., 384
Cobbs, P. M., 138
Cohen, M., 258
Cohen, O., 98
Cohn, N., 65
Coleman, C. E., 273
Coleman, J. S., 167, 170, 200, 256, 260, 278, 381, 384, 386, 388–9
Coles, R., 28, 126, 136–7, 184, 185, 189
Collins, M. E., 122, 123, 124
Colombotos, J., 147
Comstock, C., 57, 70

Converse, P. E., 180
Cook, S. W., 119, 123, 124
Cooper, E., 111
Cooper, J. M., 429
Cooper, R. M., 369
Coser, L., 148
Cottingham, S., 275
Cox, K., 269
Crandall, V. C., 381
Crandall, V. J., 381
Cressey, D. 139, 432, 434
Cressey, P. F., 216
Criswell, J. H., 35
Cross, H. J., 449
Cuber, J., 216

Dalfiume, R. M., 145
Danelski, J., 147
Darcy, N., 395
Das Gupta, J., 411
Davidson, H. H., 204
Davidson, K. S., 368, 380, 382
Davies, J. C., 161
Davis, A., 343
Davis, C. H., 196
Davis, E. E., 249, 269
Davis, F. B., 400
Davis, H., 28, 31, 181
Davis, K. E., 91
Dean, T., 334–5
Dennis, W., 34
Desrosiers, M., 429
Deutsch, K. W., 405, 407, 408, 409
Deutsch, M., 122, 123, 124, 186, 188, 194, 195, 200, 201, 353, 383–4
De Vos, G., 449
Dickens, C., 43
Dickson, L., 35
Dillehay, R. C., 59, 62, 251
Doczy, A. G., 227, 228
Dodson, D., 98
Domhoff, G. W., 323
Domnitz, M., 354
Drake, St. C., 188–9, 196, 197, 198
Dreger, R. M., 271

Du Bois, W., 282
Duncan, O. D., 293, 294, 304

Ebling, F. J., 78
Edmunds, E., 105
Edson, P., 354
Edwards, H., 154
Edwards, L. P., 161
Eilson, W. C., 34
Eisenberg, W., 165
Eisenman, R., 129
Eisenstadt, S. N., 226, 232, 235, 236
Elkins, S., 104
Ellison, R., 282
Empey, L., 139
Englemann, S., 394
Epps, E. G., 261, 262, 263, 264, 442
Erikson, E. H., 199, 271, 278, 282, 325
Ex, J., 236
Exner, J. E., 270
Eysenck, H. J., 362, 444, 445
Eysenck, S. B. G., 445

Fanon, F., 170, 180
Faris, R., 145
Faulkner, W., 152
Feld, S., 382, 384
Feldman, D., 69
Ferguson, C. A., 411
Ferracuti, F., 432, 441, 442
Ferron, O., 330
Festinger, L., 231, 317
Field, M. J., 419
Fine, M., 151
Fineberg, S. A., 130-31
Fink, C. F., 148
Fischer, J., 352
Fishman, A., 395
Fishman, J. A., 403, 410, 411, 412
Fleming, E., 28
Flowerman, S. H., 111, 113
Fodor, J. A., 394
Forrester, B. J., 274
Foster, C. C., 136
Frank, L. K., 137
Frazier, E. F., 198, 216

Frazier, T. R., 164
Freedman, M. B., 69
Freedman, P. I., 273
French, J. R. P., 116
Frenkel-Brunswik, E., 34, 38, 59, 62, 68-9, 89, 251
Freud, S., 79
Friedenberg, E. Z., 70
Friederich, C. J., 406
Friedman, S., 149
Frijda, N. H., 226, 230
Fromm, E., 62, 320
Fusco, G., 355

Gage, N. L., 62
Galanter, E., 394
Gardner, R. C., 84, 396, 398, 399
Geber, M., 334-5
Geer, J. P. van de see Van de Geer, J. P.
Geertz, C., 167
Gellner, E., 404, 405
Gergen, K. J., 86
Gibbens, T. C. N., 438, 449
Glenn, N. D., 217
Glock, C., 64
Goffman, E., 267, 269
Gold, M., 443
Goldberg, M. M., 217
Goldhamer, H., 217
Goldman, R., 343, 345, 346, 347, 351, 352, 354, 357
Goldston, A., 257
Golovensky, D. I., 217
Goodman, M. E,. 24, 26, 28, 29, 88, 181, 182, 185
Gordon, M. M., 216, 238
Gottesman, I., 361, 363, 364
Gough, H. G., 38, 68
Gove, W. R., 140
Grambs, J. D., 189, 199, 201-2, 203
Graubard, S. G., 320
Graves, M., 195
Green, A. W., 218-19
Greenbaum, C., 258, 261
Greifer, J. L., 216
Grier, W. H., 138

Grigg, C., 105
Grimshaw, A. D., 305
Grindstaff, C. F., 161
Grossack, M., 207
Guion, R. M., 453
Guttman, L., 53–4, 106, 162

Hadden, R., 440
Haimowitz, M., 140
Haimowitz, N., 140
Hallowell, I., 417, 420
Hamilton, C. V., 154, 159
Hammer, E. F., 379
Hammet, P. J., 220
Hampshire, S., 394
Harary, F., 317
Harding, J., 33
Harrell, R. F., 366
Harris, D. B., 38, 68
Hartley, E. L., 30, 116, 122, 181
Hartman, A., 269
Hattem, J., 276, 279
Haugen, E., 411, 413
Heider, F., 317
Heine, R. W., 421
Henchy, T., 258, 389
Hepple, B., 295
Hersey, J., 70–71
Hess, R., 343, 390
Heyd, U., 413
Higgin, G. W., 73
Hill, K. T., 270, 382, 383
Himmelfarb, M., 151
Hoch, E., 417
Hodge, R. W., 289
Hofstede, B. P., 226, 230
Hokansen, J. E., 280
Hollingshead, A. B., 191, 277, 281
Holmes, R., 85
Hope, J., 295
Hopkins, T. K., 408
Horkheimer, M., 62
Horowitz, E. L., 24, 34, 37, 39, 205
Horowitz, I. L., 448
Horowitz, R. E., 37

Horst, S. T. L. van der see Van der Horst, S. T. L.
Horton, J., 448
Hoselitz, B., 418
Hsien, R., 417, 420
Hughes, L., 152
Hummel, D., 132
Hung-Ming, C., 417, 420
Hunt, J. McV., 365
Huntley, C., 152
Hyman, H. H., 50

Inglehart, R. F., 405
Inkeles, A., 384
Irvine, S. H., 453, 455, 456, 458, 460, 461, 462
Isaacs, H., 165

Jackson, D., 390
Jackson, M. M., 133
Jackson, V., 390
Jaco, E. G., 420
Jacobson, A., 232
Jacobson, L., 132–3, 204, 368, 385
Jacobson, N., 352
Jahoda, G., 32, 33, 36, 86, 87, 88
Jahoda, M., 111, 298
James, J. C., 276, 279
Janowitz, M., 48, 203, 289
Jaspars, J. M. F., 87
Jeffries, V., 120
Jensen, A., 364, 371–3, 374
Jernudd, B., 413
Johnson, B. C., 29, 182
Johnson, C. S., 183, 193
Johnson, D., 421
Johnson, N., 87, 88
Johnson, R., 219
Jones, E. E., 91
Jones, J. A., 384
Jones, R. S., 200
Jowell, R., 43

Kamii, C. K., 383
Kanzer, P., 389

Kaplan, A., 44
Kaplan, B., 421
Kardiner, A., 188, 189, 198
Karemzadeh, F., 408
Karne, G., 421
Karno, M., 276
Karon, B. P., 380
Katkovsky, W., 381
Katz, B., 83
Katz, D., 103, 311
Katz, I., 121, 205, 241, 257–65, 274–5,
    277–8, 350, 367, 368, 373, 374, 377,
    380, 382, 386–8, 389
Kawwa, T., 35, 40, 345
Kecskemeti, P., 317
Kedourie, E., 406
Kagan, J., 368
Kellaghan, T., 397
Kendall, P., 111
Kendell, P. L., 224
Kennedy, W. A., 274
Kent, D. P., 227
Kerckhoff, A. C., 216, 220
Kerner, O., 320, 447
Kerr, M., 337
Kiev, A., 276, 343, 416, 420, 421, 422,
    426, 429
Killian, L., 105
King, M. L., 165
Kirk, S. A., 365
Kirscht, J. P., 59, 62, 251
Klaus, R. A., 274
Kleiner, R. J., 189–90
Kline, P., 445
Klineberg, O., 32, 59, 133, 352,
    370
Kloss, H., 396, 412
Kluckhohn, C., 315, 316
Kluckhohn, F. R., 104, 314
Knobloch, H., 272, 374
Koblitz, M. W., 133
Koch, H. L., 34
Kohn, H., 406, 408
Kosa, J., 232, 233
Kramer, B. M., 37
Krausz, E., 217

Krupinski, J., 232
Kuper L., 164
Kutner, B., 34, 36, 47, 287

La Crosse, L., 274
Lambert, J., 437, 439, 440, 447
Lambert, R. D., 115
Lambert, W. E., 32, 395, 396, 398, 399,
    400
Landreth, C., 29, 182
Lang, G., 204
La Piere, R. T., 47, 287
Lasker, B., 24, 36
Lauwerys, A. J., 355
Lederman, S., 349
Lees, H., 165
Leighton, A. H., 419
Lerner, D., 404, 407
Lester, J., 154
Le Vine, R. A., 251, 318–19
Levinson, D. J., 38, 59, 61, 66, 89, 102,
    103, 251
Lévi-Strauss, C., 77
Levitt, E. E., 68, 269
Lewin, K., 131, 207
Lewis, A., 152
Lewis, J., 382, 384
Lewis, O., 320, 422, 446
Lewit, D. W., 221
Lieberson, S., 305
Liebowitz, M., 448
Lighthall, F. F., 380, 382
Likert, R., 52, 55
Lincoln, C. E., 165
Linn, L. S., 249, 287–8
Lippitt, R., 117, 139
Lockard, D., 302
Loeb, M. B., 232
Lomax, L., 165
Lopez, F. M., 458
Lorenz, K., 78
Lott, A. J., 194–5
Lott, B. E., 194–5
Lundberg, G. A., 35
Lunt, H. G., 413
Lyle, W. H., 68

Maas, J., 276, 279, 280
McArthur, R. S., 461
McClelland, D. C., 170, 190, 378
McClintock, C., 103
McClintock, F. H., 437–8
Maccoby, E., 116, 446
McCormick, T. C., 216, 220
McCoy, J. N., 28
Macdonald, A., 463
McElwaine, D. G., 456
McEntire, D., 297–8
McEwan, P. J. M., 236
McGill, R., 165
McGinnies, E., 134
MacIver, R. M., 105, 109
McKee, J., 104
MacKenzie, B. K., 121
McKinley, D. G., 201
Macnamara, J., 393, 395, 397
McPartland, J., 386
McWilliams, C., 115
Major, C., 268, 269
Malcolm X, 323
Malherbe, E. G., 395
Mann, J. W., 121, 213, 218, 220
Marcus, L., 133
Marcuse, H., 312, 314, 324
Marinho, A. A., 419
Marrow, A. J., 116
Martin, W. E., 38, 68
Masling, J., 271
Maslow, A. H., 62, 229
Mason, P., 313
Masotti, L. H., 447
Matthews, D. R., 106
May, M., 66
Mayer, A. J., 297
Mayer, M. F., 28
Mayhew, L. H., 149
Mead, M., 322
Meier, A., 154, 156, 157, 165
Menges, L. J., 232
Merton, R. K., 100, 101, 102, 103, 224,
    287, 447
Mezei, L., 248
Middleton, R., 113, 268

Midlarsky, M., 161
Mill, J. S., 99
Miller, D., 299
Miller, G. A., 393, 394, 398
Miller, J., 37
Miller, K. S., 271
Miller, L., 152
Mills, C. W., 167
Milner, D., 88
Minogue, K. R., 406
Mitchell, G., 165
Mittnick, I., 134
Mizushima, K., 449
Molotch, H., 119, 299
Monachesi, E. D., 38
Moore, B., 168
Moore, R., 300, 446
Moore, W. E., 419
Moreno, J. L., 35
Morland, J. K., 25, 26, 27, 28, 36, 88,
    181, 182, 185
Morris, D., 78
Morris, P., 437
Moses, E. R., 435
Mosher, D. L., 38
Motz, A., 113
Moynihan, T. P., 378
Murphy, G. E., 200
Murray, H., 73
Murray, W., 193, 196
Mussen, P. H., 127, 188, 191, 379
Myrdal, G., 105, 106, 108, 322,
    409

Nagasawa, R. H., 443
Nassiakou, M., 248
Nemeth, C., 87, 88
Newcomb, T. M., 69, 116, 122, 180,
    317
Newton, H., 159
Newton, P., 176, 384
Noar, G., 132
Noel, D. L., 207, 251
Noel, J., 64
Norburn, V., 23
Norman, R., 317

Ødergaard, O., 233, 419
Ogilvie, D. H., 136
Olsen, M. E., 106
Olton, R., 396, 398, 399
Opler, M. K., 421
Oppenheimer, P., 170
Ord, I. G., 463
Osborn, R. T., 369, 371
Osgood, C. E., 54, 317
Ovesey, L., 188, 189, 198

Palermo, D. S., 188
Park, R. E., 213–14, 215, 216, 219, 220
Parker, S., 189–90
Parsons, T., 314, 426
Pasamanick, B., 272, 374
Passow, A. H., 344, 346, 352
Patterson, S., 295
Peabody, D., 62
Peace, W., 165
Peal, E., 395
Perry, A., 262, 263, 264
Peterson, R. C., 112
Pettigrew, T. F., 89–90, 127–9, 188,
    197, 199–200, 206, 273, 274, 281, 305,
    320, 350, 365–70, 374, 378, 386
Piaget, J., 31, 32, 85
Pidal, R. M., 410
Pinkney, A., 100, 252
Pollack, A. B., 73
Porter, J., 26, 29
Postman, L., 116
Preston, A., 381
Pribram, K. H., 394
Price, D. O., 273, 274, 374
Proshansky, H., 176, 180, 202, 367, 384
Prothro, J. W., 106
Proudfoot, M., 165
Pushkin, I., 23, 27, 28–9, 33, 36, 38, 39

Rabow, J., 139
Radke, M. J., 28, 31, 117, 181, 182, 183,
    184, 185, 205
Radke-Yarrow, M. see Yarrow, M. R.
Rainwater, L., 197, 198, 201, 323
Ramos, M., 394

Rankin, E., 272
Ransford, H. E., 120
Rao, S., 445
Raths, L., 113
Razran, G., 83
Reader, G. G., 224
Redl, F., 137
Redlich, F. C., 276, 280
Reich, W., 62
Reid, M., 216
Reitman, A. P., 273
Reitzes, D., 145
Rex, J., 300, 446
Rhyne, E. H., 145
Richardson, A., 230, 231, 233, 236
Richmond, A. H., 286, 287, 295, 300, 305
Riddleberger, A., 113
Riesman, D., 217
Riess, A. R., 275
Riessman, F., 384
Rim, Y., 88
Ritchie, J. E., 311, 324, 327
Robbins, R., 150
Robert, P., 442
Roberts, S. O., 261, 262, 263
Robins, L. N., 200
Robinson, A. L., 136
Robinson, J. M., 261
Robison, J. B., 159
Roen, S. R., 367
Rokeach, M., 62, 63, 247–8, 317–18
Rosario, G. del., 413
Rose, A. M., 134, 145
Rose, C., 134
Rosen, B. C., 190, 191, 192
Rosenbaum, M., 30, 140, 181
Rosenthal, B. G., 299
Rosenthal, R., 132, 133, 204, 271, 350,
    368, 385
Rosovsky, H., 136
Rotter, J., 380, 381, 388
Rowley, K. G., 350
Rubin, I. M., 138
Rubin, J., 413
Rudwick, E., 154, 156, 157, 165
Ruebush, B. K., 380, 382

Ruesch, J., 232
Runyon, E., 262

Sack, E. L., 270
Saint, C. K., 348
Sanders, J. T., 458
Sanford, R. N., 38, 57, 59, 61, 62, 70,
  89, 251
Sanseigne, A., 429
Sarason, S., 270, 275, 380, 382, 383
Sarnoff, L., 103
Scarpitti, F. R., 435
Scheff, T. J., 140
Schmelz, U. O., 441
Schrader, R., 126
Schwartz, P. A., 456, 462
Schwartz, S., 30, 181, 275
Scodel, A., 38
Seale, B., 157
Searles, R., 165
Secord, P. F., 83
Seguin, A., 419
Sellin, T., 435
Selltiz, C., 119
Selznick, G., 64
Seward, G., 178, 197
Shakor, A., 351
Shaw, G. B., 350
Sheatsley, P. B., 50–51, 53
Sheikh, A. A., 84
Sherif, C., 124
Sherif, M., 119, 124, 125, 145, 291
Shields, J., 373, 444
Shils, E., 62, 314
Shoham, S., 441, 446
Shuey, 271, 364, 373
Shuval, J. T., 236
Sibayon, B. P., 394
Sills, D., 156
Silvey, J., 462
Simmel, G., 148
Simon, M. D., 87
Simpson, G. E., 96, 145
Singer, B., 276, 279, 280
Sjoberg, G., 216
Slater, E., 373

Slavson, S. R., 140
Smilansky, S., 353
Smith, B. L. R., 168
Smith, F., 394
Smith, M. B., 379, 380
Smith, W. C., 216
Solomon, A., 135
Sparks, R. F., 437
Spearman, C., 362
Stark, R., 64
Steinberg, S., 64
Stember, C. H., 136
Stephenson, R. M., 435
Stevenson, H. W., 25, 26, 182, 183, 270
Stewart, E. C., 25, 26, 182, 183
Stoller, A., 232
Stonequist, E. V., 214–16, 217, 219,
  220, 221
Storr, A., 78, 79
Strauss, C. Lévi- see Lévi-Strauss, C.
Summers, G. F., 273
Sumner, W. G., 60, 314
Sveri, P., 442
Swanson, M. W., 301

Taft, R., 226, 227, 228, 230, 231, 233,
  235, 236, 238
Tajfel, H., 32, 76, 80, 81, 82, 83, 84, 86,
  87, 88
Tang, J., 273
Tannenbaum, P. H., 317
Tanter, R., 161
Taueber, A. F., 296–7
Taueber, K. E., 296–7
Tausch, A., 356
Tawney, R. H., 99
Taylor, F. M., 347, 352
Taylor, L. J., 448
Teryeny, F., 299
Thompson, R. H. T., 39
Thomson, S. S., 88
Thoreau, H. D., 322
Thurstone, L. L., 52, 55, 112
Tinbergen, N., 78
Tomlinson, H., 369, 371
Torrance, E. P., 351, 354

Tracy, J. J., 449
Trager, F., 113
Trager, H. G., 28, 31, 37, 181, 182, 183, 184, 185, 196
Treiman, D. J., 289
Triandis, H. C., 246, 248, 249, 269
Trist, E. L., 73
Trubowitz, J., 119
Tsujioka, B., 445
Tunstall, K., 396, 398, 399
Turner, R. M., 216, 220
Turner, R. H., 107, 180

Van de Geer, J. P., 87
Van den Berghe, P. L., 286
Van der Horst, S. T. L., 301
Vander Zanden, J. W., 165, 220
Van Vechten, C. C., 436
Vassiliou, V., 248
Vaughan, G. M., 25, 26, 27, 34, 39, 88, 272-3
Veblen, T. V., 217
Vega, M., 274
Veness, T., 23, 36
Vernon, P. E., 347-8, 462
Vitole, M. M., 280
Volkman, R., 139
Vose, C. E., 152
Vossler, K., 410

Waite, R. R., 380, 382
Walker, J. L., 159
Walker, N., 444
Walkley, R. P., 123, 124
Wallerstein, I., 408
Warburton, F. W., 445
Wardwell, W. I., 219
Warren, D. I., 120
Watson, P. F., 220, 275, 360, 362
Weber, M., 170
Weil, A., 31
Weinberg, A. A., 429
Weiner, M., 193, 194, 196
Weinstock, S. A., 233
Weisbrod, M., 165
Weisskopf, E., 367

Wentholt, R., 226, 230
West, P. S., 298
Westra, A., 327
Wheeler, L. R., 370
White, D., 134
White, R., 139
White, W., 152
Whiteman, M., 200-201, 384
Whittaker, E. M., 272
Wiener, P. L., 105
Wilkes, A. L., 81, 82
Wilkins, C., 47, 288
Williams, J. A., 105, 165
Williams, R., 113
Williams, R. M., 118-19, 289, 290
Wilner, M., 123, 124
Wilson, A. B., 384
Wilson, J. Q., 99
Wineman, D., 137
Wirth, L., 217
Wiseman, S., 348
Wolf, K., 111
Wolff, H. A., 268
Wolfgang, M. E., 434, 435, 438, 448
Wood, M. M., 216
Woodward, M., 405
Wright, P. L., 295
Wylie, R. S., 192

Yablonsky, L., 139
Yamamoto, J., 276, 279
Yap, P. M., 429
Yarrow, L., 125, 126
Yarrow, M. R., 37, 125, 126, 196, 218, 249, 367, 375
Yarrow, P., 47, 288
Yinger, J. M., 96, 145, 146
Young, J., 270

Zahran, M. A. S., 350
Zanden, J. W. Vander see Vander-Zanden, J. W.
Zigler, E., 389
Zinn, H., 154
Znaniecki, F., 403
Zubeck, J. M., 369

Subject Index

Acculturation, 215, 233, 236
Achievement motivation, 190–96, 377, 399
Action research, 131
Administration and discrimination, 146–8
Africans, 330–35, 418–19
The Algiers Motel Incident, 70, 71
American Council on Education, 133
American Jewish
  Committee, 159–60
  Congress, 159
Amsterdam, 32
Andean Indians, 419
'Anomie', 447–8
Anti-Defamation League of B'nai B'rith, 64, 159
Antilocution, 45
Anti-negroism, 64–70, 268
  see also USA, Negroes
Antipathy, group, 45–9, 93
  cognitive aspects of, 77–80
  and internal cohesion, 92–3
  stereotyping, 84–5
  see also Group relations
Anti-Semitism, 48, 59–65
  and ethnocentrism, 63, 64
  jokes, 268
  propaganda, 61, 113, 115
  see also Jews
Apartheid, 287, 292, 301
A priori scale, 51–2
Atlanta, 126
Attitudes, 242–8
  and behaviour, 248–50
  and prejudice, 250–51
  tests, 34, 274
  see also Measurement techniques
Australia, immigrants,
  assimilation of, 287, 233, 235–6, 238
  marginality of, 220
  mental illness among, 232
  as refugees, 228, 230–31
Authoritarianism
  and culture, 69–70
  origins of, 67

and parental influence, 67–9, 250–51

Baltimore, 435
'Banneker Group' project, 370–71
Bedouins, 251–2
Behaviour, social
  in race relations, 241–54, 267–83
  and attitudes, 248–50
  and examiner effects, 270–74
  and habit, 243
  and jokes, 268
  and language, 268–9
  norms, 243–6, 249
  roles, 243, 249
Bilingualism, 395, 397–9
Birmingham, England, 345, 437, 439
  Sparkbrook, 300, 446–7
The Birth of a Nation, 112
Black
  Muslims, 167, 170, 323
  Panthers, 154, 156–8, 162, 163
  Power, 100, 122, 158–9, 208, 320
  Studies programmes, 135
Bogardus,
  scale, 51–2
  Social-Distance Test, 140
Boston, 29–30, 34, 88
Bradford, 296
Brazil, 346
Bristol, 300
Britain,
  children, in
    and nationality preferences, 32, 86
    and race preferences, 88
  Community Relations Commission, 150
  franchise in, 302
  immigrants in,
    and crime, 436–40, 443
    and housing, 299–300
    and occupations, 294–5
    relation with, 35, 287–8
  Race Relations
    Act 1968, 294
    Board, 150
  violence in, 305

British immigrants
  in Australia, 230, 231, 233
  in Canada, 237
Brown, H. Rap, 154
Bureaucracy and racism, 71–2

California Ethnocentrism Scale, 134
Camberwell, 437
Canada, 84, 232, 233, 237
Carmichael, Stokely, 154, 157, 159
Catholics, attitudes towards, 30–31,
  34, 39
Chicago, 296
Child-rearing patterns, 332, 336–7,
  340–41
Children
  and achievement motivation, 190–96
  and geographical awareness, 31–3
  and group relations, 85–9, 124–6, 139
  and nationality preferences, 32–3,
    86, 90
  and racial prejudice, 23–40
    and conceptual criteria used, 29–33,
      182–6
    consistency in, 33–4
    ethnocentrism, 34–5
    and parental influence, 23–4, 37–40
      196–202
    preferences, 26–9, 36–9, 182–6
    and religious groups, 30–31
    self-identification, 26
  and racial recognition, 24–6, 86, 303–4
Chippewas, 221
Civil Rights
  Act 1964 (USA), 302
  Commission (USA), 150
  movement, 148–60
    see also Protest
  organizations, 148–60
  business firms, 149
  private organizations, 151–60
  public agencies, 149–51
    see also specific organizations
Cleaver, Eldridge, 157, 170
College
  examiners, 270–78

intake, 99
intergroup education in, 134
negro performance in, 257–65
'Colouring test', 27, 184–5
Communities Relations Commission
  (Britain), 150
Computers
  and measurement techniques, 55
Consistency theory, 317–19
Contact, intergroup, 115–29
  in schools, 131–6
  through children's camps, 124–6
  through integrated housing,
    122–4
CORE, Congress of Racial Equality,
  155–6, 162, 163, 164, 165
Crime
  and adjustment, 446–8
  'anomie', 447–8
  in Britain, 436–40, 443
  and culture, 445–6
  in Europe, 441–2
  and heredity, 444–5
  and hidden delinquency, 442–4
  in immigrant and minority groups,
    432–50
  in Israel, 440–41
  and psychology, 449–50
  and social class, 443–4
  among US Negroes, 434–6, 443
Culture
  and authoritarianism, 69–70, 74
  consistency theory of, 317–19
  and ethnocentrism, 69–70, 313–14,
    326
  and identity, 325–6
  as values, 314–17

Desegregation see Integration
Detroit, 445
Didsbury Compensatory Education
  Project, 357
Discrimination, racial
  and administration, 146–8
  and education, 303–4
  and employment, 292

and franchise, 301–2
and housing, 296–301
in psychiatric treatment, 275–6, 279–80
and law, 146–8
measurement techniques for the reduction of, 44, 96–7, 256
and minority group psychology, 168–70
against outgroup, 46
and personnel testing, 453–65
and criterion stability, 459–61
interpretation of, 456–9
safeguards, 461–5
test content, 454–6
and prejudice typology, 46–7, 100–103, 288
and psychiatric disorders, 420–21, 424–5
and public places, 302
types of situation, 103–5
see also Prejudice, racial, Racism

Dolls
use of in preference tests, 34, 36–7, 182–4
use of in racial recognition tests, 24–7, 31, 38–9, 88

Economic privilege, 105–6
Education
Black Studies programmes, 135
and discrimination, 303–4
and immigrants, 343–57
and housing policy, 351
labelling as 'backward', 347–8
language problems, 348–9
performance, 349–50
school requirements, 345–52
social education, 353–7
intergroup, 129–36
and racism, 73
and textbook bias, 133
see also Colleges, Schools, Teachers
Eichmann, Adolf, 71
Emigrants, 230–31
from Holland, 226

Employee-employer relationships, 241–4
Employment and discrimination, 292
Eskimos, 416–17
Ethnocentrism, 34–5, 63, 312–13, 317–19
and anti-Semitism, 63, 64
and authoritarianism, 69–70
in college students, 69–70
and culture, 313–14, 326
effects of, 319–24
E scale, 60, 69
and personality, 60–66
'politicalized', 66
reduction through education, 134–5
Eurasians, 214
Europe
foreign workers and crime in, 441–2
Examiners, 270–78

Family
and Negro self-identification, 196–202
father absence in, 199–200, 378, 383–4
male and female roles in, 198–201
Fascism, 61, 63, 69
Fellowship of Reconciliation, 155
Fiji, 346
Flint, Ohio, 443
Franchise discrimination, 301–2

Galvanic Skin Response, 272
Gandhi, Mahatma, 164
Geneva, 31–2
'Gentleman's Agreement', 113
Geographical awareness
in children, 31–3
Georgia, 350
Germans, 247
Gesell Development Examination, 272
Ghettos, 296, 297, 301
Glasgow, 32, 33
Greeks, 247, 248
Greensboro', North Carolina, 154
Group relations
biological aspects of, 77–80
cognitive aspects of, 77–94

Group relations – *continued*
  coherence in, 90–93
  consistency theory of, 317–19
  need for research, 171–2
  personalization of, 91
  psychoanalytical aspects of, 77–80
  recognition, 85–9
  therapy, 138–40
  see also Antipathy, group,
    Ethnocentrism, Integration,
    Minorities, Prejudice, racial,
    Race relations, Stereotypes
Guttman scale, 53–4, 106, 162

Harlem, 370
Harris surveys, 119–20, 153, 157
'Higher Horizons' project, 369, 370
'High Wall', 134–5
Holland,
  emigrants, 226
  immigrants, 230, 236, 345, 351
  migrants, 232
Hostility, group *see* Antipathy, group
Housing, 31, 183–4
  and education, 351
  and discrimination, 296–301
  and integration, 98, 122–4
Howe, Sir Ronald, 439
Hungarian immigrants
  in Australia, 228, 230, 235–6
  in Canada, 232, 233
  in the USA, 233, 445
Hybrids
  see Marginality

Identity, racial
  see Self-identification
Immigrants
  acculturation of, 233, 236
  adjustment of, 228–31, 343–5
  assimilation of, 227–8, 233–8, 351
  in Australia, 220, 227–8
  in Brazil, 346
  in Britain, 35, 48, 234, 236, 295–6,
    436–40
    African, 330–35

    Indian and Pakistani, 338–41
    West Indian, 335–8
  in Canada, 232, 233, 237
  and crime, 432–5
    in Britain, 436–40
    in Israel, 440–41
    in USA, 445
  and education, 343–57
    labelling as 'backward', 347–8
    language problems, 348–9
    performance, 349–50
    schooling requirements, 345–52
    social education, 353–7
  in Fiji, 346
  in Holland, 230, 236, 346, 352
  in Israel, 232, 235, 236, 346, 353
  marginality, 214, 218–20
  mental health, 231–2
  pluralism, 237–8
  resocialization, 224–38
    and personality, 226–7
    and social identity, 225–35
    and social norms, 224–5, 234–5
  in Rhodesia, 236
  in USA, 30, 227, 233, 237, 345
'Index of Anti-Semitic Belief, 64
Indians
Asian
  family life of, 340–41
  migration and psychiatric disorders
    among, 17
  and poverty in India, 320
  and social attitudes, 247
  and social background, 338–41
  stereotyped assessments of, 84,
    115–16
  as students in Britain, 234
North American, 421
Indonesian immigrants in Holland,
  230, 236
Industrialization
  and race relations, 292–6
  and social reorganization, 291
Information tests, 54
Integration
  economic, 105–6

goals, 96–100
housing, 98, 122–4
of immigrants, 227–8, 233–8
and nationalism, 407
of Negroes, 257–65
in schools, 126, 202–5, 256–64
  and Negro performance, 256–65
  and teacher attitudes, 203
strategies, 108–40
  and contact, 115–29
  and education 129–36
  and exhortation, 108–10
  and group therapy, 138
  and personal therapy, 136–8
  and propaganda, 110–15
in summer camps, 249–50
US opinion survey, 1963, 53
see also Civil rights
Intelligence
comparison between US Negroes
  and Whites, 363, 366–75
definition of, 362
and environment, 364–5, 369–70
and genetic influence, 371, 373
improvement of, 370–71
and personality factors, 367–9
and underachievement, 366, 377–90
see also Tests
Ireland, 397
Israel
group preferences in, 88–9
immigrants in, 232, 235, 236, 346
  and crime, 440–41

Jackson, Mahalia, 325
Japan, 247
Jews
and achievement motivation, 191
attitudes towards, 30–31, 34, 37–9, 65
and ethnocentrism, 35
as immigrants, 217, 232, 440–41
intergroup organizations among,
  159–60
and Jewish studies, 135
marginality of, 217, 221
see also Anti-Semitism

Johannesburg, 301
Jokes, racial, 268

Kentucky, 194
King, Martin Luther, 153–4, 155, 164,
  306
Kipsigis, 252

Language
and achievement motivation, 399
bilingualism, 395, 397–9
and educational psychology, 394–5
inter-racial usage, 268–9
and nationalism, 409–13
psycholinguistics, 393, 394
sociolinguistics, 393, 394
and teaching, 394–401
Latin America, 422
Law and discrimination, 146–8
Leeds, 217
Lewis, John, 154
Likert scale, 52
London, 27, 32, 33, 38, 39, 437–9
Los Angeles, 124
Louvain, 32
Lowestoft, 39–40
Lynchburg, 25–6, 36, 88

McCarthyism, 72
Maoris
attitude towards, 25–7, 34, 39
culture of, 324–5, 327–8
and examiner effects, 272–3
and group preferences, 88
and self-identification, 26, 321
Marginality, 213–22
and cultural conflicts, 213, 217–18
  and acculturation, 215
  and personality, 214, 219–22
and hybrids,
  cultural, 214
  racial, 214, 220–21
and marginal syndrome, 220
and physical appearance, 221
'and mark of oppression', 188, 379
and measurement techniques, 44–55
and computers, 55

Marginality – *continued*
  disguised, 54–5
  of ethnocentrism (E scale), 60, 63
  of pre-Fascism (F scale) 61, 62–3
  opinion surveys, 49–51
  response bias, 61–3
  scaling methods, 51–4
  unstructured, 54–5
Mestizos, 214
Mexicans, 34, 320
Minneapolis, 37–8
Minnesota, 232
Minorities
  as a threat, 290–91
  and crime, 432–50
  inadequacies of, 96
  and mental health treatment, 79–81
  psychiatric disorders in, 416–30
  psychology of, 168–70
  see also Immigrants *and* USA,
    Negroes
Mixed-bloods, marginality of, 214,
  220–21
Montgomery, Alabama, 153, 163, 164
  Improvement Association, 153
Montreal, 32, 397, 400
'Mr Biggott' cartoons, 111–12
Mulattos, 214

National
  Association for the Advancement
    of Colored People (NAACP),
    151–3, 156, 162, 291
  Association of Intergroup
    Relations Officials (NAIRO),
    148–9
  Community Relations Advisory
    Council, 160
  Conference of Christians and Jews,
    160
  Opinion Research Center, Chicago, 53
  Urban League, 154
Nationalism, 403–13
  and children's nationality
    preferences, 31–3, 86, 90
Nazism, 71, 170

Negroes
  see Africans, USA, Negroes, West
    Indians
New England, 88
New Jersey, 435
New Orleans, 28, 126
New York, 30, 121, 127, 195–6, 204
  Educational Complex, 352
  'Higher Horizons' project, 370, 371
New Zealand, Maoris *see* Maoris
Nigeria, 458–9
Nixon, President Richard, 153
Norwegian immigrants in Minnesota,
  232

Oak Ridge, Tennessee, 126
Ohio, 38
Ojibwa Indians, 417
Osage Indians, 370

Pakistanis, 296, 338–41
Parks, Mrs Rosa, 163
Personality
  and authoritarianism, 61–74
  and ethnocentrism, 60–66
  and immigrants, 226–7
  and intelligence, 367–9
  and marginality, 215
  and racist behaviour, 57–74
  therapy, 136–8
  and underachievement, 377–84
Philadelphia, 28, 30, 36, 37, 277, 438
Photographs, use in racial
  recognition, 83–4, 87, 88–9
Picture preference test, 34
Pluralism, 98, 127, 237–8
Polish immigrants in Australia, 230
Preferences, racial, in children, 26–9,
  36–9, 182–6
Prejudice, racial
  and discrimination, 46–9
  typology, 46–7, 100–103, 287
  and interpersonal attitudes, 250–51
  origins of, 313
  and personality, 65–6
  research, 67, 93
  and status, 289–90

see also Children, racial prejudice,
　　Discrimination, Measurement
　　techniques, Racism
Princeton Plan, 352
Propaganda, 73, 110–15
Protest, 106–8
　non-violent, 153, 155, 163–5
　violent, 165–8
　see also Civil Rights
Psychiatry
　disorders in minority groups, 416–30
　prevention and treatment, 425–8
　racial attitudes, 275–6, 279–81
　research, 428–30
Psycholinguistics, 393, 394
Psychophysical scale, 52

Race
　definitions of, 360–61
Race relations
　Act, 1968, (Britain), 294–5
　and behaviour, 286–307
　competitive, 286, 290–91
　paternalistic, 286
　structured and unstructured, 289
　Board, (Britain)
　and industrialization, 291–5
　and interpersonal attitudes, 241–54
　characteristics, 244, 246
　habit, 243
　prejudice, 250–51
　roles, 243, 249
　social norms, 243–6, 249
　see also Group relations
Racial
　preferences *see* Preferences, racial
　prejudice *see* Prejudice, racial
　recognition *see* Recognition, racial
Racism, 62–3, 70–73
　see also Prejudice, racial *and*
　　Discrimination, racial
'Ranks' test, 34
Rational scale, 52
Recognition, racial
　use of dolls in, 24–7, 31, 38–9, 88
　use of photographs in, 83–4, 87, 88–9

see also Children, racial recognition
Religion
　and social background, 331–2, 337–8
Religious groups, 30–31
'Religious Symbol' picture test, 30
Resocialization of immigrants *see*
　　Immigrants, resocialization
Rhodesia, 236

St Louis, 370, 371
San Francisco, 350
Schizophrenia, 423
Schools, USA,
　and integration, 126, 202–5, 304
　language-teaching in, 394–401
　and Negro performance, 192, 257–65
　　and race of teacher, 259–61
　and segregation, 119–20
　　Supreme Court ruling against, 145
　see also Education *and* Teachers
Schools Council
　'race kit', 40, 135
SCLC, 153–4, 164
Seattle, 442–3
Segregation
　arguments for, 127–9
　in housing, 296–301
　in public places, 302
　see also South Africa, *apartheid*,
　　USA, segregation
Self-identification
　and culture, 324–6
　Maori, 26, 321
　Negro, 26, 176–80, 206–9, 282, 379
　　achievement orientations, 190–96
　　and action groups, 208
　　conflicts, 186–90, 196
　　development of, 180–81
　　and the family, 196–202, 377–8
　　hostility, 188
　　'passing' as white, 189, 324
　　personality adjustment, 187
　　racial conception, 180–81
　　racial evaluation, 180, 182–6
　　self-rejection, 185, 187
　of minority groups, 282

Sharpeville, 305
'Show Me' test, 34
Skin-colour, 29–30, 181, 189
Slang, 268–9
Smith, Gerald L. K., 115
SNCC, 154, 156
Social norms
  and behaviour, 243–6, 249
  and immigrants, 224–5, 234–5
'Social Situations' test, 34
Sociolinguistics, 393, 394
South Africa
  apartheid in, 287, 292
  and Coloureds, marginality of, 220, 221
  and discrimination, 292–3, 300–303
  group attitudes in, 89
  and industrialization, 292
  and *Terrorism Act*, 293
  and violence, 304–5
  Sharpeville, 305
South America, 421
Southern Christian Leadership
  Conference (SCLC), 153–4, 164
Sparkbrook, Birmingham, 300, 446–7
Status
  equality, 121
  and prejudice, 289–90
Stereotypes, 33–4, 47–8, 183
  as categorization, 80–85
  assimilation of, 85–90
  breaking of, 121
  hostile, 84
  as interchangeable, 48
  national, 80–81
  Negro, 324–5
  test, 34
Student National Coordination
  Committee (SNCC), 154
Student Nonviolent Coordinating
  Committee, 154, 156
Summated ratings, 52
Summer camps, 49–50, 367, 375

Tabor, Mr and Mrs Michael, 157
Teachers
  attitudes, 203–4

  influence, 304
  race of, 59–61
  segregation of, 132
  and social education, 354
  see also Education *and* Schools
Tests
  attitude, 34, 273
  'colouring', 27, 184–5
  Galvanic Skin Response, 272
  Gates Reading Test, 200
  Gesell Development Examination,
    273
  IQ, 276, 348, 362–5, 368
    and personnel discrimation, 453–65
      criterion stability, 459–61
      interpretation, 456–9
      safeguards, 461–5
      test content, 454–6
  'Ranks', 34
  Raven's Progressive Matrices, 455
  Reinforcement History
    Questionnaire, 382
  'Religious Symbol' picture, 30
  Rorschach, 276, 324–5
  'Show Me', 34
  'Social Situations', 34
  Stanford-Binet intelligence test, 274
Test Anxiety Questionnaire, 275
  382
Thematic Apperception Test, 188,
  191, 275, 325
  see also Dolls *and* Photographs
Thurstone scale, 52
Toda, 241–5
Tunisia, 417–18
Twins
  and IQ, 363–4, 373

USA
  Americans, marginality of, 217
  Chippewas, 221
  crime figures, 433–6
  cultural revolution, 322–4
  ethnocentrism, 324
  foreign service and racial etiquette,
    267–8

Greeks, 218–19
immigrants, 227, 233, 237
Indian reservations, 421
Jews, 217
Negroes
  attitudes towards, 33, 50–51,
    89–90
  children's attitudes towards, 24–31,
    34, 36–40
  and crime, 434–6, 443
  and education, 131–6, 192, 382–6
  educational performance, 257–66
  examiner effects, 263, 271–9
  housing, 122–4, 296–301
  intelligence, 360–76
  intergroup contact, 122–9
  internality, 380–82
  inter-racial behaviour, 256–66
  in the US Army, 121–2, 295
  marginality, 214, 217, 219
  'mark of oppression', 188, 379
  and mental health, 138, 279–81
  Poles, 218–19
  police, 70–71

preferences, 26–9
protest, 163–8
and race riots, 305–7, 320
segregation, 28–30, 119–20, 127–9,
  296–9
'slave mentality', 321
stereotypes, 324–5
underachievement, 366, 377–90
vocational aspirations, 192–5
see also Anti-negroism and
  Self-identification, Negro
see also Civil Rights, Discrimination,
  Integration

Value orientations, 314–17
Vienna, 90
Violence, 46, 304–7, 320
Virginia, 34, 88

Washington 'talent search', 370
West Indians, 335–8
Wilkins, Roy, 152

Young, Whitney, Jnr, 155